Le Corbusier's Practical Ae the City

MW00668112

Set within an insightful analysis, this book describes the genesis, ideas, and ideologies which influenced *La Construction des villes* by Le Corbusier. This volume makes this important theoretical work available for the first time in English, offering an interpretation of the ways and the extent to which his 'essai' may have influenced his later work.

Dealing with questions of aesthetic urban design, *La Construction des villes* shows Le Corbusier's intellectual influences in the field of urbanism. Discontent that his script was not sufficiently avant-garde, he abandoned it soon after it was written in the early 20th century. It was only in the late 1970s that American historian H. Allen Brooks discovered 250 pages of the forgotten manuscript in Switzerland. The author of this book, Christoph Schnoor, later discovered another 350 handwritten pages of the original manuscript, consisting of extracts, chapters, and bibliographic notes. This splendid find enabled the re-establishment of the manuscript as Le Corbusier had abandoned it, unfinished, in the spring of 1911.

This volume offers an unbiased extension of our knowledge of Le Corbusier and his work. In addition, it reminds us of the urban design innovations of the very early 20th century which can still serve as valuable lessons for a new understanding of contemporary urban design.

Dr Christoph Schnoor is Associate Professor at Unitec Institute of Technology in Auckland, New Zealand. Having published extensively on modernist architecture, with specific focus on the work of Le Corbusier and architectural critique by Colin Rowe, his intellectual biography on Austrian émigré architect Ernst Plischke has been published in 2020.

Le Corbusier's Practical Aesthetic of the City

The treatise 'La Construction des villes' of 1910/11

Christoph Schnoor

Routledge
Taylor & Francis Group

LONDON AND NEW YORK

First published 2020
by Routledge
2 Park Square, Milton Park, Abingdon, Oxon OX14 4RN

and by Routledge
52 Vanderbilt Avenue, New York, NY 10017

Routledge is an imprint of the Taylor & Francis Group, an informa business

Manuscript translation from French and essay translation from German © Kim Sanderson

The translation was produced in collaboration with the author

British Library Cataloguing-in-Publication Data
A catalogue record for this book is available from the British Library

Library of Congress Cataloging-in-Publication Data
A catalog record has been requested for this book

ISBN: 978-1-4724-4564-3 (hbk)
ISBN: 978-1-315-59173-5 (ebk)

Typeset in Gill Sans and Olympian
by Swales & Willis, Exeter, Devon, UK

Contents

Le Corbusier's Practical Aesthetic of the City

Introduction

La Construction des villes

La Construction des villes could have become Le Corbusier's first publication in 1910. Yet he did not grant his first text on city planning the attention it deserved. Furthermore, a certain coyness about his sources means others' knowledge of this key step in his urban education has remained severely limited.

As a rule, Le Corbusier's life and work are so well known that there is little chance of uncovering new material of his. His time in Germany in 1910/11 is now one of the most heavily researched periods in his life. It is therefore all the more astonishing that significant material could still be uncovered, providing important insights into his intellectual formation. The complete 1910/11 manuscript of *La Construction des villes* only came to light in 1999. This handwritten text by Le Corbusier remained in an unfinished state, yet it supplies new discoveries and information on how his convictions about urban planning emerged. The manuscript also constitutes a remarkable counterpart and counterpoint to his later urban design ideas, as in the 1922 *Ville Contemporaine* or the 1925 *Plan Voisin*, published that year as part of *Urbanisme*. It is fascinating to witness the work which young Charles-Edouard Jeanneret (later known as Le Corbusier) was doing in 1910 and 1911, following his apprenticeship with Auguste Perret in Paris and prior to the *Voyage d'Orient*. The work is so fascinating and revealing because Jeanneret formulates ideas in *La Construction des villes* which he later came to reject, and often vehemently denounce. Yet at the same time, these theories form major building blocks in his emerging philosophy of urban design and architecture.

Jeanneret's work is of historical significance because it engages intensively with the debate on aesthetically oriented city planning in Germany at the time. The full range of themes and diversity of arguments in this debate are reflected in *La Construction des villes*. The manuscript has its roots in a large number of books on urban design, not least Camillo Sitte's 1889 *Der Städte-Bau nach seinen künstlerischen Grundsätzen* (*City Planning According to Artistic Principles*), which triggered the whole discussion of aesthetic planning.[1] These books represent key positions taken in the German-language professional discourse during that era. Many of their writers saw themselves as Camillo Sitte's successors, but approached his theories critically and moved beyond them, notably

---

1 Camillo Sitte, *Der Städte-Bau nach seinen künstlerischen Grundsätzen* (Vienna: Carl Graeser, 1889); English translation entitled *City Planning According to Artistic Principles* included in *Camillo Sitte: The Birth of Modern City Planning*, eds. George Collins and Christiane Crasemann Collins (New York: Rizzoli, 1986).

architects and art historians like Karl Henrici, Paul Schultze-Naumburg, Hermann Muthe-sius, Albert Erich Brinckmann, and Joseph August Lux. Above all, Jeanneret develops in his work an understanding of the concept of space and of spatial perception.

Jeanneret may have been overwhelmed by the wealth of literature available, but his engagement with it was so deep that it bears detailed examination. Despite the thorough research already undertaken into Le Corbusier's younger days, little firm knowledge is available about *La Construction des villes*.[2] Thus analysis of this early work provides an opportunity to glimpse 'behind the scenes' of Le Corbusier's cultivation of his own image as a self-made man and innate genius. A precise investigation of his urban design source material provides us with a clearer lens through which to view his later work, be it *Urbanisme, Précisions* or *Vers une architecture*.[3] We are now in a better position to see the many and varied sources which Jeanneret collated for his texts. It is true that many of his intellectual sources were already known; yet new perspectives do open up, especially in urban design, since the present essay identifies beyond doubt some 70 works which Jeanneret read on architectural and urban design topics.

In early 1910, Charles-Edouard Jeanneret launched himself into a project which grew into something almost unmanageable. Charles L'Eplattenier, his teacher at the *Ecole d'Art* in La Chaux-de-Fonds, had suggested that Jeanneret prepare a study on the current state of city planning in Switzerland, to be presented in September 1910 at a conference of the *Union des villes suisses*, to be held in La Chaux de Fonds.[4] L'Eplattenier had intended this study as a way of disseminating within Switzerland a new, artistic city planning movement based on the ideas of Viennese architect Camillo Sitte, who had died in 1904.[5]

Jeanneret was just 22 years old and had been seriously engaging with architecture for some four years. He had never studied city planning, yet he now intended to publish his study from a standing start. He did not see it as a simple essay but planned to provide answers, aiming to spark an aesthetic reform in his homeland of Switzerland, which he saw as dominated by administrative planning. This project expanded throughout 1910, until the planned study became a putative book. Jeanneret collated a large volume of

2 Hence Antonio Brucculeri, writing in 2002 about a 1987 essay by Werner Oechslin, said that Jeanneret prob-ably learned about French theories of the Enlightenment and ornament via Albert Erich Brinckmann prior to 1915. Antonio Brucculeri, "The Challenge of the 'Grand Siècle'", in *Le Corbusier before Le Corbusier*, ed. Stanislaus von Moos and Arthur Rüegg (New Haven/London: Yale University Press, 2002), p. 104. Brucculeri references Werner Oechslin, "Allemagne. Influences, confluences et reniements", in *Le Corbusier: une ency-clopédie*, ed. Jacques Lucan (Paris: Centre Georges Pompidou, 1987), pp. 33–39.

3 Le Corbusier, *Vers une Architecture* (Paris: Crès, 1923); English version: *Toward an Architecture*, trans. John Goodman, with an introduction by Jean-Louis Cohen (Los Angeles: Getty Research Institute, 2007); Le Corbu-sier, *Urbanisme* (Paris: Crès, 1925), English version: *The City of To-Morrow and its Planning*, trans. Frederick Etchells (New York: Payson & Clarke, 1929); Le Corbusier, *Précisions sur un état présent de l'architecture et de l'urbanisme* (Paris: Crès, 1930); English version: *Precisions on the present state of architecture and city planning*, trans. Edith Schreiber Aujame (Cambridge, Mass.: MIT Press, 1991).

4 In the end, it was L'Eplattenier who wrote a contribution for the conference: Charles L'Eplattenier, "L'Esthé-tique des villes", in [Résumé de l'intervention de Ch. L'Eplatt. à] l'Assemblée générale des délégués de l'Union des villes suisses réunis à La Chaux-de-Fonds à l'Hôtel de Ville, les 24 et 25 septembre 1910, in *Compte-rendu des délibérations de l'Assemblée générale des délégués de l'Union des villes suisses, 1910*; Sup-plement to the Schweizerisches Zentralblatt für Staats- und Gemeinde-Verwaltung 11 (1910), pp. 24–31.

5 Sitte, *City Planning According to Artistic Principles*.

materials, drafting chapter after chapter. By spring 1911, his manuscript had grown to a hefty 600 pages. And still Jeanneret did not end up publishing the manuscript.

Originally, Jeanneret had planned to find work with an architect, as had been his intention in Vienna and Paris in 1908/09. With the help of L'Eplattenier, he had also secured a grant for a study of the applied arts in Germany. Yet between April and October 1910, he dedicated his time in Munich almost exclusively to urban design, and began to draft the proposed study under the heading *La Construction des villes*. In November 1910 he took up a position in Peter Behrens' office in Berlin for five months, and although the study was not yet complete, Jeanneret's work there took precedence. By March 1911, Jeanneret had drafted most of the manuscript, but set it aside. He was uncertain about its quality and objectives, so he postponed any publication indefinitely. At the end of March 1911, Jeanneret left Behrens' employ; he finally undertook the research on the applied arts for which he had received a grant to stay in Munich.[6] He was also preparing for a long journey to the Balkans and beyond from May to late October 1911 with the young art historian August Klipstein, who was almost exactly the same age and whom Jeanneret had met in Munich in 1910.

In the following few years, Jeanneret did not address urban design issues. Instead, he designed the *Maison Blanche* for his parents in La Chaux-de-Fonds in 1912, and published his *Etude des arts décoratifs en Allemagne*. During the First World War, Jeanneret returned to the unpublished manuscript for *La Construction des villes*. In July 1915 he travelled to Paris and spent seven weeks researching enthusiastically in the Bibliothèque Nationale. This trip bore plenty of fruit in the form of sketches, excerpts, and a detailed bibliography, which have largely remained unrevised.[7] Yet Jeanneret was no longer interested in the German-language aesthetics of perception, and concentrated instead on French architectural and planning theory from the 17th and 18th centuries. After returning to La Chaux-de-Fonds, Jeanneret did not incorporate this new material into his existing manuscript, but left *La Construction des villes* as it was, aside from a few minor edits. Thus even with this new élan, Jeanneret did not finish what he had started. It could be argued that this new research no longer forms part of *La Construction des villes*; that it instead marks the beginning of *Urbanisme*, published in 1925 under the name of Le Corbusier. This is a very different work to *La Construction des villes*. Its objectives are modernist, if not avant-garde, and are tailored to 1920s society and technology. Yet *Urbanisme* should not be considered independently of *La Construction des villes*, which sheds new light on the 1925 book.

Le Corbusier stayed stubbornly silent about *La Construction des villes*. Towards the end of his life he mentioned to Jean Petit that he had composed "un livre un peu idiot": a silly book about urban design he had started writing in 1910.[8] That he would say this

---

6 Jeanneret's first published work appeared the following year: Charles Edouard Jeanneret, *Etude sur le mouvement d'art décoratif en Allemagne*, La Chaux-de-Fonds 1912 (Reprint New York: Da Capo, 1968); English version: *A study of the decorative art movement in Germany*, ed. Mateo Kries (Weil am Rhein: Vitra Design Museum, 2008).

7 Philippe Duboy, "Charles Edouard Jeanneret à la Bibliothèque Nationale", in *Architecture, Mouvement, Continuité* 49 (1979), pp. 9–12, and Philippe Duboy, *Architecture de la ville: culture et triomphe de l'urbanisme. Ch. E. Jeanneret, «La Construction des villes», Bibliothèque Nationale de Paris, 1915* (Paris: pour la ministère de l'urbanisme, du logement et des transports, 1985). The unrevised excerpts and the sketches are filed under B2-20 in the archive at the Fondation Le Corbusier (FLC), Paris.

8 Jean Petit, *Le Corbusier parle* (Paris: Forces Vives, 1967; rev. ed. Lugano: Fidia Edizioni D'Arte, 1996), p. 9.

is understandable, given the view on urbanism which Le Corbusier had adopted since the 1920s. The path this earlier work treads is very different from the route he took in his later designs and utopian visions for the *Ville Contemporaine*, the *Athens Charter*, or Chandigarh. Yet I cannot agree with Le Corbusier here: even in its incomplete state, *La Construction des villes* represents some of Le Corbusier's most successful writing.

The work is deficient in many areas. As well as being incomplete, Jeanneret has copied directly from his sources too much and too often; he contradicts himself, repeats himself and wanders off into poetic reveries. Nevertheless, this early work is more tightly structured and developed than most of Le Corbusier's later works of comparable size and scope. And although *La Construction des villes* is more conservative on key points than Le Corbusier's later, published works, it is still innovative. In structure and objectives, it even anticipates parts of Cornelius Gurlitt's *Handbuch des Städtebaues* (1914/1920).[9]

The most important aspect is Jeanneret's appreciation of space in terms of urban design. This is central to *La Construction des villes*, and one of its greatest strengths. The whole study hinges on space in the city, its aesthetic and functional characteristics. Through investigations into these issues, Jeanneret is laying the foundations for the deep understanding of the nature of space he would later develop. In his study, this understanding remains a theoretical framework and has not developed into applied knowledge, but it nevertheless proved a valuable source of knowledge to feed into his later architecture and urban designs. In particular, the villas La Roche-Jeanneret, Savoye, and Stein-de-Monzie demonstrate a spatial complexity reminiscent of dense picturesque historic town centres, and would not have emerged without Jeanneret's early-career study of urban design.[10] Why did *La Construction des villes* remain incomplete, when Jeanneret had made such progress in 1910? The comprehensive correspondence with his mentor, Swiss writer and art critic William Ritter, indicates that Ritter encouraged and indeed pushed Jeanneret to finalise and publish an account of his journey to the East, while setting aside his interest in what Ritter referred to as the "alleged ugliness of industrial cities".[11]

Hence urban design faded into the background once Jeanneret had returned from Istanbul, Athens, and Rome. The *cubes blanches*, white cubic buildings from the Mediterranean region, had sparked Jeanneret's imagination and now loomed larger than his systematic treatment of urban design. In around 1912, after his journey to the East, Jeanneret drew up a first vision of his future architecture. *La Construction des villes* on the other hand, originally conceived to provoke change in the existing planning in La Chaux-de-Fonds, was no longer sufficiently visionary to maintain Jeanneret's enthusiasm. His neglect of *La Construction des villes* might also be related to his increasingly tense relationship with L'Eplattenier, whose original idea the study had been. Several ways of interpreting this neglect are explored below in more detail. In any event, the incomplete project became increasingly burdensome.

9 Cornelius Gurlitt, *Handbuch des Städtebaues* (Berlin: Architekturverlag Der Zirkel, 1920).

10 Richard Etlin was the first to note that Le Corbusier worked elements of the picturesque city plan into his villas. See Richard Etlin, *Frank Lloyd Wright and Le Corbusier. The Romantic Legacy* (Manchester: Manchester University Press, 1994).

11 William Ritter, "De la prétendue laideur de La Chaux-de-Fonds", in *Feuille d'Avis de La Chaux-de-Fonds*, 17 and 24 March 1917.

The fate of *La Construction des villes* may have been sealed by its coming both too early and too late. It came too early for Jeanneret, whose heroic research mission in 1910 ran out of steam two-thirds of the way through, and too late for the debate on urban design. Others were already disseminating the theories which Jeanneret posits in his manuscript. He was unable to add new insights: his innovation lay only in his presentation of these theories. Although his propositions were at the forefront of the debate in 1910 – witness the urban design exhibition in Berlin that same year – they were sound and reasonable rather than revolutionary. All in all, *La Construction des villes* is an outstanding, realistic analysis with considerable artistic merit, but it is no utopian vision. Later, Jeanneret developed a taste for provocation and gaining notoriety: a recurring theme in his work. Thus when, as Le Corbusier, he looked back critically from the 1920s over the 'sins of his youth', he was correct in one assessment: *La Construction des villes* would not have helped make his name as an avant-garde architect.

His urban study suffered the same fate as many other works that emerged immediately before the First World War: it was overtaken by events. The war and ongoing modernisation in Europe overturned all the existing models of civil society and aesthetics, and raised new urban design questions which *La Construction des villes* was unable to answer. But while this means it was very much 'of its time', *La Construction des villes* can also be seen as timeless. The analyses it contains of urban public space within squares and streets – which Jeanneret adopts from Schultze-Naumburg, Henrici, and Sitte and reassembles in his own way – are universal in their assessment of the aesthetics of perception, transcending historical periods and styles.

Jeanneret's early exploration of German-language urban design around the turn of the century made an impression on him which lasted well beyond the point when he began to call himself Le Corbusier. While he may ultimately have rejected Sitte's ideas as retrograde and narrow-minded, as Le Corbusier he was nevertheless aware of the power behind the ideas and theories he had so painstakingly collated in 1910. He would later draw on the rich seam of knowledge he had mined at that time, while disassociating the ideas from their sources so they could only be traced back by readers familiar with those original sources.[12] Herein lies the great potential of *La Construction des villes*. It provides access to the knowledge Le Corbusier gained, and enables researchers to explain formulations in *Urbanisme* or *Vers une architecture* which have hitherto remained opaque or inexplicable. The sources traced in *La Construction des villes* may grant access to a range of research that remains outstanding.

The present research

Everyone who gets to know Le Corbusier's urban design and architecture is confronted with a contradiction: between his monumental, simplifying, Beaux-Arts-inspired urban planning on the one hand, and the internal complexity of his residential projects on the other. This is an astonishing contradiction which prompts one to investigate the reasons behind it, in the hope of resolving it – or at least showing it in a new light. The

---

12 For example, in *Urbanisme* Le Corbusier adopts almost verbatim some of Albert Erich Brinckmann's ideas as developed in *Platz und Monument*. See Albert Erich Brinckmann, *Platz und Monument. Untersuchungen zur Geschichte und Ästhetik der Stadtbaukunst in neuerer Zeit* (Berlin: Wasmuth, 1908), reprint with an afterword by Jochen Meyer (Berlin: Gebr. Mann, 2000).

dissertation which forms the basis for the present book began as a comparison between Le Corbusier's urban design theories and those of Camillo Sitte. *La Construction des villes* emerged as the interface between these starkly contrasting viewpoints. My research on *La Construction des villes* became a matter of detective work.

Immediately after Le Corbusier's death in 1965, it was not clear whether *La Construction des villes* even existed, occupying this middle ground between irreconcilable positions. Although Stanislaus von Moos and Paul Venable Turner had stated, in 1968 and 1971 respectively, that there could be an early, as yet unknown tract by Le Corbusier on city planning, they lacked the necessary sources to verify this.[13] The evidence was uncovered when Harold Allen Brooks, who had been gathering material for a biography of Le Corbusier's formative years since the early 1970s, discovered a substantial manuscript in private ownership in around 1977, comprising some 250 pages. This was Le Corbusier's unpublished work on urban design entitled *La Construction des villes*. Brooks made two photocopies of it, depositing one at the Bibliothèque de la Ville in La Chaux-de-Fonds (BV), where it can still be consulted, and keeping the second for his own research purposes. In 1982 he published an essay, entitled "Jeanneret and Sitte: Le Corbusier's Earliest Ideas on Urban Design", in which he provided an overview of the structure and contents of the manuscript; he went on to discuss the manuscript in later essays.[14] Thus Brooks was able to prove beyond doubt that Le Corbusier had studied Camillo Sitte's theories, and he assumed that Jeanneret's tract largely followed Sitte.

In his 1982 essay, Brooks does cite other authors who appear in *La Construction des villes*, but does not go into further detail about the position Jeanneret may have taken with regard to their ideas.[15] In 1984, Giuliano Gresleri published Jeanneret's travel journals from his journey to the East under the title *Viaggio in Oriente*, together with letters from 1910/11, both to his parents and to William Ritter, and photographs Jeanneret took on his travels at the time.[16] Although Gresleri does reconstruct Jeanneret's travels through Germany, he appears to consider these and Jeanneret's extended periods in Munich and Berlin as preparations for his journey to the East: hence he almost entirely

---

13 See Stanislaus von Moos, *Le Corbusier. Elemente einer Synthese* (Frauenfeld/Stuttgart: Huber, 1968), p. 48 (our translation): "Even after the war had broken out, Jeanneret occasionally travelled to Paris, mainly to continue his studies using the old engravings in the Bibliothèque Nationale. The problem of the big city was on his mind even then, and he worked on a study of urban design which was never published." See also Paul Venable Turner, *The Education of Le Corbusier* (New York: Garland, 1977, originally PhD diss., Harvard University, 1971). Both authors were following up hints they had seen that there might have been an unpublished study by Le Corbusier on urban design. In 1969/70 Paul Venable Turner researched Le Corbusier's personal archive up to 1920, and presumed that von Moos was referring here to Jeanneret's Carnet *A2* dating from 1915 in which there are some notes on cities, but also on individual architecture. See Turner, *The Education of Le Corbusier*, p. 121 and footnote 42, p. 220. Turner states: "Whether Le Corbusier was really referring to a completed book, or simply to an outline for a book, I was not able to find any evidence for such a project dating from 1910 in Le Corbusier's effects."

14 Harold Allen Brooks, "Jeanneret and Sitte: Le Corbusier's Earliest Ideas on Urban Design", in *In Search of Modern Architecture*, ed. Helen Searing (Cambridge, Mass.: MIT Press, 1982), pp. 278–297. This essay was republished with additional illustrations in *Casabella* 514 (1985), pp. 40–51, and in German in abridged form as Harold Allen Brooks, "Jeannerets Auseinandersetzung mit Sitte", in *Archithese* 2 (1983), pp. 29–32.

15 "Sitte's followers are also accorded praiseworthy mention in the text. These include Werner Hegemann, Karl Henrici, Theodor Goecke, Paul Schultze-Naumburg and Sitte's son Siegfried." Brooks, "Jeanneret and Sitte", p. 285.

16 Giuliano Gresleri, *Le Corbusier. Viaggio in Oriente* (Venice: Marsilio Editori, 1984), in German: *Le Corbusier. Reise nach dem Orient* (Zurich/Paris: Spur Verlag and FLC, 1991).

skates over the existence of *La Construction des villes*.[17] In 1985, Philippe Duboy compiled the first overview of all those sketches belonging to *La Construction des villes* that can be found in the Fondation Le Corbusier (FLC) in Paris.[18] In 1992, Swiss architect Marc Albert Emery prepared the first published edition of *La Construction des villes*, for which he wrote an introduction.[19] Emery made some editorial decisions for that edition which in turn raised questions about the actual structure of the manuscript.[20] Brooks' major biography *Le Corbusier's Formative Years. Charles-Edouard Jeanneret at La Chaux-de-Fonds* appeared in 1997. He describes Jeanneret's architectural education very vividly, as well as the emergence of *La Construction des villes*.[21] Yet his analysis of the manuscript dates back to 1982, and was not updated to reflect new findings: it is a summary of his own previous research.[22]

The new edition: In translation

The Manuscript presented here is a translation of the version published by gta Verlag in Zurich in 2008. Before going into detail about the translation itself, it would be worth discussing the 2008 edition briefly.

First of all, one might ask why a new edition was necessary if Emery had already compiled the material in 1992. Should the existing edition of this work not suffice, given that its author had already declared it to be lacking? This was not the case here. My own research into *La Construction des villes* began by comparing the two publicly accessible versions of the manuscript: both the photocopy that Brooks had made in the late 1970s and Emery's 1992 edition. These two documents should have been congruent, but they were not. Each version contains large parts that the other does not. I made enquiries of both Brooks and Emery, which did not resolve these incongruities: I therefore needed to return to the original.

This research was more difficult because the original manuscript is in private ownership and the owner wishes to remain anonymous. Thankfully the owner made the original available for my research; it emerged that the original not only contains all the elements not common to both the published edition and the photocopy, but also a wealth of additional material. On top of the approximately 300 pages already known, more than

17 Gresleri merely refers to an essay "agreed upon with L'Eplattenier shortly before he left [for Germany]" but mentions neither the title *La Construction des villes* nor Brooks as his source; I assume nevertheless that Gresleri had access to Brooks' essay while writing his book. Gresleri, *Le Corbusier. Reise nach dem Orient*, p. 34.

18 Duboy, *Architecture de la ville*.

19 Marc Albert Emery, *Charles-Edouard Jeanneret: La Construction des villes* (Lausanne: L'Age d'Homme, 1992).

20 Unfortunately, Emery presents the manuscript in a way which involves major editorial intervention. This includes correcting not only Jeanneret's spelling but also his formulations, occasionally completing sentences which appear incomplete, and omitting passages Emery considers unnecessary. He does not consistently document these interventions. Emery also divides the manuscript into parts which Jeanneret still considered usable in 1915, and others which he no longer deemed acceptable; this is done in the hope of fulfilling Jeanneret's wishes. Yet I cannot identify any such sorting of the manuscript on Jeanneret's part, and Emery does not document his decisions.

21 Harold Allen Brooks, *Le Corbusier's Formative Years. Charles-Edouard Jeanneret at La Chaux-de-Fonds* (Chicago: The University of Chicago Press, 1997).

22 Brooks, *Le Corbusier's Formative Years*, p. 201.

300 additional pages came to light. These first appeared to be mostly notes, but in fact the newly discovered material also contained chapter texts, complete excerpts from relevant urban design texts, and draft texts for *La Construction des villes*. This unexpected find of several hundred completely unknown manuscript pages, combined with the enlightening and fruitful analysis which I undertook as part of my PhD, made it apparent that a new critical edition of the now-complete Manuscript should be produced.

While the present book is largely a translation of both my own 2008 essay and Jeanneret's Manuscript as published at that time, I would like to point out some differences. The 2008 edition presented Jeanneret's original French text alongside a German translation. However, for this edition we decided to simply present his text in English translation. The aim was to render the Manuscript as readable and accessible as possible, while reflecting Jeanneret's source text. This meant that the 'diplomatic transcription' technique applied to demonstrate Jeanneret's thought processes in the 2008 edition has not been employed here. Admittedly this means that readers of the present book have access to less information overall; readers who require more detail should consult the original Manuscript text, as available in the 2008 gta Verlag edition.[23]

One significant difficulty with translating this work into English lies in the fact that *La Construction des villes* is a piece of writing in which the German and French languages are closely intertwined; this is because Jeanneret read most of his sources in German, then translated them into French and rewrote them for his own purposes. Very few of the texts he read were originally written in French.[24]

Jeanneret's aim and focus was not translation per se, nor was he an experienced translator, and his renderings often bear traces of the German source texts, sometimes including the source language word order. At times he includes German words which he feels unable to translate, or renders words by using a calque on the original term or another close equivalent; at times he invents new words. On occasion, this leaves the meaning of the Manuscript unclear to a reader with no knowledge of German, or distorts the meaning of his translated text. Again, less information is available overall to the English reader, but the English Manuscript will be more readable at times, and convey more of Jeanneret's intended meaning in places, than the French.

The whole Manuscript involves interplay between these two cultures and languages. As it happens, the English language does not fit neatly into this picture. Often, terms which have close equivalents in French and German, such as *place/Platz* (square), lack one in English. It also became clear that, while in the 2008 edition it made sense to set the German source text and Jeanneret's French rewrite alongside one another, allowing the reader to study the way Jeanneret adopted and reformulated ideas, this would be problematic if all the material was translated into English: how would one translate both

---

23 Christoph Schnoor, *La Construction des villes. Le Corbusiers erstes städtebauliches Traktat von 1910/11* (Zurich: gta Verlag, 2008).

24 See Christoph Schnoor, "Le Raum dans « La construction des villes » de Le Corbusier. Une traduction aux multiples strates linguistiques et culturelles", in *Traduire l'architecture. Texte et image, un passage vers la creation?* eds. Jean-Sébastien Cluzel et al. (Paris: Picard, 2015), pp. 135–144.

Kim Sanderson, "In pursuit of the intangible: A translation on Le Corbusier's early urban planning work", https://www.academia.edu/8804938/In_pursuit_of_the_intangible_A_translation_on_Le_Corbusier_s_early_urban_planning_work?source=swp_. Translated into French by Pierre Fuentes as "À la poursuite de l'intangible," *Traduire*, no. 227 (2012), pp. 47–52. http://journals.openedition.org/traduire/477; DOI: 10.4000/traduire.477

the source text (from German) and Jeanneret's version of the same text (from French), while still showing the differences between the two? It would mean artificially creating differences between the two versions, whereas Jeanneret had sought to keep his version close to the original. Hence although the present translation may appear to have been simplified, it is a highly complex work in its own right.

In some cases where Jeanneret quotes material from a book or journal, as with Muthesius' *Das englische Haus* or Laugier's *Essai*, an English translation already exists. In such cases we have used the existing English translation, indicating any points where Jeanneret's version deviates significantly from the meaning of the original. This inevitably leads to some contrasts in style from one part of the translated Manuscript to the other.

Furthermore, some of the sources we quote are written in US English, and therefore follow different spelling and grammar conventions. The quotations from Collins and Crasemann-Collins' translation of Camillo Sitte are a case in point. It should also be noted that they chose to translate 'Platz' ('place' is Jeanneret's equivalent in French) as 'plaza'; this is the cognate term, and they justify their choice by stating that 'square' is unsatisfactory when describing something which is not necessarily a regular geometric square, and may even be star-shaped. We feel that 'plaza' is not suitable in UK English, and have therefore opted for 'square' in our translations, sometimes adding a descriptive term such as 'market'. On occasion, inaccuracies or unhelpful terms and expressions in translated quotations have been amended (where this is the case, we have noted it in a footnote).

Individual words which Jeanneret uses in German are generally kept in German in the English translation. Some of the German terms which Jeanneret employs stand out because they represent key concepts in architecture and planning, and as such are of interest to the reader. We have left these in German; it often becomes clear from the context what they mean. In the Essay, some explanations of key terms are included. However, where Jeanneret retains whole German phrases, or several words in a single sentence, we could not reflect these while also ensuring the English reader would be able to understand their content. We therefore chose to translate these parts into English in their entirety. Similarly, for ease of reading, we have chosen not to reflect instances where Jeanneret uses German word order in his French writing.

In practical terms, a number of edits have been carried out to ensure the English translation of the Manuscript is easier to read. Names and references which Jeanneret had misspelled have been corrected, so readers can follow them up. Words which Jeanneret abbreviates, such as 'dans' written as 'ds', and 'un/une' as '1', are translated by their English equivalents, written out in full. We have also expanded Jeanneret's shorthand where we believed its meaning would not be obvious to the English reader, such as 'M.A.' (for 'Michel Ange') into 'Michelangelo'. Where his notes are too 'telegrammatic' to be translated meaningfully as they stand, these have also been expanded slightly in English. Text crossed out by Jeanneret is generally omitted in the English translation, provided the sections are brief and do not convey a significantly different meaning from the remaining text. Only where the crossed-out section is long or significant is it included in the English version.

Although my own essay has largely been translated as it was in 2008, some amendments have been made: both where I felt earlier formulations could be improved on, and where new findings had altered or superseded the ideas originally presented. Equally, the footnotes have been updated, both to reflect publications that have appeared in the interim and, where possible, to provide the reader with references to English versions of the relevant texts.

Thus the present book comprises an essay on and translation of Jeanneret's text, both of which aim to make his ideas accessible to an English-speaking audience. His ideas are not outdated. He may have decided they were no longer avant-garde by the time he published *Urbanisme* in 1925, but in a sense they are timeless. As such, these ideas are highly relevant today, when theorists of urban design are reflecting once again on the user's experience of cities.

In 1960, Kevin Lynch brought the experience of the passer-by in towns back into the debate with the *Image of the City*, to which Gordon Cullen added his well-known publication *Townscape* in 1962, promoting an understanding of towns and cities through serial vision techniques. In *Collage City* (1978), Colin Rowe and Fred Koetter discussed the need to understand cities from the starting point of urban space. And then for a long time the discussion died down.

More recently, Danish urban design expert Jan Gehl has brought people's experience of cities to wider attention once again with his many publications, including *Cities for People* (2010) and *Life between Buildings* (2011). Perhaps Le Corbusier's earliest attempt at addressing the experience of urban space can now also contribute to this renewed debate and offer insights relevant to today's urban design questions.

First of all, I would like to repeat my thanks to everyone who supported this complex project through the stages of my PhD, as a research project funded by Gerda-Henkel Foundation in Düsseldorf, and the publication with gta publishers in Zurich. I would like to name Prof Fritz Neumeyer, Stanislaus von Moos, and the gta publication team, in particular the late Andreas Tönnesmann.

I am grateful for the perseverance of Kim Sanderson, her thoroughness and patience which have brought this marathon of a translation to a good end.

Thanks to the publishers, starting with Valerie Rose of Ashgate, who declared her interest in this project and began working with us, this was then transferred to Routledge, for whom Grace Harrison is now looking after the book production.

I am very grateful to the manuscript owner for their kind permission to republish Le Corbusier's *La Construction des villes* in English.

Auckland, December 2019
Christoph Schnoor

Essay

Chapter 1

Jeanneret's reading and work on the Manuscript

The task: A study of urban design

Charles-Edouard Jeanneret was apprenticed to Auguste Perret in his Paris office between March 1908 and December 1909.[1] In mid-December 1909, he returned to La Chaux-de-Fonds for a few months. Here, his teacher Charles L'Eplattenier apparently told him of a conference to be held in La Chaux-de-Fonds by the *Schweizerische Städteverbund* (Swiss confederation of municipalities) in September 1910. They agreed that Jeanneret would compile a brochure on the current state of urban planning in Switzerland, with the aim of promoting alternative approaches both for Switzerland as a whole and for La Chaux-de-Fonds in particular, in line with the ideas of Camillo Sitte. This was also the thrust of an essay published by L'Eplattenier in February 1910 entitled "Le Renouveau d'art" (Renewal in art).[2] La Chaux-de-Fonds is very suitable as a focus for the theoretical exploration of urban design, since a third of the town was destroyed by a major fire in 1794.[3] Little was left of the old village, which dated from the late mediaeval period. Abraham Louis Girardet developed an initial plan for its reconstruction, the *Plan de la Nouvelle Chaux de fonds*. In 1835 a plan by Charles-Henri Junod, which could be called radical, ultimately supplied the basis for further development.[4] L'Eplattenier criticises this plan in his essay, based as it is on a schematic grid which does not respond to the local topography. Jeanneret spent part of that winter alone, and part with friends, in a farmhouse he rented on Mont Cornu close to La Chaux-de-Fonds. He visited his parents only occasionally (Fig. I), but was in regular contact with Charles L'Eplattenier.[5] His teacher secured Jeanneret a grant to write a study on the applied arts in Germany.[6] As Jeanneret explained to his parents, he also wanted to find work with an architect; thus several reasons lay behind his departure for Germany. He would initially spend a good six months there, from April until early November 1910: months dedicated almost exclusively to research on urban design.

---

1 On Jeanneret's time in Paris, see Brooks, *Le Corbusier's Formative Years*, pp. 151–183, and Pierre Vaisse, "Le Corbusier and the Gothic", in Von Moos and Rüegg, *Le Corbusier before Le Corbusier*, pp. 45–53.

2 Charles L'Eplattenier, "Renouveau d'art", in *L'Abeille*, La Chaux-de-Fonds, 20 February 1910, p. 1. See Chapter 2, 'Proposition – The collective and the universal genius'.

3 See Jacques Gubler, "La Chaux-de-Fonds", in *Inventar der neueren Schweizer Architektur*, Vol. 3, ed. Gesellschaft für Schweizerische Kunstgeschichte (Zurich: Orell Füssli, 1982), pp. 127–218.

4 Junod's extremely rationalist planning was tempered slightly from 1856 onwards by Charles Knab's plans. Gubler, "La Chaux-de-Fonds", p. 143.

5 See Brooks, *Le Corbusier's Formative Years*, pp. 185–196.

6 This *Etude sur le mouvement d'art décoratif en Allemagne* would be the first work by Jeanneret to appear in print (in La Chaux-de-Fonds in 1912).

Fig. 1 Charles-Edouard Jeanneret with parents and brother Albert, ca. 1910 (LC 108-269 BV)

Taking stock of the material

Jeanneret never completed *La Construction des villes*: it remains a collection of fragments. Yet these fragments can be largely reconstructed, and we can also deduce how Jeanneret planned to complete the Manuscript in 1910. Before we look at Jeanneret's studies in 1910 and 1911, it makes sense to begin with a relatively detailed stock take of the relevant material. The material is almost as it was when Jeanneret worked on it in 1910 and 1911. Although some photographs and at least one of his notebooks have gone missing, the bulk of Jeanneret's Manuscript has been preserved; since large sections of this resurfaced in 1999, it is all now available for research. Thus it is not only possible to reconstruct much of the Manuscript, but it is also legitimate to describe the extant material as complete (with minor exceptions).

What exactly do we mean by 'the Manuscript of *La Construction des Villes*'? In its present form, the Manuscript comprises three very different parts, the contents of which are intricately interlinked: a loose-leaf folder in A4 format, 13 cahiers (notebooks), and the body of illustrations. Photocopies of the loose-leaf folder and notebooks are preserved in the Bibliothèque de la Ville in La Chaux-de-Fonds (BV), with the originals in private ownership. Some of the original illustrations are held by the BV and some by the Fondation Le Corbusier (FLC) in Paris.

The loose-leaf folder (MA for 'MAnuscript folder') contains exclusively handwritten, mainly single-sided A4 pages sorted into chapters using paper folders, all gathered together in paperboard. In the photocopy of the Manuscript made in La Chaux-de-Fonds in 1999, this folder contains 251 pages. It is worth mentioning the number of pages in the photocopy because the Manuscript is still available for research in the BV in this format.[7] The loose-leaf folder is largely composed of finished chapters for *La Construction des Villes*. Most of these texts have been edited and a fair copy made, in some cases by Jeanneret's mother Marie Jeanneret-Perret (Fig. II).[8] Jeanneret looked through and corrected these texts again after the fair copy had been made.[9] Some chapters are still rough drafts and show evidence of several revisions. The loose-leaf folder also contains individual pages of notes or other types of text, especially in the Annex.

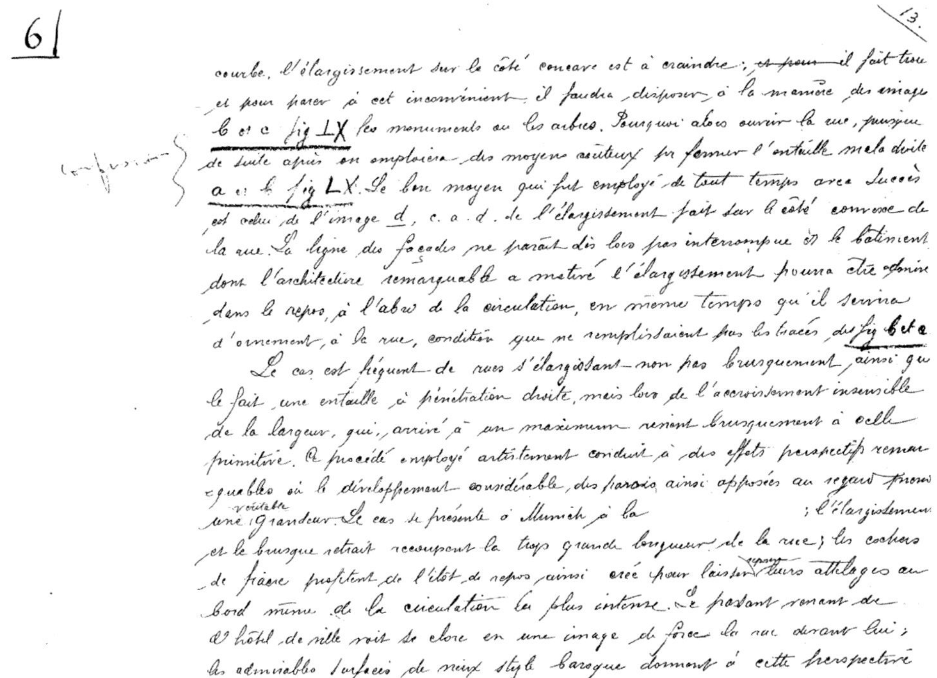
61

13.

courbe, l'élargissement sur le côté concave est à craindre; ~~et pour~~ il fait tiré et pour parer à cet inconvénient il faudra disposer à la manière des image b et c fig LX les monuments ou les arbres. Pourquoi alors ouvrir la rue, puisque de suite après on emploiera des moyens [illegible] pr fermer l'entaille mals dite a et b fig LX. Le bon moyen qui fut employé de tout temps avec succès est celui de l'image d, c. a. d. de l'élargissement fait sur le côté convexe de la rue. La ligne des façades ne paraît dès lors pas interrompue et le bâtiment dont l'architecture remarquable a motivé l'élargissement pourra être [illegible] dans le repos, à l'abri de la circulation, en même temps qu'il servira d'ornement à la rue, condition que ne remplissaient pas les tracés des fig b et a

Le cas est fréquent de rues s'élargissant non pas brusquement, ainsi que le fait une entaille à pénétration droite, mais lors de l'accroissement insensible de la largeur, qui, arrivé à un maximum revient brusquement à celle primitive. Ce procédé employé artistement conduit à des effets perspectifs remarquables où le développement considérable des parois ainsi apposées au regard [illegible] une véritable grandeur. Le cas se présente à Munich à la ; l'élargissement et le brusque retrait recoupent la trop grande longueur de la rue; les cochers de fiacre profitent de l'îlot de repos ainsi créé pour laisser reposer leurs attelages au bord même de la circulation la plus intense. Le passant venant de l'hôtel de ville voit se clore en une image de force la rue devant lui; les admirables surfaces de vieux style baroque donnent à cette perspective quelque chose d'imposant; et si, dépassant cet enclos il se retourne, l'impressi.

confusion

Fig. II Page from the chapter On Streets, handwritten by Mme Jeanneret (LCdv 108)

7 The original comprises 224 sheets, a few of which have writing on both sides; single-sided photocopies were made of all the writing.

8 Brooks comes to the conclusion that Jeanneret's mother made a clean copy of his completed chapters during his summer stay in La Chaux-de-Fonds. Brooks, *Le Corbusier's Formative Years*, p. 228.

9 Some of these corrections date from 1910; some corrections in the Manuscript are from 1915.

The cahiers are school exercise books, in A5 format, with handwriting on both sides of each page. There are 13 notebooks in all, some entirely filled with notes, others only partly so; these cover 346 pages in their photocopied version. They encompass a wider range of text types than the folder: notes of various sorts, as well as tables of contents, excerpts, transcriptions, and translations (Fig. 118). Some of the cahiers are similar in nature to Jeanneret's *Carnets de voyages*; three contain the text of chapters (Fig. III).[10]

Immediately after coming across the cahiers, I decided to number these consecutively, despite the risk of making a premature decision which might later be contradicted by a more precise dating. This initial numbering has largely withstood subsequent scrutiny,

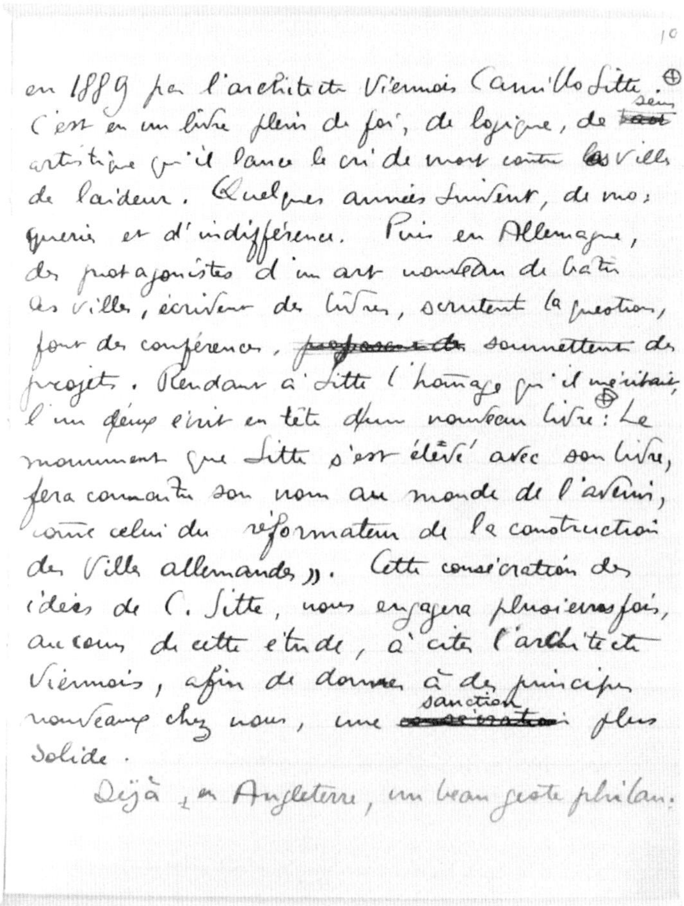
10

en 1889 par l'architecte Viennois Camillo Sitte. ⊕
C'est en un livre plein de foi, de logique, de ~~tact~~ sens
artistique qu'il lance le cri de mort contre les villes
de laideur. Quelques années suivent, de mo-
queries et d'indifférence. Puis en Allemagne,
des protagonistes d'un art nouveau de bâtir
les villes, écrivent des livres, scrutent la question,
font des conférences, ~~proposent et~~ soumettent des
projets. Rendant à Sitte l'hommage qu'il méritait, ⊕
l'un d'eux écrit en tête d'un nouveau livre: Le
monument que Sitte s'est élevé avec son livre,
fera connaître son nom au monde de l'avenir,
comme celui du réformateur de la construction
des Villes allemandes ». Cette considération des
idées de C. Sitte, nous engagera plusieurs fois,
au cours de cette étude, à citer l'architecte
Viennois, afin de donner à des principes
nouveaux chez nous, une ~~consécration~~ sanction plus
solide.

Déjà, en Angleterre, un beau geste philan-

Fig. III Page from Cahier C.1 *Considérations générales* (LCdv 37)

10 See Le Corbusier, *Les Voyages d'Allemagne. Carnet*, ed. by Giuliano Gresleri (Paris/Milan: FLC/Electa, 1994 [English edition 2002]), and Le Corbusier, *Voyages d'Orient. Carnets*, ed. by Giuliano Gresleri (Paris/Milan: FLC/Electa, 1987 [English edition 2002]).

with one exception: the cahier *General Considerations*, although initially numbered C.1, was actually started in October 1910. The cahiers *City II*, *City III*, and *City IV*, dating from April to June, were numbered C.2 to C.4; unfortunately, the cahier *City I* is missing. The cahier *Trees Monuments* was numbered C.5, which appears to be chronologically consistent. The cahier *Cities VI Squares Gardens I* was numbered C.6, following Jeanneret's numbering. The two cahiers which contain long sections of the chapter On Squares, *Squares Text I* and *Squares Text II*, were numbered C.7 and C.8. These were followed by two cahiers containing notes and excerpts on cemeteries and garden cities (*Garden Cities Cemetery I* and *II*), originating in or around October 1910, which I numbered C.9 and C.10. The last three cahiers, containing excerpts from texts by Theodor Fischer, Roland Fréart, and Marc Antoine Laugier, were numbered C.11–13 in line with the dates Jeanneret attributed to them.[11]

In accordance with the above cahier sequence, I also consecutively numbered those pages of the cahiers with writing on, from p. C.1, 1 to C.13, 346. The loose-leaf folder was also numbered consecutively, with page numbers preceded by 'MA', ranging between MA 1 and 251. However, this sequence has been altered in the present edition of the Manuscript so that the notes and texts are ordered thematically: the pages of the Manuscript were given the prefix LCdv and numbered LCdv 1 to 544. Pages from the Manuscript are therefore always cited with this prefix.

The illustrations which Jeanneret intended to include in *La Construction des villes* are also integral to the Manuscript. This body of illustrations comprises sketches, postcards, and photos. It is not clear exactly how many there would have been in his book, since Jeanneret's notes only occasionally indicate clearly which of his many photos of important urban design situations and postcards of urban layouts he actually intended to use to illustrate the Manuscript. Often, all that can be documented is that Jeanneret planned to use a particular subject or postcard as an illustration at some stage. A significant number of his photographs of urban situations have clearly been lost. Jeanneret mentions 20 to 30 photographs of La Chaux-de-Fonds which he took in spring 1910 and wanted to have sent to Munich. The photographs can no longer be traced and have therefore been replaced in this volume by comparable views of La Chaux-de-Fonds from around 1910, taken from the collection at the BV. The illustrations which can be most precisely identified are those from Jeanneret's collection of his own sketches and drawings, comprising over 70 sheets. These are kept at the FLC in Paris, with additional sketches from 1915.[12] Some further sketches can be found in the loose-leaf folder and the cahiers. In most cases it is possible to ascertain which illustration should be used where, as Jeanneret allocated many of the drawings and sketches to particular points in the text. Jeanneret's collection of postcards and photos is archived in the BV. We cannot enter into a detailed analysis of this portion of the illustrations; it merits a separate investigation. Therefore in some cases we can merely indicate which photographs and postcards Jeanneret apparently planned to use for the Manuscript.

11 Numbering the cahiers 1 to 13 was an attempt to take account of two factors: the chronological sequence in which they were produced, and Jeanneret's own numbering of cahiers *Ville II* to *IV* and *VI*.

12 Jeanneret carefully stored the sketches between the pages of the 1914 *Schweizerisches Bau-Adreßbuch* (Swiss Construction Address Book). They are to be found under B2-20 FLC. Brooks indicates that Jeanneret put a stamp on his 1915 sketches in order to distinguish them from those made in 1910. See Brooks, *Le Corbusier's Formative Years*, p. 404. Additional criteria exist by which to check the time they were made, such as the style of the sketch or references to library shelf marks.

The work in its latest form: Jeanneret's final table of contents

A very comprehensive table of contents for the Manuscript can be derived from the information on five title pages contained in the loose-leaf folder. These pages supply the latest of Jeanneret's many draft tables of contents from 1910. The texts in the loose-leaf folder are ordered thus:

Proposition

FIRST PART

FIRST CHAPTER
General Considerations

§1.-   Purpose of this study
§2.-   General principles
§3.-   Present state of the debate
§4.-   Fundamental error

SECOND CHAPTER
On the Elements of the City
§1. Overview or Introduction
§2. On Blocks
§3. On Streets
§4. On Squares
§5. On Enclosing Walls
§6. On Bridges
§7. On Trees
§8. On Gardens and Parks
§9. On Cemeteries
§10. Garden cities[13]

THIRD CHAPTER
On Possible Strategies

SECOND PART
Critical application
La Chaux-de-Fonds

Annex[14]

As shown above, Jeanneret begins his Manuscript with the Proposition. The first chapter in the first section comprises General Considerations on urban design around the turn of

---

13 LCdv 55. The last line appears to have been added later. It does not contain the article "des", and the handwriting is different. The observations detailed below would seem to indicate that Jeanneret decided in October 1910 – i.e. late in his working process – to include garden cities as part of the analysis, and therefore to include them under the 'constituent parts of a city'.

14 This overview was compiled on the basis of pages LCdv 23, 24, 55 and 359.

the century. He divides this chapter into four subsections, entitled The Aim of the Study, Guiding Principles, The Present State of the Debate, and A Fundamental Error.[15] In the second section of his study, Jeanneret presents what he sees as the constituent parts of a town or city (*les éléments constitutifs de la ville*). Jeanneret has planned ten subsections: an introduction, residential blocks, streets, squares, enclosing walls, bridges, trees, gardens and parks, cemeteries and garden cities.[16] Yet Jeanneret only succeeded in completing half of the subsections he had planned: those on residential blocks, streets, squares and enclosing walls, and the introduction that goes with them.[17] For the sections on bridges, trees, gardens and parks, cemeteries and garden cities, Jeanneret compiled a substantial amount of material and made some comments, but did not rework this material into finished texts. The second chapter in the second section is dedicated to *les moyens possibles*: an approximate translation of this would be 'possible strategies', in the sense of potential planning methods and theories to be employed.[18] In the third section of the study, Jeanneret addresses urban development and the state of his home town, La Chaux-de-Fonds.[19] The Annex rounds off the text, and contains material for a second part of the chapter on La Chaux-de-Fonds, which was never written.

To Munich

Jeanneret left La Chaux-de-Fonds for Munich on 7 April 1910. He travelled via Karlsruhe and Stuttgart, stopping for one day in each place, and Ulm, where he broke his journey on 10 April; he arrived in Munich that evening. Here, he stayed overnight with his Swiss friend Octave Matthey; he found a room at No. 3 Lotzbeckstraße the very next day, where he stayed (with some breaks) until 17 October, almost exactly six months. Jeanneret started work on the study of urban design immediately. He researched in the *Königliche Hof- und Staatsbibliothek zu München* (Royal Bavarian Library, RBL) and the small library at the *Bayerisches Nationalmuseum* (Bavarian National Museum, BNM).

A search for the earliest-dated entries in the Manuscript leads us to the Cahier Jeanneret called *City III*, which he had bought especially for his library research. Why *City III*, if these are the earliest entries? First, it is plausible that there was a notebook entitled *City I*, though none has been preserved; this may have contained excerpts from Sitte and Henrici. Second, although it is surprising that the entries in notebook *City II Bridges* were not made earlier than those in *City III*, our findings indicate that we can realistically assume some entries in *City III* were made between 10 and 15 April. These are: a brief initial table of contents; a short bibliography; and an outline spanning several

---

15 These four subsections are: Destination de cette étude, Principes guides, Etat actuel de la question, Une erreur fondamentale.

16 These ten subsections are: Vue d'ensemble ou Introduction, Des Chésaux, Des Rues, Des Places, Des Murs de Clôture, Des Ponts, Des Arbres, Des Jardins et Parcs, Des Cimetières, Cités-Jardins.

17 Jeanneret denotes these parts on individual urban design topics as subsections within the second chapter ('paragraphes'). Yet they are as long as entire chapters; for this reason and for ease of reference I will refer to them below as 'chapters'.

18 The heading, which on p. LCdv 23 remains Les Moyens utiles modernes possibles, becomes Des Moyens possibles in the actual chapter heading (LCdv 326).

19 LCdv 359: Application critique. La Chaux-de-Fonds.

pages, which Jeanneret enclosed in a letter to L'Eplattenier dated 16 and 18 April.[20] The initial table of contents reads:

> Proposition. (a) philosophical point of view. (b) satisfaction point of view.
> (a) in which there is a dream of shared living to make [__] easier (b) listing the plastic, utilitarian, hygienic and moral characteristics.
> La Ch-de-Fonds before the fire
> The town created over the past 20 years: critique
> Conclusion[:] Proposed new features. remedies[21]

Thus Jeanneret intended to begin the study with a 'proposition' investigating the formation of towns and cities from two different angles: (a) the philosophical viewpoint (which turns out to be more anthropological or sociological); and (b) the practical, i.e. technical and architectural, viewpoint. In the next chapter, divided into two parts, he analyses and assesses La Chaux-de-Fonds past and present. In his conclusion, Jeanneret plans to suggest improvements to the urban design situation in La Chaux-de-Fonds. The following page of the cahier contains the bibliography, which already features several titles of significance for *La Construction des villes* (Fig. IV):

> Camillo Sitte.
> Claudel: L'Arbre (la Ville)
> V. Cousin. Le vrai, le beau, le juste. [Sic, for: Du vrai, du beau et du bien]
> Henrici Aesthetik im Städtebau. 47$^{\underline{id}}$
> Berlepsch-Valendas. Eine Studie über Städtebau in England.
> Muthesius das Englische Haus. –
> buy G. Le Bon. Psychologie de l'éducation, Baedeker Süddeutschland 2.50 [illegible] von der Tann)[22]

Under the title of Karl Henrici's *Beiträgen zur Ästhetik im Städtebau*, Jeanneret noted down the shelf mark in the Royal Bavarian Library. This is the first fully referenced book to appear in the Manuscript, and the shelf mark establishes beyond doubt that Jeanneret's research took place in that library. Jeanneret purchased Victor Cousin's philosophical work on truth, beauty, and goodness *Du Vrai, du beau et du bien* in May 1910.

---

20 "I enclose a sheet summarising an initial idea of the small work we discussed: you could return it to me, adding in the margin corrections and additions. Do I dare ask you to show this letter to my parents? This is so that I don't have to rewrite the same things twice." Jeanneret to L'Eplattenier, 16/18 April 1910 (E2-12-53 FLC). His request that L'Eplattenier show the letter to his parents indicates that the Jeanneret-Perrets are aware, at least in principle, of their son's work on a study of urban design; yet they are truly astonished when Edouard reports in detail on the project, in a letter dated 29 June.

21 LCdv 424.

22 LCdv 426. The full titles are: Camillo Sitte, *Der Städtebau nach seinen künstlerischen Grundsätzen* (Wien: Carl Graeser, 1889). Paul Claudel, *L'Arbre. Tête d'or. L'échange. La ville. La jeune fille Violaine. Le repos du septième jour* (Paris: Mercure de France, 1901). Victor Cousin, *Du Vrai, du beau et du bien* (Paris: Didier, 1853). Karl Henrici, *Beiträge zur praktischen Ästhetik im Städtebau. Eine Sammlung von Vorträgen und Aufsätzen* (Munich: Callwey, 1904). Hans-Eduard von Berlepsch-Valendàs, "Eine Studie über Städtebau in England – Hampstead", in *Kunst und Kunsthandwerk* 12 (1909), Vol. 5, pp. 241–284. Hermann Muthesius, *Das Englische Haus: Entwicklung, Bedingungen, Anlage, Aufbau, Einrichtung und Innenraum*, 3 vol.s (Berlin: Ernst Wasmuth, 1904/1911). Gustave le Bon, *Psychologie de l'éducation* (Paris: E. Flammarion, 1909).

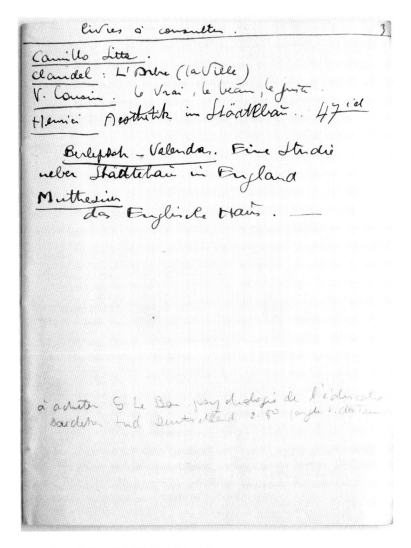

Fig. IV Bibliography in Cahier C.3 *Ville III* (LCdv 426)

Astonishingly, this is the only work which Jeanneret listed in his bibliography or used for *La Construction des villes* that coincides with Paul Venable Turner's 1971 bibliography of books Le Corbusier owned! Yet Jeanneret was not especially interested in its contents; Turner establishes that he had not even cut its pages.[23] Equally, Paul Claudel's collection of writing on urban design literature is not significant here (but Jeanneret did read Claudel in 1910 with great interest). Even Gustave le Bon's *Psychologie de*

---

23 Turner, *The Education of Le Corbusier*, p. 82f. The book held at the FLC bears the inscription 'Mai 1910' in
     Jeanneret's handwriting.

l'éducation is not mentioned again in the Manuscript, although Le Corbusier's personal library contained a whole series of Le Bon's works.[24]

It is particularly noteworthy that, at this early stage, Jeanneret planned to work on Hermann Muthesius' *Das englische Haus* and Hans-Eduard von Berlepsch-Valendàs' essay on Hampstead Garden Suburb. Brooks assumes that the idea of looking at gardens, garden cities, and other 'green' issues in urban planning came from L'Eplattenier, and should be dated back to the summer when Jeanneret was in La Chaux-de-Fonds.[25] However, the presence of these two titles here indicates that, from the very beginning, Jeanneret envisaged writing a wide-ranging study of urban design. The central entry in the bibliography is of course the work by Camillo Sitte. We shall explore it in greater detail below.

Mid-April 1910: Approaching the material

Immediately after listing these books in the Cahier *City III*, Jeanneret includes an initial comprehensive overview of ideas and roughly subdivides his material. This is the outline which he enclosed with his letter of 16/18 April, for L'Eplattenier's approval. It comprises three major sections, Thèse (Proposition), La Ville and La Chaux-de-Fonds. It helps if we look at the subtitles of these sections in more detail. The following table of contents does not appear anywhere in the Manuscript in exactly this form, but it is a summary of the titles which appear in the overview, from which we can extrapolate the logical plan for the Manuscript's structure.

> A Proposition 1-12
> B 1. What is a city? a) useful b) hygienic c) beautiful. Summary – the 3 cities, their limits and crossover. 2. Conclusion – (put at the end)
> Summary – Sacrifice of self, for all.
> Critical and practical study. La Chaux-de-Fonds from 100 years ago. La Chaux-de-Fonds of today.[26]

This overview will be discussed in more detail in Chapter 2 of the present essay. Whereas it was initially divided into two main sections, the Manuscript has now been divided into three, with the Proposition acting as an introduction. Jeanneret placed great importance on describing the three necessary properties of urban design as he saw them, through the filter of his current urban design and architecture knowledge. Following a summary which adds no further detail, he launches into the critical study of La Chaux-de-Fonds, the real reason behind the entire investigation. A list of possible illustrations was also among the first work done on *La Construction des villes*; these are noted in an annex to the overview.[27] Here, Jeanneret only lists squares and streets which he has visited for himself.[28] (Fig. V)

24 "I spent a superb evening yesterday re-reading Claudel: La jeune fille Violaine. I do believe it was the first time since I have been in Munich that I have savoured a cosy hour of poetry." Jeanneret to L'Eplattenier, 7 July 1910 (E2-12-70 FLC). For an overview of Le Corbusier's own library, see Arnaud Dercelles, "Présentation de la bibliothèque personnelle de Le Corbusier", in *Le Corbusier et le livre*, exhibition catalogue (Barcelona etc.: COAC, 2005), pp. 6–78.

25 Brooks, *Le Corbusier's Formative Years*, p. 229.

26 LCdv 427–429.

27 LCdv 430.

28 Hence 'Plan of Stuttgart', 'New district of Stuttgart', 'Curjel and Moser church//Rue Billing//Plan of Karlsruhe' – these subjects date from his journey to Munich (via Karlsruhe, Stuttgart and Ulm); 'Plan of Siena

Fig. V Zytglogge tower in Solothurn. Photo by Jeanneret, ca. 1910 (LC 108-297 BV)

The introductory text 'La Ville!' spans six pages of *City III*, as described below.[29] Jean-neret probably wrote this immediately after 18 April, since he quotes Victor Cousin's *Du Vrai, du beau et du bien* incorrectly, as he does in his bibliographical list, indicating that he had yet to receive a response from L'Eplattenier about the title of the book.

On Saturday 16 April, Jeanneret visited Theodor Fischer at his studio. He was impressed by the buildings Fischer had designed, which he had seen in Stuttgart and Ulm. Fischer was unable to offer Jeanneret a position at his studio immediately, but invited him to his house on Sunday, 17 April. Jeanneret reported back enthusiastically

(Palio square, longitudinal section of cathedral (baptistery square)//Piazza Signoria Florence//Pisa' might be references to Sitte, but Jeanneret did visit all of these places on his travels in Italy in 1907. The same is true of the 'Plan of the Ring in Vienna', which can be found in Sitte's book but was also known to Jeanneret from first-hand experience. It goes without saying that Jeanneret had seen the Swiss examples himself.

29 LCdv 10–15.

on this visit, in a letter to L'Eplattenier dated 16/18 April.[30] Unfortunately not much is known about the technical part of their discussion, which must have ranged beyond the question of obtaining a position in Fischer's office. The two men certainly discussed urban design, and probably also named books on the subject. Nevertheless, in his work on *La Construction des villes* Jeanneret is remarkably reticent about Fischer's work. One might expect Jeanneret to incorporate Fischer's 1903 booklet *Stadterweiterungsfragen*, on questions of urban expansion, into his bibliography after their discussion: he does not. Jeanneret's only direct reference to the booklet is in a note he made in *City III* in May. Surprisingly, he did not take any excerpts from *Stadterweiterungsfragen* straight away,[31] but instead waited until November 1910 – after he had left Munich.

An attempt to date Cahier *City II Bridges*

In April, Jeanneret also began the Cahier *City II Bridges*. To prove this date, we must take a small argumentative detour; it will prove worthwhile as it will allow us to clearly date some of Jeanneret's most important reading. The very first entry Jeanneret made in *City II Bridges* states: "Ask L'Eplattenier for photos of La Chaux-de-Fonds."[32] He does so in a letter which is not dated, but nevertheless provides evidence within the first few lines to date the Cahier very precisely to the last week of April 1910:

> I am writing to you again because, since Fischer was away last week, nothing has been decided on that score – I am busying myself with the brochure we discussed. I need to gather the necessary material. Firstly, I found in the library where I am working several interesting works – which I must translate, thus learning German, but making slow progress.[33]

This dating is based on Jeanneret's statement "I am writing to you again," as the last dated letter to L'Eplattenier is from 16/18 April. If Jeanneret is apologising like this, the letter in question may have been written around a week later; it is probable that he had yet to receive an answer from his teacher. Another aid to dating this letter lies in Jeanneret's words "since Fischer was away last week". As Jeanneret visited Fischer on 17 April, this letter must date from the following weekend at the earliest, i.e. around 24 April. Jeanneret asks L'Eplattenier in the course of the letter for photographs, plans, and drawings of both La Chaux-de-Fonds and other Swiss towns and cities:

---

30 E2-12-61-64 FLC. See Brooks, *Le Corbusier's Formative Years*, p. 213.

31 "Translate Theodor Fischer page 16", LCdv 443. The excerpt directly preceding this shows that it must refer to *Stadterweiterungsfragen*: here, Jeanneret translates a passage on the character of a city from the book by Johann Hubatschek, *Die bautechnischen Aufgaben einer modernen Stadt* (Linz: E. Mareis, 1905). On p. 16 of *Stadterweiterungsfragen*, Fischer describes the "Steigerung des Charakteristischen", the idea of "Intensifying characteristic aspects": Theodor Fischer, *Stadterweiterungsfragen* (Stuttgart: DVA, 1903).

32 "réclamer L'Ep photos Ch-de-Fds" (LCdv 404).

33 "München, Lotzbeckstrasse 3, IIIst. [third floor] Mon cher Monsieur, Je vous écris de nouveau, car Fischer ayant été absent la semaine dernière, rien n'a été décidé de ce côté-là – je m'occupe de la brochure dont nous avons parlé. Il me faut réunir les matériaux nécessaires. D'abord, j'ai trouvé à la Bibliothèque où je travaille chaque jour quelques ouvrages intéressants – que je suis obligé de traduire, apprenant ainsi l'allemand, mais avançant lentement." Jeanneret to L'Eplattenier, circa late April 1910 (E2-12-72–73 FLC).

I thought as well that, instead of employing the great famous monuments in cities as examples, like Sitte did, it would be more politically astute to utilise almost exclusively beauties which appear in our Swiss towns, well-known ones which everyone has seen or could see. The question then is to get hold of useful documentation. As regards La Chaux-de-Fonds, I would like to have one or two plans dating from before the fire [pre-1794] and several views relating to this, prints, woodcuts or engravings, which could be found in the historical Museum or the archives. [...] I have a number of postcards of Berne, Solothurn etc., which do not thrill me. I find that photographs do not illustrate very well that which we intend to emphasise. Oh how I regret not having bothered about this problem before; had I bothered, I would have brought back amazing documentation from my travels. [...] To summarise: I need precise materials, useful materials. Could you acquire some for me on La Chaux-de-Fonds? Shall I write to Berne, or do you think you would get better results? Could I have one set of prints from the photographs of La Chaux-de-Fonds which I took in March?[34]

If the undated letter originated on or around 24 April, then the first entry in *City II Bridges* must have been made prior to that letter. It is however impossible to date this entry more precisely.

There are two works of major importance to Jeanneret that do not feature in the initial bibliography described above. These are Albert Erich Brinckmann's 1908 historical investigation on squares and monuments, entitled *Platz und Monument*, and a 1906 book with the title *Der Städtebau*, part of Paul Schultze-Naumburg's series of cultural works *Kulturarbeiten,* which spans several volumes.[35] It is clear from the cahiers that Jeanneret did in fact study both books very soon after arriving in Munich: on the first few pages of *City II Bridges* Jeanneret takes excerpts and translates from Schultze-Naumburg's *Kulturarbeiten Städtebau*; he also notes down excerpts from *Platz und Monument* on the following pages, and after the initial overview of contents in *City III*.[36] It is here that the somewhat laborious dating of the opening remarks in *City II Bridges* proves its worth, as the excerpts from Schultze-Naumburg can therefore be dated with relative certainty towards the end of April.

This is an opportune moment to mention the missing Cahier *City I*. It is remarkable that none of the available cahiers contains even a single excerpt or translation from

---

34 "J'ai aussi pensé qu'au lieu d'employer comme exemple démonstratif les grands monuments célèbres des grandes villes comme l'a fait Sitte, il serait dans un esprit plus politique de se servir à peu près uniquement des beautés que nous offrent nos villes suisses, celles très connues, que chacun a vues ou pourra voir. La question est donc de se procurer des documents utiles. Pour ce qui concerne La Chaux-de-Fonds, j'aimerais avoir un ou deux plans datant d'avant l'incendie et quelques vues y relatives, estampes ou gravures, que l'on doit trouver au musée historique ou aux archives. [...] J'ai une certaine quantité de cartes postales de Berne, Soleure etc., qui ne m'enchantent pas. Je trouve que la photo n'illustre pas bien ce que nous pensons souligner. Combien je regrette de ne pas [m'être soucié] de ce problème; autrefois, j'eusse rapporté de mes voyages des documents épatants. [...] Je me résume donc: il me faut des matériaux précises, utiles. Pouvez-vous me procurer ceux sur La Chaux-de-Fonds; dois-je écrire à Berne, ou pensez-vous obtenir meilleur résultat en le faisant? Pourrai-je avoir 1 série d'épreuves des photos de La Chaux-de-Fonds que j'avais prises en Mars?" Jeanneret to L'Eplattenier, circa late April 1910, E2-12-72–73 FLC.

35 Brinckmann, *Platz und Monument*. Paul Schultze-Naumburg, *Der Städtebau*, vol. 4 of *Kulturarbeiten* (Munich: Callwey, 1906).

36 See LCdv 405–413, and LCdv 431ff.

Sitte's *Künstlerischer Städtebau* or Henrici's *Beiträge*, despite Jeanneret's early inclusion of both books in his bibliography; as we will see in Chapter 3, he also refers to them frequently. Perhaps excerpts from these two books were contained in the Cahier *City I*, which has not survived. Unfortunately, due to a lack of evidence this remains mere supposition.

Jeanneret studies Sitte's *Städtebau*

Before Jeanneret left for Munich, L'Eplattenier certainly told him about Camillo Sitte's *Der Städtebau nach seinen künstlerischen Grundsätzen*. Perhaps Jeanneret had already read parts of L'Eplattenier's own copy, back in La Chaux-de-Fonds. Did he already know it well, and therefore not need to list the full title in his reading list? He did not seem to know the German title, as L'Eplattenier owned the French edition. It is therefore only logical for Jeanneret to ask in his first letter to L'Eplattenier, dated 16/18 April, not only for the correct title of Cousin's text but also for precise details of Sitte's book: "could you please give me the exact title of the book by Victor Cousin 'Du Beau... (?)' and the publisher of the work by Camillo Sitte?"[37] On the other hand, it is hard to understand why Jeanneret did not seek this information from the library. And why would L'Eplattenier know who published the German edition if he himself owned the French? The two had obviously discussed Sitte and his book; the name will also have cropped up in Jeanneret's conversations with Theodor Fischer. Why did Jeanneret not simply borrow the book in the library reading room, which he could have done from the beginning of April onwards?

To answer this question, we must first look at which edition Jeanneret was working on in Munich, especially given the speculation on this issue to be found in the literature.[38] Collins and Crasemann-Collins claim, and maintain in the new edition of their book on Camillo Sitte dated 1986, that Jeanneret was misled by the French edition entitled *L'Art de bâtir les villes*. Its translator and editor Camille Martin added his own romanticising chapter on curved streets, which they say Jeanneret believed to have been penned by Sitte himself.[39] Jeanneret, however, knew of the difference between the German and French versions; there is evidence that he used both versions during his work on *La Construction des villes*. The illustrations which Jeanneret copied from Sitte's book clearly show that he used the German edition for this, as he mainly adopts Sitte's German-language captions. Furthermore, in many cases the

---

37 "Pourriez-vous s.v.p. me donner le titre exacte du livre de Victor Cousin: 'du Beau ...(?)['] de même que l'éditeur de l'ouvrage de Camillo Sitte." Jeanneret to L'Eplattenier, 16/18 April 1910, E2-12-61 FLC.

38 Brooks could have clarified this issue in 1982: he believes that Jeanneret was familiar with the German edition of Sitte's *Der Städtebau nach seinen künstlerischen Grundsätzen*, but does not substantiate this. See Brooks, "Jeanneret and Sitte", p. 279.

39 See the landmark work on Sitte, containing comprehensive critical material: George Collins and Christiane Crasemann Collins, *Camillo Sitte: The Birth of Modern City Planning* (New York: Rizzoli, 1986), a reworking of the first edition: *Camillo Sitte and the Birth of Modern City Planning* (New York/London: Random House/Phaidon, 1965), which contains a slightly updated version of the English translation of Sitte's *Städtebau*, first published as: Camillo Sitte, *City Planning According to Artistic Principles*, trans. George R. Collins and Christiane Crasemann Collins (New York: Random House, 1965). To differentiate between these two editions of the translation, we refer to the 1986 translation as Sitte, "City Planning According to Artistic Principles". The French edition of Sitte is: Camillo Sitte, *L'Art de bâtir les villes. Notes et réflexions d'un architecte traduites et complétées par Camille Martin* (Geneva: Eggiman, 1902).

illustrations Martin uses differ from Sitte, so Jeanneret's source is obvious. The fact that Jeanneret also referred to the French edition, *L'Art de bâtir les villes*, is confirmed by several quotations for which he states the page numbers in his Manuscript. This is unusual for Jeanneret's way of working: nowhere else on pages of text in the Manuscript did he quote page numbers – he only did so in the notes he made on pages containing illustrations, and in the cahiers, if he needed the information to find the page again himself. In four cases, Jeanneret quoted page numbers from *L'Art de bâtir les villes* for the same reason: not quoting in full, he required the precise details in order to find the quotations later.[40] These instances, with often only the first line of text, and then only page and line numbers, prove that Jeanneret used the French edition of Sitte's book alongside the German edition for his work on the Manuscript. In 1910, he read both versions and worked with both at different levels of intensity: the German edition in Munich and the French in La Chaux-de-Fonds. It is clear even from a superficial comparison that Jeanneret does not refer to Camille Martin's chapter 'Des Rues', in his own writing: Jeanneret's chapter on streets does not, as Martin did, mention streets in Bruges, Geneva, and Lübeck, either as illustrations or in the text. And although the theories which Jeanneret formulates about streets and their layout are similar to Martin's ideas, the detail differs too much for him to have taken them from Martin – unlike the formulations from Brinckmann and Schultze-Naumburg, which are still recognisable even after Jeanneret has translated them into French.[41]

When did Jeanneret begin to work with the German edition of Sitte's *Städtebau nach seinen künstlerischen Grundsätzen*, and what evidence is there to support this? In the undated letter from late April described above, Jeanneret writes to L'Eplattenier:

> That is why I thought, noting that many authors cite Sitte's book as the monument which has renewed architecture in German cities, that I could easily and fairly frequently draw on him for quotations. I will thus have questions of capital importance

40 Two examples will illustrate Jeanneret's way of quoting. First, in the chapter On Possible Strategies (LCdv 352) Jeanneret refers to a section from Sitte's book which he would like to quote. Yet he does not cite the exact point in the text, simply noting: "Sitte 145" and "page 145 (Sitte)". Emery assumes this page number refers to the French edition, see Emery, *Charles-Edouard Jeanneret: La Construction des Villes*, p. 159. This is indeed correct: the German p. 145 does not marry with Jeanneret's observations here. However, it is almost impossible to provide any further or conclusive proof, since Jeanneret fails to note where the quotation begins and ends.

Second, Jeanneret quotes Camillo Sitte in the chapter On Streets (LCdv 96). Here, he is more precise: he states the page and line numbers for the passage which he plans to quote, although not where it ends: "let us quote some lines from Camillo Sitte [. . .]: "[W]hat architect is afraid of an irregularly shaped building lot?" Sitte page 130 line 14." See Sitte, *Der Städtebau nach seinen künstlerischen Grundsätzen*, p. 97; Collins and Crasemann Collins, *Camillo Sitte: The Birth of Modern City Planning*, p. 225; Sitte, trans. Martin, *L'Art de bâtir les villes*, p. 130. Jeanneret's section of text corresponds fully with Martin's text, proving that Jeanneret has taken this detail from the French edition.

One of these examples is found in the text which Jeanneret's mother wrote up; the other was noted by Jeanneret himself, but in an unedited draft version of the text for On Possible Strategies. This means that both quotations date from summer 1910 in La Chaux-de-Fonds, and that Jeanneret had access to the French edition of Sitte's book, probably Charles L'Eplattenier's copy.

41 This refutes Collins' theory that Le Corbusier's dislike of the picturesque street layout stems from the chapter Martin added. See Collins and Crasemann Collins, *Camillo Sitte: The Birth of Modern City Planning*, p. 116.

resolved by a master and that will enable me to avoid the excessive lengths to which I always go to express myself.[42]

It emerges from this part of the letter that initially, Jeanneret was not working with Sitte's book but instead with authors who quoted Sitte, in his role as "the monument which has renewed architecture in German cities". This formulation belongs to Karl Henrici, whose book Jeanneret was clearly already reading at this stage.[43] He did not ask to borrow L'Eplattenier's edition of Sitte until 19 May:

> I'm not giving up, but I have had no luck. I had requested Cousin and Sitte. I have received the Cousin, but I am told the Sitte is out of print. Now I need that book, but I've been left high and dry. I must therefore ask you to send me your copy [...].[44]

On 2 June, Jeanneret asked L'Eplattenier for the book again.[45] Why did he repeatedly ask his teacher for his French edition of Sitte? In his foreword Karl Henrici states how important Camillo Sitte has been for German urban design, and Schultze-Naumburg and Brinckmann also refer to Sitte. It must have occurred to Jeanneret that he could save himself a lot of arduous argumentation by quoting directly from Sitte; hence he asked L'Eplattenier whether he agreed with this approach. Yet if he was to quote Sitte word for word, and avoid the unnecessary effort of retranslating him into French, Jeanneret needed the French edition.

We can assume that by the end of April, Jeanneret had access to the German version, as he wrote to L'Eplattenier that he wanted to describe Swiss towns and cities, which would lend the study greater local relevance, "instead of employing the great famous monuments in cities as examples, like Sitte did". It is interesting that Jeanneret does not appear to have believed L'Eplattenier's claim that Sitte was the central figure in the movement to reform German urban design until he learned this from other authors.[46] Jeanneret's request for the French edition was left unanswered, for reasons which remain

42 "Aussi ai-je pensé, constatant que beaucoup d'auteurs citent le livre de Sitte comme étant le monument qui à rénové l'architecture des villes allemandes, que je pourrais facilement et assez fréquemment lui emprunter des citations. J'aurai ainsi des questions d'importance capitale résolues par un maître et cela m'évitera les longueurs que je fais toujours pour m'exprimer." Jeanneret to L'Eplattenier, circa late April 1910, E2-12-72–73 FLC.

43 In Cahier C.1, General Considerations (LCdv 34), Jeanneret uses this quotation again: "To render unto Sitte the praise which he is due, one of them writes at the start of the new book: 'The monument which Sitte erected with his book, will make his name known in tomorrow's world, as the reformer of German city planning.' This consecration of C. Sitte's ideas will engage us several times, during the course of this study, to quote the Viennese architect, in order to give principles which are new to our country, firmer approval." This is indeed very close to Henrici's formulation in German – "Das Denkmal, welches sich Sitte mit diesem Buch gesetzt hat, wird der Nachwelt seinen Namen künden als den des Reformators des deutschen Städtebaues." It proves that Jeanneret used Henrici as a yardstick when verifying the importance of Sitte's ideas: a necessary safeguard against Jeanneret blindly following L'Eplattenier on Sitte's importance for urban design.

44 Jeanneret to L'Eplattenier, 19 May 1910, E2-12-65 FLC.

45 "It's just that I really need the Sitte now. My approaches to bookshops have remained fruitless, the work is no longer to be found. Since you will not miss yours, you would be doing me a great favour if you could send it to me." Jeanneret to L'Eplattenier, 2 June 1910, E2-12-66 FLC.

46 Jeanneret to L'Eplattenier, circa late April 1910, E2-12-72–73 FLC.

unclear; apparently L'Eplattenier did not respond to his pupil's requests, and on 10 July, as he was almost ready to return to La Chaux-de-Fonds, Jeanneret wrote:

> I have heaps of documents, and it would now serve no purpose to send me anything as I am soon to return to the sticks, with my work done and hoping to check it through with you.[47]

Thus it was only in La Chaux-de-Fonds that he could access the French translation of Sitte. Until then, he was obliged to work with the original German. But which of the four editions did he use (1st ed. 1889, 2nd ed. 1889, 3rd ed. 1901, or 4th ed. 1909)? From the illustrations which Jeanneret copied after Sitte, it is clear that it could not have been either the first or second edition, both dated 1889: in these editions Sitte shows the Acropolis in elevation and not, as copied by Jeanneret, in plan view with detailed description of individual buildings.[48] Not until the fourth edition in 1909 did the annex 'Großstadtgrün' on green spaces appear, to which Jeanneret certainly does refer.[49] This edition is certainly in contention as his source, since the Royal Bavarian Library acquired it in November 1909.[50]

When we say that Jeanneret based his work around Sitte, what do we mean by 'Sitte'? The history of how Sitte's *Städtebau* was received certainly makes for entertaining reading in the full and expert account given by Collins and Crasemann-Collins.[51] Even in his own era, Sitte was held up by some as an authority and rejected by others. In the twenty-odd years between the publication of his book in 1889 and Jeanneret writing his urban design study, Sitte had gathered a large following, but also attracted some dissenting voices. For example, in *Platz und Monument* Albert Erich Brinckmann heavily criticised Sitte for his romantic views. Yet architects and urban designers such as Karl Henrici, Theodor Fischer, Paul Schultze-Naumburg, and others admired Sitte and – as Sitte himself only realised a few urban designs – undertook to implement Sitte's principles in his stead. Thus Sitte's reception was necessarily beset with imprecision, meaning that by 1910 'Sitte' already stood for a wide variety of sometimes contradictory positions. Hence Brinckmann's rejection of Sitte as overly romantic must be taken with a pinch of salt, since Sitte himself argued in favour of the baroque monumental style which Brinckmann advocated – albeit with a different focus. Indeed, Brinckmann was one of the first German authors to present French *classicisme* for appreciation in the

---

47 Jeanneret to L'Eplattenier, 10 July 1910, E2-12-70 FLC.
48 Sitte, *Der Städtebau*, (4 ed. 1909), Fig. 4, p. 9.
49 See the section On Trees.
50 Sitte, *Der Städtebau nach seinen künstlerischen Grundsätzen*, 4th ed. 1909 in the RBL (shelf mark 'A. civ. 82 ua'); the relevant index card started on 26 November 1909.
51 See Collins/Crasemann Collins, *Camillo Sitte: The Birth of Modern City Planning*; for more on the situation of urban design in Germany and Sitte's role: Giorgio Piccinato, *Städtebau in Deutschland 1871–1914*, [Bauwelt-Fundamente 62] (Braunschweig: Vieweg, 1983). A critical assessment can be found in Gerhard Fehl, *Kleinstadt, Steildach, Volksgemeinschaft*, [Bauwelt-Fundamente 102] (Braunschweig/Wiesbaden: Vieweg, 1995). It positions Sitte as part of traditionalist petit-bourgeois planning, and interprets him as a precursor to architecture and urban design under National Socialism. The spectrum of knowledge on Sitte has been broadened by Michael Mönninger, *Vom Ornament zum Nationalkunstwerk: Die Schriften von Camillo Sitte zu Kunsttheorie, Pädagogik und Gewerbe* (Wiesbaden: Vieweg, 1998; also PhD diss., HfG Karlsruhe, 1995), and Gabriele Reiterer, *AugenSinn. Zu Raum und Wahrnehmung in Camillo Sittes ‹Städtebau›* (Salzburg: Pustet, 2003).

German-speaking world, and interestingly this also meant that it was ultimately better received by the French, who gained a new perspective on their own past through German art history.

Gathering material in Munich's libraries

Once Jeanneret had determined the general direction his study would take, he was evidently very productive between May and early June 1910. He did not leave Munich, and sat in one of the two libraries every day poring over the books already mentioned, as well as current issues of the journals *Der Städtebau* and *Süddeutsche Bauzeitung* from which he took individual essays or illustrations for his Manuscript. Other works listed in his bibliography are not significant in terms of *La Construction des villes*.[52]

On 29 April 1910, Jeanneret made an entry in the lending register at the library of the Bavarian National Museum.[53] We cannot check when he went there again, as readers were only required to sign in on their first visit. However, Jeanneret will have visited several times after 29 April: he took great care to trace individual urban views from several issues of *Topographiae* by Matthäus Merian circa 1650, intended to illustrate the topics discussed in *La Construction des villes*.[54]

Jeanneret's single-mindedness and selection of reading material commands admiration from the present-day reader. With no experience in urban design, he clearly absorbed almost all the German-language urban design discourse of his era, albeit with a clear bias towards aesthetic aspects. Sitte, Henrici, and Schultze-Naumburg are the most important authors Jeanneret dealt with at this time, and they have therefore had the greatest influence on the completed chapters of the Manuscript. However, in April Jeanneret also began to take lengthy excerpts from Brinckmann's *Platz und Monument*, although he was not able at the time to establish the right approach to Brinckmann's position, which differs slightly from that of Sitte.

The clearest illustration of this difficulty can be seen in Jeanneret's chapter On Squares, which is in two parts. The first part can be found in the loose-leaf folder and relates to Sitte, Schultze-Naumburg, and to a lesser extent Theodor Fischer. The second part, written later, in detail, is in the Cahiers C.7 and C.8 and focuses mainly on Brinckmann's book. Jeanneret took a series of suggestions from this book for his bibliography: for example he noted Charles Buls' 1893 *Esthétique des villes* in the Cahier *City III*, but did not borrow it.[55] At this early stage, Brinckmann's book was already broadening Jeanneret's urban design horizons in crucial ways: with the comment "books from which

52 For example, Jeanneret lists "Du sens chromatique dans l'antiquité by Dr. N-P Bénaky. Paris, publisher A. Maloine 21 place de l'École de Médecine, 1897". LCdv 437.

53 Entry in lending register for BNM: "[Entry made by library employee:] 103/29. IV. [1910]/Jeannerat Charl. Eduard [sic] Architect Lotzbeckstr. 3/III [Signature:] Ch. E. Jeanneret".

54 Jeanneret notes on the drawing of Burg Fleckenstein (B2-20-366 FLC): "Vautry histoire des Evèques de Bâle, I or II volumes, the same castle after Merian (in the library at the national museum Munich 1910[)]". Drawing from Matthäus Merian, *Topographia Alsatiae, &c. Completa, Das ist Vollkömliche Beschreibung und eygentliche Abbildung der vornehmbsten Städt und Oerther im Obern und untern Elsaß auch den benachbarten Sundgow Brißgow Graffschafft Mümpelgart und andern Gegenden...* (Frankfurt am Main: Merian Erben 1663; repr., Kassel and Basel: Bärenreiter, 1964), illustration after p. 18.

55 Note on p. LCdv 440. "Charles Buls, *Esthétique des villes*, Brussels: Bruylant-Christophe 1893". Jeanneret could have read Buls in the German edition (*Ästhetik der Städte*, Gießen: Roth, 1898) in the RBL (A. civ. 18 ^{mi}).

Brinckmann draws constantly", he added to his bibliography Patte's *Mémoire sur les objets les plus importans de l'architecture* of 1759 and Laugier's 1765 *Observations sur l'architecture*.[56] He also noted "La Théorie et la pratique du jardinage Paris 1747 Daviles et d'Argenville", again taken from Brinckmann.[57] Jeanneret did not read these books in 1910 – indeed, he would not read Patte's book on Parisian architecture until his stay in Paris in the summer of 1915, when he sketched many of its illustrations.[58] However, he also noted: "{page 140} Laugier said: 'There must be regularity and whimsy, relationships and oppositions, chance elements that lend variety to the tableau, *precise order in the details*, and confusion, chaos and tumult in the whole.'"[59] As Le Corbusier, he would use this quotation from Laugier's 1765 *Observations* in *Urbanisme* (1925) to justify the *Ville Contemporaine* design, his 'contemporary city'. But by early 1911, Jeanneret would return to Laugier, this time to the 1753 *Essai sur l'architecture*.

The undated letter to L'Eplattenier, probably written at the end of April, indicates that Jeanneret did initially plan to write about Switzerland: he requested plans and elevations, said he needed his photos of Switzerland, and wrote to Swiss towns and cities requesting postcards, which he ultimately rejected as unsuitable for his purposes. Whether suddenly or gradually, this process seems to have altered the character of his study: he did not manage to gather the requisite material, so the focus of his writing shifted from Switzerland to Germany, supported by his visit to the *Städtebau-Ausstellung* in Berlin – the grand urban design exhibition of 1910.[60] Was that one reason why, by September, *La Construction des villes* was no longer being considered for the conference in La Chaux-de-Fonds?

Between the end of April and the beginning of June 1910, an outline emerged for the first chapter of *La Construction des villes*. On Streets, so heavily based on Henrici, dates back to May 1910. The evidence for this date can be found in a small, unassuming booklet containing some details relating to the chapter. In May, a lecture came to Jeanneret's attention which had been given by an architect from Linz in 1905: Johann Hubatschek's *Bautechnische Aufgaben einer modernen Stadt*, an attempt to combine the artistic and practical aspects of urban design.[61] This is perhaps the most practical work with which

56 "C Livres où puise constament Brinkman P. Patte, Mémoire sur les objets les plus importants de l'architecture; Paris 1759 – M. A. Laugier, observations sur l'architecture. La Haye 1765", LCdv 433, and note "La Théorie et la pratique du jardinage Paris 1747 Daviles et d'Argenville", LCdv 435. These are: Pierre Patte, *Mémoire sur les objets les plus importans de l'architecture* (Paris: Rozet, 1769); and Marc Antoine Laugier, *Observations sur l'Architecture* (La Haye/Paris: Desaint, 1765).

57 LCdv 435. Antoine-Joseph Dézallier d'Argenville, *La théorie et pratique du jardinage* (Paris: J. Mariette, 1709). Reference is made to the fourth edition of Brinckmann, dated 1747: "Lenautre [sic] hatte praktisch die Grundzüge in bewundernswerter Weise ausgebildet, die theoretische Fixierung dann u. a. wie Daviler ausführlich von d'Argenville in La théorie et la pratique du jardinage." Brinckmann, *Platz und Monument*, p. 136.

58 These illustrations – and those from 1910 – can be found under B2-20 at the FLC. In 1915, Jeanneret read Pierre Patte's *Monumens érigés en France à la gloire de Louis XV* (Paris: Auteur et al., 1765), among other texts.

59 "{page 140} Laugier disait: Il faut de la régularité et de la bizarrerie, des rapports et des oppositions, des accidens qui varient le tableau; *un gd ordre ds les détails*, de la confusion, du fracas, du tumulte ds l'ensemble." LCdv 436. Brinckmann also quotes Laugier in French. Brinckmann, *Platz und Monument*, p. 140.

60 See for example the letter to L'Eplattenier dated 4 July 1910: "Oh those bloody administrators! Our brochure will give them a dose of their own medicine! As for the results of my approaches to Swiss towns and cities, I have had to deem them unsuccessful due to the dreadful postcards which they sent. [...] I would have liked to use Swiss places as proof; too bad." E2-12-69 FLC.

61 Jeanneret notes: "Bautechnische Aufgaben einer modernen Stadt Joh.[ann] Hubatschek. 1905 Druck et Verlag E. Mareis (Linz)"; LCdv 437.

Jeanneret came into close contact. Most of the books and essays to which he refers address artistic, aesthetic, and experiential aspects of urban design, and barely touch on social or technical questions. In contrast, Hubatschek combines Sitte's theories with highly pragmatic explanations, even down to issues such as types of pavements and drainage channels. The only similarly practical work relevant here is Joseph Stübben's 1890 handbook *Der Städtebau*. Jeanneret did have this to hand in Munich, but only copied a few drawings from it, and not until he returned from Berlin in June.[62] Otherwise, it is clear that Stübben's book with its encyclopaedic approach did not interest him. This is no surprise, since Stübben advocates just that sort of tasteless historicism which urban design reformers were rejecting, and which Jeanneret himself vehemently condemned.

One of the early, still-incomplete draft tables of contents in the Manuscript can be dated, albeit cautiously, to the period between late April and early June.[63] Here, Jeanneret places a foreword (*Avant-propos*) before the main body of his study. He then plans to present his Proposition (*Thèse*). He is already clear that this initial chapter will contain five subsections, but does not describe these in any more detail. Jeanneret's focus has now shifted to the second section, where he intends to present the development of La Chaux-de-Fonds (*La question du développement de la ville de la Chaux-de-Fonds*), and the third section, where he will discuss garden cities and cemeteries (*Quelques mots au sujet des cités-jardins. Cimetierres* [sic]); the work will end with an annex. Jeanneret would later rank garden cities and cemeteries simply as 'constituent parts of a city', yet at this stage they occupy an important position in his work. To give such prominence not only to garden cities but also to cemeteries could be a sign of the great interest in cemeteries Jeanneret displayed at the time. He documented cemeteries through visits, photographs, and sketches from all his travels circa 1910, whether to Pisa, Munich, or Constantinople.[64] The outline table of contents can be dated as early as this because Jeanneret does not, and possibly is not yet able to, name the topics for the five subsections which were to constitute his first chapter.[65]

It is highly likely that Jeanneret spent most of his time researching in the Royal Bavarian Library. All but one of the works which interested him were held there; Hubatschek's booklet, for example, is still available for loan there to this day.[66] In contrast, the library at the Bavarian National Museum contained none of the books Jeanneret was looking for that could not be found in the Royal Bavarian Library; Jeanneret's

---

62 Joseph Stübben, *Der Städtebau. Handbuch der Architektur*, Part 4, sub-volume 9 (Darmstadt: Bergstrasser, 1890). From this, Jeanneret copies several sketches of Berlin squares, ground plans for parks and church squares. See Fig.s 68, 20, 83: B2-20-321, 342, 347 FLC and LCdv 269. Cahier C.5 *Trees Monuments* shows that Jeanneret only turns to Stübben after his return from Berlin: "Look in Stübben for famous squares which have been ruined by trees." LCdv 233.

63 LCdv 521.

64 See On Cemeteries.

65 It is nevertheless conceivable that, despite having already established them, he merely omitted to state the topics here because this was not where his focus lay at the time. The table of contents would then be dated later, yet certainly no later than the urban design exhibition, since on his return from Munich in late June Jeanneret began to address new topics which would surely have appeared in the table.

66 See the bibliography of all works consulted by Jeanneret, p. 503. Except Georg Metzendorf's *Denkschrift über den Ausbau des Stiftungsgeländes* (Essen: Petersen, 1909), the RBL holds all the books which Jeanneret intended to work with in Munich. Hubatschek 1905 has the RBL shelf mark: A. civ. 50^lg. To my knowledge, very few other German libraries hold this text.

research there must have been restricted to copying the cityscapes from Merian's *Topographiae*. Unfortunately, the Royal Bavarian Library does not hold a lending register as some small libraries do, and therefore, with rare exceptions, Jeanneret's loans cannot be dated precisely.[67]

Nevertheless, two loan tickets from the Royal Bavarian Library are extant. The first dates from 4 June 1910, for Jeanneret's loan of Armand Thiéry's work *Über optisch-geometrische Täuschungen* (On optical-geometric illusions).[68] Unfortunately it cannot be established with certainty that Jeanneret really did work on Thiéry's text, as no reference to quotations from it is made in the Manuscript. However, he did sketch a series of geometric-optical illusions in one of the carnets from his *Voyages d'Allemagne*, without stating his source; in any event, only part of this series could be traced back to his reading of Thiéry.[69] The second loan ticket, for a book on Bavarian bridges which Jeanneret seems to have worked with, is confusing in terms of its date: Jeanneret entered the date as 23 October 1910, although he was no longer in Munich on that date. The library stamped the ticket with the date "I 24. SEP."[70]

The urban design exhibition in Berlin

Jeanneret met the Swiss writer and critic William Ritter through L'Eplattenier in Munich at the end of May.[71] He had asked his teacher on 16 April "if you see fit, could you possibly give me the address of William Ritter again?", and backed up his request in the undated letter from late April, saying: "I don't know anyone interesting here and it will be a while yet before I can get to know people."[72] In no time at all, Ritter and Jeanneret became friends; they would maintain a lifelong friendship. This was an exception for Le Corbusier, as it seems most of his friendships suffered due to the strength of his personality. In Ritter, however, with a strong personality to match his own, Jeanneret found the most important – and underestimated – *maître* for the period leading up to his final departure from La Chaux-de-Fonds. He was a mentor, friend, father figure, and even occasional therapist.[73]

67 The Royal Bavarian Library kept a 'Visitors' register' (Fremdenverzeichnis) in the 19th century and into the 20th century (now in the section for handwritten texts). However, there is a gap in this register between 1902 and 1919, meaning it is not possible to verify the exact dates of Jeanneret's work in the RBL.

68 "[Munich,] 4. Juni 1910//Thièry//Üeber geometr. Täuschungen//Leipzig//1895//Ch. E. Jenneret//Math. A./2³⁸ⁿ." LCdv 422. The library stamped this ticket with the date '5-7-10', or 5 July. The Manuscript Department at the Royal Bavarian Library stated that it assumes the stamp denotes the end of the loan period rather than the date the volume was requested.

69 Carnet 4, pp. 21–27.

70 LCdv 423: "[Munich,] 23. Oktober 1910//Brückenbauten//von der Staats-Bau-Verwaltung//M.//1906.//Ch. E. Jenneret//4°/Bavar./1775 f." Of course it is impossible to ascertain in hindsight whether these discrepancies arose from the library stamping the date on which a book was borrowed, meaning that Jeanneret noted down the wrong month in both cases, or whether the librarian used the wrong stamp.

71 William Ritter (1867–1955) came from Neuchâtel. He was a music and art critic for various Munich newspapers, and an author. He also gave Jeanneret a copy of his book *L'Entêtement Slovaque* (Paris: Bibliothèque de l'Occident, 1910).

72 "Vous pourriez peut-être si vous le jugez bon me redonner l'adresse de William Ritter." and "...je ne connais ici personne d'intéressant et ça ira toujours un moment jusqu'à ce que je puisse me faire des relations." Jeanneret to L'Eplattenier, 16 April (E2-12-62 FLC) and end of April 1910 (E2-12-72–73 FLC).

73 On the relationship between Jeanneret and Ritter, see Brooks, *Le Corbusier's Formative Years*, passim; Klaus Spechtenhauser, "The Mentor: William Ritter", in Von Moos and Rüegg, *Le Corbusier before Le Corbusier*,

William Ritter's life partner Janko Cádra apparently mentioned the Berlin urban design exhibition to Jeanneret, who then reflected to L'Eplattenier on 2 June that he was considering a trip to Berlin via Prague and Dresden.[74] Jeanneret did indeed travel to Berlin and attend the *Allgemeine Städtebau-Ausstellung*, where exhibits from throughout Europe and North America were displayed alongside the winning designs from the urban design competition for Greater Berlin, announced in March. His travel journals contain many entries about this exhibition.[75]

Jeanneret's assessment of the competition entries for greater Berlin is significant here, because it clarifies which of the prevailing tendencies he preferred. Jeanneret was excited about Hermann Jansen's designs, and even chose him as one of the architects for whom he would like to work. Immediately after the journey, he wrote to L'Eplattenier that he would like a work placement with Jansen, the winner of the competition for Greater Berlin, once he had gained work experience with Behrens and Bruno Paul.[76] Jansen represents a school of urban design that is exemplary in its ability to implement Sitte's imagined pictorial cityscapes, with façades demonstrating an unobtrusive homogeneity (Fig. VI).[77] Jeanneret's appreciation of Jansen's work contrasts with his reaction to the monumental designs by Bruno Schmitz, which had been well received by architects: he was appreciative, but unenthusiastic about the monumental aspects. He wrote to William Ritter:

> This is what the exhibition of projects for greater Berlin demonstrates, with a fully realistic project by Jansen and a much more utopian one by Bruno Schmitz, which takes as its motto 'where there's a will there's a way', but whose architectural solutions tend towards the grandiose.[78]

pp. 260–263, Christoph Schnoor, "Soyez de votre temps – Le Corbusier et William Ritter", in *Le Corbusier. La Suisse, Les Suisses*, XIIIᵉ Rencontre de la Fondation Le Corbusier, ed. FLC (Paris: Editions de la Villette/ FLC, 2006), pp. 105–127, and Marie-Jeanne Dumont (ed.), *Le Corbusier, William Ritter. Correspondence Croisée 1910–1955* (Paris: Editions du Linteau, 2014).

74 Jeanneret to L'Eplattenier, 2 June 1910 (E2-12-66 FLC): "M. Csadrà m'a parlé d'une énorme exposition de l'habitation à Berlin. Je prends des informations, et suivant ce que c'est, il est possible que j'y aille, passant par Prague, Dresde etc."

75 See in particular Le Corbusier, *Carnets de Voyage d'Allemagne 1910–1911*, carnet 1, pp. 56–78.

76 "J'ai été voir Peter Behrens, Muthésius et Bruno Paul. J'aimerais faire 1 stage chez le Ier et chez le dernier. Puis faire 1 stage encore chez Jansen l'arch. de villes qui a été primé au concours pour Gross-Berlin." Jeanneret to L'Eplattenier, 27 June 1910 (E2-12-68 FLC).

77 See the exhibition catalogue, *Führer durch die allgemeine Städtebau-Ausstellung in Berlin 1910* (Berlin: Wasmuth, 1910). Werner Hegemann subsequently published *Der Städtebau nach den Ergebnissen der allgemeinen Städtebau-Ausstellung in Berlin...*, 2 volumes (Berlin: Wasmuth, 1911/1913). See Wolfgang Sonne, "Ideen für die Großstadt: Der Wettbewerb Groß-Berlin 1910", in *Stadt der Architektur. Architektur der Stadt. Berlin 1900-2000*, eds. Thorsten Scheer, Josef Paul Kleihues and Paul Kahlfeldt (Berlin: Nicolai, 2000), pp. 67–77, and Vittorio Magnago Lampugnani, "Moderne, Lebensreform, Stadt und Grün. Urbanistische Experimente in Berlin 1900 bis 1914", in Scheer, Kleihues and Kahlfeldt, *Stadt der Architektur. Architektur der Stadt*, pp. 29–39.

78 Le Corbusier, *Carnets de Voyage d'Allemagne 1910–1911*, p. 66f. "Bruno Schmitz qui a 1 faible pour le colossal emploie tout à coup 1 énorme gratte ciel qui pourra devenir 1 point de repère capital, (beau en même temps)", and p. 68: "arch. à citer. Möhring Jansen. Gessner Bruno Schmitz". Section of letter to William Ritter dated 21ˢᵗ June 1910 (R3-18-4 FLC): "C'est ce que montre l'exposition des projets de Gross-Berlin, av. projet essentiellement pratique *Jansen* et celui d'1 caractère plus utopique de Bruno Schmitz qui a comme motto Wo ein Will, da ein Weg, mais av. des solutions architectoniques tendant au grandiose."

TEMPELHOFER FELD. *Geschlossener Architekturplatz mit Ausblick auf den Erholungsplatz | bis zu 180 m. breiter Parkgürtel |. Auf diesen münden die einzelnen, zwecks Durchlüftung durch Torbauten geöffneten langen Baublocks mit ihren Frontseiten. Im Vordergrunde liegt die große Hauptstr., in der sich die 2 Diagonalstr. vereinigen. Architekt herm. Jansen Berlin. 20 Dec. 1910*

Fig. VI Hermann Jansen, Design for the Tempelhofer Feld, Berlin 1910 (Berlinische Galerie)

The only book Jeanneret notes in his travel carnets as one he wants to use for *La Construction des villes* is Raymond Unwin's work *Town Planning in Practice*.[79] He does not employ Unwin's work in his texts, but it is possible that Unwin's proposal for a station forecourt influenced Jeanneret's own design of such a square in La Chaux-de-Fonds (Fig.s VII and VIII). In Berlin, besides visiting the urban design exhibition, Jeanneret perused an exhibition devoted to the materials clay, cement, and lime; attended the Werkbund congress; and saw the sights – the centre, Tiergarten, and new residential

---

79 "Grundlagen [des] Städtebaues von Raimond [sic] Unwin Verlag Otto Baumgärtel Berlin contient page 126 2 propositions pour la réfection de la place du Dôme à Ulm." This is a reference to the German edition of Raymond Unwin, *Town Planning in Practice. An Introduction to the Art of Designing Cities and Suburbs* (London: Fisher Unwin, 1909).

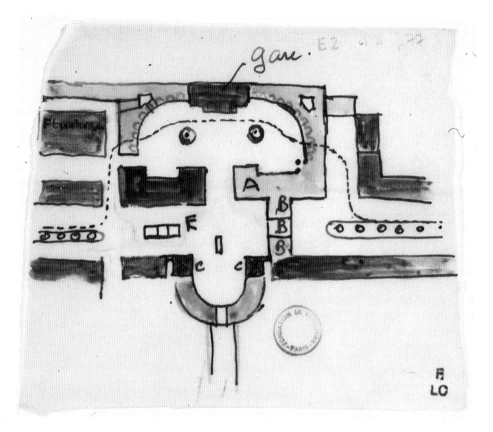

Fig. VII Jeanneret's design for the station square in La Chaux-de-Fonds, 1910 (E2-12-77 FLC)

colonies in Nikolassee, Treptow, and Potsdam.[80] Now armed with a wealth of impressions, he returned to Munich in a journey of many stages, which took him to 11 German towns and cities between 21 and 25 June. Jeanneret carefully photographed, sketched, and bought postcards of major urban design subjects. In a change to his plans, he travelled from Berlin to Munich via Wittenberg, Halle, Naumburg, Weimar, Jena, Lichtenfels, Coburg, Bamberg, Würzburg, Rothenburg, and Augsburg.[81] Although

80 See Brooks, *Le Corbusier's Formative Years*, pp. 218–223, and Le Corbusier, *Carnets de Voyage d'Allemagne 1910–1911*, carnet 1, passim.

81 On the cover of carnet 1, Jeanneret documents his journey so precisely that it can be reconstructed to the minute with the aid of railway timetables from the period! For example, here Jeanneret describes possible train connections for the first two days of his return journey:
    Return from Berlin to Munich, Tuesday 21st June 1910: "Tuesday 21. 8 o'clock station. 10 o'clock Wittenberg. 1 o'clock: Halle; 4 o'clock/Naumburg. 9 o'clock Weimar." – Berlin Anhalter Bahnhof. depart (Z4) 8:25. Wittenberg arrive 9:54. Stay of 2 hours. Wittenberg depart (Z58) 12:05. Halle/Saale arrive 13:06 Stay of 2 1/2 hours. Halle depart (Z10) 15:36. Naumburg arrive 16:32. Stay of 4 hours. Naumburg leave (Z94) 20:37 Weimar arrive 21:22.

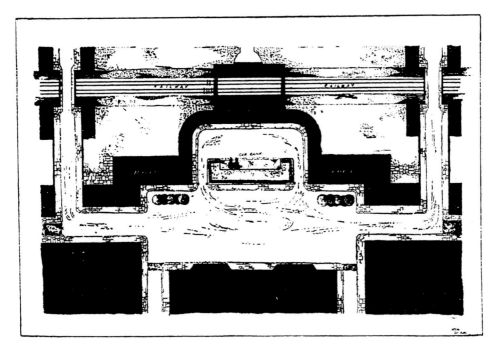

Fig. VIII "Suggestion for a station place." From Unwin, *Town Planning in Practice*, fig. 117

most of these places lie directly on the fast train line between Berlin and Munich, their selection was no accident: these stop-off points were designed to provide pictures of examples from Schultze-Naumburg's *Kulturarbeiten Städtebau*, for use in *La Construction des villes*.

To that end, he sought out the same sites and the same photographic perspectives Schultze-Naumburg had used, thus reproducing the subjects of his illustrations. This is shown most clearly with the examples of the Burkader Kirche (Church of St. Burchard) in Würzburg and the market place in Lichtenfels (Fig.s IXa/b and Xa/b). In other instances, Jeanneret contented himself with subjects that were similar to their predecessors. In view of the great effort he went to, it is astonishing that he failed to explicitly allocate his photographs to the relevant passages in the Manuscript text. Today, it is only possible to allocate these illustrations to approximate places in the text. The focus which Jeanneret applied to this journey is demonstrated by the

Wednesday 22nd June: "Wednesday visit Weimar, then Van de Velde school. 2 1/2 hours. Train to Jena. University. 5 hours on train to Coburg/Coburg 9 o'clock" – Evening of 21st and morning of 22nd in Weimar. Weimar depart (Z197) 14:56. Jena arrive 15:29. 1 1/2 hours in Jena. Jena depart (D46) 17:17. Lichtenfels arrive 20:00, depart (Z468) 20:21. Coburg arrive 21:00.

See *Reichs-Kursbuch. Übersicht der Eisenbahn-, Post- und Dampfschiff- Verbindungen in Deutschland, Österreich-Ungarn, Schweiz sowie der bedeutenderen Verbindungen der übrigen Teile Europas und der Dampfschiff-Verbindungen mit außereuropäischen Ländern* (Berlin: Julius Springer, August/September 1910); the June copy is no longer available via inter-library loan.

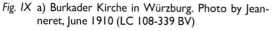

Fig. IX a) Burkader Kirche in Würzburg. Photo by Jeanneret, June 1910 (LC 108-339 BV)

Fig. IX b) Burkader Kirche in Würzburg. From: Schultze-Naumburg, *Kulturarbeiten Städtebau*, fig. 62

Fig. X a) Lichtenfels in Bavaria, market place. Photo by Jeanneret, June 1910 (LC 108-298 BV)

Fig. X b) Lichtenfels in Bayern. From Schultze-Naumburg, *Kulturarbeiten Städtebau*, fig. 180

mammoth undertaking of visiting 11 towns and cities in five days. In some cases, such as in Wittenberg, Halle, or Lichtenfels, he only stayed for two hours. We can therefore assume that he planned this journey meticulously, and during his visits worked consistently from a more or less well-defined programme.

What would be the scope of the study?

Jeanneret returned to Munich exhausted, but very satisfied. The trip to Berlin had broadened his urban design horizons and, more importantly, confirmed his views and his choice of reading material in terms of both authors and topics. Hence he wrote to his parents immediately he returned: "Just imagine what supreme importance the urban design exhibition held for me. It brought, I am most ecstatic to report, the total vindication of all that I had written. Never in all my short life have I spent months as enriching as these last three."[82] These words are remarkable given Jeanneret's later attempts to conceal how much he had learned during this period in Germany. They were motivated by the need to justify himself: his parents had been waiting impatiently since April for the news that their son had found employment with an architect; thus far, Edouard had repeatedly attempted to placate them with the argument that his job hunt would take some time and that he was unable to say what he was working on. Only in his letter dated 29 June did he acknowledge his plans, because his parents' questions had become too insistent:

> This is no 'colossal' work as Papa says, but simply a study on the art of building cities. This study ends with a robust criticism of the strategies applied in La Chaux-de-Fonds and aims to completely transform them. This study will be published as a brochure, the importance of which has exceeded my expectations. It has been an exciting matter for me and I have great faith in it having direct results.[83]

Jeanneret downplays the scope of his work here: his father's assumption that this was a colossal task was in fact accurate. Indeed, the task eventually expanded to such an extent that he was unable to complete it.

Jeanneret now had barely a month left in Munich before the summer holidays. He was becoming impatient, and even before travelling to the exhibition had written to L'Eplattenier that the study was finished: "I am writing the brochure. What hard work! My God, I really am good for nothing. In a fortnight I hope it will be ready. [...] Then I could begin publication, and it might come out in September or October."[84] And on 7 June, the eve of his departure for Berlin, he wrote again:

> I finished writing my poor text a few days ago, I have collected together all my illustrations, but I now ask myself if I should be doing them very carefully, or just making quick sketches, the better to tally with my hardly everlasting prose style.[85]

---

82 Jeanneret to his parents, 29 June 1910: "Vous pensez donc bien que le Städtebauausstellung fut pour moi d'l importance capitale. Elle apporta, j'en suis tout joyeux, la consécration complète à tout ce que j'avais écrit. Je n'ai pas encore ds ma courte vie passé des mois aussi nourris que ces 3 derniers." RI-5-21 FLC.

83 "Ce n'est point à l ‹colossal› travail comme dit papa, mais tout simplement à l étude sur l'art de bâtir les villes. Cette étude se termine par l critique vigoureuse des moyens employés à La Chaux-de-Fonds et a pour but de les faire transformer du tout au tout. Cette étude sera publiée en l brochure, dont l'importance dépasse mes prévisions. Ce fut pour moi l passionnante question et j'espère bp en ses résultats directs." RI-5-19 FLC.

84 "J'écris la brochure. Quelle peine! Cré nom, je ne suis décidément bon à rien. Dans 15 jours ce sera prêt j'espère. [...] Alors je pourrais mettre en train la publication laquelle pourrait paraître dans les mois de septembre ou octobre." Jeanneret to L'Eplattenier, mid-May 1910. See Marie-Jeanne Dumont, *Le Corbusier. Lettres à ses maîtres tome II. Lettres à Charles L'Eplattenier* (Paris: Editions Linteau, 2006).

85 "J'ai fini d'écrire depuis quelques jours, mon pauvre texte, toutes mes illustrations sont rassemblées, mais je suis en train de me demander si je dois les faire aux petits oignons, ou simplement en croquis rapides afin de

Directly after he had returned from Berlin, on 27 June, Jeanneret announced, "I intend to come and finish off my brochure with you."[86] Thus he postponed completion and expressed his hope to go through his work with L'Eplattenier in La Chaux-de-Fonds. Two days later, in a letter to his parents, he said: "documenting everything took a long time, and a lot of effort. Now everything is almost ready."[87] We see here the contradiction between what he tells L'Eplattenier and what he tells his parents. What is more, all of Jeanneret's predictions prove to be excessively optimistic when set against the dates and facts to be gleaned from the Manuscript material.

These statements can be explained by the pressure Jeanneret was under. He had agreed with L'Eplattenier that he would complete his study for the conference of Swiss municipalities, *L'Assemblée générale des délégués de l'Union des villes suisses*, to be held on 24 and 25 September 1910 in La Chaux-de-Fonds. This was what the study was designed for, and the date was an absolute deadline. Ultimately, Jeanneret would not meet this deadline, or even attend the conference; instead, L'Eplattenier gave a talk of his own.[88] We must therefore assume that the study was far from finished and that Jeanneret was painfully aware of this fact.

Our intention in examining Jeanneret's somewhat pompous justifications is not to criticise him, but relates instead to an important question about how independent this work was. Did Jeanneret act on his own initiative or on the advice of L'Eplattenier in expanding the scope of his Manuscript to include green areas in urban design? Even the first bibliography dating from April contains two works relating to the 'green' elements of Jeanneret's urban design ideas – trees, gardens, parks, cemeteries, and garden cities: Muthesius' *Das englische Haus* and Berlepsch-Valendàs' essay on Hampstead garden suburb. Jeanneret also includes a joint section on garden cities and cemeteries in the table of contents dated (with reservations) to May 1910. Thus it appears that when he stated the study was finished, this may have been to pacify his parents and declare his intentions; it may not provide us with much information on the actual progress of his work. In fact it would be strange if the urban design exhibition, with its many new designs for parks, cemeteries, and other green spaces, did not spur Jeanneret on to further investigation.

Accordingly, there is another table of contents, in which Jeanneret orders all the chapters into a sequence, which may belong to this period. The table of contents can be found on a loose sheet in Cahier C.2 *City II Bridges*:

blocks
squares → Streets. (1)
enclosure
      Bridges.
      the tree
4   Gardens and Parks.
      cemeteries.

---

    mieux concorder av. le style peu éternel de ma prose." Jeanneret to L'Eplattenier, 7 June 1910 (E2-12-67 FLC).

86 "J'ai l'intention de venir terminer ma brochure av. vous." Jeanneret to L'Eplattenier, 27 June 1910 (E2-12-68 FLC).

87 Letter from Jeanneret to his parents, 29 June 1910: "La documentation fut longue, me coûta passablement de peine. Aujourd'hui tout est presque prêt." (RI-5-20 FLC)

88 L'Eplattenier, "*L'Esthétique des villes*".

~~+2~~   General Considerations
        5   Garden cities → [after 6.]
3   useful strategies
        6   La Chaux de Fonds
                "   II
        ~~6~~ 7   Conclusion.

After corrections, the sequence would be:
1 Blocks, Streets, Squares, Enclosure
2 General Considerations
3 Useful Strategies
4 The Tree, Garden and Parks, Cemeteries
5 Garden Cities
6 La Chaux-de-Fonds I and II
7 Conclusion[89]

Until now, Jeanneret had always begun the contents of *La Construction des villes* with a Proposition on the city, followed by an account of how it could be applied in practice. His aim to systematically describe the urban design elements in a city is new here, as is his move beyond the 'stone-built' topics he had worked on thus far to include 'green' issues. Jeanneret was clearly seeking to place the chapters in a sensible sequence; they are not yet in their final order, but are nevertheless all listed. The initial sequence here includes residential blocks, squares, and enclosing walls.[90] Jeanneret then adds streets, after blocks. Next he lists: bridges, trees, gardens and parks, and cemeteries.[91] After these would come his overall *Considérations générales*, followed by garden cities, the Possibilities for Intervention (here *Moyens utiles*, or Useful Strategies, but later *Moyens possibles*, Possible Strategies), then the chapter on La Chaux-de-Fonds, which Jeanneret clearly planned to split into two sections.[92] Jeanneret then listed his *Conclusion*, which he had yet to formulate.

Following these changes, the *Considérations générales* were placed after residential blocks, streets, squares, and walls; Possibilities for Intervention came third and only after these bridges, trees, gardens and parks, cemeteries, and garden cities, followed by La Chaux-de-Fonds and the conclusion. It is strange to see what was already a very specific chapter followed by a general chapter, then another specific one, and after that the description of the situation in La Chaux-de-Fonds, with proposed improvements to the town. Perhaps this can be explained as Jeanneret hesitating to allocate a single section for all the urban design elements he has chosen, which vary so greatly in size. Later, enclosing walls would share a chapter with garden cities, despite the obvious difference

89 LCdv 523.
90 These three issues can all be found in Schultze-Naumburg, whom Jeanneret clearly began to read at an early stage in his research.
91 It is possible that the 'Großstadtgrün' chapter of Sitte's *Städtebau nach seinen künstlerischen Grundsätzen* inspired Jeanneret to group together the various green elements in urban areas at first.
92 The quotations in the Annex from Georges de Montenach's *Pour le visage aimé de la Patrie* bear the inscription 'II'. This is a further indication that Jeanneret clearly intended to divide the chapter on La Chaux-de-Fonds into two parts: an analysis and a proposed solution.

in dimensions which would place them in different categories. This loose sheet is difficult to date; it may describe the state of play around July 1910.[93]

There is further evidence that Jeanneret did indeed deal with 'green' urban topics in Munich in July. On the first pages of Cahier C.6 *Squares Gardens I*, Jeanneret draws up a very detailed structure for the chapter On Squares. If I am right to assume that this structure was drawn up before the chapter was finally drafted, it would be possible to date these pages to July. It is reasonable to conclude from this that the initial collation of ideas on gardens, which follows on from the above-mentioned structure in Cahier *Squares Gardens I*, also dates from July. Yet it is very difficult to pinpoint the date when Jeanneret created On Squares. Strictly speaking, his work on this section spanned the entire period between his first and last days in Munich – between April and October. It will not be possible for us to find an exact date during that time when he created the structure described above. If Jeanneret did indeed begin the Cahier *Squares Gardens I* in July, the closely related Cahier C.5 *Trees Monuments* would also date from that time.[94] Thus the question of when Jeanneret began to work on topics of green urban areas cannot be settled for sure. Nevertheless, I tend to think that it was Jeanneret himself who expanded the scope of his study to include these issues, although he might have needed support from his teacher to shape them clearly into individual chapter sections.

Some bibliographical details

Jeanneret used the time leading up to his return to La Chaux-de-Fonds to follow up the leads he had found in Berlin. Thus in the Cahier *City IV* he translated the article which Berlin reformists Walter Lehweß and Robert Kuczynski published in the journal *Städtebau*, in which they attempt to prove that five-storey perimeter blocks combined with detached and semi-detached houses on the interior would prove just as viable as the current tenement blocks.[95] Although this new proposal clearly belongs in the chapter On Blocks, Jeanneret makes only hesitant attempts to link it with that chapter, as we will see below. The earliest he could have been aware of the essay is June, when it appeared in *Städtebau*. Around the same time, he visited the exhibition and prepared a sketch of the plan by Lehweß and Kuczynski. It is probable that Jeanneret only started the detailed translation of the article in a new notebook on his return from Berlin, that is, no sooner than July.[96] During this period,

---

93 However, it may be that Jeanneret remained unclear about this part of the study and only began to formulate chapters focusing exclusively on urban green space once L'Eplattenier had asked him to do so. If that is the case, Jeanneret may have drafted this table of contents in La Chaux-de-Fonds in August or around that time.

94 Jeanneret worked on Cahiers C.5 and C.6 simultaneously. The proof of this is that, in C.5, LCdv 234, he notes: "write to the architect of the parks in Hamburg or Düsseldorf, requesting photos" ("écrire à l'architecte de jardins de Hambourg ou Dusseldorf [Max Läuger] qu'il m'envoie photos") – a second, almost identically worded note can be found in C.6, LCdv 239: "écrire architecte des Jardins à Dusseldorf ou Hambourg, pour envoyer photos modernes".

95 Walter Lehweß and Robert René Kuczynski, "Zweifamilienhäuser für Großstädte", in *Der Städtebau* 7 (1910), no. 6, pp. 67–72.

96 But why did Jeanneret not include this reformist design in the chapter On Blocks, which he was editing in La Chaux-de-Fonds over the summer? It either indicates that Jeanneret did not deem it very important (which is unlikely, as he translated the entire essay into French), or perhaps that Jeanneret did not translate the essay until he had returned from Munich to La Chaux-de-Fonds, when the chapter On Blocks had already been completed. Equally, the Annex to the loose-leaf folder, where Jeanneret establishes a connection between C.4 and

he ended the Cahier *City III* with several notes relating directly to designs displayed at the urban design exhibition.[97] Jeanneret also captured a direct response to what he had seen in Berlin on pages LCdv 355–358 of the loose-leaf folder, which do not belong to any particular chapter.

On occasion, Jeanneret lists books in his bibliography on the strength of their illustrations alone. Hence in a note he made under a drawing at the end of June, he states "inspired by book Renaissance und Barockvilla in Italien. Bernhard Patzak, Verlag Klinkhardt & Biermann, Leipzig".[98] Of the volumes which make up this work by Patzak, the first to appear was Volume III in 1908, on the Villa Imperiale in Pesaro.[99] From this volume, Jeanneret not only copied a section through the Rovere building at the Villa Imperiale (Fig.s XI, XII), but also began to sketch while copying, and in doing so noted down the following remarkable thoughts:[100]

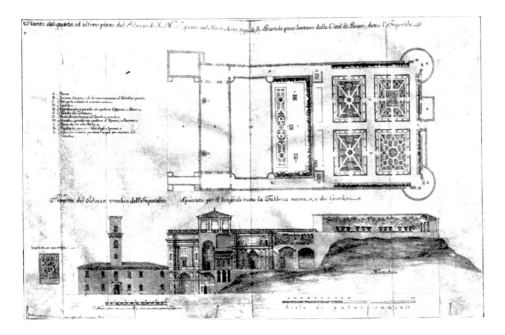

Fig. XI Palazzo Imperiale in Pesaro. From Patzak, *Renaissance- und Barockvilla III*, p. 80

On Blocks, dates from August/September in La Chaux-de-Fonds; this would place the translation of this article before August.

97 LCdv 445.

98 LCdv 446.

99 Bernhard Patzak, *Die Renaissance- und Barockvilla in Italien.* Vol. III: *Die Villa Imperiale in Pesaro. Studien zur Kunstgeschichte der ital. Renaissancevilla und ihrer Innendekoration* (Leipzig: Klinkhardt & Biermann, 1908). (The Villa Imperiale in Pesaro. Studies on the Art History of the Italian Renaissance Villa and its Interior Decoration). Volumes I and II did not appear until 1912/13.

100 Furthermore, Jeanneret ascribes a drawing he made of the Villa Madama in Rome to this book by Patzak, yet it contains no such illustration. Jeanneret notes: "Book by Bernard Patzak Renaissance Barock Villa/Villa Madama, Rome, Sangallo/what is striking is a wall__ " B2-20-349 FLC.

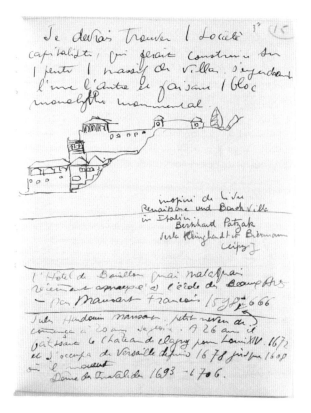

Fig. XII Handwritten page from Cahier *Ville III* with Jenneret's interpretive drawing, following Patzak
(LCdv 446)

I should find a joint-stock company which would build a block of villas on a slope,
each seeming to produce the other and forming a monumental monolith.[101]

On two loose sheets in Cahier C.5 *Trees Monuments*, Jeanneret noted book titles and shelf
marks from the Royal Bavarian Library. On the first he cited the shelf mark for Brinckmann's *Platz und Monument*, and on the second Albert Gessner's work *Das deutsche
Miethaus* of 1909, Fritz Burger's *Villen des Andrea Palladio*, and the *Elenco degli Edifici
Monumentali in Italia*.[102] However, Jeanneret did not read Gessner's text in 1910, and only
copied a single illustration from Burger's book on Palladio: a floor plan and front elevation

---

101 LCdv 446. See the letter to L'Eplattenier dated 1st October 1910 quoted below, in which he writes of his
     ideas for villas to be built on the slopes of La Chaux-de-Fonds (E2-12-75 FLC). It would be very interesting
     to see a design by Le Corbusier which integrated an urban housing block with the topography. The convent
     of La Tourette perhaps comes closest to this concept.
102 "Berlin 1908. 8. 17 ^{9}//Brinkmann." LCdv 537. Fritz Burger (ed.), *Die Villen des Andrea Palladio. Ein Bei-
     trag zur Entwicklungsgeschichte der Renaissance-Architektur* (Leipzig: Klinkhardt & Biermann, 1909).
         Albert Gessner, *Das deutsche Miethaus. Ein Beitrag zur Städtekultur der Gegenwart* (München: Bruck-
     mann, 1909). Ministero della Pubblica Istruzione (ed.), *Elenco degli Edifici Monumentali in Italia* (Roma:
     Cecchini, 1902).

for the Villa Pisani in Bagnolo (Fig. XIII). Furthermore the *Elenco* was no use in terms of additions to the bibliography since – as the title suggests – this is merely a directory of monumental buildings in Italy, without any extra information on the buildings, and was therefore of no value to Jeanneret.[103] In Cahier C.5, Jeanneret continues: "An interesting book for a study of monuments is: Handbuch der Architektur Vierter Teil. Geschichte des Denkmales. By Albert Hofmann 18 x 22cm. 700 pages, lots of illustrations."[104] Jeanneret cites Hofmann's book in Cahier C.9, the first cahier dedicated to cemeteries and garden cities, in order to note down some details on the history of Asian monuments.

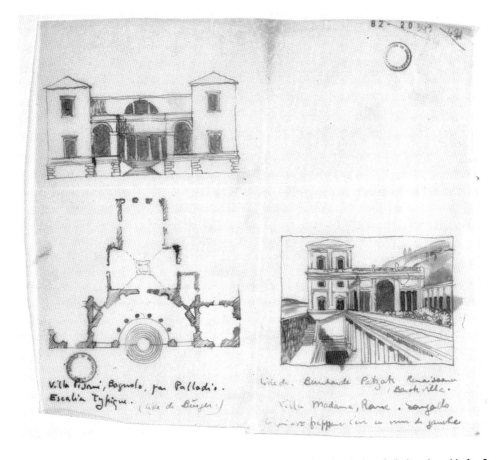

Fig. XIII Palladio's Villa Pisani in Bagnolo. From Burger, *Die Villen des Andrea Palladio*, plate 11, fig. 3, and Patzak *Renaissance- und Barockvilla III* (B2-20-349 FLC)

103 The date of this loose sheet is not at all certain. However, it is probable that Jeanneret added these books to the bibliography around early July.
104 Albert Hofmann, *Geschichte des Denkmals*, part 4, sub-volume 8, no. 2b of *Handbuch des Architekten* (Stuttgart: Kröner, 1906); LCdv 271.

Was any reference made at the Berlin exhibition to Joseph August Lux? In late June, Jean-neret added Lux's *Der Städtebau und die Grundpfeiler der heimischen Bauweise* to his bibli-ography and proceeded to take excerpts from the work on a wide variety of themes.[105] It appears that Jeanneret was not working on *La Construction des villes* as much as before, and was instead enjoying a little leisure in Munich for the first time.[106] He translated excerpts from a brief overview of the exhibition, by Walter Lehweß.[107] Lehweß stresses that urban design is where the struggle for art will be played out in future: a view which Jeanneret him-self supports at several points in the Manuscript.[108] However, in his selection of illustrations and further reading, Jeanneret made scant reference to this essay, although it contains many excellent illustrations. In autumn he did return to the subject of the Waldfriedhof (woodland cemetery) in Munich, designed by Hans Grässel, which he saw at the exhibition and which was also mentioned by Lehweß. Again we can confirm that, fundamentally, his choice of projects and books of interest for *La Construction des villes* was truly independent.

La Chaux-de-Fonds: Editing the Manuscript

On 21 July, Jeanneret interrupted his work on *La Construction des villes* and travelled with Octave Matthey to Garmisch, visited the Zugspitze and travelled back via Mittenwald, Seefeld, and Innsbruck to La Chaux-de-Fonds. He arrived at the end of July. The summer was spent here, and he would only leave for Munich in mid-September. During those seven weeks in La Chaux-de-Fonds, he stayed with his mother and brother Albert in a holiday home at 149/150 Boulevard des Endroits, perched just above the town. We know that Jeanneret edited the Manuscript, and his mother helped by writing out a clean copy of several whole chapters: the Proposition, part of the General Considerations, On Streets, Enclosing Walls, and part of On Possible Strategies. Thus Jeanneret must have made sufficient progress on these chapters for her to copy them into what was by and large their final form. However, we do not know what came of Jeanneret's wish to work with his teacher on improving the Manuscript. The extant parts of the Manuscript contain no entries or corrections that might be in L'Eplattenier's hand.

Jeanneret did indeed finish the first half of the chapter On Squares in August or early September, and also completed the first part of his *Application critique: La Chaux-de-Fonds*, the real reason behind the whole study. He then began to compose a second part of the Critical Application in which he planned to include the proposals for improving urban design. Two works in French by Swiss authors feature in this part of the Manu-script: Georges de Montenach's *Pour le visage aimé de la Patrie!* which praises German 'Heimatschutz' (the protection of the country's cultural heritage) and calls for it to be applied in Switzerland, and Guillaume Fatio's *Ouvrons les Yeux!*.[109] Jeanneret excerpts

---

105 LCdv 445. Joseph August Lux, *Der Städtebau und die Grundpfeiler der heimischen Bauweise* (Dresden: Kühtmann, 1908).

106 See the letter to L'Eplattenier dated 10 July, E2-12-70 FLC, in which Jeanneret writes that he has had time to dedicate to poetry for the first time in months.

107 Walter Lehweß, "Architektonisches von der Städtebau-Ausstellung zu Berlin", in *Berliner Architekturwelt* 13 (1910), pp. 123–125 (followed by some 40 illustrations).

108 See Proposition, LCdv 9, or On Possible Strategies, LCdv 326–380.

109 Georges de Montenach, *Pour le visage aimé de la patrie. Ouvrage de propagande esthétique et sociale* (Lau-sanne: Sack-Reymond, 1908). Guillaume Fatio, *Ouvrons les Yeux! Voyage esthétique à travers la Suisse* (Geneva: Atar, 1904). Jeanneret mentions both works in Cahier C.1, in which he writes out the second half of his chapter General Considerations, without pursuing any of the arguments made by Fatio or Montenach.

many pages from Montenach, which he places in what he called the Annex: in the loose-leaf folder next to the designs for La Chaux-de-Fonds. It would seem that *Pour le visage aimé de la Patrie!* was not available in the Munich libraries in 1910.[110]

Shortly before leaving for Munich, Jeanneret drafted yet another table of contents, which can be viewed as a checklist charting the latest progress made on his work:

Proposition:
1/2   General Considerations.

                              Introduction
                              Blocks
    Revise.   Streets
1/2   squares.   1/2 Squares
    tree   Walls.
    garden and Park.
    bridges
    cemetery
1/2   useful strategies.   1/2 Useful strategies
    La Chaux-de-Fonds. black
    the style   white
    garden cities.
    Conclusion[111]

It follows that – in contrast to Jeanneret's premature claim in his letter to L'Eplattenier of 10 July – he had only completed half of the General Considerations, the Introduction, On Blocks, On Streets, half of On Squares, Enclosing Walls, and half of On Possible Strategies (still called Useful Strategies). He adds the word 'revoir' above all the other chapters he planned: they needed revision, checking – or in fact had yet to be written. There was no further indication, once Jeanneret had left for summer in La Chaux-de-Fonds, that he would participate in the conference of Swiss municipalities on 24/25 September, let alone that his text was to be presented there. This appears to have been glossed over by both Jeanneret and L'Eplattenier without a word. Before the conference had even begun, Jeanneret travelled back to Munich for further work on *La Construction des villes*. It is therefore reasonable to assume that L'Eplattenier encouraged Jeanneret to broaden the study, possibly with a view to making it into a well-rounded, standalone work.

One final month in Munich: Green space in the city

On 17 September, Jeanneret left his home town for Munich once again, for one last, intensive month of work on *La Construction des villes*. He drafted the missing third and fourth subsections of the *Considérations générales*, attempting to paint a comprehensive picture of developments in urban design over the past 80 years. This text is more advanced and sophisticated than the hitherto known parts of the Manuscript. The tone here is less accusatory than for example the chapter on La Chaux-de-Fonds, and in terms

---

110 Since Jeanneret did not own a copy either, we must assume that he borrowed it from L'Eplattenier. But
    when? Probably not before July 1910, when Jeanneret came to La Chaux-de-Fonds to edit the Manuscript.
111 LCdv 522.

of content Jeanneret demonstrates an ability to trace the history of German-language urban design theory circa 1910 in just a few sentences, keeping an astonishingly professional distance.[112]

Jeanneret also wrote the second half of the chapter On Squares, which derives almost entirely from Brinckmann's *Platz und Monument*, at this time.[113] He added many excerpts to the chapters On Trees, On Gardens and Parks, On Cemeteries, and On Garden Cities. Jeanneret was now referring frequently to publications by Joseph August Lux: he translated several chapters from the author's 1908 *Der Städtebau und die Grundpfeiler der heimischen Bauweise*, as well as essays on garden cities, cemeteries, and monuments.[114] To the bibliography, Jeanneret added journal articles by Lux, who favoured an approach to garden design based on Heimatschutz.[115] Perhaps Jeanneret also read Lux's *Ingenieur-Aesthetik*, which appeared in print in 1910.[116] The role played by Joseph August Lux in the German-language urban design debate is little known.[117] Born in Vienna in 1871, he studied history of art and philology, edited the journal *Hohe Warte* from 1904, and wrote many publications on urban design; the basic thrust of these varies widely. In his 1908 work, *Der Städtebau und die Grundpfeiler der heimischen Bauweise*, he argued strongly in favour of Heimatschutz, largely on the basis of sentiment. By 1910 in *Ingenieur-Aesthetik* he was advocating an industrial-technical ideal which in fact foreshadowed the rhetoric of the 1920s. In terms of garden design, he entered the debate on the landscaped garden versus the architectural garden, and called for the Lenné school of landscaped gardens to be replaced by an architectural garden, in parallel with Muthesius and Schultze-Naumburg.[118] In *Der Städtebau und die*

---

112 Two details confirm that the notebook definitely belongs among the Munich Cahiers: all three of the Berlin Cahiers (C.11 to C.13) have labels featuring a small printed 'Berlin bear' as part of the manufacturer's seal; in contrast, C.1 has a label with a curved border, as do most of the other Munich Cahiers. And three pieces of blotting paper can be found at the beginning of the notebook, stamped with the following text: "Joh. Huber/Buchbinderei u. Schreibwarenhdlg./München/Augustenstr. 104/Eingang/Schellingstr." (Joh. Huber/ Bookbinder and stationer/Munich [. . .]). One of these pieces shows part of the text to which the paper has been applied: "Carl – Henrici – Aachen", text which can be found at LCdv 34. This piece of paper was therefore in the Cahier, which originated in Munich, from the start.

113 Cahiers C.7 and C.8. These two Cahiers continue On Squares, the chapter half-written in La Chaux-de-Fonds. They fit seamlessly together, and should therefore be considered as two halves of a whole.

114 These are from Lux, *Der Städtebau und die Grundpfeiler der heimischen Bauweise*, sections on the decline of monumental sculpture (LCdv 271–273), pp. 88–92; the chapter "Parkpolitik" (parks policy) (LCdv 248–252), pp. 72–76; a section on cemeteries (LCdv 275), p. 94f., and the chapter "Gartenstädte" (garden cities), which Jeanneret translates in Cahier C.9, LCdv 312–320.

115 Joseph August Lux, "Die Gartenkunst und die Landschaftsgärtnerei", in *Süddeutsche Bauzeitung*, 17 (1907), no. 3, pp. 21–23. Jeanneret adds this essay to his bibliography twice: see LCdv 240 and 242. He probably also read Joseph August Lux's article: "Alt-Wiener Vorgärten" (Front gardens of old Vienna), in *Süddeutsche Bauzeitung*, 17 (1907), no. 36, pp. 286–288. See On Gardens and Parks.

116 Joseph August Lux, *Ingenieur-Aesthetik* (Munich: Lammers, 1910). Jeanneret was unable to find this work by Lux in the RBL, using the shelf mark Techn. 139^{vd}. We assume on the basis of statements made in the chapter General Considerations that Jeanneret read *Ingenieur-Aesthetik*, but have no clear evidence of this.

117 Joseph August Lux (1871–1947), Austrian writer and journalist. Founding member of the Deutsche Werkbund, publisher from 1904 onwards of the journal *Hohe Warte*, head of the Lehrlingsschule für Kunstgewerbe (apprentice training school for applied art) from 1907 to 1910 in the garden city of Hellerau near Dresden, then freelance writer in Munich. See entry on Lux in *Deutsche Biographische Enzyklopädie*, eds. Walther Killy and Rudolf Vierhaus (Munich: Saur, 1997). See also Mark Jarzombek, "Joseph August Lux. Werkbund Promoter, Historian of a Lost Modernity", in *JSAH*, 63 (2004), pp. 202–219.

118 See On Gardens and Parks.

Grundpfeiler, however, Lux does not advocate any firm architectural approach. It is therefore no surprise that, for example on the issue of open or enclosed block form, he rejects both extremes as clichéd and calls for a return to earlier, simpler methods which treat each house individually and yet also create a coherent built environment.[119] It is equally clear that Lux makes some demands of urban design which are logically inconsistent with one another. These are: retaining, unchanged, the existing old suburbs and city centres; decentralising cities; separating business streets from residential streets; considering the former layout of the city and the traditional character of old buildings; long-term land policy; and promoting the building of detached houses.[120] What distinguishes Lux from the other authors whom Jeanneret cites, and connects him with Hans von Berlepsch-Valendàs, is his engagement with architecture as a social responsibility: for example in his chapter on garden cities. Although Jeanneret could hardly have used the structure of *Der Städtebau und die Grundpfeiler* as an example, he nevertheless took excerpts from three of its chapters: those on parks policy, monuments, and garden cities.

Cemeteries and garden cities

The topic of cemetery design, which had appeared in various draft tables of contents in the Manuscript since the spring, now came into its own: on 1 October Jeanneret visited the new Waldfriedhof in Munich which had been designed by Hans Grässel, and translated a whole article by Franz Zell in the *Süddeutsche Bauzeitung* of 1907, entitled "Die Münchener Friedhof- und Grabmalreform" (Reform of cemeteries and tombs in Munich).[121] He also translated articles on other cemetery projects, for example on a competition for a new cemetery in Osterholz, near Bremen, and on two projects by Max Läuger – for the Stadtpark in Hamburg and also for the Osterholz cemetery.[122] Jeanneret then turned to the detail of Georges Riat's *L'Art des Jardins*, which he borrowed from the Royal Bavarian Library.[123] In Riat's historical survey, which appeared in 1900 and is largely unknown, Jeanneret found just what he was looking for: poetic descriptions of gardens and parks from European and Oriental history, to act as an example and compensate for the disappointing park designs of his contemporaries. Having added Hermann Muthesius' *Englisches Haus* to his bibliography in April, he did not tackle it until the last week of September.[124] He noted illustrations of interest, where Muthesius shows the floor plans of English country houses and thus demonstrates how a house is married with a garden layout, and translated excerpts from a long passage by Muthesius on the architectural

---

119 Lux, *Der Städtebau und die Grundpfeiler der heimischen Bauweise*, p. 33.

120 Lux, *Der Städtebau und die Grundpfeiler der heimischen Bauweise*, p. 17–19.

121 Franz Zell, "Die Münchner Friedhof- und Grabmalreform", in *Süddeutsche Bauzeitung*, 17 (1907), no. 33, pp. 257–261.

122 Fritz Encke and Reinhold Hoemann, "Der Bremer Friedhofswettbewerb", in *Die Gartenkunst*, 12 (1910), no. 4, pp. 51–57, and August Grisebach, "Max Läugers Entwürfe zum Hamburger Stadtpark und zum Osterholzer Friedhof bei Bremen", in *Die Kunst – Angewandte Kunst 22* (1910), pp. 489–503. See LCdv 300 310.

123 Georges Riat, *L'Art des jardins* (Paris: L. Henry May, 1900).

124 In Cahier C.6, LCdv 248, between the excerpts from Riat, Lux, and Muthesius, Jeanneret notes: "Mardi 4 1/2 devant Brakl". According to Brooks, he visited the Villa Brakl with William Ritter on Tuesday, 4 October 1910; see Brooks, *Le Corbusier's Formative Years*, p. 231. '4 1/2' should be read as half past four in the afternoon. The fact that Jeanneret noted the appointment without stating the date indicates that this entry was made the previous week (between 26 September and 4 October); otherwise it would not have been clear, even to him, which Tuesday he meant.

nature of the garden.[125] Jeanneret was also now intensively collating material for the chapter On Gardens and Parks; he felt able to write to L'Eplattenier, on 1 October:

> I have just visited a garden city and the Waldfriedhof. I will have ideas to note in respect of both. [...] To perpetuate the genre of little villas scattered in the greenery is tedious. I dream of superb machines on our sloping land.[126] [...] My documenting of gardens is not going too badly. Nor of cemeteries. But as for bridges, I can't find anything and don't know what to say. If you have any documents or ideas on the subject, please do let me know.[127]

Jeanneret did find several books showing bridges, but they may have struck him as both too technical and not sufficiently detailed. None of these works contains any theoretical claims in relation to either the design of bridges or the aesthetic role they play in the urban landscape; Jeanneret investigates and ultimately describes these in his exploration of urban design elements. It is curious that he does not read the article "Brücken im Stadtbilde" (Bridges in the cityscape) by Gustav Ebe, which appeared in *Städtebau* in 1906. This contains many examples of bridges, throughout the history of Europe, which combine with their urban surroundings to form an ensemble.[128] Nevertheless, in his bibliography in the Cahier *City II Bridges* Jeanneret does list three works on bridges: *Architecture civile et militaire*, the first part of Camille Enlart's *Manuel d'archéologie française*, in which two illustrations of mediaeval stone arch bridges catch his eye; a two-volume publication by the royal Bavarian building authority which describes its streets, bridges and harbours; and an essay from the *Süddeutsche Bauzeitung* of 1907, in which another stone arch bridge is presented, this time a contemporary project.[129] Jeanneret notes the latter project with particular interest, and we can therefore assume that this is something approaching the ideal form he is looking for.[130]

A second bibliography can be found in the Manuscript, just as brief as the first; this one dates from late September or early October 1910. It is filed in the front part of the loose-leaf folder, under the heading 'Conclusion'. Here, Jeanneret primarily lists a series of books relating to garden cities:

---

125 The translations from Muthesius can be found in C.6, LCdv 253–258.

126 See illustrations XI and XII.

127 Jeanneret to L'Eplattenier, 1st October 1910 (E2-12-75 FLC).

128 Gustav Ebe, "Brücken im Stadtbilde", in *Der Städtebau*, 3 (1906), no. 12, pp. 159–162.

129 Camille Enlart, *Manuel d'archéologie française*. Part 1, vol. 2: *Architecture civile et militaire* (Paris: A. Picard, 1902–1904), listed in the bibliography on LCdv 230 and 415. Jeanneret notes on LCdv 230: "{taken from} book, both tracings of bridge in Tournai and bridge in Cahors." These refer to Fig.s 271 and 272 from Enlart's work, the Pont Valentré in Cahors and the Pont des Trous in Tournai. On the second request slip from the RBL to be preserved, Jeanneret writes: '[Munich,] 23rd October 1910//Brückenbauten// von der Staats-Bau-Verwaltung//M.//1906.//Ch. E. Jeanneret//4°/Bavar./1775 f. [bears library stamp: 'I. 24. SEP.']; C.3,49. The full book title is: Königlich Oberste Baubehörde, *Von der Staatsbauverwaltung in Bayern ausgeführte Straßen-, Brücken- und Wasserbauten* (Munich: Piloty & Loehle, vol. I 1906, vol. II 1909). He also lists: Arthur Speck, "Die Kronprinzenbrücke über das Spreetal in Bautzen", in *Süddeutsche Bauzeitung* 20 (1910), no. 14, pp. 105–110; LCdv 231.

130 "Completely remarkable as a beautiful huge modern bridge linking to the town. (Write and ask for a photo). The central arch has a span of 35m. The others 27"; LCdv 231.

AUTHORS	Reference	BIBLIOGRAPHY	Publisher
Berlepsch-Valendàs		Bodenpolitik und gemeindliche Wohnungsfürsorge der Stadt Ulm. (with many illustrations) Munich	E Reinhardt
Ebenezer Howard		Garden Cities of To-morrow	
Jos. Aug. Lux.			
Metzendorf. Essen		Brochure on Margarethe [Krupp] Stiftung, Essen	
		Catalogue of Städtebauausstellung Berlin 1910	
		Journal: Städtebau Berlin	
	Cahier M p16	Süddeutsche Bauzeitung – (journal)	
	Cahier M p16	Gartenkunst (journal)	
Schultze-Naumburg		Kulturarbeiten	Kunstwart Munich[131]

This is an unusual bibliography: it was written so late in the work on *La Construction des villes* that one would expect it to be an almost complete list of the works Jeanneret was examining – or perhaps a list of books and essays yet to be dealt with. The latter is closer to the truth, but why does Jeanneret note down Schultze-Naumburg's *Kulturarbeiten*? Is he referring himself to the other volumes, or merely recording the one he has already worked on: Volume IV, *Städtebau*?

Citing the first two texts was probably purely a declaration of intent: nowhere in the Manuscript is there any evidence that Jeanneret worked with these books.[132] Yet he might have been expected to, particularly in the case of Berlepsch-Valendàs' book on Ulm. Jeanneret noted in the bibliography that it contained "lots of images" – which he could have used for *La Construction des villes*, but did not.[133] In noting the name Lux, Jeanneret was most probably referring to the author's *Der Städtebau und die Grundpfeiler* from which he translated almost the whole chapter on garden cities. Next, Jeanneret references the example of a garden city he had seen at the urban design exhibition: Georg Metzendorf's design for a garden suburb at what was later named Margarethenhöhe in Essen. Jeanneret translated an abbreviated, but nevertheless detailed version of Metzendorf's own description of the design.[134] It is not clear where Jeanneret found this short book, as it appears in neither the catalogue of the Royal

131 LCdv 536. Jeanneret writes "Cahier. M p 16" on the Cahier C.9.M *Garden-Cities Cemeteries I*, on p. 16 of which (LCdv 293) he lists the two journals cited – "Extract from Süddeutsche Bauzeitung page 257 1907. Some models of tombs in the ancient world have been published – see my tracings. A very instructive article in Gartenkunst. 1st April 1910." This short bibliography must therefore have been written after page LCdv 293, probably in early October 1910.

132 In any case, both works are available at the RBL: Hans Eduard von Berlepsch-Valendàs, *Bodenpolitik und gemeindliche Wohnungsfürsorge der Stadt Ulm* (Munich: E. Reinhardt, 1910) (RBL: 4 Germ sp 24p) and Ebenezer Howard, *Garden Cities of To-morrow* (London: Swan Sonnenschein, 1902) (RBL: A. civ. 239 ͥ, acquired 1909).

133 On the last page of the book, the publisher advertises: "Vor kurzem erschien: [...] Gartenstadt München-Perlach" (recently published: [...] Munich Perlach garden suburb). This may have prompted Jeanneret to borrow Berlepsch-Valendàs' book on the Munich Perlach project.

134 The translation can be found in Cahier C.10, LCdv 321–325. Georg Metzendorf, *Denkschrift über den Ausbau des Stiftungsgeländes* [*Margarethenhöhe*] (Essen: Petersen, 1909).

Bavarian Library nor that of the Bavarian National Museum.[135] Jeanneret had bought the urban design exhibition catalogue for William Ritter, and there is no evidence that it was in Le Corbusier's possession at a later date.[136] Only Werner Hegemann's subsequent publication of *Der Städtebau nach den Ergebnissen der allgemeinen Städtebau-Ausstellung* in 1911 appears in his estate.[137] In the cahiers and the *Carnets de Voyage*, Jeanneret occasionally quotes numbers from the urban design exhibition catalogue which relate to the urban designs displayed there. We can assume that Jeanneret did not purchase a second copy of the catalogue for himself, but was reminding himself to borrow the catalogue again for reference purposes.

Thus Jeanneret's final month in Munich was once again full to the brim: with research on bridges, gardens and parks, cemeteries and garden cities, and with drafting the second half of the chapters General Considerations and On Squares.

At Behrens' studio: No time for urban design

On 17 October, Jeanneret left Munich for Berlin, impatient to start work. He had yet to receive word that he could work in Peter Behrens' studio and did not know what awaited him in Berlin. With stops in Regensburg and Donaustauf, he arrived in Berlin on Tuesday, 18 October.[138] Only a week later did he learn he would be able to work with Behrens from 1 November. Despite this uncertainty, and his intention to visit his brother Albert in Dresden – he took a trip there between Friday 21 and Tuesday 25 October – Jeanneret undertook some research in Berlin's Royal Library as early as the 20th. Thus he continued his work on *La Construction des villes* uninterrupted. At the library, Jeanneret transcribed in French an encyclopaedia article on the Roman Emperor Trajan, the source of which he cites thus: "(Gde encyclopédie) – Koenigliche Bibliothek Berlin 20 Oct 1910". On the following pages, he takes excerpts from an article on Augustus, noting the author as Camille Jullian.[139] There is also the beginning of an excerpt from French theorist Roland Fréart's *Parallèle de l'architecture antique av.*[ec] *la moderne* of 1650, probably made on the same day. Jeanneret broke off after a few pages, apparently because Fréart's text was thoroughly unhelpful in terms of

---

135 Clearly only a very few copies of the *Denkschrift* were published; today only a single copy is available for inter-library loan in Germany (at the University of Cologne).

136 "[...] I just received your card and as I will not be able to visit you before 27th June, I wonder if I shouldn't send you the two catalogues I bought for you straight away[:] I. Urban design exhibition II. Major Berlin exhibition" Jeanneret to Ritter, 17 June 1910. "Je reçois votre carte à la minute et comme je ne pourrai vous rendre visite avant le 27 juin, je me demande si je ne devrais pas vous envoyer de suite les 2 catalogues que j'ai acheté pour vous[:] I. Städtebauaust. II. Grosse Berliner Aust." (R3-18-1 FLC)

137 See Arnaud Dercelles, "Présentation de la bibliothèque personnelle de Le Corbusier", in *Le Corbusier et le livre* (Barcelona: Collegi d'Arquitectes de Catalunya, 2005), pp. 6–78.

138 The 'green' carnet, which only contains entries from this brief trip, is held in the BV.

139 LCdv 463–465, with under the last page: "(Camille Jullian. Gde Enyclopédie)". This would be a trivial detail, were Jeanneret not to make repeated notes on the great rulers under whom certain works of art were made. Thus at the start of Cahier C.2 *City II Bridges* there is a short excerpt from the 1905 report by a Russian archaeological committee on the artistic treasures of ancient Samarkand. Jeanneret devotes several lines to the warlord Tamerlane. What is more, at the beginning of the Manuscript he explicitly emphasises the importance of this great ruler in terms of art.

urban design.[140] Also on the same day, he requested at least two books which he was not able to borrow:

Jos. Aug. Lux. *Die Stadtwohnung* Charlottenburg 1910.
Die Entstellung unseres Landes von Schultze-Naumburg *Flugschriften des Heimatschutzbundes 2.*[141]

In all likelihood, the only reason we have learned of these requests is because they were not fulfilled: Jeanneret did keep a few request slips, but sadly none of these relate to especially relevant tomes. The lending slips tell us that Jeanneret is staying at 36 Dessauerstraße. This is unlikely to be the Dessauerstraße in the southern suburb of Lichterfelde, but more likely to be the Dessauer Straße near the Anhalter Bahnhof close to Potsdamer Platz, where Jeanneret will have rented a hotel room while he looked for somewhere to live.[142] His gloomy letter to his parents, dated the same evening, in which he complains about the unpleasant atmosphere in the city, fits with this version of events: "Berlin has not won me over, and when one leaves the immense avenues, there is only disgust and horror."[143] Once he had returned from Dresden, Jeanneret not only learned that he would be employed in Behrens' office, but also found himself a room in Neubabelsberg straight away: on 28 October he even told his parents and L'Eplattenier his new address, 83 Stahnsdorfer Straße. (Fig. XIV) The next day, Saturday, 29 October, Jeanneret had returned to work at the Royal Bavarian Library. He ordered four books as below, two of which he borrowed:

Berlepsch-Valendàs. The Garden City of Munich Perlach.
A. E. Brinckmann, The Practical Significance of ornament engravings for the Early Renaissance in Germany ['Study on German art history 90' added by librarian] Strasbourg 1907.
A. E. Brinckmann. *Late mediaeval town design* [in the south of France]. Berlin 1910.
Old Holland by Jos. Aug. Lux, Leipzig 1908 [added by librarian: 'Cultural sites 10'][144]

---

140 LCdv 466-470.
141 Joseph August Lux. Titles translate as: *The urban apartment* Charlottenburg 1910; *The distortion of our country* by Schultze-Naumburg, *Leaflets from the Heimatschutz association, 2.* See also the request slips (LCdv 451 and 454).
142 He writes to his parents: "En cas d'engagement il faudrait habiter Neu-Babelsberg même, c-à-d, la pleine campagne. [. . .] Pendant 8 jours encore, il me faut donc vivre en hôtel et voilà pourquoi mes capitaux ne suffisent plus." "If I am employed I will have to live in Neu-Babelsberg itself, i.e. right out in the country. [. . .] I must therefore live in a hotel for eight more days, that is why my funds are insufficient." Jeanneret to his parents, 18 October 1910 (R1-5-67 FLC).
143 "Berlin ne me conquiert pas, et dès que l'on sort des immenses avenues, c'est de l'écœurement, de l'horreur." Jeanneret to his parents, 21 October 1910 (R1-5-68 FLC).
144 Hans Eduard von Berlepsch-Valendàs and Peter Andreas Hansen, *Die Gartenstadt München-Perlach* (Munich: E. Reinhardt, 1910); Albert Erich Brinckmann, *Die praktische Bedeutung der Ornamentstiche für die deutsche Frührenaissance* [Studien zur deutschen Kunstgeschichte 90] (Straßburg: Heitz, 1907, also PhD diss., University of Heidelberg, 1907); Albert Erich Brinckmann, *Spätmittelalterliche Stadtanlagen in Südfrankreich* (Berlin: Schenck, 1910); Joseph August Lux, *Alt-Holland* [Stätten der Kultur 10] (Leipzig:

Fig. XIV Jeanneret in his room in Neubabelsberg, April 1911 (LC 108-800)

The text on late mediaeval town layouts, *Spätmittelalterliche Stadtanlagen*, was on loan, and the book on the Munich Perlach garden suburb could not be loaned for reasons which are unclear. Although Jeanneret did not ask to borrow the text until he reached Berlin, he had certainly already looked at it in Munich.[145] Nevertheless, as far as we can ascertain, he did not redeploy any information from this book in his own work. The line it takes is similar to Berlepsch-Valendàs' other work on land policy and municipal welfare in the city of Ulm, dated 1909.[146] Jeanneret had certainly come into contact with

Klinkhardt & Biermann, 1908). The request slips for these four books have also been preserved, see LCdv 452–453 and 455–456.

145 The RBL holds Berlepsch-Valendàs' *Die Gartenstadt München-Perlach* (Munich: E. Reinhardt, 1910) at shelf mark '8⁰ Bavar. 299 ⁰'.

146 Eduard von Berlepsch-Valendàs, *Bodenpolitik und gemeindliche Fürsorge der Stadt Ulm* (Munich: E. Reinhardt, 1909).

this text already, as he not only noted alongside its entry in the bibliography that this was a book "av[ec] b[eaucou]p d'illustrations" (with many illustrations), but also cited 'the Ulm case' elsewhere in the Manuscript, referring to the city's policy on workers' housing. However, this case is not explored in detail in the Manuscript of *La Construction des villes*.

In contrast, Jeanneret was able to peruse both Brinckmann's book on ornament engravings and Lux's volume on 'Old Holland' in Berlin. What was he hoping to find in these books? They bear no obvious relation to *La Construction des villes*. We assume they were not what Jeanneret had expected, especially since he mistakenly wrote 'Ornamentische' (ornamental matters) rather than 'Ornamentstiche' (ornament engravings) on one request slip. Whatever he hoped to find, the research Jeanneret undertook during his first few days in Berlin was clearly not very focused, and no particular topic emerged which he wanted to pursue.

When he joined Behrens' studio, Jeanneret had his first experience of working full-time, as Brooks notes.[147] Brooks therefore assumes Jeanneret was no longer working on his Manuscript. However, it is clear from the Berlin cahiers that Jeanneret did seize any rare opportunities that arose for further study in the library. Hence Jeanneret wrote underneath the excerpts from Theodor Fischer's booklet on matters of city expansion *Stadterweiterungsfragen*, "le 12/11/10", Saturday, 12 November. Finally, after a good six months, he took excerpts from Fischer's booklet. Why had he not done so in April or May, straight after his discussions with Fischer? After all, Jeanneret had long since included the professor's views in the Manuscript. Perhaps the excerpts were a sort of belated *hommage* to him, in contrast to Jeanneret's treatment of Peter Behrens, whom – as far as we can see – he rejected from the start.

Spring 1911: Big plans and a Laugier excerpt

Despite the thorough nature of Brooks' research into Jeanneret's *Formative Years*, he provides amazingly little detail on Jeanneret's time in Berlin: in part because he had no access to important letters from Jeanneret to his parents. These are now available for research at the FLC, and, coupled with our research on *La Construction des villes*, allow us to paint a fuller picture of these months.[148] Jeanneret was fundamentally disappointed about the atmosphere, mentality, and work ethic in Behrens' studio. He complained repeatedly about his colleagues' laziness and messing around. In his letter of 11 November 1910, he complained that he had been given practically no responsibility. Then, on New Year's Day 1911, he wrote a cheery, almost cocky letter to his parents: while staying with his brother Albert in Dresden, he had visited Heinrich Tessenow in Hellerau at the end of the year, and in his office looked at plans for the Jacques Dalcroze Dance Institute.[149] Edouard was clearly unsettled and full of plans. Hence we learn in the same letter that he was already considering a 'petite maison':

---

147 See Brooks, *Le Corbusier's Formative Years*, p. 236.

148 Rémi Baudouï and Arnaud Dercelles, *Correspondance Le Corbusier. Edition établie, annotée et présentée par Rémi Baudouï et Arnaud Dercelles* ([Fondation Le Corbusier] Gollion: Infolio, 2011–).

149 "Et jeudi, – comment? Jeudi tu ne travaillais donc point, petit Salaud? – jeudi je retournai à Hellerau où je fus présenté à l'architecte Tessenow qui me montra ses plans pour l'institut Jacques [Dalcroze]." Jeanneret to his parents, 1ˢᵗ January 1911 (R1-5-94 FLC).

You know that I have sometimes dreamed of a little house, the first one I would build when I returned. I want it to be astonishing, to amaze people. Do you know which piece of land I dream of for it? One of the best is that one behind the Aubert house. So for example I'm thinking about that one. [That is where the *Maison Blanche* now stands.] And the idea I had for the construction is changing. I would do things differently now. I have had such extraordinary inspiration, a super-duper idea! It is so extraordinary that it is sure to change again tomorrow![150]

Jeanneret did interrupt his work on *La Construction des villes*, beginning again in January 1911; only then did he return to work on Marc Antoine Laugier's *Essai sur l'architecture* in the Royal Bavarian Library. This is surprising, and it is fascinating to see how Jeanneret dealt with Laugier's treatment of the intellectual basis for architecture: being primarily interested in urban design matters, Jeanneret took detailed excerpts from Laugier's plan for urban improvements and his examination of the garden architecture at Versailles, but completely ignored questions such as the orders of columns. Jeanneret copied out excerpts from the *Essai* onto 40 pages of Cahier C.13 *Laugier*. By this stage, Jeanneret was also dating his excerpts, which unfortunately had not been the case in Munich. Thus we learn that on Thursday. 26 January and Thursday, 16 February 1911 he was working in the Royal Bavarian Library, and on Sunday, 12 March 1911 he was at home, drafting a concluding comment on the *Essai*.[151] The fact that Jeanneret clearly had time for his studies on Thursdays is surprising. However, it does not seem to mean that he was not fully occupied at the studio, since he reported proudly to his parents on Friday, 17 February (the day after a visit to the library) that Behrens had granted him a generous pay rise. Furthermore, Jeanneret's letter to his parents dated 9 March describes relations with Behrens: they were now nowhere near as bad as he claims elsewhere: "My situation had got back to normal. I now have the trust of the boss [of the studio] and of Peter. I feel I have reached the level of my colleagues, if not in terms of drafting, then at least in terms of practical results for Peter."[152] He also reports being involved in drawings for Behrens' St. Petersburg embassy:

Happily I am now as rich as Croesus, as Peter has, in view of all my willingness, suddenly raised my consideration: 80 marks, almost enough to get married. To show my appreciation, I have painstakingly cobbled together a large perspective drawing

---

150   "Vous savez que je m'occupais parfois à songer à une petite maison, la première que je ferais à mon retour. Je la voudrais épatante, afin d'éblouir les foules. Vous savez pour quel terrain je la rêverais? Un des plus beaux est celui derrière chez Aubert. Alors je pense à celui-là par exemple. Et l'idée que j'avais eue {sur la construction} change. Maintenant je ferai ça autrement. Il m'est venu une inspiration extraordinaire une idée zépatante! Elle est si extraordinaire, que demain elle changera sûrement! ..." Jeanneret to his parents, 1st January 1911 (R1-5-94 FLC).

151   See LCdv 495, 513, 516–519.

152   "Ma situation s'était cependant ramenée à la normale. J'ai la confiance du chef et de Peter. Je me sens grimpé à la hauteur des collègues, sinon en patte, du moins en résultats pratiques pour Peter." Jeanneret to his parents, 9 March 1911 (R1-5-96 FLC).

in charcoal showing the future German embassy in St. Petersburg – the drawing is to be submitted this coming Tuesday, to Mr. Sandoz-Lehmann![153]

This adds nicely to the otherwise scant evidence of Jeanneret's time with Behrens; the only other proof which has been unearthed is of his work on the Elektra boathouse.[154] However, despite all the minor successes in Behrens' studio, Jeanneret had long been contemplating calling a premature halt to his work there. Thus he explained to his parents on 17 February that he had decided to turn his back on Behrens' studio, a decision which caused him some heartache:

> Tralala! Gee up horsie, I'm nearly there. Hope is on the horizon, the hope of hop-ping it, the final push! And since I decided that, I am a new man. [...] Leaving the charming Peter behind me, I turned alone into the wind and let myself be enclosed by the dark dome of pines.[155]

He is not merely announcing his decision here; he finds himself obliged to justify it to his parents later in the letter. They appear to have reacted with just as much anger as he expected. In the next letter, he defends himself:

> Well, you wondered about what you call the hasty departure from Peter's place. I learned a lot in those five months. I came to understand his principles. What does his approach matter? As for the rest, the milieu was pretty unpromising.[156]

Jeanneret had learned a lot at Behrens' studio, but hardly had any time for *La Construction des villes*. Was there any connection between his office work and his research? Unfortunately, we can say very little on this issue. Did the work on Laugier arise not only from Jeanneret's own interest, but also from his office work? That would perhaps explain the dates of his research at the library in Berlin. But even if this were the case, we can be certain that Jeanneret's interest in Laugier originally stemmed from Brinckmann's *Platz und Monument*.[157] We will explore in more detail below how

153 "Heureusement que me voilà riche comme Crésus, puisque Peter considérant toute ma bonne volonté, me hausse d'un coup aux honneurs les plus hauts: 180 marks c'est de quoi se marier presque. Pour le remercier, je lui ai fricoté aux petits oignons, une grande diablesse de perspective au fusain, représentant la future léga-tion allemande de St. Petersburg, – laquelle perspective doit être soumise mardi qui vient – a Monsieur Sandoz-Lehmann!" Jeanneret to his parents, 17 February 1911 (R1-5-95 FLC).

154 Brooks describes Jeanneret's collaboration on the Elektra boathouse in Oberschöneweide (Berlin) and his interest in the Wiegand house. Brooks, *Le Corbusier's Formative Years*, pp. 240–243.

155 "Tra la la ou ti! Hue, la Grise, on est bientôt en haut. L'Espoir luit à l'horizon, l'espoir de la décampée, l'ouf! définitif. Aussi depuis que me voilà décidé, je suis un nouvel homme. [...] Et laissant cet affable Peter, je m'enfonçai seul dans les sillons du vent, et me laissai couvrir par le dôme noir des pins." Jeanneret to his parents, 17 February 1911 (R1-5-95 FLC).

156 "Mais au fait, vous vous êtes étonnés de ce que vous êtes appelez le départ subit de chez Peter. Ça fait cepen-dant 5 mois, où j'ai beaucoup appris. Ses principes je les ai compris. Que m'importe sa manière. Le milieu du reste était très défavorable..." Jeanneret to his parents, 9 March 1911 (R1-5-96 FLC).

157 See Jeanneret's note in C.3, LCdv 433: "Books from which Brinckmann draws constantly[:] P. Patte, Mém-oire sur les objets les plus importants de l'architecture, Paris 1759 – M. A. Laugier, Observations sur l'archi-tecture, The Hague 1765." Jeanneret knows from Brinckmann's *Platz und Monument* not only of Laugier's *Observations*, but also of his *Essai sur l'Architecture* (Paris: Duchesne 1753), even though he does not add the latter to his bibliography until early 1911. Brinckmann repeatedly quotes from both of Laugier's works.

Brinckmann investigated the content of Laugier's work, and how this may have influenced Jeanneret. The Laugier excerpts marked a provisional end to Jeanneret's research for his study on urban design. In the period that followed, and especially on his *Voyage d'Orient*, he continued to collect illustrative material for his discussion of urban design issues, in the form of sketches and photos. Yet from this point until 1915, no further work was done on the Manuscript. Thus March 1911 saw the end, not only of Jeanneret's time with Peter Behrens, but also of his work on *La Construction des villes*.

Chapter 2

The material in detail

Proposition and General Considerations

Jeanneret did not draft a single introduction to his tract, but instead wrote many introductory chapters. In so doing, he approached the concept of built form in the city step by step, proceeding from general considerations about cultural history to the principles of structuring society. Since many theories and basic ideas are repeated here, it would make sense to treat these chapters together: they represent Jeanneret's attempt to capture the phenomenon of 'the city' and its design within the limited time he had available for *La Construction des villes*. To begin with, Jeanneret's arguments in the various chapters will be presented and traced back to their sources wherever possible, in order to elicit commonalities and contrasts. The order of the chapters in Jeanneret's study will also be discussed, since it is highly likely that these chapters were not all intended to sit alongside one another, with some being intended to supersede others. Jeanneret uses the chapters Proposition and General Considerations, and the introduction to the longer section on The Elements of the City, as routes into the issue of urban design. The loose-leaf folder and the cahiers contain several versions of some of these chapters, at various stages of development.

The finished form of the Proposition features in the loose-leaf folder.[1] The draft for this chapter, which forms an initial overview of the whole study, can be found in Cahier C.3.[2] A sort of general introduction also exists, still in sketch form and beginning with the exclamation "La Ville!"; Jeanneret may have intended for it to precede the Proposition.[3] Another completed chapter is General Considerations, the first two sections of which can be found in the loose-leaf folder, with sections three and four in Cahier C.1.[4] The Introduction has also been drafted in full, and can be found in the loose-leaf folder.[5] Its content bears some similarity to the introductory chapters; however, it will be analysed later because Jeanneret uses it as an introduction to The Elements of the City.

In the loose-leaf folder, sections one and two of the General Considerations are directly followed by four pages on which Jeanneret attempts to define the three terms hygiene, modernity, and beauty. Although these were found under the heading General

---

1 LCdv 2–9.
2 LCdv 427. This overview shows the whole of the planned content of the tract, including the other chapters.
3 LCdv 10–15.
4 LCdv 24–27 and LCdv 28–46.
5 LCdv 56–62. Jeanneret also calls this chapter variously "Vue d'ensemble" (Overview) or "Avant-propos" (Foreword).

Considerations, they certainly do not belong there. However, it has not been possible to find anywhere in the Manuscript where they definitely do belong. They are directly followed by one page headed "Conclusion" and four further pages of text.[6] It is not clear whether Jeanneret intended these pages to act as a conclusion for the General Considerations, or even for the entire Manuscript – they do contain a summary and assessment of what emerged from the urban design exhibition in Berlin. Perhaps Jeanneret did intend to sum up his work on the basis of these notes; several draft tables of contents for the entire Manuscript indicate as much. If this was indeed his intention, Jeanneret must have abandoned the idea at a later stage, as he failed to complete the Conclusion section.

Proposition – The collective and the universal genius

The first page of the Cahier *City III* is devoted to an overview entitled *Thèse* (Proposition). This is followed by a brief supplement entitled *Résumé* (Summary), and a collection of notes for the chapter on La Chaux-de-Fonds over the next two pages.[7] Jeanneret arranges this overview into two columns. In the left-hand column, he attempts to describe in keywords how cities emerged from an anthropological perspective, moving from the original formation of human societies to a peaceful, utopian future. These keywords correspond to the contents of the finished Proposition in the loose-leaf folder.[8] The right-hand column contains a highly attractive definition of the ideal city of the future, which he later expanded into the text of the Introduction. Parts of the basic positions stated here can be found throughout the tract. On these three pages, Jeanneret composes a sort of table of contents complete with commentary, but does not allocate these contents to particular chapters. First, he makes clear his intention to proceed from a very general introduction to a development of specific theories on the necessity of collective living, beauty, and functionality. He then plans to turn these theories into broadly applicable, or even ideal, requirements for a city, and finally to apply them to La Chaux-de-Fonds.

In contrast to Brooks' claim, this particular arrangement of the contents and broad-brush approach have little in common with Camillo Sitte's *Städtebau nach seinen künst-lerischen Grundsätzen*.[9] Indeed, the long general introductory chapters of *La Construction des villes*, with their sketch-like format, prefigure their later counterparts in *Urbanisme*. Yet in *Urbanisme*, Le Corbusier was to make very few calls for concrete action, instead presenting more of an overall vision for society.

As elsewhere in the Manuscript, Jeanneret is very preoccupied with questions of egoism and altruism.[10] Here, he initially considers the survival instinct as a precondition for forming a society, coupled with the – not necessarily obvious – assumption that societies coalesce as a means of supporting the weakest among us. Thus Jeanneret's latent social Darwinism is deployed to counterbalance an altruism influenced by Christianity, which might in turn have been bolstered by his reading of Ruskin. He states that this altruism provides the motivation for making laws; the laws bring increased security,

---

6 LCdv 355–358.
7 LCdv 427–429.
8 LCdv 2–9.
9 See Brooks, *Le Corbusier's Formative Years*, p. 201.
10 LCdv 18–21.

which will in turn elicit a striving for beauty. He believes this is how earlier cities emerged, but that the 19th century has gone astray due to industrialisation and social crises. However, one should not necessarily conclude that it is impossible to improve the general situation: indeed, the 'new era', the 20th century, promises greater power for public institutions and greater participation in society by the general populace. The city of the future will adopt a political character. For Jeanneret, this means the interplay of three factors in urban design: the construction of public buildings, the design of public spaces, and – as a precondition – beauty in urban design. It is remarkable that Jeanneret links politics with beauty here. His apparent intention is to use aesthetics to achieve political education. Jeanneret concludes that this will result in greater morality and respect for one's native land. Thus Jeanneret links Sitte's national conservative idea that patriotism arises from the beauty of the urban environment to the socialist ideas with which he has grown up in La Chaux-de-Fonds.

Next in the Manuscript comes Part B, which can be regarded as a precursor to the Introduction. Jeanneret's three basic requirements of a city are: utility – it must be useful and practical, it must be functional; hygiene – which Jeanneret uses as a very wide-ranging term, encompassing, as explored below, more or less everything which makes city-dwellers' lives worth living from a technical, urban design, and architectural perspective; and last but not least, beauty.[11] Being the third basic requirement, beauty should be seen as directly connected to hygiene: Jeanneret considered the aesthetic and practical aspects of urban design to be inextricably linked.

Jeanneret demands that urban areas be arranged according to their functions, with residential, commercial, and industrial areas separated from one another; he also wants to provide sunshine and fresh air, and avoid irksome winds. The beginnings of the later modernist call for "Licht, Luft und Sonne" (light, air, and sun) can be detected here. A central square in the city should be dedicated to beauty. Jeanneret notes in particular that squares which are too large therefore lose their impact. He speaks of the "three cities", meaning the three key functions of a city, how they need to be separated and where they overlap. Jeanneret emphasises the collective, and the need for the individual to make sacrifices on behalf of society as a whole. Finally, even at this early stage, Jeanneret presents in brief the main requirements for improving the urban design of La Chaux-de-Fonds. He calls for a contoured map of the town, so that future town plans can consider the topographical situation, and states his intention to improve the planning of streets and squares, which he considers too open.[12]

Jeanneret drafted this overview during his first days in Munich. To a certain extent, it represents an intellectual starting point from which he was to progress considerably in terms of broadening his knowledge about and attitude towards urban design, thanks to theory from Germany and Austria. He already had very firm views, which were commensurate with the modern era: he wanted to align residential blocks to face the sun, separate factories from residential areas according to the prevailing winds, arrange a beautiful built environment around the central square, and embed residential areas in green spaces. With a little imagination, one can picture the *Ville Contemporaine* whilst listening to these stipulations.

In this, Jeanneret is in fact surprisingly close to the more technically minded German urban designers such as Joseph Stübben or Reinhard Baumeister. As shown in the plans

11 LCdv 47–50.
12 LCdv 427–429.

for Greater Berlin of 1910, German urban design of the early 20th century dealt intensively with the separation of the city into a central business district, a belt of tenement
blocks, and residential zones set in green, open spaces; industrial districts were also separated off.[13] However, Jeanneret's comment that the squares built in his era were too
large points towards picturesque urban design, which was indeed crucial for him in
1910. This tendency of his certainly arose from Sitte's theories, with which Jeanneret
was already familiar thanks to L'Eplattenier. His teacher's influence should not be underestimated; it is therefore appropriate to look, for a comparison, to L'Eplattenier's essay
"Renouveau d'art" on the need for renewal in art, which appeared in February 1910.
Here, L'Eplattenier laments the lack of art in public life, and calls for it to be reintro-
duced into our everyday existence. He examines urban design in La Chaux-de-Fonds and
bemoans the monotonous form of the town (Fig. XV), in particular the gridded street
layout, which does not take into account the geographical situation or the uneven terrain:

Fig. XV Temple Indépendant in La Chaux-de-Fonds. Photo ca. 1900 (P2-4461 BV)

13 See Wolfgang Sonne, *Representing the State. Capital City Planning in the Early Twentieth Century* (Munich:
   Prestel, 2003), and Gerhard Fehl (ed.), *Stadt-Umbau. Die planmäßige Erneuerung europäischer Großstädte
   zwischen Wiener Kongreß und Weimarer Republik* (Basel and Berlin: Birkhäuser, 1995).

In fact, in its layout and architecture La Chaux-de-Fonds does not present such a magnificent example of good sense and taste as so many other Swiss towns and cities. The aberration, which it would be puerile to try and deny, arises primarily from the fact that the street plan fails to respect the shapes and undulations of the landscape. Our precipitous streets fly in the face of common sense. The rectilinear plan, whatever advantages it may bring, generates in its monotony similar constructions without any element of surprise. The variety in plans from the olden days meant that each house needed to be given a different architecture, whereas our long rectangular *massifs* allow speculators to repeat ad infinitum the classic humdrum block of flats. The planning officials, for their part, have not exploited the real advantages presented by the straight streets, which can form a magnificent framework for group-funded buildings. Most of our churches and public buildings are lost among the rows and disappear.[14]

These theories, which are manifest in Jeanneret's words "to draw up a street plan one needs as a minimum a map of the area with contour lines in three dimensions", also appear elsewhere in the Manuscript.[15] L'Eplattenier's article is valuable to us because it appeared in February 1910, shortly before Jeanneret left for Munich. It is therefore fair to assume that Jeanneret had some concept of good and bad urban design before he arrived in Munich, and that this concept could be largely attributed to L'Eplattenier, who in turn looked to Camillo Sitte. This provided Jeanneret with a clear pattern to follow, although he had yet to ascertain what concrete implications it had for urban design.

The Proposition is very similar to the overview in Cahier C.3.[16] It can be reduced to two main thoughts: first, that the community should be valued more highly than the individual, and second, that a new type of community will produce a new sense of beauty, improving life for everybody. Jeanneret maintains that the city is the outlet for these new artistic movements. Art for art's sake will not work; instead, art must be integrated into everyday life. Equally, functionality is useless without beauty. The aim therefore is to design a hygienic, practical city which is also beautiful.[17] This is the *Gesamtkunstwerk* which will, by its very nature, improve life. These, then, are the main statements made in the Proposition; they reappear, formulated slightly differently, in other parts of the text. L'Eplattenier's influence can also been seen here, in the finished version of the Proposition. In "Renouveau d'art", he writes of how little linkage there is between art and life:

14 "La Chaux-de-Fonds, en effet, ne présente pas dans son plan et dans son architecture le magnifique exemple de bon sens et de goût de tant d'autres villes suisses. Le mal, qu'il serait puéril de vouloir cacher vient d'abord de ce que le tracé des rues n'a pas respecté les formes et les accidents du terrain. Nos rues à pic sont un défi au bon sens. Le plan rectiligne quelque avantage qu'il puisse avoir, engendre par sa monotonie des constructions semblables sans imprévu. La variété des plans d'autrefois obligeait de donner à chaque maison une architecture différente, tandis que les longs massifs rectangulaires permettent aux spéculateurs de répéter à l'infini le type banal des maisons locatives. De son côté, l'édilité n'a pas su profiter des avantages réels que présentent les rues rectilignes qui peuvent être des cadres magnifiques pour les édifices de fonds. La plupart de nos temples et nos édifices publics sont perdus dans le rang et effacés." Charles L'Eplattenier, "Renouveau d'Art", in *L'Abeille*, La Chaux-de-Fonds, 20 February 1910, p.1.
15 Quotation from LCdv 429. See also On Possible Strategies, especially LCdv 331f.
16 LCdv 474–429.
17 "Une ville hygiénique, une ville utile, et alors conçue en beauté." LCdv 46.

It is painful to admit that art and beauty are increasingly disappearing from the surroundings in which we live. Art, which used to make our existence more beautiful,
has withdrawn into the narrow confines of the painting on its easel.[18]

L'Eplattenier varies this statement in several ways in the following lines, and Jeanneret
adopts the idea in his Proposition. However, this is a view borrowed rather directly from
Sitte's formulations, especially those from the chapter "Artistic Limitations of Modern
City Planning", where he bemoans precisely this withdrawal of art from public life.[19]
   In contrast to the Proposition, in the sketch entitled "La Ville!" Jeanneret shifts his
focus to the suffering of human beings and the passionate feelings stirred up by urban
life and the transformations wrought by industrialisation. "La Ville!" may be the first
fully formed draft Jeanneret ever completed of his Proposition, and certainly constitutes
a highly romantic, poetic introduction to the subject of the city.[20] Some of the themes
employed by Jeanneret in his later version of the Proposition first appear here, albeit in
a slightly different context.[21] He goes into greater detail about the reasons behind the
change in city living: industrialisation. However, unlike William Morris or John Ruskin
but in line with the aims of the *Deutscher Werkbund*, Jeanneret clearly responds positively to progress and the advent of the machine age, exclaiming: "The feverish, modern,
intensive city, the city of toil, of factories, of electricity [...] will deflower this firmament [...] with the invasion of new machines [...], for words and lamentations cannot
stop the wheels of the chariot of progress."[22] This also provides us with an early indication of his later enthusiasm for machines, which is particularly evident in *Vers une architecture*, but which also emerges in one other part of *La Construction des villes*: the third
section of the General Considerations.[23] In 1922, Jeanneret wrote to William Ritter, with
the benefit of hindsight: "You will see my ideas on architecture in it and remember that
when I was twenty my nickname at the school was 'the ocean liner'."[24] He would heed
the call for "La Ville!" in *Urbanisme*, albeit then as Le Corbusier and in subtly different
terms: "A city! It is the grip of man upon nature. It is a human operation directed against
nature, a human organism both for protection and for work. It is a creation."[25] This contrasts with the general tone of *La Construction des villes*: here, the concept of the

---

18 "Il est pénible de constater que l'art et la beauté disparaissent de plus en plus du milieu dans lequel nous
    vivons. L'art qui, autrefois, embellissait l'existence, s'est retiré dans le cadre étroit du tableau de chevalet."
    L'Eplattenier, "Renouveau d'Art", p. 1.
19 See Sitte, *Der Städtebau*, p. 116f.; Collins and Crasemann Collins, *Camillo Sitte: The Birth of Modern City
    Planning*, p. 243f.
20 LCdv 10–16.
21 It is not clear that *La Ville!* should be allocated to the *Thèse*. However, the closing lines of this introduction
    indicate that Jeanneret planned to place it before the actual *Thèse*. On p. LCdv 15, Jeanneret uses the heading
    'I partie' and begins a text, the first lines of which are very similar to the first sentences in the final version of
    the *Thèse* found in the loose-leaf folder.
22 LCdv 12.
23 LCdv 29–33.
24 "Vous y verrez mes idées sur l'architecture en vous souvenant qu'à l'école à 20 ans, on m'avait surnommé
    'Paquebot'." Jeanneret to William Ritter, 7th April 1922, R3-19-389 – 391 FLC.
25 Le Corbusier, *The City of To-morrow and its Planning*, trans. Frederick Etchells (New York: Payson and
    Clarke, 1929), p. XXI. See Le Corbusier, *Urbanisme* (Paris: Crès, 1925), p. I: "Une ville! C'est la mainmise
    de l'homme sur la nature. C'est une action humaine contre la nature, un organisme humain de protection et de
    travail. C'est une création."

Gesamtkunstwerk and the philosophy of *Heimatschutz* ring out from many of Jeanneret's statements.

Jeanneret pins his hopes on reinforcing the community, on the anonymous artist rather than the individualist. Yet in this he is inconsistent, as he both praises the anonymous craftsman of the Middle Ages and looks to the artist, the universal genius, to achieve the betterment of humanity through improved urban design. It is interesting to note how clearly this contradiction appears in several parts of the Manuscript. Turner has already pointed out this conflict of collectivism vs. the individual genius: it is present in the work of Henri Provensal, whose text *L'Art de demain* Jeanneret had read prior to 1907, and continues unresolved throughout Le Corbusier's writing.[26] Turner and Brooks indicate that, in addition to conversations with L'Eplattenier, Jeanneret's reading of Ruskin, Provensal, Schuré, and possibly Nietzsche's Zarathustra are relevant here.[27] No notes exist for this introductory chapter: Jeanneret is clearly drawing on reading and discussions which predate his stay in Germany in 1910/11.

General Considerations – The situation of urban design circa 1900

The purpose of this study – Character and unity in the city

At the beginning of the chapter, Jeanneret explains that his study is intended as a reminder of those urban design techniques that improve urban living.[28] If architects would only work to design harmonious urban ensembles, rules might be established for a style that could create peaceful unity through the effort to express whole swathes of streets harmoniously. This would inevitably give the city its own character. However, if developments continued to be left to specialists, art would disappear from public life. Jeanneret believes in taking the lead from geniuses such as Ramses, Tamburlaine, or Charlemagne since, despite their somewhat gruesome reputations, they helped art achieve true greatness. The key words in these opening lines are without a doubt 'harmonious ensemble', 'unity', and 'character'. These lines indicate the influence of Theodor Fischer, whose 1903 lecture *Stadterweiterungsfragen* (questions of city expansion) explains the meaning of the terms 'unity' and 'character' in the context of urban design.[29] The *harmonische Einheit* (harmonious unity) which Fischer calls for is reflected in Jeanneret's wording "ensembles harmonieux".

26 See Turner, *The Education of Le Corbusier*, p. 17: "It is worth simply mentioning here that in the thinking of both Le Corbusier and Provensal, there is an apparent contradiction between this ideal of collective, impersonal endeavour, expressing a common mass spirit, and the elitist concept of the individual, inspired artist, whose duty, as we saw in the case of Provensal, is to reveal his wisdom to the mass of humanity and 'see that it is admitted and respected'. These two attitudes are to be found in various forms throughout Le Corbusier's writings, and to remain essentially as unresolved as they are in Provensal." The fact that Jeanneret at least consults Provensal when working on *La Construction des villes* is proven by a note (LCdv 381), stored as an annex to the loose-leaf folder. Here, Jeanneret copies out a section from Henri Provensal, *L'Art de demain* (Paris: Perrin, 1904), p. 299, so he can use it for the chapter on La Chaux-de-Fonds.

27 See Turner, *The Education of Le Corbusier*, and Brooks, *Le Corbusier's Formative Years*.

28 LCdv 24. The first two sections of the General Considerations can be found in the loose-leaf folder (LCdv 23–27), whereas sections three and four make up the whole of Cahier C.1 (LCdv 28–46).

29 Fischer, *Stadterweiterungsfragen*.

General Principles – *The artist shapes the city*

Jeanneret describes the role of art as one of generating profound feelings. Since he considers the city to be the place where society will either stand or fall, the key to designing the city lies in finding forms which elicit feelings. The artist who is planning a city should seek to deploy rhythms of form and colour which evoke feelings, just as a musician does with notes, or a painter with colour choice.

The urban designer is also seen as akin to the sculptor, since both deal with plastic form. Jeanneret explains that cities are made from the same materials: stone, mortar and iron, whether they are planned well or badly. The city could be likened to diamond, with rough diamond representing the real world, while perfectly polished diamond stands for the ideal. Jeanneret uses this unusual comparison to explain the value of planning – the careful polishing of the raw material. He goes on to describe urban design as an art form which, like others, operates in accordance with certain rules. Rules of order, balance and variety all apply. Fighting against what Jeanneret sees as the illness of the epoch, namely the aesthetic overloading of designs, he states that a city plan should attempt to achieve a lot with just a few, intelligently deployed design moves: "the city planner is faced with one of the noblest tasks: that of bringing his fellow citizens the joy of living in a city where the living is good."[30] It emerges clearly from Jeanneret's words here that he sees the city as a *Gesamtkunstwerk*, which can – and should – be designed like a musical score for a symphony. Such analogies, which may partly grow out of his family's familiarity with music, re-appear in *Urbanisme*.[31] It becomes evident in the above example, and in relation to urban squares, that where Sitte sees designing a city in its entirety – as if cast from a single mould – as a problem, Jeanneret senses an opportunity. His later project for the *Ville Contemporaine* is merely the logical expression of this attitude, which is informed to a large extent by the baroque monumental style of the kings of France, as conveyed by Albert Erich Brinckmann. Jeanneret's statement that "much can be achieved with few resources" appears in a similar form in Brinckmann's text: "The beauty of a city depends not on the number, but on the situation of its superb buildings. Several beautiful, well-sited constructions can improve the overall impression given by the city immeasurably."[32]

Etat actuel de la question – *Reforms in architecture and urban design*

The content of this section is divided into two parts. The first traces the development of architecture through the 19th century. Here, Jeanneret explores the conflict between academic architecture and civil engineering. He takes the view that 19th-century architectural thought and practice have become detached from their roots, which lie in the building materials themselves. According to Jeanneret, whereas engineers provide solutions to the construction problems they face at the time, proceeding logically from the materials, architects merely create masks: façades weighed down with history. Engineers are therefore the true master builders of the period. With the arrival of a new material, reinforced concrete, a new, perfect beauty can emerge. While decadent architects used to

---

30 LCdv 27.
31 See Chapter 3, Towards urbanism.
32 Brinckmann, *Platz und Monument*, p. 138.

despoil their materials with ornament and conceal their true form, the new material deter-mines its own form quite naturally.[33] Jeanneret concludes that this is effectively the advent of an architectural renaissance, which will inevitably influence urban design.[34]

In his discussion of civil engineering, the line Jeanneret takes is close to that of Joseph August Lux in his 1910 *Ingenieur-Aesthetik* (Engineering Aesthetics). There are many indications that Jeanneret knew Lux's short book, which mentions: the under-used opportunities for building with iron; the machine hall at the 1889 world exhibition in Paris; bridges; and the fantastic new option of building with concrete. However, our assumption that Jeanneret did read the 1910 text *Ingenieur-Aesthetik* cannot be con-firmed. First, he does not refer to it at any point in the Manuscript – either in his notes or in the body text – and second, he names *Der Städtebau und die Grundpfeiler der heimischen Bauweise* as the source of his key statement that the engineer is the true master builder of the 19th century; he had made an in-depth study of this text for his work on *La Construction des villes*. The fact that Jeanneret had already photographed the machine hall in Paris in 1908/09, and therefore knew it from his own experience, makes it even more difficult to prove that he had read Lux's text. Also, Jeanneret was already examining concrete as a building material independently of any suggestions to be found in Lux's work.[35] Nevertheless, it seems plausible that Jeanneret had come across *Ingenieur-Aesthetik*, published in Munich in 1910, before he wrote sections three and four of the General Considerations, especially as he deals in some detail with books by Lux in his research.

In investigating how Jeanneret arrived at his position, the relevance of one crucial sen-tence should not be overlooked. In 1908, Lux states: "Today it is an open secret, albeit unspoken, that in the related field of architecture, engineers are the true master builders of our era."[36] In 1910, he expresses himself more concisely: "I have stated it before somewhere: the true architect of the modern era is the engineer."[37] Whereas in 1908, in *Der Städtebau und die Grundpfeiler*, Lux still adopts a sceptical position, by 1910 in *Ingenieur-Aesthetik* he is reaffirming his admiration of civil engineering. Whether this sentiment is expressed in *Ingenieur-Aesthetik* or in *Städtebau*, Lux is indisputably the source which we hear echoing through some crucial phrases of *Vers une architecture*:

Engineers construct the tools of their time. Everything, except the houses and rotten boudoirs. [...] Engineers are healthy and virile, active and useful, moral and joyous.

33 LCdv 33.
34 LCdv 33.
35 Jeanneret borrowed *Eisenbetonbau* by Emil Mörsch from his friend Max Du Bois in 1909. It had just been translated into French. See Emil Mörsch, *Der Eisenbetonbau, seine Theorie und Anwendung* (2nd edition Stuttgart: Wittwer, 1906). An English translation by Ernest Payson Goodrich was published three years later: *Concrete-Steel Construction* (New York: Engineering News Publ. Co., 1909). Brooks states that Jeanneret showed little interest in this book: "[...] Max Du Bois [...] had lent him a copy that he thumbed through, thought might be useful, but had not read." Brooks, *Le Corbusier's Formative Years*, p 175. This would sup-port the assumption that Lux's *Ingenieur-Aesthetik* had indeed inspired Jeanneret.
36 "The triumph of industrialism is in fact already achieved in gravestone sculptures. We must be thankful that industry has made progress, that it has exposed and dissolved to this extent an imposter posing as an art form, because this destroys the burden of old beliefs and opens the field for new developments. Today it is an open secret, albeit unspoken, that in the related field of architecture, engineers are the true master builders of our era." Lux, *Städtebau und Grundpfeiler*, p. 89.
37 Lux, *Ingenieur-Aesthetik*, p. 14.

[...] Engineers make architecture, since they use calculations that issue from the laws of nature, and their works make us feel harmony.[38]

In the second part of this section, Jeanneret switches context abruptly to discuss the state of urban design. He links Camillo Sitte's revival of urban design with recent works of civil engineering, using the idea that a renewal is under way in both disciplines. However, he overlooks the fact that, although Sitte did not argue against the city *per se* in *Städtebau*, he did clearly state his reservations about the new technologies. One man who *could* be said to personify the link between the new techniques in architecture and those in urban planning is the Viennese architect Otto Wagner.[39] Yet Jeanneret appears completely ignorant of his writing: nowhere in *La Construction des villes* is Wagner mentioned.

Jeanneret rightly claims that it was Camillo Sitte who took the first step towards renewal in urban design, and that he did so earnestly and in good faith, with great logic and artistic integrity, speaking out against ugly urban design. Sitte had also been praised by many other authors; Jeanneret stresses that he intends to rely on Sitte as an authoritative source for his study, referring to him as and when appropriate.[40] Meanwhile, entire new towns such as Bournville und Port Sunlight had been constructed in England since the publication of Sitte's work.[41] Oddly enough, this innovative spirit seemed absent from the Latin countries, where all eyes remained firmly fixed on Paris. Jeanneret claims that, in contrast, Germany was fortunate because no single philosophy set the agenda there at that time.[42] Instead, architects were eagerly redeploying the Middle Ages as their yardstick –according to Jeanneret, this proved that the dissemination of Sitte's theories was unparalleled – but some took this redeployment further than Sitte. Unfortunately anyone who, like Brinckmann, had already turned against what he saw as the excesses of this movement, risked confusing the general public who were ignorant of the academic discourse.[43] Jeanneret quotes from several authors who refer to Sitte: Karl Henrici, Joseph Stübben, and Paul Schultze-Naumburg.[44] He also quotes Albert Erich Brinckmann, whose work *Platz und Monument* he praises and whose critical reaction to Sitte he certainly registers. Jeanneret states that Brinckmann is merely rejecting an all-too-eager mimicry of those mediaeval towns that Sitte presents as examples, and that

---

38 Le Corbusier, *Toward an Architecture*, ed. Jean-Louis Cohen, trans. John Goodman (Santa Monica: Getty, 2007), p. 94f. "Les ingénieurs construisent les outils de leur temps. Tout, sauf les maisons et les boudoirs pourris. [...] Les ingénieurs sont sains et virils, actifs et utiles, moraux et joyeux. [...] Les ingénieurs font de l'architecture, car ils emploient le calcul issu des lois de la nature, et leurs œuvres nous font sentir l'Harmonie." Le Corbusier *Vers une architecture* (Paris: Crès, 1923), p. 6f.

39 See Otto Wagner, *Modern architecture: a guidebook for his students to this field of art*, introd. and transl. by Harry Francis Mallgrave (Santa Monica: Getty, distributed by the University of Chicago Press, 1988).

40 LCdv 34. See Jeanneret's letter to L'Eplattenier dated late April 1910 (E2-12-72 FLC): "That is why I thought, noting that many authors cite Sitte's book as the monument which has renewed architecture in German cities, that I could easily and fairly frequently draw on him for quotations. I will thus have questions of capital importance resolved by a master and that will enable me to avoid the excessive lengths to which I always go to express myself."

41 LCdv 35.

42 LCdv 35f.

43 LCdv 36f.

44 LCdv 32 and 34.

Brinckmann's rejection of such mimicry could be misinterpreted by the uninitiated as a rejection of Sitte himself.

Indeed, it is hard not to misinterpret Jeanneret here. On the one hand, he does not consider Sitte to be backwards-looking at all, and is aware of his importance as a proponent of a new, modern conception of urban design. On the other hand, he believes that to adopt picturesque urban design principles too eagerly would be to mistakenly apply a new panacea. In Cahier C.3, Jeanneret expresses his view more clearly:

> At the beginning of my work, where I stated Carl Henrici's opinion of Sitte: add "In conclusion, we will look at Brinckmann's opinion of Sitte." Having spoken somewhat vehemently, I must now calm down and conclude, say that now we are convinced a wrong has been done, we should not content ourselves with a new formula as this would only substitute one wrong for another, but we should instead be interested in and excited about and follow the comings and goings of the leaders of the [reform] movement.[45]

Thus it appears Jeanneret now considers his own initial enthusiasm for Sitte to be somewhat suspect, especially since he has read Brinckmann and registered both his criticism of Sitte and of excessively picturesque urban design. By distancing himself in this way, Jeanneret shows that he really has read and understood his source material – contrary to his claim that his German was not good enough for him to grasp the finer points of the discourse. That is why discovering Cahier C.1, the second part of the General Considerations, has proved so valuable: here, Jeanneret provides an overview of his take on German and Austrian urban design, and to some extent shows how he rates its representatives. Yet Jeanneret's attitude to picturesque urban design is ambivalent; here as throughout the study, it vacillates between approval and disapproval.

Jeanneret concludes this section by warning that every small town in Switzerland now wants to copy the major cities, building its own three- or four-storey buildings and straight boulevards.[46] He continues: "The despoiling of our traditions was so complete that some people, clearly examining the future and speaking not only in the name of art but above all in the name of our economic future, sought to clear the scales from our eyes and rouse our feelings," citing Georges de Montenach and Guillaume Fatio.[47] Jeanneret also mentions Montenach in more detail later on, particularly in his chapter on La Chaux-de-Fonds. As Jeanneret puts it, Montenach's study aims to instil better taste in "Monsieur Tout le Monde" (the everyman).[48] Overall, this section of the text provides the reader with a rare glimpse of Jeanneret naming his sources – a whole series of works ranging from Lux to Schultze-Naumburg, from Stübben, Henrici, and Brinckmann to Montenach and Fatio.[49] In no other chapter of the Manuscript does such a complete bibliographical list appear.

---

45 LCdv 441.
46 LCdv 38.
47 LCdv 38f.
48 LCdv 38.
49 These are Lux, *Der Städtebau und Grundpfeiler*, Schultze-Naumburg, *Kulturarbeiten Städtebau*, Henrici, *Beiträge*, Stübben, *Städtebau*, and Brinckmann, *Platz und Monument*, as well as Montenach, *Pour le visage aimé de la patrie* and Fatio, *Ouvrons les Yeux!*

Une erreur fondamentale d'aujourd'hui – *A love of the drawing board*

There are two methods for planning a city, Jeanneret explains: one right and one wrong. The right method is organic and led by instinct, satisfying both practical and aesthetic requirements; it has always existed.[50] Jeanneret does not know whether the wrong one reigned in the past, but he believes it prevails in the early 20th century. The exceptions to the rule are countries where planning offices have been reformed.[51] Here, in line with the calls made by Sitte, a link with former traditions is being restored and a new species of urban designer is being born.[52] Jeanneret takes the view that good urban design had been performed 'in space' ("la conception dans l'espace"), in accordance with the local topography – from which the planner had derived benefit both practically and aesthetically.[53] The urban designer used to be a sculptor, since he thought in spatial terms, in three dimensions; and he was a poet, because he created surroundings for people which fulfilled the laws of nature, thus making life in cities pleasant.[54] However, Jeanneret considers that poor urban design has been elicited by bureaucracy, which has in turn emerged due to over-specialisation in the organisation of public works. He claims the problem is due to the way planners work in an office (rather than outdoors), at set times, without being responsible for their actions.[55] In the chapter On Possible Strategies, he takes up this topic in greater depth, quoting Camillo Sitte at length: he describes the evolution of the typical, subservient official whom he holds responsible for poor decisions and boring plans.[56] Jeanneret criticises the official's penchant for drawing and alienation from practice: "Beauty of a drawing on a sheet of paper, naïve admiration of a fine graphic, this, in short, is the whole error which each page of this study will combat."[57]

Les Eléments constitutifs de la ville – **The Elements of the City**

Under this heading, Jeanneret first tackles in his Introduction the interplay of individual urban design elements, thus providing an overview of the entire city as he sees it. Next he discusses, in order: residential blocks, streets, squares, and enclosing walls (*Des Chésaux*, *Des Rues*, *Des Places*, and *Des Murs de clôture*), formulating quite different opinions from those stated in his Introduction. The planned chapters on bridges, trees, gardens and parks, cemeteries, and garden cities (*Des Ponts*, *Des Arbres*, *Des Jardins et parcs*, *Des Cimetières*, and *Des Cités-jardins*) consist entirely of excerpts and notes, yet these are also discussed below, in the order Jeanneret intended. The aim here is to ascertain what Jeanneret knew about these matters and to document any particular theoretical stance he took.

50 LCdv 41f.
51 LCdv 42.
52 LCdv 43.
53 LCdv 43.
54 LCdv 43f.
55 LCdv 45.
56 LCdv 354.
57 LCdv 46.

Introduction

Jeanneret's Introduction forms part of the most comprehensive Manuscript section, the discussion of those built elements that constitute a city. However, it bears so many similarities to the Proposition and the General Considerations that this Introduction in fact acts as a bridge between the introductory chapters and the Elements of the City. Jeanneret states here that the task urban planners are faced with is both technical and artistic.[58] He explicitly states that, to achieve a functional urban design, planners must arrange the individual parts of the city according to the climatic conditions, prevailing wind, etc., so that factories are not in a position to pollute the rest of the city.[59] On some commercial streets, heavy traffic is necessary. Such streets should be designed as broad, functional urban arteries, flanked by three- to five-storey residential blocks and with *allees* of trees to catch the dust. These streets could be intersected at intervals by perpendicular buildings, with broad passageways underneath, which would provide shelter from the wind.[60] The residential areas would be protected by a building law to prevent the incursion of shameless speculators, and populated by detached or semi-detached houses or terraces. Here, Jeanneret pictures peaceful garden courtyards, curved roads, and buildings oriented towards the sun.

He takes the view that the three different areas of the city – industrial, commercial, and residential – are distinct and cannot be combined. Planners must therefore ensure that these areas are situated appropriately in relation to one another. They must then attempt to allow both cars and pedestrians to proceed as quickly as possible, and intersect without obstructing one another.[61] Jeanneret emphasises the importance of landmarks as a means of orientating oneself in the city. Public buildings should serve as landmarks through their architecture and proportions, and be located according to their function. They can succeed as landmarks provided they are designed to be beautiful. A task of this scale requires an urban expansion plan flexible enough in its details to adapt to a variety of requirements. Jeanneret believed only a familiarity with the art and activities of urban design – *la construction des villes* – would facilitate such planning, and he planned to discuss these.[62]

Thus Jeanneret keeps the promise he made in his first sketch (Cahier C.3, LCdv 427) and provides further details on the brief claims he had made there. But when could the Introduction have been written? Is this merely Jeanneret's answer to the question of defining urban design? If so, he had already found an answer by early April, and the Introduction might date to a time before Jeanneret's stay in Germany. However, a clear similarity emerges between the Introduction and a slim volume which Jeanneret had read and quoted from in Munich in May 1910: it is therefore possible that for his Introduction Jeanneret referred to this text by the Austrian architect Johann Hubatschek.[63] The lecture on "Construction tasks for a modern city", which Hubatschek gave in Linz in 1905 to homeowners with no

---

58 LCdv 56.

59 LCdv 58.

60 LCdv 59.

61 LCdv 61.

62 In an overview of the *Introduction* which Jeanneret drafts in Cahier C.6 (LCdv 533), these theories appear again in an abbreviated form.

63 Johann Hubatschek, *Die bautechnischen Aufgaben einer modernen Stadt. Vortrag gehalten im Vereine der Hausbesitzer der Landeshauptstadt Linz a. D., 28. Jänner 1904, von dem Architekten und Baumeister Johann Hubatschek, Bauwerkschuldirektor a. D. in Tetschen a. E., hrsg. auf Veranlassung des Vereines der Hausbesitzer der Landeshauptstadt Linz* (Linz: E. Mareis, 1905).

specialist knowledge of architecture, combines an emphasis on the artistic approach to urban design – primarily influenced by Sitte, Fischer, and Henrici – with Hubatschek's own technical experience of urban design. Practical issues are therefore given relatively broad coverage: Hubatschek even cites specific types of road surface and their respective costs. Jeanneret, who notes extracts from Hubatschek's lecture in Cahier C.3 *City III*, adopts some of the latter's formulations in various chapters within *La Construction des villes*. However, it is the Introduction which bears the most distinctive hallmark of Hubatschek's work, as well as covering some basic axioms of early 20th-century urban design. Hubatschek states:

> As a result of studying old city layouts on the one hand, and considering our modern economic questions and technical achievements on the other hand, today's requirements for the expansion and creation of modern cities and suburbs can be summarised as follows: requirements for traffic, health (hygiene), dwelling or type of construction, and beauty.[64]

Hence Jeanneret's 'minimum requirements' for urban design correspond exactly with Hubatschek's requirements. Jeanneret's particular emphasis on hygiene at the beginning of the Introduction also correlates to the way Hubatschek values hygiene.[65] It should nevertheless be noted that Hubatschek does not grant hygiene absolute priority over the aesthetics of shaping the city, but instead seeks to achieve a harmonious balance between functionality and beauty.[66] Jeanneret may also have found in Hubatschek's text a call to divide the city into different zones, according to use:

> The rapid expansion of the cities and the development of industrial firms alone [...] would soon usher in a new requirement, namely that of division [into] areas to be built differently (into business districts, residential districts, areas for industrial buildings, workers' quarters etc.), which has found ample expression in codes regulating buildings according to different designated zones (Vienna and Berlin) and codes categorising and regulating buildings according to height (Magdeburg and Wiesbaden).[67]

It is characteristic of Jeanneret that he chose not to deepen his knowledge of such requirements by reading texts in which urban planners such as Baumeister or Stübben lay down technical rules for urban design in detail. Jeanneret did not read Reinhard Baumeister's 1874 volume *Stadterweiterungen* (urban extensions) at all, and Joseph Stübben's *Städtebau* (City Planning) was clearly of little interest to him.[68] He did copy a few

---

64 Hubatschek, *Die bautechnischen Aufgaben*, p. 14.

65 Hubatschek, *Die bautechnischen Aufgaben*, p. 3.

66 Thus Hubatschek notes at the start of his lecture that every town and city had a unique style which identified it. Yet this style had disappeared in the 19th century, and a combination of the "nadir of all cultural efforts in the first half of the previous century" with the technological progress made in urban expansion had, for the most part, left only rational principles to guide urban construction, which was therefore undertaken "mainly in accordance with the requirements of traffic and hygiene". Hubatschek, *Die bautechnischen Aufgaben*, p. 6.

67 Hubatschek, *Die bautechnischen Aufgaben*, p. 6f.

68 Joseph Stübben's *Der Städtebau* was translated into English by Adalbert Albrecht in 1911 as *City-Building*; his unpublished translation is available at the Frances Loeb Library, Harvard University. Emily Talen and Julia Koschinsky have recently made this (flawed) translation available online: https://urbanism.uchicago.edu/page/joseph-stübbens-city-building.

drawings from the latter book, but did not explore its content any further. Except for its inclusion in the bibliography in Cahier C.1, there is no indication that Jeanneret read Stübben's *Städtebau*.[69] In contrast, in Cahier C.3 Jeanneret takes several extracts from different places in Hubatschek's *Bautechnische Aufgaben* dealing with these very questions of building regulations, differentiated zones with a maximum building height, and the division of the city into functionally separate zones. Hence Jeanneret notes down a few lines in which Hubatschek describes the difficulty of accommodating the necessary services and craft firms for a residential district made up of more expensive, detached housing.[70] The original continues by stating:

> Yet it was thus that some shortcomings and difficulties emerged, for example the fact that in districts of villas or cottages it became almost impossible to accommodate craft and commerce, which is why the attempt was made in Wiesbaden to intersperse the open manner in which such districts were built with islands built in the closed manner, so that the latter might provide for the daily and hourly needs of the villas' inhabitants in terms of trade and commerce.[71]

Jeanneret also notes down Hubatschek's subsequent remarks on the code introduced by Theodor Fischer which set out regulations for Munich imposing maximum building heights for different zones (*Staffelbauordnung*).[72] Distinguishing between different built-up areas in terms of height represents one of the major innovations in the emerging discipline of urban design at the end of the 19th century.[73] It is therefore highly remarkable that Jeanneret did not work this particular extract into the text of one of his chapters (either the Introduction or elsewhere); the idea of building height zones might have been usefully applied to the problems of urban design in La Chaux-de-Fonds.

Another idea with which Jeanneret is concerned can also be found in Hubatschek, namely the requirement for urban planners to be both artists and engineers. There is, however, a crucial difference in the way the two authors treat this idea: while Hubatschek emphasises cooperation between the two professions, Jeanneret is inclined to focus on the 'universal genius', and prefers to envisage a single person fulfilling both roles.[74]

---

69 See Cahier C.1, §3, LCdv 29–41.

70 "A Wiesbaden ds les quartiers de Villas et Landhäuser, il fallait bien loger les ateliers et les ouvriers nécessaires pour 1 tel quartier. C'est précisément la grande difficulté dans ces problèmes-là. On fit donc des îles (Inseln geschlossener Bebauung) pour loger ces services là av. leur personnel. (Hubatschek page 7)". LCdv 436. The solution is said to be "islands (islands built in the closed manner)".

71 Hubatschek, *Die bautechnischen Aufgaben*, p. 6f.

72 LCdv 436f.

73 See Winfried Nerdinger, *Theodor Fischer. Architekt und Städtebauer* (Berlin: Ernst & Sohn, 1988).

74 Hubatschek believes the plan regulating a city should not be considered the work of an administrative planner or an engineer alone, but that architects and engineers must work together "in the closest harmony". Urban designers should demonstrate enthusiasm, artistic invention and ambition. "[...] in brief, everything which characterises the true artist must be present to create a work for which such narrow boundaries are set and of which so much is expected." Hubatschek, *Die bautechnischen Aufgaben*, p. 10f. See also Jeanneret's description of the urban designer in On Possible Strategies, LCdv 351.

Jeanneret sets great store by the correct orientation of streets and buildings to the wind and sun; dust is mentioned repeatedly, from the Introduction onwards. This should come as no surprise, since La Chaux-de-Fonds is indeed exposed to the prevailing winds. Such mentions of dust and wind can also be found in Hubatschek, but it does not follow that Jeanneret simply adopted his principles of hygiene from Hubatschek.[75] Almost all the authors whom Jeanneret studied in detail, especially Joseph August Lux, Paul Schultze-Naumburg, and of course Camillo Sitte, repeatedly call for a reduction in noise, dust, and dirt on the streets – albeit in relation to the aesthetic aspects of urban design. To sum up, during his work on *La Construction des villes*, Jeanneret's only contact with the practical questions of urban design and with technical and planning legislation came via Hubatschek's short text. Although Jeanneret repeatedly emphasises the importance to the city of hygiene and technology, at key points in his work he adopts an artist's viewpoint.

Four Manuscript pages on Hygiène, Modernisme, Beauté

On these four pages, Jeanneret attempts to explain certain key terms from the contemporary discourse on urban design. These are sketches, and not allocated directly to any particular chapter. Jeanneret repeats himself several times, deletes whole paragraphs, begins again. He contrasts his own definition of fundamental terms in urban design with the current interpretation of the terms by grid-focused administrative planners. In this way, he sets himself apart from the predominant doctrine of 'administrative' urban design. For Jeanneret, the key terms are: hygiene, modernism, beauty, and utility, but not with the meaning those planners give them. He also attacks the terms balance and simplicity, which he sees as synonymous with uniformity and poverty (of imagination etc.).

> But today it is necessary to attack and deny *this* hygiene, *this* utility, *this* beauty, *this* modernism and we will leave the administrative geometers with only their geometry, to which we will apply the epithet lazy, *their* simplicity which we must equate with poverty, *their* balance which signifies uniformity.[76]

Hence the content of these pages is similar to that of the Introduction. At the same time, they contain the beginning of a modernist urban theory in his writing, going beyond the generally conservative stances of *La Construction des villes*. Jeanneret does not discuss central terms of what is to become the modernist urban design discourse anywhere else in his Manuscript (other than at the beginning of On Possible Strategies). The definitions he presents on pages LCdv 47–50 should be approached with some caution, as he is only just developing his understanding of the terms here, and they are not logically watertight yet. Still, sketchy and inconsistent as they are,

---

75 "Uneven terrain, water courses or paths already present should not be forcibly removed, but rather retained as a welcome reason to interrupt the street etc. These irregularities not only increase the pictorial effect, but also make orientation easier and are of value from a hygiene perspective in that they block and deflect the winds. [...] Vitruvius even recognised that the compass direction and above all the prevailing winds should be considered, but the modern urban designer has forgotten this." Hubatschek, *Die bautechnischen Aufgaben*, p. 13.

76 LCdv 47.

they are nevertheless immensely significant as they allow comparisons: with his own later opinions (as Le Corbusier) which have long been labelled 'classic modernism', and with those of colleagues like Walter Gropius and Adolf Behne.

For some in the modernist movement, good urban design is restricted to matters of technical and hygienic necessity; for Jeanneret, hygiene means more than just street cleaning and disease prevention. Here, Jeanneret defines hygiene as enabling people to live well and happily.[77] Besides the common good, it also means individual hygiene in the form of good living conditions: a good, pleasant place to live. Thus, as described above, hygiene is closely associated with aesthetics and expresses overall well-being. In Jeanneret's terms, the usefulness or fitness for purpose of a city (*utilité*) is not dictated by its technical infrastructure but rather by the possibility – as facilitated by construction – of travelling quickly and without obstruction in the city, using whichever mode of transport.[78] He repeatedly explains the term as something more akin to *circulation*. When Jeanneret writes, in his overview on page LCdv 533, that his three overall requirements for urban planners are "hygiène, circulation, beauté", *circulation* means much more than 'traffic'. It seems to encompass all movements within the city, and to stand for the city's function (*utilité*). With one eye on the future, one might ask whether for Jeanneret in 1910 the operation and practical purpose of the city was already defined primarily by the aspect of movement.[79]

Jeanneret explains modernism as both an investigation of contemporary issues and the most direct solution to them:[80]

> Modernism means striving to realise general questions raised by today's life forces, these are called utopian questions but acknowledged as beneficial to the community.[81]

The third term, beauty, is considered here from a rational point of view. Jeanneret states that "beauty obeys laws which are independent of emotion which belongs to the individual sphere but depend on reason which relies on Nature and which every day is checked by nature."[82] These emerging definitions will be investigated in more detail below, as they are important for our interpretation of Le Corbusier's theories.

---

77 LCdv 48f.
78 LCdv 49.
79 Are these the foundations being laid for the *promenade architecturale*, the motorway on top of houses and the inner-city airport?
80 LCdv 48. Elsewhere, Jeanneret uses "compréhension des grandes idées générales" to describe modernism: "understanding our major common ideas"; LCdv 49.
81 LCdv 48.
82 LCdv 49.

Des Chésaux – On Blocks

In this chapter, a mere nine pages long, Jeanneret depicts the ideal urban block. In so doing he touches on the source of some controversy in the urban design literature circa 1910. Jeanneret investigates the options in terms of their hygiene and form, since he considers some block forms to be ideal, and some less than ideal. He aims to determine the ideal shape for the urban block, which should achieve a number of things: first, it should present its largest area of façade to the street; second, it should save space on the street itself; third, it should have an aesthetically pleasing footprint. Jeanneret also wants a block to be suited to architectural solutions, and to combine both commercial resources and pleasant living.[83] Jeanneret distinguishes between five block shapes, four of which he rejects – either because their floor plan makes them difficult to build (due to acute angles) or because they would engender monotonous or even ugly solutions, such as hexagonal blocks or the shape which predominates in La Chaux-de-Fonds. The urban block in the 19th-century extension of this town constitutes one of the earliest examples of what would later be known as modernist *Zeilenbau*: a single line of three-storey residential buildings is situated at the front of the block, with the rear façade separated from the street by a yard or garden.[84] However, Jeanneret's ideal block is a perimeter block: a well-proportioned, slightly elongated square with a large courtyard in the middle (Fig. VI, 1). Everything seems to fit: the ground floor can house offices and shops, while the upper floors are reserved for living quarters. As the large courtyard is protected from noise and dust, it can house a children's play area and one or two public tennis courts. Jeanneret believes that mothers will be content in the knowledge that their children are safely removed from the dust and fumes of the street. An oblong shape is preferred to any other.[85] This passionate argument of Jeanneret's for such a standard block type is less of a surprise when set against the less desirable type chosen in La Chaux-de-Fonds in the 19th century, after the great fire.

The bulk of Jeanneret's theories on the best block shape cannot be traced back to Camillo Sitte, since Sitte does not take an interest in the ideal shape of an urban block.[86] Here, Jeanneret was influenced more by Karl Henrici. In his *Beiträge zur praktischen Ästhetik im Städtebau* (Contributions on practical aesthetics in urban design), Henrici decides that oblong is the preferred block shape.[87] He points out that these blocks are easy to build and therefore advocates an "elongated shape and right angled corners, while parallel sides, their straight or curved shape are only of secondary importance for construction."[88] Henrici explains:

---

83   Lcdv 65.

84   LCdv 68.

85   LCdv 68f.

86   The only exception to this is Sitte's vehement rejection of hexagonal blocks; See Sitte, *Städtebau*, p. 115; Collins and Crasemann Collins, *Camillo Sitte: The Birth of Modern City Planning*, p. 242. Brinckmann also mentions this shape: "the redundant theoretical flourishes of some urban architects, such as streets with set-backs or 'redans' (Hénard Paris), hexagonal blocks (America) are scarcely worth a mention. These are meaningless games played out on paper." Brinckmann, *Platz und Monument*, p. 157.

87   Henrici, *Beiträge*, here from the chapter: "Der Individualismus im Städtebau" (Individualism in urban design), p. 71ff.

88   Henrici, *Beiträge*, p. 73.

Admittedly, elongated block forms have an advantage over squat forms as they bring a relatively low number of corners, as the depth of the building plots can be regulated more easily as required, and as the total length of façade is relatively greater than with square or other squat forms.[89]

In contrast, Henrici considers that acute angles gave rise to a larger number of "not fully fledged plots, on a corner", i.e. sites for which the acute angles in the block's footprint pose a problem. Equally, he notes that the shape of the block also conditioned the shape of the street, "and it is always such a burden to travel or walk round a sharp corner; they are unsuitable for half of all points where thoroughfares must turn."[90] Jeanneret has clearly appropriated these thoughts of Henrici's and added a discussion of the perimeter block, with a central courtyard or garden (Fig. 2). He also adopts Henrici's comment that the need for right angles relates to the corners of sites rather than the block shape as a whole, so that a block with right-angled corners could nevertheless be flexible in terms of its overall shape:

> At all times, the elongated oblong has been preferred to other block forms. It is of capital importance that the corners are right angles, whereas whether the sides are parallel, whether straight or curved, is only of significance to the street layout. Figures *b* and *c* [...] show two derivatives of this form which, while retaining all the known advantages of form *a*, are also suitable for laying out streets which we will come to recognise as the most useful and beautiful.[91]

Thus Jeanneret comes out in favour of picturesque urban design, as represented by Sitte and Henrici, and rejects the acute angles of Beaux-Arts-inspired perimeter blocks.

Later in his chapter On Blocks, Jeanneret addresses the issue of passageways – which he explores in more detail in the chapter On Streets, and which will therefore receive only a brief mention here. Using an illustration from Matthäus Merian, Jeanneret shows that the ideal block form was deployed as early as the 14th or 15th century, during the first expansion of Berne (Fig. 3).[92] Jeanneret describes buildings grouped around large gardens, which could be made public by creating a passageway between two opposing walls of the block; this would also enable pedestrians to avoid the dull streets.[93] The shape inside the block is vital for Jeanneret. It is therefore only logical that he should cite an article from the journal *Der Städtebau*, in which Siegfried Sitte, the Viennese architect and son of Camillo Sitte, presents seven illustrations featuring reformist models for a school building (Fig.s 4, 5). The proposed building would be free of the need to have a façade with an air of authority around its perimeter. Instead, the school building itself would be relocated into the interior of the block, leaving only the

---

89 Henrici, *Beiträge*, p. 72f.
90 Henrici, *Beiträge*, p. 72.
91 LCdv 69. These Figures *a*, *b* and *c* correspond to Figures 10, 11 and 12 in Henrici, *Beiträge*, p. 72. Despite often doing so elsewhere, Jeanneret does not copy out these particular diagrams. See Fig. 2.
92 B2-20-310 FLC. Berne, bird's eye view of the mediaeval town, in Merian, *Topographia Helvetiae, Rhaetiae et Valesiae: Das ist Beschreybung und eygentliche Abbildung der vornehmsten Staette und Plätze in der Hochlöblichen Eydgenossenschafft Graubündten Wallis und etlicher zugewandten Orthen...* (Frankfurt am Main: Merian, 1654; repr., Kassel/Basel: Bärenreiter, 1960), p. 24.
93 LCdv 69f.

stairwell and administrative premises facing directly onto the street.[94] Jeanneret describes the advantages of this option as: protecting the classrooms from street dust and noise; orienting them towards the sun; and reducing the amount the municipality was required to spend on the building. Its architecture could be considerably more economical than had previously been the norm, given its modest style and avoidance of showy façades. One comment in particular provides further proof of Jeanneret's interest in the space inside the block – although he did not copy it across from his drawing into his Manuscript text: "Fig. 9 remarkable for its green spaces and quick passage through the block."[95]

What is missing from the Manuscript is a distinction between blocks in cities and those in suburbs and small towns. Jeanneret approaches the question of the right shape for a block without making any such distinction, directly comparing the block forms used in a variety of developments. However, for its final discussion this chapter returns to the interior of the block, this time approached from a different angle. Jeanneret asks whether the open or enclosed system of development is more practical. It is clear from his source here that he is discussing blocks in residential areas akin to garden suburbs; Jeanneret compares two different types of development, using descriptions from Paul Schultze-Naumburg's *Kulturarbeiten Städtebau*. The first is a detached house on a plot of land, with a garden at the front and clearance strip at each side; the second is a terraced house with no front garden, but a long back garden (Figs. 6.1, 6.2). The detached house is situated such that four small, impractical gardens are created; the terraced house not only has a good room layout, but also good garden facilities and a long view. Since the opposing terraces are some distance apart, there is no concern that either will block the other's light, and their gardens are also protected against dust and noise from the street.[96] Jeanneret explains that this beneficial development model has been widely used in new garden cities and suburbs such as Hellerau, Bournville, and Hampstead, citing Paul Schultze-Naumburg as his source. In a chapter about suburbs, Schultze-Naumburg explains the general perception that health must take precedence over beauty in building practice. However, he argues that beauty and health are not at odds here, which means that the more beautiful solution is also the more hygienic one, since detached houses bring no advantages in terms of hygiene; thus his proposed solution is a row of terraced houses.[97] Schultze-Naumburg shows that arguments had been made elsewhere against open coverage:

> It is interesting that certain proponents of hygiene, such as Nussbaum, arrive at the same end point from the opposite direction, by which I mean purely from the point of view of health care. Nussbaum claims the very fact of leaving a clearance strip has certain aesthetic benefits – yet I would entirely dispute the claim that this building method has precisely those benefits.[98]

94 See Jeanneret's note on B2-20-298, Fig. 4.

95 "La figure 9 remarquable avec ses squares et passages rapides au travers d'un massif. – (Städtebau 1906 page 130)", B2-20-298.

96 LCdv 71f.

97 Schultze-Naumburg, *Kulturarbeiten Städtebau*, p. 342f.

98 Schultze-Naumburg, *Kulturarbeiten Städtebau*, p. 354.

The author in question is Hans Christian Nußbaum, who across several issues of the journal *Der Städtebau* in 1904 debated with Joseph Stübben the pros and cons of an enclosed pattern of development.[99] Nußbaum argued that enclosed coverage would more or less double the depth of the remaining plot behind the buildings,

> and it also, when handled properly, tends to increase the length of the front gardens, so that the angle of incidence of the light striking all façades with windows is very considerably more favourable. What happens is in fact the opposite of what J. Stübben claims. At the same time, that form of parkland is created inside the block which I consider ideal for inhabitants of the block: a deep garden, shielded against storms, traffic noise, road dust and being overlooked, only subdivided by low fences between individual sites.[100]

It cannot be proven that Jeanneret had read Nußbaum's article, yet the similarity of his formulations to Nußbaum's is so striking it shows that he was au fait with the contemporary discourse. Furthermore, his conviction that enclosed coverage is to be preferred over open coverage, when combined with Jeanneret's other statements, shows that he was guided at the time by a spatial understanding of urban areas.

Cahier C.4 City IV: Semi-detached houses for cities

Although Jeanneret did not ultimately incorporate this material into his edited chapter text, the content of Cahier C.4 apparently belongs to the chapter On Blocks. The Cahier contains Jeanneret's near-complete translation into French of "Zweifamilienhäuser für Großstädte" (Semi-detached houses for large cities), an article from the journal *Der Städtebau*.[101] In this article, the Berlin-based advocate of hygiene Robert Kuczynski and the architect Walter Lehweß attempt to prove that perimeter block development with detached and semi-detached houses inside the blocks is at least as economically efficient as the practice – current at the time – of building tenement blocks which are five storeys high from the external façade right back to the courtyard, as particularly prevalent in Berlin (Fig. 7). The article appeared in the June 1910 edition and is associated with a joint contribution by its authors to the Berlin urban design exhibition. Jeanneret went further than merely translating the article: he also drafted an introductory explanation to enable him to incorporate it into his own Manuscript.[102]

In this edition, Cahier C.4 has been allocated to the chapter On Blocks because it presents a new design concept for dealing with blocks in Berlin. Yet it is astonishing that, in his chapter On Blocks, Jeanneret does not mention any such design by Kuczynski and Lehweß. However, the connection between the text of the chapter and the translated article in Cahier C.4 can be established by means of two passages elsewhere in the looseleaf folder. The first is one page found between the sheets of the introduction, containing

---

99 Hans Christian Nußbaum, "Verdient die offene oder die geschlossene Bauweise den Vorzug?" in *Der Städtebau*, 1 (1904), no. 1, pp. 29–31 and no. 3, pp. 42–45.

100 Nußbaum, "Verdient die offene oder die geschlossene Bauweise den Vorzug?", p. 31.

101 Robert René Kuczynski and Walter Lehweß, "Zweifamilienhäuser für Großstädte", in *Der Städtebau*, 7 (1910), no. 6, pp. 67–72.

102 LCdv 76.

a mere three lines of writing: "In a more detailed study, specialists have found unexpected resources in the rectangular block, acknowledged to be the most advantageous: Messrs R[obert] Kuczynski und W[alter] Lehweß have made the following promising suggestion:"[103] The text breaks off at this point. Second, the annex contains – sandwiched between different pages altogether – a further direct connection between the chapter text and the article. Pages LCdv 74 and 75, which in the original form two sides of the same sheet of paper, contain an amended version of a section from the chapter On Blocks. Here, Jeanneret describes the advantages of an enclosed perimeter block development using the example from Schultze-Naumburg's *Kulturarbeiten Städtebau*. He adds a comment that there is now a new solution for developing blocks.[104] Thus Jeanneret twice begins to establish a connection between the chapter On Blocks and Kuczynski and Lehweß's article, and twice breaks off. The urban design innovation of building detached houses inside blocks did not feature in his final Manuscript. It has not been possible to clarify why it was ultimately omitted.

Only rarely do connections arise between Jeanneret's travel carnets and *La Construction des villes*. In this case, there are notes and sketches in the *Carnets de Voyage* connected to a very similar design by Berlin architects Bruno Möhring and Rudolf Eberstadt (Fig. XVI) which Jeanneret saw at the international urban design exhibition in Berlin. The design was one part of Möhring and Eberstadt's prize-winning contribution to the 1910 design competition for Greater Berlin.[105] It is not clear whether the innovation described by Kuczynski and Lehweß was their own idea, or if they were merely investigating the economic viability of the project by Möhring and Eberstadt, as postulated by Theodor Goecke in the journal *Städtebau*.[106]

Interestingly, in 1979 historian Julius Posener indicated a possible connection between Kuczynski's ideas and Le Corbusier's urban design concepts:

> Kuczynki's contribution is of particular interest to us because he identifies the Hobrecht grid plan [for Berlin] – very deep blocks between streets of equal width, with good surfaces – as the source of all evil and proposes to remedy this by reducing the size of the plots and creating different classes of street: this anticipates Le Corbusier's *classement des rues*.[107]

---

103 LCdv 78.

104 LCdv 74–75.

105 Jeanneret notes in his travel carnets: "Greater Berlin. Project (et in Terra Pax) / Concentric / trees / radiating out // Previous // the same plot better /employed for large rented blocks on the outside with / detached houses inside / A. main street" [our translation]. Le Corbusier, *Les voyages d'Allemagne Carnets* (English), p. 44f. Giuliano Gresleri, who published the carnets, explains: "The urban plans of Walter Lehwess ('government building contractor') were laid out with the motto 'Et in Terra Pax'. Further down, J[eannere]t points out the advantages of aggregating mixed typologies based on the clear separation of vehicular and pedestrian traffic [...]." Le Corbusier, *Les voyages d'Allemagne Carnets* (English), p. 44. However this is not correct: the design Jeanneret sketches in Carnet 1 is by Bruno Möhring and Rudolf Eberstadt. Their winning competition entry for Greater Berlin is entitled "Et in Terra pax", but Kuczynski and Lehweß's design is not. Yet Möhring and Eberstadt do propose to reshape the Berlin block in a very similar way to Kuczynski and Lehweß.

106 Theodor Goecke, "Allgemeine Städtebau-Ausstellung Berlin 1910", in *Der Städtebau*, 7 (1910), no. 7/8, pp. 73–92, here p. 84.

107 Julius Posener, *Berlin auf dem Wege zu einer neuen Architektur. Das Zeitalter Wilhelms II.* (München/ New York: Prestel, 1979 (^{2}1995)), p. 245. Our translation.

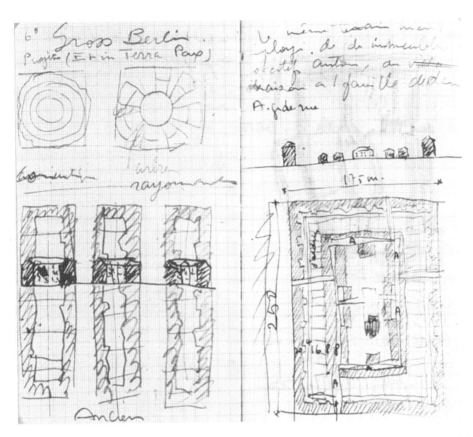

Fig. XVI Möhring/Eberstadt, competition design for Greater Berlin, 1910. From *Les Voyages d'Alle-magne. Carnets,* Carnet 1, p. 60–61

Is Posener suggesting that Le Corbusier appropriated the idea of classifying streets from Kuczynski? I think it more likely that Jeanneret derived the idea of classifying streets from Hubatschek and Schultze-Naumburg's considerations. After all, Hubatschek formulates precise requirements for the width of main and side streets, and Schultze-Naumburg describes the city as a human-like body, with main arteries and subsidiary channels. We will clarify below how Jeanneret arrived at his *classement des rues.*

Des Rues – On Streets

In this chapter, the longest in his study after On Squares, Jeanneret seeks formal solutions to the layout of streets in urban areas.[108] He sees the question as twofold, involving both the practical utility and the pedestrian's perception of a given road system.

---

108 Notes and excerpts for On Streets seem to have been kept in a Cahier "N" which no longer exists; initial letters on the sketches belonging to the chapter on streets and roads indicate this. Jeanneret may have noted down his translations of Henrici there.

Jeanneret's overall comments at the beginning of the chapter set the tone for his treatment of the pedestrian's perception:

> This is the most important chapter, since the appearance of a city's streets produces the impression of its charm or ugliness. It is in travelling a city's streets that one will either find cause for enthusiasm, daydreams and enjoyment or feel a dreary lethargy creeping in to paralyse one's legs and leave for ever a hateful memory of the city thus glimpsed.[109]

It is therefore revealing that the first topic tackled is: boring streets – normal streets – pleasing streets (*rue ennuyeuse – rue normale – rue plaisante*). It is no coincidence that Karl Henrici's *Beiträge zur praktischen Ästhetik im Städtebau* contains a chapter with a very similar heading: Jeanneret had translated and reproduced verbatim the first four pages of that same chapter, "Boring and pleasing streets".[110] In his chapter, Jeanneret discusses formal questions relating to curved streets, crossroads, intersections, passageways, road levelling, streets on slopes, and broad, straight boulevards. Jeanneret intended to subdivide the topic, and as the relevant headings make sense we apply them here to designate these as subsets of equal importance, even if he merely planned and did not actually execute this subdivision.

In the first section of the chapter, Jeanneret sets out three theories. First, he argues alongside Camillo Sitte for sites with irregular footprints. Second, Jeanneret argues that the width of streets should vary according to their function, underpinning his arguments with statements from Hubatschek. The lack of such variation partly explains why he rejects city plans based on grids as unhelpful. Third, Jeanneret declares the grid to be impractical for a different reason: its alleged efficiency actually proves highly obstructive to rapid movement through urban areas. In fact, an organic city plan as evidenced in old towns could permit more rapid progress; Jeanneret adopts this argument from Schultze-Naumburg. Thus Jeanneret appropriates formulations from three different authors and combines them into an independent train of thought.

In anticipation of protests against the revolutionary modernity of the theories he is proposing, Jeanneret begins his chapter with a line from Camillo Sitte's *Städtebau nach seinen künstlerischen Grundsätzen*.[111] Sitte argues that some architects' fear of architecture being impoverished by irregular sites is unfounded; such plots require individual solutions and therefore encourage artful designs. According to Sitte, the areas left over on such plots can in fact be used to accommodate facilities such as building services and storerooms. Initially, Jeanneret does not address this issue in any more depth and instead uses the quotation as a basis on which to establish his own argument. He admits that streets must meet certain criteria, because they are public property and may be used by everyone: "Thoroughfares must be created that are easy and practical to use, firstly for the beasts that transport heavy burdens, and then to save mankind tiredness and tedium."[112] In addition to being entertaining, streets must be economical. And if the land

---

109 LCdv 96.
110 Henrici, *Beiträge*, p. 85–88, "Langweilige oder kurzweilige Strassen".
111 In Camille Martin's French edition of Sitte: p. 130, line 14; in the original (4th ed. 1909) page 97, line 21. Since Jeanneret does not give the end of the quotation, it is not clear how much of Sitte's formulations (in Martin's translation) he intended to reproduce.
112 LCdv 96.

is sloping, the planner must think in three dimensions, since a 'chequerboard' plan will not be possible.[113]

> For business, spacious arteries will be provided. The main places with intensive commerce will be identified; these will be linked in a well-planned network. For pedestrians, narrower streets will be created, a finer mesh with very direct intermediate links, a veritable network of capillaries bringing life to all parts of the organism via the shortest route.[114]

From this, Jeanneret derives his first rule of thumb: "... the width and slope of streets can and must vary, and systems with streets all of equal width are to be rejected."[115] He argues that streets are often either too narrow or too wide for the traffic using them. In support of this argument, Jeanneret cites the example of London Bridge, which has to accommodate a large volume of traffic despite its modest width.

This is one of the few points in the Manuscript at which it is possible to trace several steps of the method deployed by Jeanneret to draft *La Construction des villes*. Some of the phrasing which he uses in the edited Manuscript text is outlined, in this case in the form of translated quotations, in Cahier C.3 *City III*. The relevant passage from Johann Hubatschek is quoted in the original German; Jeanneret cites his *Bautechnische Aufgaben einer modernen Stadt* in the same Cahier.[116] In order to gain an understanding of how Jeanneret's urban design theories developed, it is important to note that he saw in Hubatschek's requirements a model for his own thoughts on the *classement des rues*. These included adapting the width of streets to their function – while keeping them as narrow as possible. This contrasts starkly with the practice in La Chaux-de-Fonds, where roads with different functions were all allocated the same, excessive width. Jeanneret considered that grids arose automatically from the practice of drafting with a set square and a T-square:

> Figure XXXIV shows this chequerboard subdivision: it would be hard to find a city in Europe without entire new districts planned like this. The development of cities will continue to be hampered by such procedures for some time to come, applied in the name of speed and hygiene. [...] It is said (see Figure XXXIV) that the shortest route from one point to another is a straight line, that fundamental axiom of elementary geometry.[117]

Jeanneret counters this theory by showing that, in the case of a chequerboard grid, what would appear to be the shortest route is in fact the most complicated, because – due to the lack of a direct diagonal connection – all possible routes are the same length. This observation can be traced directly back to Schultze-Naumburg, from whose *Kulturarbeiten Städtebau* Jeanneret lifts the principles of the organic urban plan practically word for word, as well as the sketch used by Schultze-Naumburg to illustrate his point, along with its peculiar combination of letters and numbers (Fig.s 8, 9).[118] Schultze-Naumburg explains the disadvantage of the grid by positing an imaginary pedestrian at one corner of

---

113 LCdv 96f. See §4, General Considerations, LCdv 43f.
114 LCdv 97.
115 LCdv 97.
116 LCdv 443f.
117 LCdv 97f.
118 B2-20-307 FLC corresponds to: Schultze-Naumburg, *Kulturarbeiten Städtebau*, Fig. 26, p. 67.

the chequerboard, who wishes to walk to the corner diagonally opposite and finds that all the possible routes are of equal length, even where the pedestrian walks the two shorter sides of the imaginary triangle instead of the apparently shortest and most direct route along the hypotenuse.[119] Schultze-Naumburg makes a comparison with an old town and its street layout, which would be of more practical use in this case, then concludes:

> One can examine the ground plan of an old town, as in [...] [Fig.s XVII, XVIII], from the same viewpoint.[120] It will be clear that, rather than an ossified geometric figure, such a plan resembles organic growth and these difficulties cannot arise. Here, the streets run through the town like great arteries; countless small commercial passageways, pedestrian and road bridges and thoroughfares always provide inter-connections via the most direct, natural route.[121]

 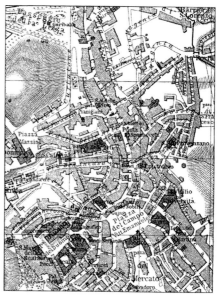

Fig. XVII Town centre of Erfurt, showing organic street layout patterns. From Schultze Naumburg, *Kulturarbeiten Städtebau*, fig. 27

Fig. XVIII Town centre of Siena. From Schultze Naumburg, *Kulturarbeiten Städtebau*, fig. 28

119 "To date, engineers designing cities have known no different and wherever possible made a right-angled intersection of every street with another street, which not only causes boredom through uniformity, but also the worst conceivable traffic conditions. A brief observation will serve to explain. Imagine a city built entirely of right-angled residential blocks, as indicated in Fig. 26. In order to travel from point a to point c, it is necessary to take route a-b, b-c, unless one prefers route a 1 2 3 4 5 6 7 c, which is of course equal in its total length to ab+bc." Schultze-Naumburg, *Kulturarbeiten Städtebau*, p. 66.

120 Figures 27 and 28 show city plans of Erfurt and Siena, drawings which Jeanneret did not trace. They illustrate a street network denoted as organic, with main streets and ancillary routes. For Jeanneret's translation, see LCdv 100.

121 Schultze-Naumburg, *Kulturarbeiten Städtebau*, p. 66.

Jeanneret incorporates this explanation of the geometric disadvantages of grids into his Manuscript, barely changing a word.[122] While Schultze-Naumburg uses the layouts of Siena and Erfurt as examples to show organic patterns, Jeanneret employs a plan of Antwerp and refers to plans of other towns such as Ulm (Fig. 11).[123] Thus he obligingly adopts Schultze-Naumburg's arguments against a grid-based plan and in favour of an organic plan. Yet in so doing he does not rely solely on this single source, instead combining Hubatschek's calls for streets of different widths with Schultze-Naumburg's argument for an organic urban plan. He also puts forward Sitte's argument in favour of irregularly shaped plots, as required by organic street layout. Jeanneret has two basic requirements: the width of streets must vary in relation to their function (commerce, pedestrians); and they must form networks of connections both large and small, which interweave to produce a functioning system. Thus the groundwork was laid in *La Construction des villes* for the argument which he would later posit as Le Corbusier, namely that the different transport systems must operate independently of one another. Furthermore, it seems plausible that Le Corbusier's use of terminology relating to organisms can also be traced back to Schultze-Naumburg, at least in part; after all, his was the clearest voice to use the analogy of the human body in relation the city.[124] For example, the illustrations of human blood circulation to be found in an annex to Le Corbusier's *Urbanisme* are merely concrete depictions of Schultze-Naumburg's theories. Le Corbusier's application of this analogy came to fruition in the drawings of city forms he produced for urban design projects of the 1920s and 1930s, such as the *Plan Obus* for Algiers or the designs in *Précisions*, and to a certain extent also in the *Ville Contemporaine*.[125]

Boring streets – pleasing streets – normal streets

The section on 'boring streets' is Jeanneret's full and direct translation of a text from Karl Henrici's *Beiträge zur praktischen Ästhetik im Städtebau*.[126] For his source material, Jeanneret used the first four pages of Henrici's chapter 'Langweilige und kurzweilige Straßen' (Boring and pleasing streets), which originally appeared in the June 1893 edition of the journal *Deutsche Bauzeitung*.[127] Jeanneret hardly omits any of Henrici's statements nor adds any material, apart from a reference to one of his own later chapters. As this passage is pure translation, like many others in the Manuscript, it contrasts with the previous section in which Jeanneret linked several authors' opinions together. To accompany the text, Jeanneret copies the diagrams in which Henrici explains the optical

---

122 LCdv 98.

123 "Fig. VII shows the plan of part of the city of Antwerp in the 17th century." LCdv 99. Emery shows a plan of Antwerp, which Jeanneret copies out during his 1915 research at the Bibliothèque Nationale. There is no plan of Antwerp drawn by Jeanneret in 1910; perhaps there never was.

124 On terms relating to organisms, see Matthias Schirren, *Hugo Häring: Architekt des Neuen Bauens, 1882–1958* (Ostfildern-Ruit: Hatje Cantz, 2001), and Caroline van Eck, *Organicism in Nineteenth-Century architecture. An inquiry into its theoretical and philosophical background* (Amsterdam: Architectura et Natura Press, 1994).

125 See Le Corbusier, *Urbanisme*, "Appendice", no pagination, after p. 287. In the English edition, this appendix was omitted – possibly because it felt out of kilter with the rest of the book.

126 LCdv 100–103.

127 Henrici, *Beiträge*, "Langweilige und kurzweilige Straßen", pp. 85–98. Jeanneret translates pp. 85–88 of the chapter into French for this section. Jeanneret translates "kurzweilig" as "plaisant", which we have translated as "pleasing".

phenomena he describes. This procedure leaves little room for Jeanneret's own ideas to shine through. It is therefore no wonder that the Manuscript as a whole yokes together conflicting content, as Jeanneret is quoting directly from a variety of authors, placing their texts shoulder to shoulder without having reworked them.

Henrici takes the view that the leisurely pedestrian, or *flâneur*, provides the measure by which streets should be designed. A street will therefore be "*boring* if a pedestrian on that street gets the impression that his route is longer than it actually is; I would call a street *pleasing* if the opposite is the case." According to Henrici, all possible urban design measures should be taken to ensure that streets are as pleasing as possible, since:

> The less one sees of the street surface and façades when one takes a perspective view of the street, the shorter the street will appear, but also the more boring; the more one sees of the surface and façades, the longer the street will appear, but the more pleasing it will be to walk through.[128]

Jeanneret then continues with a paragraph which slightly abridges Henrici's text, making it difficult to understand. Henrici is discussing the 'normal street', which is neither boring nor particularly stimulating. He believes that its neutral impact arises from its proportions, and defines these precisely:

> Midway between the pleasing street and the boring street lies the *normal street*. This is very straight, is level or has a very even gradient, and is flanked by *uninterrupted*, precisely parallel façades. I call such streets normal since one is not deceived about their length. The eye correctly gauges their dimensions, *provided they are not longer than is clearly visible from one end to the other and that the proportions of everything in and on the street can be correctly anticipated.*[129]

Although Jeanneret translates this paragraph almost in full, he omits that very detail which Henrici emphasises. As a result, Jeanneret's reader would not be able to grasp the argument without a knowledge of Henrici's original, and would instead be left to wonder what the actual difference was between normal and boring streets.[130] For Henrici, the qualitative distinction to be made between streets is whether or not a passer-by can perceive the sizes of and proportional relationships between the elements of the street, and can relate to these and to the dimensions of the street. Jeanneret had identified this question precisely, despite his sloppy rendering of Henrici's text. As Le Corbusier, he repeatedly incorporated this particular question into his lines of argument.

Henrici claims that any type of change, such as hump-backs in the carriageway or interruptions in the facing walls, would immediately cause a 'normal' street to appear boring, as these changes would make it appear shorter than it actually was.[131] In both cases, the impact

---

128 Henrici, *Beiträge*, p. 86. For Jeanneret's translation, see LCdv 100.
129 Henrici, *Beiträge*, p. 86.
130 Henrici, *Beiträge*, p. 86f. For Jeanneret's translation, see LCdv 101.
131 "However, the straight street with parallel walls will immediately cease to be worthy of the name 'normal', it will immediately become 'boring', if at any moment it appears shorter than it is. This happens if one or more humps are present on its surface, or if its walls are interrupted on both sides. These two instances have the same effect on its perception, for one and the same reason. In both cases, spaces open up out of sight, and

would be based on the same factor: the spaces created are hidden from the observer and thus the street appears shorter. Henrici explains this phenomenon in detail, and Jeanneret follows it, reproducing Henrici's arguments precisely in French, and making use of his diagrams.[132] For today's reader, what is astonishing about Henrici's argument is that – contrary to the expectation that interrupting the frame will enliven the image and thus combat monotony and boredom – Henrici instead investigates the relationship between the expected and the actual length of the street from a pedestrian's perspective. Hence the contradiction which emerges within Henrici's own assessment of boulevards – in his chapter "Großstadtgrün" on green spaces in the city, he had rejected them, but here he embraces them:

> However, means exist by which even long, straight streets with parallel but interrupted walls can be relieved of their boring characteristics. The first of these consists of marking the continuous vanishing perspective with rows of trees, lanterns or similar [...] [Fig. 14]. The second is a concave curvature to the surface of the street along its length. The street surface will then appear to the eye to have less of a shortened perspective, so that one can see more of it than if it had an even gradient, and the disagreeable apparent shortening effected by the set-backs to the sides can to a certain extent be cancelled out.[133]

This is one point on which Henrici receives no support from Sitte, who fought doggedly against boring tree-lined boulevards. Henrici also advocates avoiding intersections, instead recommending staggered junctions. He further finds that concave walls facing the street are helpful, as they eliminate boredom without the need for costly tree planting. However, Henrici is sure to emphasise that "to introduce curved streets for their own sake, just so as to have both straight and curved streets" would be as idiotic as "to have one coat tail cut straight, and the other rounded, purely in order to possess both shapes."[134]

Rues courbes – *Curved streets*

As Henrici had done before him, Jeanneret focuses next on the curved street. He argues in favour of the aesthetic and functional benefits of curved streets, taking his formulations largely from Henrici's chapter *Langweilige und kurzweilige Straßen* (Boring and pleasing streets), and directly following the thread of Henrici's reasoning.[135] Jeanneret also quotes some of the wording from Schultze-Naumburg's *Kulturarbeiten Städtebau*.[136] He describes two aspects of the curved street as beneficial: first, the façades on the long outer, concave

---

these can only be discerned once one has reached the top of the hump or the point at which there is a set-back on both sides." Henrici, *Beiträge*, p. 87. For Jeanneret's translation, see LCdv 101.

132 "The illusion about the true length of the street therefore occurs [...] because (See Figures 2 and 3) for viewers at points *aa*, points *b'b'* appear to be directly adjacent to points bb, whereas distances *bb'* and *bb'* [sic] only come to the pedestrian's attention, and annoy him, once he reaches points *bb*." Henrici, *Beiträge*, p. 87. For Jeanneret's translation, see LCdv 102. Figures 1–4a on p. 88 in Henrici's book correspond to Jeanneret's copies on sheet B2-20-314 FLC. To identify these figures in his tract, Jeanneret uses the number LVII. See Fig.s 13, 14.

133 Henrici, *Beiträge*, p. 88. For Jeanneret's translation, see LCdv 102.

134 Henrici, *Beiträge*, p. 89.

135 Henrici, *Beiträge*, p. 89f.

136 However, this cannot be proven with the same certainty as the Henrici quotations; Jeanneret uses Henrici's illustrations to accompany precisely this bit of text.

side appear to unfurl before the observer's very eyes, and second, those on the short inner, convex side appear to alter quickly.

> Instantly their appearances are infinitely varied; the concave street-front will present to the eye a great development in the surface and allow all the buildings to be seen by the passer-by, whereas the convex street-front will offer entertainment in its rounded surfaces with rapid, changing perspective views.[137]

Le Corbusier's concept of a *promenade architecturale* even makes a brief début here: the viewpoint is that of a *flâneur* wandering the city, or around a house. This concept is of course especially attractive in a city designed using a picturesque approach to urban design. Jeanneret's description is very similar to a passage in *Kulturarbeiten Städtebau*, in which Schultze-Naumburg also emphasises the advantages of a curved street layout:

> With this arrangement, the house-fronts appear to unfurl before our eyes, not only allowing the houses to be identified, but also creating lively interactions and distinctive forms in all parts of the street scene. Imagine the houses on the opposing side, as if in response, forming a convex curve in contrast to the concave curve on the other side. This row of fronts must naturally do the opposite of unfurl: the row of houses must vanish so that the first houses on this street appear to shift forward like scenery and thus in the most effective manner form the other side of the picture, as in [Fig. XIX].[138]

Jeanneret adds the reservation that curved street-fronts running parallel to one another will leave the observer unmoved; if however the width of the street changes as it curves, the varied resulting picture will be pleasing to the eye.[139] To illustrate this situation, he cites a figure he has copied from Henrici (Fig.s 15 and 16).[140] This proves that Jeanneret is quoting the formulation from Henrici, who writes:

> The curved street will only be pleasing if one creates it, not in the routine manner with parallel fronts, but if one curves these fronts so that, as they progress, they elicit the desired pleasing and stimulating variety. [...] Accordingly, the neutral curvatures in Figures 5 and 6 leave us rather unmoved, whereas the relatively greater concave curves in Figures 7 and 8 achieve decidedly more favourable effects.[141]

Jeanneret expands on this idea, stating that a good street layout elicits in the observer a pleasant feeling of being between the walls of a large room, hung with changing tapestries.[142] Yet he does not believe modern cities prompt the observer to perceive their street-fronts at all.[143] This echoes Schultze-Naumburg almost word for word:

---

137 LCdv 103.
138 Schultze-Naumburg, *Kulturarbeiten Städtebau*, p. 44f.
139 LCdv 103.
140 B2-20-308 FLC. The sketch numbers correspond to Figures 5–8 in Henrici, *Beiträge*, p. 90.
141 Henrici, *Beiträge*, p. 90.
142 LCdv 103.
143 LCdv 104.

Fig. XIX Street in Göttingen, "house-fronts appear to unfurl before our eyes." From Schultze Naum-
    burg, *Kulturarbeiten Städtebau*, fig. 24

It is a wholly undeniable observation that in our modern streets, which are all
designed dead straight or with a few unwarranted bends, nobody recognises the
façades of the houses any longer. A person merely advances through these immense
shafts towards the point where the lines vanish, without resting his gaze on the
street-fronts to the left or right [...][144]

Here, with the help of Schultze-Naumburg, Jeanneret is attempting to establish why
a curved street is more beautiful than a straight street. It *is* something, it is visible. This
may sound somewhat peculiar, but it makes a specific point: the value of picturesque
urban design is that it works with the effects of three-dimensional elements, with setbacks and projections, to stimulate the eye and shape the space. It is only when
a straight street *is* something, when its perspective is closed, that it can appear
beautiful.[145] Schultze-Naumburg also supplies an example:

144 Schultze-Naumburg, *Kulturarbeiten Städtebau*, p. 71.
145 LCdv 104.

Observe [...] [Fig. XXa/b].[146] Here, a street straight as a die leads to a church. Its effect is outstanding. This seems to be because the many vanishing lines converging on a single point steer the eyes towards a major goal and appear to lead it. Indeed, this causes the street fronts as such to retreat and the narrowing prospect becomes the principal matter. However, if these hard, straight lines continue without end, boredom sets in [Fig. XXIa/b]. This then is a case of two opposing principles. In the one case, the housing fronts are the main matter, and push themselves into view; in the other case, the housing fronts retreat to reveal a point of closure in the middle.[147]

Jeanneret evokes this interplay of elements for his reader using the example of the Marktgasse in Berne. He describes how the gently curving street, aesthetically formed façades, and decorative fountain – together with the fact that the street creates a "feeling of perfect volume" by ending with the magnificent Käfigturm – combine to give an over-all impression of beauty.[148] It is not the beauty of the façades, but that of the space alone, [le] *parfait volume de la rue*, which can in turn enable the façades to contribute to the street's beauty (Fig. XXII). Jeanneret could not have made a clearer statement on the quality of abstract space. This confirms the supposition that Camillo Sitte influenced Jeanneret's fundamental understanding of urban and architectural space both directly and indirectly.[149] Yet this section definitely does not contain any references to Camille Martin, who translated Sitte's *Städtebau* into French – despite the fact that Martin added a chapter

Fig. XX Street in Kassel, "vanishing lines converging on a single point." From Schultze-Naumburg, *Kulturarbeiten Städtebau*, fig. 18

146 Schultze-Naumburg, *Kulturarbeiten Städtebau*, p. 56. The text for the illustration states "Street in Kassel. Example of good straight street layout ending with the church. Perspective lines lead the eye towards this goal."
147 Schultze-Naumburg, *Kulturarbeiten Städtebau*, p. 55.
148 LCdv 104.
149 LCdv 104. The sketch on page B2-20-315 FLC on which Jeanneret wrote "for closed streets" may well be the most suitable illustration of this, but he does not mention it here (Fig. 17).

Fig. XXI Street whose "straight lines continue without end." From Schultze-Naumburg, *Kulturarbeiten Städtebau*, Abb. 19

entitled *Des Rues* to his translation, in which he advocated a curved street layout. This is clear from the fact that Jeanneret makes no mention whatsoever, in either illustrations or text, of the streets in Bruges, Geneva, and Lübeck, which Martin discusses.

Streets which widen briefly or with repeated projections

Jeanneret uses a variety of examples to describe a widening of the street for aesthetic reasons: for example to attract the eye to a monumental structure or divide a long, straight street into individual sections (Fig.s 18–22). He continues to translate directly from Henrici's chapter on boring and pleasing streets. Henrici discusses the aesthetic qualities of different ways of widening streets, and criticises the tendency of routine planners (*Schematiker*) to forbid any gradual widening of only one side of the street – intended to emphasise a building – which they believed to be arbitrary.

> Indeed moreover, they meet with no opposition and believe they are undertaking an artistic act if they create an indent on both sides [Jeanneret's LIXc], or if they bring themselves to create a beautifully symmetrical square as in [Jeanneret's LIXd]; for even at the very first glance the 'greatness' of this configuration can be identified, as befits a metropolis of the future, and as demonstrated using important

Fig. XXII Berne, showing Marktgasse and Käfigturm. Postcard, owned by Jeanneret (L5-9-46 FLC)

perspectives, grand squares, fascinating street scenes and picturesque groups of buildings.[150]

If Jeanneret were to continue replicating Henrici's text uncritically word for word, as he had done thus far, then he would also need to criticise those symmetrical indents in streets that Henrici denigrates with veiled sarcasm. However, Jeanneret's text does not adopt a clear stance on this until he introduces the example of the Promenadeplatz in Munich and states frankly that "it has an undeniably fine appearance"[151] (Fig. 19). Either Jeanneret has not fully grasped Henrici's position, or he takes a different view and is incorporating his own approval into his version of the argument.

Elaborating further on cases where attention is to be drawn to a building located on a bend in a street, Henrici believes that this building should not be sited on the outside of the curve because it would interrupt the visual guideline for the curve, that is the curved façade. It would cause this street-front to appear foreshortened – something

150 Henrici *Beiträge*, p. 90f.
151 LCdv 107.

which Henrici condemns because it would be wearying for pedestrians. Jeanneret follows Henrici in this argument, and concludes:

> Why then open up the street, since costly strategies will be employed straight afterwards to close the clumsy cut-out *a* and *b* Fig. *LX* [Fig. 20b, c]. The right strategy which has been employed successfully since time immemorial is that in image *d* [Fig. 20d], i.e. with the widening carried out on the convex side of the street.[152]

The illustrations which Jeanneret has copied for this section of his text all come from Henrici's chapter on boring and pleasing streets.[153] Where is Henrici heading with this line of argument? The underlying theory is as follows: where objects are arranged incorrectly or unfavourably in a space, the observer does not perceive spatial depth. It is important to Henrici that overall rules be set out to determine which urban design shapes are good or poor, varied or boring from the pedestrian's perspective. Thus as in previous cases, Henrici establishes firm rules for aesthetic arrangements but does not base these on specific examples from the built environment, as Sitte does. Instead, he aims for them to be generally applicable in urban design practice. However, this comes with the attendant risk that these rules ultimately become the very thing which both Sitte and Henrici reject: solutions which can be copied in a schematic manner, in accordance with a rulebook, and applied to all conceivable urban design situations. At the end of the paragraph, Henrici argues against a formulaic interpretation of his explanations, perhaps sensing that others might tend to construe them that way. Paul Schultze-Naumburg, whom Jeanneret also quotes in this context, does not present such rules but instead shows various pictures of successful examples, thus avoiding the risk of a dogmatic approach.

Jeanneret goes on to discuss short widenings in a street (*élargissements momentanés*). He takes the idea of a building with a monumental appearance, standing on one side of the street but facing a little square created by widening the street. Seen from the front, the building's façade presents itself symmetrically to the small square (Fig. XXIII). In this direction the street does not widen abruptly, but in a gentle curve or at a slight angle which leads towards the building. Jeanneret is truly thrilled by this example – the shorter side of the square-like space created in this case would be particularly useful in highlighting the façade of the monumental building:

> It is often the case that streets widen not abruptly, as with a right-angled set-back, but with an imperceptible increase in breadth which, once it has reached its maximum, abruptly reverts to the original breadth. This procedure, if deployed artistically, causes remarkable perspective effects in which the significant expanse of the street fronts thus exposed to our view takes on a true grandeur.[154]

---

152 LCdv 108.
153 The sketches at Jeanneret's *LIX* (Fig. 18) show limited widenings in streets, B2-20-317 FLC. In Henrici, *Beiträge*, these are Fig.s 9, 10, 9a, 11 (in that order), p. 90. A second series of sketches shows a scheme for monumental structures placed in a widening of the street, *LX a-d*. B2-20-308 FLC. Henrici shows five sketches, of which Jeanneret adopts only four. These are Henrici Fig. 13, p. 91, and 13a, 13b and 14, p. 92.
154 LCdv 108.

Fig. XXIII Sketch drawing belonging to fig. XXIV (B2-20-319 FLC)

Here, Jeanneret is discussing a sketch of Neuhauser Straße in Munich, the source for which has not been unearthed (Fig. 24).[155] He describes how these setbacks in the buildings provide islands of peace for horse-drawn vehicles, and how a façade at right angles to the direction of travel on the street is impressive enough to draw the observer's attention, particularly in this special urban design situation where the towers of the Frauenkirche loom imposingly above the buildings from behind.[156] Jeanneret is signposting a scene from his own experience, and there is therefore no requirement to track down its source. However, it is interesting to consider what prompted him to note this urban design device. Although Henrici does not mention this type of street widening, Schultze-Naumburg discusses in two different chapters of *Kulturarbeiten Städtebau* how this architectural device is used in urban design. The connection with Jeanneret's writing can be established via a small sketch which Jeanneret copies from *Kulturarbeiten Städtebau*, showing how the square is formed in a Prague street to provide a grand entrance for a baroque building (Figs XXIII, XXIVa/b).[157] This unprepossessing example is taken

155 Fig. B2-20-300, Fig. LVIII: Combination of several situations of urban design interest. As the text here is written from Jeanneret's own viewpoint, it is probable that he drew the accompanying sketches himself.
156 LCdv 108f.
157 B2-20-319 FLC, from Schultze-Naumburg, *Kulturarbeiten Städtebau*, Fig. 30, p. 72.

Fig. XXIV Street in Prague, showing the square-like widening of
a street. From Schultze-Naumburg, *Kulturarbeiten
Städtebau*, fig. 30

from a section in which Schultze-Naumburg addresses the spatial quality of such cases
where streets widen into squares:

> The pictorial, interesting and enlivening aspects are clear to all observers from [Fig.
> XXVa/b]; it is also easy to imagine how pleasant the corner spaces are inside the
> various buildings which project, externally enriching the street scene through new,
> interesting oriel and window motifs.[158]

Schultze-Naumburg goes on to advocate the advantages of a projecting or indented
building alignment, both for traffic and for the cityscape in general (Fig. XXVI
a/b):

---

158 Schultze-Naumburg, *Kulturarbeiten Städtebau*, p. 74.

Fig. XXV Example for staggered façades. From Schultze-Naumburg, *Kulturar-beiten Städtebau*, fig. 29

Fig. XXVI Rudolstadt, showing setback to enliven the street front. From Schultze-Naumburg, *Kulturarbeiten Städtebau*, fig. 156

Since the building to the side recedes far behind the street-front here, the house on the corner forms the closing prospect to the street and thus gains much greater visibility than if it had retreated into the frontage, even if it were detached.[159]

Jeanneret's discussion of buildings which project to develop a façade perpendicular to the street includes his reflections on how urban planners in earlier times cleverly closed the perspective of a street. One such example is the Karlstor at the end of Neuhauser Straße in Munich, which attracts the viewer's gaze, preventing it ranging over the adjacent expanse of square.

He also describes attractive layouts on a map of Ulm dating from 1808, which include closed perspectives, setbacks from streets and a church built at a T-junction at the end of a street (Fig.s 10, 11). These are all examples of enclosed street shapes.[160] The topic of the *rue fermée*, the very essence of which lies in its spatial enclosure, also comes into its own here, as illustrated by Jeanneret using the Marktgasse in Berne.[161] Although Jeanneret is rarely explicit in using the word 'space' – whether *volume* or *corporalité* – his attention is certainly focused on spatial phenomena.

Building on his deliberations about the principle of setbacks, he reflects on 'serrated' street widenings. Turning rows of houses away from the axis of the street front, as had been occasionally practised in the past, would give many shops a façade almost twice as long. Buildings laid out thus would also increase the length of their rear façades. Jeanneret planned to illustrate this with two Fig.s, which do not appear to have been preserved.[162] It is probable that he intended to use Eugène Hénard's impressions of a *boulevard à redans* and a *boulevard à redans triangulaires/à alignements brisés* (boulevard with setbacks, boulevard with triangular setbacks/with offset alignments).[163] Not only had Hénard's *Etudes sur les transformations de Paris* appeared prior to 1910, but more importantly some of his contributions had been shown at the Berlin urban design exhibition, and it is highly likely that Jeanneret saw them there. One further, peculiar passage in Jeanneret's text addresses the issue of 'urban design with the kerb'. This may seem an unlikely urban design element, but it is in fact central to the distinction between types of road users, as already discussed. Jeanneret explains that although the kerb cannot be deemed to be an urban design element, it is nevertheless an item with which German architects work. The edge of the pavement forms "the boundary between the moving, dangerous sphere of fast vehicles and the quieter sphere of pedestrians. It is, in some ways, the parapet on a pier surrounded by the sea."[164] The kerb, he explains, forms a guideline for pedestrians and smoothens out the projections and recesses in the pavements which might otherwise arise where alignment was varied.[165] This argument may be

---

159 Schultze-Naumburg, *Kulturarbeiten Städtebau*, p. 282.

160 LCdv 111f. Plan of Ulm, 1808: B2-20-312 FLC, from: *Der Städtebau*, 6 (1909), plate 79.

161 See also B2-20-304 (Fig. 24), a drawing from Merian which Jeanneret does not assign to any particular place in his text.

162 Spaces have been left in the Manuscript for the numbers of the illustrations; there is no further indication of which illustrations Jeanneret planned to place here.

163 Eugène Hénard, *Etudes sur les transformations de Paris*, ed. Jean-Louis Cohen (Paris: Editions L'Equerre, 1982), pp. 32–42.

164 LCdv 110.

165 LCdv 110.

based on Henrici.[166] The strong image of the pier which Jeanneret uses to distinguish firmly between pedestrians and vehicles indicates, as the introduction to the chapter did, that this initial distinction between road users would not be his last: there would be a final, more radical one. The logical conclusion of this argument would be the complete separation of pedestrian and vehicular routes which he undertook as Le Corbusier, some 15 years later.

Overall, despite presenting a wide variety of projections and setbacks used in urban design, Jeanneret's opinion is clear: streets with suitably erected edifices should be enclosed in such a way that they make a spatial impact, becoming tangible spaces.

Passages

Once he had gleaned from the urban design literature the significance of enclosed perspectives, Jeanneret looked for contemporary places in which to deploy the traditional architectural forms of gateways and passageways, rather than merely copying from earlier examples. One such useful new application of this motif was in the passageways which could be seen in the new towns and cities, in a variety of guises. He dreamed up a passageway through several blocks of housing, which would provide pedestrians with a shortcut through the city. The plan cited by Jeanneret shows the rich architectural possibilities of this form, in which spatial beauty is combined with great practicality:

> Figure [...] [25] shows one application of this in Munich; the very heavy traffic granted the buildings considerable value; instead of sorry courtyards the very architectural ploy of four enclosing walls granted very pretty aspects. – Large bays with flowered galleries and shops on the ground floor, cafés or bookshops which benefit from the constant stream of passers-by; – books and engravings can be laid out in the shade or sheltered from the rain.[167]

Jeanneret points out two further types of passageway. These are, on the one hand, an arcade in a city – such as the Kaisergalerie between Unter den Linden, Friedrichstraße, and Behrenstraße in Berlin – and on the other hand a cut-through for traffic: "The street is simply closed by a large building through which a vast archway is opened, allowing access to cars and pedestrians."[168]

Schultze-Naumburg illustrates this scenario in *Kulturarbeiten Städtebau* using the Burkader Kirche (Church of St. Burchard) in Würzburg, which has a vaulted tunnel underneath the choir.

---

166 "It is advisable whenever possible to shape those lines that delimit the vehicle track (kerbs or pavements) as straight or at least unbroken lines, so that the eye does not lose its guidelines. Such elements of the street and its frontages that act as guidelines may well contain interruptions on one side without causing that illusion, as continuity on a single side is sufficient to allow one to appreciate the extension of the set-back or interruption on the other side. Single-sided street openings or widenings [...] [Fig. 18] do not therefore have such an unfortunate effect as crossroads or precipitous widenings of the street on both sides." Henrici, *Beiträge*, p. 88f.

167 B2-20-355 FLC; Passageway through a residential block in Munich; Jeanneret notes: "An excellent means of shortening the pedestrian's route. Passages through a courtyard which thus regains the status of street and increases in rental value. An advertising column gains much attention because it is the only thing – and shops do very well in terms of trade as these passageways are very busy – a tree always contributes great charm." The text for the illustration is a rough draft of the Manuscript text, LCdv 112f.

168 Schultze-Naumburg, *Kulturarbeiten Städtebau*, cites this example: see Fig. 60, p. 114. LCdv 113.

Jeanneret photographed this subject on his way from Berlin back to Munich in June 1910, albeit from a different angle, thus demonstrating how thoroughly he had internalised Schultze-Naumburg's suggestions (Fig. IXa/b).[169] Finally, Jeanneret describes – with reference to the Limmatquai in Zurich and Prinzregentenstraße in Munich – a phenomenon which made such a lasting impression that it inspired him to produce design sketches and descriptions. These can be seen on the final pages of Cahier C.2. Here, Jeanneret sketches buildings which bridge a commercial street, forming an enclosed street space.[170] His draft text states:

> Street goes under a block of old buildings through passageways. In an old town, it would be possible to design wide 'commercial' streets which were almost or completely straight, and passed through blocks of housing. Straight through, using passageways driven through the blocks situated on the street's route – and no longer dumbly demolishing the precious encyclopaedia of a town's tradition.[171]

A design by Theodor Fischer for building over the Neumünsterplatz in Würzburg, as shown in Schultze-Naumburg's *Kulturarbeiten Städtebau*, may have provided the major impetus behind Jeanneret's suggestion (Fig. XXVIIa/b).[172] Here, Fischer develops a building complex which shapes the space in the square, standing directly opposite the Neumünster church and allowing pedestrians and cars to pass through arcade-like gateways. Thus Jeanneret casts his vote, alongside Camillo Sitte, for 'enclosed' rather than 'open' urban layouts.

The section on *passages* is likely to have been based on the third chapter in *Kulturarbeiten Städtebau*, in which Schultze-Naumburg speaks at length about the spatial qualities of passageways. He deals only in passing with arcades as often understood today – covered shopping streets – looking instead, much more generally, at routes through the city reserved exclusively for pedestrians. Schultze-Naumburg emphasises that passages and arcades are beautiful architectural motifs, which moreover are beneficial for commerce and practical for pedestrians, who can make rapid progress through the city, unhindered by vehicles. He believes they are deployed much too rarely, for spurious reasons.[173] Although Jeanneret handles passageways in much shorter order, he advances almost the same arguments in their favour as Schultze-Naumburg: their beauty, the peace for the pedestrian, the shortcuts and cloistered calm in which cafés and shops will flourish. Jeanneret even retains Schultze-Naumburg's sequence – first come passages for pedestrian shortcuts, then commercial passageways, and finally arcades. However, he drops the subject of architecturally developed courtyards, which Schultze-Naumburg discusses at the end of his chapter. This is astonishing because the subject of enclosed courtyards was known to be a major architectural element, and features repeatedly in Jeanneret's travel sketches from the *Voyage d'Orient*, as well as in his own designs. Perhaps Jeanneret first grasped the significance of the courtyard during his Journey to the East.

---

169 Jeanneret does a similar thing with other subjects from Schultze-Naumburg's *Kulturarbeiten Städtebau*, such as stairs in Würzburg and other cities, the marketplace in Lichtenfels (Bavaria), etc. The photographs are shown in Giuliano Gresleri, *Le Corbusier. Reise nach dem Orient* (Zurich: Spur Verlag; Paris: FLC, 1991), p. 139.

170 Unfortunately, the sketch is so faint it cannot be reproduced here.

171 LCdv 418f.

172 Schultze-Naumburg, *Kulturarbeiten Städtebau*, Fig. 100, p. 180.

173 Schultze-Naumburg, *Kulturarbeiten Städtebau*, p. 113ff.

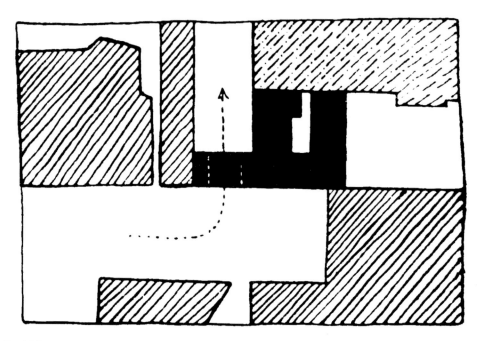

Fig. XXVII Design by Theodor Fischer, building over the Neumünsterplatz in Würzburg. From Schultze-Naumburg, *Kulturarbeiten Städtebau*, fig. 100

Road levelling

The two following sections are based overwhelmingly on Schultze-Naumburg's sixth chapter in *Kulturarbeiten Städtebau*, differences in level (*Niveauunterschiede*).[174] Here, Schultze-Naumburg describes the multitude of architectural possibilities provided by a hilly topography, and argues vehemently against the prevailing efforts made at the turn of the 20th century to compensate for differences in level by banking up and excavating such hills. Jeanneret does reorder his chapter, and begins by discussing two examples of levelling work. The accompanying illustrations are drawn onto a sheet of tracing paper from the examples in *Kulturarbeiten Städtebau*. One shows an example of levelling works which Schultze-Naumburg deems necessary, and one an example which he deems unnecessary.

The first instance is a section through a street running parallel to the slope, with villas built on both sides (Fig.s 28 and 29).[175] He proposes that the plots be terraced, so that the gardens need not follow the slope; the houses on the lower side of the street would be reached via small bridges. The villas on the higher side would be built several metres above street level, with a wall shoring up the garden on the street-facing side. According to Schultze-Naumburg, this street would be significantly more aesthetically pleasing than a street with plots designed to follow the slope.[176] Jeanneret's text, based on Schultze-Naumburg, asks: "Searching for the most advantageous orientation can bring one to design a district of villas or houses with gardens, following the contour lines of a hill; what would be the most judicious use of the land here?"[177] He responds by describing the first example (adopted from Fig. 114 in Schultze-Naumburg), where the slope of the land remains unchanged and he says the impression created is empty and bare. As the gardens would be difficult to work because of the slope, he believes they would be uncomfortable and unpleasant. Terracing would be a more expensive alternative, but would bring such benefits in terms of attractiveness and usefulness that the local authorities might even jointly finance this improved solution.[178] Jeanneret continues:

> Sketch *b* speaks for itself: it shows the monumental aspect of the large wall on the right-hand side, crowned with detached houses and vegetation; it emphasises the variety of approaches the architect could take to the house entrances lower down, on the left; we can discern the generous prospect of the street, all shaded, with its wide pavement, where benches allow pedestrians to enjoy the street between the groups of villas.[179]

174 Jeanneret does not continue to subdivide the remaining pages of the chapter On Streets using headings. However, he does note in the margin of page LCdv 115: "Insert paragraph relating to levelling" and writes above the relevant paragraph in the text "For sloping streets". The paragraph for insertion is on an additional page, and its subject matter is connected with the previous theme. It is therefore possible to deduce that the text may be divided into two sections in terms of content: *Nivellement des rues* (road levelling) and *Rues en pente* (sloping streets), even though Jeanneret did not himself subdivide it thus. These headings are included here because they help us identify the content. See Schultze-Naumburg, *Kulturarbeiten Städtebau*, pp. 184–278.

175 Schultze-Naumburg, *Kulturarbeiten Städtebau*, Fig.s 114–115, p. 205.

176 Schultze-Naumburg, *Kulturarbeiten Städtebau*, p. 204–206.

177 LCdv 114.

178 LCdv 114.

179 LCdv 114.

This brings to mind Jeanneret's *Maison Blanche*, the house designed for his parents in La Chaux-de-Fonds in 1912, situated on a sufficiently steep slope for Jeanneret to create a levelled garden. It also evokes Le Corbusier's later accounts of deriving pleasure from the peace and view at the Villa Savoye, as Colin Rowe noted in his essay "Mathematics of the Ideal Villa".[180] Here, in his poetic lines, Jeanneret paints a more detailed picture of the urban design situation outlined in the illustrations, supplementing his description with several photos which Schultze-Naumburg has used.[181] Jeanneret adds to this explanation details on the use of pavilions, which Schultze-Naumburg shows in various illustrations as part of his volume II *Gärten* (Gardens). Jeanneret would go on to design a pavilion for the *Maison Blanche* in 1912 (Fig.s XXVIII and XXIX).

Fig. XXVIII Garden pavilion. From Schultze-Naumburg *Kulturarbeiten. Vol. II Gärten*, fig. 14

180 Colin Rowe, "The Mathematics of the Ideal Villa", in *The Mathematics of the Ideal Villa and Other Essays* (Cambridge, Mass.: MIT Press, 1976), p. 12. Compare with Jeanneret's chapter On Gardens, which demonstrates his interest in Renaissance gardens.
181 "The uniformity of most streets on sloping terrain today is all the more regrettable as it offers the possibility of forming two extraordinarily beautiful motifs, as shown in Section 114, with the higher side indicated in Fig.s 242, 243 and 259, with Fig.s 266, 184 and others showing options for the lower side." Schultze-Naumburg, *Kulturarbeiten Städtebau*, p. 206.

Fig. XXIX Charles-Edouard Jeanneret, Maison Blanche in La Chaux-de-Fonds, after restoration 2006
(photo by C. Schnoor)

Jeanneret goes on to discuss the converse scenario, in which contemporary planning administrations commonly undertake excessive levelling work (Fig.s 28 and 30). He adheres closely once again to Schultze-Naumburg's text, even down to the use of some individual terms, yet without referring to the sketches he has traced from *Kulturarbeiten Städtebau*.[182] Jeanneret criticises planning administrations' unhelpful desire to regulate and level everything, and condemns the idiocy of moving large masses of earth on the sole basis of a desire to eradicate gentle undulations in a residential street. In contrast to Schultze-Naumburg, who describes this procedure in qualitative terms, Jeanneret provides the reader with the precise quantities of earth that must be moved. In so doing, his style is close to that of a tabloid journalist advocating the interests of individuals who want to build their own homes. He complains that, once they have bought a cheap plot of land, the poor housebuilders now face the extra cost of levelling work – which might instead have bought them an exotic holiday to Egypt or the Canary Islands.[183] For Schultze-Naumburg, the key question is the immense effort expended on such levelling work, which would also erase the slightly irregular beauty of the site. Jeanneret also accepts this argument, but places even stronger emphasis on the lack of practical benefit brought by such work: "The most striking thing is that this unjustified regularisation, which deprives towns of a certain charm, is of no use to traffic – especially in the case of sloping streets."[184]

---

182 B2-20-295 FLC. The sketches in question are from Schultze-Naumburg, *Kulturarbeiten Städtebau*, Fig.s 108–110, p. 198; Jeanneret designates them as *a, b, c.*
183 LCdv 116.
184 LCdv 116.

Sloping streets

Jeanneret devotes this section to his famous *leçon de l'âne*. He gives a voice to this beast of burden, who requires variation in gradients when travelling uphill and will therefore, given the choice, snake its way up a slope. Jeanneret believes that streets for vehicles should similarly adopt this lateral approach to hills. However, steps should also be built for pedestrians, fitting harmoniously into the landscape. Karl Henrici's *Beiträge zur praktischen Ästhetik im Städtebau* is the source for all the illustrations which Jeanneret intends to use here (Fig. 33).[185]

As Le Corbusier, he came to reject the donkey's teachings in 1925, stating instead in *Urbanisme*:

> Man walks in a straight line because he has a goal and knows where he is going; he has made up his mind [...]. The pack-donkey meanders along, meditates a little in his scatter-brained and distracted fashion, he zigzags in order to avoid the larger stones, or to ease the climb, or to gain a little shade; he takes the line of least resistance.[186]

But back in 1910 the donkey had yet to be displaced by the motor vehicle as a mode of transport. Jeanneret remained accepting of donkeys, and spoke accordingly, as in the chapter On Streets:

> We will not forget the demonstration given to us one rainy day by an ass pulling a heavy load. We were at the window of a building which closed off the top of a street with a steady gradient. The rain that had just fallen had made of the carriageway a uniform covering, in which the wheels of the cart pulled by the donkey made two shining stripes. At the bottom of the road these furrows started parallel to the pavement; but, soon after, they neared one side, then the other, then the first again, and so on for some hundred metres. The winding line loosened somewhat; the bends became less sharp, it regained a line parallel with the pavements. Then the donkey stopped; but as he was whipped, he regained a very winding route which became increasingly so until, once he had reached the top of the street, both donkey and cart disappeared.[187]

The poetic language of the quotation and the narrative tone indicate that this section represents Jeanneret's own point of view. After this very personal anecdote, Jeanneret allows the donkey to address the reader:

185 B2-20-316 FLC matches Henrici, *Beiträge*, p. 102, Fig.s 1–4. Jeanneret refers to Fig.s 5–6, p. 103, but does not copy them. He also notes on the above-mentioned sheet of sketches (traced from Schultze-Naumburg for the section on road levelling, B2-20-295 FLC) several illustration numbers from the latter's book.

186 Le Corbusier, *The City of To-morrow*, p. 5. There, Le Corbusier reasons against the 'cult of the donkey', as on p. 12: "The winding road is the Pack-Donkey's Way, the straight road is man's way. The winding road is the result of happy-go-lucky heedlessness, of looseness, lack of concentration and animality. The straight road is a reaction, an action, a positive deed, the result of self-mastery. It is sane and noble."

187 LCdv 115b.

The donkey's lesson should be remembered. Indeed, if this long-eared beast had been in the planners' office, he would have suggested: "My dear geometers, when it comes to streets that climb, please consider us as much as you can: the poor beasts condemned to pull very heavy burdens. We do not like your continuous slopes which you draw so very straight [...]. We would prefer a slope which is somewhat steep, then levels off a little, possibly completely. Afterwards we would begin the normal slope once more and, if necessary, we would put our backs into it for several minutes. [...] A little variety in the strain on our muscles will be less tiring."[188]

Jeanneret's reading of Henrici is likely to have been an influence here, resonating as it did with his personal experience. Karl Henrici was similarly interested in the beast of burden, arguing against a steady slope and for a zigzag as a means of gaining altitude:

For easy traffic on sloping streets another factor should be considered: there is nothing more tiring for humans than being required to walk continually uphill at the same gradient, and it is less tiring if, to attain the same height, steeper slopes are used in alternation with horizontal or gently sloping stretches. I cannot believe that our domesticated beasts feel any different in this respect than we humans do [...]. It should not therefore be seen as a particular achievement to construct slopes of a constant incline in the case of long stretches of road which lead upwards. Carts in such cases always seek out a longer, gentler ascent or descent [...].[189]

Thus the connection is made very clearly between Jeanneret's own experience – the donkey cart tracks in the rain – and Henrici's ideas, culminating in the *leçon de l'âne*, as cited above. Jeanneret's donkey acts as a mouthpiece for Henrici's heartfelt words; further investigation into the significance of the donkey as an image for Jeanneret/Le Corbusier is certainly warranted. As proof that Henrici's words are the likely source, we note that Jeanneret goes on to discuss a change in gradient combined with a fork in the road: Henrici tackles the same issue immediately before his other discussion of changes in gradient. Jeanneret also uses Henrici's illustrations.[190]

In this section, having considered the necessary incline for a street, Henrici comes to the conclusion that a hump back is a particularly ugly solution, although it cannot always be avoided. In such cases, creating a fork in the road would minimise the optical impact of the hump.[191] Jeanneret embellishes Henrici's thoughts and adds a discussion of the particular view afforded from a house at what Henrici calls the 'culmination' of the street, and of how a particular style of façade or fountain could turn this area into an urban design artwork. Jeanneret also considers the enclosure of the space – to which Henrici only grants limited attention – and emphasises in his own words the impression

188 LCdv 117.
189 Henrici, *Beiträge*, p. 102f.
190 Henrici, *Beiträge*, chapter entitled "Einiges zur Beachtung bei Anlage von Strassen, Plätzen und Gebäuden auf unebenem Gelände" (Observations on designs for streets, squares and buildings on uneven terrain), Fig.s 1–4, p. 102. Jeanneret copied these sketches and translated Henrici's captions, including a description of the gradient of the relevant streets, into French (B2-20-316 FLC).
191 Henrici, *Beiträge*, p. 101f.

created by an enclosed, pictorial solution, to which he is especially partial: "But still a wish persists to close off the image at the point where the two slopes meet."[192] Jeanneret continues to refer to Henrici, who states that pavements and streets should actually interweave:

> and if one has reason and opportunity to design such routes for pedestrians, and interrupts these with rest stops, then as per the schemes in [...] [Fig. 33], the stepped or terraced form runs alongside or intertwines with the hairpin bend. The relevant example is a street designed for traffic which runs up in large bends to the crest of a hill, crossed by a footpath following a shorter line.[193]

This appeal of Henrici's links back to Jeanneret's previous consideration, taken from Schultze-Naumburg, of an arterial network for the organic urban system:

> In the network of streets leading up to an elevation, the path for vehicles will always be the longest; the path for pedestrians, the shortest. This is where capillary networks come into play, as discussed in our comparison of a city's streets with an arterial system.[194]

Henrici further demands that the connection between winding streets and direct pedestrian routes be clearly identified; he believes this holds the key to providing a wide range of charming architectural vistas:

> With such public planning, it is important for the overall impression given that the connection between the two motifs, the sinuous route and the steep ramp, steps or terrace, be recognisable; lively intersections of the various lines arise, and the impact can be heightened fully by introducing architectural pieces, sculptural or garden ornaments.[195]

He further explains how this system of streets and steps should be treated in a densely built environment. For reasons of clarity, both elements should be handled separately, and the way the steps resemble a slide, which is daunting when seen from above, should be remedied using construction solutions such as offsetting the line of steps from the axis, or including rest stops. Extensive quotations from this section have been included here because they provide a possible key to Le Corbusier's later thinking: the similarity of Henrici's description to the ramp architecture of Villa Savoye is unmistakable – this also shows in the corresponding sketches. The Villa Savoye plays with the coexistence of two means of bridging the gap between levels: a ramp and a steep spiral staircase. The ramp is almost horizontal, whereas the staircase strongly emphasises the vertical (Fig. XXX). I propose the following interpretation: Jeanneret's early, patient collating of urban design situations as a source of inspiration ultimately produced architecture which transposed pictorial urban design traits onto the scale of the individual house. Evidence to support this interpretation lies in the fact that Jeanneret takes up Henrici's wording, citing Henrici's sketches as "image LXII a and b". His description is of diagrams; these are not present in Schultze-Naumburg, but the description does fit the only illustration of street layout on hilly terrain in Henrici's chapter which Jeanneret has

192 LCdv 119.
193 Henrici, *Beiträge*, p. 103f.
194 LCdv 119.
195 Henrici, *Beiträge*, p. 104.

Fig. XXX Le Corbusier, ramp and stair in the Villa Savoye, Poissy 1927–1931 (photo by C. Schnoor)

not traced elsewhere (or which has not survived). The sketches which Jeanneret designated as "image LXII a et b" are most likely Figures 5 and 6 from Henrici's page 103. They show stairs which run across a winding road (Fig. 33).

> The stairs shown as a diagram in image [33] could be placed either as independent motifs drawing their beauty from a happy alternation of landings and flights, according beautifully with the neighbouring houses, or passageways piercing the very bulk of the buildings and thus sheltered from rain and snow. The light they enjoy, the way they enter the housing, the way they open onto and close off streets, there is a fine balance needed where it is possible to create beauty.[196]

196 LCdv 119f.

Paul Schultze-Naumburg is also cited again. As Henrici does, he calls for uphill stretches, streets, and pavements to be separated from one another; to him the aesthetic quality of the resulting stairways is more important than their function. He contests the argument that black ice makes stairs unusable. He sees the difficulty in overcoming the related, widespread prejudice against steps due to the seemingly significant risk of falling; it is the reason ramps are often used instead of stairs, although he does not believe this to be justified.[197] The fact that Jeanneret uses Schultze-Naumburg as a source alongside Henrici is illustrated by Jeanneret's words:

> In countries where there is a dread of black ice or snow, this fear will cause master builders to increase the ingenuity of their solutions. There is no lack of variety when it comes to solutions, with all their picturesque or monumental aspects.[198]

In order to illustrate his argument, Schultze-Naumburg shows photos of some successful urban designs for stairs. Jeanneret sets out to use three of these pictures in his Manuscript, noting (Fig.s XXXI–XXXIII): "on stairs crossing a slope cite Schultze-Naumburg Fig.s 105, 106 and 107."[199] He does not make any related drawings of his own. During his research, Jeanneret also notes down in one of the cahiers the title of an essay from the *Süddeutsche Bauzeitung* dated 1903. This essay presents a design by Theodor Fischer for a stairway in Kempten, which could have served as a further illustration for this section (Fig. XXXIV).[200]

The broad boulevard

The last section of the chapter On Streets is divided into two. In the first part, Jeanneret summarises and emphasises the planner's responsibilities. These include taking into account the significance and specificities of the topography for planning purposes. Jeanneret believes the charm of any town or city lies in the diversity and richness of urban design approaches applied. He now quotes for the first time Laugier's dictum praising order in detail and variety in the whole, which he knows from Albert Erich Brinckmann's *Platz und Monument*: "Laugier said: Regularity and whimsy are needed, relations and oppositions, chance variation in the picture; *a great order in the details*, confusion, clashes, a tumult in the whole."[201]

---

197   Schultze-Naumburg, *Kulturarbeiten Städtebau*, pp. 186–191.
198   LCdv 119.
199   B2-20-295 FLC: "à propos d'escaliers coupant 1 pente citer Schultze-Naumburg Abbildung 107 106. 105". These are: Schultze-Naumburg, *Kulturarbeiten Städtebau*, Fig. 105, p. 190: "Treppenanlage am Dom zu Erfurt" (Flight of stairs at Erfurt Cathedral); Fig. 106, p. 192: "Treppenanlage in Prag" (Flight of stairs in Prague); Fig. 107, p. 193: "Treppenaufstieg in Pirna" (Stairway in Pirna).
200   LCdv 230: "Very pretty staircase by Fischer to be found in Süddeutsche Bauzeitung 1903 N° 22". It features in the article "Treppe zu Kempten" [Stairs at Kempten], in *Süddeutsche Bauzeitung*, 13 (1903), No. 22, pp. 169–170.
201   LCdv 436. See Brinckmann: "All effects are relative. In the case of architecture, this emerges from the situation. Nothing is achieved by inserting something into, or building something in, a city: it all depends on How. From the various partial beauties results an overall beauty in the city, from the well-formed harmonious details will develop a large, rich, diverse overall picture. "*Il faut de la régularité et de la bizarrerie, des rapports et des oppositions, des accidens qui varient le tableau, d'un grand ordre dans les détails, de la confusion, du fracas, du tumulte dans l'ensemble.*" Laugier, quoted in Brinckmann, *Platz und Monument*, p. 140.

Fig. XXXI Public stairs leading up to Erfurt minster. From Schultze-Naumburg *Kulturarbeiten Städtebau*, fig. 105

Fig. XXXII Public stairs in Prague. From Schultze-Naumburg *Kulturarbeiten Städtebau*, fig. 106

Fig. XXXIII Public stairs in Pirna. From Schultze-Naumburg *Kulturarbeiten Städtebau*, fig. 107

 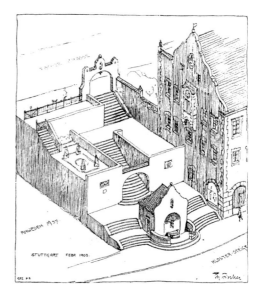

Fig. XXXIV Theodor Fischer, design for public stairs in Kempten, from *Süddeutsche Bauzeitung* 13 (1903), no. 22, p. 169

Jeanneret exhorts planners to shoulder their responsibility, for they will determine residents' later happiness or dissatisfaction with their urban environment.[202] Hence he is stating indirectly that planners have the power to mould cities to their own convictions. They are universalist designers, who can help the whole population of a city to be happy – provided that they have artistic skill and act responsibly. Thus another theme of the modern age comes into play: the artist who aims to change the world. It is not a huge leap from here to an urban design utopia.[203]

It is interesting to see how Jeanneret next weighs monumental and picturesque urban design against one another. He begins by deflecting the potential allegation that he is simply advocating *pittoresque* urban design: he says the authorities in Swiss towns and cities should consult the latest designs, such as those found in Germany and published in the journal *Städtebau*, which happen to be picturesque in nature. These would confirm that there was a reputable movement emerging, which countered the tendency in Switzerland to build *à l'américaine*.[204] The strongly forward-looking, self-justifying nature of Jeanneret's statement here is abundantly clear. It is reinforced by his claim that a city built on a gridiron system would ultimately disappear, to be replaced by another form of urban design.[205] But then Jeanneret makes an about-turn; his language becomes avidly poetic:

202 LCdv 122.
203 See the discussion in the literature, for example in Colin Rowe, *The Architecture of Good Intentions* (London: Academy Press, 1994); Rowe's essay "The Architecture of Utopia" in Rowe, *The Mathematics of the Ideal Villa*, pp. 205–223.
204 LCdv 122.
205 LCdv 123.

Then, and only then, will the straight street take its rightful place: a place of the greatest beauty. The straight line is the elegant line par excellence in nature, but also rightly the rarest. The rigid solemn columns of pine forests; the horizontal line of the sea; the vast magnificence of the plain; the grandeur of the Alps seen from a summit, when all harshness melts away into a vast expanse of peace![206]

Jeanneret extrapolates from the straight line in nature to reach a conclusion about the impact and aesthetic opportunities provided by straight, broad avenues: they can create an impression of both greatness and beauty.[207] He explains how the grandiose impression is created by immense proportions, a gently concave curve in the street and at its upper end a stately building. Jeanneret cites some shining examples of such street layout: firstly the Champs-Elysées, but also the Siegesallee with its Siegessäule and the Bismarckstraße in Berlin.

Jeanneret believes the beautiful effect of the straight street is achieved, as in the case of the Avenue de l'Opéra in Paris, where an impression of *corporalité* is created, where closed coverage lends the space a physical presence. In contrast to the grand straight avenue, the enclosed street will appear rather shorter, the perspective effects being less significant.

Beauty is rhythm, proportion, harmony. The street will only be beautiful if all the buildings are intimately related, if architects understand that it is mutually beneficial for each to heed the other so all can harmonise to create an *ensemble piece*.[208]

Jeanneret is definitely referring to Albert Erich Brinckmann here, who in *Platz und Monument* similarly describes the straight street as the most elegant urban design element:

The straight line and the right angle remain the most elegant elements of architecture and the straight broad street and the regular architectural city square will also retain their value within urban design. They form the core and backbone of the city, the most monumental shaping of space. The contrast between such streets and the irregular districts gives the city a pattern, an intensification, a rhythm.[209]

From his comments on the straight street, Jeanneret draws a general conclusion covering the entire chapter: towns (rather than cities) must avoid grand, monumental streets. In anticipation of a future architectural style, he hopes planners will make only limited use of straight streets.[210] The monumental style should therefore be an instrument reserved for cities; towns should stick to the picturesque. As with the overall Manuscript, Jeanneret has tailored this pronouncement to the urban design situation within Switzerland, which he clearly considers to be largely a question of towns. He would not therefore wish to deploy the full range of design instruments available to cities, as these would not

206 LCdv 123.
207 See LCdv 123 and compare with the sketchier version in LCdv 425.
208 LCdv 124.
209 Brinckmann, *Platz und Monument*, p. 169. See also Jeanneret's overall design for the city in the Introduction, with straight, broad commercial streets and picturesque residential streets.
210 LCdv 125.

all be appropriate to the Swiss situation. This becomes especially clear in his chapter Critical Application.

On Streets is one of the chapters which Jeanneret bases most strongly and directly on his textual forebears. These are: Schultze-Naumburg, *Kulturarbeiten Städtebau*; Henrici, *Beiträge zur praktischen Ästhetik im Städtebau*; Sitte, *Der Städtebau nach seinen künstlerischen Grundsätzen*; and Brinckmann, *Platz und Monument*. Henrici proves particularly influential on this chapter, with his rules focused on direct implementation. However, Jeanneret does not limit himself to writing up this previous literature, but instead develops something original: both by compiling these authors' texts and by distinguishing between towns and cities. The distinction Jeanneret makes between picturesque and monumental urban design is determined here by the size of the urban area. Yet Jeanneret returns to this dichotomy in the following chapter, proposing that a picturesque style be used for gradual development, and a monumental style for those rare opportunities when an entire district is designed at once.

Des Places – On Squares

Not a single line of text is devoted to the urban square in *Urbanisme*, yet here in *La Construction des villes* Jeanneret's treatment of squares forms the longest section of his study – despite his emphasis on the street as the most important theme. As discussed above, the chapter On Squares appears in two different parts of the Manuscript: on 18 pages in the loose-leaf folder and in Cahiers C.7 and C.8.[211] The first question which arises is therefore whether these constitute two versions of the same text, or whether the content of one section follows on from and complements the other. Investigation of the two parts reveals a somewhat convoluted situation, showing that the two versions both add to one another and overlap. Ideas in one also contradict those in the other.

The first fact which stands out is that Jeanneret prepared several tables of contents for this chapter, as a way of dealing with his complex subject matter. This contrasts with On Streets, in which he simply worked through the relevant subjects one after the other. He applies a similar internal order in both parts of the chapter, comparing the various instances of the picturesque style with the monumental and positioning the monumental at the end of each part, thus lending it particular emphasis. The tables of contents for On Squares can be found in both parts of the Manuscript: in the loose-leaf folder and in Cahier C.6 *Squares Gardens I*.[212] A total of five of the extant cahiers contain material for the chapter On Squares: as discussed Cahiers C.7 and C.8 contain the finished text; then there is Cahier C.6 *Squares Gardens I*, with its detailed outline table of contents; and finally Jeanneret devotes some 20 pages of Cahier C.2 *City II Bridges* and C.3 *City III* to extracts from Albert Erich Brinckmann's *Platz und Monument*, a key source of information on squares. Here, he also focuses on two further sources: Sitte, *Der Städtebau nach seinen künstlerischen Grundsätzen* and Schultze-Naumburg, *Kulturarbeiten, Städtebau*.[213]

---

211 LCdv 130–167 and LCdv 168–215.

212 The structure in Cahier C.6 is the most detailed, extending over five pages of the notebook: LCdv 527–531.

213 The cahiers in which Jeanneret would have noted extracts from these two sources no longer exist. In the case of Schultze-Naumburg, excerpts from the *Städtebau* volume of his *Kulturarbeiten* can be found in Cahier

Another factor contributes to the lack of clarity in On Squares: in Cahier C.5 *Trees Monuments*, Jeanneret begins to collect excerpts and references to texts on monuments (in the sense of statues). At first it seems as if he wants to write his own chapter on the subject, but he ultimately fills a mere three pages with relevant material.[214] Nowhere in the tables of contents for the Manuscript is there a reference to a chapter on monuments. Instead, much like Brinckmann's *Platz und Monument*, Jeanneret addresses the square and the monument together and attempts to structure his chapter in a way which simultaneously answers both the question of the right shape for a square in urban design and the position of a monument within the square.[215] Jeanneret's thought process is shown particularly clearly in the table of contents found in the loose-leaf folder, which can be understood as a supplement to the five-page listing in C.6.[216]

Once he has divided urban squares into three categories (the square as a place of rest, the square in front of a building, the square for traffic), Jeanneret discusses the various *Eléments plastiques*, the architectural criteria which mould a square. He identifies four factors affecting the physical presence (*corporalité*) of a square: unity (*unité*); enclosure (*clôture*); orienting the square in order to highlight a building or buildings (*mise en valeur d'édifices spéciaux, d'où orientation de la place*); and increasing the impact made by a square through the inclusion of a monument (*complément des impressions par la présence d'un monument*). He summarises this theory with reference to the commemorative square (*place de gloire*), moving on to discuss the geometric square and what he considers its exemplary deployment in the 17th and 18th centuries (in France) and questionable use in the 19th century. Jeanneret concludes that a square built over time requires an irregular plan, whereas a square built all at once may create a geometrically pure solution with a sublime character.[217]

Even a rough comparison between the table of contents and the actual content of the chapter shows that Jeanneret did not keep to his own plan when drafting his text. This is all the more confusing because the original, planned order would have been more logical than the order in which he actually arranged the text. However, such a comparison also shows that the text in the loose-leaf folder and the text in the cahiers are not two very different versions of the same text, but are instead two complementary texts. It is not possible at this stage to confirm why Jeanneret behaved so inconsistently when writing up his text on squares, when he had previously taken a consistent approach to describing streets. His train of thought never quite reaches its final destination, as announced in the five-page table of contents: a clear distinction between types of square.[218] The impression on the reader is that the second part of the chapter – in which Jeanneret refers

C.2, although not in relation to streets and squares, but mainly featuring regulatory measures and criticism of the building authorities.

214 LCdv 271–273.

215 This is particularly clear on two pages in the loose-leaf folder on which Jeanneret subdivides his chapter On Squares. The second page is headed "Monuments", and covers a large part of Cahiers C.7 and C.8, which are based almost exclusively on Brinckmann's *Platz und Monument*. LCdv 525 and 526.

216 On the table of contents page (LCdv 525) and in the long table of contents in Cahier C.6 (LCdv 527–531), Jeanneret uses combinations of letters and numbers to identify individual ideas or arguments. The order of these shows that page LCdv 525 was written later than the very detailed table of contents in Cahier C.6; Jeanneret rearranges the arguments again on p. LCdv 525 and refers for his own purposes to those places where he can find the full wording for each theory.

217 LCdv 525.

218 LCdv 527–531.

mainly to Brinckmann – is a more thorough investigation into some of the themes which he had already addressed in the first part.[219]

The classification of squares

Jeanneret begins his chapter on squares with a three-pronged attack on 19th-century planners: he believes they have caused traffic chaos, problems with residential housing and ugly cityscapes.[220] In contrast, Camillo Sitte's book had researched very precisely the factors that contributed to the shaping of squares prior to the 19th century. Sitte did much to rehabilitate 'irregular' squares. Jeanneret now wanted to present the fundamentals in the form of optical phenomena, aesthetic principles, practical requirements (i.e. function), and formal conventions (*convenance*) which remained the basis for determining the shape of a square.[221]

When explaining what constitutes a square, Jeanneret cites as his first criterion a clear vision of *le but poursuivi*, the desired goal, which he finds is not normally sufficiently well established. Jeanneret also stipulates a formulation and classification of the function of squares, and asks that a distinction be made between types of squares according to their function; this would replace the status quo in which "the most contradictory elements have been brought together in one and the same square."[222] Jeanneret begins by asking why squares are planned. In his response, he isolates three possible reasons for their existence: first, as a public square; second, as a square in front of a (public) building; and third, as a traffic intersection.

1. In order to obtain, amidst the dense street network, a peaceful area where markets or public gatherings can be held, or very simply for the sole purpose of (within the confines of a city) parting the walls of the buildings to arrange a greater pocket of free space. This square would because of its purpose be kept free from traffic.
2. A building with a particular character is to be emphasised: this is an opportunity to arrange a well-proportioned space in front of its façade. Amplifying the impression of beauty is the desired goal here.[223]
3. A square grows up of its own accord when several streets meet at a single point. This square is called a roundabout, a crossroads. The intent behind its creation is to ease the comings and goings of people and vehicles.[224]

Jeanneret divides the square up into its basic functions; he dissects it, but does not put it back together again. None of the authors whom he uses as a source mentions such a strictly functional distinction, although a debate was indeed under way in the early 20th century about distinguishing between squares according to their function, as illustrated in the competition for Greater Berlin held in 1910. Two matters are significant in this context: first, Jeanneret appears to be (perhaps unconsciously) taking a view that

---

219 In contrast to the previous chapter, Jeanneret wrote On Squares with no subdivisions. I have therefore added a heading for each new thematic section.
220 LCdv 131.
221 LCdv 132.
222 LCdv 132b
223 LCdv 132b.
224 LCdv 133.

belongs more properly to the forthcoming modernist movement, namely advocating that separation of functions, one which would later culminate in squares only intended to fulfil a single function: for instance that of traffic hub. Second, Jeanneret's dissection takes no account of the fact that all three phenomena may in some cases be inextricably linked. Historically, a place where trade routes met had tended to become a town square. This square would then become the site of markets and gatherings. A particular building that required emphasis, often the town hall, was frequently found on such a central square because this was a convenient meeting place, and vice versa. It can be established without going into further historical detail that squares often simultaneously perform more than one of the functions listed, and have done so for many centuries. However, Jeanneret attempts in his discussion to present precisely this versatility of function as a disadvantage which is due to poor planning. He writes that, especially in the 19th century, squares had erroneously been designed with multiple functions in mind, although planners might have known better. These squares were intended to fulfil all three of the functions Jeanneret identifies, acting as a resting place, a square in front of a building, and a transport hub.

> Due to the lack of clear intent, and as part of a synthesis which was believed to be skilful but which only proved disastrous, these squares were merged into one: the square created for its own sake (i.e. an island of peace), the square to serve a building [... and] the crossroads (i.e. all traffic compressed into a single point). And thus this standard type was obtained, with an appearance repeated 20 times in the same city, a type spread across every continent: a noisy knot where trams and vehicles rumble, where the network of electric cables blocks out the sky, where lamp posts stand in disharmony, where buildings present the shabbiest of impressions, where flowering shrubs wilt away in banal designs. This is the modern, pulsating, dust-ridden square where pedestrians fear to tread.[225]

This quirky, ahistorical argument is difficult to grasp. No source has been found for this wording to date, although – when compared with other sources cited by Jeanneret – it does seem that this passage could well have been directly adopted from one of the urban design authors he has consulted. Jeanneret cannot have based his passage on Sitte, as while the latter criticises "unholy knots of streets"[226] masquerading as squares, and states that the urban design system is "a system that, relentlessly condemning all artistic traditions, has restricted itself exclusively to questions of traffic", he does not speak of combining functions, as Jeanneret does.[227] Schultze-Naumburg, whose words Jeanneret has often quoted, compares the marketplace to a "large, open-air state room", thus combining the various aspects of the square just as Jeanneret seeks to separate them:

> One thinks on this matter [of the market square] of an intimate, enclosed square giving the impression of a large room, the walls of which are formed from the façades of the houses. Sitte analyses in detail how the marketplace as a site developed through history, and how it became a large, open-air state room for the town

---

225 LCdv 133f.
226 Our translation of Sitte's "Undinge von Strassenknoten".
227 Collins and Crasemann Collins, *Camillo Sitte: The Birth of Modern City Planning*, p. 234.

in question. If we look today at later town and city squares, we will note at first glance that they bear no trace of this market atmosphere.[228]

Schultze-Naumburg goes on to criticise the large size and open nature of these newer squares, which no longer feel enclosed but are experienced merely as extended intersections. He explains that the art of making a square feel enclosed hinges on the streets leading up to the square: these should not be straight, unbroken lines but rather be cleverly shaped to allow as few junctions as possible to be visible.[229]

The 19th-century square

After setting out his unconventional classification, Jeanneret describes several cases in which squares have been developed during the 19th century, primarily referring to illustrations from Schultze-Naumburg's *Kulturarbeiten Städtebau*. Jeanneret uses scrawled sketches in the margin of his Manuscript to remind him which illustrations to reference in writing. These can be found in his collection of illustrations, along with Schultze-Naumburg's accompanying text (Fig. 34).[230] Jeanneret begins by describing the typical urban square of the 19th century: a large, right-angled open space approached by roads on all four sides, and not therefore suitable as a place of rest.[231] Next he looks at another typical arrangement, the placing of the church (or other prestigious edifice) in a detached position within the sort of open square described above. He maintains that it is usual and widespread practice to install within a square a building to be presented as prestigious, and to issue a regulation requiring that the surrounding buildings stand at a uniform height of some 20 metres. This was believed to increase the impact of the imposing edifice. Yet Jeanneret states that the observer's perception would in fact be quite the reverse; thus he notes beneath the accompanying illustrations a translation and adaptation of Schultze-Naumburg's caption (Fig. 35a/b): "the church and buildings compete, and the church appears smaller and the buildings larger."[232] As a variation on this theme, Jeanneret quotes a passage from the chapter *Der Individualismus im Städtebau* (Individualism in urban design) from Henrici's *Beiträge zur praktischen Ästhetik im Städtebau*:

> I would like to draw attention to a weakness with the grandstanding which occurs frequently in newer town and city plans, as shown in Figure 7. Observe the display object *B* from any point on Street *A*, in the axis of which the construction is prettily planted (observe for example from point *a*), and parts *cf* and *eg* of the intervening street-fronts will disappear from view. Point *c* will appear joined to corner *b*, and *e* [will appear joined] to corner *d*.[233]

228 Schultze-Naumburg, *Kulturarbeiten Städtebau*, p. 80.
229 Schultze-Naumburg, *Kulturarbeiten Städtebau*, p. 80f.
230 B2-20-330 FLC.
231 LCdv 134.
232 "Church building constructed haphazardly in a large square, stands there very unhappily. Houses and churches are fully unconnected with one another, both internally and externally." Schultze-Naumburg, *Kulturarbeiten Städtebau*, Fig. 79, p. 145 (Fig. 35a/b). See Jeanneret's comment (Fig. 34): "the houses and the church compete with one another and the church appears miniscule and the houses bigger".
233 Henrici, *Beiträge*, chapter entitled "Individualismus im Städtebau" (individualism in urban design), p. 69f.

Thus, Henrici analyses the viewpoint of a passer-by as they approach. Jeanneret sketches the illustration in question in the margin of his Manuscript, although it does not feature among his collection of illustrations (Fig. 36). He provides a broad-brush description, enabling the reader to do without an illustration. Nevertheless, he presents the same idea as Henrici, concluding:

> However the desired effect will sadly not be achieved; the pedestrian moving along the street, at point *a* for example, will see nothing of the square's side walls *fc* and *eg*, and the building, which remains some distance away, will not appear to him at its full size. Having arrived on the square, this impression is diminished yet further; for from the end of the street his eye will be accustomed to the view of the major building, which will henceforth lose all power to move him emotionally.[234]

Thus Jeanneret substantiates in detail, using illustrations and texts from two different authors, a claim which these authors have in turn taken from Sitte. This is one of many points in the Manuscript at which Jeanneret's reception of Sitte can be seen to occur 'in stereo' – both directly and indirectly.

For positioning a prestigious building, Jeanneret proposes two solutions. If the impact of a major street is to be enhanced, the building at the end of this street should form the optical conclusion to the vista. However, if the impact of the building itself is to be heightened, then the entrances to the square should be laid out with this aim in mind. First, he discusses the third type of square: that designed for traffic. Jeanneret rejects star-shaped traffic intersections. The great spectacle of all different modes of transportation meeting – pedestrians, cyclists, trams, and more – would merely spur on the straight-line planners, who would then plan further squares with even more streets feeding into them.[235] In view of his criticism of the 19th-century trend towards squares with multiple functions, this seems a strange objection to make: such a square would after all have a single, uncompromised function. Yet Jeanneret adopts de facto Sitte's ironic criticism of the square as intersection (Fig. 37):[236]

> But what marvelous traffic conditions arise when more than four thoroughfares run into each other! With the addition of just one more street opening to such a junction, the possible vehicle encounters already total 160, which is more than ten times the first case, and the number of crossings which disrupt traffic increases proportionally.[237] Yet what shall we say about traffic intersections where as many as six or more streets run together from all sides, as in Fig. 84?[238] In the center of a populous town, at certain busy times of day, a smooth flow of traffic is actually impossible, and the authorities have to

---

234 LCdv 135.
235 LCdv 136.
236 Sketches in the margin indicate that Jeanneret intended to use B2-20-338 (Fig. 37) as an illustration here.
237 Sitte has calculated in detail on the previous pages the number of possible encounters between vehicles at a crossroads in order to demonstrate the disadvantages of this layout. See Collins and Crasemann Collins, *Camillo Sitte: The Birth of Modern City Planning*, p. 232ff.
238 Jeanneret refers to this sketch "Kassel: in der Kölnerstraße" next to the Manuscript text; it can also be found on sheet B2-20-338 FLC, a collection of six inopportune square layouts from Sitte and Henrici.

intervene, first by stationing a policeman who, with his signals, keeps the traffic precariously moving. For pedestrians such a place (Fig. 85) is truly hazardous [...].[239]

Jeanneret also adopts one fundamental idea from Camillo Sitte, who states in relation to the evolving use of squares: "We cannot change the fact that public market users are increasingly withdrawing from squares, some into artless utilitarian buildings, some dispersing altogether due to deliveries directly to homes."[240] When Jeanneret goes on to state that in days gone by, squares had been used for a town's public meetings, and nobody thought to separate art from everyday existence, he is contradicting himself once again: he had previously criticised the contemporary combination of art and everyday living which had come to urban squares in the 19th century.[241]

Jeanneret leaves his reader somewhat in the dark here as to which squares belong in which category. Which can be classed a *place pour elle-même*, a 'square for its own sake'? Can a square in front of a building such as a town hall or marketplace can be classed a public square, or does it merely serve to emphasise the beauty of the building? However interesting this attempt at typology may be in principle, Jeanneret is inconsistent in describing the types, which in turn creates uncertainty as to their interpretation: it is impossible to grasp his intention. His stated conclusion is that the square as an island of peace, 'for its own sake', is no longer strictly necessary. Instead, more space should be given over to plantings of trees, in order to challenge the tedium of stone-built wastelands. Nevertheless, the square built for the sake of beauty should remain. As a result of new construction technologies, this category of squares could be elevated to a previously unseen level of beauty. Jeanneret uses a poetic formulation: "Architecture, which is an illustrated book of the epoch's thought processes, will lend the square all the greatness of powerful and generous dreams which will come to fruition over the coming decades."[242] What Jeanneret repeatedly refers to as the *place pour elle-même* cannot to my mind be identified as a public square such as a marketplace. Instead it is that last type of square Jeanneret mentions, a square of noble, artistic design, which can be said to exist for its own sake. It remains unclear why Jeanneret insisted on distinguishing between these two categories of squares, especially as one of his examples, the Piazza della Signoria in Florence, fits into both categories: it is an artistically designed square which functions as a public, political arena.

Yet two points emerge clearly upon reading this chapter: first, Jeanneret contradicts himself and argues inconclusively because he is compiling from an eclectic mix of sources. He places quotations directly alongside his own assertions, which occasions some further contradictions. Second, as will be clear at the end of the present chapter, the only square which truly interests him here is the geometric square as a place of prestige, as an artistic statement. Brinckmann had led him directly to this subject by holding up the example of the royal squares in Paris, with which Jeanneret was evidently fascinated.

---

239 Collins and Crasemann Collins, *Camillo Sitte: The Birth of Modern City Planning*, p. 234f.
240 Collins and Crasemann Collins, *Camillo Sitte: The Birth of Modern City Planning*, chapter entitled "Artistic Limitations of Modern City Planning", p. 243f.
241 LCdv 137.
242 LCdv 139.

The artistically designed square

Initially, Jeanneret maintains that the key requirement for the aesthetic impact of a square is *corporalité*. He uses the term as a synonym for the character and volume of a space, and explains:

> If a square is not a room with large panelled walls, with carefully placed furniture, with windows giving onto beautiful views, then in no way whatsoever can it claim to be beautiful. It is like a long, straight street which is not enclosed: a volume that does not exist for the eye, and consequently remains expressionless.[243]

This formulation is based not on Brinckmann, but directly on Sitte's chapter *Die Geschlossenheit der Plätze* (the enclosure of squares):

> Aesthetically speaking, a great deal would still have to be added in embellishment, in meaning, and in character. However, just as there are furnished and empty rooms, so one might also speak of furnished and unfurnished plazas, since the main requirement for a plaza, as for a room, is the enclosed character of its space.[244]

Jeanneret summarises the necessary spatial characteristics of a beautiful square as follows: the spatial quality of the square will be beautiful: if the relationship between the plan and walls or façades of the square shows a unity of design; if the view is not diverted outwards through many openings, but instead the walls of the square capture the view using the greatest possible length of façades; if the auspicious shape of the square helps to emphasise a building; and if the addition of a monument contributes an intimate feel to the abstract architectural lines of the square.[245] This particular combination of aspects which in Jeanneret's view makes a square beautiful cannot be found in Sitte, in Schultze-Naumburg, or in Brinckmann. It appears Jeanneret has consolidated statements by these three authors into a single formulation. Jeanneret further explains that a square will only be unified if the different architectures in the square obey the same principles: if the square is built all at once, the use of lines and materials should accord with one another, and if it is built over time, the newer buildings should respect the existing ones. Jeanneret believes that this is no longer common practice, with new buildings disregarding existing ones and paying no heed to local traditions: this is the result of a universalist mentality or architectural language.[246] The calls he makes for a unified treatment of the façades in a square may well have originated in this passage by Brinckmann:

> Again and again [in 18th-century France] good design of squares is required above all to be 'bien percée', and this should in densely built-up cities be understood as follows: one wishes to grant the gaze freedom of movement. But the openings in the walls of the square will never, ever destroy the spatial impact of square; for, to emphasise this decisively: the lasting quality of its space does not rely on the

---

243 LCdv 139f.
244 Collins and Crasemann Collins, *Camillo Sitte: The Birth of Modern City Planning*, p. 170.
245 LCdv 140.
246 LCdv 140f. Jeanneret quotes Montenach, *Pour le visage aimé de la patrie*, p. XVf., who quotes this statement himself but unfortunately fails to cite his source.

surrounding buildings being uninterrupted, but rather on the treatment of the walls. Even squares with frequent interruptions will have a spatial impact due to the striking, unified formation of their façades, and the views out through the streets will only expand the space, provided they are in the proper proportion to the square. Indeed, much relies [...] on the proper relationship here.[247]

Openings onto the square

Jeanneret now turns to the point where streets enter the square, as the most important among the elements giving an impression of enclosure. He sketches in the margin of his Manuscript here an image very similar to Sitte's drawing of a 'turbine square', and comments that this principle of positioning the openings asymmetrically at each corner of the square like turbine arms is both the simplest and the closest to perfection.[248] A pedestrian entering the square would see only façades directly adjoining one another. The cathedral square in Ravenna operates on this principle; Jeanneret had already visited the square on his first journey to Italy in 1907. He can therefore confirm from his personal experience that a beautiful, enclosed impression is indeed created, although the architecture of the individual buildings is by no means outstanding.[249] Thus Jeanneret combines his own experiences with examples from the literature. He copies the sketch of the cathedral square in Ravenna from Sitte's Städtebau, as well as many other figure.-ground plans of mediaeval squares (Fig. 41).[250] Sitte says of this example:

> The whole secret consists in the fact that entering streets are laid out at an angle to our lines of sight instead of parallel to them. This is an artifice which, in another context, was employed from the earliest Middle Ages by builders [...] often with the greatest refinement, when they wanted to conceal joints in stone or wood [...]. Of the examples shown here, the purest type of this ingenious system is the cathedral square in Ravenna [...]. Similarly arranged are the plaza of the Cathedral of Pistoia and many others are also laid out thus.[251]

Jeanneret goes on to emphasise that such squares do not need to be built with a full set of right angles; as he had already stated, the eye would not detect slight deviations from the regular.[252] Examples of this would include the Piazza San Marco in Venice (Figs. 47, 48), the Piazza della Signoria in Florence, and the Piazza del Campo in Siena (which he refers to as the Palio).[253] In this section, Jeanneret initially follows Camillo Sitte, who devotes the whole chapter Unregelmäßigkeiten alter Plätze to proving this point (The Irregularities of Old Plazas).[254] Jeanneret then examines the case where two streets meet at the corner of

247 Brinckmann, Platz und Monument, p. 105.
248 See Collins and Crasemann Collins, Camillo Sitte: The Birth of Modern City Planning, p. 276, Fig. 108.
249 LCdv 141f.
250 B2-20-340 FLC contains 14 small sketches of figure-ground plans from Sitte, on the themes Irregular squares, Street openings, Building with several squares, etc.
251 Collins and Crasemann Collins, Camillo Sitte: The Birth of Modern City Planning, p. 172.
252 See Jeanneret's comments on this in On Streets, LCdv 106.
253 LCdv 142.
254 Collins and Crasemann Collins, Camillo Sitte: The Birth of Modern City Planning, p. 185.

a square, and uses five sketches to show one undesirable and four practicable solutions (Fig.s 34 and 41).[255] These solutions were taken from Schultze-Naumburg's book. He discusses the issue of streets opening onto a square in significantly more detail than Sitte, as well as presenting picturesque examples of enclosed square layout across some 20 pages.[256] Schultze-Naumburg's theory is that certain forms of junction are particularly well suited to an enclosed square layout, although his arguments relate purely to aesthetics, not to the volume of traffic. Jeanneret on the other hand uses Sitte's model to assess the practicability of junctions, asserting that it makes sense to split a crossroads into two T-junctions immediately next to one another; this avoids queues of traffic.[257] Jeanneret then adds his own aesthetic argument: having discussed the undesirable layout, he explains using the practicable solutions how a square can retain its enclosed effect even with two junctions:

> The plan adopted in this case, in our era, is shown in Fig. [a]: opening the square up at that precise point where its enclosed character should be accentuated, thus invalidating the most important aesthetic condition of the square. What is more, this will create much more significant traffic congestion than is caused by the designs in Fig.s b, c, d and e.[258]

In the illustrations b to e cited above, the openings of streets onto the square are either set back or forwards away from the corner in a variety of ways which ensure that the enclosed corner is affected as little as possible. Thus an important architectural design principle is translated into urban design. Jeanneret describes another unsuitable model which was often used: placing road junctions in the middle of squares (Fig.s 38, 40).[259] The marketplace in Dresden provides a counterexample to this (Fig. 43a/b). Here, the curve of the streets ensures the square appears completely enclosed although many streets open onto it.[260] Jeanneret also uses the example of Stuttgart marketplace, although no source has been found for his drawing of it.[261] The Stuttgart marketplace also features on one of Jeanneret's postcards, entitled "view of the Stiftskirche", although this is taken from a viewpoint which only reveals some of the square's spatial qualities (Fig. XXXV).

255 LCdv 142. Jeanneret decorates the five different sketches of solutions for squares with arrows showing vehicles turning off, à la Sitte, to demonstrate the practicability of the individual variants. Figure a) has no equivalent in Schultze-Naumburg's text, although Figures b), c), d), e), – in that order – are the counterparts to Schultze-Naumburg's sketches Figures 44, 43, 45, 72. See B2-20-330 FLC, No. 5, and B2-20-346 FLC, c), d) and f).

256 Schultze-Naumburg, *Kulturarbeiten Städtebau*, pp. 81–111.

257 Collins and Crasemann Collins, *Camillo Sitte: The Birth of Modern City Planning*, p. 232ff.

258 LCdv 142.

259 Here, Jeanneret refers to a figure without stating a number. The sketch positioned next to the text would indicate that he is referring to Fig. 81, p. 103, from Sitte's *Städtebau* ("Lyon: Place Louis XVI"), which Jeanneret sketches on sheet B2-20-340 FLC as No. XLI [a].

260 "The marketplace in Dresden, Fig. [45], is a similar case, but the view is certainly sufficiently enclosed by the concavity of the streets", LCdv 144. Once again, Jeanneret does not give a number for the figure to which he refers. He is probably referring to Figure 35 on p. 82 in Schultze-Naumburg, *Kulturarbeiten Städtebau*, a painting of the Altmarkt in Dresden, to which the accompanying caption reads: "Altmarkt in Dresden in the 18th century. Example of a fully enclosed square."

261 Neither Schultze-Naumburg, Sitte, Brinckmann, Henrici nor Fischer employs such an illustration. It is possible that Jeanneret is applying his own experience.

Fig. XXXV Stuttgart, view from the Stiftskirche. Postcard, owned by Jeanneret (LC 105-1112-28 BV)

Jeanneret states that geometrically perfect shapes used for squares often incorporate streets opening precisely into the middle of the square. This form is almost always used, he believes, because his contemporaries forget that the master builders of old used to close off the view of the streets entering a square within a few hundred metres of that square, by means of a large building. Thus the square appeared to extend up to the façade of that building, which in turn contributed its beauty to the overall quality of the square. This was a style of construction cultivated under Louis XIV and his successors; Jeanneret states his intention to devote a separate study to it (or perhaps a chapter).[262] He refers here to Brinckmann, who writes:

> The ideal completion for the monumental star-shaped circus would be to cap off the streets radiating out from this circus, well-proportioned as they are in relation to it, with significant architectural pieces and not to leave this enclosure up to perspective and the pictorial dissolution of form. French urban design practice ensures such capping of streets, although it has yet to create this type of star-shaped circus. Even where squares [play a] minor role in forming space, this model would elicit good spatial effect and this design will perhaps still have a future.[263]

The issue of the monumental square in France is addressed by Jeanneret in more detail later on, in Cahier C.7 (see below).

262 LCdv 145.
263 Brinckmann, *Platz und Monument*, p. 107f.

Jeanneret continues by quoting examples which demonstrate the enclosing effect of arched gateways. In order to prevent a street leading up to a square from piercing the square's sense of spatial enclosure – and, as Jeanneret adds, for structural reasons – such openings were in the past often spanned by stone arches, sometimes even complemented by a second arch a few hundred metres from the square. Jeanneret lists five well-known squares as examples: the forum in Pompeii (Fig. 45), the Piazza del Campo in Siena, the Louvre courtyard and the Place des Vosges in Paris, and the Piazza San Marco in Venice. Jeanneret also cites an example in Antwerp. All these examples are very different; in some, the building sits over the arch, in some the arch is treated as a freestanding architectural subject, and in some it plays a primarily structural role.[264] Only some of these illustrations can be traced back to Jeanneret's own collection of drawings.[265]

The square in front of a monumental building

Jeanneret now moves on to the next category of square. It is not clear how he decided that squares in front of monumental buildings constituted a category of their own. Yet we can see that he found a stimulus for this notion in Schultze-Naumburg, who treats the layout of monumental buildings in squares as a separate category in his *Kulturarbeiten: Städtebau*. However, Schultze-Naumburg considers the relationship between square and structure from a different angle, starting with the monumental building and asking how it can be presented in its urban surroundings. Hence for him the main principle is to lend the building in question the right sense of scale:

> It is also one of the main requirements in laying out all monumental buildings that they do not remain without scale, but instead can be sized up in relation to their surroundings. The ancients always understood this instinctively, or perhaps even knowingly. In the case of almost all monumental buildings erected prior to the 19th century, the source of their impressive effect can be traced. These are often buildings whose actual dimensions are not extraordinarily large. Yet almost every small town hall in our old towns gives an extraordinarily impressive effect [...].[266]

Jeanneret begins this section by discussing the emotional character which the planned square is to radiate.[267] Planners would have to ask themselves whether the square was to give an overall impression of 'beauty' or 'utility', and whether the square was likely to be beautiful. The next consideration would be whether the ensemble should be 'pretty' or 'grand', then whether its dimensions should be monumental or require refinement, and whether the materials chosen should help to create the desired impression. Thought must also be given to whether the surroundings in which the building is to be built would contribute to the desired impression. Having considered all these factors, the shape selected for the

---

264 LCdv 145–147.
265 The examples of Pompeii and Venice are in all likelihood taken from Sitte; illustrations for the examples of Antwerp and the Place des Vosges can be taken from sketches Jeanneret made – but not until 1915. This explains why these two illustrations do not feature here; nor does that of the Piazza del Campo in Siena. There is a small sketch of the Louvre courtyard, the provenance of which is unclear (Fig. 46, Louvre: B2-20-325 FLC).
266 Schultze-Naumburg, *Kulturarbeiten Städtebau*, S.132f.
267 LCdv 148.

square should be that which provides the best support for the character of the building.[268] This type of approach was always observed in great periods of art, whereas "spineless creations of smugly satisfied, parvenu 19th century architecture" had been created in the recent past, which stood in strange contrast to the artistic knowledge from long ago.[269] Jeanneret illustrates his claim with two opposing examples in which the shape and size of the square, the building itself, its shape and materials combine to reinforce the desired character. He compares the Frauenkirche in Munich with Saint Mark's basilica in Venice. Jeanneret states that in Munich the design for the 15th century Frauenkirche, the red brick which only allows for an abstracted form of ornament, the grey sky, harsh climate, and the city's desire for a powerful display all come together (Fig. XXXVI). In contrast Venice, which was at the height of its historic importance and aimed to crown this position of power, used the most valuable stone shipped in from far and wide.[270] Jeanneret deploys magnificently colourful descriptions of how church and square could be read as a single unit, and how the form and colour, position and outlook of the churches could express their individual characters.[271]

Jeanneret's use of the term 'character' is a nod to Theodor Fischer's 1903 lecture *Stadter-weiterungsfragen*. In this talk on questions of city expansion, Fischer emphasises two aspects

Fig. XXXVI Frauenkirche in Munich. Pencil sketch by Jeanneret, 1910 (LC 105-1067-06-1 BV)

268 LCdv 148ff.
269 LCdv 149.
270 LCdv 151.
271 See Rowe, *Mathematics of the Ideal Villa*, chapter "Character and Composition", pp. 59–87, on the use of 'character' in the 19th and early 20th century.

which re-emerge in Jeanneret's juxtaposition of the two church squares: first, Fischer's theory that "enhancing characteristic qualities" must be a major principle underlying urban design, and second, the idea that what makes an aesthetic impact in urban design is "combining all parts into a single unit".[272] However, Jeanneret is not merely following Fischer here, but is also referring to Sitte; he deduces from the comparison of Venice with Munich that despite the very different architectural formulations, in both instances the formal rules according to which the churches are situated have been derived from the 'feelings' which their master builders wished to elicit from observers: "All Sitte's book proves this; by studying all the beautiful squares which past eras have left us, the aesthetic principles leap out at the reader of their own accord."[273] In his representation of the Piazza San Marco, Jeanneret does not rely on Sitte's formulations, instead describing the square from his own memory and focusing on its materials and proportions. Although his aim is the same, namely to describe the artistic interplay of all parts, Sitte emphasises a different aspect: the successful siting of the campanile to join the individual squares:

> If we were to examine the means by which this unexcelled grandeur was achieved they would, indeed, prove to be extraordinary: the effect of the sea, the accumulation of superlative monumental structures, the abundance of their sculptural decoration, the rich polychromy of S. Marco, the powerful Campanile. However, it is the felicitous arranging of them that contributes so decidedly to the whole effect. [...] After all, the two things do go together: beautiful structures and monuments, and the correct placement of them. The grouping of the Piazza S. Marco and its adjoining squares is really perfect in the light of all the rules mentioned so far – and particular note should be taken of the placing of the Campanile to one side so that it stands guard at the juncture of the larger and smaller plazas.[274]

From the example of the Frauenkirche in Munich among others, Jeanneret derives the rule that, historically, the square in front of a cathedral has always been smaller than the façade itself. Thus the cathedral in Rouen forms three squares around it, before the front and each of the transepts, which mean an observer cannot see the façade until they are close to the cathedral.[275] This is an example which Jeanneret draws from his own experience to illustrate Sitte's chapter on groupings of squares.[276]

Jeanneret believes that in the Middle Ages, space inside the city walls was so valuable and in such short supply that squares in front of cathedrals were small, and towers high.[277] Jeanneret's initial arguments are aesthetic: the powerful effect of the cathedral is greatly heightened by the contrast between the height of the towers and the size of the

---

272 Fischer, *Stadterweiterungsfragen*, p. 18. and p. 9.

273 LCdv 152.

274 Collins and Crasemann Collins, *Camillo Sitte. The Birth of Modern City Planning*, p. 197.

275 LCdv 153.

276 Jeanneret photographed Rouen Cathedral in 1909. The pictures he took fail to illustrate the effect he mentions.

277 LCdv 154. This view opposes that of Brinckmann: "Thus those people [the inhabitants of the mediaeval town] will not have experienced the narrowness of its streets and squares as unpleasant; this did not arise from a lack of land, as the walls often enclosed sizeable areas of unbuilt land." Brinckmann, *Platz und Monument*, p. 2.

squares.[278] The administrative planners of the 19th century did not value this sort of staging for a building, and set about freeing up the cathedrals, for example Notre Dame in Paris (Fig. 50):

> The *little* houses which surrounded it, and gave it *grandeur*, were demolished. The parvis built in front of it was exactly *seven times* larger than the square for which its façade – unfinished as it was – was built – seven times larger![279]

Jeanneret then cites two fundamental principles against which to assess a church square:

> If the planned façade rises to a height greater than its width, the square at its foot will extend to a greater depth. [...] If the façade extends widthways, the square will match its character by taking a shape broader than it is deep.[280]

Jeanneret employs several examples to illustrate these principles but does not insert illustration numbers into the Manuscript, instead leaving blanks.[281] There is certainly no doubt that Sitte was Jeanneret's source. Yet the basic rule which Jeanneret cites was, for Sitte, merely a preliminary to more precise consideration of the dimensions of urban squares. Sitte very cautiously states suitable dimensions, which he derives from his investigations. The appropriate depth for a 'plaza in depth' would be one to two times the height of the monumental building, and for a 'plaza in breadth' the dimensions stated in the plan would not be as crucial as the perspective effect on the observer.[282] In order to elucidate the rule on the relationship between a church façade and a church square, Jeanneret also takes the example of the Minster in Ulm. He compares the spatial situation before and after the square was cleared:

> On plan *a* drawn from an engraving dated 1808, the parvis took the shape of the Frauenkirche parvis in Munich and the former parvis at Notre-Dame in Paris [Fig. 10].[283] It was very small, and contributed for all it was worth to the large triangle of façade topped with a heavy unfinished spire. No open street in line with the cathedral [Ulmer Münster] prepared the traveller for this powerful apparition.[284]

---

278 LCdv 154
279 LCdv 156.
280 LCdv 157.
281 Emery cross-refenced these blanks with a sheet containing 14, mostly very small, figure-ground plan sketches from Sitte's *Städtebau* (B2-20-340 FLC, Fig. 40). See Marc Albert Emery, *Charles-Edouard Jeanneret: La Construction des Villes* (Lausanne: L'Age d'Homme 1992), p. 217, Fig. 38.
282 Collins and Crasemann Collins, *Camillo Sitte: The Birth of Modern City Planning*, p. 192f. It should however be noted that none of the five examples Jeanneret mentions – the Cathedral in Verona, San Siro in Genoa, Sant'Andrea in Mantua and San Giovanni in Brescia, and the Minster in Ulm which Sitte did not mention – can be found in the corresponding chapter in Sitte, 'The Size and Shape of Plazas'. Sitte only provides two illustrations there: Florence (Santa Croce) and Modena (Piazza San Domenico).
283 E. Braun, "Eine deutsche Stadt vor hundert Jahren", in *Der Städtebau*, 6 (1909), no. 10, p. 135–137, with Plate 79 depicting the city plan for Ulm dating from 1808. Jeanneret carefully copied this plan using tracing paper: B2-20-296 FLC and – almost identical – B2-20-319 FLC.
284 LCdv 158f.

Jeanneret also explored the architectural impact of the Minster square with its large trees and enclosing wall, which accentuated the space in the square and connected the Minster to the surrounding buildings. The strongest defining factor for the square was an irregular block in front of the western entrance of the Minster, which together with the surrounding buildings formed the three-sided place described. Yet this had all gone:

> Now one fine day some 30 years ago, all was destroyed: enclosure, warehouses; the trees were replanted in neat rows, and the area of the parvis *quadrupled* with the demolition of a whole block (Fig. [51] *b*). Finally, ripped from its natural setting, the fountain in the parvis disappeared into a museum![285]

Jeanneret believed this destruction was compounded by the subsequent completion of the Minster's tower in a gothic style. In order to show the overall destructive impact, Jeanneret refers to two illustrations showing the Minster square before and after (Fig. 51). It is likely that these are two figure-ground plans of the Minster square published in two separate essays.[286]

Jeanneret digresses from his theme here: spurred on by the late 19th-century decision to complete the Ulm Minster, he devotes several manuscript pages to the question of completing historic structures. He saw his contemporaries' desire to finish off incomplete structures from other eras in the spirit of those bygone eras and took this as evidence they had forgotten they were living in the 20th century while the structure came from another intellectual era. Some of them falsely believed that paid workers could, without further ado, rekindle the poetic zeitgeist of 600 years ago.[287] It is interesting to see that, although elsewhere he displays a fascination for Viollet-le -Duc, here Jeanneret rejects the French architect's proposal that historic monuments should be reconstructed stylistically 'purer' than they had been initially. Jeanneret instead considers this an opportunity either to leave the structure incomplete or to complete it in the 20th-century spirit, provided one possessed sufficient inspiration to do so.[288] In so doing he is following John Ruskin's lead, without admitting as much. Instead, a later addition by Jeanneret cites Georges de Montenach, a Swiss author and proponent of heritage protection, who bemoans the fact that art, such as statues and frescoes, is protected by law while buildings, groupings, and landscapes are not.[289] Thus Jeanneret enters into the domain of heritage protection discourse, centred around the figure of Paul Schultze-Naumburg who, as chair of the *Heimatschutzbund*

---

285 LCdv 159.
286 Theodor Fischer, "Der Münsterplatz in Ulm", in *Süddeutsche Bauzeitung*, 15 (1905), no. 16, pp. 125–128; Carl Hocheder, "Gedanken über das künstlerische Sehen im Zusammenhange mit dem Ausgange des Wettbewerbes zur Umgestaltung des Münsterplatzes in Ulm", in *Der Städtebau*, 5 (1908), no. 2, pp. 15–18.
287 LCdv 161.
288 LCdv 162. See Pierre Vaisse, "Le Corbusier and the Gothic", in von Moos and Rüegg, *Le Corbusier before Le Corbusier*, p. 48: "He [Jeanneret] was also to remain faithful to Ruskin over Viollet-le-Duc in his abhorrence for the restoration of architectural monuments, a hatred that he would articulate again in *Quand les cathedrales étaient blanches*, in which he speaks of Périgueux Cathedral in terms that recall the sixth of Ruskin's 'lamps', the 'Lamp of Memory'."
289 LCdv 161f.

at the beginning of the new century, exercised a great influence over the protection of typical regional buildings and the use of traditional building forms.[290]

Jeanneret believes that Ulm has been degraded by the intervention described. However, a competition had recently been launched to reinstate the fountain removed from the Minster square and to fill the oversized new square with buildings. Jeanneret not only knew Ulm from his own experience but also followed in the specialist press the competition to develop the Minster square. Three articles appeared in 1905/06 in the *Süddeutsche Bauzeitung* reporting on the square and the competition, including an essay by Theodor Fischer.[291]

Freestanding buildings

Jeanneret now turns to the formation of squares using freestanding buildings: "A single building presents itself to all sides as a single entity and creates several squares by being cleverly situated, considerably enriching urban views."[292] Yet the 19th century had created squares in geometric shapes which were too simple, and placed buildings in the middle. Thus the views of both buildings and squares from all sides were too similar, which resulted in monotony.[293] This is one of Camillo Sitte's basic theories:

> We do not seem to think it possible that a new church can be located anywhere except in the middle of its building lot, so that there is space all around it. But this placement offers only disadvantages and not a single advantage. It is the least favorable for the building, since its effect is not concentrated anywhere but is scattered all about it. Such an exposed building will always appear like a cake on a serving platter. To start with, any lifelike organic integration with the site is ruled out. Also excluded is any successful achievement of perspective effects, for which it would be necessary to have deeper space – a plaza of a shape similar to a theater stage so that the façade of the building could be viewed as the backdrop to a stage.[294]

We have now come full circle, back to the beginning of the section on squares in front of monumental buildings, in which Schultze-Naumburg was quoted as saying that the building to be emphasised should be tied in with the surrounding built environment. Continuing on from that quotation, Schultze-Naumburg states in line with Sitte's theory:

---

290 If Jeanneret did indeed plan to write a chapter "On Style", as one of the tables of contents suggests, it is most likely to be located here, between heritage protection and a discussion of 'character' (See Posener, *Berlin auf dem Wege zuu einer neuen Architektur*, chapter "Vereinfachung"; on Schultze Naumburg, see: Norbert Borrmann, *Paul Schultze-Naumburg, 1869-1949, Maler, Publizist, Architekt. Vom Kulturreformer der Jahrhundertwende zum Kulturpolitiker im Dritten Reich* (Essen: Richard Bacht, 1989)).

291 These are the two essays mentioned above, by Theodor Fischer in the *Süddeutsche Bauzeitung* and Carl Hocheder in *Städtebau*, plus the article "Wettbewerb zum Ulmer Münsterplatz" in *Süddeutsche Bauzeitung*, 16 (1906), No. 50, pp. 393–396, and No. 51, pp. 401–403.

292 LCdv 165.

293 LCdv 165.

294 Collins and Crasemann Collins, *Camillo Sitte: The Birth of Modern City Planning*, p. 166.

The surest means of removing [a sense of] scale from a building is to place it in the middle of an open square, i.e. to isolate it. Misdirected construction activity in the 19th century made the most extensive use of this technique. Indeed, it went so far as to 'release' from their natural framework buildings which the ancients with their certain knowledge in artistic matters built into groups which lent them scale, and thus deprive them of this scale.[295]

To that end, Schultze-Naumburg also presents a series of photographs and supplementary figure-ground sketches. Jeanneret copies all these sketches; the example of a relatively small, historicist church in a broad square is particularly significant (Fig. 35a/b). The church is surrounded by five-storey perimeter block construction which Schultze-Naumburg describes in the caption as: "Church structure built haphazardly in the middle of a large square, sits very awkwardly. Buildings and church have been combined without any internal or external connection whatsoever."[296] Jeanneret does not translate literally, instead stating: "The houses and the church compete with one another, and the church appears smaller and the houses larger."[297] Jeanneret adds that buildings used to be located asymmetrically in such a way that four different squares with a rich variety of views were created. As an example of this he uses a figure-ground sketch from Sitte's *Städtebau* showing the church of San Michele in Foro, in Lucca, Tuscany: a freestanding church which is cleverly positioned within the city plan, forming three very different spaces around itself (Fig. 40).[298]

The chapter On Squares in the loose-leaf folder ends very abruptly, with two more examples of prestigious buildings which form several different spaces around themselves: the Town Hall in Schweidnitz (now Świdnica in Poland, Fig. 52) and the Cathedral in Vicenza.[299] Jeanneret might also have added to the list his own drawing of the Cathedral and its square in Salzburg, as this illustrates very well how space is formed by a single building (Fig. XXXVII).[300] The last two manuscript pages in this chapter contain a draft and a fuller version of the last page of text. In the draft, Jeanneret ends his train of thought with a full stop and new paragraph, whereas in the final version the last sentence on the page ends in the middle of a word; it can therefore be assumed that the text of the chapter would have continued further.[301]

295 Schultze-Naumburg, *Kulturarbeiten Städtebau*, p. 133.

296 Schultze-Naumburg, *Kulturarbeiten Städtebau*, p. 145, Fig. 79.

297 B2-20-330: "les maisons et l'église se font 1 concurrence et l'église paraît minuscule et les maisons plus grandes" – from Schultze-Naumburg, *Kulturarbeiten Städtebau*, Fig. 79, p. 145.

298 LCdv 167. The example of Lucca on sheet B2-20-340 FLC: 14 figure-ground sketches from Sitte, *Der Städtebau*, here Piazza San Michele in Lucca, Fig. 18, p. 33.

299 On B2-20-343, Jeanneret notes: "Schweidnitz // Remarkable as a group of public buildings with fountains and street *ab*, and the long building which spans a whole block // emphasise *en passant* that the tower is freestanding." From: Matthäus Merian, *Topographia Bohemiae, Moraviae et Silesiae* (Frankfurt am Main: Merian 1650; repr., Kassel/Basel: Bärenreiter, 1960), part of the plate overleaf from p. 176. And on B2-20-340 FLC, the Cathedral Square in Vicenza, in Sitte, *Der Städtebau*, Fig. 19, p. 33.

300 B2-20-331 from Sitte, *Der Städtebau*, Fig. 71, p. 85. See also B2-20-339 (Fig. 58).

301 LCdv 166f. Text does exist in Cahiers C.7 and C.8 which may have continued on directly from here, and indeed Emery adopted this text as a continuation in his 1992 edition.

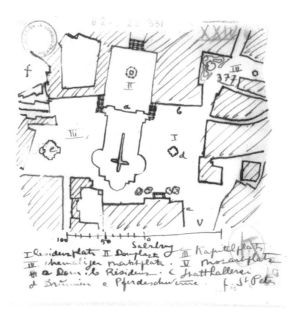

Fig. XXXVII Cathedral and its square in Salzburg. Drawing by Jeanneret, copied from Sitte, *Städtebau*, fig. 71 (B2-20-331 FLC)

On Squares in Cahiers C.7 and C.8

Adjoining squares on different levels

Before Jeanneret examines the commemorative *place de gloire*, he begins a new Cahier (C.7 – entitled *Squares Text §4 I*) by explaining the wealth of urban design possibilities which arise from two adjacent squares at different heights. He believes such squares are invaluable for areas built on slopes, and provide many resources for the planner: the wall which encloses the upper square or the row of trees atop this wall; one or more sets of stairs; the monumental or picturesque effects of these stairs as they link the two levels; the difference in character between the two squares – with the lower as a living forum and the upper as an island of peace, removed from traffic – and the grouping of the buildings surrounding the two squares.[302] Jeanneret bases his text on a passage from *Kulturarbeiten Städtebau*, in which Schultze-Naumburg discusses the urban design possibilities of two squares at different levels; he also copies the latter's sketches (Fig.s 53, 54a/b, 55a/b).[303]

Erecting monuments in commemorative squares

Next Jeanneret describes the geometric *place de gloire*, which he describes with reference to the French Royal squares he so admires. This new subject does not fit easily into

---

302 LCdv 169.
303 B2-20-354 FLC.

Jeanneret's own categories of squares for their own sake, squares in front of a monumental structure and commemorative squares. The commemorative square might best be described as a square for its own sake. Jeanneret really wanted to discuss in this cahier the "powerfully artistic synthesis of all the plastic elements", but chose first to analyse in more detail the erection of artworks within a square.[304]

To depict the square, Jeanneret uses the image of an 'open-air room' in which a monument, fountain, or statue in the square is treated as an item of furniture.[305] He believes two different types of rooms are relevant to the perception of squares: an intimate private space in which one lives, and a state room for official occasions. The private space is full of irregularities; it needs to contain variety within a unified whole, encompassing both simplicity and extravagance. In contrast, the public room requires a simplicity and clarity of expression; it must also reflect the character of the object presented there. Jeanneret can now emphasise the main point he wanted to make: that a table in such a state room would need to be positioned in the middle.[306] Transposed onto an urban scale this means that, unlike in picturesque urban design, a monument in this kind of square belongs in the middle. Camillo Sitte had pointed Jeanneret in the direction of the analogy between room and square, but whereas Jeanneret presents the character of a room and the architecture of a square as inextricably linked, Sitte did not present this connection as clearly. For example, Sitte describes the Forum Romanum: "In short, the forum is for the whole city what the atrium represents in a single-family dwelling: it is the well-appointed and richly furnished main hall," and continues later "one might speak of furnished and unfurnished plazas, since the main requirement for a plaza, as for a room, is the enclosed character of its space."[307] Jeanneret goes one step further in his thinking and combines Sitte's formulations on art and the nature of a room or square with Brinckmann's words on the French symmetrical squares of the baroque. While Brinckmann uses the 'spatial sense of an epoch' as a basis – a fundamental underlying stance each era takes towards architecture – Jeanneret and Sitte believe the style and nature of each square should be chosen individually, and adapted to its particular purpose.[308] Jeanneret may not have known it, but in selecting from either the picturesque mediaevalist or monumental classicist schools, depending on the situation, his approach was markedly eclectic. None of the urban design theorists quoted here states as clearly as Jeanneret does, when he likens the square to a room, the need for the architecture of a square to be handled in different ways, depending how public it is.

Jeanneret insists that, in any case, any ornament or sculptural decoration whether in private or public rooms must be intimately linked to its surroundings.[309] The decorative element or monument must embody the *esprit du lieu* (this is equivalent to Sitte's *genius loci*); thus a monument ornaments the public square. Jeanneret goes on to ask what that thing is which used to be called ornament, and which has lost meaning for us for the past century.[310] At this point Jeanneret begins to develop a theory of art which is rooted,

304 LCdv 170.
305 LCdv 170.
306 LCdv 171f.
307 Collins and Crasemann-Collins, *Camillo Sitte: The Birth of Modern City Planning*, p. 146 and p. 170.
308 "... there is a lack of recognition that this changing architectural form is merely the expression of a changing sense of space". Brinckmann, *Platz und Monument*, p. 153.
309 LCdv 172.
310 LCdv 174.

among other places, in his reading of Henri Provensal's *L'Art de demain*.[311] He believes ornament is something objective, independent of the subjective idea behind it, and depends on only three criteria: colour, *ligne* (outline), and volume. He further states:

> An ornament is something *which does good*, ahead of expressing any message; this involves ideas of balance – but not necessarily symmetry – and rhythm: an exaltation of colour, or shapes playing in beautiful volumes under the caresses of light, an exaltation and a beauty which will only be born of the interplay of balance and rhythms – which appeal to our visual sense – a rhythmic balance united in following a *line* which, effectively symbolising willpower, is pleasing for our minds.[312]

This is the earliest known formulation of Le Corbusier's now-famous statement "Architecture is the masterful, correct and magnificent play of volumes brought together in light" from *Vers une architecture*.[313] At this stage, it does not seem to apply to architecture as a whole, but only to ornament. Yet the now-familiar reduction of a work of art (or ornament) to an ideal of simple, essential shapes can be heard loud and clear in this statement. After a further paragraph in which Jeanneret calls for art to be guided by the knowledge of the past (which he later crosses out as superfluous), he returns abruptly to the issue of urban design.[314] He states that the fundamental considerations listed above will help with the ideal positioning of monuments, and makes a most pragmatic appeal:

> The first thing to obey is free movement of traffic. A monument should never be set against the normal to and fro of cars: it must be precisely situated in such a way that one can admire it from all sides without being disturbed. A very simple law, of which we take no account today, dictated the – ever felicitous – siting of monuments in the past; this is the law of the 'dead point'.[315]

Thus Jeanneret combines his definition of ornament, based on Provensal, with Sitte's requirement that the middle of a square be kept free in urban design. On this issue, Sitte states:

> To the ancient rule of placing monuments around the edge of public squares is thus allied another that is genuinely mediaeval and more northern in character: to place monuments and especially market fountains at points in the square untouched by traffic.[316]

Then, much as Sitte had done, Jeanneret describes how certain parts of the square remain free of traffic at all times because they are untouched by the routes connecting

---

311   See Brooks, *Le Corbusier's Formative Years*, p. 70.

312   LCdv 175.

313   Le Corbusier, *Toward an Architecture*, p. 102. Paul Venable Turner cites as Jeanneret's source Provensal's description of the emerging 'cubic' architecture: "The opposition of light and shade, full and empty, the cubic conclusions of its three dimensions, are one of the most beautiful plastic dramas in the world." Henri Provensal, *L'Art de Demain* (Paris: Perrin, 1904), p. 159, quoted after Turner, *Education of Le Corbusier*, p. 21.

314   LCdv 176.

315   LCdv 176f.

316   Collins and Crasemann-Collins, *Camillo Sitte: The Birth of Modern City Planning*, p. 162.

one street to another; to portray this situation he cites the same illustration Sitte did: "Sitte claims to have observed that, in winter, children in villages always instinctively build their snowmen at the 'dead point'."[317] Jeanneret states that artists in the past designed monuments in direct relation to the square as a whole, so they could be considered in the context of, and in contrast to, these surroundings. As examples, he lists fountains in Swiss marketplaces in general, and the Place de l'Arsenal in Solothurn (Fig. XXXVIII) and the fountain in front of the Minster in Berne in particular.[318]

Jeanneret considers the best examples to be the equestrian statue of Gattamelata by Donatello in Padua, and Michelangelo's David in the Piazza della Signoria in Florence (Fig.s XXXIX, 56). He knew these two monuments from his journey to Italy. He found relevant pictorial and textual descriptions in Brinckmann's *Platz und Monument*.[319] His text begins by following Brinckmann in a poetic account of how Donatello interposes

Fig. XXXVIII Place de l'Arsenal in Solothurn. Photo by Jeanneret, ca. 1910 (LC 108-338 BV)

317 LCdv 178. Collins and Crasemann-Collins, *Camillo Sitte: The Birth of Modern City Planning*, p. 159f.: "It is significant that when children at play follow unhindered their own artistic instincts in drawing or modeling, what they create bears a resemblance to the unsophisticated art of primitive peoples. One notices something similar with regard to children's placing of their monuments. The parallel is to be seen in their favorite winter pastime of building snowmen. These snowmen stand on the same spots where, under other circumstances and following the old method, monuments or fountains might be expected to be located."

318 Jeanneret planned to include an illustration of this fountain, but I did not find one in his extensive collection of postcards, in his own photos, or among the sketches in B2-20 FLC.

319 Brinckmann, *Platz und Monument*, p. 10–12 and 18–23.

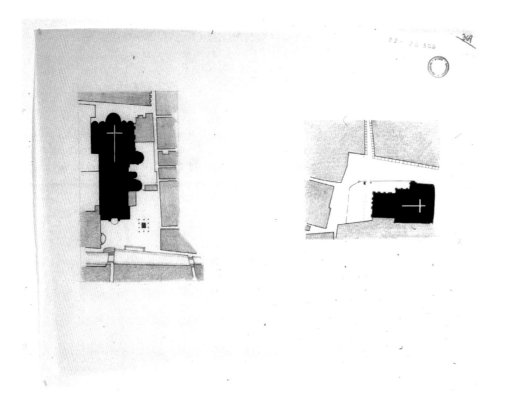

Fig. XXXIX Colleoni monument on the Piazza San Giovanni e Paolo and Gattamelata monument on the Piazza del Santo, Venice. Drawings by Jeanneret, copied from Brinckmann, *Platz und Monument*, fig. 4 and 2 (B2-20-326 FLC)

the dark image of the horse and rider between the observer and the sky by means of a high plinth, thus achieving maximum contrast.[320] At this point, Jeanneret begins to part ways with Brinckmann – he does not repeat his observation that the pedestal for Donatello's monument was white so that it would set the monument apart from the ground. Instead, he emphasises the horizontal nature of the statue and the imagined movement of the rider, which contrast with the soaring verticality of the cathedral. Independently of Brinckmann, Jeanneret draws on his own memories to formulate these key points. He goes on to report on the debate surrounding the positioning of Michelangelo's David, based on his reading of the relevant section in *Platz und Monument*.[321]

---

320 Brinckmann, *Platz und Monument*, Fig. 3, p. 13. Jeanneret copied the accompanying plan drawing (Fig. 2, p. 11) B2-20-326, FLC (Fig. XXXIX).

321 This is one of the few instances where several stages of Jeanneret's working method can be traced using the Manuscript. The corresponding excerpt from Brinckmann can be found in Cahier C.2, LCdv 412f; it discusses the attention Donatello paid to the interplay between a monument and its location.

An exception: The monument in the middle of the square

Once again, Jeanneret emphasises that throughout history, the centre of squares has been kept free and monuments have been placed against the outside walls. Sitte had already proved this as a general rule, with only one exception: the regular royal squares built under the kings of France, with a statue of the king in the middle. Jeanneret initially repeats his previous lament that square and circular public spaces with monuments placed precisely at the centre are so widespread; he labels such monuments as tasteless. In his view, neither the square in itself nor its monument will impress the observer in this case, because the powerful *sentiment du volume* had been lost in the 19th century. The classicism practised in that period rang hollow; it merely made formulaic use of tested formats. In a state of hypnosis occasioned by the French royal squares, designers in the 19th century had copied this system without filling it with either life or art. The embodiment of space – *corporalité* – as part of sensory perception had all but disappeared.[322] Having already complained elsewhere in similar terms, Jeanneret's cause for complaint here was neither Sitte nor Schultze-Naumburg, but Brinckmann's *Platz und Monument*.[323] With the help of Brinckmann, Jeanneret turns towards the artistically designed model, the regular, strictly geometric square with a monument located precisely in the centre. "This square, be it the Place des Victoires, Place Vendôme, the Louvre courtyard or derivatives thereof, in Nancy and elsewhere, was perfectly beautiful and still worthy of our greatest admiration"[324] (Fig.s 59[325] and 57[326]). Yet this admiration of French squares should not be considered to conflict with the above-mentioned principles for the layout of squares (based on theories from Sitte and Schultze-Naumburg). On the contrary, Jeanneret thought these French squares represented the ultimate embodiment of those same principles. He ruled out enforcing a counter-formula in place of an artistic principle, as this would ultimately mean aping the dogmatic classicism of the 19th century. To prescribe the design of irregular, artistic squares as a universal norm would be to fall into that same trap. Jeanneret concludes that:

> Building squares is a matter of remaking a work of art, a work of beauty; and to that end, having analysed the principles which determined the admirable squares we spoke of, we must identify them in these now-classic examples from the 17th and 18th century.[327]

The major difference between the squares Jeanneret investigated initially and those built under Louis XIV and XV is that the royal squares were designed and built all at once.[328] According to Jeanneret, the greatest argument in favour of this type of layout is unity;

---

322 LCdv 188–191.
323 Brinckmann, *Platz und Monument*, p. 153. Jeanneret refers to this point in the text in Cahier C.3, LCdv 434: "noter que le Raumgefühl change av. les époques page 153 au milieu".
324 LCdv 194.
325 B2-20-335 FLC. The Place Royale (now Place Stanislas) in Nancy, after Brinckmann, *Platz und Monument*, Fig. 40, p. 119. Brooks assumes that this is a drawing from Patte, *Monumens érigés en France à la Gloire de Louis XV*, which Jeanneret studied in Paris in 1915. However, the scale of the drawing and the legend prove that Brinckmann was the source. See Brooks, *Le Corbusier's Formative Years*, p. 406.
326 B2-20-329 FLC. Place des Victoires after Brinckmann, *Platz und Monument*, Fig. 34, p. 103.
327 LCdv 196.
328 LCdv 196.

for him it embodies Louis XIV's absolutist dictum, 'L'Etat, c'est moi'. At this point Jeanneret is speaking in general terms, attempting to derive clear principles, rather than describing specific squares dedicated to the glory of individual figures. In so doing, he uses – but does not copy – Brinckmann's descriptions: he generalises and summarises them. Whereas Brinckmann describes with precision the development of individual French baroque squares, in line with his overall aim to demonstrate differences in culture and epoch, Jeanneret drills down to general principles, and in this he is closer to Sitte.[329]

The first of these principles is that repetition of a motif on all the façades in the square results in architectural unity. The second is that the square acts as a reception room in front of the palace; it is 'inhabited' by the master of the house, who features in a central monument – usually on horseback. The third principle is that the scale of the monument is carefully coordinated with that of the square. Finally, the monument is visible over long distances along the streets that lead up to the square.[330]

Jeanneret also focuses on the design aspect of these streets opening onto the square: either the view of these streets are blocked by buildings within a short distance of the square, or porticos spanning the entrance to the streets are used to create unity in the square's façade, as in the project for a Place Louis XV. This was an ideal star-shaped design by Rousset which Brinckmann had included in his publication (Fig. 60).[331]

Next, Jeanneret revisits the importance of architectural unity in squares, looking at the Italian baroque squares which were based on principles similar to those used in France. Here the square, paving, palace, and monument came together to form a whole and gave the impression that they were cast from a single mould. The examples he uses are the Capitoline Hill, and St. Peter's Square in Rome (Fig. 60), which he compares to the Place des Vosges.[332]

The human scale in urban design

To conclude his chapter, Jeanneret calls for urban design to accommodate the human scale. He describes how, for all his immense power, Louis XIV still took this into account when designing his squares:

> This King who had created the orderly gardens at Versailles covering [__] thousands of square metres, from scratch, was content with his architectural squares being [__] or [__] square metres. His architects had preserved the feeling of a *human scale* from the healthy gothic tradition. In erecting palais of limited height, they were wary of the shrinking effect of perspective and achieved grandeur precisely through the small dimensions of their squares.[333]

---

329 For Brinckmann's view, modelled on Heinrich Wölfflin, see Jochen Meyer, "Die Stadt als Kunstwerk", afterword to *Platz und Monument* by Albert Erich Brinckmann (Berlin: Gebr. Mann, 2000), p. 206.
330 LCdv 196ff.
331 B2-20-328 FLC. Plan for a Place Louis XV, after Brinckmann, *Platz und Monument*, Fig. 35, p. 107.
332 LCdv 201. Jeanneret concludes by discussing the Place des Vosges, but this description is completely based on Brinckmann and is therefore not material to the present line of argument. LCdv 201ff. See Brinckmann, *Platz und Monument*, p. 94f. and Jeanneret's excerpt from this part of the text in LCdv 412f.
333 LCdv 204f.

Equally, he describes how the size of the monuments in these squares is consistent with the squares themselves and the buildings surrounding them. In contrast, he believes the size of the Bismarck monument before the Reichstag in Berlin is not consistent with the size of the building: the square, the Reichstag, and the monument are all excessively large. It is not possible to perceive the true size of these objects through observation alone: comparative calculations are required. The square has a detrimental effect on the Reichstag, which in turn overpowers the monument. The monument itself makes the excesses of the new Berlin architecture look paltry.[334] It is likely that Jeanneret's criticism here was inspired by Brinckmann; in his chapter on Germany since 1700 he wrote:

> In most contemporary attempts to create an effect for the monument by relying on architecture, either architecture or monument, or even both, are compromised. [...] The prominent Bismarck monument (1901) obstructs the façade of the Reichstag building, which itself falls apart, floundering miserably in that it breaks all framing constraints.[335]

Jeanneret's criticism of the Reichstag design and its lack of scale are reminiscent of Sitte's (and subsequently Schultze-Naumburg's) objections to such freestanding constructions, on the basis that both square and buildings destroy the sense of proportion which each creates for the other.

Besides Berlin, Jeanneret believed that such loss of proportion could also be observed in Paris – for example in the Place de l'Étoile with the Arc de Triomphe, built under Napoleon. As with the Reichstag, Jeanneret regrets that the true size of the Arc de Triomphe cannot be determined immediately in situ, and instead is only evident through a careful comparison of its dimensions. Only from a distance, perhaps from the Tuileries, the actual size of the Arc de Triomphe can be perceived.[336] Thus any sense of scale is lost; Jeanneret goes on to lament that anything adjacent to these squares looks ridiculously petty and distant in comparison with the vast areas and spaces themselves. The observer can no longer perceive the space which the square embodies (its *corporalité*). Jeanneret argues that the resulting emptiness is anti-aesthetic, and the impact of a project such as the square in front of the Reichstag in Berlin will therefore be mediocre at best.[337] At this stage Jeanneret does not replicate Brinckmann's statements word for word, but instead applies his statements on the decline of German urban design during the 19th century to the situation in Paris. In the course of Brinckmann's chapter on Germany since 1700, several formulations appear which may have served as a basis for Jeanneret's words, for example his criticism of Munich:

> The triumphal Ludwigstraße, 1225m long, 37m wide, with a building height of 18–21m, is in itself well proportioned. However, despite the striking emphasis effected by the Feldherrnhalle and Siegestor at either end, the distance between these structures is too great to secure them an impact on the whole street, since a monumental

---

334 LCdv 205f.
335 Brinckmann, *Platz und Monument*, p. 162.
336 LCdv 207f.
337 LCdv 210. See the textual outlines in LCdv 219f.

enclosure pales into insignificance in a very long street, and the very opposite of a monumental situation is achieved.[338]

Jeanneret expands on the situation in France: the star-shaped public squares from the time of Louis XIV have been retained, but modern traffic overlooked:

> The intense traffic in our modern cities can only be reasonably resolved where their dimensions are abnormally inflated. Only squares with the diameter of the Place de l'Etoile in Paris will suffice. – What use is there then in summoning up the scale of grandeur if one ends merely with a stopgap solution?[339]

This final theory in Jeanneret's chapter is also taken from *Platz und Monument*, where Brinckmann claims: "Only star-shaped squares with the diameter of Place de l'Étoile in Paris, and a large raised central portion, can impose sufficient order for modern traffic. The design of these squares, surrounded with discordant apartment blocks, is of no merit."[340]

Jeanneret responds by designing his first 'Modulor'. He provides a comparative overview of the dimensions, and above all the proportions, of eight French squares (all are in Paris except the Place Royale in Nancy). However, since some of the figures are missing, he can only demonstrate the ratio of street openings to enclosing façades and not the ratio between the square's diameter and the height of the buildings. Another value he is able to establish is the ratio of *vide* ('open space': width of street openings) to *plein* ('filled area': width of façades); this ranges from 1:0.56 for the Place de l'Étoile to 1:27 for the Place des Vosges. For most of the other squares, the ratio is close to his average of 1:7.[341]

By way of conclusion, Jeanneret establishes a principle which, from an urban design standpoint, is certainly eclectic. If a square is to be surrounded by buildings which are designed by different architects at different times, with their functions that are not established from the outset, the applicable aesthetic principle should be that of the irregular square, according to which each new building should adapt to the context of the existing buildings. This adaptation will be straightforward, since requirements on individual buildings' appearance will not be so strict, and picturesque elements such as porticos, setbacks, and projections may be deployed. In contrast, if a square is to be built all at once or circumstances allow the square to be planned as a whole, the unified approach makes a monumental solution possible. Jeanneret explains that such opportunities are rare in the history of a city; they should be grasped as a happy chance to construct harmonious, geometric squares in accordance with the rules he formulates.[342]

Finally, Jeanneret presents a paean to the commemorative squares which have been created in various cultures throughout history:

> To round off this study of the square, we must recall that in certain eras peoples smitten with beauty created 'squares to glory'. We do not consider this term to be

---

338 Brinckmann, *Platz und Monument*, p. 154.
339 LCdv 210f.
340 Brinckmann, *Platz und Monument*, p. 156. Jeanneret takes excerpts from this part of the text in Cahier C.3, LCdv 439.
341 LCdv 217.
342 LCdv 212f.

out of place, for when we evoke the cities where these peoples' genius is displayed, a sumptuous picture, exalted in nobility or gleaming with splendour, appears immediately before our eyes. The glory of these peoples appears to us straight away in the objective form of their artistic creations, remaining through diseased decadence, as an irrefutable testament to a healthy, harmonious organism.[343]

His examples here include the Piazza San Marco in Venice, the ancient forums in Pompeii and Rome, the Acropolis in Athens, and Jerusalem's Temple Square – he includes a long list spanning the whole history of building and a variety of cultures.[344] The major characteristics of these squares, which Jeanneret lists in note form, are:

> Grouping together rather than dispersing; commercial life kept at a distance, with its rumbling, noisy profanity. These squares in their meditation are temples to beauty. Do not disperse, unite! At the edge of the enclosure, halt the brutal flow of modern life. We should do the same, when we wish to do things properly![345]

Thus at the end of the chapter, as well as rejecting the early 20th-century metropolis as noisy, messy and chaotic, we find Jeanneret expressing a preference for monumentality hitherto only evident in his description of the straight boulevard. Yet Jeanneret's enthusiasm for the monumental is still kept in check by his overriding concern for achieving a human scale.

Murs de clôture – On Enclosing Walls

Compared with the previous chapter, On Enclosing Walls is like a chapter in miniature. Its origins can be traced back to Paul Schultze-Naumburg's remarks on enclosing walls in his chapter on urban streets in *Kulturarbeiten Städtebau*. Jeanneret begins by describing how, due to a recent preoccupation with utilitarianism, the poetry of one very simple architectural and urban design component had been overlooked – the enclosing wall:

> Among modest assemblies of stones, there is one especially likely to evoke the most varied of emotions: the enclosing wall. It is capable of beauty even in its crudest form, and can achieve splendour. Nowadays, if we employ enclosing walls, we create ugliness. Two neighbouring owners are unable to agree in order for a little harmony to reign in the walls that will run alongside the street, enclosing their properties.[346]

A comparison of the above with Schultze-Naumburg's wording clearly shows the similarities between the two:

---

343 LCdv 213f. Jeanneret drafted the model for these few sentences in Cahier C.2, p. LCdv 414. Jeanneret's discussion of the rise and fall of city civilisations reflects a cyclical, biologistic view of history very typical of his time, spreading as it did with the popularisation of social Darwinist theories and apocalyptic scenarios in the late 19th century. Oswald Spengler's *Untergang des Abendlandes* (1918), translated into English as *The Decline of the West* by Charles Atkinson (New York: Knopf, 1926–28), places a central focus on the cyclical downfall of ancient cultures. Thanks to Stephanie Warnke for alerting me to this.
344 A comparable formulation can be found in *Urbanisme*. See Le Corbusier, *The City of To-morrow*, p. 72.
345 LCdv 215.
346 LCdv 226.

The fact that walls can be advantageous not only for the garden which they enclose, but also for the street scene, is shown in Fig. 253 [Fig. XL] in which a very happy harmony is created using building, yard and wall which must give the passer-by a wonderful impression, if of course he is able to read the discernible appearances presented by the world. [...] The wall is not simply a stiff, rigid enclosure which is also very ugly yet unavoidable in some places because it is the only completely solid type of enclosure resistant to any encroachment from outside. It is in fact the most noble and beautiful type of enclosure there is. The wall is alone in permitting that homely feeling of being within one's own four walls to be extended into the open air and shared in some sense with those standing outside it.[347]

Both Jeanneret and Schultze-Naumburg present the enclosing wall as a design element which, even in its crudest form, emphasises and even elicits beauty. Schultze-Naumburg writes: "the feelings which a wall inspires in us are so extraordinarily varied that only an extreme coarsening of our visual perception can explain how this massed uprising against it can have occurred."[348] Jeanneret stresses that the 18th century and the First French Empire had built beautiful, peaceful walls in many towns and villages as an unassuming means of enclosing parks and yards. He emphasises the significance of cheap, simple, uniform walls (and takes photographs of some such walls, for example in Basle, which are very similar to Schultze-Naumburg's photos, Fig.s XLI, XLII).[349] Jeanneret believes that walls are currently being built too low and beset with too much wrought iron, without this benefiting either the street or the homeowner desiring peace and quiet. Jeanneret uses an example to illustrate the 3–4-metre height he deems necessary, positively enthusing: "What a calm their uniform surfaces bring to a great courtyard where water springs from a fountain!"[350] He states that buildings are often isolated, in disarray, but a wall could create a good connection between them. This is precisely what Schultze-Naumburg states:

> Earlier it was the happy custom to continue the straight lines of monumental structures with walls, as we can see in the example of Figure 264 [Fig. XLIII]. Today's habit of setting a monumental structure in the middle of a square and then surrounding it with 'planting' proves the lack of imagination in our times.[351]

Jeanneret cites two examples of different walls which combine beauty and utility: the 15-metre-high wall surrounding the Cathedral, Baptistery, and leaning tower in Pisa, and the wall surrounding the Camposanto there.[352] He evokes the contrast between them: the high wall is uniform, brutal, and crenelated, whereas the other has a roof, is carefully crafted, and clad in the finest marble. He states that walls are beautiful not only because of their sculptural shape, but also due to the feelings associated with them, such as comfort, delicacy (*délicatesse*), power, or brutality; they can be

---

347 Schultze-Naumburg, *Kulturarbeiten Städtebau*, p. 429.
348 Schultze-Naumburg, *Kulturarbeiten Städtebau*, p. 429.
349 LCdv 226.
350 LCdv 227. Unfortunately it is not clear which image Jeanneret is referring to here.
351 Schultze-Naumburg, *Kulturarbeiten Städtebau*, p. 435/441.
352 Pisa often appears as an example in *La Construction des villes*. See the section On Cemeteries.

Fig. XL "a very happy harmony is created using building, yard and wall." From Schultze-Naumburg
Kulturarbeiten Städtebau, fig. 253

forbidding or inviting, and they sometimes hide secrets.[353] His statements are variations on Schultze-Naumburg's theme.

In conclusion to this short chapter, Jeanneret describes three examples of good enclosing walls in France.[354] He employs colourful language to depict the wall of the Archives Nationales in Paris, "which rises bare and cold, aristocratic and austere", the enclosure of the Hôtel de Cluny, also in Paris, and the Cour des Libraires at the Cathedral in Rouen.[355] These vivid descriptions of courtyards surrounded by high walls are similar to the excerpts which he takes from Georges Riat's *L'Art des jardins* in Cahier C.6. It is no wonder that Jeanneret employs much more poetic language here than in the sections describing streets and housing blocks; this indicates that he cares very much about these oases or, as Schultze-Naumburg calls them, hidden 'paradises' in the city.[356]

353 LCdv 227.
354 Jeanneret planned to show at least one illustration, referred to as 'XLLIV' and showing the Cour des Libraires in Rouen; the identity of this image is unknown.
355 LCdv 227f.
356 In the margin of the last page of the chapter, Jeanneret noted later: "in Suleimanie, along the glorious major road to Stamboul, in Kazanlak, at the Acropolis, the Erectheion. But speak about the wall enclosing the smallest cottage in the smallest of towns." (LCdv 229). Yet he did not expand this into full text; this is probably an addition made in 1915, when Jeanneret read through the entire Manuscript again and added comments and minor corrections.

Fig. XLI Theaterstraße in Würzburg. Photo by Jeanneret, 1910 (LC 108-337 BV)

Fig. XLII Enclosing wall in Basel. Photo by Jeanneret, ca. 1910 (L4-19-173 FLC)

Fig. XLIII "Earlier it was the happy custom to continue the straight lines of monumental structures with walls." From Schultze-Naumburg *Kulturarbeiten Städtebau*, fig. 264

The unfinished chapters: Green elements in the city

The following five chapters are at least partly fictitious: Jeanneret did collate material on bridges, trees in the city, gardens and parks, cemeteries, and garden cities; he did not turn his excerpts, notes, and drafts into coherent chapters. Nevertheless, the material he did gather is very revealing. Besides demonstrating which theories and arguments he collated, the material on these individual topics is presented here in light of how Jeanneret planned to use them: as sections 6 to 10 of the chapter The Elements of the City.[357]

Des Ponts – *On Bridges*

Jeanneret's Cahier C.2 opens with notes on the topic of bridges, although these amount to a mere two pages. It seems he found very little satisfactory material on which to base his own writing about bridges in the city. Yet it is interesting that he did not restrict himself to the engineering aspects of bridges: once again, he addresses questions of perception. Thus Jeanneret mainly focuses on collecting illustrations of bridges. In addition to several subjects which his friend Octave Matthey is to photograph for him – "Dire à Octave à faire 1 photo…" – such as the Pont Royal in Paris and a railway bridge in Solothurn, and several other bridges to be used as illustrations such as the Pont Notre-Dame in Paris, Jeanneret looks through two books on the subject in the Staatsbibliothek in Munich. In the first part of Camille Enlart's *Manuel d'archéologie française*, which deals with architecture, Jeanneret finds two illustrations of mediaeval stone arched bridges (Fig.s 62 and 63), which appear so remarkable to him that he sets out a letter to the Mayor of Cahors on a tiny slip, asking for photographs of these bridges.[358] Indeed it appears he even received a response: in a letter to his parents dated 11 November 1910, Jeanneret notes with astonishment his correspondent's kindness:

> The other day I wrote to the mayor of Cahors to ask him for a postcard of a magnificent 13th century bridge which is located there. So he sent me 25 postcards, each more beautiful than the last and a four-page covering letter which he signed 'Mr X, Prefect of the Lot'. I was really touched.[359]

Unfortunately, these postcards have not survived. An extant request slip however proves that Jeanneret ordered the following from the Hof- und Staatsbibliothek:

> [Munich,] 23. Oktober 1910 // Brückenbauten // von der Staats-Bau-Verwaltung // M. // 1906. // Ch. E. Jeanneret // 4o / Bavar. / 1775 f.[360]

---

357 Although Jeanneret clearly drafts The Elements of the City as a chapter divided into sections, I deviate from his designations since the sections are, for the most part, every bit as long and substantial as entire chapters.

358 Camille Enlart, *Manuel d'Archéologie française. Première partie. Architecture. II. Civile et militaire* (Paris: A. Picard, 1902 1904). See LCdv 230. "taken from book, both tracings of bridge in Tournai and bridge in Cahors." These are Figures 271 and 272 in Enlart's *Manuel*: the Pont Valentré in Cahors and the Pont des Trous in Tournai. See also the letter on p. LCdv 415.

359 Jeanneret to his parents, 11 November 1910, R1-5-46 FLC.

360 LCdv 423. As mentioned earlier, the library stamped the slip with "I 24. SEP.", which is probably the date the request was received – on 23 October Jeanneret had already left Munich. The full title is: Königlich Oberste Baubehörde, *Von der Staatsbauverwaltung in Bayern ausgeführte Straßen-, Brücken- und Wasserbautenrückenbauten* (Munich: Piloty & Loehle, vol. I 1906, vol. II 1909).

Jeanneret would have been able to take some illustrations from the two-volume work on roads, bridges, and waterworks which this request relates to. The book shows new engineering projects in Bavaria circa 1900; most are stone arch bridges and very aesthetically appealing. Jeanneret also takes notes from an article in the *Süddeutsche Bauzeitung* about a bridge in Bautzen, the Kronprinzenbrücke (now known as the Friedensbrücke, Fig. XLIV).[361] His commentary is short and to the point: "Completely remarkable as a beautiful huge modern bridge linking to the town."[362] A design which Jeanneret would enter into a competition for the Pont Butin over the Rhône near Geneva in 1915 (Fig. XLV) bears a great similarity to this bridge which he noted with such care. The similarity does not seem to be coincidental. Brooks relates how Jeanneret submitted this design with the assistance of engineers Max Du Bois and Juste Schneider; Le Corbusier later stated that one of his main sources of inspiration had been the arches in Roman baths.[363] But perhaps this is yet another instance of his characteristic reluctance to reveal his influences. In any case, it is striking that Jeanneret mainly selected stone arch bridges as illustrations in 1910, in place of their more modern-looking iron counterparts: especially given that *Vers une Architecture* displays iron constructions. This choice reflects an attachment to tradition which Jeanneret demonstrates throughout *La Construction des villes*. It is less clear why, as mentioned above, Jeanneret does not use the 1906 *Städtebau* article "Brücken im Stadtbilde" (Bridges in the Cityscape) by Gustav Ebe as a source. This essay would have aligned perfectly with what Jeanneret was searching for, since Ebe deals with the aesthetic impact of bridges on the city.

Fig. XLIV Kronprinzenbrücke across the river Spree near Bautzen. From *Süddeutsche Bauzeitung* 20 (1910), no. 14, p. 106

361 LCdv 231. The article by Arthur Speck which is mentioned is: "Die Kronprinzenbrücke über das Spreetal in Bautzen", in *Süddeutsche Bauzeitung*, 20 (1910), no. 14, pp. 105–110.
362 LCdv 231.
363 "Masonry construction was prescribed (thus precluding concrete, iron or steel) with special attention given to its ornamental qualities. [...] These prerequisites suggested Roman forms and Jeanneret immediately asked Du Bois to research aqueducts and other viable solutions. Later he acknowledged that the vaulting of Roman baths had been a major inspiration." Brooks, *Formative Years*, p. 382f. See also Stanislaus von Moos' speculation that the Pont du Butin might be inspired by the Halenbrücke in Berne of 1910: Stanislaus von Moos: "Switzerland II", in von Moos and Rüegg, *Le Corbusier before Le Corbusier*, p. 198.

Fig. XLV Charles-Edouard Jeanneret and Max Du Bois, competition design for the Pont Butin across the Rhône near Geneva, 1915 (30279 FLC)

Des Arbres – Trees as sculptural elements in the city

Of the five chapters for *La Construction des villes* which were planned but never written, four address the issue of green space in the city. Thus the materials collated in the cahiers inevitably overlap in terms of content. Jeanneret actually intended to include one chapter each for trees in the city, gardens and parks, cemeteries, and garden cities, and accordingly allocated a separate cahier to each theme. However, the urban design discourse Jeanneret studied did not conform to these distinctions, and ultimately he did not do so himself. For example, a long passage appears in Cahier C.5 *Trees Monuments* about the uselessness of front gardens; this passage would fit much more readily into *Gardens and Parks*.

Jeanneret only adds a few lines of notes about trees to Cahier C.5 *Trees Monuments*. However, the cahier contains many requests that his friend Octave take photos, and shows that he plans to seek out illustrations of trees in city squares, especially in Potsdamer Platz, Leipziger Platz, and Pariser Platz in Berlin. Jeanneret also set himself the task of searching through Stübben's *Städtebau* for squares which had seen their aesthetic quality destroyed by trees.[364] Hence Jeanneret sketches Pariser Platz and Leipziger Platz in Berlin, after Stübben (Fig. XLVI).[365] He notes a list of requirements for the use of trees in urban design. He considers the tree to be a decorative element in the city, with aesthetic impact arising from its inherent contrasts: the round mass of the tree's crown contrasting with its dark, straight trunk (as it appears in cities), and the delicate branches contrasting with the dense foliage. However, the unwavering repetition of tree-lined boulevards across entire city districts generates uniformity, destroying the decorative effect of the individual tree. Jeanneret also states that a central row of trees is more

---

364 "Rechercher dans Stübbe[n] les places célèbres qui ont été abîmées par les arbres." LCdv 234.
365 B2-20-321 FLC.

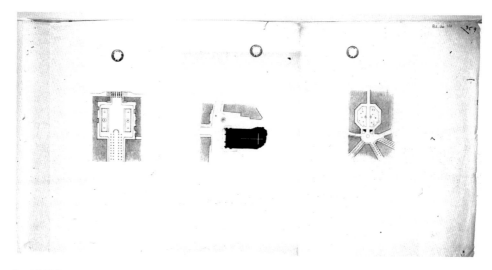

Fig. XLVI Leipziger and Pariser Platz in Berlin, fountain at the St. Lorenz-Church in Nuremberg. Drawings by Jeanneret, copied from Stübben, *Städtebau*, figs. 437, 438 and 710
(B2-20-321 FLC)

aesthetically pleasing than a row at either side of the road, and that the trees planted
alongside many of the boulevards could be more usefully planted as a wood or in
parkland.[366]

This short list of items and ideas leaves more room for interpretation regarding its
possible sources than the material for the other chapters we have discussed. Assuming
that Jeanneret is not merely reciting an opinion which he held prior to his travels in Germany, these ideas can probably be traced back to two sources. Some of his formulations
can be found almost word for word in these familiar places: Camillo Sitte's *Städtebau
nach seinen künstlerischen Grundsätzen* and Karl Henrici's *Beiträge zur praktischen
Ästhetik im Städtebau*.[367] It seems that as with other topics, Sitte acts as a role model for
Jeanneret in his approach to green space in the city. Only one of Jeanneret's stated
requirements is attributable to Henrici – the idea of an *allee* of trees in the middle of
a street. The others are most likely to have originated with Sitte. Interestingly, Henrici
refers directly to Sitte and largely repeats the latter's theories. His chapter bears the
same title as Sitte's: "Großstadtgrün" (Greenery within the City, part of *Beiträge zur
praktischen Ästhetik im Städtebau*). He explicitly indicates that he is merely engaging
with Sitte's ideas and exploring them in greater depth.[368] Yet Sitte and Henrici argue
their cases in very different ways. Here, as in the section On Streets above, Sitte is more
general and less prescriptive than Henrici, who formulates precise directives for layout.
Sitte states that, for reasons of variety and economy, boulevards lined with trees on both

366 LCdv 234–236.
367 As noted above, from the fourth edition of Sitte's book in 1909 onwards, the chapter "Großstadtgrün" was
    appended; Jeanneret must therefore have read one of the latest editions available to him in 1910.
368 Henrici, *Beiträge*, p. 179.

sides are not recommended, although he sees a single row of trees on the sunny side of the street as advantageous. His main emphasis lies on planners adapting to the local conditions and not merely following their own scheme. In contrast, Henrici attempts to draw up exact rules, such as: it is not appropriate to line commercial streets with trees.[369]

Sitte praises individual, picturesque-looking trees which he claims are good for the soul. He attempts to prove that the modern 'hysteria for oxygen' is unfounded, as scientists have proved that the difference between oxygen levels measured in cities and in the countryside is minimal. The requirement to provide a specific area of green space per head of urban population, deemed a necessity into the mid-19th century, therefore no longer applies. Instead, he seeks to satisfy city dwellers' spiritual needs and longing for nature:

> This whole matter of vegetation as presumably beneficial to physical well-being can then be ruled out. There remains only the psychological factor, rooted in the imagination. We should not, however, underestimate this, since it is a well-known fact that one's state of mind can cure not only imagined ailments but even real ones.[370]

This might even be achieved with just a few, well-placed trees. Sitte explores the issue over several pages and explains the picturesque and poetic influence of 'single' trees on the city.[371] Thus he applies the same aesthetic criteria to the (picturesque, if not always poetic) impact of a tree or group of trees on the city as he does to that of a monument:

> One can see that the matter is really quite simple: such a tree or group of bushes, just like a fountain or a monument, belongs near the plaza's edge at points free of traffic or in a secluded corner. It is only that the incorporation of greenery is more difficult than that of fountains and monuments, since the latter, because of their material and their architectonic form, merge more easily with their architectural setting.[372]

And it is here that we find the possible model for Jeanneret's reflections on the decorative nature of trees, and for his idea of adding trees to buildings or squares. Sitte goes on to state that a tree-lined *allee* represents a completely different principle from an individual tree. The former is derived from the country road or from the approach to a baroque castle, with its pompous perspective layout, and Sitte concludes: "All tree-lined streets are tedious but no city can do completely without them because the endless sea of houses necessitates every conceivable motif that can break its eternal monotony, articulate the whole, and help people to find their way."[373] As mentioned above, Sitte dismissed twin lines of trees along the street, preferring a single row of trees lining the sunny side of the street on which the buildings had front gardens; the rails for horse-drawn trams could then be placed on the shady side. This was an asymmetric layout

369 Henrici, *Beiträge*, p. 187, Collins and Crasemann Collins, *Camillo Sitte: The Birth of Modern City Planning*, p. 314.
370 Collins and Crasemann Collins, *Camillo Sitte: The Birth of Modern City Planning*, p. 307.
371 Collins and Crasemann Collins, *Camillo Sitte: The Birth of Modern City Planning*, p. 308f.
372 Collins and Crasemann Collins, *Camillo Sitte: The Birth of Modern City Planning*, p. 311.
373 Collins and Crasemann Collins, *Camillo Sitte: The Birth of Modern City Planning*, p. 312.

tailored to the local conditions rather than a purely schematic approach.[374] Jeanneret's acute observation that the ubiquitous repetition of tree-lined boulevards made both the streets and the individual trees appear banal cannot be found in either Sitte or Henrici. Yet it is more than likely that he became aware of this issue through his critical analysis of the other two architects' writings on tree-lined streets. He formulates it thus: "Making street views banal by planting with avenues of trees, complete absence of distinctive appearance in whole districts. This is widespread neutralisation."[375] Hence Jeanneret puts a finer point on a question which Sitte and Henrici also bemoan in general: monotony arises despite the tree being a lively 'urban design element'. Herein lies the basis for the calls made both by Sitte and by Jeanneret for an artistic solution to particular urban design situations, using individual trees, which should be deployed for their sculptural effect in a similar way to monuments. Jeanneret is convinced that most of the trees planted in rows alongside streets could be better used elsewhere: "With the trees which line the streets to so little avail, one could make whole forests. [...] The narrower street width would save space, it could be made available in welcome parks."[376] A comparison of this section with Sitte's wording shows that Jeanneret was probably prompted by Sitte:

> If we take the average distance between trees to be [7 m] and the average length of a circumvallating boulevard or avenue in a large city to be [4,200 m] [...], the total of the double file of trees on both sides is about 2,400 trees, that is to say, an entire forest if they were not distributed in rows. Surely this would suffice to lay out two or three parks.[377]

As pointed out above, the only thought not to originate with Sitte is Jeanneret's idea of a central row of trees, which is more in line with Henrici's line of argumentation. Perhaps Jeanneret is also closer to Henrici's vehement rejection of tree-lined streets than he is to Sitte's more moderate view. Henrici complains that streets planned in advance with a line of trees are considerably broader than is necessary for traffic or health. The surplus area they occupy, which could be freed up for private ownership, is therefore wasted.[378] He does however concede that it may be justified to plan lines of trees in some cases:

> Now it cannot be denied that above all in long stretches of dead straight road even an *Allee* of young trees is better than nothing at all which could give shade, and where we encounter such streets which are extremely wide it may be excusable if, in our confusion, we plant them with rows of trees. There should be no doubt about the fact that, where lines of trees exist, there is no better place for them than the

---

374 Collins and Crasemann Collins, *Camillo Sitte: The Birth of Modern City Planning*, p. 314.

375 LCdv 234.

376 LCdv 234f.

377 Collins and Crasemann Collins, *Camillo Sitte: The Birth of Modern City Planning*, p. 313. The distances in yards have here been replaced by metres.

378 "Let us speak initially of *Allee* planting along streets. Many streets are planned in advance as tree-lined roads, and one is obliged to grant them significantly greater breadth for this purpose alone than would be necessary for traffic and health. Thus long strips of valuable land are lost to street surface, which would otherwise be usefully employed for yards and gardens in front of and behind buildings." Henrici, *Beiträge*, p. 183.

dead straight street. But then one must meet the conditions for them to flourish and ensure a sufficient amount of light and air is available to them from all sides.[379]

Thus Henrici believes if tree-lined boulevards are to be planned at all, they should only be planned along roads that are broad. Furthermore, if trees are planted beside the street, front gardens should also be planned, so that the growing trees do not come too close to the buildings. Without front gardens, the trees would be better planted along the middle of the street. Yet both possibilities have disadvantages. With trees at the side of the street, the pavement will be too wide, and therefore the distance between road and house too long, and also the trees will obscure the façades and the outlook of the houses. With trees in the middle, the street will appear divided and no longer be perceived as a whole or experienced as a single space.[380] Henrici also concludes that in streets with heavy delivery traffic, i.e. main commercial streets, tree planting should be completely rejected.[381] He recommends instead following Sitte to a greater extent and planning into the city artistic trees or groups of trees. For today's reader, this rejection of the tree-lined boulevard for functional reasons is hard to understand, especially if we consider the pleasant effect of the trees lining streets in a large city like Berlin. Perhaps there is a parallel here with Laugier's criticism of tree planting in Versailles: Jeanneret suspects that Laugier would be converted from criticism to praise if he could see, 180 years on, the impressive canopies of foliage which the trees had created. Just as Laugier was not convinced by the young trees in Versailles, the trees planted along boulevards in many cities at the start of the 20th century must initially have appeared puny and wretched to contemporary observers, especially given the difficult growing conditions (polluted air, gas pipes in the ground, etc.).

It is appropriate here to clarify a major classification which Sitte makes. He advocates a distinction between planting trees for health and for aesthetic reasons:

> It follows from this discussion that all vegetation in a city can be divided into two strictly separate categories, completely different in effect and therefore also totally different as to application: that is, the so-called *sanitary greenery* and the *decorative greenery*.[382]

He calls for streets and squares, as public social spaces, to be planted with trees for aesthetic reasons; he does not disregard health-giving greenery, as the beginning of the chapter might suggest: he merely believes it should be hidden from view. Only a few years later, Martin Wagner's 1915 dissertation *Das sanitäre Grün der Städte* broadened the debate and established a precisely researched knowledge base on the importance of public green spaces in the city. However, Wagner brought back together the areas which Sitte had separated, and not only calculated the necessary size and location for green spaces in the city – close to residential areas – but also designed parks which adopted

---

379 Henrici, *Beiträge*, p. 185.
380 Henrici, *Beiträge*, p. 186f.
381 Henrici, *Beiträge*, p. 187.
382 Collins and Crasemann Collins, *Camillo Sitte: The Birth of Modern City Planning*, p. 319.

Sitte's requirements for a spatial understanding of the city and are akin to Fritz Schumacher's designs for Hamburg.[383] In 1910, Jeanneret did not make this distinction between health-giving and decorative green spaces, nor did he discuss parks with regard to health: for him the aesthetic point of view was paramount.

Des Jardins et Parcs – On Gardens and Parks

Jeanneret collected plenty of textual and illustrative material for On Gardens and Parks, another chapter which he did not write out in full. This material paints a clear picture of the chapter he planned. Not only does this chapter on gardens and parks quite naturally touch on the role of the tree in urban areas (as discussed above), but it also relates to the chapter on cemeteries, since both tie into the same architectural discourse: gardens seen as green space to counterbalance built-up areas. Can the planned chapter on garden cities be considered a potential synthesis of the green and the built-up elements of urban design? We will return to this question later (under On Garden Cities).

Jeanneret recorded almost all his excerpts about gardens in Cahier C.6 *Squares Gardens I*. Six pages of this notebook are occupied by a table of contents for the chapter on squares; over 35 pages are taken up with gardens. In these, Jeanneret dealt mainly with three works: Georges Riat's *L'Art des jardins*, Hermann Muthesius' *Das englische Haus*, and Joseph August Lux's *Der Städtebau und die Grundpfeiler der heimischen Bauweise*. From Lux's work, he took a whole series of excerpts – some on other themes. Jeanneret also consulted articles from the *Süddeutsche Bauzeitung* which advocate architecturally influenced garden design as opposed to 'landscape gardening'. Cahier C.5 *Trees Monuments* contains further notes which would suit a chapter on gardens. Jeanneret approaches the topic from two different angles: first via the history of garden design, and second with reference to contemporary positions. Once again, as in his analysis of 'built-up' aspects, he backs the reform and heritage protection tendencies, both influenced by the English Arts and Crafts movement.

Jeanneret planned to include a large number of illustrations in this chapter. Notes on these can be found at the beginning of the Cahier *Squares Gardens I*. One list includes "My photo of Versailles // ditto of Potsdam. Würzburg. // See my postcards on the garden at // Chantilly. Nymphenburg etc. // Lago Maggiore. Isola Bella. Isola Madre."[384] Some of these subjects can still be found in his collection of photographs and postcards (Figs. 66–71). In Munich, Jeanneret also copied down a map of the Englischer Garten, through which he often walked during his stay, especially since it is situated between the Staatsbibliothek and the Bayerische Nationalmuseum (Fig. XLVII). It is astonishing that Jeanneret does not at any point in his Manuscript add any further detail about this park, such a significant presence in his life at that time. He copies from Stübben's *Städtebau* two further plans of park designs, on which he also fails to comment (Fig. XLVIII,

---

383   Martin Wagner, *Das sanitäre Grün der Städte. Ein Beitrag zur Freiflächentheorie* (Berlin: Heymanns, 1915). See Vittorio Magnago Lampugnani, "Moderne, Lebensreform, Stadt und Grün: Urbanistische Experimente in Berlin 1900 bis 1914", in Scheer, Kleihues and Kahlfeldt, *Stadt der Architektur*, pp. 28–39, and Hermann Hipp, "Schumachers Hamburg. Die reformierte Großstadt", in *Moderne Architektur in Deutschland 1900 bis 1950. Reform und Tradition*, ed. Vittorio Magnago Lampugnani and Romana Schneider (Stuttgart: Hatje, 1992), pp. 151–184.

384   LCdv 239f.

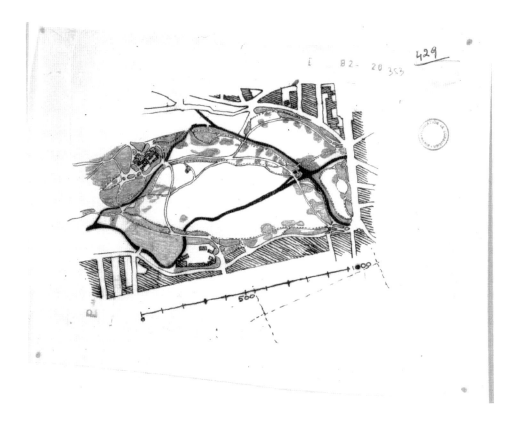

Fig. XLVII English Garden in Munich. Sketch by Jeanneret (B2-20-353 FLC)

Fig. 80).[385] Jeanneret copies small drawings such as that of a vine trellis (Fig. 79) from Riat's *L'Art des jardins*, and plans to adopt almost a dozen illustrations from among the volumes of Muthesius' *Das englische Haus* (Fig. 73–78).[386]

Riat – The Paradise Garden

The majority of Jeanneret's excerpts on gardens can be traced back to his reading of Georges Riat, whose 1900 work *L'Art des jardins* provides a historical overview of the world's major gardens. Jeanneret quotes a remark by Riat about Roman gardens, which can be taken as emblematic of the early 20th-century discourse on garden architecture:

385 LCdv 269. "Site plan of a new people's garden in Cologne", Fig. 841, in Stübben, *Städtebau*, and B2-20-347 FLC, "Part of an English park design (after: Czullik, A., *Behelfe zur Anlage und Bepflanzung von Gärten*, Vienna 1882–85)", in Stübben, *Städtebau*, Fig. 815, p. 478.
386 "Gardens of English villas {beautiful illustrations} in Muthesius I[0] page 212 // Book II. pages 110, 109, 102, 100 87 85 {plan for publication} [Arrow to 'Book II'] 84 83". LCdv 248.

Fig. XLVIIII Drawing by Jeanneret, copied from Stübben, *Städtebau*, fig. 815 (B-2-20-347 FLC)

All the organisation is jealously guarded by the architect. We must not forget, in fact it is impossible to emphasise enough, the idea that the Roman garden is the work of an architect; everything in it is dependent on architecture.[387]

This remark bridges the gap between Jeanneret's historical and contemporary interests in gardens. The proposition that the garden forms part of architecture contrasts starkly with the views of many garden designers around 1900, who wished to model the garden or park on nature wherever possible. The excerpts from Riat document the architectural side of the argument. Jeanneret collates textual extracts with which to prove and demonstrate two points: first, the significance of architecture for the garden; and second, the beauty of old gardens, which to him contrast starkly with contemporary park designs, and which he intends to take as models for new schemes. Indeed, he states this aim explicitly: "Need to find a selection of poetic quotations so that, by quoting them, can make the contrast felt with our hopeless gardens today."[388] The extracts he compiles

---

387 "Tout est ordonné avec un soin jaloux par l'architecte. Il ne faut pas oublier, en effet, et on ne peut assez insister sur cette idée, que le jardin romain est œuvre d'architecte; que tout y est subordonné à l'architecture." Georges Riat, *L'Art des jardins*, p. 44. See LCdv 258.

388 LCdv 261.

from *L'Art des jardins* do exactly that: these are poetic descriptions of the most beautiful gardens in history, beginning with Babylon and ending with the Renaissance. To begin with, Jeanneret quotes an extensive depiction of the second Wonder of the World, the Hanging Gardens of Babylon.[389] This describes the technical ingenuity of the construction supported by pillars and of the clever hydraulic irrigation system, which form an ideal combination with the beauty of the many and varied plants and flowers. Jeanneret seems very impressed by this: on the final pages of his Cahier C.2 he designs terraced buildings, which he describes as having terraces linked by steps and covered with trees.[390] This would suggest that the image of gardens resting on pillars contributed to Le Corbusier's later development of *pilotis*, his trademark pillar constructions. Max Adolf Vogt has suggested that the discovery of prehistoric pile dwellings beside Swiss lakes explains Le Corbusier's invention of *pilotis*; this theory is, however, based on assumptions, and no proof has emerged to support his conclusion.[391] It is likely that the idea of *pilotis* emerged from a wider range of sources than the single one Vogt cites. In this case, the Hanging Gardens of Babylon and the columns of the Parthenon are also possible sources of inspiration.

Jeanneret also notes examples of outstanding rose gardens. These include the mythical mediaeval rose garden in Worms – which, as Riat indicates, Kriemhilde is said to have designed around a giant linden tree. He also describes the extensive gardens surrounding the Hôtel St. Pol, designed under Charles V of France according to a highly regular cruciform architectonic layout, with many arbours composed of trellises and climbing plants.[392] His excerpts become increasingly brief as he notes down quotations from the Odyssey, references to ancient Egypt, Arabia, and elsewhere. This gives the impression that his impatience was growing. He repeatedly lists descriptions of particularly lovely garden scenes and sacred groves, or for example the irrigation skills from Arabia which had turned the gardens at the Alhambra in Granada into a paradise in Andalucia.[393] The following excerpt appears especially significant, particularly in relation to his later Villas Savoye and Stein-de-Monzie. Having worked his way onwards through history towards the Renaissance, with the help of Riat, Jeanneret notes extracts about the Italian Renaissance garden:

> The garden of Italian Renaissance villas is in effect the Roman garden, but adapted with intelligence and artistry to the new conditions of life. It met all the requirements of the time. To summarise, the Italian Renaissance garden is inspired by the gardens of Imperial Rome; it and the villa jointly make a framework for the wishes of their owners: gentlemen, courtiers, antique dealers and Italians. Their layout is panoramic and symmetrical, using many terraces and flights of stairs; it is suited to the special nature of the chosen site; architectural lines dominate the general outline of the beds

---

389 LCdv 245.

390 See LCdv 418f., sketch and text.

391 See Max Adolf Vogt, *Le Corbusier, the Noble Savage. Toward an Archaeology of Modernism*, trans. Jacques Gubler (Cambridge, Mass.: MIT Press, 1998). Vogt takes the view that Le Corbusier was heavily influenced by the late 19th-century craze for piles. The first pile constructions had recently been discovered by lakes in southern Germany and Switzerland, and were included in the Swiss primary school curriculum around the turn of the century. Charles-Edouard Jeanneret would therefore have encountered the idea of buildings on stilts at an early age. He claims that this fact, along with his observation of traditional Turkish constructions (yalı and köşk), elicited his idea of *pilotis*.

392 Riat, *L'Art des jardins*, p. 64f., see LCdv 260.

393 See LCdv 260–263.

and copses, and the play of the water; straight lines are the rule; statues and marbles, deployed knowledgeably, breach the uniformity without destroying it. The *allees* lead to interesting viewpoints. Here, art is added to nature, and not nature to art – as at Versailles for example.[394]

Here, he highlights the reception in the Italian Renaissance of such ancient Roman gardens in a way which is similar to Colin Rowe's later attribution of the influences for Le Corbusier's villas. In his famous 1947 essay "The Mathematics of the Ideal Villa", Rowe compares Le Corbusier's villas with those of Palladio with regard to their architecture and their attitude; after having quoted Palladio's lyrical account of the Villa Rotonda, Rowe writes: "No less lyrical but rather more explosive, Le Corbusier is describing the site of his Savoye House at Poissy." And: "If architecture at the Rotonda forms the setting for the good life, at Poissy it is certainly the background for the lyrically efficient one; and, if the contemporary pastoral is not yet sanctioned by contemporary usage, apparently the Virgilian nostalgia is still present."[395] It is impressive to see how clearly Rowe identifies in his comparison (which Rudolf Wittkower has so strongly rejected) a connection which he cannot actually prove from the evidence available to him.[396]

In his notes, Jeanneret condenses Riat's descriptions by reducing the length of the excerpts. This gives the impression that he is describing a single garden using ever-changing words, as if he was on a quest for the ideal garden: a paradise garden which stands in ever sharper contrast to the metropolis, which Jeanneret describes repeatedly as dusty and draughty. We can also see here the contrast between Nordic and Mediterranean countries, which Le Corbusier would later emphasise so firmly: the cold, grey, dusty northern city as against the multicoloured paradise garden of the South. The contrast between the two could hardly be greater.

Muthesius – The garden as an extension of the house

In two long excerpts, Jeanneret picks up the contemporary discourse: the first is a section from Hermann Muthesius' *Das englische Haus*, and the second a chapter from Joseph August Lux's *Städtebau und Grundpfeiler* entitled 'Parks policy' (Parkpolitik). Jeanneret does not take any notes from Muthesius' work relating to the architecture of the English country house, only passages about the English garden. This concept, which the Arts and Crafts movement developed out of English traditions, was introduced into the German discourse by Muthesius at the turn of the century. Architects including C.F. A. Voysey and Thomas Mawson had already been implementing William Morris' dictum that the garden should look like part of the house, both in plans and in reality.[397] Since the fundamental layout and history of this garden, as presented by Muthesius, bore

---

394 Riat, *L'Art des jardins*, p. 98 and 104. See LCdv 263f.

395 Rowe, "The Mathematics of the Ideal Villa", p. 2f.

396 In the foreword to the 1998 translation into German of *The Mathematics of the Ideal Villa*, Rowe comments on the origins of his original essay and, recalling that Rudolf Wittkower was "not amused" by this "jeu d'esprit", seeing it instead as a flippant, impossible comparison. See Colin Rowe, *Die Mathematik der idealen Villa und andere Essays*, trans. Christoph Schnoor (Basel: Birkhäuser, 1998), Foreword, p. 8.

397 "After 20 years, Morris' dictum that a garden should look like part of the house [...] had been deeply assimilated by turn-of-the-century architects." Peter Davey, *Arts and Crafts Architecture* (London: Phaidon 1995), p. 129.

little resemblance to the contemporary understanding of the English garden as a landscaped park, Jeanneret decided not to use that particular expression to describe it:

> Use the term *landscape garden, instead of English garden which would cause confusion.* To support what I say about English and French gardens, cite Nymphenburg which is half of one and half the other, perfectly beautiful; one is constantly drawn back to the French-style part, there is an attraction.[398]

What was Muthesius' argument? "House and garden have been inseparably linked at all periods of human civilisation." Only when surrounded by garden will a house be worthy of human habitation; the garden brings joy to the home. "Thus the garden is only a part of man's habitation, the wider dwelling-place wherein the smaller, the house itself, is situated."[399] Jeanneret omits a page or so of this text, in which Muthesius discusses the opposition between traditional English gardens on the one hand and 19th-century landscape gardening on the other – which attempted to imitate the "caprices" and "wild nature" and which ruled out regular garden designs.[400] Yet the tide of opinion was beginning to turn, back to traditional garden culture: this was aristocratic in nature, with very luxurious designs. Just as society had changed, so gardens would also have to change.

> The feature of the old garden that modern designers, leap-frogging the art of the landscape-gardener, have felt bound to revive, is its ordered, that is to say, its formal plan. As a natural creation of the human hand and therefore a creation that has become absolutely natural, the garden has an inherent tectonic form, which in fact it had had at all periods until the false sentimentality of the eighteenth century wrought a change.[401]

With their designs, humans brought regularity, form and rhythm to the coincidences of nature. Muthesius rejects landscape gardeners' attempts to show nature 'in the raw', which he believes are doomed to failure. Gardeners merely create an impression of nature, forgetting that although they do not shape the bushes and hedges, they still mow the lawn. In other words, Muthesius says: designing a garden will always be interfering with nature, and designers must be fully aware of this artificiality. The following two quotations reflect this view:

> The ordered human plan makes the curved straight, the sloping even, the irregular regular, it creates rhythm in place of inconsequence, calculated effect in place of the accidental. For men to decide to try to imitate, to concentrate and heighten the caprices of nature within the small framework of the garden is a wholly unnatural situation. Those in search of nature will find it in plenty outside the garden walls.[402]

---

398 LCdv 241.
399 Muthesius, *Das englische Haus*, part II, p. 82; Hermann Muthesius, *The English House*, ed. and introduction by Dennis Sharp, preface by Julius Posener, translated by Janet Seligman (New York: Rizzoli, 1979). The edition used is the first paperback ed. (New York: Rizzoli, 1987), p. 105.
400 Muthesius, *Das englische Haus*, part II, p. 83; Muthesius, *The English House*, p. 106.
401 Muthesius, *Das englische Haus*, part II, p. 84; Muthesius, *The English House*, p. 106. See LCdv 254.
402 Muthesius, *Das englische Haus*, part II, p. 84; Muthesius, *The English House*, part II, p. 106. See LCdv 254.

The period of landscape-gardening marks a kind of realistic transitional phase of garden that, like most realistic movements in art, meant a revision of technical means. But the end was bound to be the formal garden-plan, just as rhythm is the end of all art.[403]

After landscape gardeners had shown such great interest in exotic plants, they were now increasingly endeavouring to use native plants. The contemporary view in Britain favoured adopting regular garden designs once again. Although not pursuing the decorative details of an aristocratic garden, "great care is lavished on flower-beds, lawns, fruit and vegetable gardens, which are all divided into sections in the manner of the old gardens and kept clearly separate from one another".[404] All parts of the garden should be horizontal, the paths straight, and where the land sloped it should be made level using terraces, with clear geographic boundaries created using either walls or hedges. "Each part of the garden lies close to that part of the house to which it belongs, the kitchen-garden to the domestic wing, the flower-garden to the drawing-room, while the lawns lie facing the residential front of the house."[405] Thus Muthesius' emphasis falls both on a functional arrangement and on a very architectonic treatment of the various areas of the garden. The garden is considered to be an extension of the rooms in the house, with each individual part a self-contained and precisely delineated external room. "Thus the garden extends the house into the midst of nature."[406] The garden frames the house, linking the building with nature. From an aesthetic point of view, the garden forms the pedestal onto which the house is placed like a statue and displayed. Hence the garden is not a reproduction of nature in miniature, but instead an artificial, cultural work which forms part of the architecture: it joins the house to the natural environment. This is precisely the point of view which Jeanneret adopted in 1910: that much is clear from his own sporadic comments here, sometimes formulated as instructions to himself. For example he is in agreement with Muthesius: "Say that the garden adjoining a residence must not be a reminder of nature, but a continuation of the reception rooms, halls etc., cool or sunny rooms."[407] Jeanneret visited the major villas built by Muthesius in Berlin-Nikolassee, where – as it is at Behrens' studio in Neubabelsberg – the garden is treated as architecture. His lived experiences would combine with the convictions he gleaned from reading Muthesius, Schultze-Naumburg, and others, to become built reality in 1912 with the *Maison Blanche*.

Joseph August Lux and the landscape garden controversy

For his putative chapter on landscape gardening, Jeanneret made an effort to translate almost the entire chapter on 'Parks Policy' from Lux's book. Lux considers modern parks policy, or the increasing efforts made by cities to create public gardens, to be motivated by several, related factors: "[t]he expansion of cities, the disappearance of

---

403 Muthesius, *Das englische Haus*, part II, p. 84; Muthesius, *The English House*, part II, p. 106. See LCdv 255.
404 Muthesius, *Das englische Haus*, part II, p. 85; Muthesius, *The English House*, part II, p. 107. See LCdv 257.
405 Muthesius, *Das englische Haus*, part II, p. 85; Muthesius, *The English House*, part II, p. 107. See LCdv 257.
406 Muthesius, *Das englische Haus*, part II, p. 85; Muthesius, *The English House*, part II, p. 107. See LCdv 258.
407 See LCdv 246.

gardens belonging to houses, the rational exploitation of building lots".[408] Every city currently had three types of park or garden. There were: baroque gardens, like those created for castles and open to the public; domestic gardens in the suburbs forming part of the forest and meadow belt surrounding the city; and finally the new public park facilities which contrasted with the other two types. Lux saw these facilities as a failed attempt to combine the English and French garden traditions:

> hemmed in by wretched wire netting, a patch of lawn represents the meadow, and an uneven mildewed collection of bushes [represents] the forest. French carpet beds, and curved paths leading in many different directions, are characteristic of these haphazard designs which consequently often appear cheerless.[409]

Lux believes this new type of urban garden has lost its connection to a vernacular tradition which demonstrates "a secure artistic spirit" in both large- and small-scale designs:

> In the layout of public gardens situated in the middle of buildings and streets, a memory for tradition would be beneficial, since *it teaches us that the smaller its area, the more architecturally a garden must be designed.* Old gardens with pruned arbours and bowers set an excellent example.[410]

The phrase set in italics was also highlighted by Jeanneret: probably because Lux's statement so precisely describes the desolate situation of the small parks in La Chaux-de-Fonds, which each occupy one block.[411] Jeanneret's emphasis on this principle makes it clear how important it is for his position, and shows not only that he believes it is necessary for gardens to be architecturally designed, but also that the smaller the garden, the more necessary this is. Perhaps this phrase explains the apparent discrepancy between the masonry-based architectural gardens in his villas and multi-storey *Maisons Dom-Ino* on the one hand, and his use of a more 'English' landscape garden or an organically shaped free plan in his major urban schemes on the other, for instance in the parks within the *Ville Contemporaine* or the *Ville Radieuse*.

The type of garden to which Lux refers most often is the rustic front garden. In 1907, he published an article in the *Süddeutsche Bauzeitung* on traditional Viennese front gardens; here, he praises the natural beauty of these gardens, which were gradually disappearing at the time.[412] He discusses the unforced natural style of such front gardens for small houses in the suburbs of Vienna, their modest architecture, and the fact that they appear to be part of the living space. Lux professes that the true secret of this seemingly simple layout is little known; he attempts to unearth the secret by describing the materials and plants employed. He cites wooden fences, whitewashed stone walls, and cut hedges; he sees rose bushes, laburnum, ivy, and grapevines in his mind's eye and evokes idyllic moments sitting out in front of the house at evening time, listening to birdsong. "Things have emerged as they had to, out of necessity. They grew wild, but

---

408 Lux, *Städtebau und Grundpfeiler*, p. 72. LCdv 248.
409 Lux, *Städtebau und Grundpfeiler*, p. 74. See LCdv 249f.
410 Lux, *Städtebau und Grundpfeiler*, p. 75. See LCdv 250. Emphasis by Lux.
411 See Critical Application. La Chaux-de-Fonds.
412 Joseph August Lux: "Alt-Wiener Vorgärten", in *Süddeutsche Bauzeitung*, 17 (1907), no. 36, pp. 186–288.

seemingly nature turned artist itself."[413] Lux extols the virtues of a thoroughly *bieder-meier* concept of 'nature', echoing the Austrian writer and creator of idylls, Adalbert Stifter. He states that simple people – in this case farmers and the petty bourgeois in the villages around Vienna – have a better feel for beauty than academics. This notion bears a certain similarity to William Ritter's interest in the authentic architecture of Eastern Europe, which exerted a lasting influence over Jeanneret, throughout and beyond his *Voyage d'Orient*. Just as Ritter saw the old, simple cultures dying out, Lux's article on old Viennese front gardens ends on a resigned note, with a prediction that these simple gardens will disappear. However, he warns against simply replicating them, "since copying them will not sound the right note; intention can never replace that relaxed, yet rule-bound essence of nature."[414] Yet he does hope for positive developments in future – in part because the regularisation which he saw in its infancy would continue and, coupled with artistic resources, would create a new and different type of garden art.

While Lux argues at the end of his chapter on park policy that the existing old gardens should be maintained, he hesitates when it comes to the design of new garden schemes:

> In Vienna, the creation of a 'belt of meadows and forests around Vienna' is under consideration, in other cities parks policy will have to deal with similar things. However, in all cases it would be reasonable not to deal so much with new creations as with maintaining what is already good, that is to say a sort of 'Heimatschutz' [heritage protection]. Hence parks policy has an important and contemporary cultural role to play in all towns and cities. When creating new parks and gardens, we should wait in those semi-rural and often charmingly beautiful suburbs until the good old subjects from our local heritage (which we have indicated in this connection) are worked up artistically such that, finally, gardens will emerge once again which just like the old ones, as [Francis] Bacon [, Baron] of Verulam said, are the source of pure joy.[415]

The photos which Lux displays in this article are very similar to the pictures Jeanneret would later take on his voyage to the East, in which he repeatedly snaps simple houses, gardens, etc. in villages. The pictures from the area surrounding Tirnovo (now known as Veliko Tarnovo) in Bulgaria are one example of this: simple rural houses are shown complete with enclosures, courtyards, and front gardens.[416] The intellectual basis for Jeanneret's interest in these would appear to come from both Lux and Ritter.[417]

---

413 Lux: "Alt-Wiener Vorgärten", p. 287.
414 Lux: "Alt-Wiener Vorgärten", p. 288.
415 Lux, *Städtebau und Grundpfeiler*, p. 76. Lux's emphasis. See LCdv 251f.
416 See Gresleri, *Reise nach dem Orient*, p. 172ff.
417 It should be noted that there is no definitive proof Jeanneret did read the article by Lux on front gardens. His notes are inconclusive; hence in Cahier C.6 he writes in two different places: "Article by Jos. Aug. Lux in Süddeutsche Bauzeitung. page 21 1907, id. p. 281" and "Article {which is good} by Jos Aug Lux. in Süddeutsche Bauzeitung 1907 page 21 in the same year *Garten und Park in künstlerischer Gestaltung* page 281 293, 301 326" (LCdv 240 and 243). The article described as "page 21 1907" is entitled "Die Gartenkunst und die Landschaftsgärtnerei"; the other article "p. 281" is not by Lux, but by Ludwig Fuchs, although the title is as noted by Jeanneret. Lux's article on old-fashioned Viennese front gardens is therefore not expressly cited. However, it is highly likely that Jeanneret read the article, since it follows directly on from the essay by Ludwig Fuchs, which he definitely did read.

There is one article by Lux of which Jeanneret was certainly aware, and which also appeared in the *Süddeutsche Bauzeitung* – "Die Gartenkunst und die Landschaftsgärtnerei". It comprises a response to criticism, which also appeared in the journal, from Frankfurt's director of garden design Carl Heicke.[418] An academic dispute was fought in this journal about the true direction for garden design to take, which can in some respects be compared with the disputes between Baumeister and Sitte, or Stübben and Henrici, about the right kind of urban design. At issue was the role of art within garden design, a discipline which wanted to be seen as self-sufficient and not secondary to architecture – just as within modernism, urban design emerged as a discipline and also wanted to be independent of architecture. Garden design aspired to self-determination, applying the internal logic of gardening work. This dispute went beyond Carl Heicke, Ludwig Fuchs, and Joseph August Lux to draw in almost all garden designers of the period. For the 'gardeners', Carl Heicke adopted a position in his 1906 article in *Süddeutsche Bauzeitung* attacking those architects – such as Muthesius and Schultze-Naumburg – who saw garden design as an *artistic intervention* and opposed the replication of nature, shored up with scientific justifications, which they saw happening in landscape architecture.[419]

Heicke's article "Rückständige Gartenkunst" (retrograde garden design) is a polemic against artists and architects who he sees as meddling with the gardening profession. He names Schultze-Naumburg, Muthesius, and Lichtwark in particular, calling them garden design reactionaries. He recommends reading books by these three architects to hear their almost complete silence on gardens; to him this demonstrates their incompetence and disinterest. Heicke's main material argument against these three is the accusation that they are ignorant and incorrect in their use of straight lines in garden design:

> I now ask: did I dream it, or have all people with artistic sensibilities been caught up for several years in the increasingly fierce fight against straight lines in city planning? Was it not in fact the artists who campaigned against the considerations advanced by engineers, fitness for purpose and for traffic? And who called for the picturesque to be emphasised more in city planning? [...] Are we now to believe the theory that connecting two points by a straight line is logical, and therefore the only workable solution, only applies to gardens?[420]

Two points emerge from this: first, despite Sitte's best intentions, the debate on renewal in urban design is reduced here to the question of whether curved or straight streets are justified. Second, Heicke assumes that urban design and garden design run in parallel – that what is true for one must be true for the other: "Or must it [the garden path] be

---

418 Carl Heicke (1862–1938) was director of garden design for the city of Frankfurt and editor of the journal *Gartenkunst*.

419 See Uwe Schneider, *Hermann Muthesius und die Reformdiskussion in der Gartenarchitektur des frühen 20. Jahrhunderts* (Worms: Wernersche Verlagsgesellschaft, 2000). Schneider investigates Muthesius' influence on the garden reform movement at the beginning of the 20th century. He concludes that Muthesius was swayed in England by arguments in favour of the regular architectural garden made by Reginald Blomfield, Thomas H. Mawson, and Gertrude Jekyll, but that his own influence was more limited than had previously been assumed.

420 Carl Heicke, "Rückständige Gartenkunst", in *Süddeutsche Bauzeitung*, 16 (1906), no. 46, pp. 364–367, and no. 48, p. 379–383. Here p. 379.

straight because there is no trace of rectilinearity in the vegetation which fills the garden?"[421] This is precisely the reason Jeanneret gives in his own definition of garden design (see below), probably without even reading Heicke. Heicke feels it is illogical for "informal lines" in gardens to be considered as "a momentous derailment of modern artistic sensibilities", and warns against the garden being considered part of the human habitat and therefore also part of architecture:

> The garden must follow a regular plan, because it is extended dwelling, we are told. But that is of course not the case! We do not live in the garden, at best perhaps on the veranda – and even if that were the case, would it only be possible to live in a garden which had a regular plan? [...] The garden is not an extension of our living space, but rather it is part of nature into which we build our living quarters [...]; it is a place where we walk and move around for relaxation, and for this purpose paths with thin, curved lines are more comfortable than those with sharp corners.[422]

Thus Heicke dismisses out of hand the fundamental design basis on which Muthesius, Lux, and other architects had built their understanding of the garden. Heicke received responses from both Joseph August Lux and Ludwig Fuchs in editions of the *Süddeutsche Bauzeitung* published the following year; Jeanneret followed this debate with interest.

Jeanneret's view of garden art

From his collection of excerpts and translations on garden art, Jeanneret gleaned one idea above all: the garden has throughout its history adopted an undeniably architectural quality, as something that has been *constructed*. It has been inextricably linked to the house, villa, or palace. As Muthesius states, it is actually the garden which gives the house a foothold in the landscape. Yet one particular question arises amidst the countless poetic illustrations of sublime gardens: what has all this got to do with urban design? Are the examples Jeanneret employs not taken almost exclusively from private gardens belonging to houses or palaces? This also applies to the long passage he quotes from Muthesius, describing the English country house and its garden in such detail. Which aspect of these gardens does Jeanneret believe should be employed in urban design? The answer to this question lies, at least in part, in the chapter on park policy from Lux's *Der Städtebau und die Grundpfeiler*. Lux establishes the connection: he distinguishes between the dreary, boring park designs of the late 19th century and the ancient gardens, for example in Rome, which could be used as blueprints for modern parks in terms of beauty and architectural order. This contrast is what Jeanneret emphasises in a note he makes: "Need to find a selection of poetic quotations so that, by quoting them, can make the contrast felt with our hopeless gardens today."[423] Thus Jeanneret is clearly looking for historical examples which could help

---

421 Heicke, "Rückständige Gartenkunst", p. 380.
422 Heicke, "Rückständige Gartenkunst", p. 381.
423 "Il faudrait trouver tout 1 choix de citations poétiques afin de faire en les citer sentir le contraste désolant de nos jardins actuels." LCdv 261.

produce a new type of architecture for urban parks and public gardens. Naturally, this search for good designs also encompasses private gardens.

It is abundantly clear that Muthesius and Schultze-Naumburg made their mark on *La Construction des villes*, but what about Behrens' view on the architecture of gardens? There is no question that, while at Peter Behrens' office, Jeanneret will have learned lessons about handling the tangible spatial quality of a garden and its role as a room outside the house. This is evident in relation to the villa which Behrens built for the archaeologist Theodor Wiegand, in the Dahlem suburb of Berlin: Jeanneret sketched its peristyle and took a drawing of it home to La Chaux-de-Fonds.[424] He may also have learned from the garden which Behrens had designed for his Neubabelsberg studio to overlook "a geometric extension of space, featuring carefully placed benches, latticework pergolas, and statuary as intermediaries between the viewer and the verdant background of the heavily wooded neighborhood".[425] As Jeanneret had already grappled with the theories of Muthesius, Grisebach, and Läuger, his experience of this garden may have prompted him to incorporate the architectural garden into his repertoire, thus paving the way for the *Maison Blanche*. However, Behrens' key essay "Der moderne Garten" (the modern garden) did not appear until June 1911, too late to be reflected in *La Construction des villes*.

One further possible reason for Jeanneret's interest in gardens is the connection they establish between two urban design elements which he had previously discussed. For Jeanneret, gardens and squares are intimately linked. The evidence for this is twofold: first, Cahier C.6 is given over to both categories, and Jeanneret worked simultaneously on excerpts relating to both these themes – within the cahier, gardens and squares alternate. Second, in his view similar principles applied to both squares and gardens. Both were types of 'open-air room': one built from stone, the other from vegetation. This view emerges when Jeanneret, albeit enigmatically, applies to the garden his definition of the square as a public room:

> We must confirm this: as for GARDENS, they are rooms – with in fact a floor, walls and ceiling – and not houses. And it is necessary to create volumes which one can enter into, not where one remains outside oneself [?].[426]

In conclusion, Jeanneret formulates a definition of the architecture of gardens which attempts to reconcile the apparent discrepancy between picturesque urban design on the one hand and strictly regular architectural garden art on the other. Thus in some ways he answers Heicke's question as to why architects prefer sweeping, picturesque lines for urban areas while deploying strictly rectilinear forms in gardens:

> The garden is a construction made with trees and flowers, these elements which in their structure contain irregularity, chaos, disorder. This is true not when you take a single tree, which is almost always marvellously ordered – a true palmette – but when compared with the means at the disposal of city architects:

---

424 Both Brooks, *Le Corbusier's Formative Years*, p. 241ff., and Barry Bergdoll refer to Jeanneret's interest in the Wiegand house. Barry Bergdoll, "The Nature of Mies's Space", in *Mies in Berlin*, ed. Terence Riley and Barry Bergdoll (Munich: Prestel, 2001), p. 66–105, here p. 77.

425 Bergdoll, "The Nature of Mies's Space", p. 74.

426 LCdv 244.

streets and squares – strongly accentuated, brutal forms, geometric volumes, etc. Hence to avoid dryness, the planner of streets and squares uses curves; to avoid chaos, splintering, nothingness, the gardener uses straight lines which allow him to align elements along [intangible?] perspectives in plan which in elevation are open to imaginative [handling] – and thus to create an architecture made from living materials: architectures being order, will, power, *a feeling that this was intended*.[427]

The excerpts which Jeanneret collates stand in sharp contrast to his descriptions of the dirty, draughty urban area of his day – be it La Chaux-de-Fonds or Berlin. He explicitly states that in gathering these examples he wants to counter the sorry situation in which parks and gardens currently find themselves. At the same time, the examples provide him with a vision of a life in paradise and as such can be contrasted with the dreary, boring contemporary city as a means of injecting these paradisiac qualities. It is not possible to state conclusively whether Jeanneret is taking this stance because he feels drawn towards the Mediterranean and away from Northern Europe; this is often said to be the case – not least by Jeanneret himself. Perhaps the topic always remains a constant for him, a longing for a 'paradise' and thus the formulation of urban design with utopian qualities.

Des Cimetières – The architectural possibilities of cemeteries

In the Cahiers C.9 *Garden Cities Cemetery I* and C.10 *Garden Cities Cemetery II*, Jeanneret gathers materials on the topics of cemeteries and garden cities. The texts included in these cahiers are almost all book chapters or journal articles which Jeanneret has translated. Five of these texts address contemporary issues in cemetery design:

1. "Der Bremer Friedhofswettbewerb" (the Bremen cemetery competition) by Fritz Encke and Reinhold Hoemann from the journal *Die Gartenkunst*.[428]
2. "Die Münchner Friedhof- und Grabmalreform" (Munich cemetery and memorial reform) by Franz Zell from the *Süddeutsche Bauzeitung*:[429]
3. A short excerpt from the *Handbuch der Architektur, Geschichte des Denkmales* (Handbook of Architecture, History of the Monument) by Albert Hofmann including a description of the Avenue of Giants [or 'spirit path'] in Nanking (now Nanjing).[430]
4. A one-page excerpt about cemeteries from Lux's book *Der Städtebau und die Grundpfeiler der heimischen Bauweise*.[431]

---

427 LCdv 266f.
428 Fritz Encke and Reinhold Hoemann: "Der Bremer Friedhofswettbewerb", in *Die Gartenkunst* 12 (1910), no. 4, pp. 51–57. See LCdv 293–297.
429 Franz Zell: "Die Münchener Friedhof- und Grabmalreform", in *Süddeutsche Bauzeitung* 17 (1907), No. 33, pp. 257–261. See LCdv 280–292.
430 Albert Hofmann, *Geschichte des Denkmales*, part 4, sub-volume 8, no. 2b of *Handbuch des Architekten* (Stuttgart: Kröner, 1906). See LCdv 276–280.
431 Lux, *Städtebau und Grundpfeiler*, p. 94f. LCdv 275.

5. Translated excerpts from a text by art historian August Grisebach, who reported in *Gartenkunst* about two projects by Max Läuger – one for the Osterholz cemetery on the outskirts of Bremen and the other for the Stadtpark in Hamburg.[432]

There is also a page containing reflections about the floral decoration of graves, which may have been drafted by Jeanneret himself.[433] Jeanneret adds to the bibliography an essay by Franz Seeck entitled "Neuzeitliche Friedhofsanlagen" (modern cemetery design) from the journal *Angewandte Kunst*.[434] He further notes an illustration which turns out to be from another article: one volume of the journal *Moderne Bauformen* contained illustrations of a cemetery design by Wilhelm Kreis (Fig.s 85 and 86).[435] This design was displayed at the exhibition of Christian art in Düsseldorf in 1909. In Cahier C.9 there are also two pages containing small sketches of monuments and cemetery designs (Fig.s 84 and 87).[436]

The topic of cemeteries clearly preoccupied Jeanneret. He repeatedly made notes, copied sketches, and photographed cemeteries over a period of years, whether on his voyage to Italy in 1907, in Germany in 1910, or the following year on his voyage to the East. Harold Allen Brooks is astonished by this:

> I have no explanation for Jeanneret's fascination for cemeteries and tombstones, or why so many of his sketches, postcards, and particularly photographs are of them. His notes and letters frequently speak of them. See letter of July 18 to L'Eplattenier wherein he mentions how Léon Perrin will find this documentation interesting, but this hardly explains the vast amount of time and energy Jeanneret devoted to them.[437]

It is indeed astounding that while in Munich Jeanneret collated such a goodly number of texts on cemeteries – although it must be emphasised that the essays he translated deal mainly with garden design rather than the buildings in cemeteries. It may be that Jeanneret saw cemetery garden design as closely related to that of gardens and parks; he certainly saw major architectural potential in cemeteries as well as gardens. He was clearly fascinated by the architectural treatment of nature – both plants and terrain. It is clear that Jeanneret wished to engage with contemporary discourse about landscaping and architectural design, not only in relation to gardens and parks but also in relation to cemeteries. After all, cemeteries are also associated with the subject of paradise, with which he was preoccupied: they are gardens where people may rest in peace.

---

432 Grisebach, "Max Läugers Entwürfe". See LCdv 300–310.

433 LCdv 299. Unfortunately we found no indication of the source from which this text could have been translated. The style here does differ from the style in which Jeanneret penned his own thoughts in the cahiers, indicating that this is indeed a translation.

434 "1 article sur cimetierres nouveaux ds Die Kunst 1908 1909 page 521". The article in question is: Franz Seeck, "Neuzeitliche Friedhofsanlagen", in *Angewandte Kunst* 20 (1909), pp. 521–536. See LCdv 311.

435 The relevant article is an introduction by Max Schmid, "Baukunst und Innendekoration auf der Ausstellung für Christliche Kunst in Düsseldorf 1909" in *Moderne Bauformen* 8 (1909), No. 9, pp. 385–455. See LCdv 275.

436 LCdv 274 and 298.

437 Brooks, *Le Corbusier's Formative Years*, 267f.

The Munich Waldfriedhof – Grässel's cemetery reform

Jeanneret translated the article by Franz Zell about the Munich woodland cemetery, only omitting a few lines. In this article Zell describes in detail the reform of cemeteries and monuments undertaken by the Munich council architect Hans Grässel, which led to a new way of designing cemeteries (Fig.s XLIX and L). Zell states that in the past, cemeteries had only been granted the opportunity to design artistically attractive burial sites in exceptional cases, for example where these were close to buildings. Elsewhere, the sites had been lamentable:

> In other places, the familiar confusion of modern municipal cemeteries reigns; despite all the lines of trees, which are also bare in winter (because only deciduous trees thrive in Munich), they resemble large gravestone depots.[438]

Zell concedes that successful grave monuments do exist in cemeteries, but adds that these hardly registered among the "great preponderance of inferior, clichéd monuments". He concludes: *"Thus the beautiful individual shape of grave monuments is in no way sufficient to achieve a harmonious effect in cemetery design."*[439]

Fig. XLIX Munich woodland cemetery. From Seeck, "Neuzeitliche Friedhofsanlagen," p. 522

438 Zell, "Die Münchener Friedhof- und Grabmalreform", p. 257. See LCdv 281.
439 Zell, "Die Münchener Friedhof- und Grabmalreform", p. 257; Zell's emphasis. See LCdv 282.

Fig. L Munich woodland cemetery. Postcard, owned by Jeanneret (LC-105-1112 BV)

For the first time, there was an attempt at an all-encompassing new type of cemetery design, which represented a breakthrough in terms of reform. Grässel's idea was that for a large urban cemetery to create a positive impression, it should be divided into smaller individual cemeteries, separated from one another by abundant cultivated areas. "In the Munich woodland cemetery, Grässel largely found the abundant vegetation which he required, and he used patches of virgin forest and newly created woodland meadows, each half a hectare in size, to create the individual cemeteries."[440] Zell states that, in order to not detract from the harmonious overall effect, Grässel required each area of graves to have its own type of monuments and use its own materials. Grässel had established a number of regulations to ensure unified design, which relate among other things to the materials used for monuments. Thus stone, wood, or iron was only to be used in the individual section or sections allocated for this material. Gravestones were required to have matt surfaces made of materials such as tuff, trass, nagelfluh, muschelkalk, granite, or granular limestone. As with gravestones, Grässel insisted that plants should be appropriate to the type of woodland. For example, he advocated using ivy, moss, fern, box, juniper, or Virginia creeper instead of "ornamental varieties".[441] Jeanneret translated all these prescriptions without commenting on them; he also visited the Waldfriedhof, sketched from nature and noted down his thoughts on the design which, despite the strict prescriptions from Grassel as described above, he still judged to have too little unity and control:

---

440 Zell, "Die Münchener Friedhof- und Grabmalreform", p. 258. See LCdv 283.
441 Zell, "Die Münchener Friedhof- und Grabmalreform", p. 261. See LCdv 292.

On the Waldfriedhof, in order to break up the excessive length of the wall and to achieve a step up in height at A, a shrine splits the excessive length of the enclosing wall. In clearings 15, 26 and 33 etc., where the tombs in rows are, and in the large allées, the planting of too many sorts of shrubs was permitted. The result is a tiresome bric-à-brac, in the midst of which the tombs rise up poorly and no longer have a powerful effect. I would suggest using large walls with an architectural appearance. Only the names would be engraved on this, and at its foot would be a lush expanse of ordered flowers.[442]

It is worth noting Jeanneret's call for architectural strictures here because it brings to mind his use of Pisa as an example. The use of the attribute "powerful" here is striking: it evokes its modern counterpart, Aldo Rossi. At the cemetery of San Cataldo in Modena, Rossi's 'city of the dead', or ossuary, embodies Jeanneret's recommendation "I would suggest using large walls with an architectural appearance". This phrase of Jeanneret's expresses an enormously strong, rigid creative will, which even extends into the realm of the dead. Perhaps this is the spiritual equivalent of his modernist urban design.

Albert Hofmann – The history of burial sites

Jeanneret takes excerpts from the comprehensive handbook by Berlin architect Albert Hofmann *Geschichte des Denkmales*, which discusses the burial constructions with which cultures around the world have honoured the dead. These excerpts describe a few examples which have obviously impressed him: hence he translates several lines on the Avenue of Giants near Nanking in China. According to Hofmann, the last journey of rulers in the Ming Dynasty was along this 2-kilometre route flanked with animal figures which were supposed to protect the deceased from evil spirits.[443] At the start of the Avenue stand two turtles carrying obelisks, which are followed by lions, camels, and horses, both reclining and standing. At the end of the boulevard are two warrior figures reclining, and two standing. Jeanneret summarises as follows:

All this lies or stands in the middle of the deserted countryside, in short grass, overlooked by mountains, and the figures are worked and of such style and size that they possess the greatest emotive strength. (Cite this as the type of thing that, with the help of natural elements, makes the deepest of impressions. Similarity to Egypt (to Miletus, sacred way and Roman 'Via Campana'). – We must then contrast with the modern cemetery which cannot make such preparations but which must be entrenched behind ramparts so it can be a place of rest.[444]

---

442 Le Corbusier, *Voyages d'Allemagne*, Carnet 3, p. 13–15: "à Waldfriedhof pour interrompre la trop grande longueur du mur et faire un ressaut dans la hauteur en A un oratoire coupe la trop grande longueur du mur de clôture à l'extérieur dans les clairières 15 26, 33 etc. où sont des tombes en lignées, – et dans les grandes allées, on a toléré la plantation de trop de sortes d'arbustes. Il en résulte un aspect fatiguant de bric à brac au milieu duquel surgissent mal les tombes qui ne font plus un effet puissant. Je proposerais l'emploi de grands murs à tenue architecturale. Seuls des noms seraient inscrits et au pied s'étendrait la folie des fleurs riches et ordonnées".
443 Hofmann, *Geschichte des Denkmales*, p. 750.
444 LCdv 277. The meaning of the end of the text is unclear.

As in Jeanneret's assessment of the Munich Waldfriedhof above, he takes the view that a cemetery, like a room, should be enclosed by a wall. This reinforces the impression that Jeanneret considers the cemetery to be a *hortus conclusus*, an enclosed garden.

Cooperation between architect and landscape gardener

An article by Fritz Encke and Reinhold Hoemann reports on the competition to design a cemetery in Osterholz at the outskirts of Bremen.[445] Using this as an example, they expound their theory that cooperation between architects and landscape gardeners is highly beneficial.

> The view taken by the competition [...], a view often attacked but equally vigorously defended, was that garden artists and architects should work together, that a solution was required for the layout as a whole, including the architecture. We hold such cooperation to be thoroughly desirable. The spatial design of land which is later to be occupied by buildings may, for a wide area around these buildings, only be acquitted well and with character when it is combined with both a detailed floor plan and the architecture of these buildings.[446]

They indicate that such cooperation could have disadvantages if one party, either the architect or the garden designer, was not actually skilled in his discipline – as was the case with the Osterholz competition. However, they see the advantages of cooperation as much greater: for these two interdependent professions, cooperation brought an improved understanding of one another's perspectives; for the authority holding the competition it provided the possibility of identifying, from the point at which the tenders were submitted, which artists would be in a position to collaborate and arrive at a realistic design.

Initially, the expansion of earlier churchyards outside the town had created a soulless, chequerboard distribution. Later attempts had then been made to mitigate this negative effect by introducing the 'landscaped' cemetery, which took the shape of the ubiquitous mid-19th-century park. This resulted in confusion and a waste of space. In the recent past, a type of cemetery reform had emerged which involved neither parkland nor chequerboard designs: "It [...] arises from requirements and is thus an individual arrangement, with its own character clearly showing how it was determined."[447] Now the shape of a cemetery did not need to be restricted to a single form. The possible types ranged from the woodland cemetery to the monumental cemetery, in which plants are used as a sculptural mass from which the space is formed. According to Encke and

---

445 Encke and Hoemann, "Der Bremer Friedhofswettbewerb". See LCdv 293–297. On the role of Encke and Hoemann in garden design reform in the early 20th century, see Uwe Schneider, *Hermann Muthesius und die Reformdiskussion in der Gartenarchitektur des frühen 20. Jahrhunderts* (Worms: Wernersche Verlagsgesellschaft, 2000). According to Schneider, both designers represented a moderate approach granting legitimacy to both the landscape and architectural garden design trends. One quotation from Fritz Encke illustrates this: "I believe this means the question as to whether domestic gardens should be designed in a strictly architectural or an informal manner is redundant. It is my view that rules and philosophical utterances should not shape the domestic garden; its character should instead be established by the needs and wishes of the client". Fritz Encke, *Der Hausgarten* (Jena: Diederichs, 1907), p. 14; quoted in Schneider, *Hermann Muthesius und die Reformdiskussion*, p. 247.

446 Encke and Hoemann, "Der Bremer Friedhofswettbewerb", p. 51. See LCdv 293.

447 Encke and Hoemann, "Der Bremer Friedhofswettbewerb", p. 55. See LCdv 296.

Hoemann, Friedrich Ostendorf's design for Osterholz was a fitting example of the latter type. The authors' willingness to compromise on the debate between design theories is illustrated in this proposal to combine the two extremes:

> The type of cemetery design most suitable for fulfilling the usual practical requirements and the aesthetic sensibilities of large swathes of the population lies somewhere in the middle: a tectonic cemetery which however is neither terribly symmetrical nor given a monumental treatment, with paths that are clearly designed in conjunction with the organic forms of the construction, and which provides good orientation and creates smaller spaces within the overall area, approaching in its spatial impact the churchyards of old.[448]

It stands to reason that the authors gladly advocated the prize-winning design by Hermann Grage and Kurt Winkelhausen. In this, the city of Bremen had found a "beautiful, practicable, we would even say deeply rooted cemetery project".[449] Nevertheless this design was never realised: the project implemented was by Berlin team Franz Seeck and Paul Freye. As before, Jeanneret does not comment on this excerpt.

Max Läuger's cemetery and garden projects

Jeanneret translated, in slightly abbreviated form, the article by art historian August Grisebach on two cemetery and garden projects by the architect Max Läuger, who worked in Karlsruhe. In the article, Grisebach expresses his regret that two of Läuger's competition submissions, the Osterholz cemetery near Bremen and the city park in Hamburg, failed to win despite being far superior to the rival designs as overall architectural entities. Grisebach takes as his theme the conflict between garden design and landscape gardening, and speaks of the compromises which some have made, while attacking the middle way and favouring instead the same trenchant approach which Läuger adopted as a garden architect:

> People take no heed of the fact that the essential part of a garden lies in a sharply defined contrast between an open, clearly arranged area (be it floorscape or pool) with a raised, enclosed mass (hedge or thicket). In other words: the *spatial* effect – perhaps the most important element which fell victim to the pictorial tendencies of landscape gardening some 150 years ago – eludes the designs by garden architects who take the 'middle way'.[450]

According to Grisebach, in his competition entries for the park in Hamburg and the cemetery in Bremen Max Läuger had demonstrated an architectural approach, for which he sadly received no credit from the jury; once again, landscape gardening had taken precedence.[451] Grisebach goes on to describe both of Läuger's designs in detail, turning

---

448 Encke and Hoemann, "Der Bremer Friedhofswettbewerb", p. 56. See LCdv 297.
449 Encke and Hoemann, "Der Bremer Friedhofswettbewerb", p. 57. See LCdv 297.
450 Grisebach, "Max Läugers Entwürfe", p. 489. Emphasis by the author. See LCdv 302.
451 The second prize in the 1908 competition for the Stadtpark in Hamburg was awarded to Gebrüder Roethe and W. Bungarten. Fritz Schumacher, as building director for the city of Hamburg, and chief engineer

for comparison to Fritz Schumacher's revised design for the Stadtpark in Hamburg. He repeatedly emphasises the spaces which Läuger literally cuts from the forest in his design for the park: some are individual sports pitches, but one is a large central grassy area intended as a public park.

> The open space formed in the middle of the woodland is reminiscent of the shape of the communal garden from the Middle Ages, which we can reconstruct from literary and visual representations: a flower meadow, surrounded with regular rose trellises, behind which rises an arboretum. These, the oldest public gardens in Germany, were naturally much more primitive and modest in scale than a park for modern day Hamburg could possibly be. I am merely keen to indicate the similarity in principle, since some take the opinion that a formal composition is the least suitable for a public park.[452]

Läuger's drawings give the impression of an aesthetically appealing park, which in fact is decidedly spatial or architectural in appearance, and also follows strict design principles. It is therefore unsurprising that the jury in 1908 opted for a less uncompromising design. Furthermore, in the case of the Osterholz cemetery, Läuger submitted a serious design which Grisebach believes skilfully arranged the various areas such as the cinerarium and burial ground alongside each other to form a unified whole. Finally, Grisebach indicates the difficulty facing such formal designs in that the plants take time to grow:

> Criticism is raised against the bleak divisions and lack of luxuriant foliage and shaded walkways, which of course the plentiful shrubs of a landscaped park produce more quickly. As with today's fashion for discovering and raising a genius overnight, so demands are made that gardens immediately appear in their final forms. How does it benefit us if future generations enjoy them![453]

Franz Seeck – modern cemetery designs

In one of the cahiers, Jeanneret made a note referring to an article by Franz Seeck, who came second at the Osterholz competition. It discusses the theoretical basis for architectural and landscaped cemeteries and collaboration between architect and landscape architect.[454] It appears that Jeanneret did not have time to translate this before he left Munich. However, we can assume that he did read it – however fleetingly. In contrast to Max Läuger and his supporter August Grisebach, Seeck shows greater willingness to compromise in the dispute between garden theories.

Sperber were jointly responsible for revising and realising this design. In the 1910 competition for the cemetery in Osterholz near Bremen, Hermann Grage and Kurt Winkelhausen from Hamburg won first prize; however, the second prize design by Franz Seeck and Paul Freye from Berlin would ultimately be realised. See also Theodor Goecke, "Der Wettbewerb um Entwürfe für den Osterholzer Friedhof in Bremen", in *Der Städtebau* 8 (1911), no. 8, pp. 89–91.

452 Grisebach "Max Läugers Entwürfe", p. 498. See LCdv 304.
453 Grisebach "Max Läugers Entwürfe", p. 503. See LCdv 310.
454 "Article on new cemeteries, in Die Kunst 1908 1909 page 521", LCdv 311. This is Seeck, "Neuzeitliche Friedhofsanlagen".

According to Seeck, there are three groups into which modern-day building tasks can be divided:

> those which emerge in conditions that have remained the same for centuries; those for which the plans have changed and expanded as requirements have changed; and finally those for which there had previously been no need at all, the need having emerged in the present era.[455]

For Seeck, small cemeteries belong to the second group of buildings, but the large central city cemeteries can be seen as completely new creations, for which two things must be achieved: "constituting a particular type and finding for this type its own form of artistic expression".[456] He finds that the design for a cemetery bears similarities to the layout of a town plan.[457] In both cases, it is not merely a question of meeting the practical requirements.

For towns as for cemeteries, Seeck sees it as important to respect the "sequence of spaces", the beauty of the cityscape, although in cemeteries the possibilities for shaping space in the absence of built mass are more limited than with urban planning.

> It is therefore clear that, if at all possible, the necessary cemetery buildings must be given an excellent location and this should be given as dominant a position as possible in the overall layout in relation to any other important volumes.[458]

He states that, in the age of urbanisation, a larger number of buildings are required and the possibilities have therefore expanded.

Seeck states that two main types have emerged, "the architectural and the landscape, or more accurately woodland, type". These can be described as artificial and natural cemeteries. He finds that the second type takes into account the cemetery's role in providing an "atmospheric space" for the veneration of the dead.[459] According to Seeck, the natural cemetery adopts the prevailing mood in nature and uses this directly; the architectural cemetery first has to create a mood. The major, architecturally designed cemeteries by Hans Grässel in Munich are presented as "textbook examples of generous designs", both in their conception and in their implementation, which despite an "apparently exaggerated luxury" in their use of space were actually very economical.[460] Seeck believes that the overall artistic concept has been neglected in many cemetery plans. Only recently has this cultural requirement been heeded with greater care, and his verdict is: "it speaks volumes that these attempts began on the basis of the landscape type and only much later paid any attention to the architectural type."[461]

---

455 Seeck, "Neuzeitliche Friedhofsanlagen", p. 522.
456 Seeck, "Neuzeitliche Friedhofsanlagen", p. 522.
457 See Laugier, who says: "Il faut regarder une ville comme une forêt." Laugier, *Essai*, p. 222. Marc Antoine Laugier, *An Essay on Architecture*, trans. Wolfgang and Anni Herrmann (Los Angeles: Hennessy and Ingalls, 1977), p. 128.
458 Seeck, "Neuzeitliche Friedhofsanlagen", p. 523.
459 Seeck, "Neuzeitliche Friedhofsanlagen", p. 523.
460 Seeck, "Neuzeitliche Friedhofsanlagen", p. 524.
461 Seeck, "Neuzeitliche Friedhofsanlagen", p. 524.

Seeck believes that, in order to combine the buildings and green elements in a cemetery and produce a successful whole, the competitions for new cemeteries should be presented in such a way that garden designers and architects submitted their entries jointly; he states that this is now often the case. Seeck does acknowledge, however, that the competition winners are often not ultimately awarded the contract to implement the work. He states that a sharp distinction cannot always be drawn between landscape and architectural cemeteries, and often a combined approach is appropriate – for example, where the site is already partially covered in woodland.

The Camposanto Monumentale in Pisa as an example for Jeanneret

The articles compiled by Jeanneret on the issue of cemeteries do not display a consistent theoretical stance. None of them explicitly advocates the landscape theory, although both Encke and Hoemann and Seeck propose a compromise between the two potential extremes. August Grisebach and his preferred architect Max Läuger both favour a strongly spatial, architectural approach to garden design. However, none of the expert voices in these articles calls to turn the clock back beyond the reformist attitude represented most clearly by Hans Grässel's Munich woodland cemetery project, whose major characteristics are simplicity and spatial treatment of the individual burial grounds, while incorporating the existing wooded area into a landscaped layout.

Jeanneret's own view during these years is distinctive, despite him voicing it only briefly here. Even on his first journey to Italy in 1907 he had visited the Camposanto Monumentale in Pisa, and there can be no doubt that it influenced him greatly. He appears to measure modern cemeteries against the yardstick of that powerful architectural expression which he observed in Pisa. He notes to himself that he should cite the Camposanto as a positive example in his chapter On Cemeteries:

> Discuss the Campo Santo in Pisa where there were no personal tombs but where everything was for a more intense exaltation of being moved with emotion. The corpses shrouded in 'holy ground' and then great emotion, cries, tears, joy, blessings, comfort expressed on the walls, in a calm, moving atmosphere, in the touching atmosphere of beauty.[462]

It is increasingly clear, both here and in Jeanneret's already-cited note, that Pisa was his main prime example of a good cemetery: "We must then contrast with the modern cemetery which cannot make such preparations but which must be entrenched behind ramparts so it can be a place of rest."[463] This would indicate that Jeanneret had not reached any conclusions by reading about cemeteries in 1910 which he had not already reached on the basis of his earlier experience. As previously in 1907, he believed the 'correct' model was the strictly architectural Mediterranean cemetery, which allowed for little individual expression and instead formed a greater artistic whole, was for him the 'correct' model. However, it is also possible that Jeanneret reached certainty on this position only once he had engaged with the issue in Munich, on reflection as it were.

---

462 LCdv 310.
463 LCdv 277.

Can any further conclusions be drawn here? Perhaps only that he had a preference, as expressed elsewhere in *La Construction des villes*, for greater collectivity and artistic unity. It is not possible to ascertain the precise extent to which Jeanneret was actually swayed by Grässel's calls for cemeteries to be divided into individual areas according to the materials used for the tombstones: a stance that is close to the modernist separation of functions. It is clear, however, that Grässel's rigid rules did not go far enough for Jeanneret – who stated that Grässel created confusion instead of a unified whole, or *unité*. In terms of content, it is clear that there are great similarities between the issues of cemeteries and gardens. Equally, both the reform movement and emergent modernism played major roles in terms of cemetery design, with their respective calls to involve local traditions, greater honesty, and simplicity.

Des Cités-jardins – On Garden Cities

Jeanneret did not collate very much material for his chapter about garden cities. He translated excerpts from Georg Metzendorf's memorandum (*Denkschrift*) on the Margarethe-Krupp-Stiftung development in Essen, and from the chapter on garden cities in Joseph August Lux's *Der Städtebau und die Grundpfeiler der heimischen Bauweise*. As with his previous chapter, Jeanneret used Cahiers C.9 and C.10 for these notes and extracts. He also added books to his bibliography which he did not work on: *Die Gartenstadt München-Perlach* and *Bodenpolitik und gemeindliche Wohnungsfürsorge der Stadt Ulm* by Hans-Eduard von Berlepsch-Valendàs, and *Garden Cities of To-morrow* by Ebenezer Howard.[464] The other materials which Jeanneret collated were a promotional leaflet from the German Garden City society (Deutsche Gartenstadtgesellschaft), and drawings of Hampstead Garden Suburb copied from an essay by Berlepsch-Valendàs which appeared in the journal *Kunst und Kunsthandwerk* (Fig. LI–LV).[465]

Lux – Garden cities

Joseph August Lux devotes a chapter of his book *Der Städtebau und die Grundpfeiler der heimischen Bauweise* to garden cities. Jeanneret made extensive use of the entire work, translating almost the whole of this chapter in which the author explores the concept of the garden city in some detail.[466] Lux believes the reasons behind creating garden cities are the urban overpopulation and rural depopulation caused by so many people migrating to work in cities. He states that people are now beginning to move back out into the countryside. Lux describes the beginnings of ideal towns springing up in many places, initiated by social organisations within industry. To him, the most significant of these is First Garden City Ltd., the company established to build Letchworth Garden City in conjunction with industries relocating to the countryside. The founding father of this movement, Ebenezer Howard, wrote in his book *Garden*

---

464 [Hans-Eduard von] Berlepsch-Valendàs und [Peter Andreas] Hansen, *Die Garten-Stadt München-Perlach* (Munich: E. Reinhardt, 1910); Berlepsch-Valendàs, *Bodenpolitik und gemeindliche Wohnungsfürsorge*; Ebenezer Howard, *Garden Cities of To-Morrow*.

465 Berlepsch-Valendàs, "Eine Studie über Städtebau". The references for the illustrations are B2-20-357, 362, 363, 364, 365 and 367 FLC.

466 Lux, *Städtebau und Grundpfeiler*, chapter entitled "Gartenstädte", pp. 96–103. See LCdv 312–320.

Fig. LI "Colonie de Hampstead." Drawing by Jeanneret, copied from Berlepsch-Valendàs, "Eine Studie über Städtebau in England – Hampstead," p. 273 (B2-20-367 FLC)

Fig. LII Enclosing wall in Hampstead. Drawing by Jeanneret, copied from Berlepsch-Valendàs, "Eine Studie über Städtebau in England – Hampstead," p. 282 (B2-20-363 FLC)

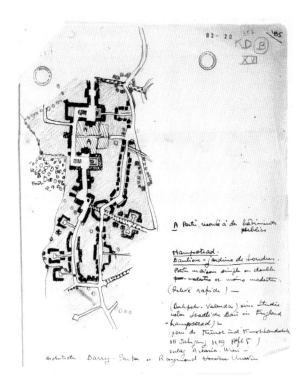

Fig. LIII "Hampstead. Banlieue-jardins de Londres." Drawing by Jeanneret, copied from Berlepsch-Valendàs, "Eine Studie über Städtebau in England – Hampstead," p. 245 (B2-20-357 FLC)

Fig. LIV Houses in Hampstead. Jeanneret, Drawing by Jeanneret, copied from Berlepsch-Valendàs, "Eine Studie über Städtebau in England – Hampstead," p. 259 (B2-20-364 FLC)

Fig. LV Houses in Hampstead. Jeanneret, Drawing by Jeanneret, copied from Berlepsch-Valendàs, "Eine Studie über Städtebau in England – Hampstead," p. 277 (B2-20-362 FLC)

Cities of To-Morrow about the possibility that these new developments would alleviate poverty among urban workers. Lux reports in detail on the establishment and planning of Letchworth: from the purchase of suitable land some 35 miles north of London, to the planned low population density of 9 people per hectare outside and 35 people per hectare inside the city, to the projected total overall population of 35,000. The city's residents would enjoy hygienic facilities, support for arable farming, and the knowledge that increased yields from the land would directly benefit them. As shareholders in First Garden City Ltd., residents would share in the profits.[467]

Lux presents the plan in great detail, showing the lay of the land and even individual trees. He is probably referring to the 1904 plan by Barry Parker and Raymond Unwin, which shows a radial street layout derived from Howard's original concentric diagrams.[468] Lux is sceptical about this type of planning and would prefer to see the principles of picturesque urban design being implemented. Yet he defends the plan in the context of the English countryside:

> In order to understand or endorse this, we need to picture in our mind's eye the wonderful English landscape with its hazy far horizons, pictures by Gainsborough. To see the city surrounded by such natural vistas, visible from the central intersection of all its streets, is an idea which has much merit.[469]

467 Lux, *Städtebau und Grundpfeiler*, p. 101.
468 See for example Standish Meacham, *Regaining Paradise: Englishness and the Early Garden City Movement* (New Haven and London: Yale University Press, 1999), pp. 95ff. and Fig. 22.
469 Lux, *Städtebau und Grundpfeiler*, p. 102.

He immediately goes on to stress that the layout of streets in other places must necessarily be different. It is not for him a question of whether straight or curved streets are more beautiful, but rather a question of laying out front gardens or grassy areas between houses and streets in accordance with the position of the sun and the prevailing wind.

> Besides the centre which was originally established, new neighbourhood centres are formed for later developments which will in turn constitute each wider district as an architectural unit. Hence a network of new garden cities will be created, all located amidst woodland and fields, separated by sufficient open space and satisfactorily connected by modern means of transport! [...] A giant park will form the focal point of the city, and schools, museums, theatres and other public buildings will have their place there.[470]

It emerges that the principle behind Unwin and Parker's plan for Letchworth is similar to that behind the Munich Waldfriedhof – both are cases in which islands of homogenous development are sited amidst untouched landscape (meadows or forest), something which Lux had advocated for cemeteries. Urban design and garden design (including cemetery design) clearly provided inspiration for one another.

It is astonishing that Jeanneret, elsewhere so thorough in his translation of this particularly woolly chapter, omitted the last page – particularly as it contains a description of the garden city, which is significant for urban design. Why would he omit precisely those few concrete lines of text that relate to architecture? Is it because this particular design does not speak to him, so he does not want to use it as an example? This omission from the translation shifts its focus onto the preservation of trees, onto landscape and onto Lux's observation that commercial urban design, built according to artistic principles, cannot fail to be healthy, fit for purpose, and beautiful.[471] This central observation turns the standard sequence of events on its head. The argument others made in the early modernist period was that fitness for purpose itself creates beauty, whereas Lux argues here that beauty creates fitness for purpose. This maps exactly onto Jeanneret's approach elsewhere in the Manuscript: he emphasises that it is the artist who will liberate people. The artist alone has the ability to make the necessary social reform movement a success, as the only one who can provide people with the prerequisites for such success: hygiene, practicability, and simple beauty.[472] Thus Lux's work foreshadows the messianic importance and world-healing powers which the modernists in general, and Le Corbusier in particular, would accord to the artist-architect.

Metzendorf – the Margarethenhöhe in Essen

The garden suburb in Essen developed by the Margarethe-Krupp-Stiftung, later dubbed the Margarethenhöhe, was of particular interest to Jeanneret (Fig.s 85–87) – as illustrated by two notes made in Cahier C.9. In one, Jeanneret states: "Read the Metzendorf brochure and the

---

470 Lux, *Städtebau und Grundpfeiler*, p. 102f.
471 Lux, *Städtebau und Grundpfeiler*, p. 103.
472 See On Possible Strategies.

catalogue for the Städtebauasstellung."[473] A few pages later, he notes: "Garden city at Essen-Metzendorf will be remarkable for the way in which its master plan is drawn, in broad sweeps, and only the part currently built has small, defined streets. Städtebau July August [1910] Tafel 46[I]."[474] This is a reference to an article by Theodor Goecke in which he summarises the events of the Berlin urban design exhibition.[475] There is scant information about the Margarethenhöhe in Goecke's article, but when combined with the illustrations Jeanneret saw in Berlin it was apparently sufficient to sustain Jeanneret's interest. In the first of his notebooks on his travels through Germany, Jeanneret made notes on the Margarethen-höhe; these appear to be a very slightly abbreviated version of Goecke's wording.[476] He also got hold of Metzendorf's brochure; thus in Cahier C.10 Jeanneret translates a significant part of the *Denkschrift* which Georg Metzendorf had written in July 1909.[477] Jeanneret translates those passages that relate to the topographical peculiarities of the settlement, to the basic design concept for its streets and marketplace, and the integration of houses and gardens.

Whereas Lux's chapter on garden cities provided more of an overview, Jeanneret found in Metzendorf's text a concise summary of almost all the major principles in mainstream contemporary urban design, using Essen as an example. As for the topo-graphical situation, a gorge separated the west of Essen from the future garden suburb. Hence, as Metzendorf describes, the first construction task was to build a bridge big enough to take trams and motor vehicles across the gorge. This bridge would set the architectural tone and be an aesthetic boon for the new suburb, linking two parts of the town while also conferring on the new suburb the status of a self-contained world, which would be both unified and secluded. This bridge was bound to be monumental, and as such should wear a crown; Metzendorf planned a large building at the entrance to the town, through which two small arcades would pass to form a powerful gateway. The mass of the building would be connected to the buildings on the outside of the suburb by the 'city walls'. Thus the suburb would only be revealed once the visitor had entered the gateway.

Two smaller pavilions flanking the bridge would further underline its powerful character, provide an aesthetic contrast to the massive construction, and act as waiting rooms for the tram. Two fountains would stand between these pavilions and the entrance to the city, with a large flight of 15 steps running between them up to the gatehouse building. To the left and

---

473 The "Metzendorf brochure" is a memorandum on the expansion of the Margarethenhöhe by Georg Metzen-dorf, *Denkschrift über den Ausbau des Stiftungsgeländes* (Essen: Petersen, 1909). On the Margarethenhöhe, see also: Rainer Metzendorf, *Margarethenhöhe – Experiment und Leitbild. 1906-1996* (Bottrop/Essen: Pomp, 1997); Rainer Metzendorf, *Georg Metzendorf – 1874-1934: Siedlungen und Bauten* (Darmstadt: His-torische Kommission für Hessen, 1994; also PhD diss., Aachen 1993); and Andreas Helfrich, *Die Margar-ethenhöhe Essen. Architekt und Auftraggeber vor dem Hintergrund der Kommunalpolitik Essen und der Firmenpolitik Krupp zw. 1886 u. 1914* (Weimar: VDG, 2000; also PhD diss Darmstadt, 1999). LCdv 320.

474 LCdv 540.

475 "Plate 46I and illustrations 29–32 show the Margarethe-Krupp-Stiftung für Wohnungsfürsorge; this was a gift from Mrs Margarethe Krupp to the city of Essen. It covers a building plot measuring some 50 hectares, a belt of woodland and parks measuring another 50 hectares, and capital of a million marks. The develop-ment is to be completed in 20 years and house 12,000-15,000 people, primarily less well-off officials, includ-ing those not working at Krupp. The architect is Georg Metzendorf in Essen." Theodor Goecke, "Allgemeine Städtebauaustellung Berlin 1910", in *Der Städtebau*, 7 (1910), no. 7/8, pp. 73–92, here p. 82.

476 "Mme Krupp donne 1 million de marks pour 1 einsiedeler [sic, for "Siedlung"] ‹Margarette Krupp für Woh-nungsfürsorge›; en plus 50 ha de terrain et 1 forêt de 50 ha. en 20 ans il sera prêt et 12000 à 15000 travail-leurs seront logés. arch. {officiel} Metzendorf. Essen – Ruhr." Le Corbusier, *Carnets de Voyage d'Allemagne*, Carnet 1, p. 77.

477 LCdv 321–325.

right, long ramps would allow vehicle access. Once inside the gate, the visitor would see a perfect city vista unfold. In order to achieve this, the road into the city would curve slightly, and the gable ends of houses would face the street according to Westphalian tradition – without eliciting a picturesque mediaeval effect. They would instead be very simple, drawing the gaze pleasantly along the street. Metzendorf describes the individual houses as being connected by a continuous narrow wall, some three metres high. There would be gardens behind the houses, but no gardens in front: this would maintain residents' peace and privacy. The calm of the beautifully designed street should not be disturbed by the trams, which would run along a different street altogether. The street starting from the gatehouse would end at the marketplace, around which the church and parsonage, pharmacy, doctor's surgery, department store, and town hall would be grouped.[478]

This is an urban design solution that is highly picturesque and heavy with symbolism, a concise combination of almost all the elements which Jeanneret describes individually in *La Construction des villes*: the gently curving street leading to a square which acts as the 'city crown' of this garden suburb. Although the houses stand alone, they are connected by walls which give the impression of an enclosed space. The gardens are behind the buildings. A 'city wall' surrounds the suburb so that it becomes an entity of itself, an enclosed domain. The gorge effectively forms a mediaeval moat, which isolates the Margarethenhöhe and adds to this effect. The city gate provides a window on the surrounding world – both in practical and symbolic terms. This is an ideal embodiment of the urban design reforms and architectural methods which *La Construction des villes* is calling for. The fact that neither Metzendorf's nor Jeanneret's text mentions the issue of industry is a coincidence, insofar as Metzendorf's Margarethenhöhe is a residential development designed partly for people working at Krupp, an industry which is already present. On the other hand, it is no coincidence given that planners at the time attempted to separate residential developments from industrial sites.

Among Jeanneret's collection of photographs from the 1910/11 period are three pictures of buildings in the Margarethenhöhe development (Fig.s LVI–LVIII). However, it is not clear when Jeanneret visited this garden suburb, since he fails to mention it in his notebooks on his travels through Germany. The only realistic possibility of a visit to Essen directly connected with his work on *La Construction des villes* was on his second journey through Germany in April 1911, yet Essen does not appear in his route description.[479] His photos may date from 1914, when he travelled to the Werkbund exhibition in Cologne.

It is remarkable how significant the Margarethenhöhe continued to be for Jeanneret. In his book *Le Corbusier's Formative Years*, Brooks shows Jeanneret's 1914 design for a garden suburb on the Cretêts site in La Chaux-de-Fonds, commissioned by the investor Arnold Beck.[480] This development was never built, but it is important to note its strong

---

478 Metzendorf, *Denkschrift*, pp. 9–18.
479 Jeanneret sketches the route he travelled in April 1911 on p. 1 in Carnet 4 of his *Carnets de Voyage d'Allemagne*. He could only have taken the detour to Essen from Hagen, because he notes: "Dusseldorf. dép. 7h soir p. Hagen Mercredi dép. matin p. Brême". On Monday, 8 May he travelled directly from Düsseldorf to Hagen around 7pm, and Jeanneret was there on Tuesday (was he meeting Karl Osthaus?), early on Wednesday he journeyed on to Bremen. In 1911 it took around 2 hours to travel from Hagen to Essen by train. The detour would therefore certainly have been possible in terms of time, but cannot actually be proved; I assume that Jeanneret made the detour *in these few days* rather than in 1910; the leaves on the trees visible in the photos would indicate it was springtime, yet in spring 1910 Jeanneret was unaware of the Margarethenhöhe and construction was not yet complete.
480 Brooks, *Formative Years*, Fig.s 292 and 293, p. 370.

Fig. LVI Houses in the Margarethenhöhe garden suburb, Essen. Photos by Jeanneret, probably 1911 (LC 108-171 – 173 BV)

Fig. LVII Houses in the Margarethenhöhe garden suburb, Essen. Photos by Jeanneret, probably 1911 (LC 108-171 – 173 BV)

Fig. LVIII Houses in the Margarethenhöhe garden suburb, Essen. Photos by Jeanneret, probably 1911 (LC 108-171 – 173 BV)

similarity to Metzendorf's Margarethenhöhe (rather than – as Brooks claims – to Hellerau; Fig.s LIX–LXII, see also Fig.s 85–87). Features clearly inspired by Margarethenhöhe include the exposed gateway in Jeanneret's garden suburb design, and the enclosing wall which both separates it from the rest of the town and links together individual buildings

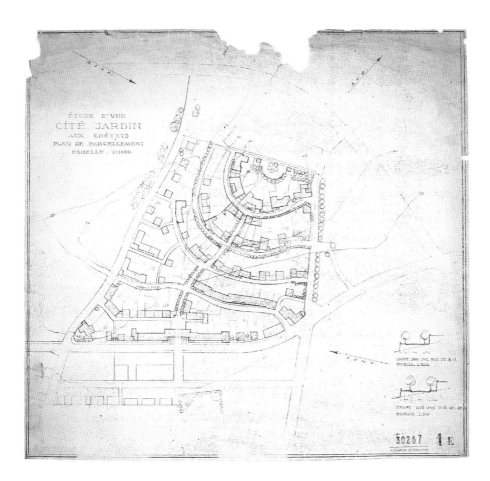

Fig. LIX Charles-Edouard Jeanneret, plan and perspective for a garden suburb on the Cretêts site, La Chaux-de-Fonds, 1914 (30267 and 30268 FLC)

and groups of buildings, which stand both parallel with the wall and with their gable ends facing it. Jeanneret's design certainly also contains ideas borrowed from other examples, such as Hampstead Garden City. Yet the main point is that, because of the exemplary way in which it fulfilled almost all the requirements Jeanneret developed while writing *La Construction des villes*, the Margaretenhöhe became a model for his later work.

Redemption through garden cities

It is safe to assume that Jeanneret did not intend to base his planned chapter On Garden Cities purely on Lux and Metzendorf, but also on descriptions of Hellerau or Hampstead. In 1910 he was very interested in these developments – Hampstead, for example, appears in the chapter On Possible Strategies. We can only speculate about Jeanneret's precise plans for the chapter, since nowhere in his Manuscript does he state which examples he actually intends to discuss. It is, however, perhaps worth comparing the texts described above with

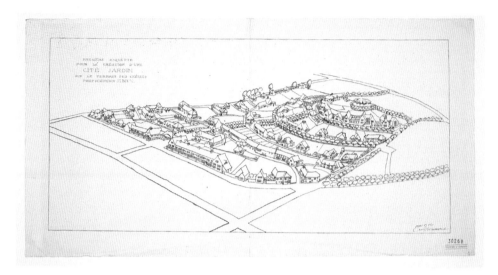

Fig. LX Charles-Edouard Jeanneret, plan and perspective for a garden suburb on the Cretêts site, La Chaux-de-Fonds, 1914 (30267 and 30268 FLC)

Fig. LXI Entry to the Margarethenhöhe garden suburb, Essen (Photos by C. Schnoor.)

Fig. LXII Entry to the Margarethenhöhe garden suburb, Essen (Photos by C. Schnoor.)

Jeanneret's 1912 *Étude sur le mouvement d'art décoratif en Allemagne*, since under the heading 'Art in the service of speculation' this contains several pages on garden cities in Germany.[481] Generally speaking, these pages can be read as an extension of *La Construction des villes*, but surprisingly not as a completion of the chapter On Garden Cities. Instead, Jeanneret's comments on garden cities focus on the economic aspects of town planning, as the heading in his *Étude* suggests. He also makes sweeping generalisations. It is surprising that Metzendorf's Margarethenhöhe, which Jeanneret considers to be an exemplary garden suburb, is not mentioned at all here. Instead, Jeanneret uses notes from his *Carnets de voyage d'Allemagne* to describe the atmosphere of a garden suburb in Berlin. In June 1910 he made comprehensive notes in Carnet 2 about his impressions of Nikolassee, a wealthy new suburb of Berlin. His concrete observations turn into general pronouncements about the role of art in life.

For Jeanneret garden cities are artistic statements which can heal people's lives, lift their morals, and improve their taste and morale. He even dreams that in future a new, stronger human race will emerge from such 'healthy' cities, which will instil "a deep, health-giving calm". During the day people wrestle with 'the infernal city', and during the evening they recover. He adds: "children raised in perfect quiet, mothers enjoying healthy nature, this is the way to develop a strong, virile people and to make immorality, languid *morbidezza*, unhealthy tastes and abnormal desires disappear." Contemporary art, with the

481 Charles-Edouard Jeanneret, *Etude sur le mouvement d'art décoratif en Allemagne* (La Chaux-de-Fonds 1912; repr. New York: Da Capo, 1968), pp. 47–51.

products of its strange imagination, will then appear to be "a peculiar mistake".[482] These words from Carnet 2 appeared in his 1912 *Étude*, in a somewhat tidier and less personal form. Jeanneret recommends the necessary housing be designed by Bruno Paul, Muthesius, or Behrens, or one of their school. "With the effect that, taking a walk one summer or spring evening in whichever one of these cities, the visitor coming from the great furnace of Berlin will be struck: he will feel himself truly living in beneficial calm." Visitors will

> think of the incomplete joys of the city, so very mixed with dissonance: exhibitions of paintings, concerts, symphonies of exhaustion and the opera. He will consider these to have been erroneous, rather like remnants of something no longer possible. He will feel the need for a more domestic, familial culture.[483]

This writing anticipates the ideal separation of city centre and suburbs, the garden city as expressed in Le Corbusier's 1925 *Ville Contemporaine*, because Jeanneret has experienced the reality of it in Berlin. In terms of Jeanneret's writing, there is an odd discrepancy between his German travel notebooks (*carnets de voyage*) and *La Construction des villes*. In the *Étude*, Jeanneret does not refer back to his work he had already done on the study of urban design; equally, there is no indication that he would have mentioned Nikolassee alongside Margarethenhöhe if *La Construction des villes* had been published. At this stage, it is not possible to explain why. However, it is possible to say that the statements on Nikolassee bear similarities to Jeanneret's outline of the Proposition, as previously discussed under the heading 'The City!'.

Des Moyens possibles – On Possible Strategies

The chapter On Possible Strategies (*Des Moyens possibles*) is closely associated with Jeanneret's chapter about their critical application to La Chaux-de-Fonds. It was therefore tempting, when ordering the material, to place On Possible Strategies

---

482 "Hier au soir, tout le long de la ligne de Nikolassee on ressentait un calme profond et bienfaisant. Une vie calme, saine, cossue, se développe autour de ces rues tracées elles-mêmes pour le repos des yeux. Il est à prévoir que dans 10 ans on fera d'admirables choses avec ces cités-jardins. Les gares sont étonnamment agencées propres et n'ayant pas 1 atome de la laideur effrayante des gares de la ville. Dans 1 telle vie, pendant le jour lutte dans l'enfer de la cité et le soir repos parfait dans 1 cité harmonieuse, – les enfants élevés dans 1 calme parfait, les mères jouissant de la saine nature, voilà de quoi développer 1 race virile et puissante, de quoi faire disparaître l'immoralité, la morbidesse les goûts malsains, les désirs peu normaux. A cela se reconnaît la grande évolution dont les arts, affirment la marche, les joies incomplètes fortement mêlées d'impressions anti-esthétiques: les expositions de peinture, les concerts, les éreintées symphoniques, et cette immense organisme de l'opéra, toutes expressions d'1 vie anormale et déséquilibrée, apparaissent alors comme 1 singulière erreur." Le Corbusier, *Carnets de Voyage d'Allemagne*, Carnet 2, p. 122–125.

483 Jeanneret, *Etude sur le mouvement d'art décoratif en Allemagne*, p. 48f.: "Les maisons seront de Muthésius ou de Bruno Paul ou de Behrens ou de la foule de leur satellites. Si bien que, se promenant un soir d'été ou de printemps dans l'une quelconque de ces cités, le visiteur qui vient de la grande fournaise berlinoise, sera frappé; il se sentira vivre vraiment dans un calme bienfaisant. Une vie saine, cossue, se développe autour de rues tracées pour le repos des yeux. Il sentira que dans dix ans on fera d'admirables choses avec ces cités-jardins, et il mesurera la répercussion certaine de cette vie nouvelle à la campagne sur les éléments mêmes de la famille; puis il pensera aux joies incomplètes de la grande ville, si fortement mêlées de dissonances: les expositions de peinture, les concerts, les éreintées symphoniques et l'opéra. Il les concevra presque comme une erreur, plutôt comme une persistance désormais impossible. Il sentira la nécessité d'une culture plus domestique, plus familiale."

after the critical application chapter. After all, in On Possible Strategies Jeanneret can also be heard criticising the authorities in charge of rebuilding La Chaux-de-Fonds in the early 19th century, and the chapter ends with his proposed solutions in terms of organisation and urban design. Yet Jeanneret himself placed this chapter before his critical application, even though it represents a synthesis which corresponds to the thesis and antithesis Jeanneret proposes as part of his dialectic, his attempt to reconcile the need for technical innovation with the need for beauty and art.[484] It was apparently more important to him that his work be presented as a progression from the general to the specific, from cities in general to La Chaux-de-Fonds in particular.

In this chapter, Jeanneret also collates many and varied sources: Viollet-le-Duc and Ruskin had already influenced his views on honesty in construction, and Ruskin (in contrast to Viollet-le-Duc) contributed to his rejection of archaeological reconstruction. Jeanneret combines his earlier convictions with his current reading of Sitte, Schultze-Naumburg, and Theodor Fischer. Other possible influences flow from the Werkbund discussion held in Berlin in 1910. Jeanneret also displays an interest in garden cities, and is influenced by sociopolitical issues from La Chaux-de-Fonds. The material for this chapter is a very interesting agglomerate, as yet raw and unpolished, a combination of contradictory ideas and tendencies. The chapter presents this material and, after some general statements on architectural theory, concludes by hailing the urban designer as a universal genius who can save society through his art.

Jeanneret is convinced that a prejudice had aggravated the ugliness of 19th-century cities: the assumption that beauty in the city was incompatible with practicality – with economy, hygiene, and functionality. He stresses that art and beauty are in fact compatible with all three of these objectives, not only in theory but also in practice, as can be seen in the examples of reforms in England and Germany. In order to illustrate this compatibility of art and economy, Jeanneret lists some examples of construction solutions which he has already described in the course of his Manuscript: the best block shape for optimising the use of space; integrating churches, schools, and other public buildings into the block; piercing the block with public passageways; accepting curved street design in order to avoid problems with expropriation and reallocation of land; dealing with the existing topography instead of levelling the land; and preserving the available trees to avoid costly replanting. He states that these measures will in turn have a positive influence on hygiene: creating large, green courtyard spaces within the block; keeping schoolrooms away from the noise and dust of the street; foiling the wind with curved or arcaded streets; improving the orientation of buildings on their sites by following the topography; and siting smoking factory chimneys all together, thus leaving residential areas with clean air. These positive solutions were not available to the old urban design system.[485]

Jeanneret asks how a traditional planner can successfully combine the many elements that make a town or city: the picturesque, monumental, and nuanced with the purely functional? Although many planners aimed to create clear and simple images, Jeanneret laments an oversimplification which caused them to overlook contours which

---

484 This chapter contains 27 manuscript pages. The first nine pages of text are a fair copy made by Jeanneret's mother. The following 18 pages are a rough draft, with many of Jeanneret's crossings-out, additions, and improvements. There is some overlap between this rough draft and the pages of fair copy.

485 LCdv 327f.

provide vital information on a three-dimensional plot. He notes that contours have always been taken into account when competitions are held in Germany, as per the reports in the journal *Städtebau*. He believes a model drawing including contours is indispensable to good planning, and a model of the terrain is also a useful means of considering all the conditions on the site, such as exposure to light and wind, during the planning process.[486]

Jeanneret considers his own age to be full of promise: there is a need for urban expansion on an unprecedented and monumental scale. If this were left to chance, it would create great confusion; he thinks chance has already ruined many aspects of the city. And although some picturesque situations have arisen by chance in the past, nobody has yet ascertained how such beauty arose. Jeanneret also notes that there has been a break with the artistic tradition of the past; a lack of rigour nowadays would no longer elicit beauty. Instead, a logical programme is now needed in order to define the future needs of the general public.[487] This is a statement from Johann Hubatschek's *Bautechnische Aufgaben einer modernen Stadt* which Jeanneret had already used for his introduction. Hubatschek refers to a landmark general assembly of the *Verband deutscher Architekten- und Ingenieurvereine* (alliance of German architects' and engineers' associations) in 1874:

> This was a concise dismissal of all preset grid systems, and thus a decisive step towards improvement, although the assumption that chance would now bring about beauty in and of itself, as it had in days gone by, is a great mistake since the former, solid artistic tradition no longer exists generally, and thus disorder and confusion would arise.[488]

Hubatschek's statement is itself a reaction to Sitte: in fact he adopts Sitte's text almost word for word, if somewhat abbreviated.[489] We could conclude that Jeanneret adopted this text directly from Sitte, but in fact this is not the case: Jeanneret noted down these precise lines by Hubatschek in Cahier *City III*, with a citation.[490] Yet it is entirely possible that Jeanneret was indeed aware that he had read Sitte's words from two different sources – a comment he made between the lines here at a later stage refers to Sitte.[491]

Jeanneret complains that planning officials are sadly indifferent to the possibilities their own discipline offers. For example, a district of the town which was particularly

---

486 LCdv 331–333.

487 LCdv 334.

488 Hubatschek, *Bautechnische Aufgaben*, p. 11. In the preceding paragraph Hubatschek mentions that the following principles were agreed by the general assembly of the *Verband deutscher Architekten- und Ingenieurvereine* in Berlin in 1874. First, a project for expanding a city consists primarily of establishing the main transport layout. Initially, the road network thus established should cover the main roads, taking into account existing route choices. The different districts should be arranged by reinforcing their character and individuality.

489 See Sitte, *Der Städtebau*, p. 135-138.

490 LCdv 442: "[Assumption that, even today,] chance would bring beauty all on its own, as in the olden days: grave mistake, for today there are no longer, as in the past, solid artistic traditions among the populace, und ein wildes Durcheinander die Folge wäre [and a confused pell-mell would be the result]." Jeanneret notes down the name Hubatschek immediately before this quotation.

491 Sitte goes into detail about the necessary preparations for expanding a city, and emphasises the need for a precise programme. Jeanneret refers to pages 150–156 and 157 of the French version of Sitte. This corresponds to pages 279 to 297 in the English translation.

well suited to becoming a garden suburb would suddenly find itself occupied by a factory and associated buildings – just because an industrialist had the bright idea of buying that particular land. Jeanneret could not understand why municipal administrations did not prevent such things from happening. This is a direct reference to events in La Chaux-de-Fonds, which he details in his Critical Application.[492] When a town or city is expanded, Jeanneret would not advocate scattering key buildings throughout the area. Instead, he believes it is better to group these together harmoniously around a particularly well-situated square, as can be seen in older settlements.[493] He cites as an example the town of Breisach, whose minster and major buildings have been gathered on a cliff overlooking the Rhine since the middle ages (Fig.s 88 and 89).

Jeanneret goes on to discuss the contemporary example of Hampstead Garden Suburb: the suburb was built by those most modern of architects Parker, Unwin, and Scott, on a large hillside site. The groups or individual buildings follow the rules for good urban design discussed in the previous chapters, and the top of the hill provides a large area reserved for the public buildings which will be required as Hampstead develops – a site for buildings suited to a monumental layout.[494] Jeanneret's source for these concrete facts was an essay by Hans-Eduard von Berlepsch-Valendàs about Hampstead, from which he carefully traced several illustrations (Fig.s LI–LV).[495] Going into greater detail about the issue of grouping buildings, Jeanneret argues the benefits of a collective society in which labour unions, being closer to the people than the government, act as a second governing body.[496] These new executive agencies of the public's will would be situated close to the established institutions. This would benefit all concerned, precisely because individuals required increasing involvement in public life. It would therefore be logical for all public services in the city to be concentrated in a single *bloc massif* – a large block or cube. Each institution could monitor and oversee the others, bureaucratic procedures could be speeded up, citizens could find the right institution more quickly.[497]

Next, Jeanneret turns somewhat abruptly to a long quotation dealing with the silhouette of the city. He notes on a separate sheet a passage by Georges de Montenach, who is astonished that contemporary architects have largely failed to consider or investigate the silhouette cast by a city – despite the aesthetic value of the city lying at least as much in its overall impression as in the details. Creating a silhouette necessarily meant reserving particular plots for particular buildings at specific heights.[498] Jeanneret then outlines a fascinating architectural vision of a cluster comprising public utilities, which could translate Montenach's discussion of the silhouette into reality:

> The principle of grouping public buildings were adopted, one could assume the growth likely to occur, one could design on a template all the services which would be grouped there in line with the close connections between them. The site deemed

492 See Critical Application.
493 The second part of On Possible Strategies exists as two parallel drafts; it is hard to tell which one is the 'final' version. The differences between the two lie beyond the scope of this study.
494 LCdv 337.
495 Berlepsch-Valendàs, *Eine Studie über Städtebau in England*.
496 LCdv 339.
497 LCdv 340.
498 LCdv 341. Montenach 1908, p. 188. Jeanneret has not worked any quotations from Montenach into his text; these remain separate. Many sheets containing quotations from Montenach, which Jeanneret plans to use for his Critical Application: La Chaux-de-Fonds, can be found in the annex to the Manuscript.

the most practical would be indicated, which would allow the most beautiful solution, and building would begin as and when required. The years would pass, bringing new buildings or successive floors, and all would respect the template as adopted. The work would complete itself, taking on a complexity as a unit due to the nuanced styles that reference the progress or regression during the periods when they were created. Then, finally, a powerful block would be born – this beauty, admired everywhere in famous cities: variety in an imposing unity. Thus the dimensions of this cube with multiple purposes would become colossal. The city would once again have its acropolis, once again its piazzetta, once again its Burg [...] – and [...] the city could be proud of itself.[499]

The picture Jeanneret paints here is so striking because it anticipates, in its own way, Bruno Taut's model of a *Stadtkrone* (city crown).[500] It also foreshadows the design of the *Unité d'habitation* and the Villa Savoye, two examples by Le Corbusier of internal diversity within external unity. Furthermore, it brings to mind other complex constructions within a unified shell: historical precedents such as the Basilica of Santa Maria Maggiore in Rome or John Soane's Bank of England in London. One possible precursor to this architectural vision of a growing group of buildings might be the École d'Horlogerie in La Chaux-de-Fonds (Fig. LXIII). Jeanneret's wording can (with some reservations) be traced back to Theodor Fischer, who in his lecture *Stadterweiterungsfragen* lists precisely those buildings that effect the city's skyline and community as a whole (an acropolis, citadel, etc.). However, Fischer doubts that the image of the Acropolis could be transposed onto the modern city skyline:

> It is of course hardly possible for a modern metropolis, an incalculable colossus, to form a single unit in the same way ancient cities could form one with their acropolis, their citadel or their minster, or in the way many of our small towns and villages can still be seen as unified today, with houses huddled at the foot of the church like a flock around its shepherd.[501]

Jeanneret is himself designing as he writes: although he addresses the examples of Hampstead and Breisach, which he clearly uses as role models to some extent, the conclusion he comes to is somewhat different. In his introduction he repeatedly writes of public buildings distributed throughout the city like landmarks. Yet now he speaks of the requirement for "complexité dans l'unité", "la variété dans unité l'imposante": complexity and diversity within a unified whole.[502]

Jeanneret then refers once again to the open space created around the Minster in Ulm and the destruction of the square there. He says it is essential to show existing buildings due respect, although the general public is often unclear how to express such respect. Should existing buildings be made safe, restored, or even expanded and completed? "Or must they let them, the old works, die their beautiful death gently, without troubling

499 LCdv 342f.
500 Bruno Taut: *Die Stadtkrone* (Jena: Diederichs, 1919; repr., Berlin: Gebr. Mann, 2002). An English version of Taut's own text in his anthology was translated by Ulrike Altenmüller and Matthew Mindrup, published in *Journal of Architectural Education*, 63, 1 (2009), pp. 121–134.
501 Fischer, *Stadterweiterungsfragen*, p. 9.
502 LCdv 342f.

Fig. LXIII Ecole d'Horlogerie in La Chaux-de-Fonds. Photo, ca. 1900 (P2-76 BV)

them in their death throes?"[503] Jeanneret states that older buildings should certainly be removed in cases where their replacement would be more beautiful, and where the old building no longer meets modern requirements. However, he believes this principle, which has applied for such a long time, has been transformed in the present day to an overly rigid menace, given the almost total lack of artistic feeling. Today the cornerstone of *convenance*, of what is artistically appropriate, has disappeared.

Jeanneret believes the situation is different when it comes to adapting buildings that are no longer fit for purpose. Here, great sensitivity is required. Germany had already acknowledged how useful urban design competitions were for this: rather than a single architect offering his solution, a choice could be made from among many proposals as to the best way of dealing with the building in question. Jeanneret is convinced that, where a competent jury is available, a competition provides the best means of achieving good solutions to such problems. He cites as an example the city of Munich, which planned to change the use of the former Augustiner-stock monastery near the Frauenkirche, and announced a design competition in 1909. Theodor Fischer undertook the conversion of this monastery into the police headquarters.[504]

---

503 LCdv 344.
504 LCdv 345f. See the essay "Wettbewerb Augustinerstock München", in *Süddeutsche Bauzeitung* 19 (1909), no. 27, pp. 209–214; no. 28, pp. 217–223. Fischer only won third prize, but was ultimately commissioned to implement the solution.

Very often, Jeanneret complains, professionals with insufficient training make decisions to 'release' old buildings, 'regulate' city centres, and straighten curved streets, all in the name of functionality; they plan precisely right-angled squares in the name of beauty.[505] Just as the building administrations have no respect for art, they fail to respect the lay of the land. Art and respecting the topography appear to be incompatible with construction as it is currently organised.[506] However, although this was alien to the grid-focused administrative planners of the present day, the example of Carlsbad (now Karlovy Vary) showed that planners of buildings had in the past adapted them to the landscape instinctively. Jeanneret finds common ground with Schultze-Naumburg here in his astonishment at how the planners of new towns sometimes design streets too steep and straight for vehicles to use. One could be sure that in such cases the issue was not particularly unfavourable terrain, but particularly poor planning.[507] Jeanneret continues by explaining:

> No longer do either a respect for the beauty of land or a respect for what that land requires instil fear in our geometers, blinded by unacceptable procedure. We say that the beauty of a town, the fruit of properly adapting all utilitarian, public well-being and aesthetic requirements, can only be realised by artists: men who feel the deep-seated responsibility of a vocation where men are passionate about this cause.[508]

Thus the artist, the universal genius, must save the city from the technocrats' iron grip. This is where Sitte's theories combine with Jeanneret's idealism and sense of his own greatness, his vocation. With his praise of city builders here, Jeanneret once again moves into the territory he occupied in the General Considerations at the beginning of the Manuscript. City planners must be equipped with the perceptions and sensibilities of a painter, but the strength of a sculptor.

> In order to undertake this arduous task, men must have noble souls. For their thankless labour demands a constant sacrifice. Their work will not be completed until years after they designed it. [...] In order to foreshadow a town's future, to discern the sense of forward progress and to satisfy it, they need the spirit of the age with modernist ideas, and a broad imagination. If we are to both change and respect the leftover beauty from ages past, then extreme tact and great knowledge of the laws of beauty will be required. In order to design beautiful streets, beautiful squares, to dictate the proper building height and proportions, to design those moving screens of buildings with changing perspectives, to balance the cubes of buildings in a proper relationship, in mutual interrelation and in a proper quantity given the voids of the walls, squares and gardens one needs a painter's sensibility, a sculptor's power.[509]

This is of course a rather lofty view of the work which Theodor Fischer achieved in Munich, but it is also – more importantly – Jeanneret's description of the professional role he himself hopes to fulfil in future.

---

505 See LCdv 345–348.
506 LCdv 348.
507 LCdv 349. See Cahier 2, LCdv 410; Jeanneret is quoting excerpts from Schultze-Naumburg, *Kulturarbeiten Städtebau*, p. 184.
508 LCdv 349.
509 LCdv 351f.

As indicated above, it is more difficult to discern the direct sources for the material here than it was with the chapters on urban design elements in the city. Jeanneret makes frequent reference to the journal *Der Städtebau*, yet most of his references are general and do not cite a particular article. Some passages could have been inspired by Henrici or Brinckmann. The main speaker in the debate on whether beauty and functionality can be combined in urban design was not Sitte but Theodor Fischer – but Jeanneret had not taken any extracts from his text *Stadterweiterungsfragen* before he drafted On Possible Strategies. It is therefore difficult to state the exact extent to which Jeanneret knew Fischer's arguments at the time he was writing. What is clear is that on major considerations, in particular those relating to improving the culture of planning, Jeanneret certainly references Camillo Sitte.

Application Critique – La Chaux-de-Fonds: A case study

In a sense, the last chapter of the Manuscript, about La Chaux-de-Fonds, is the key to understanding the whole work. In the search for material for his study, Jeanneret was guided by his own experiences and observations: by the plan of La Chaux-de-Fonds, with all its artistic and practical disadvantages. In order to elucidate Jeanneret's criticisms of La Chaux-de-Fonds, we will need to describe in greater detail both the town and how it formed.

La Chaux-de-Fonds is one of the main watchmaking centres in Switzerland, alongside Geneva and Biel/Bienne (Fig. LXIV); its population of 40, 000 has remained fairly stable since the early 20th century. Situated in the Jura mountains, in a high-lying valley around 1,000 metres above sea level, the town is secluded due to both its geographical and political situations. The river Doubs a few kilometres to the west of the town marks the border with France, while the folds of the Jura to the east separate the town from Neuchâtel, situated at an altitude some 600 metres lower on Lake Neuchâtel. Watchmaking has been established in the region's valleys since the late 17th century. Around 1790, La Chaux-de-Fonds and the neighbouring town of Le Locle employed some 3,500 people in watchmaking. In 1794 the town centre burnt down, destroying over 50 houses. A reconstruction plan was published immediately after the fire and is attributed to Moïse Perret-Gentil. This plan contained the essence of the later, grid-based expansion of the town; over the following 60 years, increasingly systematic planning was established, extending outwards in lines from the irregular centre, with streets running along the valley from the north-east to the south-west. Two plans were drawn up which prioritised infrastructure planning over aesthetic considerations: fire prevention had been a central tenet of construction in La Chaux-de-Fonds since 1794.[510] The first plan was by Charles-Henri Junod, inspector of bridges and roadways for the Principality of Neuchâtel (in 1835), the second by Charles Knab, engineer for the Canton of Neuchâtel (in around 1856). In their history of La Chaux-de-Fonds, Jean-Marc Barrelet and Jacques Ramseyer emphasise the importance of water supply:

---

510 See Jacques Gubler, "La Chaux-de-Fonds", in *Inventar der Neueren Schweizer Architektur. 1850-1920. Vol. 3* (Berne: Gesellschaft für Schweizerische Kunstgeschichte, 1982), p. 142f., and Brooks, *Le Corbusier's Formative Years*, p. 6f.

Fig. LXIV Rue Léopold-Robert in La Chaux-de-Fonds. Photo, ca. 1900 (P3-37 BV)

Water supply has always posed a problem in this mountain town and has become, if not a myth, then certainly a recurring theme in the history of La Chaux de Fonds. In this place where the great fire of 1794 is constantly remembered and commemorated, water is seen as the antidote to fire, and also as the great purifier, the element which will purge the town of its endemic diseases. Yet water plays an ambivalent role, in that it is also the vector for the main epidemics. Clean water therefore had the task of freeing the town from its miasma, its chronic insalubrity.[511]

La Chaux-de-Fonds has no natural supply of fresh water, so this was the main concern for the town's founding fathers until the end of the 19th century.

Bore holes were drilled, without great results; plans were outlined to convey water from the Taillères lake or the river Doubs. The idea of digging a large artificial lake was even proposed. Finally, a solution advocated by engineer Guillaume Ritter proposed that water be drawn from springs located in the Areuse gorges, near Noirai-gue, and conveyed to a large reservoir above the town via an ascending pipeline

---

511 Jean-Marc Barrelet and Jacques Ramseyer, *La Chaux-de-Fonds ou le défi d'une cité horlogère. 1848-1914* (La Chaux-de-Fonds: Editions d'En Haut, 1990), p. 104.

several kilometres long, rising from 600 to over 1,100 metres. [...] The arrival of
running water in 1887 captured people's imagination; the celebrations were impressive; the Bureau de contrôle donated a monumental fountain, a new symbol for the
town erected at the entrance to Rue Léopold-Robert.[512]

In the three decades between Knab's plan and the opening of the water pipeline in 1887,
the town swiftly took on its present shape – which Jeanneret criticised so passionately in
1910. According to Barrelet and Ramseyer, the inhabitants insisted on continuing to call
the town a village until the early 20th century, although it had been growing for over 50
years. They suggest the residents were afraid of losing their traditions:

> Uprooted, as if pushed out of their home town by the new population flowing in,
> they fear they will no longer command this place which used to belong to them.
> Others heap praise instead on this 'watchmaking metropolis', this American town
> they designed, as a challenge they threw down to the world. [...] the residents of La
> Chaux-de-Fonds have built their own history and that of their town, with the inten-
> tion of participating directly in the life of their era. They were moved by a desire to
> build an unrivalled town. These patriotic mountain-dwellers, models of republican
> virtue and obstinacy, had faith in progress and the ideologies which underpin it.
> They gave of their best to ensure that this village became a town worthy of
> admiration.[513]

The 'American' look to La Chaux-de-Fonds' layout is due to its streets being arranged
into a right-angled grid which measures a constant 25 by 40 or 60 metres. Combined
with straight rows of buildings four storeys high occupying only the downhill side of
streets running lengthways, the town takes on the character of a somewhat utopian city.
This makes Le Corbusier's later quest for ideal urban solutions seem logical, even perhaps necessary. The 'utopian' impression is also created by La Chaux-de-Fonds' isolated
position. Even today, this town without suburbs contrasts sharply with its natural surroundings, a low mountain landscape which varies from undulating to rugged. Visitors
get the impression that this town is alone in the world; Le Corbusier's *Ville Contemporaine* and subsequent projects recapture this spirit of a place centred on itself. Another
fascinating aspect of La Chaux-de-Fonds is that this town, which lives to a very great
extent from watchmaking and other mechanical industries, still houses its manufacturing
and smaller businesses in the town centre in between residential buildings, shops, and
offices. This town has become truly mixed-use, a quality which Le Corbusier did not
particularly value. Indeed, Le Corbusier was, and would remain, convinced by the idea
that buildings should be separated according to their use – an idea from progressive
German reformist urban design at the turn of the century – despite later distancing himself from that movement's other ideas.

The young Jeanneret was a long way from that view. His Critical Application begins
by quoting two lengthy passages from Paul Schultze-Naumburg's *Kulturarbeiten Städte
bau* criticising small towns which insist on using plans based on those of major cities.[514]

---

512 Barrelet and Ramseyer, *La Chaux-de-Fonds*, p. 106.
513 Barrelet and Ramseyer, *La Chaux-de-Fonds*, p. 13.
514 Schultze-Naumburg, *Kulturarbeiten Städtebau*, p. 168f.

Jeanneret plans to apply Schultze-Naumburg's approach to La Chaux-de-Fonds, showing good and bad examples of the same urban design situation. He also intends to present solutions that succeed using simple methods and simultaneously represent good urban design. Jeanneret constructs the chapter on La Chaux-de-Fonds in parallel to his Elements of the City in the first part of the Manuscript, and discusses each of these Elements in turn in relation to his home town: trees and parks, streets, residential blocks, enclosing walls, and squares. Here, as previously, he subdivides each of the themes into different categories. Using the argument he had previously set out, Jeanneret criticises the urban design of La Chaux-de-Fonds. He only picks up on negative aspects; at the end he briefly discusses the villa districts. The chapter then stops abruptly.

This last section is backed up with his collection of quotations from Schultze-Naumburg (in Cahier C.2). These introductory quotations from Schultze-Naumburg's *Kulturarbeiten Städtebau* (abbreviated here) are as follows:

> What are known as "the regulations" sound the death knell for harmonious old city layouts. [...] The main cause of all this regulatory nonsense is the founding fathers of our cities losing all sense of lively form and no longer recognising anything worthy of reverence in the traditional traits of their home cities. Instead, parvenus that they are, they are ashamed of the simplicity, and focus all their attention on assimilating into the sought-after 'metropolis'. They imagine that everything there is lovely and straight and regular. Yet the only way of achieving such a marvellous goal is with new building lines. Since as long as the building lines retain the shape of life, the rows of houses can never be arranged as beautifully as a front of soldiers. What is more, the streets must be as wide as those in major cities, since 'metropolitan traffic' is an idea that rumbles and buzzes around and around in everyone's brains.[515]

These quotations reflect the main content of the chapter on efforts to straighten streets and open up layouts ("Begradigungsbestrebungen und Freilegungen") in *Kulturarbeiten Städtebau*, which Jeanneret uses to prepare the ground for his critical remarks on La Chaux-de-Fonds. In these lines by Schultze-Naumburg, everything 'metropolitan' becomes inimical to good town planning, and he therefore ridicules small towns all the more in their attempts to adopt metropolitan forms.

Having stated his position, Jeanneret records the history of reconstruction in La Chaux-de-Fonds after the great fire of 1794. Apparently the new reconstruction plan for the town had already been established just three weeks after the fire.[516] Reconstruction was based on the elongated rectilinear grid model discussed above, which ran parallel to the valley floor (Fig. 92). Jeanneret emphasises that this produced a few streets which were excessively long and ran dead straight, parallel to the contours, plus many short cross streets linking these – some of which climbed an enormous vertical height due to their orientation. Except for a few diagonal streets, the entire reconstructed part of the town, which comprises over two-thirds of it, obeys this principle.

Jeanneret also describes the intersecting streets and other disadvantages of the grid-based plan as implemented in La Chaux-de-Fonds. It is clear from his previous chapters what he

---

515 Schultze-Naumburg, *Kulturarbeiten Städtebau*, p. 165ff. See LCdv 406–408.
516 Brooks proves that Jeanneret is wrong on this. See Brooks, *Le Corbusier's Formative Years*, note 6, p. 6f.

considers these to be: open squares, open parks, and a complete absence of public buildings which are well situated from an architectural perspective.[517] His greatest criticism in relation to this plan is that the logical urban design principles which had previously been applied are now being ignored. For example, residents had created paths at a diagonal to the rigid rectilinear axes originated by the planners, running from the middle of the valley to the mountain ridge. Furthermore, Jeanneret is disappointed that, although trees only grow slowly in the mountain climate, the new plan for the city sacrifices many trees, and it leaves only three relatively large parks in the town. He promises to include a series of illustrations comparing urban design situations in La Chaux-de-Fonds with parallel constellations in towns which treat artistic sensibilities with respect. He avoids selecting illustrations showing magnificent monuments here, because he wants to demonstrate that a town can satisfy artistic criteria even on a limited budget.[518] Jeanneret had written to a series of Swiss towns and asked them to send suitable pictures, but received only poor postcards in return and was therefore obliged to fall back on his own travel shots.[519] The comparisons between good and poor examples clearly draw on Schultze-Naumburg and his practice of comparing pictures: Jeanneret had found this exemplary during his in-depth reading of *Kulturarbeiten Städtebau*.

The expansion of La Chaux-de-Fonds was not complete by 1910; Jeanneret speculated that the future would merely bring an extension of the existing pattern:

> Hundreds of straight streets, and all of uniformly, eternally equal width. On both sides of the valley, all the streets form perspective lines, never enclosed, and continue to be oriented exactly in the direction of the very strongest wind: west-east. In summer, everyone complains about the swirls of dust which rage on days when the foehn blows. In winter, nothing stops the flurries of snow. Quite the reverse, the streets channel the wind which sweeps through without encountering the least obstacle. We have seen that, in all the towns where enclosed aspects had created comfort and beauty, straight streets of medium width were very short. 500-metre lengths were rarely seen.[520]

Jeanneret compiles a list in which he compares the streets running parallel to the valley floor in La Chaux-de-Fonds in terms of how straight they are, and details their current and future length.[521] He establishes that none of the public buildings in the town has been well staged from an architectural point of view. Almost all of them – schools, town hall, etc. – are distributed seemingly at random throughout the town's grid structure and therefore fail to stand out. Jeanneret states that the spatial effect of the intersecting streets suffers from the fact that the blocks built lengthways only occupy one side of the street, and a sort of courtyard garden occupies the downhill side, precluding any continuity in the cross-street fronts. Furthermore, the cross streets certainly enjoy an enclosed perspective, but the

---

517 LCdv 361–363.
518 LCdv 366.
519 Our reconstruction of the Manuscript has necessarily been based on speculation in this respect. Jeanneret does of course mention some travel photos, many of which show German cities. What is unclear is how he planned to compare these with situations in La Chaux-de-Fonds; further research would be required to establish this. See Gresleri, *Reise nach dem Orient*, for example pp. 131–146. BV LCi 1-589.
520 LCdv 368.
521 LCdv 369f.

impact of this is unsatisfactory because the buildings at the ends of the streets do not exploit the design possibilities which their architecture provides.[522] Generally speaking, hilly situations such as that in La Chaux-de-Fonds provide opportunities for many attractive urban design situations. Yet the grid system robs the town of these opportunities, and many ugly situations arise as a result.[523] He translates a quotation from Schultze-Naumburg's *Kulturarbeiten Städtebau* on this issue in Cahier C.2: "The steep slope of certain streets can cause astonishment. When this is the case, we can be sure that this is not due to an especially unfavourable site, but rather to a design by a poor dilettante."[524]

Jeanneret takes stock of the present and future of public squares in La Chaux-de-Fonds. Two old squares, the Place de l'Hôtel-de-Ville and Place du Marché, are successful on the whole. However, one new type of square is created simply by omitting to build on one block and designating it as a square, without making any further architectural effort:

> Neither the land nor the orientation nor the buildings which border it have been considered. [...] The Place de l'Ouest provides the least advantageous plan we have identified for a small town square, and its fountain placed in the geometric centre is a sort of signature for official building works. Hence all future squares in La Chaux-de-Fonds will be of this type, where 8 streets open up all 4 corners of the square.[525]

Jeanneret next turns to the question of presenting a public building within a square: he distinguishes between three concrete examples. The first sees a prominent, detached building placed in the middle of a plot which requires four identical and costly façades to be built. In addition, the large areas of open space surrounding the building make it look smaller, and disconnect it from its surroundings. Furthermore, the building fails to contribute to the perspective of the street. A second possibility lies in the detached building occupying one end of a block. The results are similar to those in the previous case. The third option used in La Chaux-de-Fonds is to slot a building in between two others. In this case, only two façades are required: but even here the building contributes nothing to the quality of the street.[526] He concludes that not one of the expensive public buildings in the town contributes anything to its overall attractiveness, since none of the streets is curved enough to provide a suitable backdrop for the building, and because none of the squares is designed in such a way that the building can be seen properly and perceived in particular.[527]

The chapter then ends abruptly in the middle of a sentence quoted from an unknown source. The first half of the sentence indicates Jeanneret's attitude towards urban design (which would also be Le Corbusier's): "The difficulty is: 'Freedom in city planning is anarchy, and as long as the public authorities fail to act, [...]'."[528] Here, Jeanneret

---

522 LCdv 373.
523 LCdv 375.
524 LCdv 410. See Schultze-Naumburg, *Kulturarbeiten Städtebau*, p. 184.
525 LCdv 376.
526 LCdv 377f.
527 LCdv 378.
528 LCdv 380.

brings anarchic designs together in an uneasy coalition with his criticism of the authorities' technical and grid-based thinking. The only conclusion one can draw from this is that the state must use its power to promote greater aesthetic flexibility for urban design, and that for their part architects must make more effort to integrate their work into the overall concept.

The Annex to the loose-leaf folder

This annex consists of a collection of sheets which do not initially appear to belong together. There are 41 pages, covering a wide variety of document types. Some are outlines of text for other chapters (for example a plan to expand On Blocks by adding the journal article about designing semi-detached houses for cities, "Zweifamilienhäuser für Großstädte"), there is a single excerpt from the French edition of Sitte's *Künstlerische Städtebau*, and there are letters and notes. Yet Jeanneret also notes down extracts from Georges de Montenach, *Pour le visage aimé de la patrie!*. Montenach was an enthusiastic supporter of the Heimatschutz movement:

> The Germans have in their rich vocabulary an untranslatable word [...]. It describes perfectly the goal of those who are striving to combat ugliness: the word is Heimatschutz. I like this word because it states our intention, defines it overall; because it provides something immediate to speak to one's intellect as well as one's heart.[529]

Jeanneret's excerpts from Montenach are highly interesting, although the vast majority of the quotations merely serve to confirm or reinforce material which Jeanneret has already drafted for his study. The similarity between Montenach's arguments and Schultze-Naumburg's is undeniable – there is clearly a reason why Montenach used the German word 'Heimatschutz' despite writing in French. His book offers Jeanneret fewer direct new insights than his other reading material on urban design does, not least because Montenach was primarily interested in politicising aesthetic arguments in order to win over his compatriots to his cause.

However, Jeanneret demonstrates a strong interest in the natural beauty of Swiss farmhouses which goes beyond what he has read on urban questions to date – and he therefore finds himself strangely suspended between L'Eplattenier's efforts to create a regional Jura style and William Ritter's romanticised anthropological interest in the authenticity displayed by the Slavic peoples. This can be illustrated with a single quotation, which also prepares the ground for a statement Jeanneret was to make when he returned from Istanbul:

> Say that there is no education in schools, that local architecture is not understood because not publicly revealed – quite the reverse – that many readers in La Chaux-

---

529 "Les Allemands possèdent, dans leur riche vocabulaire, un mot intraduisable en français et qui qualifie d'une manière parfaite le but que poursuivent les ennemis de la Laideur: c'est le mot Heimatschutz. Je l'aime ce mot, parce qu'il précise notre action, parce qu'il la définit dans son ensemble, parce qu'il lui donne quelque chose qui frappe immédiatement l'intelligence et le cœur." Montenach, *Pour le visage aimé de la patrie*, p. 466.

de-Fonds will smile when they hear us state: cubic buildings without sculptures are beautiful, and they are beautiful in our town.[530]

Yet Jeanneret failed to finalise his chapter on La Chaux-de-Fonds. Not only does it end mid-sentence, but he also omits the most important part, namely his own proposed improvements for selected parts of the town. Most of these proposals can be found as outlines in the Annex: the design to build a market hall surrounded by arcades on the Place du Marché (Fig. 112); the plan to enclose the long, straight Rue Léopold-Robert (Fig. LXV, Fig. 114) – which obviously harks back to Jeanneret's visit to the square before the church of St. Ulrich in Augsburg; several visual conclusions for small cross streets; and last but not least the design for the station square which will transform all the buildings into an enclosed ensemble, closely following Sitte's proposed improvements to the ring road in Vienna (Fig. 115).[531] It may be interesting to compare Jeanneret's design for a station square with its counterpart in Raymond Unwin's *Town Planning in Practice*, which shapes the space using a semi-circular construction in baroque style in a very similar way (Fig.s VII,

Fig. LXV St. Ulrich in Augsburg. Postcard, owned by Jeanneret (LC-105-1112-28 BV)

---

530 LCdv 385.

531 These designs have already been published in several places, including for the exhibition *La Chaux-de-Fonds avant Le Corbusier* (La Chaux-de-Fonds, 1987), and in Brooks, *Le Corbusier's Formative Years*, p. 206. Several previously unpublished precursors to Jeanneret's station square design also exist, dotted throughout Cahiers 2, 3 and 4: see LCdv 418, 438 and 402.

VIII).[532] Since Jeanneret lists Unwin's work in his bibliography but does not cite it, there is no evidence that he was aware of this design. However, the similarity between the two is so great that Unwin's design may well have provided inspiration for Jeanneret.

A draft table of contents, indicating that the chapter about La Chaux-de-Fonds was to be expanded, has already been introduced above. This draft can be found in the middle of the Annex.[533] It is not clear whether the chapter on La Chaux-de-Fonds was to have two contrasting parts or whether other parts would be added, for instance a section on garden cities and a conclusion. However, in the Annex, Jeanneret labels a series of pages 'Ch de Fds II', 'La Chaux de Fds II chap.' or 'Ch-de-Fds Chap. II'. This gives credence to the assumption that Jeanneret planned to write two chapters on La Chaux-de-Fonds. Besides the first, analytical chapter, a second would then have been added in which Jeanneret would propose improvements, and also present general stances on preserving local Swiss traditions. Thus although it is missing from the Manuscript, the groundwork for Jeanneret's outlook on the future is prepared in his notes in the Annex.

---

532 See Raymond Unwin: *Town Planning in Practice*, Fig. 117, p. 173.
533 LCdv 522.

Chapter 3

1911 to 1925

Towards urbanism

The Laugier excerpt as a turning point

Our analysis of the Manuscript itself, as composed by Jeanneret, ended when we looked at the chapter Critical Application: La Chaux-de-Fonds. However, one of his cahiers deserves particular attention, as it seems to occupy a unique position between *La Construction des villes* and *Urbanisme*. This is where Jeanneret presents extracts from Marc Antoine Laugier's *Essai sur l'architecture*, published in Paris in 1753. Laugier's theories played an important role in Jeanneret's later life: his development of the *Maison Dom-Ino* in 1914/15 can be seen as a contemporary interpretation of Laugier's primitive hut. It is therefore significant from a wider historical perspective that Jeanneret studied Laugier's *Essai* in early 1911 (Fig. 122).[1] In the context of his work on *La Construction des villes*, he did not read the *Essai* as a manifesto of classicism, as it is sometimes considered today, but rather as a tract rich in urban design proposals.[2] Hence he takes thorough excerpts from Laugier's urban design ideas, which occupy a large part of the *Essai*.

Jeanneret finds that Laugier's text covers most of the themes which he has already addressed in his own study: the structure of towns and cities, urban squares, monuments in squares, streets ending in squares, streets themselves, and, using the parks of Versailles as an example, gardens. Jeanneret's excerpts mark both an end and a beginning: the end of drafting *La Construction des villes* and the beginning of a view on urban design which ultimately leads to his designs for a *Ville Contemporaine* in 1922 and the book *Urbanisme* (1925). A closer analysis of the relevant excerpts will demonstrate just how important studying the *Essai* was to Jeanneret.

Jeanneret cites Laugier's introductory criticism of the overall condition of towns and cities: "Most of our towns have remained in a state of neglect, confusion and disorder, brought about by the ignorance and boorishness of our forefathers."[3] Laugier also

---

1 On the title page of notebook C.13 (LCdv 475), Jeanneret notes: "Laugier. Borrowed from the Koenigliche Bibliothek Berlin January 1911". On the first page, he copies Laugier's title page. Three precise dates are given in the notebook: 26 January, 16 February, and a final comment under the heading "My impression of this book", on 12 March 1911. Thus it is possible to date this cahier precisely, unlike all other parts of the Manuscript.

2 As in the title of the 1989 retranslation into German, literally 'The Manifesto of Classicism': Marc Antoine Laugier, *Das Manifest des Klassizismus. = Essai sur l'architecture*, [1753 version], trans. Hanna Böck (Zurich: Verlag für Architektur, 1989).

3 Marc-Antoine Laugier, *Essai sur l'architecture. Avec un dictionnaire des termes, et des planches qui en facilitent l'explication. Nouvelle édition, revue, corrigée, et augmentée* (Paris: Duchesne, 1755), p. 209; English

criticises instances where buildings have been renovated but where street layout or the haphazard, chaotic decoration of the buildings has not. He states that the worst such chaos can be found in Paris, where the centre has remained fundamentally unchanged for some 300 years. "The beauty and splendor of a city depends mainly on three things: its entries, its streets and its buildings."[4] He then proceeds to address these themes in turn, and Jeanneret follows this pattern in his excerpts. Initially, Laugier advocates grand entrances to a city, such as Rome's Piazza del Popolo.[5] He also demands that a grand avenue should approach such entrances, lined by two or four rows of trees and capped by a triumphal arch, from which several streets radiate out towards the centre and outskirts of the city. He does not believe that this can be achieved in the Paris of his day, but thinks a plan properly designed then can be implemented by future generations.[6] Jeanneret notes that the streets of Paris are "so winding and so full of senseless bends" that this doubles the length of one's route; he adds Laugier's remark on the need to lay out enough straight, sufficiently broad streets.[7]

Laugier demands that we regard the layout of a city in the same way as the layout of a forest or park; the streets in a city are equivalent to clearings in a forest or park and must be designed accordingly. "The essential beauty of a park consists in the great number of roads, their width and their alignment." He bases this on the proviso that executing such a layout would require a Le Nôtre figure, as the qualities listed are not sufficient in themselves, but also require the presence of "at one and the same time order and fantasy, symmetry and variety".[8] Laying out cities according to a strict grid is unsatisfactory, as it is deathly boring and all the *quartiers* look alike: he states the need for change. Jeanneret notes all this down, alongside the key sentence: "Above all, let us avoid excessive regularity and excessive symmetry."[9]

In addition, Laugier asks why it should be deemed impossible for Paris to develop a grand plan to improve the appearance of the whole city in accordance with artistic criteria: after all, the city's existing variety would only be an asset to the architect of such change. He asks why this should be impossible; after all, "So many provincial towns, with meagre resources, have had the courage to contemplate rebuilding the town on a new plan, hoping to achieve it with the help of time and patience."[10] In this context, Laugier also mentions a 'pruning' of the city (a formulation which Jeanneret does not quote), repeatedly comparing the city to a large forest and the built mass to greenery, from which spaces or clearings could be cut. This is precisely how Gianbattista Nolli's plan described the built mass of Rome in 1748, and how Max Läuger or Friedrich Ostendorf designed parks and cemeteries in the early 20th century. It seems that Jeanneret had a good grasp of this fundamentally spatial approach, although he did not adopt the concept of 'pruning'.

translation, *An Essay on architecture* by Wolfgang and Anni Herrmann (Los Angeles: Hennessey and Ingalls, 1977), p. 121; LCdv 487.

4 "La beauté et la magnificence d'une Ville dépendent principalement de trois choses: de ses entrées, de ses rues, de ses bâtiments." Laugier, *Essai* 1755, p. 210; Herrmann, *An Essay*, p. 122; LCdv 479.

5 Laugier, *Essai* 1755, p. 214f.; Herrmann, *An Essay*, p. 123. See LCdv 480.

6 Laugier, *Essai* 1755, p. 219f.; Herrmann, *An Essay*, p. 127. See LCdv 483–484.

7 Laugier, *Essai* 1755, p. 221f.; Herrmann, *An Essay*, p. 128. See LCdv 488–489.

8 Laugier, *Essai* 1755, p. 222; Herrmann, *An Essay*, p. 128. See LCdv 489.

9 Laugier, *Essai* 1755, p. 223; Herrmann, *An Essay*, p. 129. See LCdv 491.

10 Laugier, *Essai* 1755, p. 225; Herrmann, *An Essay*, p. 130. See LCdv 493.

Jeanneret immediately associates 'provincial towns' with La Chaux-de-Fonds, and states in a brief commentary that his native town is the ugliest in Switzerland. Whether or not reading Laugier changed Jeanneret's view, in registering his disapproval of La Chaux-de-Fonds he stays true to form. Nevertheless, this is the first time Jeanneret has described the past as being disruptive to urban development:

> It might be stated in the chapter on La Chaux-de-Fonds that this is the youngest town in Francophone Switzerland – and the ugliest to boot. It has no past whatsoever; besides, the past becomes an encumbrance where it remains in places which continue developing due to the course of events (Geneva, Lausanne, Berlin etc.).[11]

As Laugier imagines making Paris the most beautiful city in the universe, over time, Jeanneret exclaims ironically: "So, what a magnificent dream, to make this oh-so-modernist town of La Chaux-de-Fonds into the most beautiful new town in Francophone Switzerland."[12] He would also be able to link another of Laugier's remarks to La Chaux-de-Fonds, noting that "regularity and great diversity" are essential not only to the town as a whole, but also to façades in particular. "Long streets where all houses seem to be one single building, because one has observed a rigorous symmetrical scheme, are a thoroughly boring sight. Too much uniformity is the worst of all faults."[13]

Laugier's criticism of the parks at Versailles is of particular importance to Jeanneret's understanding of gardens. Laugier believed these were boring despite their great majesty, with nature being suffocated by overblown artifice. Jeanneret takes up this criticism of the gardens' excessively strict regularity, but criticises Laugier's rejection of pruning plants and interfering with nature: "A tendentious train of thought, which would soon lead one to Jean-Jacques Rousseau."[14] Jeanneret appears completely smitten with the idea of the architectural garden. Other errors identified by Laugier in the design of the gardens at Versailles are the feeling of being too enclosed and the lack of fresh foliage. Laugier sees everything in Versailles as appearing dry and barren, due in particular to the excessive use of box trees. He also criticises the complete lack of water.[15] In contrast, Jeanneret – who after much hesitation had visited Versailles for the first time in 1908 and was enthusiastic about it afterwards – states his position in a concluding comment:

> He laments, in the gardens at Versailles at the time, the excess artificiality. But I think that today, now that 180 years have allowed us to gain an overwhelming impression of the natural beauty there, huge foliage in free forms has taken over from the slender proportions of days gone by, to powerful architectural effect – this asserts itself everywhere, given the heights it now reaches, and the physical embodiment of space, contrasts, balance, harmony between restraint and folly, flowerbeds like embroidery and marble walls with a green patina from the vases, hedges and

11 LCdv 493.
12 LCdv 494.
13 Laugier, *Essai* 1755, p. 227; Herrmann, *An Essay*, p. 131; LCdv 495–496.
14 LCdv 499; see Laugier, *Essai* 1755, p. 240. His remark may be significant in relation to Adolf Max Vogt's theory that Le Corbusier was strongly influenced by Rousseau's ideas. See Max Adolf Vogt, *Le Corbusier, The Noble Savage*, trans. Jacques Gubler (Cambridge, Mass.: MIT Press, 1998).
15 Laugier, *Essai* 1755, pp. 244–248; Herrmann, *An Essay*, pp. 136–143; see LCdv 501–503.

clipped box trees, the exuberant domes of chestnut trees, long *allees* laid out like the naves of cathedrals, etc. – I think that Laugier would alter his criticism to unrestrained praise.[16]

Although the sentence is somewhat garbled, it is clear that Jeanneret is pursuing an argument which strongly favours the type of architectural garden promoted by Muthesius, Schultze-Naumburg, and Behrens.[17] In the last four pages of the notebook, Jeanneret attempts to produce a summary and assessment of Laugier's *Essai* which is readily understandable. Here, he formulates his impression of those 150-year-old thoughts. Despite certain similarities with contemporary theories, Jeanneret must have been stirred by the clarion call to design cities on a large scale. Laugier's discussion may also have revealed to Jeanneret for the first time how much more theory was available which was worthy of consideration:

> His ideas about urban design are perfect for his era, and for art. Logical steps forward in [architectural] spectacle. Always striving for the *grand style [français]*, which is superior to the surprises and entertainment of the picturesque. [...]
>
> In the present day, when a reaction can be detected against the outdated principles of the mediaeval picturesque style developed by Sitte, Laugier speaks with uncommon force because he is of an era which has already tried and tested the *grand style* and which, having reached saturation point, but also emboldened by this extraordinary development, has turned towards charm and grace. We are emerging from our spinelessness, we have allowed ourselves to be deceived by a childish bout of romanticism and are now yearning for a style which – in order to enact the growing wisdom of our philosophy and science and the generosity of our dreams for society – adopts an adequate form of expression i.e. more abstract beauty than petty materialism, striving for *greatness*, a sign that the masses are marching in unison and overturning the picturesque, which is the mark of narrow, miserly individualism.[18]

This is clearly a new position for Jeanneret in his consideration of urban design theory. We had already seen isolated indications in the Manuscript that picturesque urban design was by no means the only position Jeanneret might take. Monumental urban design also held a tangible fascination for him; this is expressed – albeit more reticently – in his chapters On Streets and On Squares. Now, Jeanneret is quoting excerpts from an author who explicitly requires monumental urban design, complete with broad, straight boulevards, large, star-shaped squares, and triumphal arches. What impact did Laugier's view have on Jeanneret? Was he surprised by the former's vehement denial of all that is small, narrow, and picturesque? At the very least, Laugier's view confirms an opinion which he had already cautiously formulated himself. Jeanneret's words on the matter bear similarities to those of Brinckmann, whose work he studied so intensively.

Laugier's calls for monumental entrances to cities, triumphal arches, star-shaped crossroads, and broad, straight boulevards appear to have been heeded in Haussmann's reform of Paris (from 1853 onwards); Le Corbusier also obeyed them in his *Ville Contemporaine*

---

16 Lcdv 517f.
17 See On Gardens and Parks.
18 LCdv 516–520.

of 1922, which encompasses all these elements, including the triumphal arches at the entrance to the city. This goes to show that the Laugier excerpts Jeanneret took in spring 1911 do indeed occupy a key position. I would not claim that Jeanneret was fully aware of their significance at the time; the incubation period for such awareness appears to have been much longer. However, these excerpts do represent a major milestone on Jeanneret's journey from support for the mediaeval picturesque to advocacy of the classic monumental. Reading the *Essai* may even have played a part in distancing Jeanneret from his own text, *La Construction des villes*. Further factors in his 'conversion' were his reading of Albert Erich Brinckmann's *Platz und Monument*, conversations with William Ritter, and last but not least Peter Behrens, whom Jeanneret jokingly referred to as 'the bear'. All these factors conspired to bring about Jeanneret's change of heart, displacing any Ruskinian or similar convictions. Yet despite what his commentary on Laugier suggests, this was no Damascene conversion and certainly did not mean that Jeanneret had permanently distanced himself from the *malerisch* in March 1911.

It is important to note that Laugier promoted more than just monumental urban design. Indeed, in the famous quotation about the necessity of tumult on the whole and order in the detail, taken from Laugier's second book *Observations sur l'architecture*, he speaks of diversity, surprises, sudden changes to the built fabric of the city: in this, he is close to the picturesque approach.[19] Furthermore, Laugier's criticism of urban planning based on grids, as mentioned above, could easily have come from Sitte or Henrici:

> There are towns with perfectly aligned streets, but since the plan was made by uninspired people, a boring accuracy and cold uniformity prevail which makes one miss the disorder of towns of ours that have no kind of alignment at all.[20]

It should also be considered that, with his call to design the city like a forest, Laugier is starting from a basic premise that is very spatial: the space of a street is considered to have been cut from the mass of houses.

Just as Jeanneret does, Laugier is attempting in his own way to construct a balanced approach to the city, while keeping his eye on the bigger picture. Yet Jeanneret's reading of the *Essai* clearly precipitated a collapse of his own previous thinking on urban design. It may well be that it was precisely his reading this text which ultimately caused Jeanneret to set aside his own Manuscript, even at this advanced stage, as he was uncertain of his ability to continue advocating the views it expressed.

Why was *La Construction des villes* not published?

After his commentary on Laugier in which Jeanneret had become exercised about the individualism in the picturesque approach, one might suppose that he would renounce picturesque urban design from spring 1911 onwards. This supposition would not be borne out by reality, partly because the facts are more complex. In the end, *La Construction des villes* is less about the *malerisch* as a style than about it as an architectural

---

19 "Il faut de la régularité et de la bizarrerie, des rapports et des oppositions, des accidens qui varient le tableau; un grand ordre dans les détails, de la confusion, du fracas, du tumulte dans l'ensemble." Laugier, *Observations*, p. 313.

20 Laugier, *Essai* 1755, p. 222f.; Herrmann, *An Essay*, p. 128f; see LCdv 490.

treatment of urban spaces. The Manuscript deals with how to "shape spaces using buildings", as Brinckmann succinctly puts it at the end of *Platz und Monument*.[21]

This means that in the end, the question of whether the architecture is classical, baroque,
or mediaeval is irrelevant. And this is one of the fundamental misunderstandings in the
reception of Camillo Sitte. Although Sitte's focus in *Städtebau nach seinen künstlerischen
Grundsätzen* lay on examples from (German or Italian) mediaeval cities which he had
observed, it is abundantly clear from his text that he was tackling universal principles of
spatial organisation – as Alexandre Cingria-Vaneyre would emphasise in his *Entretiens de
la villa du Rouet*, which Jeanneret read with such enthusiasm.[22]

We must therefore guard against throwing out the baby with the bathwater by
assuming that Jeanneret would suddenly and completely dismiss 'Sitte'. Jeanneret was
much too full of contradictions himself to take such a step. Thus for example he wrote
to William Ritter in 1911 that his dwindling knowledge of French meant he needed to
leave Germany:

> I need to leave these Germans behind as quickly as possible and return to the
> French-speaking world. As you know, I am experiencing an attack of gothophobia.
> Nuremberg is grinding me down, and the castles on the Rhine would often appear
> loathsome were it not for the landscape. Indeed, I am unrelenting, only on this: that
> modern life has nothing to do with this built framework which has become too con-
> strained. Subsequent epochs are more satisfactory to us now. However, I would like
> to recount how [...] I was completely blown away by the cathedral in Cologne yes-
> terday and remained there for an hour to hear mass, feasting my eyes on this mas-
> terly, unitary vertical creation.[23]

However pronounced his 'gothophobia' was, it did not cause Jeanneret to abandon the
spatial principles of urban design which he had established in *La Construction des villes*.
Instead, he sought on his *Voyage d'Orient* to find confirmation of what he had written
the previous year in the anonymous indigenous architecture of south-eastern Europe. By
observing what was original and authentic, he sought to confirm the hypotheses which
he had derived from theory. Thus on this *Voyage d'Orient*, in Prague, Istanbul, and
Rome, Jeanneret dealt in detail with the principles of visual perception and the possibilities of spatial organisation which he had gleaned from the urban design literature; he
was already familiar with the principles, but continued to learn through observing them
in practice.[24] Schultze-Naumburg's *Kulturarbeiten Städtebau*, Sitte's *Städtebau nach*

---

21 Brinckmann, *Platz und Monument*, p. 170.
22 Alexandre Cingria-Vaneyre, *Les Entretiens de la Villa de Rouet* (Geneva: Jullien, 1908), pp. 347–351, esp.
    p. 350.
23 "Tout ceci prouve qu'il me faut quitter aux plus vite ces Allemands et réintégrer les pays latins. Vous me
    savez en crise de gothophobisme. Nuremberg me lasse et les burg du Rhin seraient écoeurants souvent sans le
    paysage. Au fait je suis inexorable, seulement pour ceci: c'est que la vie moderne n'a rien à faire de ces
    cadres devenus trop restreints. Il est des époques postérieures qui nous satisfont davantage. Sachez cependant
    que hier [...] je fus tout à fait emballé du dôme à Cologne et que je restai une heure à écouter la messe, les
    yeux tout pleins de cette magistrale et unitaire verticale." Jeanneret to Ritter, 8 May 1911 (R3-18-84 FLC).
24 See Christoph Schnoor, "Le Corbusier's early urban studies as source of experiential architectural know-
    ledge", in Jorge Torres et al. (eds.), *Proceedings of Le Corbusier, 50 Years Later, International Congress*
    (Valencia: Universitat Politècnica de Valencia, 2015), pp. 2064–2081.

seinen künstlerischen Grundsätzen, and parts of Henrici's *Beiträge* are excellent textbooks on architectural perception, and Jeanneret had grappled so intensively with the principles of building illustrated therein that he repeatedly sought to confirm them on his journey – by sketching and photographing flights of stairs, enclosing walls, walled gardens, and cemeteries, etc.[25]

The fact that Jeanneret showed an interest in these intensely spatial, often picturesque situations during his work on *La Construction des villes* has already been stated and is not surprising. While travelling from Berlin to Munich in late June 1910, Jeanneret made many sketches and took photos, to be considered in parallel to the urban design literature he consulted. However, Jeanneret's interest in spatially rich architectural and urban organisation, as influenced by picturesque urban design, had clearly not been extinguished – even after he had read and commented on Laugier's text. With his interest in geometrically unified, monumental urban design on one hand, and in picturesque urban design on the other, Jeanneret can be seen to hold two attitudes concurrently.

Urban aesthetics versus the *Voyage d'Orient*

On the face of it, the reason why Jeanneret set aside *La Construction des villes* in March 1911 is very mundane: after he left Behrens' employ, he simply had no more time to devote to urban design. The subsequent journey through Germany for his study on applied arts was unavoidable; after all, this study had secured him the grant for staying in Germany. Despite clearly looking forward to the journey, Jeanneret sold it to his parents as a troublesome obligation:

> First of April: I am packing my bags and breathing in the air of Neubabelsberg for
> the last time, dedicating myself body and soul to the spirit of adventure. I will begin
> with a tour of all Germanic states, exercising the dreary role of inspector which fate
> and our town councillors have thrust upon me. It appears that I will weave in some
> daydreams too.[26]

This journey and the subsequent *Voyage d'Orient*, which was what Jeanneret was really longing for, would leave no time to continue the intensive writing of his urban design study. Jeanneret and August Klipstein, the art historian he had met in Munich as a German-language conversation partner, had already begun to hatch plans for travel to south-eastern Europe. William Ritter's precise local knowledge of the Balkans helped Jeanneret plot his route to Istanbul. Originally, he had intended to continue his journey as far as Egypt, yet during a protracted bout of diarrhoea on Mount Athos he dispensed with this notion. Following his return to La Chaux-de-Fonds in November 1911, Jeanneret would have had the opportunity to devote himself to completing *La Construction des*

---

25 In parallel with the present study, Leo Schubert explores Jeanneret's practice of seeking out and photographing places that he had seen in Schultze-Naumburg's *Kulturarbeiten Städtebau*, so they were available to him for his own use, and perhaps also in order to understand them better, see Leo Schubert, "Jeanneret, the City and Photography" in von Moos and Rüegg, *Le Corbusier before Le Corbusier*, pp. 55–68.

26 "Ier avril: on fait les malles, et humant l'air de Neu Babelsberg pour l'ultime fois, on se voue corps et âme au démon-voyageur. On commence par une randonnée à travers toutes les Allemagnes, faisant ce triste métier d'inspecteur qui m'ont dévolu mon sort et nos conseillers communaux. On y mêlera apparemment quelques rêveries. [...]" Jeanneret to his parents, 17 February 1911 (R1-5-95 FLC).

villes, yet in the long term other matters were to draw him away from this task. William Ritter appears to have played a key role in this, as he took the view that Jeanneret's wrestling with the aesthetics of urban design was taking him in the wrong direction; instead, he strongly argued that Jeanneret should complete and publish his writings on the *Voyage d'Orient*.

From 1910 onwards, Jeanneret and Ritter engaged in an intensive exchange of correspondence, which they maintained during the *Voyage d'Orient* (Fig. LXVI). In this correspondence, Ritter makes some astonishing comments on urban aesthetics. In September 1911, while Jeanneret was still travelling, Ritter wrote that he would like one day to devote some quiet reflection to the question of beauty and ugliness in industrial cities: the attempts at reform currently under way were not making them more attractive, but in fact adding fresh ugliness. He explains, "Where you see merely an aesthetic question, I see a moral question. We need to start with primary schools, not with houses or other buildings."[27] It is probable that Ritter intended this as a criticism of *La Construction des villes*, which is of course largely devoted to the aesthetic side of urban design.

Fig. LXVI Jeanneret, portrait of William Ritter, 23 January 1916 (3783 FLC)

27 "Le chapitre de la laideur de vos cités industrielles nous l'aborderons de front quelque jour. Cette laideur étant, la réaction contre cette laideur ne peut être qu'une *autre laideur* et laissez moi vous dire que je la vois poindre. Du moins cette laideur toute négative est elle encore déniée de prétention, mais la laideur positive qui va vouloir la contrecarrer sera terrible pour des gens comme nous. *On a l'architecture que l'on mérite.* Là où vous ne voyez qu'une question esthétique j'en vois une d'éthique. C'est par l'école primaire qu'il faut commencer et non pas par des maisons, ou des édifices." Ritter to Jeanneret, 26 September 1911 (SLA 1922.291).

In the same letter, Ritter approaches aesthetics and taste in more detail, objecting to "false taste", which in his opinion is even worse than the "cosiness of poor taste". Indeed, by saying "we get the architecture we deserve" and stating that he shudders at the thought of what he saw at the Observatory in Neuchâtel, Ritter deals a direct blow to Charles L'Eplattenier, who had designed the interior of the Pavillon Hirsch there.[28] At the time, Jeanneret was in the throes of a conflict: whose authority would he accept, that of L'Eplattenier – who initiated *La Construction des villes* – or Ritter? This conflict, which peaked in Jeanneret's correspondence with Ritter during the *Voyage d'Orient*, has been discussed elsewhere and cannot be addressed in detail here.[29] What needs to be noted is that Ritter was keen to warn Jeanneret against following L'Eplattenier unreservedly, as this would not necessarily benefit his intellectual development – and indeed that L'Eplattenier had bitten off more than he could chew in terms of theory. Above all, Ritter states that Jeanneret must find his own, independent path: independent not only of L'Eplattenier but also of Ritter.

Ritter employs a very vivid image, possibly adapted from La Fontaine, in one of his letters to Jeanneret; it literally means: "The king, the ass or I will die." In this La Fontaine fable, a charlatan claims to be able to make any old ass – whether literal or figurative – into a great orator. The king gives him an ass for a pupil and pays for ten years' tuition, on the condition that the charlatan will be hanged if he fails to train it in public speaking. When asked why he would accept this risky challenge, the charlatan replies that, in all likelihood, within those ten years either he, the king, or the ass will die. The moral of the story is twofold: beware of charlatans, and life is short. Ritter may be warning Jeanneret against following L'Eplattenier too closely, but he is also advising him: do not cling to me either, because one day I will no longer be there to advise you.[30]

In terms of Ritter's criticism of "false taste", Jeanneret had so far been unable to see the Pavillon Hirsch designed by L'Eplattenier and his students, as it was erected during his *Voyage d'Orient*. He was, however, familiar with the crematorium in La Chaux-de-Fonds, as well as the work of L'Eplattenier and the *cours supérieur* at the Ecole d'Art. This building manifests a strong desire to produce a *Gesamtkunstwerk*, combining colour, space, decoration, symbol, and sound – a very imposing and ambitious project. However, there are obvious clashes between the styles used in some of the décor; furthermore, the desire for symbolism is manifestly excessive, and indeed downright misplaced. Ritter's criticism that L'Eplattenier had overreached himself with his comprehensive approach is entirely understandable in view of these works. He writes:

---

28 "J'aime mieux la bonhomie du mauvais goût innocent que le faux goût. J'ai *horreur* de ce que j'ai vu à l'observatoire de Neuchâtel et ailleurs, provenant de l'influence dont vous allez accepter la domination." Ritter to Jeanneret, 26 September 1911 (SLA 1922.291). See Claire Piguet, "L'Observatoire cantonal de Neuchâtel: une architecture et un ensemble décoratif Art nouveau entre terre et ciel", in *Revue historique neuchâteloise*, no. 3–4, 2003. Unfortunately, the Pavillon Hirsch is not in its original state, having had a new glass roof fitted in 1993, which means that the work of Léon Perrin and George Aubert can only be seen on the vestibule walls.

29 See Brooks, *Le Corbusier's Formative Years*, p. 289, and Schnoor, "Soyez de votre temps".

30 "Le roi, l' âne ou moi nous mourrons." Ritter to Jeanneret, 26 September 1911 (SLA 1911.291). This uses the exact words of a line from near the end of the fable, for which the English is available in Jean de La Fontaine, book 6, fable 19, The Charlatan: "Ere that, the king, the ass, or I, Shall, one or other of us, die." *The Fables of La Fontaine*, vol. 1 of Universal Library, translated by Elizur Wright (London: Ingram, Cooke, 1853), p. 168.

L'Eplattenier, who was a *good painter*, has gradually been diverted from his course by theory which he is unable to digest. He has insufficient historical culture or appropriate philosophy for his milieu, by which I mean [insufficient] for him to take charge of his environment.[31]

As Ritter was plainly concerned that Jeanneret would adopt L'Eplattenier's 'false taste', he examined in great detail the latter's view of aesthetics and the common good. In Ritter's view, Jeanneret should set himself priorities: "Make what is beautiful *for yourself*, as it pleases you," but equally "make beautiful things for your people, *things it needs*; and it will be for the people, not you, to decide what it needs."[32] In a dramatic comparison typical of Ritter's graphic way of writing, he hopes to convey to Jeanneret his view on the digestibility of art:

You may call it a paradox, but just reflect on this for a minute: it is the stomach which digests, and food is made for the stomach. Imagine food revolting against the stomach: food decides one day that its main purpose is to be beautiful. From then on, the stomach can no longer digest it and says "I don't care a damn about your beauty; beauty to me is something I can digest." The problem is not to be theoretically beautiful but to be digestibly beautiful.[33]

Ritter concludes his letter with the following observation:

If you cast pearls before swine, it is not the swine who are stupid. I am amazed that nobody appears to have realised this before. Adieu. For a pig, the aim is to be a very pretty little piggy. Your job is to help it achieve that and not to transform it into a gazelle or a guinea fowl. Take a look at the Acropolis, it will tell you whether or not I'm talking nonsense, and whether I'm just a doddering old bugger.[34]

With these comments, Ritter was astonishingly far-sighted: it is almost as if he anticipated the post-modern debate on modernist architecture. So why did Ritter reject an aesthetic approach to urban form in 1911? After all, the architects around Sitte were arguing in favour of a 'digestible' city which was pleasant for the average citizen,

31 "L'Eplattenier, qui était un *beau peintre*, s'est laissé dérouté [sic] petit à petit par des théoriciens qu'il n'a pas su digérer. Il lui manque une culture historique suffisante et aussi une philosophie adéquate à son milieu, par quoi j'entends qui lui permette de gouverner son milieu." Ritter to Jeanneret, 26 September 1911 (SLA 1911.291).

32 "Faites *pour vous* les belles choses qu'il vous plaira, faites pour votre peuple les belles choses *qu'il lui faut*, et ce n'est pas vous, mais lui le juge de ce qu'il lui faut." Ritter to Jeanneret, 26 September 1911 (SLA 1911.291).

33 "Criez au paradoxe, mais réfléchissez deux minutes. C'est l'estomac qui digère et la nourriture qui est faite pour l'estomac: représentez vous la révolte de la nourriture contre l'estomac: les aliments ont décidé un beau matin qu'avant tout il faut être beaux. La dessus l'estomac ne les supporte plus et réponds je me f. de votre beauté, la beauté pour moi c'est que je vais digérer. Le problème n'est pas d'être beau théoriquement mais *digestiblement*." Ritter to Jeanneret, 26 September 1911 (SLA 1911.291).

34 "Si l'on jette des perles aux cochons, c'est pas le cochon qui est bête, et je m'étonne que personne ne semble s'en être avisé. Au revoir. L'idéal des porcs est d'être un très joli goret: c'est votre devoir de l'y aider et non de les changer en gazelles ou en pintades. Regardez l'acropole elle vous dira si je divague ou non et si je suis un vieux c.[on]." Ritter to Jeanneret, 26 September 1911 (SLA 1911.291).

Monsieur Tout le Monde.[35] Surely Ritter should have agreed with Sitte? Was he afraid that an urban design determined by aesthetics would give everyday life too little influence in the urban sphere? This would certainly tie in with Ritter's repeated calls for Jeanneret to take life more seriously than art. He expresses these most clearly in a letter dated July 1911: "there is no masterpiece worth a single drop of blood or semen. And, besides music, there is no beauty worth as much as a sunset."[36] In the same vein, Ritter comments six years later, in 1917, on the – repeatedly criticised – ugliness of La Chaux-de-Fonds:

> About that ugliness: I hear it mentioned everywhere, by people who feel they know something about art. Now, in all modesty, I am astonished every time. One could say that we have got out of the habit of assessing an initial impression, and opening our eyes no longer seems to mean opening our mind's eye as well. Can we call it ugly if an organ is created normally and determined by its function? If we were to see it like that, would we not also call the nose ugly *per se*, and the ears beautiful?[37]

Here, Ritter apparently assumes that La Chaux-de-Fonds was optimally designed from a functional perspective. Yet there is good reason to call precisely that functionality into question – as Jeanneret states in *La Construction des villes*. He does not fall into the trap of pure aesthetics set by Ritter, despite giving aesthetics priority. Did Ritter, undeniably a faithful reader first of Jeanneret's authorial efforts and later of Le Corbusier's writings, ever actually read *La Construction des villes*? Regrettably there are no indications whatsoever to that effect. The study is not mentioned in their correspondence, as Ritter clearly perceived it to be irrelevant and headed in the wrong direction.[38] In contrast, Ritter tried with all his might to give Jeanneret's report on the *Voyage d'Orient* a friendly push in the right direction:

> You must complete this *Voyage d'Orient*, particularly as you are the last person to have seen *that* old European Turkey of late, which is now little more than a late Turkey in flames, in the way you have. Think about it: nobody worthy of the name *writer* has painted a *picture* of Adrianople.[39]

---

35 Montenach, *Pour le visage aimé de la patrie*, p. XV.

36 "Il n'y a pas un chef d'œuvre qui vaille une goutte de sang ou de sperme. Et il n'y a pas même beauté en dehors de la musique qui vaille un coucher de soleil." Ritter to Jeanneret, 9 July 1911 (SLA 1911.154).

37 "Cette laideur, je l'entends affirmer partout par quiconque se pique de bien penser dans le domaine artistique. Or j'avoue humblement que chaque fois je m'étonne. Nous avons perdu, dirait-on, l'habitude de raisonner une première impression et ouvrir nos yeux corporels semble ne plus nous ouvrir simultanément ceux de l'esprit. Y a-t-il laideur effective lorsqu'un organe se trouve normalement créé et régi par sa fonction? A ce compte-là ne pourrait-on pas aussi bien déclarer laid le nez en soi et belle l'oreille?" William Ritter, "De la prétendue laideur de La Chaux-de-Fonds", *Feuille d'Avis de La Chaux-de-Fonds*, 17 and 24 March 1917, quoted after Fernand Donzé, *William Ritter. Au temps d'une autre Europe* (Neuchâtel: Nouvelle Revue Neuchâteloise, 1999), p. 21.

38 There are one or two exceptions to this rule, such as Jeanneret's announcement in 1915 that he would complete and publish the book in Paris.

39 "Il faut le compléter ce voyage d'orient et d'autant plus que vous serez le dernier à avoir vu *ainsi* cette feue Turquie d'Europe qui n'est plus qu'une Turquie en feu. Songez donc: il n'existe d'aucun écrivain digne de ce nom une *vision* d'Andrinople." Ritter to Jeanneret, 19 November 1912 (SLA 1911.946).

Subsequently, he and Jeanneret repeatedly agreed that Ritter was to proofread the text, and Jeanneret revisited the *Voyage d'Orient* time and again, although he ultimately failed to complete even this project, for which Ritter had provided so much support – it was ultimately published posthumously in 1966.[40]

In short, at this time when Jeanneret's ties to L'Eplattenier were becoming ever weaker and his ties to Ritter ever stronger, the aesthetics of the city did not stand a chance. What is more, in order to complete *La Construction des villes*, Jeanneret would have needed to travel from La Chaux-de-Fonds to a bigger city, as only a sufficiently well-stocked library would hold the necessary material for completion. There were too many ifs and buts: Jeanneret did not attempt to complete the work. He did not discuss urban design again in writing until 1915, except in the essay "Hellerau". This appeared in the La Chaux-de-Fonds *Feuille d'Avis* in 1913, but Jeanneret was merely rehashing his previous accounts of German garden cities.[41]

France ou Allemagne? Reasons against publication

Jeanneret's interest in the unpublished Manuscript *La Construction des villes* was re-awakened in 1915, during the First World War. Plans to rebuild those French cities destroyed by war seemed to offer a possible practical application for it. On 30 June 1915 he wrote to Auguste Perret:

> I intend to come to Paris soon, for the publication of a book which I have written about city planning and expansion plans etc. A major work and at a very advanced stage, but with tortuous, narrow-minded writing. I will completely rework it. I'm coming to Paris to find a publisher. I thought that this would be the right opportunity to bring out the study and dust it down, and that my modest effort could prove very useful at present, since laws on this matter are being discussed.[42]

These lines belie a certain pride in his text, but also great dissatisfaction about the way it is drafted. How much more effort does Jeanneret believe he needs to invest in it? He continues:

> Outside the major conurbations, people are making such a hash of this question that having them consider it is far from incidental. The plan for a town or village forms

---

40 For example, on Jeanneret's return to La Chaux-de-Fonds: "You could start by producing a definitive version of your travels now your mind has had a rest. And don't forget to send me the next instalment of the published part and the manuscript of anything that isn't published!" Ritter to Jeanneret, 3 November 1911 (SLA 1911.380). Just weeks before his death, Le Corbusier looked over the manuscript for the *Voyage d'Orient* and released it for publication by Jean Petit.

41 Charles-Edouard Jeanneret, "Hellerau", in *Feuille d'Avis de La Chaux-de-Fonds*, 4 July 1913.

42 "Je pense venir bientôt à Paris, pour la publication d'un bouquin que j'avais écrit sur la construction des villes, plans d'extension, etc. Un gros travail très avancé, mais écrit dans [un] esprit étroit et tortueux. Je le remanierai complètement. Je viendrai à Paris pour trouver un éditeur, me disant que l'heure est peut-être favorable de sortir cette étude de son tiroir; et que ce modeste effort pourrait être utile, en ce moment où l'on discute de lois relatives à ce thème." Jeanneret to Auguste Perret on 30 June 1915. Marie-Jeanne Dumont, *Le Corbusier. Lettres à Auguste Perret* (Paris: Editions de Linteau, 2002), p. 145f.

the foundations on which its beauty or ugliness will be built, depending on the extent to which this essential process has been governed by a true understanding of the matter at hand. If we study the past and compare it to the present, we can see how desperately inadequate our present day methods are. Reminding the public about the methods, and indeed the planner's very alphabet, may well bring life to our somnolent and anaemic planning offices.[43]

These lines read like a reprise of Jeanneret's arguments in *La Construction des villes*; as if five years had not passed since the work was written, and as if Ritter had not fundamentally called the project into question in the meantime. Jeanneret writes to Ritter in late July 1915 that he is travelling to Paris to "finish collecting materials for my book".[44] To Perret, he states that the Manuscript for *La Construction des villes* is very far advanced, but requires reworking. When he said to Ritter that the material had yet to be fully collated, was Jeanneret being more realistic with him than with other people? Were his words to Perret merely a statement of intent, in which he portrayed himself as further ahead than he really was? He had already declared to others several times in 1910 that *La Construction des villes* was nearly finished; there may well have been 'diplomatic' reasons why Jeanneret would say this, although it was clearly not the case.

Having arrived in Paris, Jeanneret studied in the Bibliothèque Nationale. He looked in great detail at works of architectural theory, with a focus on French urban planning literature of the late 18th century. Some of his effort was devoted to two major tomes: *Topographie de France* by Gabriel Pérelle, dated 1753/66, and *Monumens érigés en France à la gloire de Louis XV* by Pierre Patte, dated 1765; the latter work may have served as inspiration for his radical treatment of central Paris in his 1925 *Plan Voisin*.[45] Antonio Brucculeri traces Jeanneret's criticism of the historically disorderly state of Paris back to Pérelle; however, as we have demonstrated, Jeanneret had actually already taken this topic from Laugier in 1911. Jeanneret's bibliography from his stay in Paris includes 80 titles; he made new sketches as illustrations and copied out extracts in tiny handwriting, to produce a full hundred pages of urban design text.[46]

Thus we are now able to qualify a statement made by Brooks:

> However, once he began library research he realized that 'La Construction des villes' was far from finished and once he started studying eighteenth-century principles of urban design his thinking underwent a radical change. This motivated his

---

43 "Cette question a été tellement gâchée, hors des grands centres, qu'il n'est pas indifférent d'y faire songer. Le tracé d'une ville ou d'un village c'est le bloc de base, sur lequel s'érigera de la beauté ou de la laideur, suivant qu'une intelligence juste des choses aura présidé à cette opération capitale. A étudier le passé, à le confronter au présent, la pauvreté de nos moyens s'avère désespérément. Remettre en mémoire du public les moyens, l'alphabet, du constructeur des villes, c'est peut-être provoquer une action salutaire sur nos bureaux de cadastres engourdis et anémiques." Jeanneret to Auguste Perret on 30 June 1915 in Dumont, *Le Corbusier. Lettres à Auguste Perret*, p. 145f.

44 "Je repartirais Mardi matin du Landeron pour finir mes affaires ici, et probablement mercredi soir pour Paris, où je vais travailler à la Bibliothèque Nationale pour compléter la documentation de mon bouquin." Jeanneret to Ritter, 25 July 1915 (R3-18-468 FLC).

45 Pierre Patte, *Monumens érigés en France à la gloire de Louis XV*, (Paris: Auteur (et al.), 1765), Gabriel Pérelle, *Topographie de France* (Paris: Jombert, 1753). See Brucculeri, "The Challenge of the Grand Siècle", and the catalogue entry "Parisian Urbanism" in von Moos and Rüegg, *Le Corbusier before Le Corbusier*, p. 200.

46 The bibliography, sketches, and excerpts are filed under B2-20 FLC.

rejection of Camillo Sitte's romantic ideas in favor of classical values such as he had already accepted in architecture and furniture design but had continued to reject (witness the project for Arnold Beck of June 1914) in town planning.[47]

On the contrary, we have seen that Jeanneret knew even before he left for Paris that *La Construction des villes* was not finished. Nor did he experience a radical *volte-face* after his arrival there in 1915. In contrast to Brooks' interpretation, we have shown that Jeanneret had already worked on French 17th and 18th-century urban design – first via the intellectual bridge of Brinckmann, then directly from Laugier. Indeed, the fruits of this labour can be seen in the 1910/11 Manuscript.

As previously stated, Jeanneret's excerpts from the Bibliothèque Nationale have yet to be fully transcribed.[48] Like the excerpts, the sketches he made in this library also await in-depth analysis. These sketches cover French urban design of the 17th and 18th centuries as well as European and Far Eastern urban design subjects spanning all eras. We are nevertheless able to establish that in 1915 Jeanneret was building on his 1910 research: a considerable proportion of the 1910 bibliography is listed again, including in particular those books he had yet to work with at all, or in any depth. These include Brinckmann's *Spätmittelalterliche Stadtanlagen in Südfrankreich*, Charles Buls' *Esthétique des villes*, Joseph Stübben's *Der Städtebau*, and Raymond Unwin's *Town Planning in Practice*, as well as Roland Fréart's *Parallèle de l'architecture antique av.[ec] la moderne* and Laugier's *Essai sur l'architecture*, from which Jeanneret had already quoted, Laugier's other work *Observations sur l'architecture*, and Patte's *Mémoires sur les objets les plus importans de l'architecture*.[49] All the major works of classical architectural theory from antiquity and the Renaissance suddenly appeared in Jeanneret's bibliography: Vitruvius, Alberti, and Palladio, alongside French theoreticians such as Blondel, Briseux, de l'Orme, and Perrault, as well as contemporary essays and works on social and technical questions in urban design. This comprehensive bibliography suggests that Jeanneret felt a need to compensate for some intellectual shortcoming – perhaps he had been piqued by his discussions with Ritter? For our examination of the 1910/11 Manuscript, two important matters arise here: why did Jeanneret choose to engage with urban design again, and why – despite this – did he not publish *La Construction des villes*?

A key question which preoccupied Jeanneret at the time can now be addressed here, namely: 'France or Germany?'. The First World War made the question of national allegiances more pressing, although it had been looming on Jeanneret's horizon for some time. In 1915, he prepared a pamphlet for publication entitled *France ou Allemagne*. Jeanneret discussed this intensively with Auguste Perret, yet as with *La Construction des*

47 Brooks, *Le Corbusier's Formative Years*, p. 403.
48 Philippe Duboy transcribed and published some of Jeanneret's notes in "Charles Edouard Jeanneret à la Bibliothèque Nationale", in *Architecture, Mouvement, Continuité* 49 (1979), pp. 9–12, and in *Casabella* 531/532 (1987) under the heading "Laugier. C.B.N. 1915".
49 Where listed in the 1910 bibliography, these appear as: Albert Erich Brinckmann, *Spätmittelalterliche Stadtanlagen in Südfrankreich* (Berlin: Schenck 1910); Charles Buls, *Esthétique des Villes* (Bruxelles: Bruylant-Christophe, 1893; Roland Fréart, Sieur de Chambray, *Parallèle de l'architecture antique av. la moderne* (Paris: Martin, 1650); Laugier, *Essai* 1753; Laugier, *Observations*; Pierre Patte, *Mémoires sur les objets les plus importans de l'architecture* (Paris: Rozet, 1769); Stübben, *Städtebau*, 1890, Raymond Unwin, *Grundlagen des Städtebaues* (Berlin: Baumgärtel, 1910). Bibliography follows the files under B2-20 FLC.

villes it ultimately remained unpublished.[50] In the booklet, Jeanneret aimed to document the superiority of French culture over German; he encountered difficulties, partly as his knowledge of German contemporary architecture and urban design was much sounder than his knowledge of the French equivalents. Brooks takes the view that Jeanneret planned the booklet as a means of obtaining a 'passport' to Paris.[51] Rather than interpreting Jeanneret's intent as nationalist, he considers that it was pragmatic (a less charitable description would be 'opportunistic').[52] Thus Brooks' view is useful here, as it prevents our position from hardening too far into what are now familiar battle lines: did Le Corbusier hate Germany, had he learned more from France – or had he gained most of his detailed knowledge during his time in Germany? Regrettably, the 'France ou Allemagne' conflict has proven so intractable that researchers from both countries continue to wage it to the present day.[53]

The idea that Jeanneret's *France ou Allemagne* was a sort of application for a passport to Paris is particularly plausible in view of the historical context. Given the increasingly antagonistic atmosphere before and during the war, it would have been hard, to say the least, for Jeanneret to publish (either in France or Switzerland) a text written in French which praised the achievements of the German-speaking world – and that is precisely what *La Construction des villes* does. We can therefore conclude that *La Construction des villes* was the victim of events. Might Jeanneret's decision to take up the project afresh in 1915 and research it in Paris prove he was attempting to adapt it to a francophone setting? If so, it is no wonder he discarded *La Construction des villes* once again: France had not begun to reform urban design to the same extent as other European countries, and the aesthetics of perception (*Wahrnehmungsästhetik*) were primarily being debated in Germany. *La Construction des villes* could not therefore simply be rebranded; Jeanneret will have recognised as much while in the Bibliothèque Nationale. From this perspective, his research here does indeed mark a new beginning. The old – *La Construction des villes* – as originally conceived was on the way out, as it no longer served Jeanneret's purposes, nor could it be readily adapted to the altered circumstances.

In the debate about *France ou Allemagne*, it should be noted that Jeanneret's short book *Etude sur le mouvement d'art décoratif en Allemagne*, published in La Chaux-de-Fonds in 1912, was reprinted in 1914 and this time found great resonance in France, elicited not least by Ritter's discussion of it in *L'Art et les artistes*. As Ritter later recounted, he wanted to surprise Jeanneret and dedicated part of his column 'Allemagne' to the *Etude*.[54] As a result, several interested parties contacted Jeanneret to obtain a copy

50 See Jeanneret's letters to Perret dated 14 December 1915, 26 and 29 March 1916, and 14 June 1916, in Dumont, *Le Corbusier. Lettres à Auguste Perret*. On *France ou Allemagne* see Jean-Louis Cohen, "France ou Allemagne? Un Zigzag éditorial de Charles-Edouard Jeanneret", in *SvM. Die Festschrift für Stanislaus von Moos*, eds. Karin Gimmi et al. (Zurich: gta Verlag, 2005), pp. 74–93.

51 Brooks, *Le Corbusier's Formative Years*, p. 409ff.

52 Le Corbusier's political views have sometimes been interpreted as opportunistic. See Mary McLeod, *Urbanism and Utopia. Le Corbusier from regional syndicalism to Vichy* (PhD Princeton 1985 [Ann Arbor, Mich.: University Microfilms International 1987]).

53 See not only Werner Oechslin, "Allemagne. Influences, confluences et reniements", in Jacques Lucan (ed.), *Le Corbusier. Une encyclopédie* (Paris: Centre Pompidou, 1987), pp. 33–39, and Winfried Nerdinger, "Le Corbusier und Deutschland. Genesis und Wirkungsgeschichte eines Konflikts. 1910–1933", in *Arch+* 90/91 (1987), pp. 80–86, but also Dumont, *Le Corbusier. Lettres à Auguste Perret*, p. 26.

54 "On that subject, for once a good old boy called William Ritter wanted to give him a nice surprise and dedicated part of his column *Allemagne* in *l'Art et les Artistes* to this rough, naïve report. Upon which various

of the *Etude*. Maurice Storez was among them.[55] In his 1915 publication *L'Architecture et l'art décoratif en France après la guerre*, Storez explores Jeanneret's reports from Germany at length. Indeed, his interpretation is that Jeanneret's *Etude* effectively fulfils the role of *France ou Allemagne*. Discussing the second edition of Jeanneret's study, Storez deems it necessary to know one's enemy's art, in order to rise above it; significantly, Storez praises German organisation, but rejects the manifestations of German art.[56]

The confrontation between Mediterranean and Germanic culture had been brewing in Jeanneret's mind since before the war broke out. His reading of Alexandre Cingria-Vaneyre's work *Les Entretiens de la Villa du Rouet* served to crystallise the conflict in his mind. Cingria's book, written in the form of dialogues, calls for Greco-Latin-inspired art to be established in francophone Switzerland in general, and in the Geneva area in particular. William Ritter had mentioned this book shortly after he and Jeanneret first met in May 1910; the latter bought and read it shortly afterwards. To what extent did the book influence his attitude?

In his correspondence with Ritter, Jeanneret sounds so taken with the book that Ritter responds in November 1910: "I am so happy you like Cingria's fine book – the finest ever written in Switzerland about art."[57] Can Ritter be serious? The book he has recommended to his protégé is certainly odd: even its author admits that it is full of contradictions and exaggerations.[58] For example, Cingria uses Gaudens, one of his key figures (the others are Clothaire and Constance), to explain his calls for an "art full of peace and order" in the Alps, then declares:

> Was it not mountainous Greece which invented the Doric order? And do not these temples, which Huysmans derides as 'big stone chalets', thus demonstrate their mountain origins? [...] But I would go further: one would have to be impervious to beauty not to understand that the mountains require on their slopes regular, calm architecture which provides a respite from the lowly disorder at their feet. That is why our Alpine valleys should be decorated by long colonnades, by calm, powerful burial places, by bas-reliefs cut into the hillside with grand, geometric technique.[59]

persons in France asked the author for this somewhat rough report, which is still very entertaining to re-read even today, written with the same spirit, the same confident vigour, in the same nimble, devil-may-care way, based on somewhat haphazard documentation, following remarks made by friends and visits to notable personages, which a comparatively limited grasp of German made less fruitful than they would otherwise have been." William Ritter: Unpublished typescript *Mes Relations avec les artistes suisses*, SLA Bern, p. XIV.18.

55 In his letter to Auguste Perret of 30 March 1915, Jeanneret writes: "Un Monsieur M. Storez, architecte diplômé à Verneuil-sur-Avre, «grand ami de Maurice Denis», m'a écrit, et va sous peu amorcer une campagne – nationaliste-roi, pourquoi? – pour révéler la formidable organisation allemande. [...] La tentative me paraît très belle et heureuse." Dumont, *Le Corbusier. Lettres à Auguste Perret*, p. 132.

56 I would like to thank Philippe Duboy for referring me to Maurice Storez's *L'Architecture et l'art décoratif en France* (Evreux: Auguste Aubert, 1915), and Jean-Louis Cohen for his kind *ad hoc* support in my research on Storez.

57 "Heureux, heureux au possible que vous aimiez le beau livre de Cingria-[Vaneyre]; ce qui a jamais été écrit de plus beau, en Suisse, sur l'art." Ritter to Jeanneret, 8 November 1910 (SLA 1910.715).

58 "J'ai exagéré, badiné, lancé des paradoxes, je le confesse; je n'ai pas fait mention des louables efforts vers un renouveau d'art que l'on sent partout poindre dans nos villes." Alexandre Cingria-Vaneyre: "Epitre dédicatoire à Gonzague de Reynold", p. IXf. of *Les Entretiens de la Villa de Rouet* (Geneva: Jullien, 1908).

59 "N'est pas la Grèce montagneuse qui créa l'ordre dorique? Et ces temples que Huysmans appelle, par dérision, de 'grands chalets de pierre', ne prouvent-ils pas par là leur origine montagnarde? [...] Mais, je dirais plus, il faut être insensible à la beauté pour ne pas comprendre que la montagne appelle à ses flancs des architectures

Cingria lets Clothaire respond for him: "But what you're saying there is a bit crazy, it's nonsense; for all that I prefer lakes to mountains, I would still suffer to see the mountains blighted in this way, even for the classical cause."[60] Since Jeanneret noted his agreement with it, Brooks also quotes this section, but he glosses over the nonsensical parts and merely states that Cingria was promoting for the Alps an architecture "of regular features and calm" which "must not imitate classical building types".[61] Nevertheless, it is worthwhile quoting the section in full to represent Cingria's book, because it is far from straightforward to abbreviate and gloss over his writing: he should be left rough and ragged, because that is how he wrote. There follows the puzzling question of how William Ritter, with his considerable literary education, could actually have enjoyed this book greatly. It is not surprising that Jeanneret was taken with it: he was open to the wildest ideas. It is fully understandable that he took some of Cingria's demands literally, however circuitously they are expressed through dialogue and complex clauses. While returning from his *Voyage d'Orient*, as he expounded on his plans for a new architecture for Switzerland (Ritter was also wonderfully ironic in his treatment of these), Jeanneret dispatched his now-famous aesthetic manifesto to Ritter from Pisa. The Cathedral, Baptistery, and Camposanto inspire Jeanneret to produce this poetic outburst: "I am mad about the colour white, the cube, the sphere, the cylinder and the pyramid, the uniform surface and the wide open space."[62] Ritter's response is simultaneously euphoric and ironic: "Bravo! – Your youth is behind you, but your work has just begun, dear friend. Good luck! ... – I can't really see those white Mediterranean cubes in your Jura ... But if it makes you happy!"[63] Thus, even though Ritter clearly takes a different view, he acknowledges that Jeanneret is finding his own path. Jeanneret asks of his poetic flights of fancy: "Can you hear the music in them?"[64] Ritter answers: "Can I hear the music in your white Stamboulachauxdefonds? What a great word! Just watch out your architecture doesn't turn out the same! The Acrop'... ouillerel! How funny! And perhaps the Styx [will flow] over the Saut du Doubs?"[65] Ritter's word 'Acrop'ouillerel' conjures up images of Jeanneret's *Maison Blanche* before our very eyes, since it was built on the slope of the Pouillerel in La Chaux-de-Fonds. However, in reality no link between the two is possible, as Ritter could not be envisioning a house here which had not yet been

---

régulières et calmes qui la reposent du désordre inférieur de ses bases. Et c'est pourquoi les vallées alpestres devraient être décorées de longues colonnades, d'hypogées tranquilles et puissants, de bas-reliefs taillés dans le roc, avec une facture géométrique et grandiose." Cingria, *Les Entretiens*, p. 262.

60 Clothaire: "Mais c'est un peu fou, ce que vous dites-là, c'est un non-sens; j'ai beau préférer le lac à la montagne, il me semble que je souffrirais de la voir mutiler de la sorte, même pour la cause classique." Cingria, *Les Entretiens*, p. 262.

61 Brooks, *Le Corbusier's Formative Years*, p. 237.

62 "Je suis fou de couleur blanche, du cube, de la sphère, du cylindre et de la pyramide du disque tout uni et d'une grande étendue vide." Jeanneret to Ritter, undated [around 1 November 1910] (R3-18-128 – 141 FLC).

63 "Bravo! – C'est fini la jeunesse, mais c'est l'œuvre qui va commencer, mon ami. Courage! ... – Vos cubes blancs méditerranéens, non je ne les vois pas dans votre jura... Mais enfin si cela vous fait plaisir!" Ritter to Jeanneret, 3 November 1911 (SLA 1911.380).

64 "Entendez vous de la musique là-dedans"? Jeanneret to Ritter, undated [around 1 November 1910] (R3-18-132 FLC).

65 "Si j'entends de la musique dans votre blanche *Stamboulachauxdefonds*? Hein, comme cela fait bien un mot comme cela! Prenez garde que votre architecture ne soit de même! Laugier'Acrop'...ouillerel! Spas!! Et le Styx au saut du Doubs [...] Détournez vous de l'art et allez vers la vie! Sans dogme nietzschéen, non plus que n'importe quel autre! Vivre, s'augmenter, se préparer une vie toujours épanouie et large ici et dans l'autre monde, auquel vous ne croyez pas, mais auquel je crois ferme, moi!" Ritter to Jeanneret, 3 November 1911 (SLA 1911.380).

designed. Because they had discussed Cingria's work – Jeanneret had asked from Florence for his address – Ritter knew what Jeanneret was driving at, and his two imaginative neologisms show almost clairvoyant powers.

Cingria's influence reinforced Jeanneret's interest in Mediterranean culture. It could also have strengthened the positions which Camillo Sitte represented: despite all his attacks on 'sentimentalisme' and 'romantisme', Cingria is clearly in favour of Camillo Sitte's urban design theories.[66] Hence Constance says to Gaudens: "Ah! I see you have read the book by Sitte, which our compatriot Camille Martin translated so nicely."[67] Cingria then has Clothaire introduce Sitte's book, since Gaudens admits he has heard great things about it but never read it himself. After a balanced exposition of Sitte's theories, lasting several pages, Gaudens asks:

> Well, it's all very ingenious, but I wonder whether all these observations aren't in danger of leading us towards romanticism and the sentimental picturesque approach which we branded a public nuisance.[68]

Clothaire responds rather elegantly that the regularity which Sitte rejects is not the harmonious regularity of classicism, but the ludicrous geometric division of cities into chequerboards.[69] This remark stems from Cingria's acknowledgement of the generally applicable artistic rules which Sitte calls for in urban design. At the same time, it seems that in his commentary on Laugier's *Essai*, Jeanneret takes up where Gaudens left off, querying Sitte's calls for the picturesque. And Jeanneret's note at the end of his copy of the *Entretiens* reads: "Finished reading 22nd November [1910] in Neubabelsberg. Totally agree with his general, inspired approach. [...] It provokes examination, and conclusions: regular, bright, crystal clear. It releases me from the grip of Germany."[70] Thus Jeanneret's reactions to reading the *Entretiens* indicate both that he agreed and disagreed with the theories he had postulated in *La Construction des villes*. Both reactions seem equally plausible. Does this supply sufficient proof that reading Cingria helped to distance Jeanneret from *La Construction des villes*? It does, to a degree. There were evidently several obstacles to the publication of *La Construction des villes*. Jeanneret was now more strongly aligned with Ritter, who viewed urban aesthetics as the wrong path and instead advocated publishing the *Voyage d'Orient*. Jeanneret was uncertain about the accuracy of the theories he himself had previously formulated, an uncertainty only reinforced by reading Cingria's *Entretiens*. And he had also realised that *La Construction des villes* promoted 'the wrong' national culture: this impression was strengthened by the war.

66 See Cingria, *Les Entretiens*, pp. 346ff., especially p. 349f.
67 "Ah! Je vois que vous avez lu le livre de Sitte, qu'a si joliment traduit notre compatriote Camille Martin." Cingria *Les Entretiens*, p. 347. NB The copy of the *Entretiens* accessible in the Swiss Literary Archives bears a handwritten inscription by Cingria to Camille Martin.
68 "Tout cela est très ingénieux, mais je me demande si toutes ces constatations ne risquent pas de nous ramener au romantisme et à ce pittoresque sentimental que nous avons dénoncé cependant comme un péril public." Cingria, *Les Entretiens*, p. 349f.
69 Brooks sees this as Sitte's "medieval romanticizing being interpreted as possessing certain Greco-Latin values and ideals". See Brooks, *Le Corbusier's Formative Years*, p. 238.
70 "Fini de lire le 22 novembre à Neu-Babelsberg. Et pleinement d'accord avec l'esprit général et génial. Les paradoxes d'ici n'en sont pas. Je le souhaite un jour vérités vécues et vivantes. Pour moi, ce livre vient favorablement aider à mon orientation. Il provoque l'examen, les déductions normales, claires, lumineuses; il desserre pour moi l'étau germanique. Dans une année, à Rome, le relirai et par des esquisses je fonderai ma discipline jurassique neuchâteloise." Jeanneret quoted in Dumont, *Le Corbusier. Lettres à Auguste Perret*, p. 169.

La Construction des villes and *Urbanisme*

In 1925, Le Corbusier published the book *Urbanisme*, which then appeared in English in 1929 as *The City of To-morrow and its Planning*.[71] It is divided into three parts, which Le Corbusier entitles 'General Considerations', 'Laboratory Work: a Theoretical Study', and 'A Concrete Case: the Centre of Paris'.[72] This very structure shows the similarity between *Urbanisme* and *La Construction des villes*.[73] In both cases, Le Corbusier begins in general terms, with an introduction and a discussion of ideal form in urban design, albeit with one major difference: in 1910 this analysis contained a mixture of historical and contemporary precedents, whereas in 1925 only a single design was discussed – Le Corbusier's own *Ville Contemporaine*. He ends each book with a design for a specific place. In 1910, it was La Chaux-de-Fonds, and in 1925 the centre of Paris, where the *Plan Voisin* was to be implanted. One major difference between the two volumes lies in the choice of illustrations. Brooks claims Le Corbusier re-used many of the 1910 illustrations in 1925, "but in a textual context that gave them exactly the opposite meaning."[74] Yet of the 180 or so illustrations for *Urbanisme*, Le Corbusier only includes two drawings from 1910, some ten sketches from the *Voyage d'Orient* (particularly from Istanbul), and around 20 additional drawings prepared in Paris in 1915.[75] While it is certainly true that Le Corbusier revised his earlier convictions, this certainly puts Brooks' claim into perspective.

Urbanisme and Le Corbusier's preparatory work for it have yet to be investigated sufficiently, although the subject is broached in Thilo Hilpert's *Die funktionelle Stadt*, and in the work by Philippe Duboy and Antonio Brucculeri on Jeanneret's 1915 research at the Bibliothèque Nationale in Paris.[76] We are only able to provide an outline of the link between *La Construction des villes* and *Urbanisme*, fleshed out by individual observations, and thus to identify a possible thread of continuity running through Le Corbusier's theories. While the two works are comparable, 1920s Paris was very different from Munich or Berlin in 1910. The car was becoming established as a mode of transport, there was a great need after the war to construct economical, efficient housing, and the European architectural avant-garde was busy proposing building methods in line with the zeitgeist. Society had undergone a significant shift since 1910, and if he was to get his urban design noticed in Paris, Le Corbusier would need to employ drastic methods: cue his 1922 *Ville Contemporaine* (Fig. LXVII).

---

71 Le Corbusier, *Urbanisme* (Paris: Crès, 1925). The version used here: Paris: Flammarion, 1994. The English version is entitled Le Corbusier, *The City of To-morrow and its Planning*, and was translated from the 8th French edition of Urbanisme with an introduction by Frederick Etchells (New York: Dover, 1987 [New York: Payson & Clarke, 1929]).

72 "Avertissement/Débat général/Un travail de laboratoire, une Etude théorique/un cas précis. le centre de Paris".

73 See Brooks, "Jeanneret and Sitte".

74 "Interestingly enough, however, many of the illustrations prepared for the 1910 manuscript were published in 1925, but in a textual context that gave them exactly the opposite meaning." Brooks, *Le Corbusier's Formative Years*, p. 207.

75 These are: the 1808 plan of the city of Ulm and an engraving of the town of Altdorf, copied by Jeanneret from: Merian, *Topographia*. Le Corbusier, *The City of To-morrow*, p. 7 and 26.

76 Hilpert, *Die funktionelle Stadt*; Duboy, "Charles Edouard Jeanneret à la Bibliothèque Nationale"; Brucculeri, "The Challenge of the Grand Siècle". See also Barry Bergdoll, "Paris: Le Corbusier and the Nineteenth-Century City", in *Le Corbusier. An Atlas of Modern Landscapes*, ed. Jean-Louis Cohen (New York: Museum of Modern Art, 2013), pp. 246–249.

Fig. LXVII Bird's eye view of the *Ville Contemporaine*. From Le Corbusier, *Urbanisme*, p. 140

Camouflage

In the foreword to *Urbanisme*, Le Corbusier picks up the trail of his unpublished tract *La Construction des villes*; he refers to his own learning process:

> Fifteen years ago, in my extensive travels, I felt the all-powerful might of architecture, but many and difficult stages were in front of me before I could find an adequate frame for it. Much of architecture lay buried deep under meaningless and incoherent traditions which had to be dug through before any enthusiasm could be evoked, and then only to a limited degree. On the other hand, when an architecture was genuinely appropriate to its environment it gave a pleasing sensation of harmony and was powerfully moving. Only when this was so, and without recourse to text-books, did I feel the presence of one essential factor; URBANISM, a word I only learnt later. I was devoted to art.[77]

This paragraph can only be fully digested in a biographically informed 'translation': "fifteen years ago" was 1910. When he describes "meaningless and incoherent traditions", Le Corbusier is referring to historicism, about which he understandably felt little enthusiasm. Does he include Greek or Roman classical architecture in his rejection? It appears to suit his purposes to leave this question open. The "long journeys" he mentions refer primarily to the *Voyage d'Orient*, but also to his previous travels to Italy and Vienna and long stays in Paris and Germany. By "architecture [...] genuinely appropriate to its environment", Le Corbusier means the many modest rural dwellings he has seen, such as those in the Balkans – William Ritter had taught him to appreciate their aesthetic.[78] Equally, he may be alluding to the simple, yet imposing farmhouses in La Sagne, a settlement neighbouring La Chaux-de-Fonds, which he photographed carefully circa

---

77 Le Corbusier, *The City of To-morrow*, Foreword, XXIV. Translation adapted.

78 William Ritter, who had an interest in the indigenous cultures of the Austro-Hungarian Empire and the Balkans, as his novels and many drawings attest, had provided initial travel tips for the Voyage d'Orient in 1910: see Spechtenhauser, "The Mentor: William Ritter", and Schnoor, "Soyez de votre temps".

1910.[79] It is doubtful that Jeanneret intended to include in this category German reformist architecture of the early 1900s, dedicated though it was to the *genius loci* and to attempts at embodying regional spirit using simplified forms, and therefore pursuing precisely that goal which Jeanneret and L'Eplattenier had first identified for Swiss Architecture.

Le Corbusier's claim that he only learned the word 'urbanisme'[80] some time later may at first appear nonsensical, but this would be a misunderstanding arising from the translation of the term. Frederick Etchells used the term 'Town Planning' in his translation of *Urbanisme*, since this was the British English equivalent and a common term at the time. But it is worth pointing out that Le Corbusier did not use an English or German term like 'town planning' or 'Städtebau', but a recent French coinage: *urbanisme*. This term was coined in 1910, but was slow to find widespread acceptance in the French-speaking world.[81] It is therefore perfectly possible that Le Corbusier did not absorb that specific term into his vocabulary until later.

On the other hand, Le Corbusier is certainly also attempting to give the impression that he knew nothing of urban design (by whatever name) in 1910: "Only when this was so, and without recourse to text-books, did I feel the presence of one essential factor; URBANISM."[82] This flowery formulation, intended to indicate that he intuitively grasped the significance of urban design issues, actively disguises his intensive work on German *Städtebau* and the British garden city concept. Subsequently, Le Corbusier states in much more concrete terms:

> Later, I read Camillo Sitte, the Viennese writer, and was affected by his insidious pleas in the direction of picturesque town planning. Sitte's demonstrations were clever, his theories seemed right; they were based on the past, and in fact WERE the past, but a sentimental past on a petty scale, like the little wayside flowers. His past was not that of the great periods, it was essentially one of compromise. Sitte's eloquence went well with that touching rehabilitation of 'the home' which was later, paradoxically enough, to turn architecture away, in the most absurd fashion, from its proper path ('regionalism'). [...] Decorative art is dead. Modern town planning comes to birth with a new architecture. By this immense step in evolution, so brutal and so overwhelming, we burn our bridges and break with the past.[83]

In an inappropriate simplification – after all, Le Corbusier knew better – he links together the very different strands of regionalist architecture (Heimatschutz) on the one hand and a historicist, picturesque attitude on the other. Yet there is a striking comparison to be made with his March 1911 commentary on Laugier's *Essai*, the thread of which he appears to be taking up here. In that commentary, he turned strongly against the picturesque, associating it with small- and narrow-mindedness. In 1911, almost siding with Laugier, he hoped for urban design to become collective, modern, and *great*:

---

79 A series of photos taken by Jeanneret around 1910 is dedicated to the simple farmhouses in La Sagne, a small linear village just a short distance from La Chaux-de-Fonds, where Jeanneret spent at least one summer. See also Brooks, *Le Corbusier's Formative Years*, p. 74f. The photos are archived under LCi 419–429, BV.

80 Translator's note: although this is rendered as 'TOWN PLANNING' in Etchells' translation above (which we have adapted), in keeping with the period, elsewhere in this essay we have used the term 'urban design'.

81 See *Le Petit Robert*, "Urbanisme", and Dumont, *Lettres à Auguste Perret*, p. 147f.

82 Le Corbusier, *The City of To-morrow*, Foreword, XXIV.

83 Le Corbusier, *The City of To-morrow*, Foreword, XXIV–XXV. Translation adapted.

We are [...] now yearning for a style which – in order to enact the growing wisdom
of our philosophy and science and the generosity of our dreams for society – adopts
an adequate form of expression i.e. more abstract beauty than petty materialism,
striving for *greatness*, a sign that the masses are marching in unison and overturning
the picturesque, which is the mark of narrow, miserly individualism.[84]

Fundamentally, the formulations Le Corbusier chose in 1911 and 1925 are not so very
different, albeit Le Corbusier expresses himself in a much briefer and less circuitous
manner in 1925. His design language in the two periods also differs greatly. Yet here, as
elsewhere, it emerges that he has *not* made a clean break with his earlier views, but
rather shifted his emphasis. The same two sides of the debate are present, both the picturesque and the classical/monumental, but the representations made on behalf of each
side differ.

The technical debate about whether Le Corbusier's *Ville Contemporaine* is a city
designed by an artist or one which obeys functional principles is not a new one.[85] But
by tracing *La Construction des villes* back to its source material, we are nevertheless
able to outline the continuity of certain statements and theories. In *Urbanisme*, Le Corbusier describes the soul of the city:

> Though I shall, later in this book, allocate a very important place to the mechanism
> of the city, it is more necessary to state now that this mechanical adjustment lies
> apart from the definite and profound feelings which belong to our emotions and
> sensibilities, which hold the secret form of our happiness or our misery. A form of
> town planning which preoccupied itself with our happiness or our misery and which
> attempted to create happiness and expel misery would be a noble service in this age
> of confusion.[86]

Later, he becomes more emphatic:

> The city which is to be will contain *in itself* a formidable mechanism, a powerful
> bull, a workshop containing innumerable and precise implements, a harnessed tem-
> pest. The forms we are discussing are the eternal forms of pure geometry and these
> will enshrine in a rhythm which will in the end be our own, going far beyond the
> confines of formulae and charged with poetry, the implacable mechanism which will
> pulsate in it. The eye is capable of both being battered into submission or of being
> caressed. The soul too may be sunk deep or lifted high. I give a *problem of form*
> which should be entered in the agenda of all Municipal Councils: "A decision must
> be arrived at in regard to the prohibition of certain injurious forms and the encour-
> agement of stimulating forms".[87]

Indeed, the *Ville Contemporaine* is no purely functional city: its motivation has deeply
aesthetic roots. Moreover, although knowingly contradicting himself, here Le Corbusier

---

84 LCdv 520.
85 See Hilpert, *Die funktionelle Stadt*.
86 Le Corbusier, *The City of To-morrow*, p. 58f.
87 Le Corbusier, *The City of To-morrow*, p. 64f. Translation adapted.

writes explicitly of the emotional qualities of a city, and therefore those questions of perception that had exercised the artists and architects around the turn of the century, not least Sitte, Henrici, and Schultze-Naumburg.

As indicated above, Le Corbusier's *Ville Contemporaine* appears to embody many of Laugier's requirements. Le Corbusier even realises Laugier's ideal triumphal arches as entrances to the city. He echoes Laugier's criticism of enclosed and overly narrow squares and winding streets. Thus the *Essai* is undoubtedly one of the major models for Le Corbusier's urban utopia, and for the idea of approaching the city as a forest or park. Although Laugier refers to the even expanse of a French hunting forest, we need only substitute this with the English landscape garden, the park as landscape, to find the basis for Le Corbusier's *Contemporary City* with its green, open spaces: an artificial landscape to envelop the Cartesian order of architecture.

Is it not somewhat strange that a plan from the 1920s, based on 18th-century ideas from Laugier, should appear more avant-garde than the modern ideas which German urban designers produced at the turn of the century? Yet it does indeed appear as if Haussmann – who followed Laugier's approach – was not radical enough in his treatment of Paris: for Laugier's vision of avenues, uniform blocks, and star-shaped squares to be implemented, Le Corbusier's complete *tabula rasa* would be needed. In *Urbanisme*, Le Corbusier repeatedly quotes Laugier on the necessity of tumult in the whole and order in the detail, and explains his understanding of this formulation:

> We have now formulated an ideal and precise aim. Already, in the time of Louis XIV, the Abbé Laugier had propounded the following axioms: 1. *Chaos, disorder and a wild variety in the general lay-out* (i.e. a composition rich in contrapuntal elements like a fugue or symphony). 2. *Uniformity in detail* (i.e. reticence, decency, 'alignment' in detail).[88]

This begs the question: where in the composition of the *Ville Contemporaine* are the elements of counterpoint? Le Corbusier himself exclaims: "And in every direction we have a varying spectacle: our 'gridiron' is based on a unit of 400 [metres], but it is strangely modified by architectural devices! (The 'set-backs' are in counterpoint, on a unit of 600 x 400 [metres])."[89] The reader is left to judge for themselves – I do not consider the *Ville Contemporaine* to be a contrapuntal composition; instead, it resembles a lavishly orchestrated major chord. It contains no internal contradictions or tensions intentionally created by the composition, much less any sequence of forms varying over time. The uniformity of detail across individual buildings has been criticised in the literature from the very beginning, and would appear to need no further exploration. And yet any spatial richness in Le Corbusier's city plan arises more from the individual dwellings than from the overall scheme. In some respects, Le Corbusier seems to have inverted Laugier's requirements: he creates order and uniformity in the scheme as a whole, but variation and counterpoint in the designs for his dwellings. Yet however interesting these observations may be, they are not directly related to *La Construction des villes*.

---

88 Le Corbusier, *The City of To-morrow*, p. 72 (italics by Le Corbusier/Etchells). Although totally different from the *Ville Contemporaine*, would Hermann Jansen's designs for Berlin circa 1910 not meet these requirements, and perhaps even more satisfactorily than Le Corbusier's designs?

89 Le Corbusier, *The City of To-morrow*, p. 178.

What is Le Corbusier arguing against in 1925? "Present-day reality does not accord with the first of these axioms [about chaos in the general lay-out]; since those who make our bye-laws for us demand streets which can never be anything but corridors."[90] Is this not practically a word-for-word repetition of his 1910 criticism? On the redevelopment of La Chaux-de-Fonds, he had asked: "What does the future hold in store for us? Hundreds of straight roads, and all uniformly, eternally equal in width."[91] How can he honestly square this – justifiable – complaint with his rejection of Sitte? In 1925, Le Corbusier takes the criticism further:

> And it gives us the contrary of our second axiom; for we are constantly assailed by incongruous details. And our decorative town-planners, the lovers of wrought iron gates and of highly individual shop-fronts and so on, thrust us still deeper in error.[92]

It might reasonably be assumed that he is referring here to the picturesque approach to urban design, which he has already criticised. However, advocates of urban design reform such as Paul Schultze-Naumburg, Theodor Fischer, and even Albert Gessner and Hermann Jansen argued against excessive embellishment; they aimed for a basically picturesque stance, without descending into kitsch ornamentation. Whether or not Le Corbusier chose to recall this fact, he had already made the case against such excesses in *La Construction des villes*, calling precisely these architects as his chief witnesses. Le Corbusier is right to criticise the "decorative town-planners" in *Urbanisme*, but this criticism would be better directed at Joseph Stübben, for example, who presented over-ornamented advertising columns, lamps, and even urinals in his work *Städtebau*. Yet the illustrations in Henrici's *Beiträge* shed light on Le Corbusier's criticism: the depictions of Henrici's urban design sketches are replete with towers, oriels, and wrought-iron ornament.

For Le Corbusier, the question is not one of rejecting the past *per se*, nor of rejecting historical urban design, as the following quotation illustrates:

> *Past realities* do fit in with our axioms, as far as the so-called 'art' cities are concerned: Bruges, Venice, Pompeii, Rome, old Paris, Siena, Stamboul and the rest: here we find certain large-scale intentions for the whole, and a remarkable uniformity of detail. *Yes, of detail!* In those fortunate epochs the methods of construction were uniform. Right up to the nineteenth century, a window, a door were 'holes for men', that is to say, elements on the human scale [...] *They had an astonishing unity. [...] There was a universal standard and complete uniformity in detail.*[93]

This shows that simplicity and uniformity, the *unité* which Le Corbusier is advocating, do not in his view contradict the efforts of urban designers like Jansen or Fischer, and he is unwilling to relinquish these rich sources of knowledge and experience. But at the same time, he had lost the taste for fine distinctions by 1925: what purpose would they serve anyway, since his readers would not perceive a difference between work by Joseph Stübben and Hermann Jansen?

---

90 Le Corbusier, *The City of To-morrow*, p. 72.
91 LCdv 366ff.
92 Le Corbusier, *The City of To-morrow*, p. 72.
93 Le Corbusier, *The City of To-morrow*, p. 72f. Translation adapted.

Curved or straight streets revisited

Contrary to expectation, the debate on correct street layout plays a major role in *Urbanisme*, just as it had in *La Construction des villes* (Fig.s LXVIIIa–c). In *Urbanisme*, Le Corbusier opens the subsection entitled 'Winding Roads and Straight Roads' with an attack on Camillo Sitte:

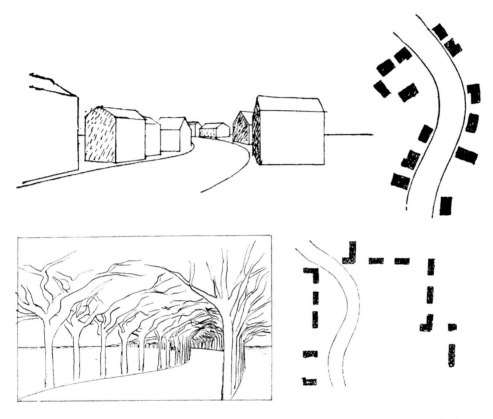

Fig. LXVIII Discussion of the relationship between curved streets and houses. From Le Corbusier, *Urbanisme*, p. 174

Twenty or thirty years ago Camillo Sitte explained to us that the straight road was a stupid thing, and the winding road the ideal. The straight road, he said, was really the longest path between two points, the winding road the shortest; his demonstration, which was based on the maze-like cities of the Middle Ages (cities which became so by accident, see: 'The Pack-Donkey's Way,' Chap. I), was ingenious but specious. He forgot that the cities he quoted were less than a kilometre long and that their charm was the result of something quite apart from town planning. He put forward and brilliantly sustained his paradoxical argument and the fashion was set. Munich, Berlin and many other cities began to build these mazes in their very midst.[94]

---

94 Le Corbusier, *The City of To-morrow*, p. 207. Translation adapted.

However, our exploration of *La Construction des villes* showed that the demonstration which Le Corbusier criticised did not originate from Camillo Sitte. Instead, it stemmed from Paul Schultze-Naumburg: he argues that a city laid out on a strict chequerboard grid often makes for longer routes than a model using curved streets, since the curved routes trace the most frequently used connections and thus incorporate the local realities more flexibly than a grid.[95] Jeanneret took up this idea enthusiastically in 1910, and in his chapter On Streets defended the organic ground plan of older towns and cities, as postulated by Schultze-Naumburg, with its main trunk arteries and capillary links. It is of no consequence to Le Corbusier in 1925 that it was not Sitte who made this point, as he now takes Sitte to represent the whole of reformist urban design.

The troubling aspect of Le Corbusier's line of argument in this chapter is that he ends up criticising both curved or straight street as an end in itself, independent of any local context, and that this criticism is also aimed at Camillo Sitte. However, as can be seen clearly in *La Construction des villes*, he had understood in 1910 that reformist urban design was an attempt to break free of unyielding geometric principles and schematic urban design, rather than a promotion of the curve as an end in itself.[96] Back then, he correctly described how German urban design, embodied by Henrici, overshot this basic principle and slipped back into inflexibility, as with 'the curve as an end in itself'. Brinckmann was one reformist voice who warned against just such an overreaction. However, in 1925 Le Corbusier would reject this sort of nuanced position, as this was the only way to promote his new picture of the city. Nevertheless, he remained aware of many of the arguments he had read 15 years earlier. In *Urbanisme*, he therefore deals in detail with the question of correct street layout and, during his explanation, reins in his rigorous stance:

> We should also be right in saying that a straight street is extremely boring to walk through, it seems never to finish; the pedestrian feels he is never advancing. The winding street, on the other hand, is interesting because of the variety of succeeding shapes; we must remember this in our attempt to get the matter clear. The straight street is dead boring to walk in. Admitted.[97]

Astonishingly, Le Corbusier now reaches straight for formulations from Henrici's essay 'Boring and pleasing streets', as quoted almost verbatim for his 1910 chapter 'Des Rues' in *La Construction des villes*. Earlier in his text, Le Corbusier had stated:

> But, if it is true that the straight road is often extremely depressing because the houses which border it are ugly, how painful is the inevitable disorder in a winding street where the houses on either side are detached. Everything then seems at sixes and sevens. The eye cannot see the curve as originally drawn on the plan, and each individual façade has its own restless importance: such housing schemes give one the impression of a field of battle or of the after-effects of an explosion.[98]

95 Schultze-Naumburg, *Kulturarbeiten Städtebau*, p. 66f.
96 See General Considerations, and LCdv 28–46.
97 Le Corbusier, *The City of To-morrow*, p. 208.
98 Le Corbusier, *The City of To-morrow*, p. 208.

It is evident that Le Corbusier sees this clearly: as he stated in 1910, a solid, curved façade has the quality of a film playing out before the pedestrian's eyes, constantly providing new impressions. Now, however, he conflates curved streets with streets with clearance space between buildings – a model the reformist architects of the early 20th century rejected.

Indeed, he concedes a few pages later:

> Yet the architect can create agreeable effects with curving streets by building continuous façades along them; for thus he would create forms eminently plastic, though their frequent repetition would quickly end in boring the observer. But in towns a road of this sort, which makes it impossible to see any distance ahead, would quickly paralyze all motor vehicles.[99]

Once again, we get the impression of a concerted argumentative effort. It appears that Le Corbusier wants to free himself forcibly from architectural principles which he has already acknowledged as effective. Thus his efforts to dismiss them are somewhat forced. In contrast to 1910, he is no longer able to acknowledge a general justification for streets that are anything other than dead straight, and now feels he has to restrict their *raison d'être* drastically.

What does Le Corbusier hope to achieve? It would appear that Brinckmann is his unacknowledged role model here. In 1910 he had read Brinckmann's chapter 'Moderne Bestrebungen im Städtebau' in *Platz und Monument* very attentively, and even in 1925 in *Urbanisme* he closely follows a section from Brinckmann:[100]

> But if it is a street for work, then [elevated trains], trams, buses and motors can get along it quickly just because it is straight. Therefore let us adopt the curve if we want streets to walk in, little countrified walks, where there is no architecture, and the result will be a sort of small park or laid-out garden for promenaders and nursemaids. *The curved street has every justification for itself if no architectural effect is aimed at, and if the surrounding countryside, or at least the trees and grass, are picturesque and not overborne by any striking creation of man.* Clearly we are dealing in this case with roads for strolling in or walks winding through a garden city. [...]
>
> ([...] On varying levels the curve has prior rights, since here it is a question of climbing evenly by winding about: to aim at the picturesque in such a case is necessary, and the architect's problem is how to discipline the natural disorder and bring about that unity which is indispensable to every feeling of harmony and aesthetic.)[101]

Brinckmann's critique of picturesque street layout anticipates Le Corbusier's phrasing in *Urbanisme* in terms of the distinctions it makes:

> While the irregular, curving street [...] can certainly be justified aesthetically in districts of villas or areas of detached houses, and as a contrast to the straight, open street, it cannot create a complete monumental situation.

99 Le Corbusier, *The City of To-morrow*, p. 209–10. My emphasis.
100 "Le dernier chapitre de Brinkman/N° 35 est caracteristique./Moderne Bestrebungen" LCdv 441.
101 Le Corbusier, *The City of To-morrow*, p. 208f. Translation adapted.

City plans have emerged in recent years which sport only curved streets, even on flat terrain: these are an erroneous extreme, a new form of schematism.

"It would be folly to erect curved streets as an exclusive rule" says J. Stübben; not even Sitte himself would have condoned this.[102]

It is clear from this that Brinckmann exerted a decisive, sustained influence on Le Corbusier. Thus there exists a further commonality between Jeanneret/Le Corbusier's two urban design texts: by 1910 Jeanneret was already fascinated by the straight street, and praised it enthusiastically; in his Introduction he called for commercial streets to run straight, and for residential streets to curve. Now, as Le Corbusier, he echoes this call: let us keep straight streets in cities for cars and for human beings intent on travelling from A to B; curved streets belong in the garden suburbs. The question remains: how can this be reconciled with the very different urban images which Jeanneret/Le Corbusier *draws* in each case? The drawings and sketches used in 1910 differ fundamentally from those of the *Ville Contemporaine*. The answer to this question may very well lie in his different treatments of urban space. However, we must first recognise that both texts are characterised by internal contradictions, which can be seen particularly clearly here. In 1925, Le Corbusier argues for an ordered, rectilinear built environment, for the avoidance of chaos, in a landscaped setting:

When the road winds, the eye can perceive but vaguely the foreshortened view. Therefore arrange the houses on either side of your winding road (so pleasant to ramble in) in blocks at right angles to each other. Standing free in space they make the view (as the eye sees it), which then becomes an ordered thing. The above theory applies to level ground. [...] To sum up the whole matter, the curving street is essentially picturesque. Picturesqueness is a pleasure which quickly becomes boring if too frequently gratified.[103]

Thus Le Corbusier employs the landscaped park as an underlay, or even a foil for his right-angled constructions. He justifies this with a demonstration from a Breton village: "The street curves amid the rectangular alignment of the houses. The direction of the prevailing wind determines the orientation of all the houses. This uniformity is pleasant."[104] At the same time, he warns his reader against the 'street as corridor'. In the chapter 'The Urban Scene', he puts forward a very artistic view of the city. He demands that the contours of houses against the sky be ordered as opposed to jagged, forming a straight, even line: "I repeat that the silhouette against the sky is a determining factor in our feelings; it is exactly the same thing as profile and contour in sculpture."[105] Yet the 'street as corridor' must be avoided:

We must break up the corridor-street and, properly speaking, we must create the *broad vista* in the urban scene. That must be our aim, and not the monotony of the narrow depth which the corridor-street gives us. In designing my Blocks of Dwellings with 'set-backs', I have provided wide vistas to right and left, and by constantly getting back to the longitudinal axis my composition takes on an architectural character; the hitherto

102 Brinckmann, *Platz und Monument*, p. 167f.
103 Le Corbusier, *The City of To-morrow*, p. 209–10. Translation adapted.
104 Le Corbusier, *The City of To-morrow*, p. 211.
105 Le Corbusier, *The City of To-morrow*, p. 232.

dull lines of the corridor-street now become a series of prism forms which give emphasis to the recesses or to the projections; and the dry, wearing façades of the corridor have been replaced by volumes juxtaposed, or set far apart, or brought together in a monumental and lively urban landscape.[106]

In relation to whether Le Corbusier's *Ville Contemporaine* was predominantly a functional city, it is important to note that the shape of the large residential blocks was born of artistic conviction. Moreover, we can assume that these meandering blocks emerged from a principle which Camillo Sitte also advocated: after all, both Sitte and Le Corbusier rejected the urban design 'evil' of the typical monotonous perimeter block development. Sitte and Schultze-Naumburg had both tried to dispel the monotony of such developments, making them more lively for the observer and pedestrian with setbacks and projections. Le Corbusier adopted the same basic position, that built mass in urban areas should be enlivened by architectural composition. One major difference between Schultze-Naumburg and Jeanneret/Le Corbusier is the fact that Schultze-Naumburg considers setbacks from streets as individual places in a city; witness his detailed depictions and Jeanneret's sketches,. In contrast, Jeanneret treats them – even as presented in his sketches as early as 1910 – as a fixed schematic element in street layouts. The precise shape of Le Corbusier's 'meanders' may well have its origins less in small-scale picturesque urban design than in Munich's Ludwigstraße: Jeanneret bought several postcards of Ludwigstraße while in Munich, including one of Friedrich von Gärtner's 1835–40 university building. The two-winged building opens up into a sort of square with an apparently meandering setback; here we can see that the seed has been sown for Le Corbusier's later *blocs à redens* (Fig.s LXIX and LXX). However, two further factors also contributed to Le Corbusier's inspiration here: his aversion to a tightly packed, narrow city and his penchant for monumental schemes came together and expanded these schemes until they reached an outsized street scale. Le Corbusier offers an interpretation of his inspiration: he cites the Place des Vosges, Place Vendôme, or the Tuileries as examples of the *bloc à redens*, so that his French readers can picture a familiar scene which in the regularity of its façades corresponds approximately with his design.[107]

The residential block

Le Corbusier designed several blocks of stacked villas (*Immeubles-villas*) for the City of Three Million Inhabitants. These were ten-storey buildings housing comfortable maisonettes, each with a hanging garden.[108] Thilo Hilpert has compared these huge buildings to ocean liners, after a statement Le Corbusier made in *Precisions on the Present State of Architecture and City Planning*.[109] Hilpert rejected the comparison made by Françoise Choay with Fourier's utopian socialist *Phalanstères*.[110] Here, we offer a far more prosaic interpretation. As described above, in 1910 Jeanneret studied an article on the reform of the Berlin tenement block authored by Walter Lehweß and René Kuczynski, translating

---

106 Le Corbusier, *The City of To-morrow*, p. 232–36. Translation adapted.
107 Le Corbusier, *The City of To-morrow*, pp. 232–36.
108 Le Corbusier, *The City of To-morrow*, p. 186.
109 Le Corbusier, *Precisions on the Present State of Architecture and City Planning*, translated by Edith Schreiber Aujame (Cambridge, Mass.: MIT Press, 1991); Hilpert, *Die funktionelle Stadt*.
110 Hilpert, *Die funktionelle Stadt*, p. 125.

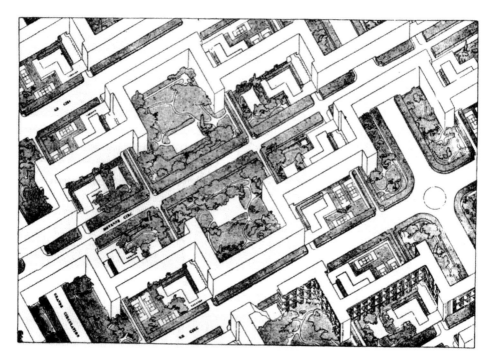

Fig. LXIX Blocs à redents of the *Ville Contemporaine*. From Le Corbusier, *Urbanisme*, p. 193

Fig. LXX Friedrich von Gärtner, Munich University (1835–40). Postcard, owned by Jeanneret
(LC-105-1112-28 BV)

the whole paper published in the periodical *Städtebau*, complete with all its figures.[111] Lehweß and Kuczynski divide up the traditional Berlin block in a new way, so that its over-all size (in one of their examples) is precisely 362 x 208 metres (Fig. 7). The size of the *Immeubles-villas* in Le Corbusier's design matches these dimensions surprisingly closely: he states them as 400 x 200m.[112] It therefore seems appropriate to compare Le Corbusier's 1925 plan with Kuczynski and Lehweß's reformist design, which attempts to overcome the problematic spatial aspects of Berlin's traditional tenement block form with its overly small, densely built-up rear courtyards (Hinterhöfe). Their intention is to keep only the outer layer of five-storey tenement blocks, to shield against noise and dust, while replacing the many layers of wings and rear courtyards with a system of two-storey detached and semi-detached houses inside the block. In Le Corbusier's plan, the outside of the block rises to twice the height, and the inside space is completely given over to greenery. The houses have migrated into the outside walls of the block, and each has received its own architectural garden: thus Le Corbusier takes the reformist idea for improving the Berlin housing block even further. Yet he omits to mention that this design allows the dreaded 'corridor-street' to persist between his *Immeubles-villas*. While the 'corridor' is not as narrow as it was at the turn of the century, at a width of 75m, it remains nevertheless.

Public spaces in the city

At first sight, it would appear that the square as a public space has vanished from Le Corbusier's designs for the *Ville Contemporaine*. All that remain are layers of terraces with restaurants, cafés, and shops.[113] That pithy definition of enclosed space, *clôture*, which Jeanneret explored in such variety and detail in 1910, seems to have disappeared without a trace in 1925. While *La Construction des villes* was dedicated to space, the 1925 work makes only fleeting reference to any means of delineating space in the city. In *Urbanisme*, Le Corbusier decrees that squares from a bygone era only have a right to remain where they were built as unified works of art. In fact, this is in line with Jeanneret's 1910 preference, as illustrated in On Squares. Here he writes with reference to Sitte:

> Nowadays, public life has withdrawn from squares. [...] In short, the square's raison d'être has evolved and the square for its own sake is now certainly subject to our requirements. [...] The square to enrich aesthetic urban heritage will survive.[114]

Reading between the lines, we can see the *Plan Voisin*, where Le Corbusier sets out his scheme of ideas on urban squares; we can see that he is already reinventing such squares as isolated monuments. In *Urbanisme*, Le Corbusier expresses his admiration for Louis XIV, despite Laugier's strong criticism of the *Place Vendôme*:[115]

> So Louis XIV issued an edict, to the effect that the Place Vendôme was small and mean; that the buildings in it were to be demolished and the materials re-used to

---

111 Lehweß and Kuczynski, "Zweifamilienhäuser für Großstädte".
112 Le Corbusier, *The City of To-morrow*, p. 182.
113 Le Corbusier, *The City of To-morrow*, p. 204.
114 LCdv 137–139.
115 See Chapter 3, "The Laugier excerpt as a turning point".

build a new Place. The plans (given above) showed the rebuilding in accordance with Mansart's designs. The façade to the square was to be built at the King's expense. The ground behind the façades was available for purchase as desired. Buyers could acquire a portion, larger or smaller, of the façade, regulated by the number of windows. Houses could extend to a considerable depth back from the frontage. The Place Vendôme is one of the purest jewels in the world's treasures.[116]

Not only does Le Corbusier single out this square as an example (Fig. LXXI), but he also retains it in the *Plan Voisin*; it thus turns into an absurd historical remnant which has lost its context – the built mass of the city – and stands isolated and exposed, as with the Marien-kirche near Alexanderplatz in modern-day Berlin. Precisely that characteristic of the Place Vendôme which Le Corbusier accurately identifies is thereby lost from the square: its ability to pry open the built density. What use is Le Corbusier's reverence if it wrests a much-valued object from its surrounding context? Nevertheless, interesting parallels can be drawn between the theoretical view of the square on the one hand, as advanced here in relation to this particular square, and Sitte's thoughts on the stylistic unity of a square on the other. In one of his designs for the Vienna ring road, Sitte aims to create a square in front of the neo-gothic Votive Church, to generate stylistic unity with the church building. The underlying principle, upheld as much by Le Corbusier as by Sitte, is: the façade belongs to the square and must be consistent with it. In contrast, the rear side of the square, the built mass itself, holds no significance for the design (for either Sitte or Le Corbusier) and may therefore obey other criteria.[117]

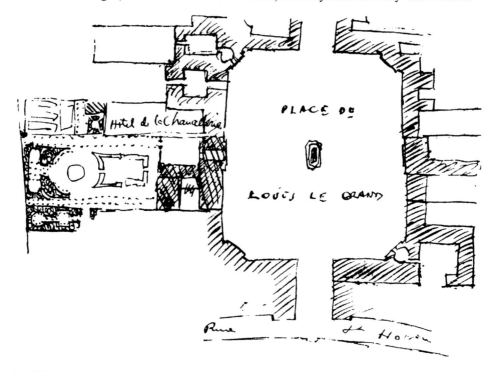

Fig. LXXI Place Vendôme in Paris. From Le Corbusier, *Urbanisme*, p. 123

116 Le Corbusier, *The City of To-morrow*, p. 154.
117 See Collins and Crasemann Collins, *Camillo Sitte: The Birth of Modern City Planning*, pp. 281–284.

Jeanneret adds to the question of public space in *La Construction des villes*:

> Instead, people are calling for vast spaces planted with trees, intended to interrupt the tiring uniformity of the 'stone desert', and parks around which buildings will happily close ranks, will constitute a good supply of clean air, in which easily-arranged fountains will provide refreshment and beautiful motifs.[118]

The counterpart piece in *Urbanisme* (Fig. LXXII) is expressed in almost the same tenor:

> The whole city is a park. The terraces stretch out over lawns and into groves. [...] Where are now the trivial *Procuracies*? Here is the CITY with its crowds living in peace and pure air, where noise is smothered under the foliage of green trees.[119]

Thus Jeanneret's idea of public space in the city as expressed in *La Construction des villes* has changed in *Urbanisme*: the concept of the park, already present in 1910, has by 1925 expanded to encompass the bulk of the public space, largely replacing any 'stone-built' urban space. Like the street, the park has developed from an enclosed space

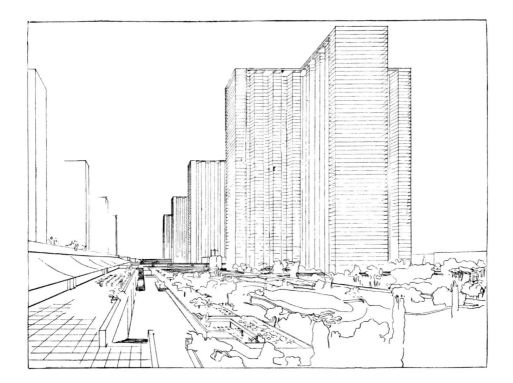

Fig. LXXII Public space in the *Ville Contemporaine*. From Le Corbusier, *Urbanisme*, p. 204

118 LCdv 138ff.
119 Le Corbusier, *The City of To-morrow*, p. 144.

into a wide open area: Jeanneret's penchant for the architectural, spatially designed park is transformed into a preference for a man-made landscape which forms the basis for the *Ville Contemporaine*.

For Le Corbusier in 1925, there are clearly two types of urban green space: first, the 'stone gardens' which, in line with Muthesius, he regards as an extra room to the dwelling. Le Corbusier considered these gardens, either on the roof or 'hanging' between floors, as a refuge for residents: a highly private space. The mid-sized back garden, which he had studied so intensively in 1910 via Muthesius' *Das Englische Haus*, and made such an exemplary reality at the 1912 *Maison Blanche*, has become an intrinsic part of the dwellings designed for the *Ville Contemporaine*. Indeed, his thoughts in 1910 foreshadowed these design solutions:

> Why not plant a tree or trees at half-height or at the very top of a building? Large and powerful trees and Virginia creepers and ivy etc. In the past, materials prevented this because the stones would be dislodged by the growing roots. Today, reinforced concrete permits it and allows all conceivable combinations.[120]

On the preceding page in the cahier, Jeanneret sketched a section through a residential block with stepped terraces, where every terrace is covered in trees (Fig. LXXIII) and noted: "Trees on all three levels thanks to reinforced concrete, streets with walkways accessed via steps running lengthways."[121]

The other sort of greenery to feature in 1925 is the 'wild' landscape running through the city. Numerous attempts have already been made in the literature to explain this.[122] The scene is based on the English-style landscaped park. As described above, 'natural' landscape is now used as a substrate for a city designed on a Cartesian grid. It is astonishing to see the conviction with which Le Corbusier promotes this version of the landscaped park in 1925, given that in 1910, he compared the French and English types of park directly, and clearly favoured the baroque French approach. Perhaps an explanation of this development in Jeanneret's thinking can begin with his description of the Tiergarten in Berlin, a large park which is more English than French in layout. Although in 1910 it lay outside the old city boundary, the Tiergarten was still in the midst of the expanding metropolis: "In the Tiergarten, we enjoy afresh the impression of great peacefulness in these large woods immediately near noisy main roads."[123] Reading his remarks on the Tiergarten with the image of the future *Ville Contemporaine* at the back of one's mind, it is possible to see Jeanneret laying the foundations here for his later large, ideal cities. The huge, peaceful park with a big, noisy city in the background – Jeanneret's description is closer to New York's Central Park than to the visions of urban parks and gardens proposed by Sitte or even Henrici, Fischer, or

---

120 LCdv 419.

121 "arbres au III étages grâce au béton armé/Rues à Promenoir auxquelles on accède par des escaliers longitudinaux" LCdv 418.

122 For example, in *Collage City* Colin Rowe devotes an entire chapter, "Crisis of the Object: Predicament of Texture" to the question of whether or not the unlimited space of the modern city represents cultural progress. See Colin Rowe and Fred Koetter, *Collage City* (Cambridge, Mass.: MIT Press, 1978).

123 "Au Thier Garten on goûte à nouveau l'impression de gde paix ds ces gds bois à proximité immédiate des gdes rues bruyantes." *Le Corbusier – Carnets de Voyage d'Allemagne 1910–1911*, English edition, ed. Giuliano Gresleri (Milan: Electa; Paris: FLC, 2002), Carnet 2, p. 122.

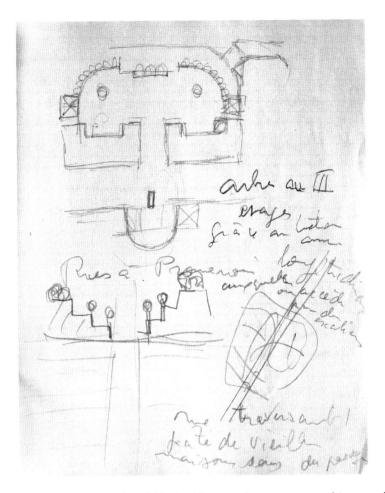

Fig. LXXIII Section through a residential block with stepped terraces covered in trees. Sketch by
Jeanneret (LCdv 418)

Schultze-Naumburg.[124] Nevertheless, in 1910 Jeanneret had yet to conceive of his
'towers in the park'.[125]

Of course, this brief comparison can only hint at the potential fruitfulness of a more
in-depth comparison between the theories and convictions Jeanneret held in 1910 and
those Le Corbusier held in 1925 in relation to urban design. Yet it is already clear that
as Le Corbusier, he retained some of the same views which he held circa 1910. We have
seen an indication that some of the authors whom Jeanneret had read in 1910 continued

124 Most closely related to this picture are Fritz Schumacher's designs for the new Volkspark in Hamburg –
which Jeanneret of course explores in *La Construction des villes*.
125 See Fig. LXXII. On the last two pages of Cahier C.12 (LCdv 472f), Jeanneret does draw a few trees that are
strongly reminiscent of the vegetation which would encircle Le Corbusier's towers in the park in 1922 (Fig.
121).

to influence his thinking into the 1920s, and seen that Le Corbusier's new theory was not without its internal contradictions. The odd coupling of artistic demands with the purported superiority of technology which can be found in the *Ville Contemporaine*, and the unresolved conflict between the picturesque and the monumental approaches, still permeate the 1925 tract: it shares these fundamental hallmarks with *La Construction des villes*, but in a mirror image. A further, surprising strand of continuity or kinship exists between the *Ville Contemporaine* and La Chaux-de-Fonds: Le Corbusier's home town embodies precisely that utopian ideal settlement, sharply delineated and embedded in the landscape, which appears so unrealistic in the *Ville Contemporaine*. This is perhaps evidence that Le Corbusier ultimately assimilated an idea which he had initially attacked rather vehemently.

Chapter 4

Conclusion

What would *La Construction des villes* have contributed to the planning debate, had it been published? We began by tracing the history of its creation, with reference to Jeanneret's library studies: this illustrated how intensely the young architect grappled with the subject matter in his Manuscript, even without being aware of the full spectrum of contemporary planning discourse. Subsequently, our in-depth analysis of the Manuscript's content documented the wide range of theories and opinions Jeanneret took on board as he read. Indeed, he adopted and adapted these ideas, soaking them up like a sponge; he tended to process the concepts straight away and transfer each into a fresh context. An overview outlining the period from 1911 showed the extent to which Jeanneret's examination of urban design issues was later supplanted by other projects. This continued until 1925 when, as Le Corbusier, he published *Urbanisme* – a book which, while deeply rooted in *La Construction des villes*, paradoxically seeks to obfuscate and outwardly deny these roots. We have proposed answers to the question of why Le Corbusier himself never published *La Construction des villes*.

Now, equipped with this new information on the chronology of events, on the connections between ideas, on the Manuscript and its sources, we approach our final analysis. The following questions will be addressed: was Camillo Sitte actually the main influence on Jeanneret's study, and conversely how much of himself did Jeanneret bring to the Manuscript? What, after all, is the Manuscript's central theme? Could *La Construction des villes* have stood its ground among the contemporary planning literature, and can it really be viewed as a treatise? Throughout this essay, we have seen that it would be difficult to concur with Le Corbusier's later assertion that *La Construction des villes* was a somewhat stupid book, "un livre un peu idiot" as he put it. But would Jeanneret's document have been well received among experts if published?

The *malerisch* versus the monumental

Jeanneret did indeed largely model *La Construction des villes* on Camillo Sitte. He does appear to have integrated some of Sitte's fundamental opinions into his work. Yet besides Jeanneret's direct dealings with Sitte's writing, Sitte's indirect influence is equally important. He exerts this via the legacy he left to sympathetic thinkers, especially Karl Henrici, Paul Schultze-Naumburg, Albert Erich Brinckmann, and Joseph August Lux. This combination of influences lends Jeanneret's Manuscript a complexity which would not have emerged if he had simply imported Sitte's theories wholesale.

Sitte scarcely devotes a single sentence of his book to the form and layout of streets and streetscapes. Yet Jeanneret states that his own chapter on streets is the most important in his Manuscript. In ascribing such importance to this topic, Jeanneret necessarily goes beyond Sitte's ideas and thus limits Sitte's direct influence on the Manuscript. Indeed, we have seen that Jeanneret's views on good street design, particularly on curved streets and skilful setbacks, primarily stem from Henrici and Schultze-Naumburg. While it is true that both architects' positions lead directly back to Sitte, he left it to his successors to complete his fundamental theories relating to the urban square. Each in his own way, Sitte's successors answer the question of how to translate these theories into an urban reality.

Although Paul Schultze-Naumburg is an avowed supporter of Sitte's theories, the metropolis is actually anathema to him. Nobody could be clearer in rejecting cities than he is in the introduction to *Kulturarbeiten: Der Städtebau*. Yet it would be wrong to conclude that Sitte was therefore also critical of the city and that his was intrinsically a theory of towns, as is often claimed in the literature.[1] There is reason enough to reject this conclusion in the simple fact that Sitte's adopted home of Vienna is a major city, the planning of which he addresses – without ever questioning the validity of the city as an entity. Furthermore, many of his examples are drawn from historic cities, and Sitte explicitly calls for urban schemes on a major city scale.[2]

Nevertheless, the conflict between town and city clearly appears in Jeanneret's study, not least because in 1910 Jeanneret is nominally writing for a conference audience in his home town, La Chaux-de-Fonds, while his practical experience lies in the cities of Munich and Berlin (and his memories of Paris). Indeed, Jeanneret is plainly aware of this discrepancy. Sitte applies the same principles to towns that he does to cities: see for example his plans for the towns of Mährisch-Ostrau, Marienthal, or Olmütz (Moravská Ostrava, Mariánské Údolí, and Olomouc, now in the Czech Republic). He consistently advocates a 'malerisch' (picturesque), or more precisely spatial-architectural, type of urban design with distinct plans adapted to the particular location.[3] Jeanneret, on the other hand, applies one principle to towns and another to cities. For example, he would grant a city its monumental, triumphantly straight avenue such as the Champs-Elysées in Paris, but deny a town the same aspiration. However, as so often in *La Construction des villes*, Jeanneret is not completely consistent and writes in his introduction that curved streets are appropriate in residential areas, while implicitly describing a shopping street as straight.[4] Here, Jeanneret abandons his differentiation between town and city in favour of a functional distinction between residential and business districts.

Indeed, it is possible to detect a certain ambivalence on Jeanneret's part. This permeates the entire Manuscript, but is most keenly felt in his handling of the most suitable shape for streets (curved or straight) and layout for urban squares (irregular or geometric). It is therefore no surprise that this conflict between street shapes continues into *Urbanisme*. Whereas in *La Construction des villes* Jeanneret advocates learning from curved donkey tracks, in *Urbanisme* Le Corbusier favours the straight line over the

---

1 See Gerhard Fehl in *Kleinstadt, Steildach, Volksgemeinschaft* and Wolfgang Sonne, *Representing the State. Capital City Planning in the Early Twentieth Century* (Munich: Prestel, 2003). Sonne is more differentiated in his approach but adopts the same basic position.

2 Collins and Crasemann Collins, *Camillo Sitte: The Birth of Modern City Planning*, pp. 251ff.

3 'Malerisch' (literally: painterly) in German; 'pittoresque' (literally: picture-like) in French. We agree with Collins and Crasemann-Collins who deem 'malerisch' (painterly) untranslatable for these purposes. At times, 'picturesque' is perhaps more appropriate, at others 'pictorial'.

4 LCdv 58–60.

curved, this time leaving the *leçon d'âne* for the donkeys. Yet even here, the conflict is not finally resolved: at the end of *Urbanisme* Le Corbusier describes the fine form of the country road. He makes an exception for its picturesque, sweeping curves and grants it a stay of execution: perhaps harking back to his roots in La Chaux-de-Fonds.

Urban space

Around 1890, at the same time that Camillo Sitte engaged in the first discussion of urban space in his book *Der Städtebau nach seinen künstlerischen Grundsätzen* (City Planning According to Artistic Principles), a branch of architectural and aesthetic theory was emerging in Germany devoted to the phenomenon of space. At the time, August Schmarsow, Heinrich Wölfflin, and Adolf von Hildebrandt were among those who helped develop the idea that space was an abstract concept with a tangible impact. New disciplines such as physiology and psychology were beginning to rub shoulders with art theory, which was also evolving.[5] Camillo Sitte himself embodies such interplay of different influences, having had both medical and artistic training which lend him a particular awareness of the observer's perception of space and the built environment.[6]

The new theories of space in architecture and urban areas focused their attention on the 'everyman' observer rather than on experts trained in art and architecture. In the words of Swiss supporter of heritage protection Georges de Montenach, written in 1908, they prioritised 'Monsieur Tout le Monde'.[7] However, it is likely Jeanneret was not familiar with the detail of these theories: nowhere in the Manuscript of *La Construction des villes* is there a mention of Schmarsow, Wölfflin, or any other art historian concerned with theories of perception. It is true that the notebooks for the *Voyage d'Orient* explicitly mention Wilhelm Worringer, to whose work *Abstraktion und Einfühlung* (Abstraction and Empathy) Jeanneret was introduced by his travel companion August Klipstein.[8] Indeed, we must remember that Jeanneret absorbed the principle of space and its impact on the observer purely via the applied 'practical aesthetics' of Karl Henrici, Camillo Sitte, Paul Schultze-Naumburg, and Albert Erich Brinckmann. From these writers, Jeanneret drew ideas such as: the enclosure of public squares and the asymmetrical organisation of monuments therein (Sitte); the impact of street space on the *flâneur* (Henrici); the significance of the opening onto the square (Schultze-Naumburg); and the observation of human scale, yet another take on the enclosure of squares, plus a major interest in the uniform, symmetrical French royal square (Brinckmann).

In all the chapters of his Manuscript, whether taking the curved or straight path, Jeanneret advocates the spatial organisation of the urban built environment, often even advocating enclosed spaces. This is true whether Jeanneret writes on the spatial characteristics of the street, on the enclosed square – be it picturesque or monumental – or even on the peculiar issue of enclosing walls. The latter is only discussed briefly, but

---

5 See Harry Francis Mallgrave and Eleftherios Ikonomou (eds.), *Empathy, Form, and Space. Problems in German Aesthetics, 1873–1893* (Santa Monica: Getty Center for the History of Art and the Humanities, 1994).

6 See Gabriele Reiterer, *AugenSinn. Zu Raum und Wahrnehmung in Camillo Sittes "Städtebau"* (Salzburg: Pustet, 2003).

7 Montenach, *Pour le visage aimé de la patrie*. Jeanneret quotes Montenach in Cahier 1, LCdv 39.

8 Le Corbusier, *Carnets de Voyage d'Orient*, Carnet 1, p. 43: "Worringer. ‹Einfühlung and Abstraktion› à lire dit Klipstein." Wilhelm Worringer, *Abstraktion und Einfühlung* (Neuwied: Heuser, 1907; new edition Dresden: Verlag der Kunst, 1996).

is nevertheless significant. Schultze-Naumburg contributes crucial suggestions here and Jeanneret draws on his equally important experience of the Camposanto in Pisa. Even where gardens are concerned, Jeanneret looks to their architectural character and the enclosed nature of their space. Although he is heavily influenced by Brinckmann, it should also be noted that Brinckmann's thoroughly critical stance on Sitte does not mean that he does not prioritise space. Quite the reverse: Brinckmann, distinguishing between historical eras, follows his teacher Wölfflin and attributes to each era its own sense of space. He concludes: "To construct cities is to shape spaces using buildings!"[9]

Although Jeanneret's focus on the question of space in urban design permeates the entire Manuscript, that question is not always formulated in Sitte's terms. Sitte believes the creation of urban spaces follows a subtractive principle, and this is the fundamental premise underlying his spatial view of the city; it is not clear that Jeanneret consistently upholds this principle.[10] This type of issue is by no means unique to Jeanneret: it affects the overall approach to urban design during the whole period before the First World War. Colin Rowe wrote in his 1978 work *Collage City* that Berlage's 1915 plan for Amsterdam South saw an abandonment of the subtractive principle in urban design, although Berlage's plan actually created powerful urban spaces. The reason Rowe gives is the lack of that "fabric" (or *tessuto*, to use the illustrative Italian term) which would facilitate the "cutting out" of a street layout – a principle clearly demonstrated by Hauss-mann's boulevards in Paris.[11] Yet Rowe also states that, where no smaller structures are behind the façades, the basic principle of spatial thinking has been relinquished.[12] The architects and urban planners who had to design whole new districts in around 1900 were of course unable to rely on this type of underlying fabric. It may therefore be purely academic to ask whether Berlage's Amsterdam plan, or comparable plans in Ger-many, had dispensed with the basic principle of spatial planning. Yet this question is not without importance. The fact that architects and theorists at the dawn of the 20th century chose space as the basis for their urban plans is not merely proof of an increasing abstraction, a gradual move away from ornament and decoration towards abstract spatial thought. This choice also shows that what was traditionally the fundamental basis for spatial organisation in urban design, namely a built fabric dating back to the Middle Ages or baroque period which would underlie any construction, no longer existed. Thus any reflection on space would be coloured by an awareness of this loss, and might there-fore feature some nostalgia; but that reflection in itself would also be critically important for urban design.

In terms of architectural theory, the most important discovery in the Manuscript of *La Construction des villes* is Jeanneret's emphasis on space and its perception. Jeanneret accurately captures the difficulties arising in the debate on urban spaces. It would appear that, in his work on the concept of urban space, Jeanneret treats architectural space as a malleable, abstract element. When dealing with spatial phenomena, he often uses the

---

9 Brinckmann, *Platz und Monument*, p. 170.
10 "These considerations bring us close to the crux of the matter. In modern city planning the relationship between the built-up and open spaces is exactly reversed. Formerly the empty spaces (streets and plazas) were a unified entity of shapes calculated for their impact." Collins and Crasemann Collins, *Camillo Sitte: The Birth of Modern City Planning*, p. 225.
11 Rowe, *Collage City*, pp. 54–56.
12 "The matrix of the city has become transformed from continuous solid to continuous void." Rowe, *Collage City*, p. 56.

French term *volume*: for example when translating from Brinckmann's *Platz und Monument*. Jeanneret also employs the astonishing term *corporalité* (embodiment of space):

> an impression of beauty! For this, the straight street must assert the feeling of *embodied space*. Its length, breadth, the height of the buildings, will fit together in such a way that perspective tapering is barely apparent. Hence the street will be very short and its ends closed off. – Beauty is rhythm, proportion, harmony. The street will only be beautiful if all the buildings are intimately related, if architects understand that it is mutually beneficial for each to heed the other so all can harmonise to create an *ensemble piece*.[13]

Why does Jeanneret employ the term *corporalité*, and where does he take it from? Is it a literal translation from the German *Körperlichkeit*, a term which plays a major role in the early 20th century *Wirkungsästhetik* movement, which investigated the aesthetics of perception?[14] Even if this is the case, Jeanneret does not employ the term to denote the physical presence of buildings as we would now understand them – as architectural objects. In fact, he consistently uses the term *corporalité* when referring to a tangible three-dimensional space, something which is apparently not adequately conveyed by the term *espace*. The word *corporalité* is rarely used in French, although it is interesting to note Voltaire's use of the term in connection with something ostensibly intangible: he writes of the "corporalité des âmes", or physicality of souls. He means precisely the same thing Jeanneret is seeking to express: actually being able to feel something which in itself is intangible.[15] We can show clearly, taking a single example, that Jeanneret did not unthinkingly ape the concept of space he encountered in the literature. The example can be found in the chapter On Streets, where Jeanneret describes the particular qualities of the Marktgasse in Berne:

> We have all experienced the enchanting Marktgasse in Berne: having been through the passageway under the [Käfigturm] tower [...]. The beauty of this street is generally attributed to the very buildings which frame it, to the superb fountains which enliven it. This is erroneous. Its beauty arises from the feeling of perfect volume in the street, and only then – as a result of this – do the façades contribute effectively to it.[16]

In *Urbanisme*, Le Corbusier has dropped the issue of space in urban design. However, in *La Construction des villes* Jeanneret clearly accepts space as a key part of urban design aesthetics.

Analysis of Jeanneret's chapter On Squares shows him tackling two different interpretations of urban squares. The first part of the chapter (as it appears in the Manuscript Folder) deals with the first of these interpretations, based on Camillo Sitte's theories, plus Schultze-Naumburg's formulations, which add several aspects. The second part of

---

13 LCdv 124.

14 See Francesco Passanti on Jeanneret's use of the term "corporalité" in his essay "Architecture: Proportion, Classicism, and Other Issues", in Von Moos and Rüegg, *Le Corbusier before Le Corbusier*, p. 84.

15 This meaning of *corporalité* is illustrated in Emile Littré, *Dictionnaire de la langue française*, first published 1863/72 "Qualité de ce qui est corporel. ‹Arnobe parle positivement de la corporalité des âmes›, Voltaire, Philosophie II, p. 336."

16 LCdv 104f.

the chapter (in Cahiers C.7 and C.8) presents the second interpretation, primarily based on Brinckmann's remarks. Reading Cahiers C.7 and C.8 gives the impression that Jeanneret is really wrestling with the shape of urban squares. On the one hand the focus by Sitte and Schultze-Naumburg on the picturesque effect of squares seems plausible to him, associated as it is with some asymmetry and irregularity. Yet on the other hand, Jeanneret is obviously so fascinated by the uniform, symmetrical, and complete shape of the French royal square that he is tempted to favour this type – perhaps because its unity amplifies the spatial impact of the square.

It seems that reading Brinckmann's *Platz und Monument* (Square and Monument) in particular prompted Jeanneret to see the structural unity of these squares as the cause of their major impact. Jeanneret describes how "Le culte du moi" (the cult of self) found expression in urbanism via the Place des Victoires and Place des Vosges. Here, the monument is placed in the middle of a square which is doubly symmetrical, surrounded by architecture whose dominant characteristic is the unity of form. It is remarkable to witness how Jeanneret, despite arguing throughout his study for picturesque solutions, singles out for particular praise the monumental, centralising, symmetrical designs for urban squares in the French baroque and early classical periods.

Jeanneret's real achievement in this connection is, as already discussed, his eclectic answer to a pressing question: should solutions to urban expansion be geometric and monumental, or picturesque? If the opportunity presents itself to plan and build a square 'en un jet' (in one go), he believes the best reference would be the monumental unity and symmetry of Paris's squares. However, if a city is developing its square over a longer period of time, the appropriate idiom would be picturesque.

Does Jeanneret's solution take him closer to Sitte or to Brinckmann? Brinckmann distinguishes between particular ways of understanding space by emphasising that, as with artistic concepts in general, they are determined by their era. He fundamentally rejects a picturesque solution, not merely because it is anachronistic, but also because even the master builder of the Middle Ages, at a time when "the necessary space is available in the old towns, with his basic instinct for order [...] strives for a square with a regular layout, without enclosed sides".[17] And Brinckmann clearly states, "Sitte writes all too often of 'picturesque effect', which is only too easily reminiscent of theatrical effect. Architects should not build for the love of theatrical effect."[18] Thus Jeanneret's compromise may be closer to Sitte. After all, as Collins and Crasemann as well as Posener have indicated, Sitte does not posit the mediaeval square as the only possible model.[19]

Sitte takes an eclectic approach, accepting the picturesque solution but also making clear that he seeks to define the artistic principles according to which spaces and squares have been and will be designed. He is eclectic in his choice of architectural styles for façades in squares, as illustrated by the Votive Church plans.[20] Sitte clearly emphasises the esteem in which he holds baroque squares, with their regular, symmetrical layout.[21] Yet he does not mention any occasions on which it would be appropriate to site

17 Brinckmann, *Platz und Monument*, p. 2f.
18 Brinckmann, *Platz und Monument*, p. 165.
19 "As we know, Sitte was not exclusively interested in how towns appeared during the Middle Ages." Collins and Crasemann Collins, *Camillo Sitte: The Birth of Modern City Planning*, p. 81.
20 See Sitte's design for the enclosure of the Votive Church in Vienna: Collins and Crasemann Collins, *Camillo Sitte: The Birth of Modern City Planning*, pp. 281ff.
21 Collins and Crasemann Collins, *Camillo Sitte: The Birth of Modern City Planning*, pp. 218ff.

a monument centrally in a square. Indeed, Brinckmann was the first in the discourse to suggest this, and it appears that Jeanneret saw this distinction very clearly in 1910 – although he would later shift the emphasis in his own urban designs towards a preference for central orientation. However, more relevant than Sitte's personal view is how Jeanneret adopted and interpreted that view. I would therefore stress once again that Jeanneret's enthusiasm for baroque and early classical layouts only emerges in the second part of the chapter On Squares, the part in which he considers Brinckmann's theories.

Beauté and utilité

The very structure of *La Construction des villes* illustrates Jeanneret's aim to harmonise beauty and utility, and in particular to prioritise artistic considerations above all others. In the main part of his book, Jeanneret constructs a unique grammar of urban design comprising basic elements. These Elements of the City: blocks, streets, squares, enclosing walls, bridges, trees, gardens and parks, cemeteries, and garden cities, are astonishing due to the seemingly inconsistent way the list is assembled. Jeanneret is undecided as to the requisite size for an 'element'; he does not list some as a subset of the others, as could be expected. Compare, for example, the tree on one hand with the garden or park on the other. The garden city 'element' sits particularly uneasily in this list, a fact of which Jeanneret himself was aware.[22] However, it would be too simplistic to condemn his way of listing elements as wholly inconsistent. The remarkable thing about it is that each individual element, including the enclosing wall and the individual tree, is considered sufficiently important to warrant being listed alongside whole blocks of houses. This shows artistic, architectural thought winning out over a purely functional approach. Indeed, these individual elements, each of which is inherently useful in its own right (a wall closes a garden off from the street, a tree gives shade in summer), are singled out for praise by architects with a 'picturesque' outlook, such as Camillo Sitte and Paul Schultze-Naumburg. They are viewed as independent elements in urban design from both artistic and spatial perspectives, placing them on an equal footing with streets, squares, and blocks.

In his General Considerations, Jeanneret defines the urban designer's job as creating art out of necessity. He views urban design as an artistic activity and not as the rational fulfilment of functions necessary for city living. In this, *La Construction des villes* differs markedly from *Urbanisme*, which begins with the provocative declaration: "The city is a tool."[23] Back in 1910, Jeanneret had stated: "The layout of a city is primarily a work of art; in order to realise it, the artist must draw inspiration from the same rules which govern the other arts: the rules of *convenance*, balance and variety."[24] In brief, he saw the urban designer's role as: "Architect, engineer, painter, sculptor and poet, the city planner is faced with one of the noblest tasks: that of bringing his fellow citizens the joy of living in a city where the living is good."[25] Beauty takes priority for Jeanneret. If, as an urban designer, he were faced with two equally practical solutions, he would choose

---

22 In different drafts of the table of contents for his text, Jeanneret vacillates between including the 'garden city' as an Element of the City and as part of his Critical Application.

23 "La ville est un outil de travail." Le Corbusier, *Urbanisme*, p. I.

24 LCdv 27.

25 LCdv 27.

the one which held the promise of greater beauty. Yet Jeanneret does not dismiss the question of utility. In fact, he repeatedly seeks a balance between the practical and aesthetic sides of urban design. In the chapter entitled *Des moyens possibles* (On Possible Strategies), Jeanneret takes German and English reformist urban design around the year 1900 as proof that beauty and utility are compatible. The philosophy is seen as an example to be adopted in Switzerland in general and La Chaux-de-Fonds in particular:

> People have always stated that art and economy or art and hygiene are incompatible. [...] The facts have disproved this 'incompatibility': the works published on the subject have disproved it from a theoretical viewpoint, and the radical reforms which have occurred in recent years in the progressive towns and cities of Germany and Britain have disproved it from a practical viewpoint.[26]

It should, however, be noted that Camillo Sitte did not believe it possible to resolve the inner conflict between the *malerisch* and the practical through discussion alone, as this conflict existed in all art forms, even those that seemed the freest.[27]

In contrast, Jeanneret aims to show that beauty and utility are far from being mutually exclusive, as in fact they determine one another. In defence of this view, Jeanneret cites extracts from Theodor Fischer's 1903 lecture on *Stadterweiterungsfragen* (Questions of urban expansion). He demands that "no major effort" be expended in pursuit of beauty, instead linking form to function in the Arts and Crafts tradition, convinced that beauty increases rather than decreases with simplicity and functionalism:

> I am going so far as to say that we could have everything at a much lower price if we made things more beautiful – and more simple. More simple, and more fit for purpose! [...] Thus I seek to link aesthetics with economy [...] and hygiene.[28]

In his attempt to combine *beauté* and *utilité*, Jeanneret does not turn against Sitte. Instead, as shown above, he turns against "bureaucratic" design, which only churns out clichéd, supposedly practical solutions that are actually both ugly and far from practical. Jeanneret unleashes an impressive tirade in *La Construction des villes* against planning officials. Although Camillo Sitte's work also contains such attacks on officialdom, Jeanneret's comments are mainly based on Schultze-Naumburg's passionate critique of "clichéd" urban design and of official solutions which are "hostile to life"; indeed, passages of his polemic are incorporated word for word into Jeanneret's Manuscript. And he contrasts the planning official with the figure of the urban designer, a position to which he clearly aspires and which he sees largely embodied in the person of Theodor Fischer.

This urban designer is an artist who does not neglect the technical and practical aspects of his role, but is first and foremost creative. Such creativity requires patience, claims Jeanneret, as the urban designer will not see the fruits of his labour – a new, functioning city or district – for many years. In the chapter On Possible Strategies in particular, Jeanneret develops the idea of a superman who can control the city's final shape. This part of the polemic against planning bureaucracy stems less from Sitte's

26 LCdv 327.
27 Collins and Crasemann Collins, *Camillo Sitte: The Birth of Modern City Planning*, p. 248.
28 See Cahier C.11, LCdv 459f.

example than from Jeanneret's own imagination, in which he is a superhuman genius; as Turner has shown, this idea began early on.[29] Elsewhere, however, Sitte and the journal he founded, *Der Städtebau* (urban design), did indeed serve as an example to Jeanneret, as demonstrated by the latter's staunch support for urban design competitions whenever extensions of cities are planned. Sitte is also the source, perhaps via Theodor Fischer, for Jeanneret's conviction that planning must take account of topography. Before the turn of the 20th century, the term *genius loci* had already been mooted – as had the concomitant concept that one should not only draw contour lines into plans, but also wherever possible make urban design models.[30]

In four of the newly uncovered Manuscript pages, Jeanneret develops a definition of sorts for 'beauty' and 'utility'. He writes that in the 19th century, bureaucrats had spoken of "geometry, utility, balance, hygiene, simplicity, beauty and modernism". Yet as applied by administrations, these fine words stood merely for poor, uniform design – hence the need for fresh definitions. In Jeanneret's formulation "the utility of a city lies in the fastest possible route through it", hygiene is "bringing the calm that comes from living in inviting homes where [people] can be happy". Hence hygiene did not just stand for street cleaning, but referred to the health of the individual urban residents. It was "synonymous with the happiness which, leaving aside other factors, a pleasant dwelling can ensure".[31] Jeanneret's definition of hygiene is not restricted to technical aspects. However, on the whole Jeanneret lacks precision in his use of terminology, and one would therefore wish to avoid unduly restricting the definition of these terms. In the section of text cited here, Jeanneret equates *utilité* with *circulation* (transit/traffic), and places *utilité* on a par with *hygiène*. Elsewhere in the Manuscript, *utilité* is used as an umbrella term covering *hygiène*, *circulation*, and *économie*, which comprise the practical requirements for a city.[32] These definitions remain imprecise; *utilité* and its various facets are only discussed superficially. Where Jeanneret approaches the practical side of urban design, he does so almost exclusively in conjunction with aesthetic questions. Thus his definition of hygiene is also drawn with a broad brush and encompasses psychological health, and therefore aesthetics in its broadest sense. Even the beauty of the city can therefore be considered part of its utility, as this beauty ensures the inhabitants' aesthetic well-being.

The architectural garden and the garden city

Green space in the city is another important topic covered in the Manuscript. However, it has not been possible to determine conclusively whether Jeanneret addressed the various green spaces in the city because of a suggestion L'Eplattenier made, as Brooks quite reasonably supposes, or whether this was Jeanneret's own initiative. I assume that both contributed: Jeanneret certainly did discuss the matter with L'Eplattenier during his stay in La Chaux-de-Fonds over the summer, but all the available evidence shows he was already examining the issue of green space in urban areas. This is hardly surprising,

29 See Turner, *Education*, p. 17.
30 See Sitte's use of the term 'genius loci' in Sitte, *Der Städtebau*, p. 102. This term is not directly replicated in the translation by Collins and Crasemann-Collins.
31 LCdv 47–48.
32 LCdv 327ff.

given that Jeanneret viewed a great many projects on parks, cemeteries, and garden cities at the Berlin urban design exhibition, and made extensive notes on these. What is more noteworthy is that, during his remaining month in Munich (mid-September to mid-October 1910), Jeanneret threw himself enthusiastically into researching urban green spaces: they were of genuine interest to him. In particular, his notes on the planned chapter On Gardens and Parks show a yearning for a 'paradise garden'; it is no exaggeration to say that Jeanneret envisaged these spaces as the setting for a true opposition of heaven and hell. He actually employed the term 'hell' ("l'enfer de la ville") to describe Berlin, a city which he criticised seriously on several occasions, for example in letters to his parents.[33]

Furthermore, Jeanneret sought – and found – in George Riat's *L'Art des jardins* many earlier examples of 'paradise gardens' which he intended to transform into contemporary solutions. Yet this is not the only time Jeanneret described something using polar opposites. His answer to the question of what an ideal garden would look like is clear: regular and architectural. In this, Jeanneret was once again allied with turn-of-the-century architectural reformers such as Muthesius and Schultze-Naumburg, who advocated architectural garden design in their academic dispute with followers of the Lenné school, including Carl Heicke.

Of all the literature and other potential sources of inspiration for Jeanneret's later designs, one urban plan in particular stands out: Georg Metzendorf's Margarethenhöhe garden suburb, built for the Margarethe-Krupp-Stiftung in Essen. It encompasses, in condensed form, almost all the urban elements Jeanneret lists in *La Construction des villes*, and is also almost the ideal plan for a picturesque town or suburb. These elements range from its gently curving streets, to the façades and garden walls which enclose the streets, to the carefully staged approach to the suburb, which suggests that the suburb is enclosed by a wall. The town centre is a traditional market square, hosting all the necessary facilities including a department store, town hall, and church. Margarethenhöhe can be reached from the city of Essen via a bridge over a gorge, and has thus been informed by the local topography; the gatehouse complex serves as an entrance to and 'reception area' for the suburb, and the simple buildings are designed around local examples from the Rhineland-Westphalia region.

In his treatise, Jeanneret lists all the above points as prerequisites for good urban design. This explains the striking similarity between his 1914 design for the garden city in La Chaux-de-Fonds (produced for the investor Arnold Beck) and the Margarethenhöhe development. Indeed, the design is much more akin to Margarethenhöhe than to Hellerau, which Brooks has cited as a possible model.[34] It was not in Hellerau, but here in Essen that Jeanneret found the urban design theories which he compiled in *La Construction des villes* embodied in a small town. It is certainly astonishing that Jeanneret's *Etude sur le mouvement d'art décoratif en Allemagne*, published in 1912, contains no mention of Margarethenhöhe. Instead, he refers back to notes made in his *Carnets de voyage d'Allemagne* for examples of garden cities as places of redemption, fostering a happy and morally sound human race.

---

33 For instance, when writing to his parents, on 18 October 1910: "Berlin extended a horrid welcome to me this morning" ("Berlin était ignoble ce matin dans son acceuil") and 21 October 1910 (R1-5-67 FLC).
34 See Brooks, *Formative Years*, p. 370.

A somewhat stupid book, "un livre un peu idiot"?

Jeanneret was commissioned to undertake a clearly delineated study, which he began in April 1910. He believed it would be dealt with quickly, but within six months the study had grown into a detailed analysis of contemporary German-language discourse on urban design. Jeanneret had launched into what amounted to an introductory immersion course in urban design based in Munich and Berlin; the main part lasted until November. The sheer volume of notes he made is impressive: Jeanneret produced around 300 handwritten chapter pages during this time, with a further 300 pages of excerpts and translations, plus some 70 drawings and sketches.

How independent was his writing? Perhaps a general remark on Jeanneret's degree of independence would be appropriate here. Le Corbusier repeatedly referred to his development as autodidactic, implying that he had trained himself, but it has become clear – as demonstrated in Brooks' *Formative Years* if not earlier – that this was not in fact the case. Brooks and others show plainly that Jeanneret was in no way an *Übermensch*, but depended instead on external stimulus and criticism. Prior to his final departure from La Chaux-de-Fonds in 1917, Charles L'Eplattenier, Auguste Perret, and William Ritter were Jeanneret's main sources of guidance. These three men acted as *maîtres* to whom Jeanneret, partly because of persistent self-doubt, constantly looked for reassurance of his own direction. Yet receiving such guidance did not prevent him from seeking and finding his own voice with great certainty and self-belief.

These two sides of Jeanneret's personality also emerge clearly in *La Construction des villes*: L'Eplattenier was present in the background as the instigator of the study, and his own preference for Sitte's theories certainly influenced Jeanneret. Jeanneret made many enquiries of L'Eplattenier in April and May 1910: this demonstrates his close focus at this stage on his teacher's ideas. However, as Jeanneret's analysis deepened, he became more independent. Above all, he expanded the range of issues under discussion in light of the diverse themes in the urban design exhibition. L'Eplattenier's letters to Jeanneret have not survived, so it is not clear whether he proposed any reading material. Jeanneret certainly asked questions, made suggestions and requests – giving us a rough impression of their discussions in terms of subject matter and intensity. However, there is no evidence that L'Eplattenier intervened directly in the Manuscript, in the form of either corrections or comments.

It is important to acknowledge that, being new to urban design matters, Jeanneret was obliged to stay close to his sources. Indeed, rather than summarising what he had read, Jeanneret often translated whole sections or even chapters from German into French, and employed these as his own words. The sources can still be identified in his workbooks, but in the finished chapters these references are generally missing. In these finished sections, his own comments are few and far between. It may therefore be difficult to ascertain the extent to which Jeanneret's own thoughts and convictions feature here.

Yet *La Construction des villes* hardly resembles the work of a clueless novice: it is an unconventional, well-thought-out compilation of contemporary theories focusing on the concept of space and its perception, the attempt to reconcile beauty and utility, and the issue of preserving historic monuments and buildings. Even the inventive, eclectic response to the conflict between the picturesque and the monumental appears to be Jeanneret's own work. Furthermore, it is worth noting that established authors such as Henrici, Schultze-Naumburg, and Brinckmann used Sitte's *Städtebau* as their theoretical foundation, just as Jeanneret did.

An answer to the question of independence now emerges: whilst Jeanneret's study was initiated by L'Eplattenier, *La Construction des villes* developed its own independent character as the work progressed. Could it be that Jeanneret initially saw the theories which he discussed in *La Construction des villes* as a purely abstract theoretical framework, which had yet to prove its practical relevance? These concepts might have remained theoretical after Jeanneret stopped working on the Manuscript in March 1911, at least until he had fleshed them out with his own life experience – for example on his *Voyage d'Orient*. I would claim, however, that he had already fathomed the concept of 'tangible' space, developing it in the light of his own experience. There is some evidence to support this, such as Jeanneret's use of the unusual term *corporalité* to describe this quality of space, primarily with reference to the Marktgasse in Berne.

What overall impression does *La Construction des villes* make, and how does this compare with *Urbanisme*? We have already outlined the structural similarities between the two, alongside some major differences. As Le Corbusier himself was so tight-lipped about *La Construction des villes*, save to declare the work pointless, we feel a counter-argument is required – to salvage some of the book's reputation. It may be incomplete, but it is certainly not "somewhat stupid".

There is no doubt that *Urbanisme* was written with greater knowledge than *La Construction des villes* was, and indeed 15 years separate the two projects. Nevertheless, I take the view that *La Construction des villes* is more accomplished in its method. First, it has been drafted with greater precision of thought: *La Construction des villes* is a treatise in terms of its structure and method, whereas *Urbanisme* is a piece of urban design propaganda. In *La Construction des villes*, Jeanneret aims to convince the reader using arguments – well-balanced, reasonable reflections – and constructs these carefully, working from the ground up. In contrast, *Urbanisme* is a promotional text, which attempts to persuade the reader. *Urbanisme* is also a surprisingly disorganised text. Le Corbusier writes about order, arguing for rationality in a polemic against chaos and sentimentality. But in doing so, he creates precisely the type of chaos he is railing against: instead of arguing logically, clearly, and precisely, Le Corbusier loses himself in clichés, vanities, and redundancy – and says much too little about the true subject matter.

The same author, writing in 1910, managed to avoid these mistakes. Jeanneret was disciplined, keeping close to the problem as stated (except in the Proposition, which he himself declared "probably useless" in 1915). In 1910 Charles-Edouard Jeanneret was still searching for the right city form, whereas by 1925 he was convinced that he had found it, and therefore took less care with his arguments. Le Corbusier did succeed in attracting the level of attention he wanted for *Urbanisme*, but most of this was probably due to his designs for the *Ville Contemporaine* and the *Plan Voisin*, to which *Urbanisme* is practically a guidebook. Without these drawings, the book would not have caused such a stir.

If Jeanneret had published *La Construction des villes* in French in 1911 as a response to the German-language debate on urban design, how much attention would it have attracted? That same year, Walter Curt Behrendt's *Die Einheitliche Blockfront als Raumelement im Stadtbau* appeared, alongside Otto Wagner's study *Die Großstadt*.[35] These texts shifted the focus of the debate on the elements which form urban space.

---

35 Curt Walter Behrendt: *Die einheitliche Blockfront als Raumelement im Stadtbau: Ein Beitrag zur Stadtbaukunst der Gegenwart* (Berlin: Cassirer, 1911); Otto Wagner: *Die Großstadt: eine Studie über diese* (Vienna: Schroll, [1911]).

Brinckmann's *Platz und Monument* had paved the way for unity to be valued more highly in the design of façades in streets and squares; Behrendt and Wagner now advocated unity throughout the city. Picturesque urban design was past its peak. *La Construction des villes*, with its search for the picturesque aspects of urban design, would therefore have arrived slightly too late. In other words, almost all the theories that Jeanneret discussed had already been digested by other people – from this perspective, his treatment of the subject would have been of marginal importance.

Nevertheless, Jeanneret's text, with its original comparison between monumental unity and individualistic, picturesque attitudes, would certainly have been able to hold its own against its contemporaries. In his presentation of *Les Eléments constitutifs de la ville*, however imperfect, Jeanneret achieved something nobody else had achieved: he began to systematise the subject matter at the heart of the debate on urban design aesthetics. This prompts us to call his work an aesthetic grammar of the city, since it defines and articulates the individual architectural and urban design elements which belong to and create the city.

Thus Jeanneret's overall achievement lies less in the originality of the thoughts he expresses than in the way they are presented. This is remarkable: his later writing often lacks such a systematic approach. In *La Construction des villes*, Jeanneret even preempts the urban design handbook drafted by art historian Cornelius Gurlitt in 1914 – which did not appear until 1920 due to the First World War.[36] Gurlitt covers more ground than Jeanneret, investigating individual functional and aesthetic aspects of urban design in greater depth, but Jeanneret's study is very similar to Gurlitt's handbook insofar as they both present an aesthetic of urban design. Hence it is no exaggeration to claim that Jeanneret's book would have earned itself a special place in the debate on urban design circa 1910. It is therefore highly regrettable that Jeanneret never published *La Construction des villes*.

---

36 Cornelius Gurlitt, *Handbuch des Städtebaues* (Berlin: Architekturverlag Der Zirkel, 1920). This book gives an overview of both the technical and artistic aspects of urban design, in the form of a detailed grammar of the city which posits an aesthetic of perception.

La Construction des villes

The Manuscript

Legend

[…]	Places where Jeanneret omits text in his excerpts or translations.
[…]	Passages omitted by the editor from the present manuscript
[__]	Blank space (for example after "Fig.")
[__]	Illegible text
{with text}	Additions by Jeanneret in the margins or above the body text
*	Notes added by Jeanneret

Proposition:

[LCdv 1] PROPOSITION
[Wrapper marked with:] Probably useless. 23 June 1915[1]

[LCdv 2] 1//PROPOSITION. –
If men came one day to band together in villages and towns, then it was indeed with the idea of improving their lot. Today one *resigns oneself* to living in a town, with the recognition that life there has become boring and tiring, often barbaric.

For too long, mutual relations between the individual and the community have bound men little by little, to an arbitrary living condition from which it is no longer possible to escape. A special mentality is born: that of the 'city dweller' which is expressed in infinitely complex needs. [Unclear how much text is crossed out here.] Now, realising these needs places the most conflicting elements into constant opposition and creates *inharmony*, a cause of the adversity in towns. This inharmony, which is more appreciable in a large metropolis, has made it very difficult to improve life there.

In order to resolve the question, certain great minds have only managed to propose destruction: obliteration of the accursed walls and the degenerate races; incredible explosion, ravages of fire and iron ... Then, after years *when* nature has reasserted itself, the problem will be *repeated*, of giving happiness, to the community by placing it in a purely harmonious setting. The systematic creators will then present their dreams ...

Although the problem proves anguished today for over-sized agglomerations, it remains *solvable* and sounds simple, for cities of smaller size. It is therefore these which we will deal with.[2]

[LCdv 3] 2)
– When the first tribes were formed, primitive man had to sacrifice something of his personality; but palpable, indisputable advantages were the aim of and reward for this infringement of his individual liberty; it was a sacrifice worth making.

Today, the question is no different. In the name of liberty, we have tolerated serious infringements of that liberty. The allures of some people, stronger, richer and more commercially inclined, sometimes of those who are less scrupulous, less rounded and less artistic, have compromised many factors in the normal life of society. In respect of the development of towns and cities, the need for individual sacrifice to the common good is axiomatic. Yet *this is no longer the case.*

{[Above the previous two paragraphs:] good}

In all eras when peoples were rising out of barbarism to their zenith, the laws dictated by the majority brought justice, power, beauty – all these relationships have been

---

1 It is no longer possible, now that Brooks, Emery and the present editor have all investigated these papers, to ascertain which part of the Manuscript this 1915 wrapper and comment refer to. I assume however that it refers only to the Proposition. Of all the chapters, the Proposition bears the clearest signs of reworking by Jeanneret in summer 1915; this text was written out by his mother, and can therefore be dated to the best of our knowledge to August/September 1910 in La Chaux-de-Fonds. The revisions are in Jeanneret's handwriting; the style of handwriting – which is already redolent of Le Corbusier's later, flowing style – would indicate a date of 1915. Jeanneret either did not edit or only sparsely annotated the other chapters his mother wrote up (On Streets, etc.).

2 This paragraph was crossed out.

retained between the ideas of the majorities of days gone by, and the ideas of today. Thus peoples of indifferent origin have bequeathed to humanity, in witness to their wisdom, such souvenirs as Thebes, Athens, Paris etc. and all the major cities, some of which still hold onto the glorious past.

That same spirit of radiating power animated provincial towns and even the smallest market towns at that time; that is why excavations and searches unearthed the purest masterpieces, all dating

[LCdv 4] Proposition//3

from the same *years* and indeed supplying proof of the general movements of peoples and not of several particular leaps forward.

There were glory days for entire peoples. This is a point which we must bear in mind. Because these countries had a major driver, which was an idea breathing life into all its surroundings.

Then after triumph came fatigue. The time of decadence dawned, causing big ideas, moral principles to topple, bastardising all that was healthy, flattering perverse instincts and leading peoples into a state of slump in which each man bemoaned his lot and in which pride was no more, in which all collective strength dried up.

However, just as spring returns after winter, so in the history of peoples, when the decades have passed over people and things, gradually that which creates mankind's very essence wells back up: his appetite to fight for an ideal goal, his need for revealed truth which, acquired at the price of combat, *leads to* joy and health.

The 19th century, after the great shock caused by the Revolution, was destined to be a chaos of highly complex torments and desires. Because of the mixing of so many races – a mixing which strengthened the weaker ones – Europe could not at that time fade and die out as Assyria,

[LCdv 5] 4

Egypt or Rome did. All the most passionate aspects of man, from the vilest egotism to the greatest magnanimity, fought, tore at one another, making *men* into peoples bruised, experiencing disgust and sometimes foolish hope. And it is due to the great tension that truth began to become detached and called – everywhere, in sometimes clumsy terms – for goodness, justice, beauty.

Pessimists may decide that it is impossible to rise again; [but] from the pernicious encroachment of industrialism, from the improper use of current forces, from the present imbalance, [we] may rise towards a great and noble idea, happiness arrives, greater for all, and especially for the dispossessed.

The 20th century heralds the power of communal institutions: the participation of everyone in public life, free entry for all into intellectual life. Forces that are currently opposed will need to educate one another.

The city will then change with the impetus from these new requirements. Beauty will inhabit the street and housing. The future will create festivals. The future will create, outside our current daily life, sanctuaries of beauty dedicated to the glory of goodness. Schools will be set up for the development of taste as much as for that of the sciences; nature will be saved from profanation so that it can always remain a temple of recollection, 'raising up' virile forces.

[LCdv 6] Proposition//5

Hence hatred will be less violent, respect of one's fellows made possible by the balance due [in turn] to sacrificing the egotistical 'self'. Respect for the masses as a whole will be reborn, and the love of homeland, which so many current factors have tarnished, will be revived in the form of a more real altruism, in the form of a justifiable local pride, pride in the work finally accomplished through the judicious use of rational forces. And just as in long-gone eras, at the touch of harmony the moral feeling of an entire people will rise up in an imposing block!

{simply say that there will be more happiness possible}

Our desire for beauty has not been properly realised for almost a century now.

The withdrawal of artists into their ivory towers has led us to the most unfortunate artistic designs; it has provoked a very regrettable conflict between the public and the producers of art so that, since then, they have been relegated to a position outside working life.

We no longer demand that art reign over our governors, and we are even ready to consider as legends those edicts – which reveal fuller governments – in which vibrant patriotism shone out in memorable terms.[1] – In response to the brutal, loud sound of armoury,

{remove[:] from the preoccupations of working life we knew how to combine beauty with costume, custom, dance, housing, furniture, fêtes etc.}

I ["]Whereas the great wisdom of a people of illustrious origin, requiring that it proceed

[LCdv 7] 6)

we knew in the past how to add a gentle, most enduring note of poetic and plastic art; very naturally the noblest buds blossomed. ... the white Panathenea unfurled along the length of the ramps on the Acropolis; Venice had emerged as the 'pearl of the Adriatic'; in the tumult of wars, the Florentine lily had shone through; while in the misty towns of the North there emerged halls, town halls where in strange silhouettes the memories were evoked of distant merchant voyages to lands with jungles and fantastic architecture. Artists are right to complain about governments' lack of interest;

[Comment continued, large area crossed out:]

in matters concerning its administration, such that the wisdom of its views shall burst forth from the works that it commissions, we hereby order Arnolfo, the leading master in our community: to design a model for the restoration of Santa-Riparata, which bears the imprint of such pomp and magnificence that human art and imagination could imagine nothing more beautiful – this being according to a resolution made through both a private and public consultation with the most able persons in the town to not undertake for the community any work, the execution of which was not required to respond to feelings which are all the more great and generous because they result from the deliberations of a meeting of citizens whose intentions in this regard only form a single, unified will." Edict promulgated in Florence by [__] in 12 [94])

[LCdv 8] Proposition//7

on the other hand, are they themselves without sin? Should they not ask themselves the question: "If art has fallen into such disrespect, if one pays slightly less attention to artists than to the incurably insane or to elderly paupers, have we not done everything we can to be considered as a luxurious category of individuals, of no use to public life? Have we successfully deployed the powerful weapon: of education? Or if we have attempted this, have we done it in the best way by wanting to transport the crowds in exhibition halls, where art sits exasperated on the walls and stands? –

We have populated some squares with monuments, busts or important groups. But we have never seen the people return time and again to feast their eyes on so much beauty, such as the simple folk in the Florentine countryside who never tire of contemplating, at the Baptistery, Basilica of Saint Mary of the Flower, the works of Pisano and the Ghibertis![3]

{Modern museums (which take up almost the entire budget for Fine Arts, and have a disastrous effect of removing painting and sculpture from their true framework and relegating architecture – the superior blossoming – to the basest rank), museums} whose walls are offered up to popular meditation, have never captured 10 people together in a joint burst of enthusiasm!

Well then, since the masses are not capable of judging art and are insufficiently educated to resonate with creations which may be superior, we have determined that the *field of activity* which we proposed does not meet current needs. – And we are not so very angry with our governments if they take a lot of persuading to fritter away public funds on superfluous works!" –

… … *Another field of activity!* That is one which controls modern life, and

[LCdv 9] 8)

the expression of which forms a succession of popular ideas.

This new field is art introduced into everyday life. The framework for this most lively artistic life is the *city*; a framework which today is so lamentable that art has escaped its bounds or has remained within and suffocated. It is this framework above all which, not only for the Arts but above all and primarily for human happiness, must urgently be transformed.

Happiness will only be found in art when concerns about the struggle for daily existence have subsided. – Campaigns in society will generally achieve a more stable balance. As for us, we must therefore occupy ourselves with offering a setting sufficient for the new living conditions: *a hygienic city, a useful city, and therefore designed with beauty.*

This is the topic of our study.

The City! *[Part or early version of the Proposition]*

[LCdv 10] 13)

The City! This is a word which opens up an unlimited, infinitely complex field to the imagination. The city, today, is almost all the life of humanity: its laws of organisation, its struggles and its needs, its dream. Man has through the centuries gradually transformed his way of living. He finds himself at the beginning of this 20th century, living a life almost totally opposed to the one he lived in the time we call 'the golden age', and yet here he is more fiercely enthusiastic still, equally determined to fight for happiness as this happiness seems, due to an accumulation of disturbances arising from the

---

3 This sentence was crossed out.

unrestrained egotism of these last centuries, to want to escape his grasp; some say they can already feel it ice cold like a corpse between their clutching fingers. –

The City. This is the broadest of subjects: it is the field in which the economist, the policeman, the jurist, the pedagogue, the moralist, the scientist, the philanthropist operate, it is also the poet's field. The late 19th century had the feeling of the active power of these colossal agglomerations of all human passions. It felt the immense suffering, the deaf and poignant lament of the city, and its poets found in it unprecedented concord, cries of real life lived, with a power equivalent to or even dominating it, the lyrical tones of outmoded dreamers – whose muse could resonate only with past memories of bygone eras in which, they sing, the sun was always brilliant, and nature pure. Our era can hear emerging, amidst the terrible tumults of all the aspirations and all the decline, a new cry, a healthy cry: joy wishes to be rediscovered: and not in plains

[LCdv 11]

{not in reactionary efforts tinged with the melancholy of past beauty,}

[LCdv 12] 15)

and mountains, in forests and oceans, irrevocably debased – but in the very nightmare that is the city! The feverish, modern, intensive city, the city of toil, of factories, of electricity whose exuberance, whose overflowing vitality [...] the open country with roads, canals, railways, and will deflower this firmament – [...] respite for tired eyes – with the invasion of new machines.

These stronger poets, whose voice is already ringing in some ears, can sense the opportunity for a joyous conquest which is certainly possible. It is these poets whom we rally round, for words and lamentations cannot stop the wheels of the chariot of progress.

Frankly, if we immediately [place ourselves] under the banner of this young phalanx, it is because we wish to reaffirm our faith in the splendour of progress, in the greatness of the human soul, in the immense beauty of its aspirations. It is because we wish for our ideals to be realised, and our faith will lie herein: the good, the just and the beautiful pushing humanity to a new zenith greater, more magnificent than all those we have known. For

[LCdv 13] 17)

this pinnacle will belong to the community, with engraved above its door the Word, finally spoken: we work for one another.

However the reason for this booklet is of a much less philosophical order. Our aptitudes do not allow us to remain at dazzling metaphysical heights. We simply wish to demonstrate common sense and set out by means of a swift classification followed by a critical view of even more limited emergence, what we think of the city, of [...] very positive [...] of houses and streets, districts and suburbs; and we will devote the major part of this short study to the question which is so pressing, so urgent: the beauty or ugliness – the reader will decide which – of our own town.

So that we avoid excessive incursions into domains beyond the question, we will design right away a plan which we will constrain ourselves to follow, giving to each its relative value.

[LCdv 14] 19)

We will quickly say what we think to be the reason for cities, and how they have in some eras shone like beacons which have yet to go out. Then having established concrete laws which made of these cities complete artworks, we will try in the IInd part to see whether the natural instinct of our ancestors guided them well and whether the instinct which inhabits us ourselves, master builders in the 19th century and beginning of the 20th, is still a natural instinct and therefore a major factor in any artistic realisation. –

[LCdv 15] 21//I Part.

Why have men organised themselves from the very beginning? It was in order to combat the hostile natural elements. Then after that it was to neutralise the too-violent needs of the strongest men, and their brutal instincts. On this basis we then created the primordial principle of all societies, and one which is still the fundamental axiom of our agglomerations: brute force of some balanced by the number [text breaks off here.]

Sketches for the Proposition

[LCdv 16]

The city overwhelms the poor man. It satisfies the rich man, who leaves when he has had enough. The ordinary man must be repatriated to the countryside in a beautiful environment.

Proposition I. first camp where there was a military superior commander – one chose a hill, the mouth of a river and put a castle then church there, and the city flowed from that.

Originally men organised themselves *out of necessity*; this remains *today* in the past as today there was one party who gained a benefit,* another who suffered from it. Today it is a question of finding a greater share of happiness for all in this organisation which is necessary.

Societies of the past which formed and extended cities were more concerned than we are with making existence in agglomerations more pleasant, and replacing natural life (countrysides) with artificial life (the city) more beautiful due to art because man in the city

[LCdv 17] 2)

had to substitute beauty found in art for the beauty of nature. It was, overall, finding a balance.

*Athens had 30,000 slaves to make beauty for others. – Basically the world does not change, but Christianity has brought charity: a feeling which will, through development far into the future, produce improved manifestations. It is only 50 years ago that this entered into practice, it had remained until then a 'fragrance' to give pleasure. It is now given outward expression, children's hospitals etc. Christianity germinated in man's heart and is flowering, and growing to improve the lot of our modern slaves. [End of comment.]

The builder of the magnificent temples in Egypt, the labourer, the Parthenon, the slave who carried the Parthenon's columns – got, besides his trouble, a very great share of happiness because he was aware that his efforts [continued in the margin, vertically:], however puny, were useful and served the glory of a superior being (his God, his [King?])

[LCdv 18] 3)

Whereas now the same worker no longer sees the fruits of his labour. Today the whip hits morale even more because we have educated the populace and have positioned ourselves as educators of the populace.

Man, no longer finding in everyday existence {recompense for his efforts}: the joy which his heart, his soul, his intelligence got from permanent contact with great noble and beautiful things, sought to find in material satisfaction that which he [no longer] finds in the great matter which was a matter for everyone.

That which was a matter for everyone [–] Pisa, Egypt, Crusades, cathedrals, no longer exists, so all their force has been granted to the cult of the self, the proof: a domestic dwelling of the past and that of today. Public matters of the past and of today, {in which each enjoyed contemplating the temple, whereas today the worker employed on a tunnel enjoys only jealousy.}

[LCdv 19]

Past noble idea, present egotism. (This seems wrong, because […] stupid teaching of history, which gives wrong ideas, instead of major wave, there are trivial details.

Type of history: 1 painting per century, with major dates and made visible to the eye. Like a dial.

1 colour for glorious facts

Another " " " opposite "

1 artist historian would then depict each century)

The Catholic church provides the poor with sensual pleasure which is within reach.

There was major enthusiasm, disgust for war. Gas factories are made which will allow a rich man to light his lounge very well. In the past the poor man said I have two eyes and the cathedral is

[LCdv 20]

for me too.

Napoleon was the last person who knew how to give to each a good quality of joy, a smart uniform.

They cried long live the Emperor, i.e. long live *enthusiasm*. All were buoyed up, poor, rich, he knew how to make heroes of all. Today all is tarnish and grumbles. –

The situation of the past and that today: generous, great-hearted men, who sense the matter of today must set their hearts on bringing back into the life of us all an enthusiasm based on very grand, very noble, very lofty idea[s]. This idea must succeed in counterbalancing our egotism.

Altruism must counterbalance the efforts which are absorbed by egotism. Art will not take a single step forward if we do not change this. There are matters

[LCdv 21]

to implement by putting into a grand setting and giving them the scope which our era can afford them.

With all our means, [with] light, one can do grand things. It is this grandeur which, by inspiring, will combat egotism.

– Incite enthusiasm! Makes Ruskin {the pacifist} say: only one thing remains: *war*.

Wonders have been made: tunnels, factories, electricity, science, – *but we no longer see these*.

General Considerations

[LCdv 22]
PART I.//FIRST PART
Chap I. General Considerations
" II Study of the element[s] of the city
" III On possible (useful) modern strategies

[LCdv 23]
FIRST CHAP.//GENERAL CONSIDERATIONS
§ 1. –   The purpose of this study
§ 2. –   Guiding principles
§ 3. –   The present state of the debate
§ 4. –   A fundamental present-day error
          (Drawing on paper.)
          Art is excluded
          no responsibilities.

§1 *Purpose of this study*

[LCdv 24] 1//I^{ST} PART//FIRST CHAPTER
General considerations.//§. 1.
Purpose of this study.//1
This study, written with no other claim than as a reminder of the procedures which make our existence in cities agreeable, is addressed in particular to the authorities.
Perhaps it will evoke in architects a concern for harmonious ensembles, a concern which, more than any other, will bring them to set out the rules for a style. The view of modern cities would then lose the inconsistency which affects our eyes and spirits. Seeking harmony in entire streets would lead inevitably to a restful *unity*, and from there inevitably to character.
These principles developed here outside of all technical form, can be understood by all; they offer each of us a foundation sufficient to follow with interest the development of cities where we are obliged to live.
This development is not always dictated by sufficient logic. The area of city planning,[4] overly monopolised by specialists who remain beyond the reach of popular criticism,

---

4 Jeanneret uses "la construction des villes" here (literally 'building towns/cities'), in an apparent calque on the standard German term 'Städtebau'.

needs to be more widely known. A matter which meets with such peremptory public interest deserves assistance from each of us, or at least requires informed assent, and not as is the case

[LCdv 25] 2
today, blind assent, unreasoning trust.

Every man needs intellectual contributions from his contemporaries – and a man who exercises a public function even more so. Otherwise he risks confining himself to a small circle of personal ideas, often mediocre and short-lived. The history of the sciences and the arts involves nothing if not constant collaboration.

The authorities hold enormous strength; either they are unaware of the generous efforts born of the masses, and their government will be sterile and sad as a barren land; or they instigate in the people noble flights of fancy; upholding that which is beneficial, they provoke a flowering of great works.

Of past eras, there remain only those works in which our spirit is immortalised in beautiful shapes and, in tacit recognition, History has passed down the names – which are like torches – of those who crowned their warrior triumphs with a garland of the arts: Ramses, Ashurbanipal, Pericles, {Titus, Augustus, Trajan,} Charlemagne, the Caliphs, Tamerlane,* the Ming Dynasties, The Dukes of Berry, Louis XIV ... Our mentality fashioned by the advanced state of socialisation

*{good} ... But the most magnificent of master builders was Timur Beg (or Tamerlane). His warrior successes in Russia, in the Caucasus, in Persia, in Asia Minor and the Indies, provided him with abundant material with which to decorate his capital Samarkand. Many caravans brought rich spoils there. When a city was taken by force, the order was given to spare the [Continues on page LCdv 26]

[LCdv 26] 1.//3
in which we find ourselves, brings us to sometimes accuse these men of being cruel and despotic; their egotism which we condemn was at the time no worse than that which reigns today, more hidden, incapable of such frank violence, but just as active: an essentially human feeling, which differs only in its outward expression. {These men whom we often understand poorly have shown themselves as geniuses; their genius was to prompt the greatest flowerings of art.}

§2 *General principles*

Feeling beautiful emotions is the joy of life. The power, the task of art is to awaken feelings which, according to the level of nobility in individuals, will be more or less profound. The city is the field of action in which society lives and dies. The problem of beautifying it will therefore be a search for designs which evoke feelings.

Forms and colours arouse sensations, and from there, provoke emotions. The artist, drawing the plan for a city, will employ in rhythms the shapes and colours which bring feelings, as does the musician with his notes, the painter with the treasures of his palette. The more or less perfect beauty of a city will depend on the level of imagination

[Continued from LCdv 25]* architects, painters, skilled workers, who Tamerlane then used to carry out his projects. Constantly playing a very active part in his constructions, Tamerlane was very hard to satisfy; he often ordered that an already finished monument be altered and personally oversaw the rebuilding he had indicated. (Meciti, the Mosques of Samarkand[5]).

[LCdv 27] 1//4.
which had presided over the grouping of the various elements. This question is a plastic one, and altogether as delicate as questions of statuary. Equally, a funerary marble is made of similar material to the usual commercial marble – a glorious city is built of stone, mortar and iron just like an ugly city.*
{[In the margin:] *(as a note)
The ideal and the real have one same, single essence. Raw diamond and polished diamond are both diamond; but raw diamond is the real; polished diamond is the ideal.}
The layout of a city is primarily a work of art; in order to realise it, the artist must draw inspiration from the same rules which govern the other arts: the rules of *convenance*, balance and variety.
Thus he will recall that what adds to the heart's emotion, the spirit's rapture, *is to do much with little*. The opposite would be madness, – the madness of our era, which confuses beauty with surfeit, which measures emotion according to the level of budget.
As he considers that a richly dressed man will appear as such only when surrounded by colleagues dressed soberly, he will know the value of contrasts.
He will know that everything is relative, that the absolute of a dimension or an impression does not exist in the play of emotions; only by a correct scene setting, and a perfect adaptation to the surroundings, will the thoughts which he wishes to inscribe in concrete forms be brought forth.
His aesthete's taste will force him to choose, when two equally practical solutions present themselves, the solution capable of more beauty.
Architect, engineer, painter, sculptor and poet, the city planner is faced with one of the noblest tasks: that of bringing his fellow citizens the joy of living in a city where the living is good.

[LCdv 28] GENERAL CONSIDERATIONS//Text.//I

§3 *The present state of the debate*

[LCdv 29] The present state of the debate. §3
[LCdv 30] 2)
Today we are in the midst of an artistic rebirth and the city, in its shape, is caught up in this. The development is also truly curious, which led to the reappearance of *Architecture*. From 1800 to 1900 – the problem had much more distant roots –, architecture had fallen into irretrievable decadence; it became excessively formulaic, to the point of being deadly, it had begun to lose sight of its own existence, its reality, its raison d'être: the

---

5 Izdamie imperatorskoj archeologiceskoj Kommissii: *Meceti Samarkanda.* (Les Mosquées de Samarcande, published by la commission impériale archéologique), Volume: *Le Gour Emir*, St. Petersburg: Éxpédition pour la confection des papiers d'état 1905. Text in Russian and French.

material. Being cultivated in shady offices where theory was king, it was gradually reduced to a harmonious and flattering graphical representation, non-viable lines traced on the drawing board. Yet this display ignored the material, often contradicting it. Besides which, science was developing, and the demands of everyday life required something other than linear fantasies: bridges were needed,

[LCdv 31] 4)

vast halls, etc. Industry supplied the iron, and this not being easily reconciled with the formulary for sculpture, architects discounted it. They could not however do without it, and being cowards they left the ignoble task to the engineers; they contented themselves with making masks. In front of the metal frame which they left unaesthetic, they erected stone walls, disfigured with useless mouldings and columns, vaults and arches; these immoral trompe-l'œil masks which constituted inadmissible trickery, a veritable blasphemy which [...] by this dressing against their own ideals engineers were modest, and undertook the ignoble task for a long time. Yet little by little, going back to study the material which the architects had abandoned, they learned its capacity for plasticity. And this ascetic school,

[LCdv 32] 6)

considering the ungratefulness of iron, one day, made it express beauty. That beauty was still lacking in generosity, and many did not understand it. There were some imposing bridges, and the immense Machine Hall at the 1889 Exhibition. Iron was decidedly lacking in *corporalité*[6], but in this persistent struggle, characters had formed and ideas changed. The impressionist painters, literary figures, symbolists had already shaken the routine structure. Leaving the morbidly Elysian fields given over to art, the end of the 19th century got back in touch with the earth, the plain material. In architecture, a writer specialising in these questions said, quite correctly: "It is today something publicly acknowledged, but not yet admitted, that in the field of architecture, engineers are the true architects of our time."*
{[On facing page:] * Der Städtebau. Jos. Aug. Lux. Dresden[7]}

[LCdv 33] 8)

Moreover, a new material has arrived since then, prodigiously rich in promise: reinforced concrete. It will, when combined with the boldest designs, afford us a new all-encompassing beauty. With the situation as such, we should not be surprised if we see the new movement asserting itself with the strength of youth. Science as a basis, the material as a tool, a powerful ideal as the engine: these are its characteristic methods. The substance logically determines the form, whereas with the Decadents ornament distorted the material and concealed the function. This architectural rebirth, passing from the industrial hall to the useful and beautiful bridge and to the residential house would inevitably have repercussions in city planning. The first effective act was accomplished

---

6 Translator's note: literally 'embodiment'. By extension 'innate architectural quality'.

7 Joseph August Lux, *Der Städtebau und die Grundpfeiler der heimischen Bauweise* (Dresden: Kühtmann, 1908).

[LCdv 34] 10)

in 1889 by the Viennese architect Camillo Sitte.* It was in a book full of faith, logic, artistic meaning that he cried out 'death to ugly cities'. Some years passed, with mockery and indifference. Then in Germany, some protagonists of a new art of building cities, write books, examine the question, have conferences, submit projects. To render unto Sitte the praise which he is due, one of them writes at the start of the new book*: "The monument which Sitte erected with his book, will make his name known in tomorrow's world, as the reformer of German city planning." This consecration of C. Sitte's ideas will engage us several times, during the course of this study, to quote the Viennese architect, in order to give principles which are new to our country, firmer approval.

Already, in England, a fine

{[On facing page:] * Der Städtebau nach künstlerischen Grundsätzen – Camillo – Sitte – Wien –
* Beiträge zur praktischen Ästhetik im Städtebau, Carl – Henrici – Aachen
Other books would be: Stübben. Städtebau and the remarkable works of Schultze-Naumburg, Kulturarbeiten.}

[LCdv 35] 12)

philanthropic gesture decreed that for the use of workers in certain large factories, entire small towns be built in the countryside; art, hygiene and comfort were adopted once again and realised here, without any speculative idea. This time the problem of the city is posed categorically, and it is artists, – and not geometers, who draw the furniture, the houses, and the streets of Bournville and Port-Sunlight.

This has provided the impetus. Remaining in the private domain, efforts increase, conferences, books, propaganda of all sorts.

Finally, here we stand 10 years after the end of the 19th century, in an atmosphere transformed; the hideousness of the city is not extinct, but energetic efforts are made to fight it.

Now, a strange thing, this progressive movement which today has been consecrated by the governments of Germany, England, Austria, Belgium and Flanders

[LCdv 36] 14)

etc., remains utterly foreign to the Latin countries. France, Italy, Spain, French Switzerland, always have their eyes fixed on Paris, and Paris, where despite the Republic, the self-satisfied last bourgeois gasp of this 'third Empire' lives off the fat of the land, does not move: what is more, still speculating on the grand crown of praise which its ancestors have bestowed upon it, Paris does not tolerate progress, in this area, refusing bread to the very numerous innovative talents, who struggle and strive there.

A characteristic sign: Germany having suffered less than France from the imposition of a centralising, obligatory and official school of architecture, of a routine, suspect office dominated, mummified and cataleptic by the immutably routine and beatific gods of the Institute, (architecture section) – Germany having accomplished, and still accomplishing, reform is already at the stage of reaction! Proof of a singular

[LCdv 37] 16)

advancement in ideas.

In fact some clumsy disciples of C. Sitte, overstepping his theories, would almost (if others had not put an end to it) have achieved a revival of the mediaeval era so brilliantly rehabilitated by this eclectic Viennese architect's book. These reactionaries – Mr. Brinckmann among others in his very fine study *Platz und Monument* – have in some sense been placed in a similar situation to that of Sitte, 30 years ago. Relishing the reforms accomplished, but already fearing a satisfaction arrived at too quickly thus invoking a fateful status quo, they discern certain unwholesome tendencies; but by denouncing them, – as Mr. Brinckmann does, – without secondary considerations, they risk disturbing the uninitiated reader, the simple distracted onlooker who does not know the heart of the matter.

[LCdv 38] 18)

In Switzerland, for the development of our towns, we have done as all the others have, looking to Paris and dreaming of major capital cities; we introduced practices which were even more useless since these models, cities of several million inhabitants, bore no similarity to our towns. Our cities set the pace, and aided by contagion, we threw away little by little our national castoffs which we believed to be shameful, and the smallest villages having heard tell of the avenues and boulevards of Paris also wanted to have a their own straight avenue and 3 or 4 storey buildings.

The despoiling of our traditions was so complete that some people, clearly examining the future and speaking not only in the name of art but above all in the name of our economic future, sought to clear the scales from our eyes and rouse

[LCdv 39] 20)

our feelings. Mr. Georges de Montenach then wrote *Pour le Visage aimé de la Patrie!* and Mr. Guillaume Fatio published *Ouvrons les yeux*.

Our modest study is a small stone supplied for building our taste in this country, as overseen by these men. Lacking we are in any literary capacity, we have edited our work accordingly. We envisaged a very precise goal, that of the very planning of cities, the laying out of streets, squares, gardens.

In matters of art, and in particular in the overlooked area of city planning, the public must have an education, – "the education of Everyman" (as Mr. de Montenach says), "because it is he who, either as a voter, or as a candidate, is called upon constantly to take sovereign decisions."

[LCdv 40] 22)

The considerable progress made in the latest period in the Germanic lands has usefully facilitated our documentation.

Our remarks or the solutions which we propose are dictated by the critical study of established works of art or, in part inspired by eminent specialist works.

We have restricted ourselves, in the choice of our illustrations, to examples from the classical lands of Greece, Italy, France etc. Periods of art marvellously more or less unknown by the public at large are still waiting for us to reveal them. – Neither opulent India, nor refined Persia, neither sumptuously mystical Cambodia, nor spiritual Japan, nor even mysterious China will lend us their architecture here, since these sun-kissed arts,

[LCdv 41] 24)

towards which the youth of tired old Europe turn, are still misunderstood by many, and disputed. This is regrettable, as perhaps they might have provided us with new and unforeseen solutions.

Our goal nevertheless remains precise: through critical study, to seek for each problem the logical and beautiful solution and, denouncing the routine procedures which are detrimental to the harmonious development of cities, bring about the creation of "things which instead of being a defect, are new finery added to the old".

§4 A fundamental present-day error

{[On facing page:] §.4.//A fundamental present-day error}

There are two ways of designing the plan for a city: the right way and the wrong way. The right way has governed since time immemorial,

[LCdv 42] 26

as it is the expression of reason and emotion; it always complies with the demands of and the laws of beauty. It is an instinctive act of a healthy organism.

We do not know if the wrong method ruled previously. But it is certain, and reality proves this, that it is today applied universally – except for those countries which, in recent years, have undertaken complete reforms in the organisation of their planning offices. – After 80 or 90 years of development, it is now at its height: thus in its hour of crisis, – an unhealthy organism born of a troubled state of society, developing like a bad tumour, in the tranquillity left for it by the struggles of the 19th century.

Today, during this period of intensive research on art, the tumour has taken on a worrying aspect. Specialists

[LCdv 43] 28

born more recently have denounced its ugliness and demanded that it be eradicated. At Sitte's call, Germany stirred itself, and the struggle was engaged with vigour; one might say that there, and in the several countries which partially followed the movement, a connection was re-established with the thread of ancient tradition. The art of building cities, after 80 years of decline, is emerging from its lethargy. The maximum ugliness attained in recent years has provoked a reaction by itself. A desire for beauty, a hope of living better, the very perseverance and nobility of great social ideas have created a new organism: city planners.[8]

The first method was *design in space*. Streets and squares were designed by considering the topography of sites, [they] benefited from the structure of the ground, from its practical, economic, hygienic resources and its

[LCdv 44] 30

capacity for beauty. Public edifices were placed where their intended purpose was fully satisfied, – intended for utility, intended for munificence. The same was true of all other edifices. – The planner was a sculptor because he saw in 3 dimensions; he was a poet,

---

8 Here, Jeanneret uses the term "bâtisseurs de ville", a direct translation of the German "Städtebauer".

because he created landscapes made by human hand, in which beauty, fully impregnated with the laws of nature, could make staying in cities agreeable and charming.

The description of the method adopted today defines it well: administrative-bureaucratic. Of what was it born? It was after the disarray at the beginning of the 19th century, the delineation of an arbitrarily exclusive silo for each public service.

The principles inherent in this delineation of a domain

[LCdv 45] 32

bounded with unjustified limits are also its undoing: rising through the grades based on your years of service, degree of obedience, and sharing the views of the boss, results in a levelling out of personalities. This results next in the imposition of a fixed formula, an immutable basis for action, a sacred code, a standard model, a sort of common measure for everyone and for all purposes. This new calling produced preachers and servants with great conviction. Its repercussions in practice were: work undertaken in a studio, at fixed hours, by irresponsible employees. These employees, in their legitimate desire of satisfying their boss, sought to perform work worthy of praise, and thus little by little an irrefutable dogma established itself, the fundamental vice: a love of plans making a fine effect on the paper, – and the compasses and set square

[LCdv 46] 34

won the day.

... ... The very goal, the *art* of building cities well, was forgotten.

This then is, in a few words, a review of these past 80 years.

Beauty of a drawing on a sheet of paper, naïve admiration of a fine graphic, this, in short, is the whole error which each page of this study will combat.

Sketches for 'General Considerations'

[LCdv 47] 4/4/1

The 19th century thus totally lost its way in the question of the design of cities; besides several strokes of inspiration which allowed the major capitals to develop, the field of the residential city has not been understood. The realisation of administrative theories is a nonsense which if it continued would lead cities to a state of ugliness such that the demoralisation which is already affecting the most dreary districts would reach entire populations.

[...]

Then section *a* first

People used this to play with the finest of words. They spoke in administrative terms of: geometry, utility,

balance, hygiene,

simplicity, beauty, modernism...

[The following paragraph crossed out] But we attack and we will deny *their* utility, *their* hygiene, *their* modernism and *their* beauty. We will leave the administrators with *their* geometry, to which we will apply the epithet lazy, *their* simplicity which we must equate with poverty, *their* balance which signifies uniformity.

But today it is necessary to attack and deny *this* hygiene, *this* utility, *this* beauty, *this* modernism and we will leave the administrative geometers with only their geometry, to which we will apply the epithet lazy, *their* simplicity which we must equate with poverty, *their* balance which signifies uniformity.

And we establish
[Whole of the following paragraph crossed out]
a) That the utility of a city lies in the most direct possible route through it, easy immediate orientation. That it is speed in commercial transactions, transit made possible and easy and pleasant for all; that for the businessman as much for the stroller, those travelling for business as much as for those travelling for pleasure, for

[LCdv 48] 2 [Whole page crossed out]
the infirm, for the old, just as for the nimble. We will prove that utility means meeting all these needs of the resident living his life in the city, which current methods do not meet.
b) That hygiene is tranquillity brought to residential places, calmly spending time in a peaceful setting, sheltered from the dust, the smoke from factories, the wind and drafts, in full sun and in the purest air possible. We say that the first condition of hygiene is to provide the residents of a city with a dwelling which is inviting, where they can, if they want – and not where they cannot despite wanting to, be happy. And we will prove that the systems employed today work against this.
c) That modernism is understanding the needs of the era and realising them as promptly as possible. To be modernist is to allow for collective needs, noble wants and individual wishes to find a satisfactory form; it is to help them even in their outward expression. Modernism means striving to realise general questions raised by today's life forces, these are called utopian questions but acknowledged as beneficial to the community. Now the plans for city extensions adopted today are predominantly [Sentence incomplete].

[LCdv 49] 3)
[Whole paragraph crossed out] For hygiene is not only cleaning streets and protective measures against the spread of diseases. There is, besides this necessary collective hygiene, that of the individual: and this hygiene of the individual is the satisfaction of living, which can produce with all the other factors a pleasant dwelling. Today's cities wear the mantle of pure dreariness.
And we will establish:
That utility in a city is the quickest route, transit made easy for all;
That hygiene is the tranquillity of living in inviting dwellings where they can if they want – and not where they cannot despite wanting to – be happy;
That modernism is above all understanding the needs of the era, their realisation, understanding of our major common ideas, their potential outward expression, and preparation of the necessary settings for these;
That beauty obeys laws which are independent of emotion which belongs to the individual sphere but depend on reason which relies on Nature and which every day is checked by nature.
That the beauty of a city is a matter of great art which therefore needs a contribution from all the resources of the human brain and heart,

and that all these common problems could not be resolved in anonymous administrations, without responsibility.

And we hardly need an epilogue on the three resources which remain on the balance sheet of dedicated systems: lazy and simplistic geometry; poor simplicity and uniformitarian balance.

[LCdv 50] 4)

We are therefore going to study the principles of city planning.[9] In order to free ourselves of all theory for its own sake, we will only pose here problems which, arising as they do every day, vary constantly according to the terrain.

We will not base our demonstrations on works from eras acknowledged as beautiful and useful, but we will underline this from the outset: those works that were produced in harmony with the tastes of the era will only serve as a bitter comparison: for today our needs are different ... only the laws of beauty and reason remain.
End of §3.[10]

[LCdv 51]

This modest work appears very timely to us. While in other countries the question of the future for cities has undergone a real revolution in the design of expansion plans, French- and also German-speaking Switzerland remains under the influence of France, which does not move and remains content with processes recognised as unfavourable; Switzerland continues to take no interest in the current problem of developing its towns and cities.

A book had appeared in French in 1902 which is now out of print. Since that time we are not aware of any others. Other countries Germany, Austria, England in particular have published numerous works on this issue ...

We believe that by benefiting from the experience of these countries we can offer the public, and not just

[LCdv 52]

men in the trade, a rich – though all too brief – summary of everything which creates beauty in cities and could better combat ugliness at home.

With a practical goal in mind we have appended here a critical study of a town in which to date beauty has not been an overriding concern. This demonstration of the principles set out in Part I will – we suppose – also interest readers from other towns and cities.

We have made no secret of our opinions on the cause of the current evil. J. J. Rousseau once said in the preface to his *Émile*: Propose what can be done.

[LCdv 53] 1.//5. [Text outline for LCdv 33; whole page crossed out]
fellow citizens the joy of living in a city where life is good.

---

9 Here, Jeanneret uses "la construction des villes".
10 "End of §3" was added later, to replace "End of §1". This might indicate that Jeanneret was unsure whether he should add these pages to §3 General Considerations or use them as part of his Introduction. The content bears more relation to the Introduction than to general remarks on urban planning.

§3. Attempts have been made to resolve this problem. Written works have initiated these. We do not know any works published in France, where banal processes continue to enjoy official approval.

Camillo Sitte, a Viennese architect in Austria, was the first in 1889 in a very strong book to cry death to the ugly city.[I] He initially met only with irony and indifference. But several years later, Mr. Carl Henrici, who with his proposal for an expansion to the city of Munich in 1892 was the first to apply Sitte's ideas, expressed the esteem in which he is held as follows.[II] "The monument which Sitte raised with this book will announce his name to the future world as the man who reformed German city planning."[11] Hence we will frequently cite the Viennese artist in the course of our study, in the aim of thus providing a firmer reinforcement of the principles, which are new here.

I.   *Der Städtebau nach seinen künstlerischen Grundsätzen*, Wien: Schroll 1889. –
II. *Beiträge zur praktischen Ästhetik im Städtebau*, München: Callwey 1904.

[LCdv 54] [Entire page crossed out] 6
More recently, the architect Mr. Schultze-Naumburg published in the collection Kunstwart 3 volumes dealing, the first with
the second with
the third with

11 Jeanneret mistranslates Henrici slightly. More accurately, it would read: "The monument which Sitte raised with this book will announce his name to the future world as the man who reformed German city planning."

The Elements of the City

§1 *Introduction*

[LCdv 55]
1st Part.

[LCdv 56] before 5//§ 1. Elements of the City.//1
Foreword
In years to come, cities will have to reverse the baleful current created by the 19th century in *the art of building cities*, and base their development on more rational procedures. It is however right and proper to give the previous century its due: the immense discoveries which illuminated it will pose the question of the city against a backdrop of a new grandeur and beauty. Being a firm foundation from which to take new flight, that century gave the city, the house and the individual one factor which was an elementary requirement: Hygiene. This forms an immense contribution – police regulations, distribution of drinking water, street cleaning, the creation of sewers, sanitary facilities etc. – for without hygiene all the practicable solutions would become unsatisfactory.
It is therefore in fact the planner who has remained behind the times. His task required that he be an artist as much as a technician. This did not arise and that is where all the current evils can be sought.
The city and its suburban region make up the field in which the planner operates.

---

1 The last line appears to have been added later. It omits 'Des' (which we translate as 'On'), and the handwriting differs from that in the previous lines.

[LCdv 57] 2)

Some elements work against him, others, instead, are in his favour; some, which could be the most valuable assets he has, will turn against him if he is not skilful. He must overcome the fumes and smells from factories and railways as well as the noise from both, to which is added that of the traffic; the winds will work for or against him, accordingly; the lie of the land will hinder him or alternatively, if he is artistic, bring him a powerful contribution to beauty. For him, the sun, the trees, and springs are so many valuable factors.

The stage on which he plays is a site which is always reduced to a minimum. By making himself master of the various elements, he must make them contribute to a useful and beautiful goal.

The wind which prevails across the countryside and the airflow engendered by the very folds of the land may remove the smoke and smells for him, if he has corralled these in a convenient place.

What of the noise? He will obey the principle that a muffled and continuous roar, a rumble will

[LCdv 58] before 5//3

cease to be heard due to its regularity. But he will be wary of unexpected noise, shrill and intermittent, and instead of providing city residents with a – very special – sort of tiresome soloists, he will orchestrate a neutralising symphony of all the piercing elements.[2]

Thus he will group the smoky, stinking, humming factories in a place within the city through which the winds sweep. He could even align them in a veritable ventilation channel. It is here that trains will arrive, warehouses, stations, garages, tram intersections will be situated – in this zone given over to labour. But through vigorous legislation, he will demand of its buildings everything which modern hygiene has to offer.

Active commerce in today's cities brings heavy traffic in some streets. Trams, cars and bicycles create an atmosphere which is less than conducive to habitation. These streets shall become spacious arteries allowing easy traffic flow, they shall be paved with material that gives off no dust, lines of large buildings shall be arranged along their pavements – uninterrupted but for penetration by cross streets –

[LCdv 59] 4)

a constant 3, 4 or 5 storeys high; trees shall be planted in *allees* to cut occasionally through the uniformity while presenting an effective obstacle to the swirls of dust. These arteries shall be oriented such that the usual winds can sweep them, or at least these long streets shall be interspersed frequently with edifices set crosswise to the carriageway, with openings in their bases for through routes – then all the noisy intensiveness of trade will be concentrated in a clearly limited area, thus leaving vast parcels of land sheltered from noise, dust, and tiring to and fro, to make these areas suitable for habitation.

In these 'businesslike' streets which intersect in the factory district and radiate out in all directions will be situated shops, offices – in a word, 'businesses'.

The residential districts protected by a 'building law' against the depredation of builders – shameless speculators – will provide city residents with calm places of rest. Garden courtyards and fountains will maintain a peaceful

---

2 Several lines of subsequent additions in the margin, illegible.

[LCdv 60]
before 5//5
and healthy atmosphere here. Buildings for one, two or more families, built in either the 'open' or 'closed' manner, that is to say free-standing or in rows, will pick out streets with useful and beautiful curves which will cut out the wind, orient the front of buildings towards the maximum sunlight, create the most successful aspects.

To sum up, the primary task for the planner will be to choose, within the site with which he is entrusted, those districts worthy of habitation and those required for the factory, the main commercial arteries delimiting properly these two irreconcilable areas.

With these major points established, he will resolve the issue of traffic which is so important and generally so poorly understood.

The lack of accord between the current means of locomotion and the design of our cities in the American style has in many places created an untenable situation. The city must be crossed easily by all, those on business or out for a stroll, by the old, the infirm as well as the sprightly.

The issue is therefore one of finding the shortest route, for vehicles on the one hand and for pedestrians

[LCdv 61] 6)
on the other: *two networks which interpenetrate without doing harm to one another*, thus best satisfying the speed of commercial transactions.

Reference or orientation points are a primary requirement. The public edifices, carefully distributed so as to meet the services which we expect of them, will all be designated by their special architecture, and by their dimensions, and their forms which may have been designed specifically with that end in mind, to be the most perfect reference points.

This huge job of implementation, based on multiple utilitarian requirements, will have no real value unless, conceived by an all-rounder, it has been *designed with beauty*.

Now the manner in which he works from day to day cannot live up to this. Such a result can in truth only be obtained due to '*an extension plan*', an approximate image of the present and future which will allow for a city, by putting down the overall outline protected by laws, scope for rational development, permitting changes to the detail over the years. This is a necessary condition which current expansion plans

[LCdv 62] before 5//7
do not meet; these render – unless great pains are taken – the building lines immovable and consequently unimprovable.[3]

Such a plan for regularisation may only be designed with a deep understanding of the science which is known as 'city planning',[4] a complex science comprising, in terms of plastic considerations alone (which this study addresses): *the block, the street, the square and its monuments, enclosing walls, bridges, trees, gardens and parks, cemeteries* etc.

end of § 1 chap. II part I

[LCdv 63] [Draft for pages LCdv 56f.]
before 5//INTRODUCTION.//1

---

3 Several lines of illegible subsequent additions in the margin.
4 As above, Jeanneret uses the term "construction des villes".

In the coming years, cities will have to reverse the baleful current created by the 19th century in 'the art of building cities', and base their development on more rational procedures. Nevertheless, it is right ~~while rebuking the city planners from this tiresome period for making this century which did not have the time, through a lack of time, left them too absorbed by other problems neglecting~~ that the previous century be given its due: the immense open terrains which illuminated it will posit the problem of the city in relation to the given situation of a previously unknown grandeur and beauty. Being a firm foundation from which to take new flight, it granted the city, the house and the individual one factor which was an elementary requirement: hygiene. This forms an immense contribution – police regulations etc. – for without hygiene all the improvements that could be proposed would remain unsatisfactory.

It is therefore in fact the planner who has remained behind the times. His task required that he be an artist as much as an engineer. This did not occur and that is where all the current evils can be sought.

The city and its suburban region, always reduced to a minimum, are the field in which the new planner operates.

Some elements work against him, others instead are in his favour; of those that could be his most valuable assets, he has and he will turn some against him unless he is skilful. He must overcome the fumes, the smells, the noise; the winds will work for and against him, accordingly; the lie of the land will hinder him or alternatively, if he is good, bring him a powerful contribution to beauty: variety. The sun, the trees, the {[in the margin:] springs represent so many valuable factors.}

The stage on which he plays is a site which is always reduced to a minimum. He must make himself master of the various elements, in order to make them contribute to a useful and beautiful goal.

§2 On Blocks

[LCdv 64] part I Chap. II//5//P//§ 2 or II//§ 2. – BLOCKS

[LCdv 65] 5//1//ON BLOCKS.

The programme for a city extension consists of laying out a given site into parcels or *blocks*, of favourable shape, inclination and orientation, leaving between them streets with a design, slope and orientation which must satisfy the services which we require of them.

Several geometric block shapes have a wealth of hygienic and plastic benefits, and are highly favourable to construction – others are poor and inconvenient, and one would avoid these in plans.

The degree to which the block forms are favourable in themselves should be considered, alongside the degree to which they detract from or add to the street.

Let us therefore seek the ideal form, which is to say one simultaneously providing the most street frontage while economising on the street area, providing the most beautiful sites for building and lending itself the most readily to architectural solutions, having both commercial resources and residential amenities.

Shapes with acute angles will be firmly rejected as, with an equal area of frontage, these angles leave a poor area for premises; they are

[LCdv 66] 2)

also hideous in terms of their architecture. Obtuse angles are of greatly improved efficiency, but generally they require an acute angle in the block opposite. The right angle remains, with all its advantages: it allows the best layout solutions inside the block and the most beautiful architectural aspects; it determines the same in adjoining blocks and creates the most favourable street intersections.

The form reproduced in Fig. [__],[5] which is that of a rectangular block the depth of one building, requires considerable street frontage, with defects as a residential block because the dwellings would find themselves drowned by the noise and dust of the street. At the outside, it could perhaps be applied when building large commercial premises or certain public buildings.

The case for a triangular block, Fig. [__] is dismissed by the block itself: the prows at *a'* and *b'* are impossible to lay out and the space between interior angle *a"* or *b"* and exterior angle *a'* or *b'* will not receive any

[LCdv 67] 5//3

direct sunlight. The ugliness of the façades generated by such a system requires no further comment.

The block in Fig. [__] is exceedingly efficient. The courtyards, provided they are of sufficient area, will open up the rooms and provide light: the surface area of façades onto the street is large and there is potential for pleasing architectural solutions. The benefits of this form struck some administrations in American cities who, seeing achieved herein the minimum road surface achieved at the same time as the maximum façades, saw fit to join together a great number of these hexagons and form entire districts from them. This produced the most melancholy sight: all stretches of street *ab* are identical to stretches *bc*, *ce*... etc. so that these cities bear the indelible stamp of the dullest uniformity. From which deduce that we should remember the hexagonal block, but only employ it as an exception.*

{[In the margin:] *The most practical and beautiful solution would be obtained by having the street pass not outside the polygon but inside. This was done in England, Fig. [__] The greatest number of windows then open onto the gardens.}

Other forms are exploited, for example that in Fig. [__] Which is merely a mid-point between the solution in Fig. [__] and that which we will propose in Fig. [__]. It consists of

[LCdv 68] 4)

entrenching the block of houses behind a courtyard or a garden, thus distancing one of the fronts from the street. But while something has been gained, this is relatively little given the monotony which this oft-repeated design engenders, and the ugliness which it produces in streets.

The block par excellence is that in Fig. **[1]**, the richest in varied solutions; it merely needs to be oriented favourably. This is the elongated rectangular shape, with good proportions, and arranged within its walls a huge courtyard which will be transformed into shady gardens. As the intended aim of choosing block shape is to accommodate the largest number of rooms, this is where it is best achieved; the ratio of corners to façades is lower than that provided by the square or any other configuration; the depth to be given to the dwellings may be varied easily as needed, and all the factors in useful, comfortable and hygienic living come together here. The ground floors can be developed as shops or offices; the

---

5 Jeanneret did not assign any illustrations to this placeholder or those below.

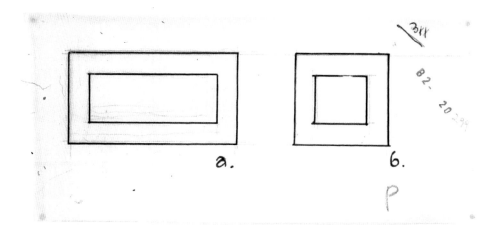

Fig. I The perimeter block. Sketch by Jeanneret (B2-20-299 FLC)

first floors will provide favoured dwellings with one façade on the street and another façade above a huge garden. There is no reason why this courtyard, sheltered

[LCdv 69] 5//5

from the wind and the dust from the streets, should not become a delicious shady retreat in the summer, with one or two communal tennis courts for all the houses and a playground for children. Such a solution would, without a doubt, bring joy to the mothers who would see their children romping around safe from carts and motor cars, in air no longer poisoned by dust and petrol vapours.

At all times, the elongated oblong has been preferred to other block forms. It is of capital importance that the corners are right angles, whereas whether the sides are parallel, whether straight or curved, is only of significance to the street layout. Fig.s *b* and *c* [2] show two derivatives of this form which, while retaining all the known advantages of form *a*, are also suitable for laying out streets which we will come to recognise as the most useful and beautiful.

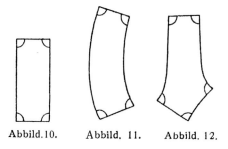

Abbild.10.   Abbild. 11.   Abbild. 12.

Fig. 2 Variations of a rectangular block. From Henrici, *Beiträge zur praktischen Ästhetik im Städtebau*, 1904, p. 70, figs. 10–12

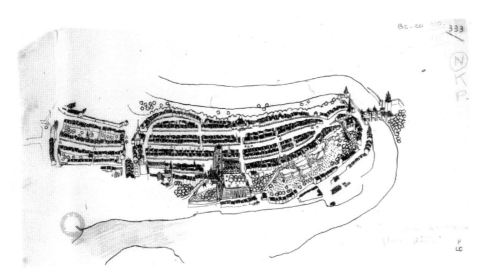

Fig. 3 Berne, bird's eye view Jeanneret, tracing from Merian, *Topographia Helvetiae*, p. 24 (B2-20-310 FLC)

When the city of Berne was extended beyond its initial enclosure, in the 15th or 16th century, the rectangular block was chosen; the left-hand part of our Fig. [3] shows the bourgeois housing grouped around large gardens.

[LCdv 70] 6)
These gardens may sometimes be part of the public domain, two passageways through the walls of the rectangle, allowing access for the enjoyment of all.[6] Thus – while facilitating transit – they intersperse those journeys through arid streets with an oasis of freshness, Fig. [__].[I]
The Viennese architect Mr. Siegfried Sitte proposes in the journal *Städtebau* a whole series of locations for school buildings, in which he makes good use of the elongated rectangular block. Renouncing the custom – which he shows to be detrimental – of placing school buildings along the length of the street with one, two or three or four façades opening onto the carriageway, he proposes the solutions represented by Figs [4, 5]: The school administration, vestibule and stairs occupy the façade facing the street, set back from the alignment of the housing, while the main body, in garden courtyards, orients its line of classrooms and corridors, cloakrooms, water-closets towards the sun, occupying the remaining space. Mr. S. Sitte thus removes the pupils from the noise of the road and from many inconveniences, and provides them with the benefit of the shade provided by the
I) Proposal by Mr. S. Sitte in the journal Städtebau 1906.[7]

6 Sketch with comment in the margin: "Perimeter block development pattern with through access and block with roads on either side [up to here in German] financial solution//more façade for individuals//Same traffic//same area belonging to the community, costs equivalent: a garden, or carriageway. *in addition*: a garden"
7 Siegfried Sitte, "Das Schulhaus im Stadtplane", in: *Der Städtebau*, Vol. 3, 1906, No. 10, pp. 130–133

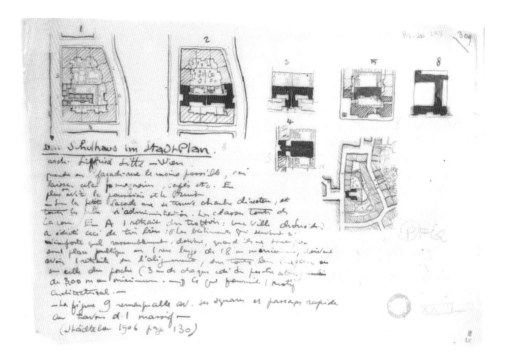

Fig. 4 Jeanneret, tracings from Siegfried Sitte, "Das Schulhaus im Stadtplane" (B2-20-298 FLC)

[LCdv 71] 5//7

neighbours' properties. The façades designed in a very sober style, almost exclusively utilitarian, provide serious savings in the budget for school buildings; these buildings have been until now a pretext for very special architectural attempts by our local councillors; the generally costly sculptural treasures of architectural officialdom would be repeated four times along the four façades, and would more certainly incur expenditure than they would make an effective contribution to aesthetic perspectives in the city.

The depth of the block greatly influences the parcelling out of plots for construction. On this, a sketch with the prettiest effect on paper and current practice both contradict the best solution. Here is one example:[1] Fig. **[6]** shows two groups of 6 plots each with equivalent areas. The standard form in image *A*, as generally applied, means placing isolated houses in the middle of each plot; 4 small gardens result: *a*, *b*, *c*, the limited size of which allied with their proximity to the street precludes any convenience; d has very little depth, is of an unsuitable shape and hardly lends itself to a successful layout.

On the other hand, Fig *B* presents great
I) From Schultze-Naumburg. Kulturarbeiten – Städtebau.

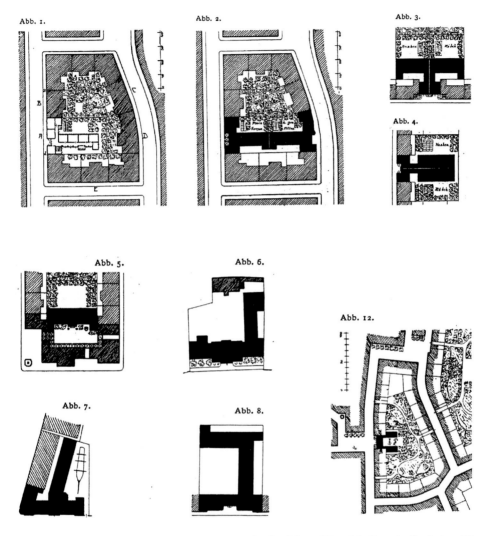

Fig. 5 Reformist models for school buildings. From Siegfried Sitte, "Das Schulhaus im Stadtplane," in: *Der Städtebau* 3 (1906), no. 10, figs. 1–12

[LCdv 72] 8)

advantages. The houses adjoin one another and are therefore more economical; with an equal surface area they extend further lengthwise than the previous type, allowing the rooms to be arranged just as favourably. And the very deep garden will inspire pretty arrangements with long perspectives. Due to the great distance which separates the two rows of buildings *M* and *N*, a lack of air and sunshine is not a concern; on the contrary, hygienists will be pleased because all the gardens are sheltered from the noise and dust of the streets.

This system in the new plans is employed all the time. It has been applied to the new town of Hellerau, near Dresden, and England's garden cities, – Bournville, Hampstead, etc. have for several years demonstrated its advantages.

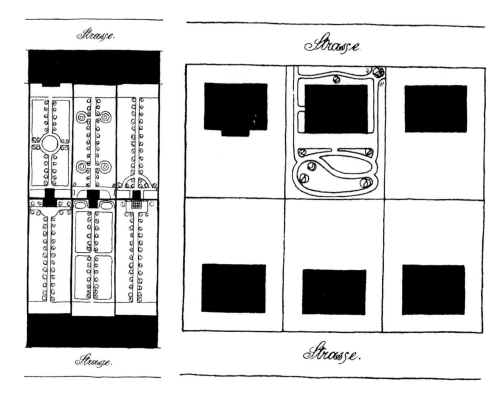

Fig. 6 Terraced and detached houses and their plots. From Schultze-Naumburg, *Kulturarbeiten Städtebau*, figs. 200 and 201

However, a type of block which is practical in itself will not be adopted if it institutes an unfavourable road system; equally, a road network will only find a useful application where it creates no plots that are unacceptable to build on. Only if the one is properly in accordance with the other will something useful

[LCdv 73] 5//9
and beautiful be produced. While respecting the requirements for a good block, this type must also yield to the requirements of good streets.

Sketches: transition to 'semi-detached houses for cities'

[LCdv 74] 5//7
The dimensions of the block bring a heavy influence to bear on the parcelling out of plots for construction. Here once again, at a glance both paper and current images are at odds with the best solution. Fig. [__] gives two groups of 6 plots, where *A*, designed in the ordinary fashion, means placing isolated houses in the middle of each plot, forming small gardens giving onto the street (*a*) and onto the sides of the building (*b, c*): – all 3

impossible to plan, due to their small size and exposure to dust from the carriageway; – the remaining plot (*d*), which has become very limited in size, precludes a convenient layout.

Fig *B* proposes a much more advantageous design; the houses adjoin one another and are therefore more economical; with an equal surface area they extend further back, allowing the rooms to be arranged just as advantageously. And the deep garden will allow pretty arrangements with long perspectives. Furthermore due to the great distance separating the two facing rows of buildings *M* and *N*, a lack of air and sunshine need not concern hygienists, and also all the gardens will be completely sheltered from the noise of the street and its dust. Such a system is employed in the new town of Hellerau (near Dresden, – in England's garden cities (Bournville, Hampstead) {[later addition:] resume page 6}

{[In the margin of the following paragraph:] put in small type as a note}

Today it is no longer sufficient to implement that formula which is deemed the best. Efforts have been made to expand the value of the rectangular block and solutions such as that which we have borrowed from Messrs. R. Kuczynski and W. Lehwess show the infinite flexibility of the strategies that can be employed

[LCdv 75]

It is a question of proving that with the uniformity being created
plus the use of the rectangular block [__] a solution full of variety and which offers great benefits.
In most German cities, and in their suburbs, the majority of the population remains …
[Text breaks off here]

[LCdv 76]

Today it is no longer sufficient in progressive circles to apply in a dry and unvarying manner that formula which is recognised to be the best. Many efforts are made and the combinations of rectangular blocks proposed by Messrs. K. [__] and S [sic] show us that, in city planning, a boldness of design can be reconciled with the likelihood of realisation. These gentlemen, with their calculations and combinations, propose the following: *to house half the population of the major capitals in detached or semi-detached houses with gardens*: with the interests of owner, tenant and local authority remaining the same; the area of land used will be exactly the same as that which capitals occupy today to house their residents in houses of 5 or 6 storeys without gardens and with unhealthy courtyards.

We have translated the essence of the solution proposed by Messrs. K and L. leaving aside the numerical tables, which

[LCdv 77]

would take us into too much depth, and will confine ourselves to showing the results.

[LCdv 78]

In a more detailed study, specialists have found unexpected resources in the rectangular block, acknowledged to be the most advantageous: Messrs R[obert] Kuczynski and W[alter] Lehwess have made the following promising proposal:

On Blocks, II – Semi-detached houses

[LCdv 79] VILLE IV

[LCdv 80] 1)//*Semi-detached Houses for Cities*
[7] In most large German cities and their suburbs, the majority of the population lives in apartment blocks 4 or 5 storeys high. Everyone is agreed that such an arrangement is detrimental to all social, hygiene, cultural, educational and moral 'considerations'. But if someone asked why a system[8] always finds applications, why in newly built districts instead of 4 or 5 storey buildings one does not construct 2 or 3 storeys, why rather than apartment blocks with lateral and transversal buildings one does not create small dwellings with 1 or two homes and gardens, – the response would be: the land is too expensive, we must construct tall buildings in order to make best use of the land and prevent rents increasing still further. We must cut deep plots so that in all cases buildings have transversal and lateral wings and so we do not therefore need to devote too much of the plot to street surface; furthermore the city would be too extensive and would be obliged to meet too many demands in terms of means of transport, establishing streets, and lighting charges. And if

[LCdv 81] 2)
anyone objected that it is possible to accommodate at least half the population in buildings of 1 or 2 dwellings with gardens, and despite that ensure: that the owner of the land received the same price; and the owner of the buildings the same rent per tenant, the same surface area of housing and the same rental price; that the district had the same population as was the case with these 4 storey rental blocks without gardens, with lateral and transversal bodies he would surely be considered mad. And yet he would be in the right.
As the basis for our example we take a plot in a suburb of Berlin which belongs to the enclosed block form 1). The dimensions are 382 metres wide and 544m long. The block will be surrounded by 4 streets 20m wide and crossed by another main road 24m [wide]. In terms of squares with green space, an area of 5,692m^2 will be provided inside the block. The price of the land as a whole is 30 marks per m^2.
[...]
I Previous System
in current construction plans over 1/3 of the
1) As a note: The most important conditions in the (Baupolizei-Verordnung für die Vororte von Berlin vom 28. Mai 1908) say: It is not permitted to build on over 5/10 of the area of a plot – for a corner plot 6/10. The height of the buildings may not exceed 18m. Residential buildings may not have more than 4 storeys – not including the attic and cellar.

[LCdv 82] 3)
block area is given over to road surface. In the present case, in order to find themselves in the most advantageous position for the owner, only roughly 30% of the total surface area will be allocated to roads. It will be accepted that, not including the broad

---

8 Jeanneret has omitted "als verhängnisvoll anerkannte" – 'acknowledged as fatal' and instead left a blank.

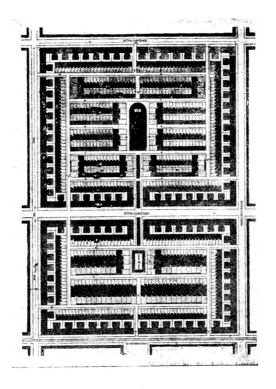

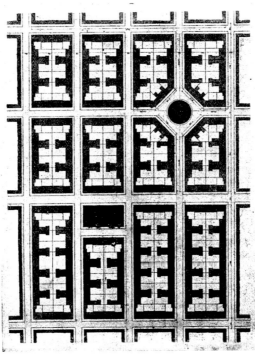

Fig. 7 Perimeter block development with terraced houses inside the block, compared with the traditional perimeter block. From Lehweß/Kuczynski, "Zweifamilienhäuser für Großstädte," p. 72

connecting street, 4 roads will run across the plot, of which 2 will be 19m wide and two 20m: thus the plot will be divided into 12 blocks, each with a depth of 76m. Each plot will have a depth of 38m. Façades, except for corner plots, will be set at 20m. – In all, the land will comprise 191 sites for 4-storey buildings. 2) The price for laying roads is 18 marks per m^2, sewerage costs 60 M per metre of façade, building costs 300 M per m^2 of built-up area or 75 M per m^2 usable area for residential floors. The rent price is set at 6 M per m^2 of usable area. A supplement for renting a shop will be a lump sum of 50,000 marks. The development of the land will therefore be calculated as follows.

[…]

2) There are 44 corner plots with an area of 684m^2 (18 x 38m) each, 8 with an area of 342m^2 each. The other 139 plots measure 760m^2 (20m x 38m)

[LCdv 83]

Zweifamilienhäuser für Großstädte [Semi-detached houses in cities] continued
by R. Kuczynski and W. Lehwess
II New system.
The old system brings with it, within the whole building zone area, absolute uniformity in the construction method: in a building area for the enclosed block form, in the Berlin suburbs for example, all apartment blocks must have the same 4 storeys, which cover 50% (or for corner plots 60%) of the area available for construction. Furthermore, the old system does not have any streets specially [designated] 'residential street', since the fact of establishing a straight row which is much wider than the 18m corresponding to the building height will [not necessarily] make the others residential streets. In order to meet the needs of the population, the new system must include special residential streets, [and] authorise a more intensive building method on the broad

[LCdv 84]

connecting streets – of which fewer are required; in residential zones […] corresponding to the height of the buildings in the […] belt, [the streets] can be considerably narrower. In the current example, the land, which not including the external streets measures 19 ha, is divided, in line with the old system, into 12 small block-shaped building lots. Each block would be built in a similar way, with four-storey buildings which would cover 5/10, and in the case of corner plots 6/10, of the site area.
According to the new system the land which is already surrounded by four large streets would be crossed by only one broad connecting street and thus divided into two blocks. In each block, only one narrow exterior zone is planned for four-storey buildings. The interior of the block, on the other hand, would only be built up with detached or semi-detached houses

[LCdv 85]

which would have, above a non-residential basement, two storeys and one attic which would cover (a maximum of) 2/3 of the ground floor.
The capacity for construction in the narrow exterior zone must, for four storeys, be the same as in the population's particularly preferred suburbs of Berlin, i.e. inside the railway's circle line [Ringbahn] – (Kurfürstendammviertel, Bayerisches Viertel). In these suburbs, the exterior zone must be sufficiently narrow that the area covered with buildings, given the same frontage, is no larger than that currently required as most beneficial, from the hygiene point of view, in suburbs outside the Ringbahn – thus something like the present example. The

buildings themselves must – contrary to the current [. . .] much more extensive method for building suburbs outside the Ringbahn – [only include] buildings with cross ventilation. Buildings within the block must have gardens. Shops or workshops

[LCdv 86]

are prohibited here. The construction method must be the same as in suburbs outside the Ringbahn with an enclosed block form.

Main streets will bring sufficient access roads into the interior of the block. For circulation within the block many minor roads will be used, whereas with the former system this was done using broad streets.

We ought to cite here the building regulations relating to this:

"Each block must be divided into two zones by an imaginary line of 26m drawn [= in parallel][9] to the exterior streets; the buildings in the first or exterior zone may not exceed four storeys intended for habitation. The maximum allowable height of the buildings is 18m. The distance between walls with openings and the edge of the neighbouring property must be at least 4m. It must be possible to ventilate all residences

[LCdv 87]

from one side to the other, which means that they must have two façades with windows, facing one another. As to the remaining conditions required, the Charlottenburg building regulations dated 22 August 1898 apply.

Buildings in the second or interior zone must contain (besides uninhabitable basements) two storeys. Attics may only cover 2/3 of the ground floor area built on, for residential use. [The houses] will be for only one or two families. The height of these buildings may not exceed 8 m. The minimum distance to the edge of the neighbouring property is 2.50m. Shops or workshops are completely prohibited. Further applicable conditions are in the building order for the Berlin suburbs dated 28 May 1907, with in addition the special requirements for detached or semi-detached houses which will also apply.

[LCdv 88]

— access roads from main roads in the interior of the zone will be at least 8m wide. All streets within the block must be at least as wide as the buildings are high."

The land under consideration could be adapted as follows in the exterior zone:

26m deep, i.e. on exterior roads, plots with a depth of 26m will have a frontage of 20m. Thus in the exterior zone 107 building lots will be created for the construction of four-storey buildings. These residential buildings will, as in example I (with the exception of corner buildings) for a 20m frontage, have a built area of 20 x 19m = 380m^2. These 107 buildings will only differ from the 191 buildings in example I insofar as it would be possible to ventilate them with a through draught and, due to the ban on shops in the interior zone of the large block, will include

[LCdv 89]

just as many shops etc. as the 191 buildings in example I. The courtyard area of the houses separately would, it is true, be smaller than in example I. However this disadvantage would be richly compensated for by the fact that the windows of the back bedrooms

---

9 Comment in square brackets inserted by Jeanneret.

would open, instead of onto a courtyard for a four-storey apartment block, onto the gardens of small houses.

The interior zone will be divided into small blocks with a depth of only 40m, or in exceptional cases 46m. In the 40m deep blocks, each plot will have a depth of 20m, with a frontage set at 6m. Across the entire 120m² will be 60m² designated for construction – for corner buildings this would be 72m². The remainder would serve as a front or back garden. The ground floor would become an apartment and the above-ground and attic floors would be for rental. In the 46m deep blocks, the plots would be

[LCdv 90]

20m deep on one side, 26 on the other. The 20m deep parts would be used in the manner described immediately above. For the 26m deep plots, the frontage would be 10m. Of the overall 260m² area, 130 would be built up – 156 for corner buildings – with the remainder serving as a front or back garden. The ground floor would once again be an apartment and the above-ground and attic floors would be for rental. In total 550 small and 100 larger semi-detached houses would be created.

Due to the lesser depth of the blocks, the interior zone will be crossed by many residential streets, as well as the 6 access roads which establish a connection with the streets on the exterior, [all] 8m wide. Other streets of the same width divide the small blocks for the benefit of traffic flow. Thus the total length of the streets in

[LCdv 91]

example II [is] greater than in example I. In both, 2,714m [sic: 2,174m] are reserved for the exterior streets and the cross street; whereas the other streets in example I have a combined length of only 1,880, those in example II including the passageways have a length of 3,434m. In both cases, the exterior streets and wide connecting streets cover an area of 26,808m² – But whereas the other streets in example I cover an area not less than 36,600m², the residential streets in example II which are so much longer and which correspond to the lowest building height because they are wesentlich [significantly] narrower than the streets in example 1 (including passageways) and only measure 27,472m², so that the overall area of streets in example II is only 54,280m² as against 63,408m² in example I.

The 5,692m² area of the square will not be as in example I divided into two large squares, serving the wide connecting streets, but it serves on the one hand to draw

[LCdv 92]

fresh air into the large block, and mainly to provide children with a playground, in the streets with little traffic, and adults with a recreation area.

As in example 1 the price of streets is 18 M. per m²; for sewerage 60 M per m of façade. Although by employing lighter paving and narrower sewerage pipes in the quieter and less densely populated streets: for the sewerage pipes a Betrag nicht unerheblich [not insignificant sum] would be saved. Accordingly the price of road building and sewerage would appear with the same Betrag [sum] in example II (1,503,600 M) as in example I (1,468,776 M), although with the same usable area, the street area as in example II is 14% smaller than that in example I, as has been shown. A construction price of the same as in example I will be 75 Marks per

[LCdv 93]

m^2 of usable area in the residential floors or 300 M per 1 m^2 of built-up area in the exterior zone, and 200 M per m^2 of built-up area in the interior zone. Once again the rental figure is 6 M per m^2 of usable area for the residential floors. The same plus a rent supplement in the shops..[10] The development of the land will proceed as follows:

New System =

. . . .

. . . .

According to the above, profitability in the new system is as per the old. In other words: the owner of the land will not suffer any losses through the application of the new system. Although it may appear

[LCdv 94]

at first glance

[Text breaks off here. The Manuscript contains no translation of the end of the article.]

§3 *On Streets*

[LCdv 95] §3. On Streets

[LCdv 96] 6) On Streets.//1

This is the most important chapter, since the appearance of a city's streets produces the impression of its charm or ugliness. It is in travelling a city's streets that one will either find cause for enthusiasm, daydreams and enjoyment or feel a dreary lethargy creeping in to paralyse one's legs and leave for ever a hateful memory of the city thus glimpsed.

Before beginning this chapter and in order to anticipate an objection which will certainly be raised (since the theories we put forward here will appear – in our homeland – a little revolutionary to those who now control the beauty of cities), let us quote some lines from Camillo Sitte – on the bête noire of bureaucratic building administrations: 'irregular' plots, i.e. plots not exactly rectangular or triangular, round or square. The principles we set out below will occasionally create such irregular plots and, as we do not consider this a cause for despair, quite the opposite, we wish from the start to preempt any objections on this matter.

"[W]hat architect is afraid of an irregularly shaped building lot?" Sitte page 130 line 14.[11]

The street belongs to all. All pay for it, all have a right to it. The right to move around freely in it, the right to safe transit through it, the right to amenity, the right to beauty.

Hence the obligation to establish organs specially adapted to the various relevant requirements.

Thoroughfares must be created that are easy and practical to use, firstly for the beasts that transport heavy burdens, and then to save mankind tiredness and tedium. All this must also be combined with the most economical solutions.

---

10 Lehweß/Kuczynski: "Provision has been made for 50,000 M. in additional income from shops."

11 George Collins and Christiane Crasemann-Collins, *Camillo Sitte: The Birth of Modern City Planning* (New York: Dover, 2006) p. 225.

[LCdv 97] 2

The land may happen to be uneven, in which case a design completed with a pair of compasses and a set square will be impossible and the city planner must become a 'geometer of space', constantly calculating in three dimensions: height, depth and width.

For business, spacious arteries will be provided. The main places with intensive commerce will be identified; these will be linked in a well-planned network. For pedestrians, narrower streets will be created, a finer mesh with very direct intermediate links, a veritable network of capillaries bringing life to all parts of the organism via the shortest route. From this, we can draw our first conclusion: that the width and slope of streets can and must vary, and systems with streets all of equal width are to be rejected. The present-day building administration does not think the same, and the latter is in fact the system it employs, thus creating some streets which are too narrow for their heavy traffic and numerous others that remain too wide, too open: sad, solitary streets where one mourns how the space has been maligned. The first corollary of such an arrangement is – a disastrous consequence of designing with the T square and set square – a rectilinear street layout, with cruciform intersections, and blocks of a picture-perfect square or rectangular shape. Fig. *XXXIV* [**8**, **9**] shows this chequerboard subdivision: it would be hard to find a city in Europe without entire new districts planned like this. The development of cities will continue to be hampered by such procedures for some time to come, applied in the name of speed and hygiene.

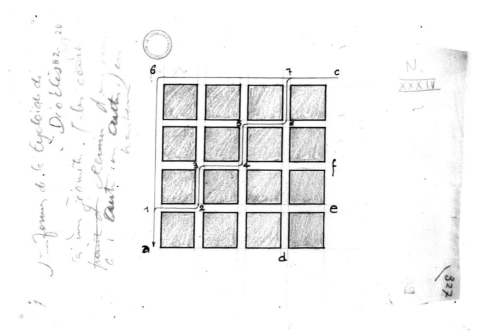

Fig. 8 Chequerboard grid. Drawing by Jeanneret, after Schultze-Naumburg (B2-20-307 FLC)

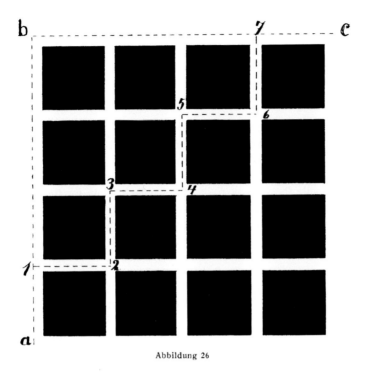

Abbildung 26

Beispiel für die unpraktische Anordnung des
Strassennetzes in Quadratform. Die Verbin-
dung zwischen a und c wird immer die Länge
von a 1 2 3 4 5 6 7 gleich a b c haben

Fig. 9 Chequerboard grid. From Schultze-Naumburg, *Kulturarbeiten Städtebau*, Abb. 26

[In the margin:] {City III, p. 12
As proof of the often poor correlation created between the width of a street and the traffic using it, one of London's busiest streets, London Bridge, is 16 metres wide while
25,000 vehicles and 125,000 people pass along it each day.}

[LCdv 98] 6//3
It is said (see Fig. XXXIV) that the shortest route from one point to another is a straight
line, that fundamental axiom of elementary geometry. Thus if one wants to take the most
direct route from *A* to *B*, route *AB* would be best, from *B* to *C* route *BC*, from *7* to
D route *7d*, and from *1* to *e* route *1e* is of course shortest. All conditions are met optimally, the problem is resolved and the solution universally applied. However, if one
were to counter that, in a city, it is infinitely more often the case that one must travel
from *c* to *a*, or from *f* to *a*, who would vouch for the shortest route? And here is some
nonsense that will cause real amazement: the pedestrian going from *c* to *a* must take the
route *c* to *b*, then *b* to *a*. The longer journey immediately stands out; as such, the pedestrian will be wary of taking it. He will be caught out by a mere illusion: instinctively, he

will try and find the diagonal, and will walk the route *c 7 b 5 4 3 2 1 a* believing this will save him time, yet he will have walked exactly the same distance as with route *c b a*. {[In the margin:] perhaps add to Blocks}

Such considerations do not stop those in charge of city planning from telling us: 'Nevertheless, the straight line is the shortest route and we shall not be satisfied with those curved and badly designed streets so abundant in old towns; they were fitting in times gone by, when people had time to waste.'

[LCdv 99] 4

Here then is a refutation of planning in straight lines. It is inconvenient because it lengthens routes. *Fig. VII* shows the plan of part of the city of Antwerp in the 17th century. It is an admirable plan, containing large numbers of practical and beautiful solutions. In order to reconcile the lines at right angles, which allow for fine building lots but lengthen routes, with diagonal lines which shorten routes but create plots for building which (as we have acknowledged) are unacceptable, city planners have in the past employed a curved, winding line. At once, they achieved both streets sheltered from the wind by the obstacle of the curved line of façades which close in on themselves like the four walls of a room, and streets full of charm with a multiplicity of pleasing, ever-varying, sometimes imposing perspectives.

In Fig. *VII*, *A* was the city's gate, and *B* its port. A major arterial road directly linked these two important points. From *A*, one could access public buildings via the shortest possible route: *A* to *D*, *A* to *I*. The furthest outlying points were optimally linked in all directions: from *E* to *I*, from *E* to *D*, from *H* to *K*, from *H* to *A*, from *I* to *H* and from *K* to *B* or to *E*, etc. etc.

Thus the question was not one of dividing the land up into a mosaic that resembled a chequerboard, but one of considering the city to be a living organism and the streets to be major arteries;

[LCdv 100] 6//5

the main points were linked by main streets, countless small commercial galleries, paths, bridges and covered walkways. These established – in the shortest, most natural way – connections between all points in the city. (See confirmation of this principle in Figures *VIII*, *XXI* and *XXXI* showing the plans of Berne, Ulm and Solothurn). [**10, 11, 12**]

[I] *Boring street – pleasing street – normal street*

According to Henrici, a street is boring when the passer-by walking there feels that the street is longer than it is in reality; if the opposite is true, the street is pleasing. The skill of the street planner is therefore to play with optical illusions to obtain advantages or disadvantages: the less street surface and façade is visible, the shorter the street is believed to be. If, however, the street creates a negative misapprehension in the pedestrian walking there, the street is boring. Yet the more street surface and side walls are visible, the longer, more spacious and important the street appears. Being shorter in reality than its clever proportions lead one to believe, the street surprises the passer-by agreeably and becomes a pleasing street.

Having the end of the street constantly before one's eyes, in vanishing perspective, but taking a long time to reach it although one expected to be transported there more quickly, is tiring and dispiriting. If however the passer-by reaches the end of the street

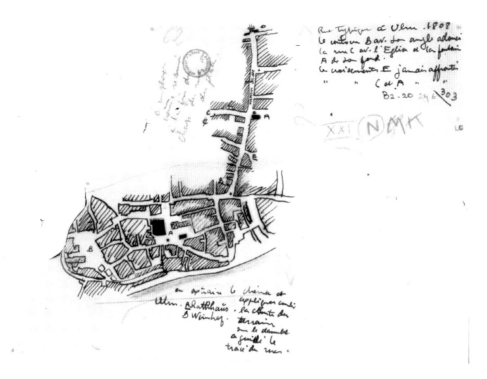

Fig. 10 Figure-ground plan of Ulm. Drawing by Jeanneret, copied from the 1808 plan (B2-20-296 FLC)

Fig. 11 Section of the plan of Ulm 1808. From *Der Städtebau* 6 (1909), plate 79

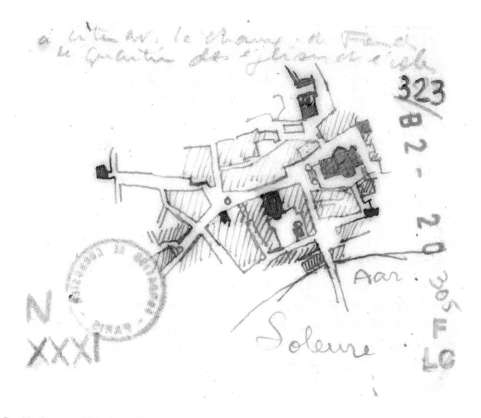

Fig. 12 Centre of Solothurn. Drawing by Jeanneret (B2-20-305 FLC)

more quickly than he thought, this is a nice surprise. The growing succession of changing impressions will transport him to an agreeable state of mind;

[LCdv 101] 6

this is certainly the best treatment for tiredness. There is general agreement that it is less tiring to walk for two hours among mountains than it is to walk a straight road for the same period, between two unrelenting rows of poplars. Would that this were taken into consideration when cities are planned!

Between the boring street and the pleasing street lies the *normal* street, i.e. the street which is straight, either flat or on a steady slope, with parallel street-fronts and with limited dimensions which allow a proper evaluation of its length. This sort of street, appearing as it really is, will be neither 'boring' nor 'pleasant'.

Straight, fairly long streets with continuous parallel street-fronts will only shed their boring nature if they appear shorter than they are. This will only occur if the view of their sides, before they meet the end wall, provides one or two points of note which provide a break and enable a precise appreciation of distance.

One special case of a long straight street with parallel frontages is the street with two slopes in opposite directions, each one a gentle continuous incline, forming a 'hump back' where they meet. The perspective is less closed than ever and even more boring, as both rows of houses will fall away behind the ridge of the hump back; and it is only on arrival at the highest point that the passer-by will perceive the second route, closely resembling the boring one he has just taken.

[LCdv 102] 6//7
Disappointment from a misapprehension about the true length of a street is caused by the fact that, to a viewer at point *a*, Fig. [**13, 14**], points *b'b'* appear to be immediately

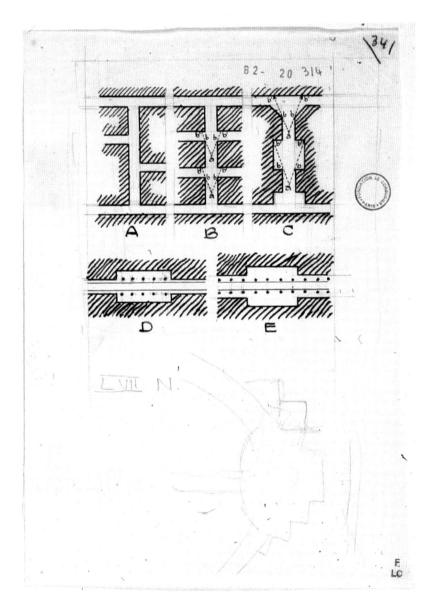

Fig. 13 Intersections and widenings of a street. Drawings by Jeanneret, after Henrici (B2-20-314 FLC)

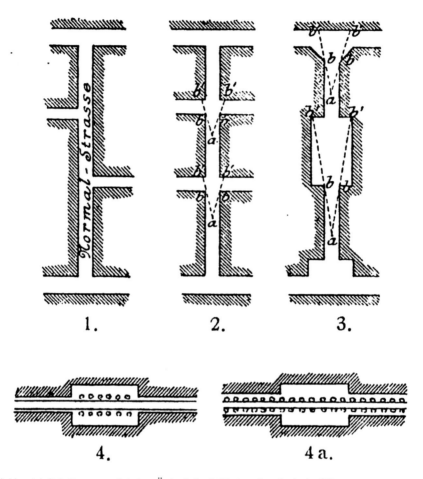

Fig. 14 Henrici, *Beiträge zur praktischen Ästhetik im Städtebau*, figs. 1–4a (p. 88)

adjacent to points *bb*, and distance *bb'* will only be revealed to the passer-by when he has almost reached points *bb*. He will then see that the street is longer by a distance of *bb'*. If this misapprehension recurs ten or twenty times in the same street, the street will become tiresome.

There are ways of lessening the negative impression inherent in straight streets with parallel frontages: one way is to partially hide the converging line of houses by planting trees. A second is to give a concave (hollow) curve to the street's surface, if circumstances allow – a curve starting at one end and finishing at the other: the eye will therefore see a greater area of street surface, certainly much more than where two continuous slopes meet to form a 'hump back'.

Another method is to avoid repeated cruciform intersections as shown in Fig. *LVIIa* [13, 14] (we will demonstrate below the serious practical difficulties caused by numerous cruciform intersections), but instead to design these differently.

Believing he is doing the right thing, the street planner often divides up excessively long straight roads as shown in Fig. *LVIIc.* But this only worsens

[LCdv 103] 8

the misapprehension shown in Fig. *LVIIa* and, if he wishes to remedy this in part, he will be obliged to employ costly measures, such as planting large trees, Fig.s *LVIIc* and *d.*

Just as the concave nature of the street surface counters the boredom created by an excessively rectilinear view, the curve of the lateral frontages will equally, or to an even greater extent, bring great charm without the need for costly measures.

II   *Curved streets.*

Instantly their appearances are infinitely varied; the concave street-front will present to the eye a great development in the surface and allow all the buildings to be seen by the passer-by, whereas the convex street-front will offer entertainment in its rounded surfaces with rapid, changing perspective views. –

However if the frontages beside a winding road are designed in parallel to one another, they will leave the passer-by rather indifferent, Fig. *LVIII* [**15, 16**]. Yet if they exaggerate a layout of a well-proportioned parallel nature, those roads will give the impression [of being] very rich in a variety of appearances; finally the eye will have something on which to alight and will be able, in seeing them, to notice the architectural motifs on the façades, Fig. *LVIII c* and *d.* Instead of being in a street as if in a desert where one's eyes have nothing to rest on but the relentless convergence of 4 lines at a point on the horizon stuck on an unlimited surface, the passer-by will have the comfortable feeling of finding himself between the walls of a great room with changing tapestries.

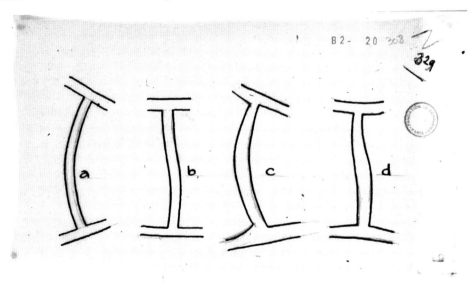

Fig. 15 Curved streets. Drawings by Jeanneret, after Henrici (B2-20-308 FLC)

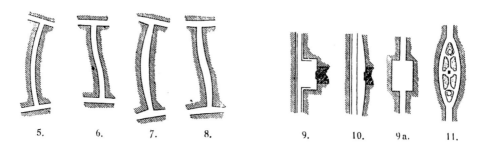

5.   6.   7.   8.   9.   10.   9 a.   11.

Fig. 16 Henrici, *Beiträge zur praktischen Ästhetik im Städtebau*, 1904, figs. 5–11 (p. 90)

[LCdv 104] 6//9

There is something truly remarkable in modern cities: the fact that one no longer sees what makes up the city – the buildings. The façades no longer offer themselves up for view; they all recede into an imperceptible surface.

Why then does the curved street have so many favourable elements? Because it obeys the first law of beauty: it is something, it can be seen. How should a non-existent or almost non-existent thing, such as a very long, straight street without a surface at the end, claim any plastic beauty? No such plastic creation has yet emerged out of empty space; until this tricky problem is resolved, the curved street remains the most harmonious; here, the images enclose themselves. Thus a short, straight street, closed at its ends, has the capacity for beauty. It will certainly require more from appearance of the surrounding edifices; that is why, although successful, it is less commonly realised.

We have all experienced the enchanting Marktgasse in Berne: having been through the passageway under the [Käfigturm] tower [**17**], one enters this very elongated, slightly curved enclosure lined with arcades and adorned with two fountains, which ends at the bottom with, initially hidden by the curvature of the street front, the clock tower [Zytgloggeturm] and its faded paintings and enormous shield displaying the coat of arms. The beauty of this street is generally attributed to the very buildings which frame it, to the superb fountains which enliven it. This is erroneous. Its beauty arises from the feeling of perfect volume in the street, and only then – as a result of this – do the façades contribute

[LCdv 105] 10

effectively to it.

We have seen – Fig.s *VII* and *VIII* – that the needs of rapid interaction imposed layouts with winding lines. We have just seen that these provide the most pleasant aspects. Where land is hilly, they win out, since the street planner must strive to find the most favourable slopes. It is very enlightening to study the paths which countryfolk take across undulating countryside to reach the town. They are clearly guided purely by utility. These paths are the best-established norm for tackling the obligations imposed by slopes, the climate, [deploying] the minimum of effort and [attaining] the maximum speed.

Now rural roads, which are laid out by the locals and not by geometers from the administration, are never drawn with a tracing-line. The route and incline they adopt is gentle and always has a decorative effect on the countryside; these lines, intimately linked to

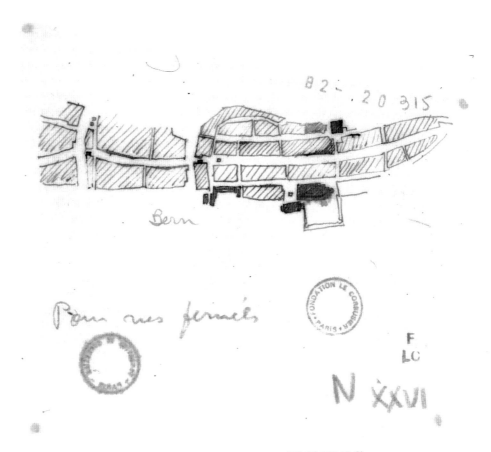

Fig. 17 Extract of the plan of Berne. Drawing by Jeanneret (B2-20-315 FLC)

the hills and dales which governed their layout, often lend the countryside an element of beauty with their white mesh accentuating the contours of the hills like a slender necklace on a curvaceous décolleté. These paths should therefore represent 'life lines', around which the city planner weaves the fabric of his streets. This is common sense, and so instructive that there are abundant examples of cities which have been sheltered from progressist devastation, and spread their exquisitely charming, lively design across the hillside; see (Fig. *XI*). The buildings may be nondescript, deprived

[LCdv 106] 6//11

of any richness, yet these cities still retain the flavour and interest of something created naturally.

Street intersections

Fig.s *LVIIIc* and *d* have obtained a greater capacity for beauty than Fig.s *a* and *b* with regular, parallel frontages. It is time, incidentally, that this optical phenomenon was established: 'that the eye is absolutely incapable of measuring certain geometric shapes in space'. Thus whereas an angle of less than 90 degrees strikes one as disagreeable, in the case of a housing block created by two streets meeting, an angle of over 90 degrees can be overlooked, or at least shocks one less; an angle less than 90 degrees is irretrievably ugly. The right angle is the most beautiful, the most monumental; the angle which is slightly greater retains great plastic effect, as it has allowed the most successful solutions when many palaces were built in Italy or elsewhere during the Mediaeval and Early Renaissance periods. As we will see below, where city squares are concerned the eye is even less capable of independent assessment. The most irregular squares will appear rather normal; in most cases, squares with monumental aspects, or very intimate squares with a pressing feel, will occasion the greatest surprises

[LCdv 107] 12
when their plans are examined. Once again the worthlessness of drawing on paper is confirmed, as is the need for the planner to see objects in space.

Streets widening temporarily or with repeated projections

If, for ordinary reasons (e.g. to create space around a public building by thinning the surrounding traffic) it is necessary to widen the street, one would be tempted to adopt the strategy indicated in image *a* Fig. *LIX* [18]. Indeed this would appear more correct than the strategy in image *b*; it will however have a second-rate effect: image *b* opens up the ample surface area of its buildings to view, and it is the street which will appear wider here, while in image *a* the widening would scarcely have any more marked effect than that of a street opening.

What if there is to be a dual widening? This will inevitably be performed along the lines of image *c* despite the inconvenient aspects demonstrated in Fig.s *LVIIc* and *d* [13]. The belief will be that something monumental has been created, and objections will be raised to image *d* due to a purported lack of merit in the design, which nevertheless allows for

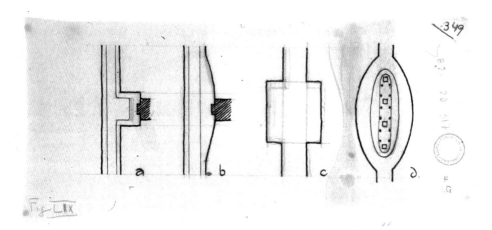

Fig. 18 Widening of streets. Drawings by Jeanneret, after Henrici (B2-20-317 FLC)

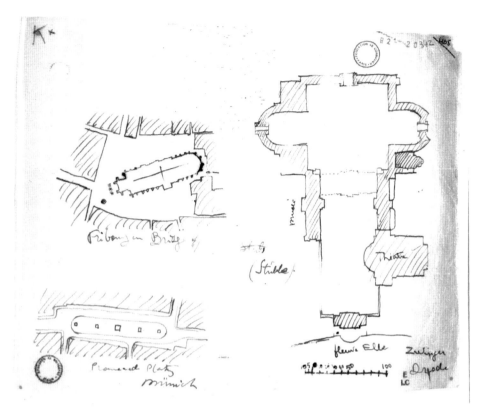

Fig. 19 Münsterplatz in Freiburg, Promenadeplatz in Munich and the Zwinger Palace in Dresden. Drawings by Jeanneret, copied from Stübben, *Städtebau*, 1890, fig. 395, 308 and 413 (B2-20-342 FLC)

the major buildings to gain grand perspectives and to be grouped beautifully. The Promenade-Platz in Munich has been designed in this way; it has an undeniably fine appearance. [19].

From the point of view of continuity in the street fronts, image a from Fig. *LVII* is satisfying because the line of buildings continues on one side of the street, without interruption. In the case of a curved street,

[LCdv 108] 6//13

widening on the concave side should be avoided: it appears as a hole and it is necessary, to make up for this difficulty, to arrange monuments or trees in the manner of images *b* and *c*, Fig. *LX* [20, 21]. Why then open up the street, since costly strategies will be employed straight afterwards to close the clumsy cut-out *a* and *b* Fig. *LX*. The right strategy which has been employed successfully since time immemorial is that in image *d*, i.e. with the widening carried out on the convex side of the street. The line of façades will not then appear to be interrupted and the building whose remarkable architecture motivated the widening can be admired restfully, sheltered from traffic, and at the same time will decorate the street, a condition which the designs in Fig.s *b* and *c* did not meet.

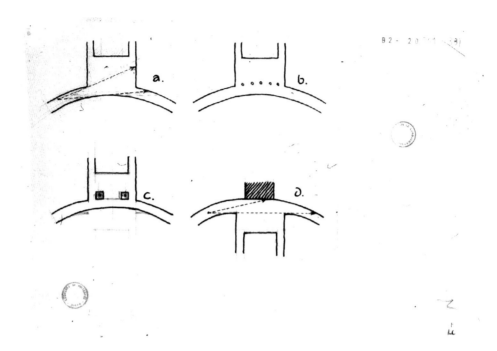

Fig. 20 Placing of monumental buildings. Drawings by Jeanneret, after Henrici (B2-20-309)

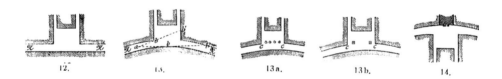

Fig. 21 Henrici, *Beiträge zur praktischen Ästhetik im Städtebau*, figs. 12–14 (p. 91f.)

It is often the case that streets widen not abruptly, as with a right-angled set-back, but with an imperceptible increase in breadth which, once it has reached its maximum, abruptly reverts to the original breadth. This procedure, if deployed artistically, causes remarkable perspective effects in which the significant expanse of the street fronts thus exposed to our view takes on a true grandeur. This is the case in Neuhauser Straße, Munich; the widening and sudden return cut down the excessive length of the street [22], carriage drivers use this island of peace to let their teams rest at the very edge of the most intense traffic. The passer-by coming from the town hall sees the street closing off with a strong image before him; the admirable old baroque-style surfaces lend this perspective a certain, imposing something. And if, having crossed this enclosure, he turns back,

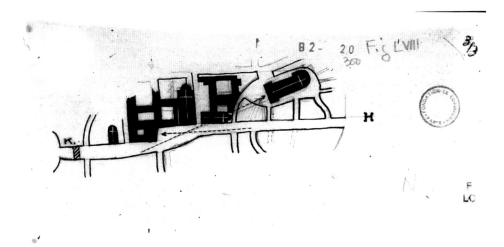

Fig. 22 Neuhauser Straße in Munich. Drawing by Jeanneret (B2-20-300 FLC)

[LCdv 109] 14

the impression made will be even greater, with the two brick towers of the Frauenkirche so shapely and original against the sky, in a strong frame.

The principle behind these widenings with projections becomes at opportune moments full of unforeseen charm if repeated. Old streets have no shortage of such designs which allow two façades to be situated on the same street. Today this style, when employed exceptionally, offers certain benefits. Shops, competing as they do in terms of the munificence of their displays, would gain the opportunity to double the area of their frontage, and the window-shopper could rejoice in these displays at their leisure without obstructing the traffic.

– Fig. [__] shows that while the area of street fronts almost doubles, the frontage facing the gardens which are provided where there are blocks, as in Fig. [__], also doubles.

{[In the margin:] add that in the case of an upward-sloping street this is very advantageous.}

It is time for a brief digression on the design of pavements.

A principle has now been established: the glance of the passer-by, who does not wish to be bored in a street, needs to alight upon real surfaces; the planner's efforts will focus on multiplying these surfaces. And although these designs inspire a grimace when viewed on paper, the artistic geometer will not shy away from them, because this grimace does not arise in reality. Yet it is necessary to show the passer-by his direction of travel with at least one line. The line of the pavements will do this. Furthermore it will harm the comings and goings of cars if the river channel provided for traffic

[LCdv 110] 6//15

has banks like the teeth of a saw. It would occasion a number of unfortunate collisions along the line of the pavements. Pavements should therefore have a continuous, direct line and one should avoid sudden jumps varying the width of the carriageway. This important consideration had already motivated the parallel pavements for widenings as per Fig.s *LVIIc* and *d*, and *LIXb*.

{for example, the pavements opposite la Madeleine, Paris}

The shape of the pavement would not seem the sort of preoccupation which is essential to the aesthetic question of planning the city. However, this is a subject of special concern to modern architects: the edge of the pavement forms the boundary between the moving, dangerous sphere of fast vehicles and the quieter sphere of pedestrians. It is, in some ways, the parapet on a pier surrounded by the sea. A poetic feeling is often associated with its shape.

See Fig. *XXXXV*, a square congested with trams, motor cars and carriages, adorned by a fountain and a monument; the latter is drowned in the noise of the vehicles; it is hard to approach and one is constantly obliged to stay on the kerbstones of the narrow pavement. The fountain has become an exquisite decoration, not because of its sculptures which are indifferent, but because it extends cool freshness, which they may enjoy, into a place accessible to pedestrians. What great joy to make out, through the dust of trams, carriages and motor cars, a cool trickle of water! The cleverly planned pavement delivers the amenity associated with a fountain in a square. What is more, a plan with a dual bend removes the square's brutal

[LCdv 111] 16.

geometric strictures.

Fig. *LVIII* showed the clever strategy of truncating a long journey along the Neuhauser Straße in Munich by clearly countering the vanishing line of the street with a large façade at right angles. Yet a great square opens up at *K*; in order to avoid the unfortunate effect of the hole made where a major arterial road enters a square in line with it (more on this subject below), the Karlstor was either retained or built – we do not have this information. This is a building made of a large arch cast over the carriageway and two smaller passageways over the pavements. – The Sendlinger Tor in Munich also repeats the same procedure with less pretentious and more successful architecture, Fig. *LII* [**23**].

On Fig. *XXI* [**10**], the streets of Ulm illustrate many interesting solutions: in *G*, that of a city gate similar to the above case. The street which opens into major artery *GF* is enclosed by a church *D* built in line with it. Thus the street intersection is very advantageous. At *E* and *F* the enclosed aspect of these two streets is obtained using a procedure frequently employed in the past, consisting of brutally closing off a major arterial road with a right-angled turn. (See Fig. *XVIII*) [**24**] This is where the master builder can bring his artistic ability to bear on the proportions he gives street widenings – with the most advantageous situation for a fountain or as in *E* {Fig. *XXI*} a skilful combination of recessed or projecting façades and the fountain acting as an end to the street.

[LCdv 112] 6//17

The use of such procedures relieves straight streets of their ugly, boring character; the first precondition is to divide their length into short sections. The examples we have just supplied, and that in Fig. *XII*, were not created with beauty in mind, but constructed for military defence; having lost their purpose, they remained because of the beauty they brought to the streets. It should be noted that in Fig. *XII* the town hall was not aligned with the street, since two important buildings standing at the ends of a straight street give the impression of banality, which the artistic eras carefully avoided.

Fig. 23 Sendlinger Tor in Munich. Drawing by Jeanneret, copied from *Süddeutsche Bauzeitung* 13 (1903), p. 218 (LCdv 417)

Passageways

It would admittedly be ridiculous to construct, in a new town, gates and towers akin to those from centuries past, simply to close off a street view. We must find a useful adaptation of this plastic strategy. One can be achieved in new town plans of different shapes: *passageways*. In the case of a block like the one in Fig. [___] (Sieg. Sitte), the passageway will be made through a building, and cars prohibited; it will sometimes be closed at night. The improvements in traffic made by these passageways will be all the greater if the procedure is repeated in several consecutive blocks. Fig. *XVIII* [**25**] shows one application of this in Munich; very busy traffic gave the buildings considerable value; in

[**LCdv 113**] 18.
place of sorry courtyards the very architectural ploy of 4 walls closing in on themselves granted very pretty aspects. – Large bays with flowered galleries and shops on the ground floor, cafés or bookshops which benefit from the constant stream of passers-by – books and engravings can be laid out in the shade or sheltered from the rain.
In another fashion, Fig. [___] which shows at *A* the above type of passageway also shows at *B* a beautiful, characterful solution. The street is simply closed by a large building through which a vast archway is opened, allowing access to cars and pedestrians.

B 2 - 2 0 304

Weissenburg

Fig. 24 Weissenburg (Wissembourg), Alsace. Drawing by Jeanneret, copied from Merian, *Topographiae Alsatiae*, fig. after p. 66 (B2-20-304 FLC)

Other passageways of all shapes have been made in cities; the standard one is like that in Fig. [ ] which crosses a covered courtyard with a glazed ceiling; all the walls are arranged as shop windows and fronts: as well as improving traffic, land which is generally sacrificed can thus be developed.

One charming solution which aims to cut down the excessive length of a street is to position a house on the pavement as a projection measuring 4, 5 or 6 metres, and open up a large archway at its base. The Limmat-Quai in Zurich provides several illustrations of this procedure. This is also the case in Munich, in Prinzregentenstraße in front of the Nationalmuseum. Fig. *XXX* [**26, 27**] shows a variation which combines in a single stroke the beauty of a square with that of the street; – it is a garden city project; – the rooms with

[LCdv 114] 6//19

their windows in these projecting blocks are exceptionally well situated.

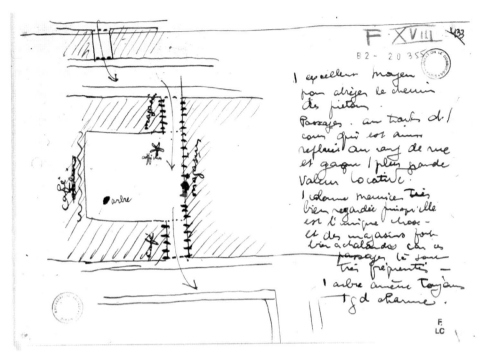

Fig. 25 Urban passageway. Sketch by Jeanneret (B2-20-355 FLC)

Searching for the most advantageous orientation can bring one to design a district of villas or houses with gardens, following the contour lines of a hill; what would be the most judicious use of the land here?

On the two layouts in Fig. [**28, 29**], the slope of the ground is shown by the dotted line *AB*. The system applied every day is that in sketch a which, being of no benefit for the owners of the villas, gives the street a very denuded appearance. The gardens on either side of the street will not be at all comfortable and will be very hard to design as they will slope. However, there would be a way to draw marvellous benefit from this same site. The cost of terracing would, it is true, be greater. For the owners this would amount to several thousand francs. But if they were given an assurance that this would be hugely offset in terms of well-being and beauty, they would doubtless consent to this additional cost. Since it would also be a question of creating a beautiful street which could become a well-used pedestrian route, the local authorities would have an interest in building the supporting walls and would contribute to the costs. Sketch *b* speaks for itself: it shows the monumental aspect of the large wall on the right-hand side, crowned with detached houses and vegetation; it emphasises the variety of approaches the architect could take to the house entrances lower down, on the left; we can discern the generous prospect of the street, all shaded, with its wide pavement, where

Fig. 26 Perspectival view of market square in Marktredwitz. Drawing by Jeanneret, copied from P.A. Hansen (B2-20-313 FLC)

[LCdv 115a] 20
benches allow pedestrians to enjoy the street between the groups of villas. Hence it is merely a matter of designing building lots with a good depth and requiring owners to build the walls and detached houses which crown them, in line with set types which are in harmony with one another.

One of the administration's quirks is its passion for levelling and making regular. We have already observed them moving – if not heaven and earth to find the most economical solution – then at least thousands of cubic metres of rubble or rock to strive for the ideal, unyielding line. Considerable sums have flowed out for this, towns and cities been made uglier, and the useful purpose stated has not been served: quite the reverse.

{[In the margin:] Insert paragraph relating to levelling}

[LCdv 116] [Jeanneret intended to insert this after the above comment 'Insert. . .']
6 annex to 20
In the course of a street 1,000 metres long, it grows convex by 2 metres in the first 500 metres, and concave by 2 metres in the subsequent 500 metres, which sets in motion the public works team, shaving off 10,000 cubic metres of earth, clay or rock just so they can deposit them further along, in a bank packed down with great care [**30**]. These two metres below and two metres above the very sweet line ruled on a bureaucrat's drawing board is said to justify moving 20,000 cubic metres of material.

Fig. 27 Peter Andreas Hansen, "Baulinienplan für die Stadt Marktredwitz," in: *Der Städtebau* 6 (1909), plate 37

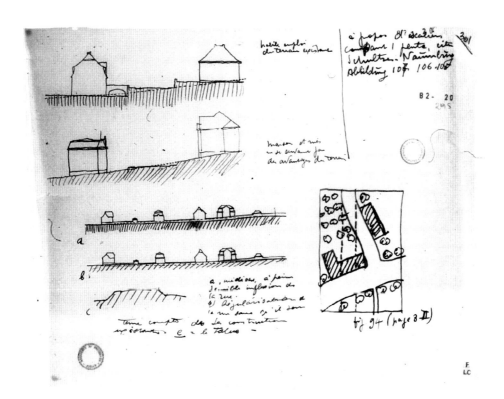

Fig. 28 Superfluous and reasonable levelling. Drawings by Jeanneret, copied from Schultze-Naumburg (B2-20-295 FLC)

BEISPIEL

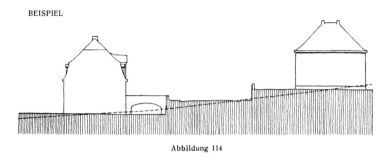

Abbildung 114

GEGENBEISPIEL

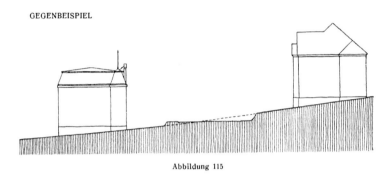

Abbildung 115

Abbildung 114: Geschickte Aus-
nutzung des vorhandenen Terrains zu Strassenanlagen mit
Terrassen. Abb. 115: Strassen-
und Hausanlage ohne Ausnut-
zung des vorhandenen Terrains.

Fig. 29 Schultze-Naumburg, *Kulturarbeiten Städtebau*, figs. 114–115

Yet the consequences aren't limited to this mean feat in itself! The cross streets and
neighbouring gardens will also be chopped off or built up and the figure of 20,000 cubic
metres could well rise to 100,000 over the years; it would be done little by little, and
nobody would dream of being surprised. An owner who has bought land measuring 20
x 30 metres to build an economical house will read on his architect's quote, without
thinking to dispute it, an excess of excavation: some 1,200 cubic metres which could
have paid for a pleasure cruise to Egypt or the Canary Isles!
The most striking thing is that this unjustified regularisation, which deprives towns of
a certain charm, is of no use to traffic – especially in the case of sloping streets.

[LCdv 115b]

Sloping Streets

We will not forget the demonstration given to us one rainy day by an ass pulling
a heavy load. We were at the window of a building which closed off the top of a street

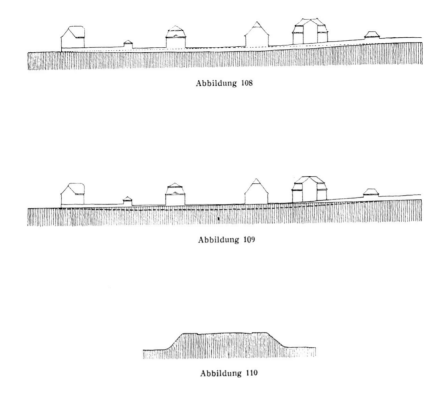

Abbildung 108

Abbildung 109

Abbildung 110

Abbildung 108: geringe, kaum
sichtbare Senkung einer Strasse.
Abbildung 109: „Regulierung"
der Strasse ohne Rücksicht auf
ihre vorhandene Bebauung.

Fig. 30 Schultze-Naumburg, *Kulturarbeiten Städtebau*, figs. 108–110

with a steady gradient. The rain that had just fallen had made of the carriageway a uniform covering, in which the wheels of the cart pulled by the donkey made two shining stripes. At the bottom of the road these furrows started parallel to the pavement; but, soon after, they neared one side, then the other, then the first again, and so on for some hundred metres. The winding line loosened somewhat; the bends became less sharp, it regained a line parallel with the pavements. Then the donkey stopped; but as he was whipped, he regained a very winding route which became increasingly so until,

[LCdv 117] 6//21
once he had reached the top of the street, both donkey and cart disappeared.
The donkey's lesson should be remembered. Indeed, if this long-eared beast had been in the planners' office, he would have suggested: "My dear geometers, when it comes to streets that climb, please consider us as much as you can: the poor beasts condemned to pull very heavy burdens. We do not like your continuous slopes which you draw so very straight, burdening your budgets so heavily as you do so; our masters, made sullen by

taxes, make us pay for these with great lashes of the whip. We would prefer a slope which is somewhat steep, then levels off a little, possibly completely. Afterwards we would begin the normal slope once more and, if necessary, we would put our backs into it for several minutes. For the love of us beasts, do not make all our four-legged kind sweat so, without a pause to catch our breath, on continuous slopes where we must give a constant effort. A little variety in the strain on our muscles will be less tiring. When it comes to you, you say: a change is as good as a rest. All the more so for us! And, if you make streets as we suggest, they will be much more pleasing, and our drivers will swoon with admiration before the ingenious combinations you produce; they will forget their whipping and God knows our backs will be glad of it."

If the donkey's lesson were heeded, we would face ingenious challenges. For here utility will result in the greatest ugliness

[LCdv 118] 22

or the most unexpected charm.

The ugliness of a straight street forming a hump back in the middle of its length has already been mentioned. – Let us now suppose that a street rising on a normal slope continues into a street with a much gentler or zero slope, or indeed continues into a descending street. This is a case which constantly occurs in hilly terrain. At the break in continuity, a very marked hump will appear and, as one climbs, one will have the impression of a large void at the end of the street: the line of houses will fall away, with an effect even more lamentable than that created by the infinite perspective of a long, straight street with parallel frontages. The geometer can make a most brilliant play of this state of affairs by bending his streets as shown in Fig. *XXVIII* [**31**, **32**]. In diagrams *a* and *b*, due to a slight widening of the street at the peak of the slope, the views will be closed off by a building which blocks the street at its end point; this surface will allow the eyes to rest, distracting from the adverse hump. The beauty of this solution speaks for itself: from the windows, the view across town and the line of the descending street will give homes here a wholly special value. The façade thus emphasised may warrant an artistic intervention; a fountain or any small plastic structure will contribute to the overall beauty.

Fig.s *c* and *d* show another ploy: two streets forming a fork.

[LCdv 119] 6//23

But still a wish persists to close off the image at the point where the two slopes meet. The coldly symmetrical design will be happily replaced by that in Fig. *d*, for instance, where one can discern the additional care taken to add beauty to the perspectives from points 1 and 2 opposite.

In the network of streets leading up to an elevation, the path for vehicles will always be the longest; the path for pedestrians, the shortest. This is where capillary networks come into play, as discussed in our comparison of a city's streets with an arterial system.

The cart routes will take the most favourable slope; the resulting streets will always be beautiful if we apply to them the architectural procedures stated above, procedures which a respect for the terrain both imposes and multiplies. More direct routes, in the form of stairs, will be provided for pedestrians. In countries where there is a dread of black ice or snow, this fear will cause master builders to increase the ingenuity of their solutions. There is no lack of variety when it comes to solutions, with all their picturesque or monumental aspects. The beauty of stairs was understood in the Renaissance and the

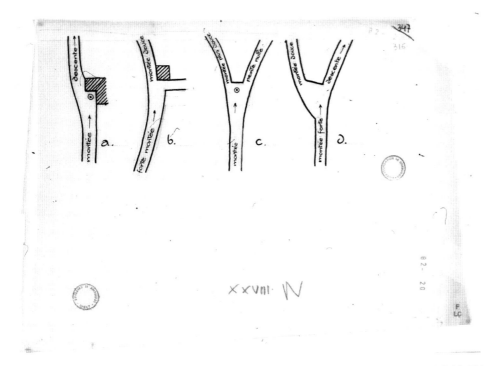

Fig. 31 Transitions between varying slopes. Drawings by Jeanneret, copied from Henrici (B2-20-316
        FLC)

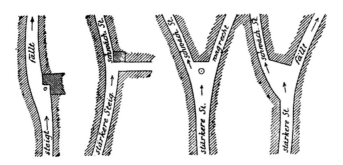

Fig. 32 Henrici, *Beiträge zur praktischen Ästhetik im Städtebau*, figs. 1–4 (p. 102)

18th century. The stairs shown as a diagram in image *LXII a* and *b* [**33**] could be placed
either as independent motifs drawing their beauty from a happy alternation of landings
and flights, according beautifully with the neighbouring houses, or passageways piercing
the very bulk of the buildings and thus

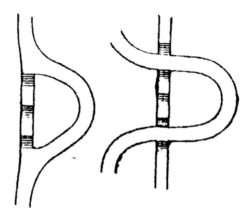

Fig. 33 Henrici, *Beiträge zur praktischen Ästhetik im Städtebau*, figs. 5–6 (p. 102)

[LCdv 120] 24

sheltered from rain and snow. The light they enjoy, the way they enter the housing, the way they open onto and close off streets, there is a fine balance needed where it is possible to create beauty.

The ring road is a type of street with origins dating back to the Middle Ages. When, finding itself too narrowly confined inside its fortified walls, the mediaeval town decided to create new districts, the initial enclosure which was of no use in peace time served as a means of communication and also a promenade. A ring, intermittently encircling the complex road network, will perform the same function; it will be an easy point of reference. Busy people will make little use of it but during leisure time, in the evening or on Sunday, this boulevard on which specialist shopping will be concentrated – meeting the demand for luxury rather than everyday needs – will be enlivened by crowds strolling. Due to their circular nature, these boulevards will vary constantly in aspect.

A few words here on the official 'parade' street, where modern building focuses its most inventive engineering. If one wants to show strength, one draws a very straight street; at each end one sites a great edifice, a church here and a school or a law court there. As these two buildings are fundamentally different in architectural character, one would expect this to increase the variety in views of the street. That is an error: the foreground and background will appear in absolutely the same frame of dimensions and perspective lines. The nature of a view in either direction will be the same; both will

[LCdv 121] 6//25

bear the seal of banality. It will be redolent of the typical parade, and interest nobody.

Let us now sum up this view of street design. Residents of a city cannot be content with monotony. The methods mentioned above must therefore never be generalised across entire districts. In the 18th century, Laugier said: "There must be regularity and whimsy, relationships and oppositions, chance elements that lend variety to the tableau, *precise order in the details*, and confusion, chaos and tumult in the whole."[12] The attractiveness of a city is said to depend precisely on the rich, intelligent combination of all the procedures imaginable. We certainly cannot claim to have listed all these methods here. The range of architectural combinations is inexhaustible. What shall guide the geometer in his work, above all, is the terrain: he shall respect the land which he is tasked with developing. He shall apply himself with the greatest modesty, with great self-abnegation. For only he can know the reality of what he creates, he sees its harmonious beauty in his mind's eye. His lot is never, or rarely, to enjoy the fruit of his labour; his designs will only be realised over the years. Indeed he must admit the distinct possibility of his dreams being destroyed by a lack of agreement among builders in the future, and by the inefficiency of excessively weak laws, [easily] bypassed. For then he will truly know that his is a noble task. Thanks to him, thousands of his fellow citizens might one day be proud;

[LCdv 122] 26

thanks to him, an entire town might live shrouded in deep indifference towards its own history. Riches might accumulate in a city which he has made a charming place to stay; conversely if this wealth leaves it, having sucked the marrow from the city's very bones, that too will be his fault. For if he is a man too quickly satisfied, he may not have understood the responsibility his fellow citizens have granted him.

Those dreaming of intensive progress and extreme modernism will indeed be outraged by the techniques we have advocated. They will reproach us with regressing to an inferior, picturesque stage. We anticipate their objections and to avoid a lengthy exposition, we will respond thus: buy the journal *Städtebau*, with monthly coverage of everything relating to city planning, and you will see that cities more modernist than our little Swiss villages have elevated the matter of development to its rightful place. You will not find a single plan which one would call progressive, a plan of our time – an American-style plan. You will see then that common sense has won out once again. That human life {[in the margin:] look at the rectilinear city, Pompeii etc.} in a town or city is not a theory, but a reality experienced every day; that humans want comfort, have ideal aspirations, and first and foremost the excusable need to live like intelligent beings. That one cannot allow oneself to be handled like an unfeeling factor in an algebraic equation; that one's dreams cannot be enclosed in a drawing

[LCdv 123] 6//27

made [purely] of elementary geometry.

The chequerboard city will therefore disappear from our lives and the vision of current administrations will be transformed.

Then, and only then, will the straight street take its rightful place: a place of the greatest beauty.

The straight line is the elegant line par excellence in nature, but also rightly the rarest. The rigid solemn columns of pine forests; the horizontal line of the sea; the vast

---

12 Translation of Laugier's phrase by Stephen Sartarelli. Cf. Manfredo Tafuri, "Toward a Critique of Architectural Ideology", in: Michael K. Hays, ed., *Architecture Theory Since 1968* (Cambridge, Mass.: MIT, 1998), p. 7.

magnificence of the plain; the grandeur of the Alps seen from a summit, when all harshness melts away into a vast expanse of peace!

Two impressions are associated with the straight street: the impression of grandeur; the
impression of beauty. Grandeur, when its exceptional use makes the street striking and its
dimensions so enormous as to be awe-inspiring. A certain slope or dip will benefit this
street, and it will always be enclosed at its upper end by a glorious monument. Its skilful
orientation will make the street even more magical. Such is the avenue des Champs-Elysées
in Paris, crowned with the immense Arc de Triomphe, behind which the sun sets gloriously.
So too in Berlin, the 'effect' of the Siegesallee at the end of which the Siegessäule stands
drowning in the crimson of the setting sun, almost mirrored in the tarmacadam

[LCdv 124] 28

polished by automobiles. – Bismarckstraße in Charlottenburg with its enormous dimensions
follows an inflexible direction for interminable kilometres, almost the only straight line
through districts which are and will be designed according to the new procedures.

Paris under Napoleon III demonstrated a type of straight street which embodies power:
fairly long; closed at both ends; and flanked by blocks of rental apartments. Lesser
towns and cities believed that this was what they must imitate. The wide streets of Paris,
such as the Avenue de l'Opéra, are only imposing both due to the unity of their architecture and due to the mass of traffic which floods their carriageways and their pavements,
like a turbulent river between two embankments whose height is well in proportion with
their breadth, where the line of the horizon against the sky is perfectly tranquil and
imposing; solid legislation has imposed this condition.

The second characteristic: an impression of beauty! For this, the straight street must
assert the feeling of *embodied space*. Its length, breadth, the height of the buildings, will
fit together in such a way that perspective tapering is barely apparent. Hence the street
will be very short and its ends closed off. – Beauty is rhythm, proportion, harmony. The
street will only be beautiful if all the buildings are intimately related, if architects understand that it is mutually beneficial for each to heed the other so all can harmonise to
create an *ensemble piece*.

[LCdv 125] 6//29

From these latter considerations on the straight street, it emerges that small towns must
renounce the grand street and that, while we await the day – perhaps in the not-too-
distant future – when a *style* will assert itself, when geometers will use the straight line
only in a much more moderate way.

{[Underneath, in pencil against several sketches:] give photo//photo of Maison des Cretêts.//compare with Nuremberg.//photo//drawing Nuremberg//plan//plan}

[LCdv 126] [From here to 129: notes belonging to the chapter on streets]
STREETS

It must be said that in Ludwigstraße there is not a single shop which makes the buildings
into pedestal-like bases, very much part of the carriageway and the pavements – worthy
of great attention.

The Leopoldstraße is typical with four rows of poplars [sketch] and arc lamps suspended
on horizontal wires along the axis of the street. Thus the wall of poplars is illuminated
and forms a formidable, severe and regular embankment.

The street continues on from Ludwigstraße which does not have a single tree but, not being dotted with shops, is an imposing, [seemingly] impossible wall of stones. The triumphal arch separates the two streets, and two rows of arc lamps on Ludwigstraße are suddenly interrupted by one wall of the triumphal arch; underneath this archway one can glimpse the single, flaming line of arc lamps on Leopoldstraße.
STREETS

[LCdv 127]

Heilmann and Littmann://Geb. Rank – tomorrow Thursday – Eisenbetongesellschaft. Tiefbau. Sendlingerstrasse 1 Leonhard Moll Hoch and Tiefbau Lindu_mstrasse 129–131

[LCdv 128]

It is in the street, said Jules Vallès, that people commune with beauty.

[LCdv 129]

Ludwigstraße 1500m long. X wide. All lined with public buildings, secondary schools, library, university, church, seminary etc. which means that no shop opens up the massive, powerful base of these buildings. Hence their perfect connection with the pavement and the asphalt carriageway.
[For further material for On Streets see LCdv 410f., 417, 425, 438–440, 443f., 447]

§4 On Squares, I

[LCdv 130] part I//Chap. II//K.//§4//§4 SQUARES
Die Kunst Oktober 1910 vil[l]as Muthesius

[LCdv 131a] 7. ON SQUARES.//1
Even more than with streets, the design of squares during the 19th century produced unaesthetic views, and similarly the utilitarian requirements which geometers invoked brought only confusion for traffic, disadvantage to residents, and ugliness in urban perspectives.
{[In the margin:] insert sheet 1a}

[LCdv 132] 7//1a
Camillo Sitte, in his book *City Planning According to Artistic Principles*, sought in minute detail the underlying reasons which dictated the design of squares before the 19th century.*
{[In the margin:] * In particular he delighted in rehabilitating the 'irregular' square, those beautiful squares derived from mediaeval principles which our current administrations ceaselessly profane with their misplaced regularisation.}
We should have liked to refer our reader to this lengthy study by a master; sadly that edition is out of print. Hence we will review the laws based on optical phenomena, on aesthetic principles, on utilitarian and suitability requirements, which emerge unchanged in even the most contradictory cases.

[LCdv 132b]

Here, as in the other areas of city planning, we lack a clear view of the goal being pursued, and hence the most contradictory elements have been brought together in one and the same square. Let us establish a classification which, although somewhat theoretical, will allow us to demonstrate precisely what we have just stated above.

Why do we create squares?

1. In order to obtain, amidst the dense street network, a peaceful area where markets or public gatherings can be held, or very simply for the sole purpose of (within the confines of a city) parting the walls of the buildings to arrange a greater pocket of free space. This square would because of its purpose be kept free from traffic.

2. A building with a particular character is to be emphasised: this is an opportunity to arrange a well-proportioned space in front of its façade. Amplifying the impression of beauty is the desired goal here.

{[In the margin:] for patriotic demonstrations, crowds etc.}

[LCdv 133] 2

3. A square grows up of its own accord when several streets meet at a single point. This square is called a roundabout, a crossroads. The intent behind its creation is to ease to the comings and goings of people and vehicles.

The above are 3 clear, distinct categories. If one studies 19th century squares one will observe the constantly poor adaptation of form to requirements. Due to the lack of clear intent, and as part of a synthesis which was believed to be skilful but which only proved disastrous, these squares were merged into one: the square created for its own sake (i.e. an island of peace), the square to serve a building (i.e. erasing the square itself in order to transfer all gazes onto a privileged highlight), the crossroads (i.e. all traffic compressed into a single point). And thus this standard type was obtained, with an appearance repeated 20 times in the same city, a type spread across every continent: a noisy knot where trams and vehicles rumble, where the network of electric cables blocks out the sky, where lamp posts stand

[LCdv 134] 7//3

in disharmony, where buildings present the shabbiest of impressions, where flowering shrubs wilt away in banal designs. This is the modern, pulsating, dust-ridden square where pedestrians fear to tread.

If it is indeed possible to ascertain, amidst the confusion which these squares' realisation brought, what their 19th century planners intended, a brief analysis will show how few of the conditions imposed on them were met.

Fig. [34] shows the simplest current example of a square as a 'place of rest'. On market days, cars cannot follow their usual route. Fig. [__] represents one of the most widespread squares in new districts, especially in cities. Given that we saw on *page* [__] the inconvenience even a simple 'crossroads' causes, what must one make of this example?

If the intention is to place an edifice in a setting worthy of the dignity we hope to display on its frontages, and to add

[LCdv 135] 4

further to the grandeur of its dimensions, then the design in Fig. [35] will be adopted. As the surface area of the square is enormous, the zealous geometer will submit for approval a building law which obliges the façades of all the neighbouring buildings to rise to between 18 and 20 metres, which he claims will amplify the grandeur of the planned church or palace!

Fig. 34 Monumental buildings in their relationship to a square. Sketches by Jeanneret, copied from Schultze-Naumburg, *Kulturarbeiten Städtebau*, figs. 69, 70, 72, 76–79 (B2-20-330 FLC)

Fig. 35 Schultze-Naumburg, *Kulturarbeiten Städtebau*, fig. 79

Or the planner may even, having designed a vast and pompous street, want to end it off beautifully with a splendid building. He will open up the end of his street into a vast square, and erect the building of his dreams along the very line of the major artery at the bottom of the square, Fig. [**36**]. However the desired effect will sadly not be achieved; the pedestrian moving along the street, at point *a* for example, will see nothing of the square's side walls *fc* and *eg*, and the building, which remains some distance away, will

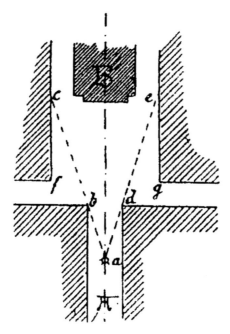

Fig. 36 From Henrici, *Beiträge zur praktischen Ästhetik im Städtebau*, fig. 7 (p. 70)

not appear to him at its full size. Having arrived on the square, this impression is diminished yet further; for from the end of the street his eye will be accustomed to the view of the major building, which will henceforth lose all power to move him emotionally.
Two clear solutions are possible: if the intention is to crown the appearance

[LCdv 136] 7//5
of the major artery, one must erect the building's façade at the very end of that street, Fig. [___].
If, on the other hand, it is the building itself which is to be shown as grand, a wise design of the openings of streets onto the square must be employed to move the viewer emotionally. But we shall examine this issue a little later; let us now return to the third type of modern square, the crossroads or roundabout.
Fig.s [**37, 38, 39**] show the image of this. These, say the geometers, are 'centres' and this is one of their favourite forms of square {which one finds in abundance on all modern town plans}. On the drawing boards in their planning offices, they trace – not without a certain pride – the majestic arrival of trams, bicycles, cars and wagons into the bottom of this funnel! At each street opening, they can picture the strict 'flick' of the baton directing traffic, constantly making busy people stop and wait. And since this spectacle appears to interest geometers greatly..., they take up their T squares and set squares with faith and conviction to plan another crossroads with even more streets opening onto it!

[LCdv 137] 6
Before we address the issue of the plastic elements, those factors for beauty in squares, it is good to set out some considerations about the usefulness and appropriateness of squares in the modern city.

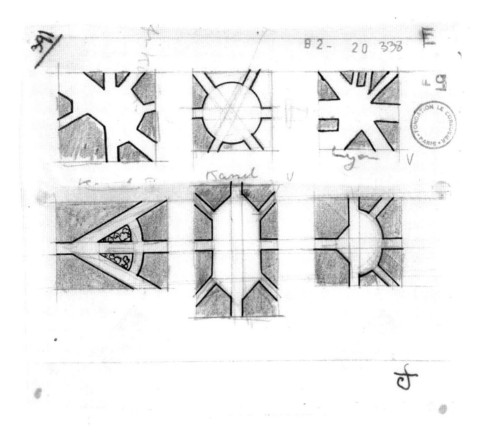

Fig. 37 Unfavourable forms of contemporary squares. Drawings by Jeanneret, following Sitte, *Der Städtebau*, figs. 84–86, and Henrici, *Beiträge*, p. 70, fig. 9 (B2-20-338 FLC)

Nowadays, public life has withdrawn from squares. {[In the margin:] We must ask ourselves if it has withdrawn because there is no more room or if for its own reasons.} In antiquity there were forums where, under a merciful sky, crowds would gather to discuss their shared interests, in which Greek and Roman citizens played a more direct part than today. The Middle Ages had common ideals which brought citizens together frequently, in large crowds. Since large halls were built, with immense effort, only for the purpose that man held most sacred – his religious faith – the rooms that were chosen for meetings were not covered, and these rooms, which were always intended to be beautiful for there was never "the idea of separating art from daily existence, and making of it something occasional and accessory"[13] – these rooms were town squares. There was the square for religious ceremonies, by the cathedral; the square for political life, by the town hall; squares for daily needs, marketplaces

13 The source of the quotation is unclear.

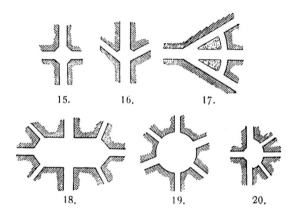

Fig. 38 Henrici, *Beiträge zur praktischen Ästhetik im Städtebau*, figs. 15–20 (p. 92)

Fig. 39 On the lack of enclosure of contemporary squares. Sketches by Jeanneret, copied from Sitte, *Der Städtebau*, figs. 81–87 (B2-20-345 FLC)

[LCdv 138] 7//7

or fairgrounds.

Markets today are best held in covered halls; under our rarely calm skies meetings are more comfortably held in vast premises, which current building methods make it easy to construct; intellectual and political life has confined itself to journals and daily newspapers. Man's only wish, having expended the best part of his active strength and powers of invention in an overly long working day at the factory, is to rediscover a bit of restorative calm in his 'home' – the fountains no longer serve a directly useful purpose; the to and fro of cars is best achieved on carriageways of constant width rather than in these sudden widenings, which are reasons to break with the fateful order to 'keep right'.

In short, the square's raison d'être has evolved and the square for its own sake is now certainly subject to our requirements. Instead, people are calling for vast spaces planted with trees, intended to interrupt the tiring uniformity of the 'stone desert', and parks around which buildings will happily close ranks, will constitute a good supply

[LCdv 139] 8

of clean air, in which easily-arranged fountains will provide refreshment and beautiful motifs.

The square to enrich aesthetic urban heritage will survive. Conversely, due to the construction methods which science allows us nowadays, the square may take on a hitherto unknown beauty. Architecture, which is an illustrated book of the epoch's thought processes, will lend the square all the greatness of powerful and generous dreams which will come to fruition over the coming decades.

As regards the third [type of] square, the crossroads, it is increasingly disappearing from designs made in a rational spirit.

The plastic elements which are essential to the beauty of a square are all derived from a crucial condition: *la corporalité* [embodied space]. We have already stated the platitude that a work of art must be concrete, perceptible to the eye. Now 19th-century squares as reviewed above do not embody space, whereas squares from all the beautiful eras had this characteristic of volume, of *chambre*,[14] to the very highest degree.

If a square is not a room with large panelled walls, with carefully placed furniture, with windows giving onto beautiful views, then

[LCdv 140] 7//9

in no way whatsoever can it claim to be beautiful. It is like a long, straight street which is not enclosed: a volume that does not exist for the eye, and consequently remains expressionless.

The square's embodiment of space will mature into beauty: when the relationship between its plan and the surrounding walls heightens the unity of design; when instead of drawing the gaze through numerous deep openings in the surface of the walls, the square holds the gaze by offering up a maximum of façade; when due to advantageous orientation the whole square helps embellish a designated building; and finally when, by adding a monument – a fountain, statue, etc. – it adds a more personal, intimate feel to the abstraction of architectural lines.

Unity will only share its advantageous impression when the architectures of the various façades which adjoin and fold in together forming an enclosure obey similar laws simi lar architectural lines, harmony in materials – and when the whole square is built at a stroke; or when, in a succession of stages,

---

14 Jeanneret uses this French word meaning 'room', in an apparent calque on the German 'Raum', which can also mean 'room', but in this context would be more usefully translated as 'space'.

[LCdv 141] 10

each new building takes account of what went before, since: "Progress has a duty to respect the things it replaces." This is no longer true today, when buildings – the work of architects who have studied away from local traditions – are thrown up without reference to one another, giving the square around which they gather an astounding atmosphere, born of a 'World's Fair mentality'.

The impression created – of comfort, of volume – is above all a result of the way the streets open onto the square. An artistic geometer will work towards the maximum visible surface area, the type proposed in the diagram Fig. [_] is by far the simplest and most perfect. A passer-by exiting any one of these streets onto the square will see only the surfaces folding together. And such squares, imbued with calm, will make the most beneficial impression on him. The cathedral square in Ravenna is one of these [**40**]; although the architecture of none of the buildings, including the cathedral itself, is [any better than] nondescript,

[LCdv 142] 11

we were overcome several years ago by the winning charm of this square, without at that time being preoccupied with town planning.

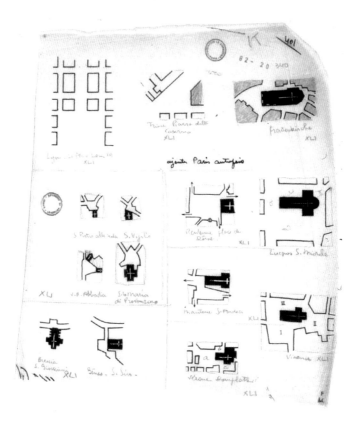

Fig. 40 Irregular squares. Drawings by Jeanneret, copied from Sitte, *Der Städtebau*, figs. 12, 18, 19, 23, 25, 40–44, 52, 78, 81 (B2-20-340 FLC)

It is of no significance that the cathedral square is shaped as in the proposed diagram, an irrevocably right-angled and regular square. As we said when looking at roads with brief widenings, this [any irregularity] is one of those things in space that the eye does not register. It is this optical phenomenon which allows our eyes not to be deceived by the Piazza San Marco in Venice, the Piazza della Signoria in Florence or the Palio in Sienna [Piazza del Campo].[15]

[Five sketches in the margin, mostly corresponding to Schultze-Naumburg's illustrations. See Fig.s **34, 41, 42**]

But not all streets can enter the square in the advantageous manner in diagram Fig. [__]. Often two streets emerge onto the square at the same angle. The plan adopted in this case, in our era, is shown in Fig. [*a*]: opening the square up at that precise point where its enclosed character should be accentuated, thus invalidating the most important aesthetic condition of the square. What is more, this will create much more significant traffic congestion than is caused by the designs in Fig.s *b, c, d* and *e*.

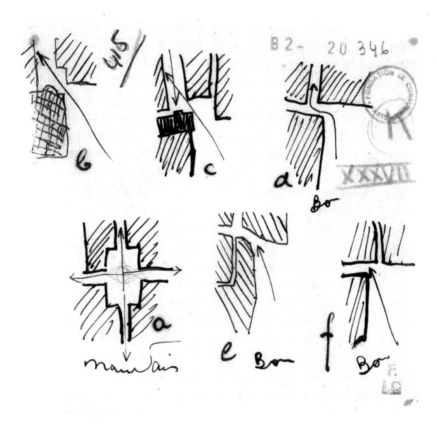

Fig. 41 Favourable corner situations of squares. Sketches by Jeanneret, following Schultze-Naumburg, *Kulturarbeiten Städtebau*, figs. 41–45, 47 (B2-20-346 FLC)

---

15 Jeanneret thinks the irregularities are not apparent as such to the viewer; however, this is not what he writes.

Fig. 42 Schultze-Naumburg, *Kulturarbeiten Städtebau*, fig. 42

[LCdv 143] 12

Design *a* appears the most normal on paper [__]; in reality it is purely a disadvantage, and if it is required by needs of any sort, the situation using Fig. *e* should be applied. This provides a welcome reminder of the case stated when we studied streets, where the excessively long perspective was broken up by a building set perpendicular to the pavement with a passageway through its base. This very solution would be charming and would allow many of our 'failed' squares to regain an aesthetic quality simply by modifying a façade.

Fig. *d* is an image which shows the pavement widening at the corner of the entrance onto the square, and also indicates the need for a small building which, with its attractive silhouette, is sufficiently interesting to make up for the poor impression of a void created by this sort of opening onto the square.

{[In the margin, before the next paragraph:] too soon}

[Text crossed out: see similar text on page LCdv 145–6]

[LCdv 144] 7//13

{[In the margin, the sketch of a square with many streets leading onto it at right angles:] This is fig.}

Where the entrances to the square are in the middle of the sides, this is much less detrimental to the beauty of the square. Less detrimental, but certainly not at all favourable! Here once again, we cannot let the practices of recent times continue, and it is by studying squares from the past that we will rediscover healthy, traditional principles. Fig. [___] showed the square opened up on all sides by the streets' rectilinear perspectives. The marketplace in Dresden, Fig. [43],[16] is a similar case, but the view is certainly sufficiently enclosed by the concavity of the streets; and the plan of the remarkable marketplace in Stuttgart, Fig. [44] emphasises in a much more characteristic manner the wish to offer the eye only an uninterrupted façade surface. Designed with an astonishing awareness of volume, this square is perfectly enclosed, from whichever point one views it, despite the number of streets and alleyways which open through its walls. This design succeeds due to the successive projections in the façades *a*, *b*, *c*. We should also state that the design of the street which climbs to the Stiftkirche, in common with many old towns, was not guided by a whim. It gives the square a strong corner,

[LCdv 145] 14
linking two major buildings via the shortest route: the church [Stiftkirche] and town hall [Rathaus].

When in the past a square provided a perfect geometric shape – a square, circle or oval – the streets often led off the square through the middle of the façades along the four main axes. Today nobody misses the opportunity to lay out a square thus, but everyone forgets that the master builders of old always brutally enclosed these streets several hundred metres from their opening onto the square, using a palace, church or other grand building. Thus the square extended its area virtually, up to the very foot of those monumental façades which, while beautifying the streets' silhouettes, also added to the beauty of the square. Indeed this ploy was taken to such a level by Louis XIV and his successors that we will shortly be looking at this separately.

Fig. 43 Marketplace in Dresden. Schultze-Naumburg, *Kulturarbeiten Städtebau*, fig. 35

16 Jeanneret is probably referring to Fig. 35 in Schultze-Naumburg, *Kulturarbeiten Städtebau*, p. 82, a painting of the old marketplace in Dresden.

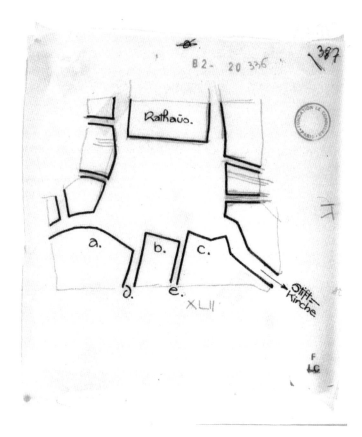

Fig. 44 Marketplace in Stuttgart. Sketch by Jeanneret (B2-20-336 FLC)

The Forum in Pompeii in Fig. [45] shows us a means, at *A*, that has been employed since time immemorial of closing off the undesirable gap left in the walls of a square by a street. That is a simple arch

[LCdv 146] 7//15

crossing the street where it opens into the square. This was carried out in the past in Verona, Siena and many cities in all countries. Although a single arch would not suffi-ciently close off the unfortunate gap, a second arch a few hundred metres in front of the first in the street would strengthen it (Fig. [__]). Sometimes 3, 4 or 5 arches are spaced out a short distance from one another. Besides their charming look, on occasion they have the advantage of consolidating the buildings among themselves, preventing the overly high walls of simple brickwork from sagging and collapsing.

{[In the margin:] say that irregular squares like Stuttgart permit uneven levels, inclines etc., hence major savings (otherwise costly repercussions for all neighbouring streets)}

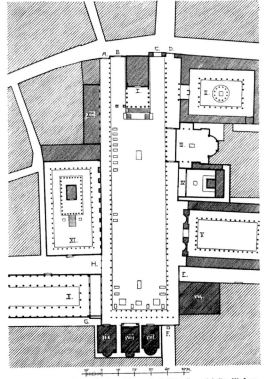

Fig. 1. Forum von Pompeji. I. Jupitertempel; II. Viktualienmarkthalle; III. Laren-
heiligtum; IV. Vespasianstempel; V. Markthalle für Wollstoffe (Gebäude der Eumachia);
VI. Comitium; VII.—IX. Amtsräume; X. Basilika; XI Apollotempel; XII. Markthallen.

Fig. 45 Forum in Pompeii. Sitte, *Der Städtebau*, fig. I

By reducing themselves to large vaulted passageways through the very mass of buildings, the street openings, as is the case in several parts of the Palio square in Siena, can
be hidden and make the view majestic due to the feeling of sudden size which the
passer-by will have, transporting them in an instant from a nondescript street into a vast,
beautifully arranged square.

The Louvre courtyard in Paris, the serene work of Pierre Lescaut, Mercier and Perrault, owes its calm imposing nature to the application of this ploy, repeated four
times. Fig. [**46**].

[LCdv 147] 16
Antwerp, Fig. [__], had shown at *D* the exceptional situation of a public building which
straddled 4 streets all at once, enclosing their perspectives. The 4 passageways opened out
behind a colonnade; this brings us to a procedure, derived from the above, which allowed
the master builder for the Place des Vosges in Paris, under Henri IV and Louis XIII, to
retain the maximum possible tranquillity in its façades. (Fig. [__]) Each time one wanted to
assert above all else a unity in the volume of the square, the powerful sober architectural
lines, one ended the streets behind the screen of a colonnade so that the eye was not

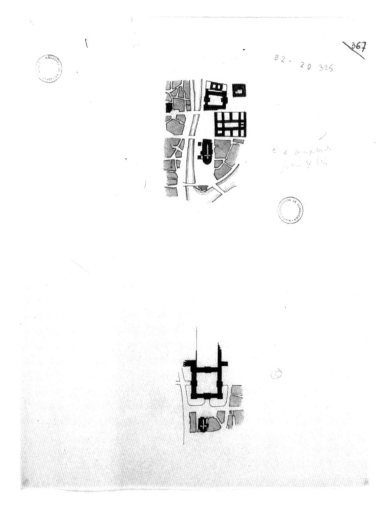

Fig. 46 Part of the Louvre and the Ile de la Cité with Notre-Dame, Paris. Drawings by Jeanneret (B2-20-325 FLC)

distracted, and as a result the feeling was more incisive. This is the way the Procuratie were built on St Marks' Square in Venice, Fig. [47], how the architects of the Forum at Pompeii thought (Fig. [45]): where the walled city was not closed off with simple arches *A*, *B*, *D* or a triumphal arch *C*, they made all the streets end behind a majestic portico.

[LCdv 148] 7//17
What we have just studied is the square for its own sake. Let us now see what becomes of a square when its purpose is purely to enhance the façade of a remarkable building. Once again the planner in the 19th century lacked a clear, strong intent and only produced drab, hybrid impressions. Here perhaps more than elsewhere, there was a need to define the cause for which an effect was to be produced; but this was not done and the result was a mess.

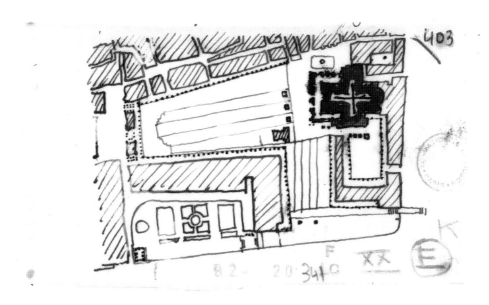

Fig. 47 Piazza San Marco in Venice. Drawing by Jeanneret, copied from Sitte, *Der Städtebau*, fig. 49
(B2-20-341 FLC)

One needed to analyse the *nature* of the emotion one aimed to elicit, to ask oneself:
'Will this all be designed for *beauty* or all for *utility*?' And to add: 'Is this task *suited to eliciting beauty*?'
And then: 'Will it be *pretty* or *grand*?' and, when considering the facts of the matter, the question would be: 'Do the dimensions at my disposal allow for something *colossal*, or do they require *delicacy*, and do the *materials* that I must use to fulfil the requirements work together effectively to create the impression for which I am aiming?'
One also needed to consider whether the *environment* in which the edifice was to be built favoured the desired sort of emotion,

[LCdv 149] 18
and weighing up all that, to choose the shape of square that would add the most to the nature of the work. For some squares make the façade of the building which they show-case appear enormous, while others make it *bijou*; and some façades oppress a square, while others give it a grand feel.
So many questions to ask, so many different solutions would have emerged as a result.
All the great artistic eras have acted with full knowledge of the facts, producing works which have characters and personalities, which stand in strange contrast to the spineless creations of smugly satisfied, parvenu 19th century architecture.
Let us take two typical examples to analyse the laws of relativity which render the abstraction of feelings tangible:
In 15th century Munich, a single material: common red brick, which only allows for brief ornamental flourishes. The climate is harsh, and the sky dull. There are plans to erect an impressive cathedral as a lasting testament to the city's power.

[LCdv 150] 24 **[48]**
Solution to enclose a square and street. Postcard after the Bellini painting.

[LCdv 151] 7//19
Venice, in its heyday, wants to crown its majestic achievements with glory. At its docks, weighed down with the fruits of its pillage and conquests, are abundant marbles, porphyry, precious stones, and the light which beams boldly on the lagoon reflects even the most modest colour as a heraldic tincture.
Munich built the Frauenkirche. **[49]**
Venice finished off St. Mark's Square.
Munich made the parvis in front of its cathedral into a little curved triangle, and Venice had the vast trapezium of the Procuratie extend to the foot of St. Mark's [basilica].
Munich added a touch of the grandiose by erecting a severe, uniform wall 97 metres high which oppresses the viewer with its dizzying surface, forcing him into a contortion to embrace, however uneasily, all the brutal lines.
Venice astonished the whole world with a fairytale accumulation of gold and marble, a gleaming basilica and the immense parvis which gives it the appearance of a fabulous oriental jewel in a sober, classic setting. The Campanile points abruptly skywards, with its thick, haughty solid red needle

[LCdv 152] 20
showing the extent of the basilica's extreme life, fluidity and splendour and, with the small chiselled white marble loggia which nestles at its foot, completely confusing its true scale!

Fig. 48 San Marco, Venice. Sketch by Jeanneret, after a painting by Bellini (LCdv 150)

MÜNCHEN   Frauenkirche

Fig. 49 Frauenkirche, Munich. Postcard, owned by Jeanneret (LC-105-1112-28 BV)

A miracle of mind over inert matter! Two peoples succeeded, in more or less the same era and by properly weighing cause and effect (using opposing strategies), in enclosing within walls the strong language of their willpower.

Despite the totally opposing characters of the two above-mentioned works, formal laws do govern the emphasis placed on an edifice: more or less complex laws depending on the case in point.[17]

These laws, as we have just seen, are the result of the very feelings which one aims to elicit.

---

17 Crossed out: "All Sitte's book proves this; by studying all the beautiful squares which past eras have left us, the aesthetic principles leap out at the reader of their own accord."

Now that popular instinct has been distorted and can no longer guide the harmonious development of beauty, we must once again, in the relationship between the building and the square,

[LCdv 153] 7//21
heed the lessons of the past.

The principle which gave the Frauenkirche in Munich its power had spread across the whole of mediaeval Europe, that is: with the intention of underlining grandeur and dominance, the square extending up to the foot of the cathedral was always smaller than the façade itself. Rouen cathedral is oppressive and captivating, presenting itself this way three times: once for its façade and once for each of its transepts. This impression is further heightened because streets are planned so that the traveller is not forewarned of their ending, and it is only once he has arrived before the dominance of the façades themselves that he sees them, like torrents raining down on his head, mixing into a jumble: initially confused, then gradually a splendidly ordered multitude of sculptures. Nor does the Palazzo Vecchio, in Florence, have the decency to announce its presence much in advance: it rises up suddenly and frightens one with its brutal overhanging belfry, seemingly ready to crash down into the square.

[LCdv 154] 22
It is no mere whim that creating an impression this way was widely adopted in the Middle Ages. The system of fortified towns encircled by walls and ditches made the land 'intra muros' infinitely precious. These were intended as a powerful expression of the common will, and since it was not possible due to land scarcity to build temples spread across thousands of metres of desert, like the Egyptians, we built upwards; this strategy, imposed by circumstances gradually became the source of a great dawning of the vertical line. Façades outgrew naves, pinnacles straddled façades, and as in Rouen towers lifted their 7 arms to the heavens. And as the walls rose to a peak in the air, at their foot the square made itself small to accentuate even further, by contrast, the power of the vertical gesture. Thus the cathedral itself determined the width and depth of the parvis in front of it.

In the northern countries where cathedral architecture

[LCdv 155] 7//23
required that a whole system of mechanics and statics be deployed – flying buttresses and such like – their master builders managed to conceal the disagreeable reduced perspective of these long, often thin arms by reducing the lateral space around the cathedrals to such an extent that only the beautiful surface of the chapels was visible, around which bas-reliefs ran and which was crowned with gables or balustrades ornamented with openwork; the pinnacles pointed skywards, the flying buttresses hidden behind the gables only showed the agitation of their hard lines in distant views of the cathedral; then, with no perspective, they appeared numerous and arranged themselves beautifully along the upturned hull of the nave.

... But – thought the office-based geometers, in that baleful 19th century – these uneducated craftsmen from the dark ages, who were unable even to construct a belfry on their palaces in line with their façades and who,

[LCdv 156] 24

due to the blatant irregularity of these façades, proved that they had never been inducted into the beauty of elementary mathematics, those master builders were incompetent yet again; they did not know how to frame their works fittingly.

... And conscientiously throughout Europe moves were made to *free space around* cathedrals.

Notre-Dame de Paris, the queen of Ile-de-France, the cradle of purest Gothic, was debased [**50**]. The *little* houses which surrounded it, and gave it *grandeur*, were demolished. The parvis built in front of it was exactly *seven times* larger than the square for which its façade – unfinished as it was – was built – seven times larger! Around this parvis, around the former north side cloister, enormous buildings were erected, with brutal, irksome volumes – fire station, general hospital, six-storey apartment blocks. Now the pinnacles which once were bold stand lower than the cornice of the apartment block in a degrading crowd,

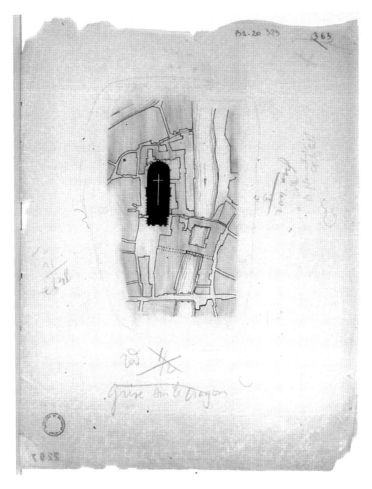

Fig. 50 Notre-Dame, Paris, before the parvis was opened up. Drawing by Jeanneret, copied from Brinckmann, *Platz und Monument*, fig. 32 (B2-20-323 FLC)

and the great façade, in all its nobility and powerful rhythm, stands at the end of the vast macadam expanse, disoriented and overwhelmed. When, on our return from Rouen, we saw [the cathedral] floundering thus, we felt that its fall from grace

[LCdv 157] 7//25

was irreversible. {[In the margin:] Refer to the spirit of the Renaissance with horizontal and spread, squares introduced by perspectives, and to age of reason and theories, to canonical proportion leading up to the Revolution.}

When the objective is not to supply the viewer with a very brutal impression of grandeur, as did the design of parvis in front of cathedrals, but instead to open up to his eyes a building in the tranquillity of its architectural forms, the study of Figures [__] to [__] brings us to posit these two general principles:

If the planned façade rises to a height greater than its width, the square at its foot will extend to a greater depth.

This is a theory which merely confirms instinctive practice. If the façade extends widthways, the square will match its character by taking a shape broader than it is deep.

The cathedral at Verona, Fig. [__], since it has a high façade justifies a deep parvis (*a*), whereas along its nave are wide squares: *b, c*.

San Siro in Genoa, Fig. [__], has a deep square, built into the very mass of houses which face it – this process of freeing up space as recommended above when widening streets makes the church part of the street's silhouette. – Same in Brescia, Fig. [**40**].

[LCdv 158] 26

{Strasbourg?}

Same with the Basilica of Sant-Andrea, Mantua (Fig. [__]), deep square before main façade, long square before lateral façade. Prior to 18xx [sic], Ulm cathedral [Ulmer Münster], Fig. [__], had a deep square before its façade and elongated spaces gave the length of its nave and its apse the most favourable views. The story of its deterioration is so typical that we will dwell on it, especially as this teaches a harsh lesson in the duty of respect we owe to the past and because it illustrates through their destruction some of the main aesthetic factors in emphasising buildings.

Guide books all speak of this marvel of German gothic art and the deep impression it makes on the traveller. Yet while that may have been true in the past, it is no longer the case:

examining the two Fig.s [**51**] will soon reveal the reason. On plan *a* drawn from an engraving dated 1808, the parvis took the shape of the Frauenkirche parvis in Munich and the former parvis at Notre-Dame in Paris. It was very small, and contributed for all it was worth to the large triangle of façade topped with

[LCdv 159] 7//27

a heavy unfinished spire. No open street in line with the cathedral [Ulmer Münster] prepared the traveller for this powerful apparition. Some large trees accentuate the two lateral courtyards separated from the square by an enclosing wall. In the circumstances, this enclosing wall was a verse added to the poetry of the place; it greatly enriched the scene which determined two squares, as distinct in their character as in their remits. To the left, to the right and behind the apse, the clear space was much reduced by an enclosure formed in places by a simple wall and in others by light constructions – stonemasons' workshops, warehouses, housing for clergy.

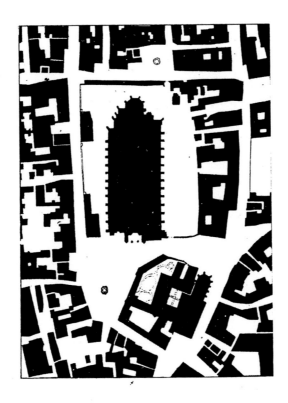

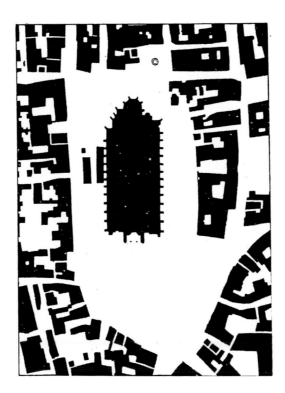

Fig. 51 Minster in Ulm, before and after having been 'freed up'. From *Der Städtebau*, 5 (1908), plates 22–23

Now one fine day some 30 years ago, all was destroyed: enclosure, warehouses; the trees were replanted in neat rows, and the area of the parvis *quadrupled* with the demolition of a whole block (Fig. [**51**] *b*). Finally, ripped from its natural setting, the fountain in the parvis disappeared into a museum!

[LCdv 160] 28

And in the very tower of that church [Ulmer Münster] a chamber of honour was dedicated to the memory of the man who presided over the massacre, putting the finishing touches to his work by *finishing the spire on Ulm cathedral in pure gothic style*. Certainly, the man cannot be guilty, as he was espousing the ideas of his era; the fashion at the time was for this type of embellishment; Florence had already, at great expense, covered the façade of Santa Maria del Fiore with disastrous stucco, which furthermore was 'in pure Florentine style'. In a deadly competition, the Shepherd's Tower as celebrated by Ruskin [the Campanile], the work of Giotto, was obliterated for ever at a stroke!

The mania for finishing off ancient buildings in an archaeological style has not yet been satisfied; men with a certain *literary* talent have for some 70 years instigated it and we fear that, in replicas of the Ulm case, the ranks of those 'freers' of cathedrals will be joined by archaeological architects with their frigid tributes, destroying the poetry of ancient art.

We want, driven by a touching modesty which may well mask our own creative forces running dry,

[LCdv 161] 29

to respectfully follow our ancestors' threads, finishing off their work in the same form in which they bequeathed it. In so doing we forget that we are living in the 20th century and that the styles of yesteryear have a language which is not only expressed in the collection of forms, but also in a frisson from their very shapeliness, in which one can still discern the caress of the artist and artisan. We forget that each one of these stones speaks of a mentality that is no more, which evokes the poetry conferred upon it by the passing of years, and we think we can revive the soul of expired eras, 600 years later, through our 20th century mentality, with the hands of our jobsworth workforce!

We once heard, in the Medici Chapel in Florence where Michelangelo's passion particularly crystallised in the formidable figure of 'Day', where the chisel dared go no further than to roughly hew the face in order to leave the ill-defined shapes to accumulate mystery, {[In the margin:] whose face was only rough hewn because the chisel stopped still before the mystery accumulating in its undefined shapes} we heard a visitor cry: "Now then, how after 400 years have they not yet managed to finish off that face?" The visitor was French!

[LCdv 162a] 30

Why does nobody laugh at people who finish off the 'face' of cathedrals?

Let them finish these off in 20th century style if they feel inspired and strong enough, or leave them unfinished if not. Let these erroneous people at least be prohibited from attacking our *universal* heritage. For each work with which man has raised himself up proudly belongs to all humanity, and not to a single municipality. (put as note: →)

[LCdv 163] As note 7. page 30.//page 119

In Europe laws are now gradually guaranteeing that historic monuments are protected. "Legislation in some places, and this is for example the case in Italy, imposes on works in individual ownership a real obligation which, without limiting some use of them, nevertheless prevents these treasures from being moved, exchanged or sold: paintings, statues, frescoes, mosaics, which thus form a sort of national inheritance.["][18] (page 119) ["]On the contrary, [...] that which constitutes the public domain i.e. the streets in a town or city, its squares, its silhouette and the pieces of natural architecture, urban or rural landscapes, is not protected in any way. As a consequence, through a strange anomaly, which has survived for too long, the law is equipped to classify and maintain a curious façade, some old loose stones in an ancient wall; on the other hand, it is not at all equipped to prevent, in a homogeneous historic setting, demolition or construction which would remove all its value and all its charm.["][19] (page 125) ... ["]It would be pertinent to add that although governments arrogate to themselves both new rights to protect natural beauty, and means

[LCdv 164]

of coercion, they must, above all, apply these against themselves: their undertakings are often poorly executed, artistically speaking.

It is the officers in our Canton chancelleries who take least account of new concerns and directions, who are still hampered by the most disconcerting routines, who affect the most cynical contempt for the rights of beauty in the state.["][20] (Georges de Montenach, – Pour le visage aimé de la Patrie!)

[LCdv 162b]

Hence Ulm deteriorated; its glory, its cathedral, is now even more lamentable than Notre-Dame in Paris, since its inferior style would not be able, on its own, to express such beauty! And the fountain indoors in a museum like a corpse ... ceased to babble!

... But since then ideas have changed. In some places, people worry and begin the struggle against those who would profane the peace of cathedrals. Some time ago, we read with astonishment in the journal *Städtebau* of this competition being held: "The municipality of Ulm wants to put the fountain currently in the museum back onto the Cathedral square. In order to furnish

[LCdv 165] 7//31

this overly large square, it is appropriate to locate a tram station and public conveniences there. On the northern side of the cathedral, new building sites will be created before it to enclose the façade, without however concealing the north porch. Space will also be found for a building containing sculptors' workshops, stereotomic design, the archives, the verger's apartment, [church] council chamber', etc. !!!

When will there be a competition for the demolition of the 'pure gothic style' 19th century spire?

---

18 Georges de Montenach, *Pour le visage aimé de la patrie. Ouvrage de propagande esthétique et sociale* (Lausanne: Sack-Reymond, 1908), p. 119.

19 Montenach, *Pour le visage aimé de la patrie*, p. 125.

20 Montenach, *Pour le visage aimé de la patrie*, p. 125.

But let us return to the matter at hand.

A single building presents itself to all sides as a single entity and creates several squares by being cleverly situated, considerably enriching urban views.

The 19th century sought geometrically shaped public squares, and generally placed buildings in the middle of these. Thus all 4 perspective views of the monument and the square itself were similar, or at least two resembled the other two, which induced monotony.

[LCdv 166] 32 [Whole page crossed out]

In the past, the building was always placed asymmetrically, thus creating, see Fig. **[40]** (Lucca), 4 different squares *a*, *b*, *c*, *d* which presented the building from multiple angles.

But there was an even more rewarding method: this was to place the building in a way that resulted in three distinct squares. This was employed in Vicenza, Fig. [__]. The city, instead of only having one cathedral square, has 3 which work together to charm the traveller. It has been acknowledged that one of the characteristic charms of cities, for example Bruges which people talk enthusiastically about, has to do with the repetition and renewal of impressions from adjoining or nearby squares (exactly what we wanted to demonstrate); they repeat in frequent succession on a short walk [and] give the impression of a great wealth of aesthetic urban views.

[LCdv 167] 7//33

In similar cases in the past, the building was placed asymmetrically; 4 squares with fundamentally different characters were created, which would present the building from different angles. See Lucca Fig. [__].

The delightful town hall in Schweidnitz [Świdnica], shown in the illustration Fig. **[52]** taken from an engraving by Merian, had a belfry erected in a particularly balanced setting. Everything came together to delight the eyes: the asymmetry of the façade favourably offset by the set-back belfry which lends the porch a welcoming character; the location of the well, the bench, the fountain; the street layout; and above all the layout of these 2 squares, all attest to what we have just explained.

Even richer still was the strategy of placing a building in the middle of an open space – or grouping housing around this – so that three very distinct squares are created. Vicenza, Fig. [__] has not just one cathedral square, it has three: and all three work together to charm the traveller. It has been acknowledged that one of the characteristic charms of cities – of Bruges, which people speak enthu- [sentence breaks off here].

§4 On Squares, II

[LCdv 168] part I//Chap. II//SQUARE.//Text.//§4 I

[LCdv 169] 1

We must note once again the very special nature of two squares with one adjoining side, separated from one another by a very strong difference in their levels (a nature rich in picturesque or powerful architectural resources); the large wall which retains the upper square, the avenue of trees, perhaps clipped, which may top it off, the picturesque or monumental flight(s) of stairs which make the link between the 2 squares, the purpose of these – the upper one abandoned to traffic, the lower one taking on the characteristics of a forum, or vice versa, its organisation necessarily full of the unexpected, buildings surrounding this dual enclosure, etc., etc., provide an infinitely rich range on the planner's

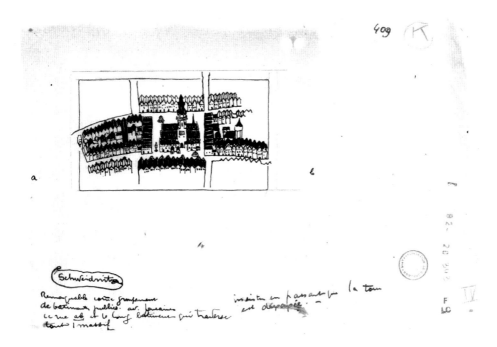

Fig. 52 Marketplace with town hall in Schweidnitz/Świdnica. Drawing by Jeanneret, copied from Merian, *Topographia Bohemiae, Moraviae et Silesiae*, plate after p. 176 (B2-20-343 FLC)

palette, a range to which the land in hilly cities would add if one were to use one's imagination [**53, 54, 55**].

We would now turn immediately to study the

[LCdv 170] 2

geometric square and the square we will call the 'square to glory' – a powerfully artistic synthesis of all the plastic elements – if it were not time to set out a few comments on the subject of what destroys the already problematic beauty of our squares, even as it beautifies them. We want to discuss siting commemorative monuments, fountains and all other objects which are intended as embellishment.

In so doing, let us return to our recent illustration which likened the public square to a great room with judiciously-made openings and well-placed furniture.

A monument or fountain is a piece of furniture, or rather a luxury item, the centrepiece of the room.

Past eras, just like modern life, show us in human habitation two types of room or hall: the room where we live, stamped with

[LCdv 171] 3

the intimacy that is dear to our hearts; the state room, parlour or *vestibule d'honneur* – the image of splendour, grandeur, which we like to display for special occasions.

The intimate room will be full of irregularities, due to the multiple tastes and wishes which it must satisfy. Variety is necessary, within a unity which is always observed:

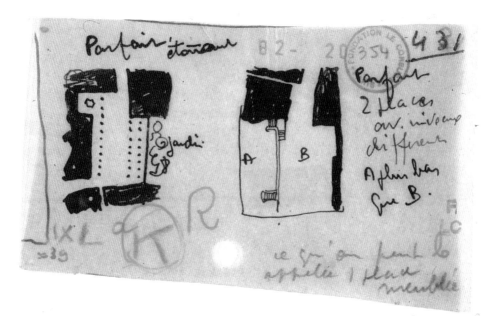

Fig. 53 Picturesque layout of squares. Sketches by Jeanneret, copied from Schultze-Naumburg (B2-20-354 FLC)

Fig. 54 Schultze-Naumburg, *Kulturarbeiten Städtebau*, fig. 53

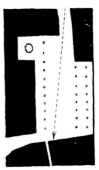

Fig. 55 Schultze-Naumburg, *Kulturarbeiten Städtebau*, fig. 54

light and dark, simplicity and bonhomie here, refined precious luxury there, delicate and intimate, preferred for reveries and meditation. There is no need for this room to reaffirm a single, clear, irrevocable will, unlike the *vestibule d'honneur* or parlour which the master of the house wants as an incarnation of his own *character*. Here, to express this determined unity, geometry will provide the clarity and unshakeable strength

[LCdv 172] 4
of its shapes: the large table in the meeting room will be placed in the axis of the room; the bust or statue, or the marble table in the *vestibule d'honneur*, will mark the middle of the main wall panel or the centre of the parquet floor, the design of which will itself help reinforce the geometric principle.
This luxury object, in a living room or in a gala hall, will always find a place where the idea which it embodies will be best revealed, spreading the benefit of its pretty shape at the corner of the chimney or near a window, amidst other beloved objects, rising up alone and imperative, in the middle of the room, imposing itself on every observer.
In both cases, it will play the role of *ornament*, but an ornament with a *raison d'être*, *living intimately alongside what surrounds it, embodied as much by what it signifies*

[LCdv 173] 5
as by its plastic shape. As this object more than any other is the most precious thing, it must carry within it the genius loci. This is so clear that people would be truly astonished to find a laboratory retort in the middle of a living room, or – as a counterpart to a painting –

[LCdv 174]
the lithographed portrait of each of the seven Federal Councillors, each a medallion set in an oak and laurel frame.

Equally, a Roman throne made of Carrara marble would look out of place at the writing desk of a gentleman wearing a top hat and frock jacket, just as a minuscule Venetian looking glass which satisfied Queens some 500 years ago would look taking the place of a swing mirror in the boudoir of a society lady.

Thus in a public square, the monument is in fact an *ornament*. But what of that which we used to call ornament, the meaning of which has been lost for a century?

It is an objective thing, independent of all subjective ideas whatsoever;

[LCdv 175] 6

it arises from just three areas: colour, line and volume. An ornament is something *which does good*, ahead of expressing any message; this involves ideas of balance – but not necessarily symmetry – and rhythm: an exaltation of colour, or shapes playing in beautiful volumes under the caresses of light, an exaltation and a beauty which will only be born of the interplay of balance and rhythms – which appeal to our visual sense – a rhythmic balance united in following a *line* which, effectively symbolising willpower, is pleasing for our minds. An ornament is created in a shape which is pressed into the service of the material, and can henceforth evoke feelings which please our hearts.

[LCdv 176] 7

These few preliminary considerations will help a lot in the search for the ideal location of a monument on a public square.

The first thing to obey is free movement of traffic. A monument should never be set against the normal to and fro of cars: it must be precisely situated in such a way

[LCdv 177] 8

that one can admire it from all sides without being disturbed. A very simple law, of which we take no account today, dictated the – ever felicitous – siting of monuments in the past; this is the law of the 'dead point'.

In any square crisscrossed by traffic, there are areas of various shapes and sizes, always set apart and deserted. These result directly from the street openings onto the square, and as long as none of these is changed, the areas or dead points will remain intact. These are easy to recognise because it is paths (carriage routes) and their intersections which determine them. Why do so many old squares, which have remained sheltered from planning devastation, offer strange undulations in their surfaces? These are grooves dug little by little by carriages passing repeatedly along the same track, making

[LCdv 178] 9

slightly raised areas which have, as if by design, become pedestals seemingly designed for siting monuments. It is precisely at these points that one should seek antique fountains, wells, wayside shrines, big trees and their stone benches, the quiet evening meeting places. Sitte claims to have observed that, in winter, children in villages always instinctively build their snowmen at the 'dead point'.

Here then is the public square divided into areas propitious for placing monuments.

But we were discussing atmosphere earlier, and asked that the monument be an ornament among the buildings. Now the square will generally have been built from day to day; each street-front will have a purpose which is alien to the others and the monument designed in a specific spirit might suit some of the façades, yet add nothing to others, or even be detrimental to them.

[LCdv 179] 10

In the design of his monuments, the artist of the past drew inspiration from the genius loci, and as the external expression of this, their shapes reinforced the atmosphere. To situate the monuments, he chose that dead point in the square which provided the most beautiful setting. It was then that the laws of contrast came into play, with which he confirmed his will and all was created *as ornament*. This brought us marvellous Swiss fountains, as stunning in their spirit as in their placement, thanks to which, their carving was added, where necessary, to contrast with the severity of the architecture.

The fountain in the Place de l'Arsenal in Solothurn motivated the architecture of the building against which it rests – or perhaps it was this façade of such exquisite proportions which prompted the sculptor to set his fountain against it. In any case, a refined taste reigns there in

[LCdv 180] 11

the contrast of this simple wall with the lively, polychromatic sculpture. The powerful Arsenal imposes its façade, while facing it the strong setting is completed by a large tower with baroque pilasters contrasting in their nervous unrest with the naked curves of the apses. And from whichever side one views it, the fountain is only ever a harmonious graphical element, an ornamental silhouette, a sculptural arabesque.

This was a time which did not know the fashion for siting a monument in line with a monumental gate, itself enriched with sculpture[s] and ironwork, so as to heap 'splendour upon splendour'. It was thought that, from this distance, neither gate nor monument could be distinguished from one another, and therefore benefit.

Fig. [__] shows us, in 17th century Berne, a fountain situated at the corner of the cathedral square. Its volume and silhouette

[LCdv 181] 12

came together to better close off the opening for the street, and put a valuable accent on the sobriety of the residential buildings. Opposite, the porches of a decadent gothic, hollowed out too deeply, display the jumble of their outlines.

But today in the middle of this small square stands the banal and international monument which commemorates a hero of the city. Plastering itself on top of already confused sculptures from the 16th century is the horrible silhouette of this posing cavalier, flanked by 4 bears, the ensemble scarcely plastic, inevitably surrounded by large cast-iron chains which ironmongers must stock in considerable numbers given that they have encircled so many monuments in Europe and elsewhere, and chained up the imagination of so many poor sculptors!

The cathedral square in Berne is ruined, a victim of people who thought they were beautifying it.

[LCdv 182] 13

This perfect adaptation to the atmosphere, and the heightening of emotions through contrasts, can be seen masterfully employed by Donatello in Padua with his Gattamelata, and by Michelangelo in Florence with his David.

Donatello was one of the last remaining great ornamental artists, and that equestrian statue links powerful evocation with the perfect beauty of ornament. Vasari teaches us that he always designed his works while considering the space that they were to occupy. He did so at length, and in minute detail. He decided that this man of war on his fearsome battle charger would be raised up on a plinth, so high that the entire mass of bronze, both man and horse, would stand out at its most beautiful angle against the luminous sky.[21] Hence this black mass was born, cut out against the azure light, with the same

[LCdv 183] 14

joy as a black Grecian palmette stands out from white marble. It attenuates the always-ugly aspects of an equestrian statue, the front and rear, the former by 'drowning' it against a backdrop of architecture, the latter by preventing it from being viewed: by the ingenious placement of the monument at the corner of a high cemetery wall – which today has disappeared. But what gave his work its genius loci was the imposing mass very close to the Santo [Basilica of our Saint], a savage and barbaric brick wall, stubbornly oppressed by its pediment. This, right next to the black palmette against the light sky, formed a dark screen which touched the firmament in an enormous, solemn *vertical*. Thus Gattamelata, this leader of armies,

[LCdv 184] 15

calm, with a bald head, imposed a *horizontal* gesture...[22]
Michelangelo had just finished his colossal David. A committee, convened by the government of Florence, met to decide about siting it on the Piazza della Signoria.[23] The architect Giuliano Sangallo and Leonardo da Vinci were in attendance. The matter was discussed, and a solution adopted. Yet Michelangelo, still a young man, did not agree at all with that assembly's decisions. He had already considered the matter and wanted to give his work the most powerful character, with a contribution from the architectural masses. And the

[LCdv 185] 16

setting he proposed, which was accepted, was disconcerting: in the very corner, where the narrow Uffizi passage opens off the square, right next to the Palazzo Vecchio, he placed his David, on the same level as the square, on a pedestal not a metre high [56]. This young marble Titan stands there like a giant descended into the crowds, and Michelangelo knew very well that by putting him into direct contact with them his stature would tower, colossal and white against the dark brown opus quadratum wall of the Palazzo Vecchio, bright against the dark backdrop of the Uffizi passageway.
It was a matter of the right proportions and, as Mr. C. Sitte says, if he could see it Michelangelo would dismiss the monument, as pitiful as it is luxurious, erected to him some years ago in the geometric centre

[LCdv 186] 17

of a huge square, on a hill with the Tuscan plain as a backdrop, melting away into the blue horizon: his David perched some 6 or 8 metres high, flanked by four great figures

---

21 In this paragraph, Jeanneret paraphrases Albert Erich Brinckmann, *Platz und Monument* (Berlin: Wasmuth, 1908), p. 11f.

22 Crossed out: "To work, having settled in Padua, Donatello shut himself away in his studio for several years, surrounding himself in the greatest mystery so as not to hear ignorant initial opinions."

23 From here to LCdv 186, Jeanneret paraphrases Brinckmann, *Platz und Monument*, pp. 19–22.

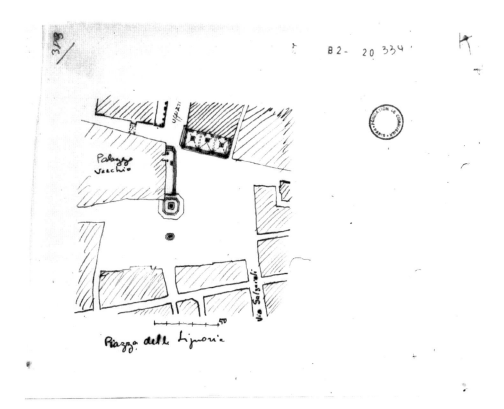

Fig. 56 Piazza della Signoria in Florence. Drawing by Jeanneret, copied from Brinckmann, *Platz und Monument*, fig. 6 (B2-20-334 FLC)

from the Tomb of the Medicis, took on all the power of a table centrepiece or an ornament on a mantelpiece![24]

But let us return to the Piazza della Signoria. Until 1594 a second statue of a giant [Hercules] could be seen standing there: by Michelangelo's rival Bandinelli, placed right beside David, in the same conditions. Then, continuing the straight line, above Donatello's Marzocco which has long held in its clawed paw the Florentine coat of arms, a fountain of Neptune which Ammanati built in 1571 at the *corner* of the Palazzo Vecchio,

[LCdv 187] Part I//Chap II//SQUARE//Text.//§4 II

[LCdv 188] 1

realising clearly that, if raised up in the middle of the square, the fountain would have segmented it awkwardly and upset the overall view. Finally, finishing off this string of

---

24 Here, Jeanneret refers to Camillo Sitte, *Der Städte-Bau nach seinen künstlerischen Grundsätzen* (Vienna: Graeser, 1889), p. 21f. Cf. Camillo Sitte, *City Planning According to Artistic Principles*, translated by George R. Collins and Christiane Crasemann Collins (New York: Random House, 1965), p. 18f.

sculptural ornaments, the equestrian monument of Cosimo I by Jean Boulogne [Giambologna] in a sense brings the façade of the Palazzo Vecchio into the open part of the square, pushing into the background the small lateral square it defines, and skilfully creating the fiction of a single large, right-angled public square which Michelangelo one day proposed, in the spirit of unity, to surround with a monumental portico continuing on from the three arches of the Loggia dei Lanzi.

Examining all the large, famous squares: the Piazza della Signoria in Florence, Piazza San Marco in Venice, the Palio square in Siena [Piazza del Campo], the marketplace [Hauptmarkt] in Nuremberg [**57**],

[LCdv 189] 2

the three cathedral squares in Salzburg [**58**], the Grand-Place in Brussels and – going further back – the forum at Pompeii and Roman forums, the huge courtyards of Egyptian temples, etc., proves to us that neither fountains, statues, triumphal arches nor obelisks occupied the geometric centre of the square. *The centre of the square was always free*, and all the monuments were in groups along its edges, a very beneficial method which allowed many works of art to be grouped together without reducing the usable area in the square. Furthermore, they gave the monuments an atmosphere and a favourable scale due to the immediate architectural surroundings, and allowed them to be viewed from several, dissimilar angles.

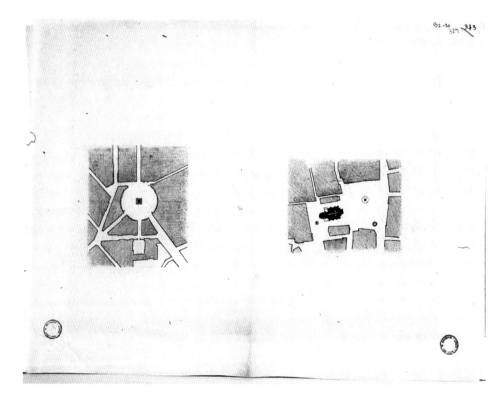

Fig. 57 Marketplace in Nuremberg and Place des Victoires in Paris. Drawings by Jeanneret, copied from Brinckmann, *Platz und Monument*, figs. I and 34 (B2-20-329 FLC)

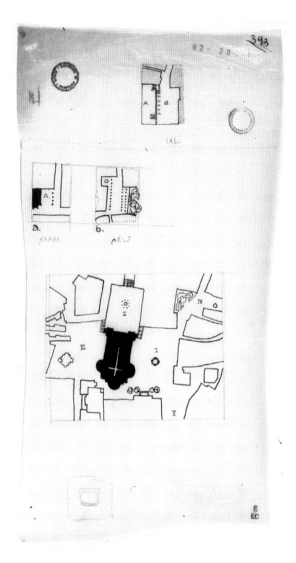

Fig. 58 Adjoining squares. Drawings by Jeanneret, copied from Sitte, *Der Städtebau*, fig. 71, and
Schultze-Naumburg, *Kulturarbeiten Städtebau*, figs. 51, 53, 54 (B2-20-339 FLC)

The rule, which Sitte proved

[LCdv 190] 3
at length, is a general one and only has one exception – a very special case which we
will see shortly.
Thus there is cause to regret the unsuccessful common practice which today dictates the
placing of monuments in our squares. It is precisely the law of the geometric centre
which prevails, as a consequence of a fanatical love of the compasses and set square,
and the total absence in our planning offices of artistic concerns. No need then, when

placing a monument, to wear oneself out weighing up the advantages of such a built backdrop, or the trouble with the view when a street opens clumsily onto a square. Whether the square is rectangular or circular, two axes – with two additional diagonals if it is irregular – will at their intersection determine the ideal place. Reason and common sense dictate this; all the buildings are

[LCdv 191] 4
then equidistant from the monument, and all should be satisfied; no self-respecting administration will delay further for more subtle considerations.
Thus Europe has covered itself in insipid monuments on amorphous squares. Now neither the square, whose area is destroyed, nor the monument, whose situation is the same in perpetuity, is impressive; the eye has become accustomed to the banal spectacle of its charms: disarmed, stunned, hampered by its ill-assorted isolation, its lack of atmosphere. *The feeling of volume* which was so powerful in previous eras disappeared in the 19th century. That century's classicism only wanted to retain from the past the lines it had employed to express itself; it lost the spirit.

[LCdv 192] 5 [Original version, later pasted over up to 'the mind –']
particular, throughout Europe and further afield, despite differing climates, tastes and customs, the abstract classicism of the 19th century offered only the dominance of dry, banal, fateful geometry: streets straight for no reason topped off with star-shaped squares, or rectangles in the centre of which stands a fountain, statue or obelisk bearing no relation to the surrounding buildings.
The memory of the impressive squares by Louis XIV and Louis XV obsessed the mind – these were soon imitated by their admirers and courtiers, provincial or foreign princes, extending their influence anywhere there was a court and some money in the treasury. The Louis XIV square, a symbol of dominant pride, travelled as far as Russia, Austria and throughout Germany;

[LCdv 193] 5 [Improved version]
As if hypnotised by the majestic memories of Louis XIV and Louis XV, our councillors made cities into constellations of star- or square-shaped spaces with monuments in the geometric centre, on the pretext that the splendid shapes handed down by the 17th and 18th centuries were no different. They forgot art when applying this dry, arid formula: that is to say they did not concern themselves either with volume, contrasts or 'human scale'; in a word, they ignored *corporalité* [the embodiment of space].
This causes us to speak of the squares which those kings drunk on absolutism, Louis XIV and Louis XV, had built to glorify their cult of the self – soon imitated by their admirers and courtiers, provincial or foreign princes, extending their influence anywhere there was a court and some money in the treasury. The Louis XIV square, a symbol of dominant pride, travelled as far as Russia, Austria and throughout Germany;

[LCdv 194 – 195] 6 [Comments marked * on left-hand page of notebook = LCdv 195]
it even invaded Italy and England; unsurprisingly, even now this square fascinates our councillors with their modest thinking, who insist at all costs*
{*on fooling themselves with grandiloquent words, conferring on their work and especially themselves a respectable and impressive appearance.}

Now the Louis XIV square was rigorously geometric in shape, and the monument with which it was always adorned was in the centre. This square, be it the Place des Victoires, Place Vendôme, the Louvre courtyard*,
{*NB: We cite the Louvre courtyard, the result of a very complex confluence of Italian and French influences, which emerged well before Louis XIV under Francis I, – because due to the issues its construction raised, it would guide current thinking towards what would later become the Louis XIV formula.}
or derivatives thereof, in Nancy and elsewhere, was perfectly beautiful and still worthy of our greatest admiration [**57, 59**].
One should not imagine that this contradicts the principles stated above. On the contrary, it provides a very particular, definitive demonstration of these. For it is not a matter, as with 19th century classicism, of restoring a formula:

[LCdv 196] 7
that of the irregular square. Building squares is a matter of remaking a work of art, a work of beauty; and to that end, having analysed the principles which determined the admirable squares we spoke of, we must identify them in these now-classic examples from the 17th and 18th century.
What completely distinguishes the squares built under Louis XIV and Louis XV from those that went before is: they were *designed in a single stroke and built all at once.*
Embodying the master's spirit, the centralising power – 'l'Etat c'est moi' – they borrowed from simple geometry inexorable lines, which

[LCdv 197] 8
by repeating a single motif all along their walls, they employed to express the language of *unity.* This square, a *vestibule d'honneur* in front of the palaces which flank it, was inhabited by the master: usually on horseback, cast in bronze with a black sheen, the King stood at the centre of the square. The proportions of the latter were calculated to emphasise as fortuitously as possible the statue which, in turn, was modelled for that very square. The dimensions of its plinth, whose height dominated the bronze, were intimately linked to the base of the palaces, the cornice of the roofs, the prominence of the colonnades. It stood centrally because the streets entered the square along the square's axes, and it was imperative that even from a distance – relatively speaking – it could be perceived, and people would say: this is the King's square. As we have said, these streets

[LCdv 198 – 199] 9 [Comments marked * on left-hand page of notebook = LCdv 199]
had little depth, and if they were not closed off after several hundred metres with an hôtel or palais (Place des Victoires and Place Vendôme) or with triumphal arches (Nancy), then the inopportune gap in the square's walls was instead cancelled out with porticos of great architectural character, which took the motifs from the façades out through the street openings, (Place Louis XV, Fig. [**60**]), thus adding to the imposing unity.
If, when idolising himself in bronze, the King did not adhere to the law of the 'dead point', it was precisely because he wanted to make his presence felt;* {*inconveniencing pedestrians somewhat did not displease him and he permitted himself to do so.}
Furthermore, the traffic, which was so minimal at the time, – Paris only had hackney carriages at the time, and the number of these was not significant – could not have been disturbed in any way.
In many of the squares derived from these or built using similar principles

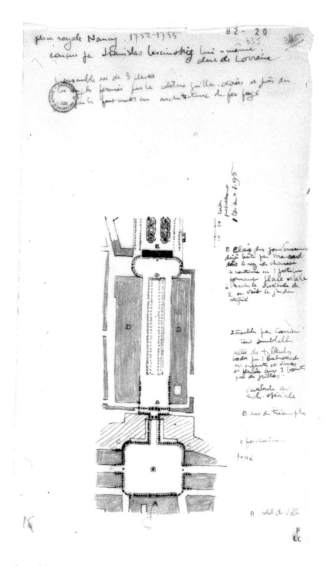

Fig. 59 Place Royale in Nancy. Drawing by Jeanneret, copied from Brinckmann, *Platz und Monument,*
    fig. 40 (B2-20-335)

[LCdv 200 – 201] [Comments marked * on left-hand page of notebook = LCdv 201]
such as the baroque Italian squares, the ground was paved and decorated with large geometric designs, emphasising the perimeter of the enclosure and at the same time accentuating the intentional, sudden soaring of the monument. Thus the square and the
monument now formed a single homogeneous block, like iron cast all at once (Place des
Vosges in Paris*, St. Peter's square in Rome etc.) {The Capitol, Rome}
{*The Place des Vosges is another square created by Henri IV which precisely marked
the rise of this clear, determined spirit which was to triumph 2 generations later}
The contrasts were highly evocative.

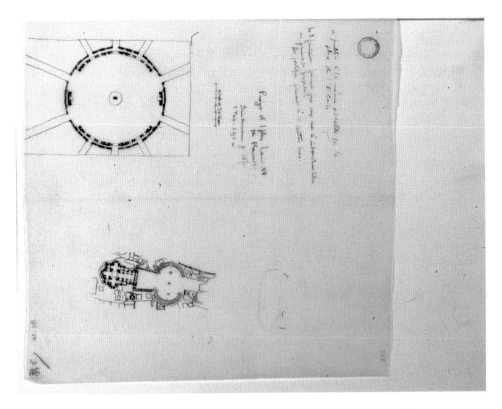

Fig. 60 Project for a Place Louis XV by Rousset, and St. Peter's Square, Rome. Skizzen Jeannerets nach Brinckmann, *Platz und Monument*, figs. 35 and 15 (B2-20-328 FLC)

The King was *alone*, at home, in his *cour d'honneur*, for everyone to see: for in this (essentially ornamental) equestrian form, he set himself up in substantial contrast with the surrounding setting. The Place des Vosges (Fig. [__]), built in the Franco-Dutch style under Henri IV and Louis XIII to a single plan, presents the observer with its façade areas: 4 orthogonal red brick sections with delicately inset vertical grey stone chains.

[LCdv 202] 11
An arcade dots the perimeter of the square with black punctuation (cite Laugier's opinion). With magnificent baroque wrought iron railings around it, the inside of the square is divided into four square segments of close-cropped lawn, separated from one another by 4 white sand paths at whose intersection stands the equestrian statue of Louis XIII. This marks the main point, in black and green bronze on a white marble plinth, underlined by its intense colour amidst this symphony of restful reds, clay-tiled roofs and bright green mown lawns. Sadly the Revolution razed the black bronze horseman to the ground; the following years replaced it with a white marble statue; the 4 squares were each divided into 4 triangular scraps of land, in the middle of which stood 4 sadly similar fountains. Finally, a destructive double row of trees was planted all around the square,

[LCdv 203 – 204] 12 [Comments marked * on left-hand page of notebook = LCdv 204] masking the pretty brick façade and, in place of the baroque railings torn up in revolutionary fervour, long vertical cast-iron bars completed the overall degradation.[25]

In another way, attempts were made in the Place des Victoires to pick out the equestrian group, that black arabesque, against a favourable backdrop. Its height was such that it did not (from any point of view) reach beyond the cornice of the roofs, and that as a whole it stood out against the strict order of the colonnades; the massive ground floor area joined forces with the monument's plinth area.[26]

{*The same was true of the Place Vendôme before the equestrian statue of Louis XV was replaced by the column to the glory of Napoleon.}

Despite all his power, Louis XIV only ever built squares of very limited size compared to those built when we wanted to flaunt our luxury. This King who had created the orderly gardens at Versailles covering [___] thousands of square metres, from scratch, was

[LCdv 205] 13

content with his architectural squares being [___] or [___] square metres. His architects had preserved the feeling of a *human scale* from the healthy gothic tradition. In erecting palais of limited height, they were wary of the shrinking effect of perspective and achieved grandeur precisely through the small dimensions of their squares.

The same was true of a statue harmonised with the walls of the square which, whether palais or hôtels, were intended to be used by humans and retained the imprint of a human presence in the dimensions of even their smallest parts. This statue hardly existed in this colossal frame, as with the well-meaning attempt in Berlin, which erected the colossal monument to Bismarck [Siegessäule] in an overly vast square before the overly immense Reichstag building.

[LCdv 206] 14

Knowing that everything there is so large requires reasoning, comparison and calculation; the square diminishes the palais, which oppresses the monument, and the monument makes even the greatest exaggerations of neo-Berlin architecture seem miserly.

The King, on his horse, often had a bare head and was always alone on his very sober plinth. No lions dying at his feet, no slaves in chains, heaps of broken weapons, crowns or garlands, sceptres or trophies, like the colossal fancy moulding – if indeed the term is appropriate for such a weight of metal – which bristles, terrible and comical, all around an emperor (Wilhelm I) in front of the beautiful façades of a Louis XIV-style imperial palace

[LCdv 207] 15

on the castle square [Schlossplatz] in Berlin.

The spirit of Gattamelata persisted in those times of good taste and tact. The feeling of 'volume' was alive; the formula had not yet become stale, dry and wizened.

When studying the projects or creations by certain architects from the latter period who wanted, using the same shapes, to pursue the route to glory traced by Louis XIV, one is soon struck by the initial vice which makes these pompous settings into mediocre works of art: on the plan, all proportions are hugely exaggerated. Napoleon I created a pernicious

---

25 Here, Jeanneret partially paraphrases Brinckmann, *Platz und Monument*, p. 94f.
26 Cf. Brinckmann, *Platz und Monument*, p. 104.

precedent by implementing around the immense Arc de Triomphe the vast Place de l'Etoile. Seen from the square, the arch hardly seems imposing; in order to be convinced of its grandeur, comparisons

[LCdv 208] 16
must be made; it is only viewed at its true size again when seen from very far away: several thousand metres, for example from the Jardin des Tuileries.

The inheritors of this distorted formula, starting in a manner of speaking with the Avenue des Champs-Elysées and the Place de l'Etoile, abnormally widened their parade streets; they increased the ordinary area of squares tenfold, took their perspectives too far. In short, thinking only of the plan, they did not design for volume. Yet their materials were no different than in the time of Louis XIV; the size of trees does not increase in line with scientific progress; palais or houses (subject to the requirements for living) are limited in height, and this limit was not linked to the sudden extension in new dimensions.

[LCdv 209] 17 [Whole page crossed out]
A monument whose very reason to be in that place is problematic will rise up suddenly in this large area, very small despite its great dimensions, and banal – very banal.

And, creating star-shaped squares in grand siècle fashion, we will forget to think of our automobiles and the vehicles congesting our carriageways. As stated at the beginning of this chapter, we will be mistaken when we call these 'squares for traffic'. The intense traffic in our modern cities will only find a reasonable solution if the dimensions are inflated out of all proportion, and if a hub of very substantial diameter is built in the middle of such squares, such as in the Place de l'Etoile in Paris. But it is not the lot of these squares to be beautiful.

So what use is there in summoning up the attributes of grandeur if this only [Sentence ends here.]

[LCdv 210] 17
Then the walls, intended to indicate for the viewer the boundaries of these disproportionately amplified spaces, appear miserly at such a distance, and the viewer presented only with distant converging lines loses all awareness of the embodiment of space. Empty space is anti-aesthetic; immense settings – the Reichstag square in Berlin, the plans by Jackson and Webb for monuments at Buckingham [Palace] in London, etc. – only achieve mediocre results.

On the other hand, creating *star-shaped squares* in grand siècle fashion, we forget to think of our automobiles and the vehicles congesting our carriageways. We mistakenly describe these as 'squares for traffic'. The intense traffic in our modern cities can only be reasonably resolved where their dimensions are abnormally inflated. Only squares with the diameter of the Place de l'Etoile in Paris will suffice. – What

[LCdv 211]
use is there then in summoning up the scale of grandeur if one ends merely with a stopgap solution?

To really feel the ratio of dimensions on which the embodiment of space in a square depends, we drew up the following table [LCdv 216], with figures which appear to speak for themselves. In it, we analyse some of the most famous geometric squares, and compare these against the prototype square for 19th century creations, the Place de l'Etoile.

The last three columns show:

I° The ratio between the empty street openings and the full area of façades; the first figure is for empty space and the second for full.

II° Where a constant building height has allowed a ratio to be established between the height of the façades and the diameter of the square, the first figure gives the diameter, the second the building height.

III° The dimensions of the squares along their main axes.

[LCdv 212] 19

In summary, all the above considerations about the beauty and ugliness of squares lead us to derive the following approach:

When planning new squares, if buildings are to be constructed piecemeal, by architects unknown to one another; if the purposes of these buildings cannot be determined in advance, and must meet the needs of commerce, residential use and perhaps some public areas, then aesthetics requires an irregular shape which allows the gradual harmonious adaptation of each new building to its pre-existing neighbours – an adaptation which will be easier the less rigid the site plan is – and if picturesque elements may be introduced: arcades, porticos, partial and total set-backs and projections. It is clear that these picturesque elements are only permitted in a plan which is irregular and therefore elastic.

[LCdv 213] 20

On the other hand, if the square is all built at once, or if the purpose of its buildings, or particular circumstances, allow it to be designed at a stroke, unity means that monumental solutions are possible. Such occasions in a city's history are rare. One must therefore grasp them with joy; they will be a reason to create geometric *places* where harmony and the plastic nature inherent in this type of square will be applied powerfully, as we have tried to set out.

To round off this study of the square, we must recall that in certain eras peoples smitten with beauty created 'squares to glory'. We do not consider this term to be out of place, for when we evoke the cities where these peoples' genius is displayed, a sumptuous picture, exalted in nobility or gleaming with splendour,

[LCdv 214] 21

appears immediately before our eyes. The glory of these peoples appears to us straight away in the objective form of their artistic creations, remaining through diseased decadence, as an irrefutable testament to a healthy, harmonious organism.

When we speak of Venice, we can see its Piazza before us, or speaking of Pompeii or ancient Rome their ceremonious forums, of Athens the Acropolis, of Jerusalem the Temple square, of Thebes or Luxor, the courtyards onto which the hypostyle halls opened. – Pisa had its square to glory, Siena and Brussels too. History evokes the marvels of the ruined countries of the Phoenicians and Carthaginians, and if we were to turn to the East, there would be a nimbus of light, a fantastic display of art which subjugates and disconcerts us, enclosed in the complete forms of architecture.

[LCdv 215]

Grouping together rather than dispersing; commercial life kept at a distance, with its rumbling, noisy profanity. These squares in their meditation are temples to beauty.

Do not disperse, unite! At the edge of the enclosure, halt the brutal flow of modern life. We should do the same, when we wish to do things properly!

[LCdv 216]
Some comparisons of famous squares.
58 x 142m = dimensions of the largest ancient squares

				Ratio of length development	
Date	Monument	Type		Façades	Street openings(s)
1685–87 Place des Victoires. by Mansard J. H. 78m diam. arterial road is closed off after 38m by the Hôtel de Toulouse. Height of façades 19m	equestrian statue in the centre	star-shaped	4 streets each 9m. 2 streets each 7m.	4 12	1 3
	Place du Roi, project by Rousset for the intersection with Rue de Buci, diam 130m	statue in the centre 2 fountains on the edges	star-shaped	6 streets each 10m. 4 streets each 7m. enclosed by arcades	7 1/3 22	1 3
1836	Place de l'Etoile. Paris. 560 m in diam.	Arc de Triomphe	star-shaped	2 streets each 142m. 6 streets each 70m. 4 " " 90 "	0.56 1.7	1 3
1701	Place Vendôme. 122m x 140m Mansard. Both streets are closed off by a church – and by buildings after 52m	equestrian statue in the centre	rectang. with cut-away corners	2 streets each 22m	9 1/3 28	1 3
1755	Place Royale in Nancy – 95 x 115 Place " " 95m x 38 both avenues are 13m wide	statue at the foot in the centre	rectangle	2 streets 1 street which is enclosed by 1 triumphal arch at around 50m	18 ½ 6 1/6 3 1/3 10} 40} 13 1/3	3 3 1
		empty	oval	enclosed all around with 2 galleries and 1 large opening along its 60m course.		
1639–	Place des Vosges 90 x 65 140 x 140	statue in the centre			2.7	1
circa 1600	x—x Place Dauphine in Paris 90 x 65 before it deteriorated	Empty			11 [?]	1
	St. Peter's square in Rome				8	
1700	Louvre courtyard					

[LCdv 217] 18//Table comparing the dimensions of some geometric squares.

Dates		Type	Monument	Number and dimensions of streets opening onto the square	Ratio of empty street openings to area full of façades	Ratio of the square's diameter to the height of the façades	Dimensions of the square in metres
Late 16th century	Place Dauphine – Paris, before it deteriorated	Rectangular	Centre clear	2 streets	1 to 16		56 x 90
1639–	Place des Vosges – Paris – 2 streets open out under galleries, behind a portico	Square	Statue in the centre	2 streets	1 to 27		140 x 140
1685–87	Place des Victoires – Paris – the main arterial road is closed off 38m away from the square, by the Hôtel de Toulouse	Circular	Statue in the centre	4 streets each 9m. 2 streets each 7m.	1 to 4	4 to ¼	diameter 78
from 1539 to 1806	Louvre Courtyard – Paris	Square	Centre clear	4 galleries			
1701	Place Vendôme – Paris. – both streets were previously closed off 52m away from the square by a church and other buildings.	Rectangular	Statue in the centre	2 streets each 22m.	1 to 9.3		122 x 140
under Louis XV	Place du Roi – Paris, plan for Carrefour de Buci crossroads – 6 of the streets are closed off with a portico where they enter the square	Circular	Statue in the centre	4 streets each 7m. 6 streets each 10m.	1 to 7.3		diameter 130
1755	Place Royale – Nancy Square in front of town hall	Rectangular	Statue in the centre		1 to 6		95 x 115
	Square in front of government building	Oval	Centre clear		1 to 8		38 x 95
1836	Place de l'Etoile – Paris	Circular	Arc de Triomphe in the centre	2 streets each 142m. 4 streets each 90m. 4 streets each 70m.	1 to 0.56		diameter 560

Material for On Squares

[As material for On Squares, see LCdv 404, 409f., 412–414, 416, 431, 433–436, 439–442.]

[LCdv 218] 6
[All paragraphs on this page crossed out individually]
Certain squares are like great halls, ceremonial rooms. Especially geometric squares or others made for a building and which that building personifies and [...] the monument comes to life and has the last word.//A
If [the] object [of the] monument is to be unexpected, striking, plan in same state of mind as cathedral façades.//B
If it is to exalt the King, monument precisely in the middle. At the route intersection. In order that it is along the route, is imposing and seen from afar. It is clear that in this case the silhouette should be very clear – a horseman –//C
In other cases, the Middle Ages for example dead point, and in tumultuous façades, seeking the most favourable backdrop.//D
Today we must once again define here the desired goal, which those committees of non-authorised persons who decide on the placing of monuments – which Michelangelo and Donatello researched for so long – never do; they are slapdash, always speak of 'common sense' and follow the strictures of [__] without examining the law of the geometric centre, placing monuments which jar against deadly backdrops of trees, in a flagrant outpouring of our modern aesthetic culture.//E

[LCdv 219]
[Whole paragraph crossed out]
In seeing the projects or the manifestations by certain architects from the latter period who wanted to pursue the route to glory traced by Louis XIV, one feels straight away what is wrong. All the proportions are forced. Napoleon had already made the Etoile. Beginning, in a manner of speaking, at the Avenue des Champs Elysées, they forced the proportions, [...] quadrupled the surface area, made the perspectives too long, and since the materials available for the elevations were the same as in the time of Louis XIV, that is trees whose volume is limited and façades whose height, to remain within the

[LCdv 220] 15 [Whole page crossed out]
residential requirements for a palace, also have a limited height barely greater than in previous eras, – the walls intended to indicate the boundaries of these disproportionately amplified dimensions appear small and miserly, as they are far away, and the eye, seeing practically nothing except [...] the converging lines of a large area barely encircled with a light belt, loses all awareness of the embodiment of space. Yet empty space is unaesthetic and the desired goal is not achieved.
The relativity of the items employed is beyond the human scale. – Lack of *convenance* once again.
One could cite certain pompous designs in Berlin.
Jackson's plan for the Victoria Monument in Buckingham Palace, London.
Webb's project for the same Monument.

[LCdv 221] 12 [Whole page crossed out]
La Piazza [della] Signoria.
A committee was [__] in January 1504 to decide where to place Michelangelo's David. Architect Giuliano da [San] Gallo, Leonardo da Vinci, and others could not agree. The

choice was ultimately left to Michelangelo himself, and he chose the square next to the door of the Palazzo [Vecchio] in front of its dark, uniform wall with its powerful *opus quadratum*. The young giant was finally placed on 18 May 1504 and it was quite an event for Florence. M. subsequently approved several small aspects of its placement: the light here, the immediate surroundings there. Vasari comments many times that it is firstly the open air, then the particular light in that place, which enable one to judge the work properly.[27]

...A figure placed against one wall of the square does not need to dominate the whole square in order to be impressive, as it would if situated in the middle of the square.

[LCdv 222] 13 [Whole page crossed out]
This type of placement presents the opportunity to position more sculptural works in the most advantageous way. Benvenuto [Cellini]'s Perseus was placed in the openwork at the corner of the colonnade. Due to his jealous vanity, Bandinelli placed his Hercules right beside the David. Realising that a fountain placed in the middle of the square would have upset the overall view, due to the deficit caused by the non-equivalence of the areas in the square on either side of its centre of gravity, Ammanati built his fountain at the corner of the Palazzo Vecchio in 1571 where, with its figure of Neptune and water horses, he created a beautiful frontal unity with the other ornaments. Sculptural: the equestrian monument of Cosimo I by Jean Boulogne, 1594, continues the line of marble figures into the open part of the square and skilfully

[LCdv 223] 14 [First two paragraphs crossed out]
sets back the reinforced part of the square by creating the fiction of a right-angled main square.[28]
Previously, Donatello's Marzocco was already situated there, and his column of Judith (which had been there since 1495) was removed to make room for the David and found a space under the arch of the loggia which opens onto the Uffizi. Michelangelo at the instigation of Cosimo I had proposed continuing the Loggia d'Orcagna [Loggia dei Lanzi] all around the square.[29]
[...]

[LCdv 224] 15 [
"This pleasure of the eyes which is one of the elements of happiness." Charles Gide
David Michelangelo transported in 1872 to the Accademia. Copy replaced in 1910, and the Tribune will be done up.

§5 On Enclosing Walls

[LCdv 225] Part I//Chap II//§5 *R*//ENCLOSING WALLS//Ready

[LCdv 226] 9//1//On Enclosing Walls
It seems that the utilitarian preoccupations of recent years have made us forget the poetry of the simplest building methods. Taste has gone astray – you could say it has been spoilt – in the service of the parvenu 19th-century bourgeoisie. Among modest

---

27 Here, Jeanneret paraphrases Brinckmann, *Platz und Monument*, p. 21.
28 Here, Jeanneret paraphrases Brinckmann, *Platz und Monument*, p. 22.
29 Here, Jeanneret paraphrases Brinckmann, *Platz und Monument*, p. 19f.

assemblies of stones, there is one especially likely to evoke the most varied of emotions: the enclosing wall. It is capable of beauty even in its crudest form, and can achieve splendour.

Nowadays, if we employ enclosing walls, we create ugliness. Two neighbouring owners are unable to agree in order for a little harmony to reign in the walls that will run alongside the street, enclosing their properties. Each one will have a complicated enclosure built at great expense, in which they bring together the most disparate materials: crude brick and artificial stone with little variation in its profile will be combined with the most parvenu of cast-iron railings. Faced with such results, it is astonishing how pedantically architects persist in making the streets ugly, although there are plenty of very convincing models. In many towns and villages, 18th-century and imperial master builders have left us some beautiful, calm and simple enclosing walls which soberly surround parks and courtyards. The examples are there, preaching their modest, simple methods to architects subject to budgetary constraints. These precious remnants are testament to the beautiful and charming appearance of large, uniform walls. A wall,

[LCdv 227] 2

some trees behind the wall, no more is needed in order provide continuity with the street in the absence of buildings. We build our walls too low and we top them with costly railings whose architectural effect is lamentable. The street gains nothing and the owner who wanted isolation fares very poorly. Why do we fear large walls, 3 or 4 metres high, if they have beautiful proportions? Fig. *IX* [**61**] shows the use of tall masonry enclosures in many places, and we can be sure that the charm of the streets would be compromised without them. What a calm their uniform surfaces bring to a great courtyard where water springs from a fountain!

Has anyone noted how several buildings often form a poor grouping, placing their isolated cubes alongside one another without any apparent connection? A sufficiently high wall will link them very satisfactorily.

The architects of past eras always managed to imprint onto a practical solution the seal of beauty, or to draw, from a form of plastic expression, practical and utilitarian benefits which justified the use of materials required. Where the master plan for buildings did not provide the cohesion which our gaze requires, seeking as it does to rest on visible surfaces, then the 13th-century architect in Pisa would create, for example in the Cathedral square, a 15-metre-high enclosure around the huge lawn where the famous cathedral, baptistery and leaning tower stand; a uniform, brutal wall, shot through with crenelations;

[LCdv 228] 9//3

then, closer, a more elaborate cemetery wall from which he would derive marvellous benefit. The brutal wall provided shelter from outlaws outside; the gateway, in the right place, made a shining gap. The wall with fine arcatures was the wall of the Campo Santo; it folds in on itself as an elongated rectangle. A roof protects its inside facing, a roof which Giovanni Pisano supported with one of the Quattrocento's most delicate marble lace [traceries]. This wall with vast surfaces would become the phenomenal illustrated book in which these grand masters of colour and rhythm, the Giottos, Orcagnas and Gozzolis of this world, would write of their faith, beatitudes and terrors.

A wall is beautiful not only due to its plastic beauty, but also because of the impressions it can evoke. It may speak of comfort, it may speak of delicacy, it may speak of strength

Fig. 61 Altdorf near Nuremberg. Drawing by Jeanneret, copied from Merian, *Topographia Franconiae*,
plate after p. 20 (B2-20-306 FLC)

and brutality; it may be repellent or welcoming; sometimes it holds mystery. A wall
evokes emotions.

How beautiful is the wall of the Archives Nationales in Paris, which rises bare and cold,
aristocratic and austere, some 8 metres high at the edge of one of those narrow roads
teeming with everyday life. How beautifully its interior facing encloses the Louis XVI
courtyard, with its bright green, close-cropped lawns which underline the supremely elegant greys in the ashlar where an expanse of fine mouldings play.

The enclosure around the courtyard at the Hôtel de Cluny raises its crenelations several
metres above the square. The large porte cochère and small

[LCdv 229] 4

service gate make two exquisitely-proportioned gaps in the perfect unity of dressed
stonework. The yard behind the wall, under a large chestnut tree, is an oasis of tranquil
cool which visitors to the museum appreciate.

In Rouen, the Cour des Libraires is also enclosed. But this is the city of sculptural folly, where the artist population inscribed on the stones the contempt in which it held effort. The church façades are reminiscent of a rockfall covered in vegetation. The Cour des Libraires extends from the foot of one cathedral transept, and as a dignified continuation of its porch, the walls bear a splendid covering. For here are some of the most beautiful sculptures from the Middle Ages. The 14th century emphasises dazzlingly the laws of serene beauty; but exuberance was already welling up from all sides, scouring the stone. The 15th century then erected between the courtyard and the street this splendid enclosure which gives us Fig. *XLLIV*. This is embellishment from a modest principle, taken to the extreme. –

We thought we were right, while still advocating the simple, beautiful solution, to show the unexpected combinations to which the modest enclosure lends itself in the hands of flamboyant gothic stonemasons.

{in Suleimanie, along the glorious major road to Stamboul, in Kazanlak, at the Acropolis, the Erectheion. But speak about the wall enclosing the smallest cottage in the smallest of towns.}

§6 Material for *On Bridges*

[LCdv 230] 11
BRIDGES
Pont Royal in Paris, tell Octave to take
a photo
Pont des Arts "   "   "   "
    " and compare with railway bridge at Solothurn
Very pretty staircase by Fischer, find in
Süddeutsche Bauzeitung 1903 No 22
also in "   "   1907 page 30
Bridge in Nuremberg.
Old engraving of Pont Notre-Dame
(postcard)
Consult {taken from} book, both tracings of
bridge in Tournai and bridge in Cahors.
    in Manuel d'Archéologie française
        Part one
            Architecture.
              II
      civil and military
          by Camille Enlart [**62, 63**]

[LCdv 231] 12
Süddeutsche Bauzeitung 2 April 1910 "Die Kronprinzenbrucke über das Spreetal in Bautzen (Ansicht von Süden)" [by] Building officer Dr. Ing. Arthur Speck (from Bautzen). Completely remarkable as a beautiful huge modern bridge linking to the town. (Write and ask for a photo).
The central arch has a span of 35m. The others 27 [**64, XLIV, XLV**]

Fig. 271. — Le pont des Trous à Tournai, fin du xiiie siècle.

(P. 556-557)

Fig. 62 Pont des Trous in Tournai. From Enlart, *Manuel d'archéologie française*, fig. 271

Fig. 272. — Le pont Valentré à Cahors (1308 à 1380).

(P. 556-557)

Fig. 63 Pont du Valentré in Cahors. From Enlart, *Manuel d'archéologie française*, fig. 272

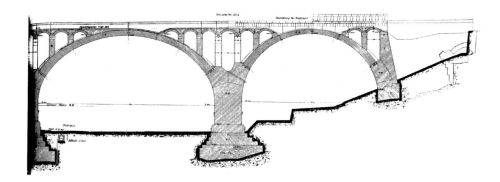

Fig. 64 Kronprinzenbrücke across the river Spree near Bautzen. From *Süddeutsche Bauzeitung* 20 (1910), no. 14, p. 105.

§7 Material for *On Trees*

[LCdv 232] [C.2,36] [Front of loose sheet]

1	ornament	2 ways	alone in addition, supplement
			grouped complete creation
2	isolated tree		
3	contemporary		removal *allee*
	history		of ornament in_pp __
4	detailed		[. . .] = ornament [arrow pointing up] addition
	study		~~screen~~ scenery
			scenery screen)

[LCdv 233] 1

The trees, map St Sulpice have destroyed everything
Cities III page 3 §4
  "   "   " 8 §3
Look in Stübben for famous squares which have been ruined by trees.
Write to the architect of the parks in Hamburg and/or Düsseldorf requesting photos.
Tell Octave to take photos in the Tuileries for me.
Find that postcard: bird's eye view of Tuileries.
Potsdamer Platz and Leipziger Platz. = a sketch filed under Squares
Pariser Platz, Berlin. No trees, but only lawns. {Sketch filed under Squares} **[65]**
ditto Place des Vosges Paris before the massacre.
Always aim to add: the tree as a decorative element: the contrast of its large, round mass. – or the contrast from its black trunk (in cities)

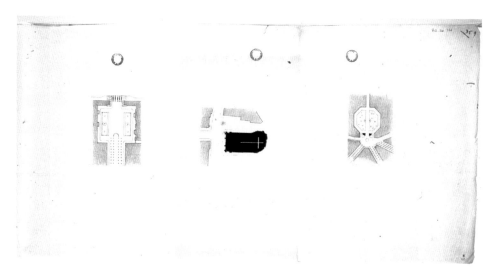

Fig. 65 Pariser and Leipziger Platz in Berlin, and square next to the St. Lorenz Church in Nuremberg. Drawings by Jeanneret, copied from Stübben, *Städtebau* (B2-20-321 FLC)

[LCdv 234]
and from all its fine branches with the gauze of leaves. On the Paris embankments, the trees make frames for landscapes where they interweave with the river water. A barge, a palais. – The Japanese print is complete at Notre-Dame.
Subscribe to Süddeutsche Bauzeitung, 18 Paul Heysestrasse = Price delivered 10 marks, appears on Saturdays
Making street views banal by planting with avenues of trees, complete absence of distinctive appearance in whole districts. This is widespread neutralisation.
A central row of trees is better than 2 parallel rows.
With the trees which line the streets

[LCdv 235] 3
to so little avail, one could make whole forests. (Quincunxes as in the [Jardin du] Luxembourg where one can play croquet etc. The narrower street width would save space, it could be made available in welcome parks.
[...]

§8 Material for *On Gardens and Parks*

[LCdv 236]
[...]
Reject small gardens in front of façades on unappealing avenues and small, unusable gardens, which get covered in dust and grow stunted. In any case who would want to settle down there having done their day's work, within sight and earshot of all the passers-by?

Nowadays we are in the habit of becoming irate about the narrow nature of certain medi-aeval routes – a fierce battle has been waged on them to make them disappear, entire districts have been gutted, showing no mercy for the memories and beauties with which they were filled. As a reaction we have designed avenues wider than the major rivers, and in fact we have gained almost nothing from all this upheaval, for with the sort of inconsistency typical of our era,

[LCdv 237]

we have taken with one hand what we gave with the other.
The modest houses of the past almost all had at the rear, if not a real garden then at least a spacious courtyard which provided the home with air and allowed families to undertake a large proportion of their habitual occupations outside the atmosphere in their rooms – blacksmiths, carpenters, cartwrights, turners, cobblers, who today are shut up ever more tightly in workshops. Thus the populus loses out, [__] and as for small gar-dens on the street front, and for broad avenues, while there has been lavish provision for the front, the back has been plundered, and "generally speaking, these neat little gardens have as counterparts meagre, lugubrious little yards,

[LCdv 238] 5

real preservers of all the deadly germs.
Let us always prefer gardens located behind buildings; *enclosed gardens*, where one may truly live and work; and if we must, to make room for these, let us reduce somewhat the width of our avenues, let us not hesitate to make this sacrifice, from which both aesthetics and the well-being of society will benefit."[30] State that sometimes trees planted inappropriately in a square play a role similar to that of flowers around beautiful fountains, in Berne or elsewhere.

[LCdv 239] 7

Gardens.

Photo of those in Granada.
Of those in Italy.
"   "   in Spain.
Tuileries. Postcard, bird's eye view.
1 sketch of the Villa Madama – Rome
                    (Filed under Trees 10)
Write to the architect of the parks in Düsseldorf
or Hamburg requesting modern photos.
Bacon's definition of art:
man adding his soul to nature
Write to the Musée Condé, Chantilly
for reproduction of painting by
Italian school in the sanctuary.
My photo of Versailles
ditto of Potsdam. Würzburg. [**66, 67, 68**]

---

30 The source for this quotation is unclear.

Fig. 66 Sanssouci Palace, Potsdam. Photo by   *Fig. 67* In the gardens of Sanssouci, Potsdam. Photo
Jeanneret, 1910 (LC 108-81 BV)   by Jeanneret, 1910 (LC 108-302 BV)

Fig. 68 Schinkel's Roman Baths, Sanssouci Gardens, Potsdam. Photo by Jeanneret, 1910 (LC 108-330
BV)

See my postcards on the garden at
Chantilly. Nymphenburg etc.
Lago Maggiore. Isola Bella. Isola Madre.
See at the exhibition Persian
miniatures showing gardens. [**69, 70, 71**]

[LCdv 240] 8
See ancient gardens by modern painters, work by Boutet de Monvel.
Get photo of Amalfi: the terrace of the garden at the Capucine monastery.
The gardens of the charterhouse in Ema {poetic contrast}.
Tell Octave {postcards} Jardin du Palais Royal. and Jardin du Luxembourg.
Ask for the Schumacher park, Hamburg [Stadtpark Hamburg].
Find in Studio [journal] and in books on Rome gardens with clipped yew trees.
Article by Jos. Aug. Lux in Süddeutsche Bauzeitung, page 21 1907, also p. 281[31]

Fig. 69 Isola Madre, Lago di Lugano. Postcard, owned by Jeanneret (LC-105-1112-12 BV)

31 Joseph August Lux, "Die Gartenkunst und die Landschaftsgärtnerei", in: *Süddeutsche Bauzeitung* 17 (1907), Vol. 3, pp. 21–23. The second article Jeanneret mentions here cannot be clearly identified. On pages 281–285 in *Süddeutsche Bauzeitung* 17 (1907) is an article by Ludwig Fuchs, "Garten und Park in künstlerischer Gestaltung". Following this, on pp. 286–288 of the same issue, is an article by Joseph August Lux, "Alt-Wiener Vorgärten".

161 — CHANTILLY — Le Grand Parterre de Le Nôtre (1665) — ND

Fig. 70 "Chantilly – Le Grand Parterre de Le Nôtre." Postcard, owned by Jeanneret (LC-105-1112-28 BV)

Fig. 71 Nymphenburg Palace and garden, Munich. Postcard, owned by Jeanneret (LC-105-1112-28 BV)

[LCdv 241] 9
Use the term *landscape garden, instead of English garden which would cause confusion.*
To support what I say about English and French gardens, cite Nymphenburg which is half of one and half the other, perfectly beautiful; one is constantly drawn back to the French-style part, there is an attraction.
By looking at lots of engravings from the time of Louis XIV, we sense that our era – in which no single man imposes a single fashion – could not remake the Le Nôtre garden. One can feel a slight surfeit when one views the images of the engravings. However, with the passage of time, these parks actually strike a more modern note, nature having stifled that which was *too artificial* by accentuating, simplifying and loosening.
In the French park, the percentage of gravelled terracing, of that part which man intended as architectural, is huge. In Marly, it is 60 or 70 or 80%.
Whereas in English gardens it is scarcely 10%. – Although small towns come in at 10% for English gardens, this is poor transposition.

[LCdv 242] 10
Say that Marly [arrow down to 'Karlsruhe'] made [Hardouin-]Mansart famous, quote extract from La Grande Encyclopédie.
If one wishes to create a leafy part in the centre of a city, then increase the number of benches, rent out chairs, follow the example of the Jardin du Luxembourg: 1 whole part in gravel, in the shade of the trees, and other vast lawns and trees.
These gardens [are] widespread: Karlsruhe; Nymphenburg; Schleißheim; Potsdam; Nancy.
More than in any other domain, the art of the garden should be revived. In the marvellous gardens of Rome, one would hate modern man if he were to dare build such a garden. The memory, the evocation is 1 of their great strengths "the beauty of Rome comes as much from what one feels as from what one sees" Montenach page 143/IV.

[LCdv 243] 11
We know that a hermitage became a palais, the work of [Hardouin-]Mansart, which was admired by all his contemporaries – La Grande Encyclopédie. – Marly –
Ictinus, Kallikrates, architects of the Parthenon.
Article {which is good} by Jos Aug Lux. in Süddeutsche Bauzeitung 1907 page 21.
In the same year, artistically designed parks and gardens page 281 293, 301 326.[32]
[Whole page crossed out] In seeing the projects or the creations by certain architects latterly who wanted to follow the road to glory taken by Louis XIV, one feels straight away what is wrong. All the proportions are forced. Napoleon had already made the Etoile. Beginning, in a manner of speaking, at the Avenue des Champs Elysées, they forced the proportions, quadrupled the surface area, made the perspectives too long, and since the materials available for the elevations were the same as in the time of Louis XIV, that is: trees whose volume is limited and façades whose height, to remain within the [continued on page LCdv 220]

32 *Süddeutsche Bauzeitung*, Vol. 17 (1907), No. 37, pp. 293–294, and No. 38, pp. 301–303: Continuation and conclusion of article by Ludwig Fuchs, "Garten und Park in künstlerischer Gestaltung". On page 326 of this issue of *Süddeutsche Bauzeitung* there is no essay on gardens or parks.

[LCdv 244]

We must confirm this: as for GARDENS, they are rooms – with in fact a floor, walls and ceiling – and not houses. And it is necessary to create volumes which one can enter into, not where one remains outside oneself [?]. [Two small sketches:] Volume offered up for view.

Volume is beyond the realm of the senses.

[LCdv 245] 16

Semiramis' hanging gardens.[33] "Strabo says it is an immense square with sides of 4 ple-thra (120 metres)" {say how small this is} "made up of several terraces, supported by cube-shaped pillars. These pillars are hollow and filled with earth, through which the biggest trees could grow." The blocks which made up the terraces were covered with overlaid layers of reeds, bricks, lead and earth, with stairs linking the levels, circling in spirals around the pillars, in many places several very advanced pieces of hydraulic equipment raised water from the river. Tamarisks and palms spread their shade across beds studded with lotus, thyme and hyssop, as worn – according to Mr. Joret (Les plantes dans l'antiquité) – by Assyrian kings on the bas-reliefs of Nineveh[34] –

In his essay on the art of gardens, Bacon explains this anomaly (that the Greeks did not know how to make luxurious gardens before foreign influences[35]

[LCdv 246] 17

arrived from Egypt, Assyria, India, Asia minor) stating: "men managed to build splendid edifices before they succeeded in making beautiful gardens, as if the latter work expressed a higher level of perfection", L'Art du jardin, Georges Riat), page 25.)[36]

Say that the garden adjoining a residence must not be a reminder of nature, but a continuation of the reception rooms, halls etc., cool or sunny rooms.

(Egyptian garden Riat page 18. Pompeii ditto 35,

a lovely illustration would be [Arrow pointing to lines above] [**72**]

extract of a painting of the thermae garden near the [. . .] gate which represents a painting of Pompeii which it would be good to track down again. (See tracing.)

"Almost everywhere", Taine says in his Voyage en Italie, "in the centre of the house is a garden like a large saloon, and in the middle of this a marble basin, a fountain flowing into it,"

[LCdv 247] 18

"and the whole enclosed within a portico of columns. What could be more charming, and simple, and better disposed for the warm hours of the day? With green leaves visible between two white columns, red tiles against the blue of the sky, this murmuring water sparkling among flowers like a jet of liquid pearls; and those shadows of porticoes intersected by the powerful light; is there a more congenial place for the body to grow freely, for healthy meditation, and to enjoy, without ostentation or affectation, all that is most

---

33 Jeanneret uses Riat's exact words (here translated by us): cf. Georges Riat, *L'Art des Jardins* (Paris: L. Henry May, 1900).

34 Riat, *L'Art des Jardins*, p. 16.

35 Riat, *L'Art des Jardins*, p. 24.

36 Riat, *L'Art des Jardins*, p. 25.

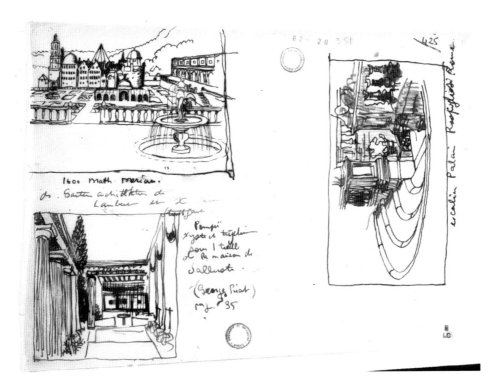

Fig. 72 Various examples for garden architecture. Drawings by Jeanneret, copied from Riat, *L'Art des jardins*, fig. 35 and Lambert/Stahl, *Gartenarchitektur*, fig. 32 (B2-20-351 FLC)

beautiful in nature and in life? Some of these fountains bear lions' heads, and sprightly statuettes, with children, lizards and wild beasts running around the lip.[37] In the most capacious of all these houses, that of Diomed[es], orange and lemon trees, similar, probably, to those of ancient days, are putting forth their fresh green buds; a fishpool gleams brightly, and a small colonnade encloses

[LCdv 248] 19
a summer dining-room, the whole embraced within the square of a grand portico."[38]
(Georges Riat, page 34)
Tuesday half past 4
in front of Brakl[39]
Look in my photos of paintings, see if there are any good gardens

---

37 Riat's words are not exactly the same as Taine's here; we have followed Riat where the two differ. Cf. Hippolyte Taine, *Italy: Rome and Naples; Florence and Venice*, Volumes 1-2, transl. by John Durand (New York, Leypoldt & Holt 1871), p. 49f.

38 Riat, *L'Art des Jardins*, p. 34.

39 This information suggests Jeanneret visited the Villa Brakl with William Ritter on 4 October 1910.

Gardens of English villas {beautiful illustrations} in Muthesius I⁰ page 212
Book II. pages 110, 109, 102, 100 87 85 {plan for publication} [Arrow to 'Book II'] 84
83 [**73–78**].

Parkpolitik.[40] The expansion of cities, the disappearance of gardens belonging to houses, the rational exploitation of building lots, have pushed this matter to the forefront of local interests, and make of it a current question. All cities present 3 sorts of gardens.

[LCdv 249] 20)

Firstly all the past creations in baroque style. – There would be a castle or palace which had a park, now made public, in which the splendid order of *allees*, beds, stairs, topiary and statues of the architecture make a marvellous whole.

II Like a green belt, in the area around the city, in the Vororte [suburbs] where there are gardens of all sorts, depending on the villas, country houses etc. in baroque or Biedermeier styles from the past. Always exquisite.

III. A sure-fire contrast is provided by the 3rd sort, the new 'public parks and gardens' – the formula is the same everywhere. A mixture of French- and English-style principles, which have not brought a felicitous outcome: a patch of lawn

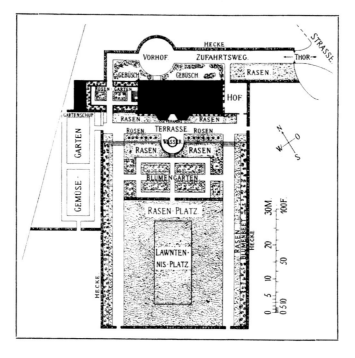

Fig. 73 C.F.A. Voysey, garden of Prior's Field Compton in Surrey. From Muthesius, *Das englische Haus*, fig. 37

---

40 From here to LCdv 252, Jeanneret follows Joseph August Lux, *Der Städtebau und die Grundpfeiler der heimischen Bauweise* (Dresden: Kühtmann, 1908), pp. 72–75, partially summarising.

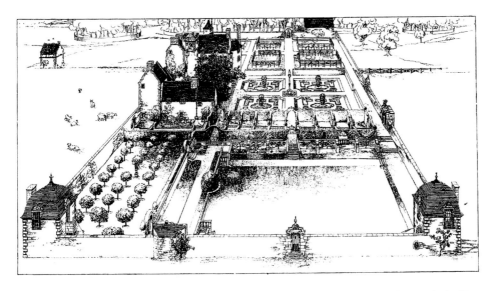

Fig. 74 R.S. Lorimer, garden of Earlshall in Fifeshire, Scotland. From Muthesius, *Das englische Haus*, fig. 54

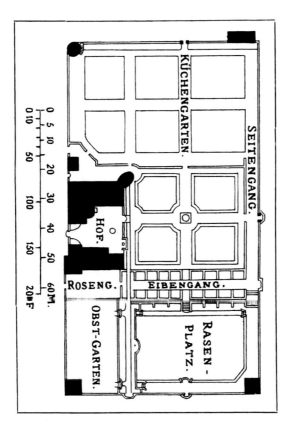

Fig. 75 Plan of Earlshall garden. From Muthesius, *Das englische Haus*, fig. 55

Fig. 76 Garden of a house near Bedford. From Muthesius, *Das englische Haus*, fig. 57

Fig. 77 Garden of Brickwall House in Sussex. From Muthesius, *Das englische Haus*, fig. 65

Fig. 78 Garden by Thomas H. Mawson. From Muthesius, *Das englische Haus*, fig. 66

[LCdv 250] 21

surrounded by a paltry strand of wire represents the meadow; a busy mass of bushes represents the forest. French-style parts, and curved paths which are completely out of tune, are characteristic of the complete absence of direction in the plan of garden and park, often appear awkward. It is regrettable that nothing from the tradition in categories I and II can be found here. In the layout of public gardens situated in the middle of buildings and streets, a memory for tradition would be beneficial, since *it teaches us that the smaller its area, the more architecturally a garden must be designed.*
Old gardens with pruned arbours and bowers set an excellent example. Even the smallest

[LCdv 251] 22

area appeared large, presented a green unity, which was like a jewel in the middle of the city's noise. But where in our modern public garden is the wall of arbours, or clipped hedges, where is the local type of garden?

One of the major preoccupations now is *the park* in the area surrounding the city. In Vienna they plan to create a belt of *forests and meadows* around the city and in other places they are dealing with similar questions this way. In all cases, according to all sound reasoning, the issue must not be *new creations* but the conservation of existing advantages: a sort of Heimatschutz. In this area cities must undertake strong and contemporary[41] educational propaganda. When creating Anlagen [areas of (park) planning]

[LCdv 252] 23
we should take care to conserve this exquisite suburban part in the middle of the city, until the beautiful traditional motifs, [...], understood and studied, [...] each garden with its soul, just as in the old gardens, so that they are, in the words of Bacon, "the purest of human pleasures".
Extract from Jos Aug Lux page 72 et seq.

Muthesius page 82 II Volume.[42]
House and garden have been inseparably linked at all periods of human civilisation. The garden has always brought joy to the house, love of the house is almost incomprehensible without love of the garden.
[...] it is mainly for the sake of having a house in its natural environment that renders the house worthy of its human occupants, [...] the garden is only a part of man's habitation, the wider dwelling-place wherein the smaller, the house itself, is situated.

[LCdv 253] 24
In the first place, the garden of the sixteenth to the eighteenth centuries [...] was an aristocratic garden, over-pompous and ornate. The mighty avenues, broad walks, the [convoluted patterns of the] flower-beds are neither to our taste today nor are they a practical possibility in modern conditions. Love of nature which men, especially the English, have now cherished for 50 years,[43] demands plants in profusion and a mass of flowers rather than the empty beds filled with vari-coloured soils and the figures clipped from box of earlier times. Just as our attitude to nature has changed, so has our way of life. We spend less time on sunny, broad terraces showing off the magnificence of our dress and the virtuosity of our court etiquette; we would rather enjoy the view from those terraces and take a healthy constitutional. As conditions have changed by comparison,

[LCdv 254] 25
so must the modern garden become a different garden from the old aristocratic one.
The feature of the old garden that modern designers [...] felt bound to revive is its ordered, [...] formal plan.

41 Jeanneret mistranslates the German "zeitgemäße" (contemporary) here as "limité de durée" (of limited duration).
42 From here to LCdv 258, Jeanneret translates from Hermann Muthesius, *Das englische Haus* (Berlin: Wasmuth, 1904–11), Vol. II, pp. 82–85. Hermann Muthesius, *The English House*, ed. and introduction by Dennis Sharp, preface by Julius Posener, translated by Janet Seligman (New York: Rizzoli, 1979). The edition used is the first paperback ed., Rizzoli 1987.
43 Muthesius writes: "a century and a half".

As a natural creation of the human hand [. . .] the garden has [. . . a] form, which in fact
it had had at all periods until the false sentimentality of the eighteenth century wrought
a change. The ordered human plan makes the curved straight, the sloping even, the
irregular regular, it creates rhythm in place of inconsequence, calculated effect in place
of the accidental. For men to decide to try to imitate, to concentrate and heighten the
caprices of nature within the small framework of the garden is a wholly unnatural situation. [. . .] The landscape-gardener pretends to compose landscape-pictures using natural
objects as his means, but he forgets that this is work on the level of the waxwork
dummy. He finds it unnatural to clip trees and hedges without reflecting

[LCdv 255] 26
that he himself mows the lawn to keep it short and tidy. He pretends to arrange the whole
layout of his garden in the way that most favours the growth and display of the plants but
forgets that he can do this just as well in the ordered garden as by imitating wild nature, nor
that this need to be his only reason for calling himself an artist. ~~It is true that during the last
hundred years when the landscape-gardener has had the reins in his hand,~~
The period of landscape-gardening marks a kind of realistic transitional phase of garden
that, like most realistic movements in art, meant a revision of technical means. But the
end was bound to be the formal garden-plan, just as rhythm is the end of all art.

[LCdv 256] 27
With its interest in plant cultivation, landscape-gardening produced many sound results
but also a number of unsound ones, such as the introduction and great predilection for
innumerable exotic plants. – (All that would be needed is some Satyriums around the
palm trees, and – reflected indoors – around our bourgeois ladies' pot plants.)[44] It is precisely against these foreign intruders, among other things, that the modern English movement in gardening is aimed. The English wish to stock their gardens once more with
native English plants, the quieter but more natural and, to us more congenial, charms, of
which had been [. . .] almost forgotten [. . .].
The modern English view of the garden is that the formal plan should be revived but
that at the same time the utmost attention should be paid to the cultivation of flowers
and plants, preferably indigenous.
Little use is made of the decorative repertoire of the old aristocratic ornamental garden;

[LCdv 257] 28
but great care is lavished on flower-beds, lawns, fruit and vegetable gardens, which are
all divided into sections in the manner of the old gardens and kept clearly separate from
one another. All the individual sections are horizontal and even, all the paths are straight,
sloping ground is terraced, the boundaries of the several sections are clearly outlined by
means of low walls or clipped hedges.
Each part of the garden lies close to that part of the house to which it belongs, the kitchen-garden to the domestic wing, the flower-garden to the drawing-room, while the
lawns lie facing the residential front of the house.

---

44 This insertion is either from the first edition or in Jeanneret's own words. It is our interpretation of "Il y aurait
à faire 1 bout de Satyres sur les palmiers, et – reflet ds l'intérieur, – les jardiniers de nos bourgeoises.".

[LCdv 258] 29

The garden is seen as a continuation of the rooms of the house, almost a series of separate outdoor-rooms, each of which is self-contained and performs a separate function.
Thus the garden extends the house into the midst of nature. At the same time it gives it the framework in nature, without which it would stand like a stranger in its surroundings. In aesthetic terms the ordered garden is to the house as the socle to the statue, the base on which it stands.

Georges Riat. Roman gardens B.C. All ordered with particular care by the architect. Indeed, we must not forget, and it cannot be emphasised enough, that the Roman garden was the work of an architect, that everything in it was secondary to architecture.[45]

[LCdv 259] 30

An architect designs avenues starting from the house – for outings on foot, in a litter; hippodromes – he erects porticos everywhere, with all aspects, for sun or shade, for the shows which nature puts on at all times of day, builds exedrae which promote conversation, rocaille grottos, etc., finally glasshouses.[46]

A linden tree growing in the middle under which 500 noble ladies could find shelter; dazzling roses filled it.
Rose gardens.[47]

The garden by Charles V at the Hôtel St-Pol: "surrounded by hedges covered with intertwined, layered climbing vines in a diamond shape, which make arbours; and these arbours were attached at either end to pavilions made in the same fashion; and there were pavilions not only at each corner of the gardens and courtyards, but also in the middle, and there were equally other arbours which crossed these and

[LCdv 260] 31

divided them into compartments." There was a maze or labyrinth; dutiful architects engraved it on the stone of cathedrals, in front of the choir, so that the faithful, following their meanders like a modern-day Way of the Cross, could also accomplish a pilgrimage while their compatriots were waging war in the Holy Land.[48]

From Bocaccio. "Whereupon they hied them to a walled garden adjoining the palace; [...] they entered, and wonder-struck by the beauty of the whole [...] In the middle of the garden, a thing not less but much more to be commended than aught else, was a lawn of the finest turf, and so green that it seemed almost black, pranked with flowers of, perhaps, a thousand sorts [...] In the middle of the lawn was a basin of whitest marble, graven with marvellous art; [...] figure which sent forth a jet of water of such volume and to such an altitude that it fell, not without a delicious plash, into the basin in quantity [...] At length, however, they had enough of wandering about the garden [...]

---

45 From here to LCdv 265, Jeanneret again follows Georges Riat, *L'Art des Jardins* (Paris: L. Henry May, 1900). Parts are isolated excerpts, but he mostly copies out Riat verbatim. Here: Riat, *L'Art des Jardins*, p. 44.
46 Riat, *L'Art des Jardins*, p. 44.
47 Cf. Riat, *L'Art des Jardins*, p. 65.
48 Riat, *L'Art des Jardins*, p. 64.

[LCdv 261] 32

wherefore they repaired to rest on the green carpet and to the beautiful fountain, around which were ranged the tables, and there, after they had sung half-a-dozen songs and trod some measures, they sat them down [...] waited for the story-telling to begin."[49]

Marcabru from the Middle Ages in the Midi. "By the orchard's spring, where the grass is green beside the bank, in the shade of a fruit tree, with its pretty white flowers and the usual spring birdsong, I came across that young woman who, alone and without companion, does not want my company."[50]

There is an exquisite illustration of an arbour after a miniature from the Decameron, which would be good as the end of a chapter (see sketched copy) – **[79]**

Need to find a selection of poetic quotations so that, by quoting them, can make the contrast felt with our hopeless gardens today.

[LCdv 262] 33

Discussing Greece

Taine: "In these beautiful islands of marble, sparkling on the azure of the Aegean Sea, is found now and then a sacred grove, the cypress, the laurel."

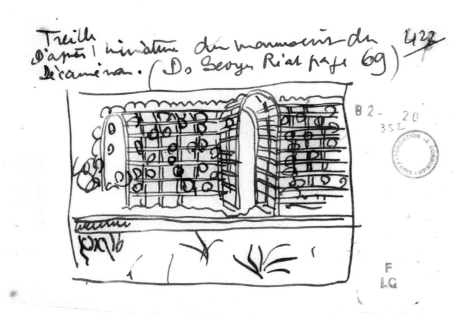

Fig. 79 Trellis from the Decameron. Sketch by Jeanneret, after Riat, *L'Art des jardins*, p. 69 (B2-20-352 FLC)

---

49 Riat, *L'Art des Jardins*, p. 61f, using an existing translation of Bocaccio, adding "to rest on the green carpet".
50 Riat, *L'Art des Jardins*, p. 60.

In the Odyssey, the "fair flowing spring, with a basin fashioned, whence the people of the city drew water. This well Ithacus and Neritus and Polyctor had builded. And around it was a thicket of alders that grow by the waters, all circlewise, and down the cold stream fell from a rock on high, and above was reared an altar to the Nymphs, whereat all wayfarers made offering."[51]

In Egypt.
The poets of Egypt revel in celebrating their gardens: "She led me, hand in hand, and we went into her garden... The bushes were verdant and all flowering. There were fruits redder than rubies; the persea fruit resembled bronze, and the groves had the lustre of the stone nashem; the half-open menni

[LCdv 263] 34
supplied their almonds to us: their shade was fresh and airy, and soft for the repose of love."[52] –

"The Arabs have taken the art of irrigation to the highest point; their hydraulic works attest the most advanced state of civilization; these works still exist; and it is to them that Granada owes the reputation it has of being the Paradise of Spain, and the fact of its enjoying eternal spring in an African temperature. An arm of the Darro has been turned out of its course by the Arabs, and carried for more than five leagues[53] along the hill of the Alhambra."[54] (Tra los Montes Théoph. Gautier)

The garden of Italian Renaissance villas is in effect the Roman garden, but adapted with intelligence and artistry to the new conditions of life. It met all the requirements of the time. (Georges Riat 98)[55]

[LCdv 264] 35
To summarise, the Italian Renaissance garden is inspired by the gardens of Imperial Rome; it and the villa jointly make a framework for the wishes of their owners: gentlemen, courtiers, antique dealers and Italians. Their layout is panoramic and symmetrical, using many terraces and flights of stairs; it is suited to the special nature of the chosen site; architectural lines dominate the general outline of the beds and copses, and the play of the water; straight lines are the rule; statues and marbles, deployed knowledgeably, breach the uniformity without destroying it. The *allees* lead to interesting viewpoints. Here, art is added to nature, and not nature to art – as at Versailles for example, G. Riat 104.[56]

The Italian garden began in 1500 – Villa d'Este 1549 – Colonna Palace, Villa Madama (Stendhal said: "I have seen Romans spend whole hours in mute admiration, pressed against a window at the Villa Lante, on the Janiculum"[57] Villa Negroni 1580. Villa Mattei 1582. Quirinal Palace after 1600 Villa [Doria] Pamphili 1680

---

51 We used an existing Odyssey translation by S.H. Butcher here, rather than translating from Taine.
52 Riat, *L'Art des Jardins*, p. 19.
53 Jeanneret writes "five leagues", as Riat does, whereas Gautier speaks of "two leagues".
54 Riat, *L'Art des Jardins*, p. 92, after Théophile Gautier, *En Espagne (Tra los Montes)* (Paris: Charpentier, 1890), p. 236.
55 Riat, *L'Art des Jardins*, p. 98.
56 Riat, *L'Art des Jardins*, p. 104.
57 Riat, *L'Art des Jardins*, p. 110, after Stendhal, *Promenades dans Rome I* (Paris: Calmann-Levy, 1853), p. 104.

[LCdv 265] 36

Besides these grandiose creations there was the individual garden, pretty images of which can be found in manuscripts and paintings.[58]

Then came decadence, small minds, tricks, little mechanisms – hidden jets of water which spring into your face when you set foot on a step, etc. – small water mills, windmills, animals copied most naturally and placed in grottos and copses. – Montaigne in his account of his voyage to Italy has abundant information of this type. It was the fashion, and he rejoiced in it wholeheartedly.[59]

In France the gardens of castles on the Loire where princes [went] to live far from Paris, Blois Chambord Chenonceaux.

[LCdv 266] 37

The garden is a construction made with trees and flowers, these elements which in their structure contain irregularity, chaos, disorder. This is true not when you take a single tree, which is almost always marvellously ordered – a true palmette – but when compared with the means at the disposal of city architects: streets and squares – strongly accentuated, brutal forms, geometric volumes, etc. Hence to avoid dryness, the planner of streets and squares uses curves; to avoid chaos, splintering, nothingness, the gardener uses straight lines which allow him to align elements along [intangible?] perspectives in plan which in elevation are open to imaginative [handling] – and thus to create an architecture made from living materials: architectures being order, will,

[LCdv 267] 38

power, *a feeling that this was intended*. ChEJt

The French garden is inspired by Renaissance Italy, very late, under Marie de' Medici with the Luxembourg (the palais and garden inspired by the Palazzo Pitti, circa 1620–28).

In Germany the influence of the Italian garden [arrived] very late in the northern lands, in the mid-17th century, and through the art of Le Nôtre.

Versailles was not made all at once, slow development of the plans.

In 1661 start of changes to the Louis XIII garden,

Le Vau orangery built. In 1663 the central *allee* was designed, which later acted as a green carpet. – 1664 the parterre nord and parterre du midi – 1665 the French arranged water effects. – 1667 the fountains were decorated by many artists. – Between 1671 and 1674, flower beds replaced

[LCdv 268]

by the *parterre d'eau* in front of the palace.

1684–1687 animal cages placed: tiger and bear, stag and dog. –

1683–1713 the *parterre d'eau* is transformed, replacing the pool compartments, 2 large pools surrounded by [__] figures with 8 groups of infants.

– the colonnade in 1688. It was in this year that the garden appears to have been finished. The changes made since then do not seem to have destroyed the park's overall layout.

---

58 Riat, *L'Art des Jardins*, p. 120f.
59 Here, Jeanneret paraphrases Riat, cf. Riat, *L'Art des Jardins*, p. 124ff.

After Versailles, the garden at the Château de Clagny then St. Cloud, Fontainebleau, and the Parc de Chantilly. The grand parterre de Nancy.
– Across the whole expanse of France, gentlemen or even simple local squires used all possible ingenuity in imitating their master and his marvels at Versailles.[60]
England adopted and exaggerated the regularity of the French garden; Germany did the same. –

[LCdv 269] [Loose sheet] [Drawing] [80]
carrousel, garden pond, restaurant terrace *à la française*! After Stübben

§9 Material for *On Cemeteries*

[LCdv 270] [Front of loose sheet; outline of letter to Max Läuger]
Dear Professor, I am at present writing (in French) a study on city planning; this area is currently developing in Germany and remains almost unknown in my own country where the habitual systems are still employed. My study will include a chapter on parks and gardens, and another on cemeteries. I am therefore writing to ask your permission to discuss your two remarkable projects, the park in Hamburg and the Osterholz Bremen cemetery, and to publish the illustrations; I enclose tracings as a reminder of your drawings. The master plan of the cemetery also seems to me a valuable document. Please tell me how I may obtain the desired plates, using the illustrations which appeared in *Die Kunst*, Vol. XI? Please tell me if I can obtain from you [...] reproductions which appeared in the journal *Die Kunst*, Vol. XI, unless you have drawings of [...]'

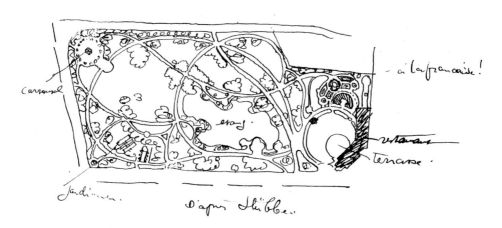

Fig. 80 Plan of a public garden in Cologne. Sketch by Jeanneret, copied from Stübben, *Städtebau*, fig. 841 (LCdv 269)

60 Riat, *L'Art des Jardins*, p. 244.

[LCdv 271]

See Gattamelata   notebook. Cities II
   David, Michelangelo   "   Garden Cities VI

"When we want to honour a man's memory, it should be with a monument and not something superfluous or disruptive. In order to honour a musician we can erect a dance hall or concert hall in his name, build a conference hall in memory of a famous orator. We can make monuments in the form of benches, beautiful portals, rose beds, children's play areas, beautiful gardens, beautiful groups of trees and tranquil ponds. And in such images which form an organic part of modern life we display greater spirit in immortalising people than in some useless sculpture."[61]

Jos Aug Lux page 92

An interesting book for a study of monuments is: Handbuch der Architektur Vierter Teil. Geschichte des Denkmales. By Albert Hofmann 18 x 22cm. 700 pages, lots of illustrations.[62]

[LCdv 272] [Front of loose sheet]

MONUMENTS

The time is almost upon us when water horses (Wasserpferde), riders and young girls [Lux: "proffering"] crowns, and similar motifs that reappear eternally in our monumental sculpture, will be made in bulk by industry. It will be possible to erect monuments according to a catalogue, with changes available ('varied at will'). The triumph of industrialism is in fact already complete with tombstone sculptures (Grabmalplastik). We should be grateful to the progress made by industry, which has unmasked and foiled this (simulated) deceptive art to such a great extent. For in so doing it has destroyed old, inopportune prejudices and left the way clear for new creative thoughts (and allowed these to be revealed) on this fallow land. *It is today an open secret that in the field of architecture, engineers are the true architects of our time.*[63] And that developers often play a deplorable role in killing off monumental sculpture in towns undergoing modernisation. The streets and public squares in all towns are congested with this academic industrialism; we are saturated and disgusted by these miserable, inorganic and disruptive things, which merely

[LCdv 273] [Front of loose leaf]

block one's route. These are things which are merely bearers of names, and which have no soul; dead stone, silent metal, where no spirit dwells. Nobody looks at them any more. Nobody feels elevated or captivated. Many people now suspect that monumental sculpture has fallen flat, but the causes of this decline and the strategies for emerging from this deep dip are still completely obscure. It is altogether certain that an art cannot survive if it becomes detached from Handwerk [craft], from Gewerbe [trade], from considering material, and wants to live purely for its own sake. – Even the ancient sculptors were stonemasons who belonged directly to the master builders' corporation. They were

---

61 Lux, *Städtebau und Grundpfeiler*, p. 92. Lux: "...display more of the spirit of the person immortalised..."

62 Albert Hofmann, *Handbuch des Architeken*, Teil 4, Halbband 8, *Geschichte des Denkmales* (Stuttgart: Kröner, 1906).

63 Lux writes: "Baumeister", master builders.

working within the discipline of architecture and architecture was working within the discipline of Handwerk (the profession, the materials, etc.)[64]
(Der Städtebau by Jos. Aug. Lux – Dresden) (page 89)

[LCdv 274]
[Three sketches of gravestones, after Franz Zell: "Die Münchner Friedhof- und Grabmalreform", in: *Süddeutsche Bauzeitung*, Vol. 17 (1907), No. 33, pp. 257–263, here p. 259, Fig.s 5, 7, 8. **[81]** See the accompanying text LCdv 280–292.]

[LCdv 275] 1//CEMETERIES.
A word about cemeteries. The cemetery can become a park, with graves as islands, which grant asylum to our dear departed! Such grave-islands *in memento mori* would oblige one to remain stillstehen amidst the hurly burly of life, and this could only have a beneficial influence. The new cemeteries, which are marked by an insensitive (geistlos) template where on every grave the conventional angel watching over it with the most painful lack of poetry is like a mark of our impoverished commercialised taste, are not edifying.
In such cases, no path leads from dire straits into the light. The heavy pain of powerlessness [will be] weighed down to a monstrous degree by the impression of general Trostlosigkeit [generally disconsolate impression]. There is no redeeming them. There is a lack of grandeur. Above all, there is a lack of art, the great redeemer.
Jos Aug Lux. p.94.*
Moderne Bauformen 1909 page 441, part of a cemetery by Kreis, Düsseldorf. (Good photo) **[82, 83]**

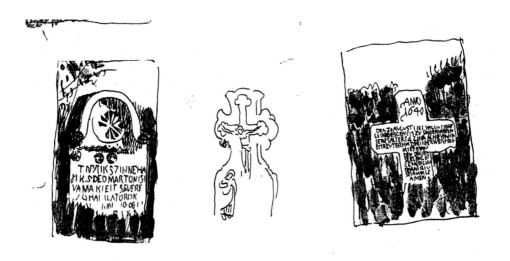

Fig. 81 Tombstones on the Waldfriedhof, Munich. Sketches by Jeanneret, copied from Zell, "Die Münchener Friedhof- und Grabmalreform" (LCdv 274)

Fig. 82 Cemetery design by Wilhelm Kreis at the exhibition for Christian art in Düsseldorf. From *Moderne Bauformen* 8 (1909), no. 9, p. 388f.

[LCdv 276] 2

In Süddeutsche Bauzeitung 1907//page 257

An article on the Munich cemetery and tomb reform.

Handbuch der Architektur IV//Monuments

Albert Hofmann: The idea of streets lined with monuments goes back to the oldest eras, it is not unfamiliar to either the art of the orient or the art of less faraway lands. – . . .[65] The avenue of some 2km called the spirit path which leads to the Ming tombs near Nanking. Along this avenue, the emperors took their last step towards the eternal resting place, and as the oriental imagination was dominated at various stages of life by the good or evil influence of spirits,[66] so the souls of great people were accompanied for their protection from evil spirits by animal figures who stood guard.[67]

65 Albert Hofmann, *Handbuch des Architekten. Teil 4, Halbband 8. Geschichte des Denkmals* (Stuttgart: Kröner, 1906), p. 749.

66 Hofmann: "to a great extent by the life"

67 Hofmann, *Geschichte des Denkmals*, p. 750.

Fig. 83 Cemetery design by Wilhelm Kreis at the exhibition for Christian art in Düsseldorf. From *Moderne Bauformen* 8 (1909), no. 9, p. 388f.

[LCdv 277] 3

At the start of the avenue stand two tortoises bearing obelisks, then lions lying down [and] standing up, roughly worked, always 2 figures facing one another; then 2 camels lying down and 2 standing. Finally 2 horses lying and 2 standing with dogs. The end of the avenue shoes 2 warriors lying and 2 standing guard, who in their appearance remind one of works from Assyria, and are similar to the figures at the imperial tombs of *Jehol.*

{by me} All this lies or stands in the middle of the deserted countryside, in short grass, overlooked by mountains, and the figures are worked and of such style and size that they possess the greatest emotive strength.

(Cite this as the type of thing that, with the help of natural elements, makes the deepest of impressions. Similarity to Egypt (to Miletus, sacred way and Roman 'Via Campana'). – We must then contrast with the modern cemetery which cannot make such preparations but which must be entrenched behind ramparts so it can be a place of rest.[68] + where the tomb of Caecilia Metella is.

---

68 Meaning of French sentence unclear. Cf. Hofmann, *Geschichte des Denkmals*, p. 750f. on the Sacred Way to the Didymaion (Temple of Apollo) near Miletus.

[LCdv 278] 4

The tombs of the Caliphs in Cairo. The cemeteries of Constantinople. Discuss stacking up in Père Lachaise, the cemeteries of Alpe [d'Huez?], all the tombs with the black cross contrasting with the bold white of the façade.

The effect of the dolmens and menhirs in arid Brittany and Britain. The immense plain, undefined and empty, and these barely worked stones rising up, forming pillars and porticoes with their rough traits that speak of fright and mystery with their ill-defined and brutal emergent forms.

[LCdv 279]

Say that accounts are kept of corpses, so it serves no purpose for them to follow one after the other, which has advantages, since one can get lost when everything looks the same.[69] We must create different sorts [of graves] according to taste, and richness so that one does not squash the other and so the names disappear in the face of the *fact,* and so that fresh consolation arises from the beauty and serenity.

Whoever introduced that silly craze for putting the name up front before everything else?

This is a sacrifice to bourgeois ways. Just because such and such an emperor or prince stated his name as a reminder to the populus in the middle of a mausoleum, that means every man, every kid, brat, etc. now does likewise, without it dawning on them that this is astonishing; ridiculous end [?] of a slow evolution of the bourgeois spirit.

Women, even if they die at the same time as their husbands, will be buried beneath them and not beside them. If they die one day later they

[LCdv 280] 29

rest 20 metres further away.

If [the deaths] are 20 days or 1 year apart, she will be at one end of the cemetery and he at the other.

Democracy in the final resting place is one of this era's most high-flown phrases, and one of the emptiest.

The Chaldrin tombs in the rock

[Sketch]

Graves framed in iron or stone destroy the lawn as ground cover.

The Stadtbaurat Hans Grässel introduced a great reform in all science in the Leichenhaus [mortuary], in technical, hygiene and artistic matters and even in such a convincing form that, in the testimony

[LCdv 281]

of many people including many British travellers, these buildings are unique, as is the way of erecting the tombs.[70]

---

69 Meaning of French sentence unclear.

70 From here to LCdv 292, Jeanneret almost completely reproduces an article by Franz Zell, "Die Münchener Friedhof- und Grabmalreform", in: *Süddeutsche Bauzeitung*, Vol. 17 (1907), No. 33, pp. 257–61. He achieves this through a mixture of translation and paraphrase. Hence not every divergence from Zell's original text is noted in the translation.

Only in the immediate surroundings of the buildings and here and there on a main *allee* was it possible, – in installing 3 new cemeteries, to keep at bay the dedicated standard job lot of modern tomb types, and to arrange some squares favourable to a unitary and artistic purpose. Outside these squares, the familiar bric-à-brac of modern urban cemeteries reigns which despite the planted *allees* are bare in winter (because only Laubbäume [deciduous trees] grow well in Munich), and appear like a large store of graveyard merchandise.

Not that there are not excellent examples of tombs from the simplest to the richest, and perhaps in greater number than in just any old cemetery, yet these do not gain the upper hand as they stand alongside others of lesser value, routine and automatic, and can therefore no more help here

[LCdv 282] 27

than the *allees* of trees can help the city of tombs – the cemetery – towards a bearable appearance full of Stimmung.

The beautiful unity of the graves does not in any way help obtain a harmonious, impressive Friedhofsanlage.

As early as 1901 a law had created an obligation, thus bringing a small improvement: a row of graves must not exceed a height of 1.15 [metres], no framing in iron or stone, no grassy mound, but treated overall as gardens. Yet reform was only truly effective with Baurat Grässel and the installation of his 4th cemetery, the Waldfriedhof, in an existing forest of fir trees of around 50 hectares, which was built starting in 1905 with part of it opening in September 1907.

[LCdv 283]

In brief, these were Grässel's thoughts.

A good urban cemetery impression lies to a great extent in a rich planting to separate isolated cemeteries, which overlook one another and from certain perspectives can be installed in artistic unity. At the Waldfriedhof the planting Grässel wanted already existed, and he deployed the existing clearings, as well as meadows obtained from forest clearance – each around 1/4 of a hectare – to establish his isolated cemeteries.

Other points of view by Grässel were:

the beautiful impression given by free nature in the forest must not in the separate cemeteries be destroyed by graves; given the small size of the area these may

[LCdv 284] 25

not be too high and damage one another in their effectiveness, that is why they will be grouped throughout the cemetery, and ordered according to materials and to type. One must encourage wood carvers, workers of wrought iron, foundry operators, just as they made graves in the past. In particular, the background formed by a lawn must remain undivided as far as possible. Stone, iron or wooden surrounds are not permitted. It is these that underline the use of the plot and the narrowness of the graves in such a disagreeable manner, and back[71] the restful impression of the cemeteries and tombs. The very shape of the planting and graves may need to chime with the character of the whole, with the character of the forest.

---

71 Zell: "restrict".

[LCdv 285]

Baurat Grässel wrote documents at the time about setting out graves and the manner in which to make the amenities at the Waldfriedhof; he spoke up for these repeatedly in public lectures, given to an audience of stonemasons who felt their vested rights were under attack, brought[72] to wide public attention the exhibition for cemeteries and grave art, and in particular got the Munich artists' society interested.

In the end, he installed the convincing models he had thus obtained, made them into a temporary installation in the Waldfriedhof and invited the public to get acquainted with them, and over the 8 days following the opening of the Waldfriedhof people rushed there in their thousands and showed great interest.

[LCdv 286] 23

So much so that gradually, recalcitrant stonemasons were won over and the magistrates, who approved the proposals Grässel made in accordance with the cemetery committee's requirements, with several changes to Article 10 concerning the judging committee requested by Grässel. Being concerned purely with the artistic question, he had requested a committee composed *only* of artists and made point *b* less strict, according to which the garish black and garish white polished tombs would not be tolerated under any circumstances.

Proposal for tombs and their layout in the Waldfriedhof:

§1. The Waldfriedhof includes rows of graves, groups of family graves, rented vaults,

[LCdv 287]

vault cells with substructure[73] or

"   "   without   "

§2 The highly atmospheric impression of unbridled nature must be preserved as far as possible when the forest is used as a cemetery, and therefore the use of the site for groups of tombs must always take account of this consideration. Nor should the impression of a natural cemetery be destroyed by damage from tombs impinging on one another and from small graveyards being enclosed.[74]

§3 To avoid them impinging on one another and with a view to obtaining an impression worthy of cemetery as a whole, we hereby state that particular requirements similar to those for the rows of graves should be observed for erecting each tomb at the Waldfriedhof. According to the divisions

[LCdv 288] 21

duly determined in the plan, each part will be for only graves with upright stones, and elsewhere horizontal stones, and elsewhere graves with wrought iron, elsewhere those made with wood, etc.

§4 Special family vaults, and groups of family tombs (Waldgräber), large gravestones may be made if they are of an artistic nature, and if with adequate planting they eliminate any risk of disadvantage to neighbouring graves.

---

72 Jeanneret's translation is hard to follow, so we follow Zell's original here.

73 Zell: "superstructure"

74 Zell: "disturbed by the funerary monuments erected on graves, the encroachment of graves on one another or their enclosure."

§5 Where mounds are tolerated on graves, these must not exceed a height, in a dome shape, of between 30 and 40cm. Box-shaped or banked mounds are prohibited. White paper wreaths cannot

[LCdv 289]

be tolerated. When planting up the grave, the character of the forest will be considered.
§6 All enclosure of graves is prohibited. This would counter the impression of freedom given by nature in the forest, and destroy the rural impression of the land.
§7 The points in the appendix must be taken into consideration by the grave's owners.
§8 Prior approval is required for all tombs to be built at the Waldfriedhof. An application for this should be made to the Stadtmagistrat, presenting a plan or model on the scale of 1:5; the name of the chosen material, the colour and inscription should be attached. Plans must be submitted in duplicate.

[LCdv 290] 19

§9 The instructions already set out on 24 February 1898 on the erecting tombs, planting trees, etc. also apply to the Waldfriedhof, notwithstanding the instructions above.
§10 A committee appointed by the magistrates monitors everything the said instructions require, and also [decides on] the requirements in §8 concerning the mandatory approval of the planned grave. This committee is formed of the speaker for the municipal council as chairman, the administration board for the cemetery, and a representative of the local authority architecture office.
– Appendix: In order for grave decoration to be appropriate to the Waldfriedhof: a) The value of a tomb will lie not in its high price,

[LCdv 291]

but rather in how it harmonises with the surrounding environment.
b) For the W.F., the particular materials designated for stone monuments are: tuff; Muschel-trass, {Nagelfluh (French word?)}, Muschelkalk {French also}[75] granite and granular limestone. Carrara marble, polished stone and any dark or black stone will only be accepted in exceptional cases, and only if the colour is in tune with the grave's location.
c) Other suitable materials include: painted wrought iron, painted oak or larch (provided the paintwork is well done), cast bronze with stone,
d) Highly artistic effects may be achieved with the application of colours and [...].
e) The tombstone inscription must be a decorative addition, and especially

[LCdv 292] 17

well arranged and not covered in ill-judged colours. Printed or sand-engraved letters will not be tolerated.
f) When an area of tombs is planned, it should be ensured that no overly major change occurs in the shape of the tombs, as order is beauty in and of itself. The way they are grouped and then their position should confer on them an artistic unity, they should take account reciprocally of what is next to them. Individuality may be fully manifest in a single shape. It is pointless to try and reproduce a unique motif by the dozen.[76]

---

75 Jeanneret makes these two comments in the manuscript.
76 Zell: "Worthless, ten-a-penny clichés are prohibited."

g) For tomb planting, the various mosses are recommended in particular, ferns, ivy, box, juniper, climbing plants like Virginia creeper, and flowers – well chosen of course; artificial plants and decorations shaped like artificial plants[77] are not allowed.

[LCdv 293]

Extract from Süddeutsche Bauzeitung page 257 1907. Some models of tombs in the ancient world have been published – see my tracings.

A very instructive article in Gartenkunst. 1st April 1910.

Competition for a cemetery in Bremen.[78]

The subject so often addressed, and yet still very much alive, was of collaboration between architect and artistic gardener, i.e. an all-round solution including architecture. The volume (presence) which the buildings will, later, adopt on the area, within a wide circumference, will only be good if this latter means of linking the details of these buildings' architecture to the overall plan [is used].

A harmonious whole cannot exist without the buildings and their details, or indeed without their architecture; the *entrance* parts of the winning project should be studied with this in mind; and where architecture becomes remarkable, the need

[LCdv 294]

for this collaboration shines through indisputably. This need certainly has disadvantages, as the arch.[itect] risks losing the design and neglecting the many different solutions which the garden would offer – and vice versa, according to the qualities of the people collaborating. But an intensive collaboration between gardener and architect brings with it, in essence, capabilities shared reciprocally. And it is most highly desirable that such work should be done, to ultimately provide solutions to questions of architecture and its surroundings.

And that is above all an advantage for the town which will receive an *executable* project which meets its conditions and demands, and it will therefore be recognising the artist(s) capable of implementing a *master plan*. For a spirit of character and individuality will always, generally, be [present] when the designer also has the execution within his gift. There were 96 submissions in Bremen.

[LCdv 295]

Some considerations about the cemetery:

The *church yard*, field of rest, Kirchhof, was originally the field for funerary rites, everywhere. When it was too small, the town or city gave God's field an additional enclosure. The larger this enclosure, the emptier and more boring it looked. The exquisite aspect of these small cemeteries was most often due to wild and free vegetation, to large trees and to the link between all this and the church, in short more a matter of chance than a matter of intent. The graves were in good taste and were not yet marked by the perversion of either taste or convenience. This character was not to be found in the somewhat larger cemeteries, and it was deemed that amends could be made for their Nüchternheit [sobriety] by creating the landscaped cemetery, inspired by the conventional park shapes

---

77 Zell: "ornamental varieties".

78 From here to LCdv 297, Jeanneret paraphrases rather than translates an article by Fritz Encke and Reinhold Hoemann, "Der Bremer Friedhofswettbewerb", in: *Die Gartenkunst*, Vol. 12 (1910), No. 4, pp. 51–57. The translation follows Jeanneret's version.

of the mid-19th century. Thus Übersichtlichkeit [clarity], convenience, economy in the use of space and primitive cemeteries were lost. In line with the contemporary taste in beautiful parkland images, very beautiful frames were gained for isolated, rich graves but in general, partly intentionally and partly unintentionally, the poor man's grave was neglected. When this error was identified,

[LCdv 296]

an error made worse by the decline of modern funerary art, attempts were made to remedy it using planting which hid [...] from view, by covering the rows of graves.

The efforts in recent years revealed a cemetery which was neither park nor field of rest (old style). They no longer show a sorry division into chequerboard squares, nor a trend towards a park with a completely different aim, but are born of requirements, take a clear, individual shape, full of character. Several points of view may influence this: ranging from the woodland cemetery where tombs are built in the middle of an almost untouched wood; to a monumental cemetery where plants will gradually relieve its brutality or pay the architecture a fine tribute of colours and latticework; and even to the point of view where the forest will provide the volume into which *rooms will be cut*, with fountains, pools, long views.

[LCdv 297]

The right strategy is a happy medium (?) which satisfies the practical needs and tastes of the masses (?!).[79] A cemetery which has lines that show intent but are not rigorously symmetrical, and which is not monumental, with a network of paths in relation to the architectural parts, which must serve as landmarks, to create small spaces over a large area, reminiscent in their volume of the old fields of rest.

There is no longer here a wide, arid plain of graves which oppress the viewer, but instead the field for the poor will be treated as lovingly as that with magnificent tombs.

In particular, it appears desirable that varied types of cemetery come together.

In particular, it is understandable that our thoughts are accurate, namely that avoiding an overly great emphasis on axes is preferable [as per] an examination of the entrances to various projects."[80]

[LCdv 298] [Two sketches of cemeteries.] [84]

[LCdv 299]

To honour the departed, there is a wish to care for their grave; and to feel that the deceased is honoured, one wishes very logically for the grave to be beautiful: it is lovingly draped in flowers, an accumulation of many beautiful flowers – sometimes with unfortunate overall effect – which is tended with care. To make the tomb beautiful is to make visible the care and emotion paid to the deceased. The new cemetery proposes to remove the individual little garden, but introduce an *overall* effect, it confers an atmosphere of beauty not only on one grave but on all graves. And then one will no longer accumulate flowers in sometimes ill-assorted clumps, but one will instead bring the flower as burnt offering as a moving

---

79 These question/exclamation marks are Jeanneret's.

80 Encke/Hoemann: "Our view that avoiding an excessively great emphasis on axes is advantageous is proven correct particularly clearly by comparing the entrance solutions in the designs shown."

Fig. 84 Cemetery designs. Sketches by Jeanneret (LCdv 298)

testament, repeated as often as desired, very simply, or splendidly opulent so one can come and honour again the memory of the deceased as often as one wants. Remember the effect of the bouquet (a few violets) on Hugo Wolf's tomb.

[LCdv 300]
Article on 2 works by Max Läuger[81]

---

81 From here to LCdv 310, Jeanneret translates selected passages of an article by August Grisebach, "Max Läugers Entwürfe zum Hamburger Stadtpark und zum Osterholzer Friedhof bei Bremen", in *Die Kunst – Angewandte Kunst*, Vol. 22 (1910), pp. 489–503. His translation often deviates from Grisebach's rather elaborate formulations.

Wherever a conflict arises between 2 aesthetic principles, there is no attempt to pursue it, and reasonable people will emerge, saying: neither party is completely in the right. Everyone thinks something correct; the truth lies in between. And a compromise style is created which is supposed to marry the qualities of the 2 opposing principles. But where some youth remains, the fight against this unreasonable demand will be fuelled by a vigorous thirst for development.

In the battle ongoing for some years in the sphere of ordering gardens, dishonest compromise[82] is the order of the day. The fundamentally opposed principles of the architectural garden and the landscape garden form the basis for this. Agreement is sometimes reached to split the architectural, geometric plan and shape the land in an architectural sense by introducing terraces, sunken beds, etc. But for the way and means in which

[LCdv 301]

this plan will be planted one will choose to follow the naturalist principles of the landscape garden. – Thus for example several groups of trees will be distributed across a geometric square of lawn, picturesque groups, as much in the shape of isolated groups as in their asymmetric interrelations. The lawn will be surrounded by a wide, floral ribbon which does not appear as a modest coloured braid,[83] but in its very structure to which the gardener has added with pleasure a mixture of climbing and springing shoots which spill over onto the path and lawn, and hide the clear lines. Above all, due to the overly vigorous, generous, charming growth of flowers – in that place the character of the planned lawn area will be destroyed. In short, gardens which are more or less planted in a landscaped manner on a geometric layout, lack the essential architectural character, the

[LCdv 302]

sense which was called the 'garden's relief' when garden art was flourishing during the 17th century. People do not realise that the essence of a garden lies in the nervous[84] contrast of a free, clear area (bed, pond), with closed, rising masses (thickets, hedges, etc.). In other words, the embodiment of space[85] – perhaps the most powerful element which 150 years ago was sacrificed for landscape garden trends – is still unknown in projects by conciliatory garden architects.

For the time being, despite many adjustments[86] and many words, we have not moved beyond a pseudo-art of gardens: the two works by Max Läuger for the park in Hamburg and the cemetery in Bremen will remain on paper. In both cases,

[LCdv 303]

the jury decided in favour of the landscaped design.

His project is built on this clearly delineated embodiment of space, with a richly unfolding perspective. The water tower presents itself from the restaurant terrace, past the great

---

82 Grisebach: "attempts at mediation are".
83 Grisebach: "belt".
84 Grisebach: "sharp".
85 Grisebach: "spatial effect"; Jeanneret: "corporalité", i.e. embodiment of space.
86 Grisebach: "good beginnings".

rectangular pool, past the vast lawn flanked by *allees*, and past the flower bed, and to the edge of the wood into whose depths the narrow waterfall path leads. The paths through the flowerbeds, the garden's area for flowers, act as a sunny walkway; the area of lawn, the 'green carpet' intended for the masses to roam on without a care, acts as the centre of the whole design. Sports and games which require distinct, quiet rooms, find satisfaction on the long sides of the meadow, separated from it by an *allee* of large trees. These areas can be found in rows.[87]

[LCdv 304]

Well enclosed clearings in the middle of the forest are reminiscent of the shape of the communal mediaeval garden as reconstructed from literature and images: a flower meadow, with a regular surround of roses, behind which is a woodland garden. All the oldest public gardens in Germany were naturally much more primitive and of more modest size than a park for the city of Hamburg could be today. I want to remind you here about this link, however, as in many people's opinions a garden for the people must contain as little formal composition as possible.[88] How good the crowd feels in an architectural garden, and how practically, easily an enormous quantity (a large crowd) moves[89] in the living spaces of the ordered gardens, is something one can observe

[LCdv 305]

every Sunday in the Parc de Versailles in fine weather.

Läuger gives the smallholders and inns[90] in his park a countenance which, in accordance with their aims, is of a plainer art[91] than the main restaurant and the cafés beside the large pool, but with fundamentally the same character, so that one feels it was made by the same hand.

In Schumacher's design, we find a smallholding (Milchwirtschaft [dairy]) to be a copy of a farm from the Vierlande. This attempt to create an artificial rural idyll stems from the same idea as the thatched cottages in the sentimental 18th century park (Petit Trianon).

It is the same phenomenon that makes these garden plans seem ill at ease: things that emerge from an artistic design are set alongside things which first and

[LCdv 306]

foremost owe their existence to a romantic idea. Läuger's buildings, on the other hand, harmonise with one another, and with the individual parts of the garden composition. It is all cast as if from the same mould.

---

87 We present Grisebach's version in full here, since Jeanneret's differs so greatly from it: "His project is built on this spatially clearly delineated perspective, full of developments: from the restaurant terrace, past the great pool, the lawn flanked by *allees* and the bed; at the edge of the wood it leads into the narrow waterfall path, which rushes towards the clearing from the water tower. As the paths through the flowerbeds – the garden's territory for flowers – serve those taking a leisurely stroll in the sunshine, so the centre of the whole design, the lawn, is intended for a crowd's rest and carefree movement. For sports and games which require a distinct space, there are rows of areas on the long sides of the meadow, separated from it by the *allees*."

88 Grisebach: "is the place least suited to a formal composition".

89 Grisebach: "how magnificent a mass of people looks".

90 Grisebach: "'rural' businesses and dairy".

91 Griebach: "type".

Osterholz cemetery, Bremen.

In the irregular plot, the main part is ordered as a large Latin cross, in such a way that its long axis creates the widest possible perspective.

It is desirable that for the installation of a city cemetery, in the practical sense of the matter, the visitor has a clear view over the overall layout. How long must one roam Parisian cemeteries before one discovers the grave one is looking for?

But above all, a view as presented here from the large chapel over the pools, towards the monument.

[LCdv 307]

Death evokes the feierlich (solemn, majestic) and ernst (serious) Stimmung [mood], which matches the character of the place.

Furthermore, the calm, mirroring water surface in straight lines gives this garden the impression of peace and rest. The *allees* intended for urns are close up to the edges of the pool;[92] they require a smaller elevation above the level of the water than the tombs, located behind them at a higher level. A marked separation between the cemeteries with graves and those with urns is desirable from all points of view However it is not necessary to set them up in 2 separate installations. Läuger makes both areas into a unified whole, finds an especially favourable solution to this issue which has arisen again in the present day. With regard to columbaria where the urns

[LCdv 308]

are aligned like flasks in a pharmacy, one can only hope that we move away from this soon.

For grouping tombs, whether a this be a quantity of places all aligned beside one another, or small areas of family tombs, attempts will be made to enclose these areas, instead of leaving these undecided shapes in a muddle, *bric-à-brac.*

For family tombs he proposes monuments which scarcely reach higher than the hedges enclosing them, see tracing *B.*

However there is nothing more unbearable in a cemetery than long walls, made of tombs aligned one against the other, temples, architectural niches, all seeking to surpass one another in size and richness. One might say individual pride (presumption) was stretching out its gurning face (folly) from beyond the grave

[LCdv 309]

without the least regard for the neighbourhood.

These two plans will not be carried out. It would have been a fine opportunity to embody some issues very much imbued with modern spirit, which would have to satisfy our modern needs, to embody them in accordance with our new architectural understanding. They would have acted as a powerful documentation of our era for our descendants. For only our descendants can weave crowns [to honour] our garden architects. For a garden will not be embodied in its designed form or fulfil all the intentions until many years later; however simplistic this consideration is, our contemporary public does not understand it. Herein lies the basis for some misjudgements of architectural gardens in

---

92 Jeanneret misconstrued this as "the alleys are tightly packed".

exhibitions. Initially one can only guess at the embodiment of space in the garden;[93] one complains of the denuded limbs and regrets the lack of pretty sprays of plants and

[LCdv 310]

shady alleys, which in any case the highly prized 'bouquet'[94] in a landscape garden could produce more quickly. Just as nowadays we discover a genius and pull him from obscurity and raise him up, we also demand of a garden that it present itself as complete from the outset. How will we benefit, if it is for future generations to enjoy? – August Grisebach – Discuss the Campo Santo in Pisa where there were no personal tombs but where everything was for a more intense exaltation of being moved with emotion. The corpses shrouded in 'holy ground' and then great emotion, cries, tears, joy, blessings, comfort expressed on the walls, in a calm, moving atmosphere, in the touching atmosphere of beauty.

[LCdv 311]

Article on new cemeteries, in Die Kunst 1908 1909 page 521[95]

§10 Material for *On Garden Cities*

[LCdv 312] 1

page 32 Ville I//page 6 Ville III §3.
Just published by Berlepsch-Valendàs, *Bodenpolitik und gemeindliche Wohnungsfürsorge der Stadt Ulm* with many illustrations. From publisher E. Reinhard – Munich.
Immigration from countryside into cities, which causes overpopulation, has created a movement in the opposite direction: cities moving to the countryside.[96]
The new movement can be observed in many places, surrounded by clear signs of hygiene in society. Some manufacturers in America, England, Holland and Germany began thus: they transported their factories out into the countryside, with their workers, to land protected from property and economic speculation, and created a {new} science with artistic, social and hygienic perspectives allied with all modern comforts.

[LCdv 313]

The first workers' colonies which were established tens of years ago were born of a humanitarian aim, without providing a major service to humanity or justice. These were normally the usual shabby buildings, painfully empty and sad, which killed beauty in the countryside and joie de vivre in the people called upon to live there.
The workers' colonies only gained any significance for social policy when the *artist* engaged with their form. The artist exercised an act of humanitarian justice in giving a man or a family what they needed given the state of modern culture. He broke with routine and freed individuality.

---

93 Grisebach: "Gartenräume", garden spaces; Jeanneret: "corporalité du jardin", embodiment of space in the garden.

94 Grisebach: "any sort of foliage".

95 Franz Seeck: "Neuzeitliche Friedhofsanlagen", in: *Die Kunst: Angewandte Kunst* 20/1909, pp. 521–536. Jeanneret neither paraphrases nor translates this article.

96 From here to LCdv 320, Jeanneret translates almost verbatim from Lux, *Der Städtebau und die Grundpfeiler der heimischen Bauweise*, pp. 96–104.

[LCdv 314] 3

He designed the home according to a family's needs, gave them the option of subsequently developing it,[97] giving the home a natural beauty corresponding to indigenous style, and giving the souls who live there the pride and joy which such beauty brings. He provided all modern, hygienic and practical arrangements and facilities which make life easy and comfortable, and banished feelings of poverty and deprivation.

Social equality[98] was perfectly able to persist within this generalised improvement in living conditions, and luxury was only manifest where costly materials were employed, without only one side dominating those resources that are necessary for life, its perfection and happiness.

[LCdv 315]

The first and best example of this type is near Liverpool: Port Sunlight. Mr. W. H. Lever, owner of the soap factory, asked artists to build his workers' colony; they had to meet all practical and hygiene requirements.

Thus in the village an architecture has been established that is inspired by the old popular architecture: and it therefore harmonises with the place. Things which employees and workers need are here reunited in ideal form. A living room and some bedrooms, with bathroom and garden.

Very similar is a colony at a chocolate factory, by G. Cadbury at Bournville near Birmingham.

[LCdv 316] 5

In neither case is the undertaking for financial gain; the rent or interest on the houses will gradually cover the price of erecting them.

Thus the possibility of a *wirtschaftlich* [economic] prosperity is supplied.

In America since the beginning[99] a general and clear knowledge of the practical, popular and aesthetic requirements. They are less pleasing than the English houses cited, but through their impeccable correspondence of form to purpose, which varies in each instance, they avoid any cliché perfectly. Kitchen, living room or hall on the ground floor, bedroom with bathroom on the first floor. The interior white or light coloured, and besides any beauty, this is one of the better colours, even if it is generally held that simplicity is the opposite of beauty.

[LCdv 317]

For 900 dollars, one can acquire such a *home*.[100]

This perfect dominance of art in life[101] without the ulterior motive of speculation signalled the start of a movement which would have great reach in society, and which would lead to a total change in the *Weltantlitz* [face of the world].

Ideal city foundations with social organisation corresponding to industry have taken their first steps here and there, and some have continued with great success, as in the Agnetapark colony near Delft.

---

97 Jeanneret misconstrues Lux's "Beziehung", relationship, as "Erziehung", education.
98 Jeanneret misconstrues Lux's "Ausgleich", equality, as hierarchy.
99 Lux: "...this movement employed...".
100 Lux: "Heim"; Jeanneret uses the English word.
101 Lux: "very practical transfer of art into life".

Above all, in Britain where social and aesthetic questions are linked, one society is working very seriously towards establishing a new town, called a 'garden city', and connecting it to the countryside and to major industries.

[LCdv 318] 7
Ebenezer Howard, the fine instigator of this movement, set out in his book *Garden Cities of To-morrow* the ways and means to help with poverty in cities and with their populations of workers.

With the current state of affairs, we can state firmly that First Garden City Ltd. bought 3,800 hectares in an excellent situation 35 miles[102] to the north of London, between Hitchin and Baldock, 42 minutes away by express train, using capital of £300,000+, in order to establish a colony there. It does not intend to house in the new town any more than 30,000 people so that the majority of the land may be kept for growing crops. Thus the population density outside the town will be 9 per hectare and inside the urban area 23 per hectare. These figures come alive

[LCdv 319]
if we compare them to the percentages for other countries.
The [city's] advantages lie:

1 In the hygiene arrangements, which provide the population with a serious* basis.
2 In the obligation to cultivate the fields, which in the new town will bring an additional aspect and become a striking place of commerce, avoiding middlemen.
3 In each city resident's knowledge that improving the soil yield will benefit the community.

An exact plan is excellent where it defines the [new] town's situation with all its main parts, and already contains several items of information on the master builders'* projects. We should underline that the site plan must be perfectly aligned with the nature of the land and must be

[LCdv 320] 9
planned with a view to improving what already exists, and to being executed without needing to fell even a single one of the existing trees or groups of trees.

Industrial villages and garden cities designed according to aesthetic principles cannot be other than healthy and harmonious, and signify a regrowth of beauty for the country.

Jos. Aug. Lux page 96–104.
Read the Metzendorf brochure and the catalogue for the Städtebauausstellung.
Conferences were held following the Städtebauausstellung.
Ist Series:
Prof. Goecke, Landesbaurat: What hopes (expectations) can we have for the result of the Greater Berlin competition?[103]

---

102 Jeanneret (incorrect): "leagues".
103 This is Jeanneret's translation of an article's title: Theodor Goecke "Welche Erwartungen dürfen wir an das Ergebnis des Wettbewerbs Gross-Berlin knüpfen?", in *Der Städtebau* Vol. 8 (1911), No. 1 pp. 2–5, No. 2 pp. 16–20, No. 3 pp. 29–31.

[LCdv 321] 1

Margarethe Stiftung. Essen[104] [85, 86, 87]

The plan was to establish in relation with the foundation's villas[105] a real garden city, intended as something following the English type.

Brückenkopf mit Platzgestaltung vor dem Langhaus.

Fig. 85 Entry to the garden suburb Margarethenhöhe in Essen. From Metzendorf, *Denkschrift*

Fig. 86 Tramway bridge between Margarethenhöhe garden suburb and Essen. From *Der Städtebau* 7 (1910) no. 7/8, pp. 73–92, fig. 30.

---

104 From here to LCdv 325, Jeanneret paraphrases Georg Metzendorf, *Denkschrift über den Ausbau des Stiftungsgeländes* [Margarethenhöhe] (Essen: Petersen, 1909).

105 Jeanneret misreads "Wille", intention or wishes, as villa. Metzendorf: "in connection with the philosophy of the foundation".

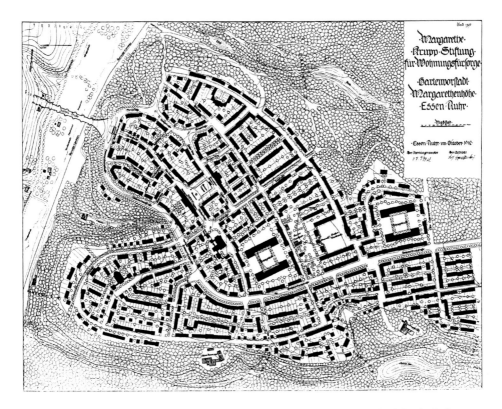

Fig. 87 Development plan of Margarethenhöhe garden suburb. From Metzendorf, *Denkschrift*

A wide ravine separates the town of Essen-West from the planned town, a railway line runs along the bottom of the ravine. It will therefore be necessary to build a large bridge to facilitate access for trams and first of all for carts. Building this will be the first thing undertaken. Besides considerably reducing the material transportation costs for the town, this bridge will be of great aesthetic value. It will be a strongly decorative element for the town. Thus its character will be emphasised. It will connect the town, but also provide separation from it, and make

[LCdv 322]

the new town a little very personal separate world, in unity and isolation.

This bridge, which will necessarily be somewhat monumental, needs to be crowned and as it is on a slope and seeks 'enclosure', a strong block will be placed at the entrance to the city, cut through with a large arcade flanked by 2 other, smaller arcades, with the block linked to the buildings on the edge of this part of the city by large enclosing walls.

Thus the town will open up beyond this door. Yet in order to emphasise the strong nature of the bridge, it will be flanked as it enters, and opposite the large block will be two small detached buildings which will of themselves provide an

[LCdv 323] 3

aesthetic contrast, and a waiting room for trams with a refreshment and catering building for practical purposes.

On the square between these detached buildings and the actual entry to the city will be 2 fountains linked by a spacious staircase with some 15 steps, while at the sides 2 shallow ramps will descend to the right and left for cars.

Beyond the gateway, the perfect aesthetic view will be provided towards the town's interior. It should offer the most impressive beauty from each viewpoint.

This will be obtained by lightly curving the street inwards; it will open up, be given order by gabled buildings in the old Rhineland-Westphalian tradition, without being picturesquely mediaeval, but

[LCdv 324]

shaped by a great simplicity. These will direct viewers' eyes nicely forwards. The buildings which are isolated are linked to one another by a narrow and normally enclosing wall about 3 metres high.

The gardens extend from the back of the building and there are no gardens on the street, since the garden, as a room for festivities and gardening after a day's work, belongs to the owner not as a piece of façade for passers-by, but – in the right season – as an extension of the dwelling itself. It does not fulfil this role unless it is used within the bosom of the family and no stranger has the right to look in.

[LCdv 325] 5

The beautifully designed street must not be troubled in its tranquillity by a tram, which is deliberately taken along another street very close by and where the houses are located according to a site plan that accords with this burden. This street will end at the marketplace,

around which will be located the church and presbytery, pharmacy and doctor's surgery, a *Kaufhaus* [department store] and a town hall.

On Possible Strategies

[**LCdv 326**] PART I//23//THIRD Chap.//On Possible Strategies.

[**LCdv 327**] 12//1st//**CHAP.** {THIRD}
{[Note in the margin:] 1 chapter on signs and advertisements}
The principles expounded in the second chapter allow us to reject overly simplistic aphorisms which have thus far been used to counter attempts at improving the development of towns and cities. Two factors have perpetuated ugliness: prejudices about the value of art – and clumsy processes in overhauling the question of building towns and cities.
People have always stated that art and economy or art and hygiene are incompatible. In accepting this incompatibility uncritically, city administrators and residents have perpetuated some practices which directly oppose general well-being.
The facts have disproved this 'incompatibility': the works published on the subject have disproved it from a theoretical viewpoint, and the radical reforms which have occurred in recent years in the progressive towns and cities of Germany and Britain have disproved it from a practical viewpoint.
The incompatibility of art and economy? Rectangular plots develop the longest street fronts and the most land for building; churches, schools or other public buildings encompassed in a block of constructions, allowing greater richness on their only façade, while making savings; – streets with public passageways penetrating into the building mass and allowing the sale of land which would otherwise have been unused; countering the infallibility of the straight line thus allowing local authorities to avoid much

[**LCdv 328**] 2
costly expropriation; respecting the beauty inherent in the land which inspires solutions no longer requiring the sums for cutting into hillsides and filling in valleys; conserving – and using – the existing trees thus dispensing with costly planting, etc. etc. – these are many areas of compatibility between art and economy.
Improving public hygiene, a consequence of courtyard gardens; schoolrooms, sheltered from noise and dust; streets curved or cut through by covered passageways which block the path of winds; the best building orientation by respecting the terrain; isolating smelly, smoky, noisy factories, leaving the residential districts with cleaner air ... ...
these are victories for general hygiene which the old systems had not achieved.
Art and utility, these two forces always in opposition instead of working together, concur in proposed plans: on making networks of the fastest roads, on the successful

development of shops and cafés, on the beneficial grouping of public services (which we will discuss soon), which result in economy and ease of use... ....

Art needs usefulness to be great, even if this is sometimes only the useful nature of its own uselessness! Yet for successful collaboration between art

[LCdv 329] 12//3.

and utility, we must discern what is likely to be beautiful – or rather, we must *know* the different types of beauty. There are buildings which are beautiful due to the very fact that they have no artistic pretensions; their beauty is that their construction perfectly suits their purpose. – As soon as a factory has a huge granite plinth, expensive steps with balustrades, painted friezes inside its halls, sculptures and mouldings on its ceilings, this will create ugliness straight away since the means are not appropriate to the end. Furthermore, a factory (or equally a warehouse, abattoir etc.) has ancillary areas – chimneys, pylons etc. – which will only lose their ugliness when stripped of all purpose other than the purely utilitarian. The contrast of brutal chimneys with moulded pilasters, steps and sculpted keystones would be intolerable. In such cases, a single type of beauty comes to the fore:*[1] once again, it is *convenance* (based on the science of beautiful proportions); this will be the beauty of a piece of machinery because no superfluity will distract us from reading the anatomy. We admire the 'temporary beauty' of a locomotive or an aeroplane, a dynamo or a racing car.

{[In the margin:] the illness afflicting architects is conceitedness}

Specially artistic treasures shall only be created where the materials and purpose justify it. The principle must be defined properly! If this means asking a factory to remain a factory, we need to ask what art will contribute for example in the case of an aqueduct, a bridge or a large above-ground reservoir. An aqueduct and a reservoir are capable of eliciting plastic beauty; their cubic volume, the materials

[LCdv 330] 4

{[In the margin:] Clarify}

they are made from – in short, their very being – calls for balance, repetition, will, simplicity: essentially architectural factors. – Towns and cities have understood this and built utilitarian factories; but they have given artistic architects the responsibility for building their bridges, water towers and sheds or aqueducts, which join the rhythm of their firm shapes to the lines of the countryside.

13

There are numerous picturesque or monumental elements, whether delicate or brutally utilitarian, which must harmonise to make a city habitable; how can a geometer tasked with an urban extension master these?

How can he make this task easier for himself, see it all in his mind's eye, since drawing has nothing but pitfalls? We understand that the matter is crushing because it is too complex. We will therefore seek help from auxiliary tools: just as an architect cuts sections through the building he is planning in order to account for its interior life which a plan completely misrepresents – an engineer must express in such clear images the reality of the sites he is to develop.

Clear images! That is what some are seeking by pushing a love of clarity so far that they settle for something unsatisfactory; in how many planning

---

1   From* onwards crossed out, comment above text 'Skip this'.

[LCdv 331]~~12.~~//13//5.

offices is the site represented using plans so simplified that only the roads and major forests, the existing buildings appear on paper! A few rare contour lines are sometimes shown: a token presence, as they are spaced so far apart and drawn in such a pale shade that they *describe* absolutely nothing of the site's relief. The pages are more or less empty, white which will allow the geometer to wield his set square and compasses without pause or any shadow of regret. Streets will therefore go their straight way, doing their best to cut across slopes. – To round off such a process, the geometer would need to mark out all the streets he had just planned on the site itself, using staffs. Once this was done, a committee would be responsible for checking the work. After multiple corrections, requiring tiring days in the sun and rain, the network would be acknowledged as sound.

But how then would one have realised, while using the surveyor's staffs, how these streets embodied space – let alone how effective the road network was?

{[In the margin:] Piazza della Signoria in Florence took 150 years' work to reorganise. – a consolation}

To set out this procedure is to state how useless it is, since it is nothing more than repeating work done on a drawing board, i.e. where all work is uncertain, where chance has ruled supreme. Now all things obey a deep logic and chance has only ever done dirty work in city design.

The German cities which introduced radical reforms in

[LCdv 332] 6

planning their expansions drew up relief plans of their suburbs; the contours are so close together that the plan speaks as eloquently as a perspective view. The trees, paths, streets and forest are picked out. When it comes to competitions, entrants must draw their road networks and squares on a relief plan supplied by the municipality, to avoid those too skilled at 'rendering' performing a sleight of hand. Then projects critique themselves. What is more, it is much more agreeable for an artist to create in full knowledge of the facts, knowing exactly what the site he is offered may yield. The artist will discover, in the lie of the land which would hinder an administrative planning employee, many unexpected solutions in which the extent of his imagination will be combined with a proper respect for the site.

{As a note: The journal *Städtebau* specially founded by Camillo Sitte and Theodor Goecke to disseminate new procedures – continuing the healthy tradition that has been neglected for too long – provides an account of these competitions and illustrates them by reproducing the winning projects.}

{[In the margin:] *Der Städtebau*, Verlag von Ernst Wasmuth, Monatsschrift für die künstlerische Ausgestaltung der Städte, nach ihren wirtschaftlichen, gesundheitlichen und sozialen Grundsätzen.[2]}

The relief plan is therefore something which all administrations wishing to protect their own interests should get drawn up. The time devoted to this lengthy job will not exceed the time lost in the endless trial and error created by the system we described above.

---

2 Monthly journal for the artistic design of cities according to their economic, health-related and social principles.

One additional strategy which seems indisputably effective is to make a model of the land in a town or city

[LCdv 333] 13//7

in any solid, washable material. It would be on a scale which gave each street sufficient width; for example, the scale of 1 centimetre to 1 metre. In the case of large cities, this model would be divided into several segments. An outline could then be drawn on this, in charcoal or wax, of the road layout and squares. How easy it would then be to correctly assess the slopes, the orientation, the light, the wind and monumental aspects then, later, to check the proposed buildings!

A conscientious architect will not finalise the plans for a large building before he has made a model. For he cannot see in space, unless with the routine eye which only a working career can give, all the relationships between volumes which his combinations create. In places where drawing is not enough, where no view is provided of objects in space, one must make up for this artificially.

So the town planner will find a model in a decent scale the best tool for sketching and checking his work at every stage.

14

We are now in a time infinitely more favourable for planning cities than any previous era. We must now

[LCdv 334] 8

plan their expansion in such colossal proportions that we cannot allow chance to come into play. Chance has spoilt more in towns and cities than it has benefited; and although it has sometimes created picturesque beauties, we have yet to define what these beauties are based on. (If we were to suppose that chance constituted the charm of these old cities – when it is merely the intelligent deployment of existing elements – and if one relied on chance to bring beauty as in the olden days, we would be exposed to cruel disappointment; for today among the masses there is no solid artistic tradition; the result would be muddle and confusion.)

{[In the margin, referring to the text in brackets:] {Clean this up!}

The current problem is the lack of a logical programme which consists of anticipating the future, making skilful calculations of a community's future needs. Leaders have a duty to prepare the site on which tomorrow's reality will come to life.

{Sitte pages 150 to 156 + last paragraph 157 [Sitte, in French translation]}[3]

Unfortunately, indifference reigns in administrations. Employees, driven by the spirit which reigns on all official premises, a prudent, conscientious spirit but without enthusiasm, draw squares, rectangles and triangles. Later, these will be churches, prisons, villas, factories, tenement blocks, schools, workers' villages; or a community centre or a market square, or a station, or a courthouse. Large factories flanked by their enormous chimneys which constantly emit black smoke,

[LCdv 335] 14//9.

built 10 years ago in the middle of the countryside, will tomorrow find themselves unexpectedly adorning a district of villas. If an industrialist chooses to acquire a plot very far

---

3 Until LCdv 336, the text has been written up by Jeanneret's mother; after that the text is sketchy, in his own hand. The content of the two parts overlaps by two pages.

from town, but already in the land registry's plans (a plot with an exceptional situation that has marked it out as the centre of a garden city), nothing will prevent a factory being built in this place, with all its corollaries. This wart will send out its roots into the landscape and contaminate everything around it. Then, 50 years or even 10 years later, we will moan: Why did the authorities not protect this site; there were many other building lots surrounding the town which could have been used for this.

The administration asks only one thing: that building lines be respected. When the suburbs are covered with all sorts of buildings erected as and when the fancy takes us, without mutual agreement or master plan, we will then see public buildings, churches, schools, theatres, meeting rooms, etc. slotted into the remaining building lots. At that point, each district will want the planned building, and claim that its own lot is superior. Quarrels between districts and in newspapers will run their course until politicians get involved and the matter moves beyond that framework.

And yet, one might easily create something similar to what the old towns had. Instead of distributing public buildings widely – this one in such a district; that one in another, to compensate – why not group them harmoniously around a square reserved in the best place?

[LCdv 336]
A single, beautiful square is enough to make a town famous!
{discuss buildings which are allowed to spring up in line with adjoining properties}
[Below this, sketch with street fronts of different heights]

[LCdv 337][4] 14//{Follows on from page 9. New}
We found in a batch of old engravings, Fig. [**88, 89**] a view of the town of Breisach in the 17th century, showing in an admirable group the church buildings to the right of the hill, to the left the ensemble of castle, chapel, main building and terraces. Can we not recreate today, with sustained and well-directed effort, what in the Middle Ages was a spontaneous expression? Attempts have been made through generous, brave initiatives with which the official bodies are not acquainted. Let us select the typical example of Hampstead in the London area, the work of the Garden-City-Association (Fig. XVI): A huge estate was bought on the side of a hill. The plan of plots and streets and the house building were entrusted – in order that this city be a model of modernism associated with hygiene, economic, social and aesthetic conditions – to the most modern and famous architects in Britain, Barry Parker, Raymond Unwin, Baillie-Scott, etc. The land was divided up into the most favourable plots; the buildings, either isolated or in groups, form squares and streets which reaffirm the laws set out in the second chapter of the present study. Then, this is the point which brings us back directly to our subject, at the top of the hill (at *A*, the shaded section on Fig. 1), a large area is reserved for public buildings which will become necessary as the City develops, so as to group together those buildings whose nature suits a monumental design in this particular situation.

{[In the margin:] place underneath the Figure that this City is intended for workers.}

---

4 This and subsequent pages mainly contain sketches for the above chapter text: partly for text already drafted, and partly for text not yet drafted. The sketches and drafted text are so closely interwoven that it was not worth separating them.

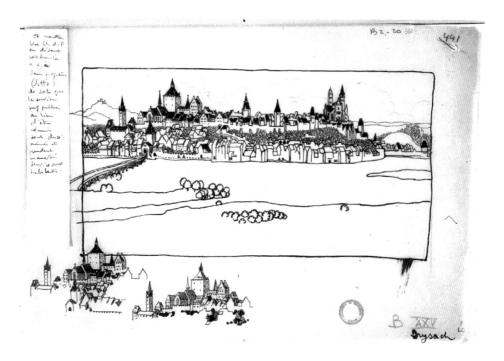

Fig. 88 Breisach on the Rhine. Drawing by Jeanneret, copied from Merian, *Topographia Alsatiae*, p. 6 (B2-20-360 FLC)

This is a first step on the issue of public services, an issue to be studied more closely today as all facts and gestures in the interests of the community must be subjected to a check by the administration.

Continued page 2a₂ ⁞14⁞

[LCdv 338] 14//2a1
But unfortunately indifference reigns in administrations.
In the drafting room, employees cover sheets of paper with geometric shapes.
{[In the margin:] poorly constructed phrase.}
Employees, driven by the spirit which prevails in all official premises – level-headed, conscientious, lacking enthusiasm – draw rectangles, triangles and squares. Later, these will be churches, prisons, villas, factories, tenement blocks, schools, workers' villages; or community centre, or market square, or fairground, or station, or courthouse. Large factories, abattoirs flanked by their enormous chimneys which incessantly emit black smoke – built 10 years ago – in the middle of the countryside, will tomorrow find themselves unexpectedly adorning a district of luxury villas! If an industrialist chooses to acquire a plot very far from town, but already in the land registry plans (a plot whose exceptional situation has marked it out to be the centre of a garden city), nothing will prevent a factory being built in this place, with all its corollaries, railway lines, large chimneys, in this case blast furnaces, workers' tenements. This wart will send out its

Fig. 89 Breisach on the Rhine. From Merian, *Topographia Alsatiae*, p. 6

deep roots into the landscape and contaminate everything around it. Then 50 years or even 10 years later, we will moan: Why has this site not been protected, there were many other building lots surrounding the town with no future which could have been used for this!

{[In the margin:] no authorities with greater foresight}

The present-day administration does not look to the future. It designs straight roads and only asks one

[LCdv 339] 2a2

thing: that building lines be respected! Later, when the suburbs are covered with all sorts of buildings erected as and when, as the fancy takes us, without mutual agreement or master plan, we will then see public buildings, churches, schools or theatres, meeting rooms, administrative buildings slotted into the remaining building lots. Then at that point, each district will want the planned building for itself, claiming that none of the other building lots is equal to its lot, etc. etc. And the district and newspaper quarrels will run their course [Jeanneret sticks the original text over the top, this the continuation of the first version:] until politicians get involved and the building is ceded to the district which has the most elected members from the majority!

And yet, *if the will was there!* ... one might create something similar to that which the old towns had: a square reserved in the best place with a group which would certainly include public buildings. Square and monument belong to all, every district needs them. Why instead of distributing them* widely {*of distributing public buildings}, this one in such a district, that one in another to compensate, {why not arrange them in [arrow pointing to 'a group']} why not arrange all the public services around that same square? – A single, beautiful square may be enough to make a town famous!

This issue of public services should be studied very closely today as all facts and acts in the interests of the masses must be subject to checks by the administration. The centralisation of all efforts is a symbol of our era. The individual is increasingly becoming part of others' lives. The unions, the active driver of the masses, are a second government closer to the people than the government in the constitutional chambers. Through them, each convulsion has a repercussion.

[1st strip of notes, glued on top of the original text:]
14 (3ba)
We found in a batch of old engravings a view of the town of Breisach in the 17th century which shows an admirable group of church buildings, to the right of the hill which accentuates the majestic cube to the left, the ensemble of castle, chapel, main building, cellars and terraces. Can we not recreate today, with sustained and well-directed effort, what in the Middle Ages was a spontaneous expression?*

[2nd strip of notes, glued on top of the original text:]
14 (3a)
to secure beautiful and hygienic rental properties at derisory prices. Straight away, the land on the hill at Hampstead was divided up into the most favourable plots. The buildings, either isolated or in groups, create squares, and perfect streets where the laws we cited in the II part of the present study were confirmed; but here is the point in which we are currently interested: at the peak of the hill, at *A*, a large area is reserved (shaded on our figure) for the public buildings that will become necessary as the city develops. - *

[On the back of one of the notes pages stuck in:]
This is not an insoluble problem; cities where a generous spirit prevails have already addressed it. It is worth stating that these rebellious initiatives did not emerge from within the administrations. It was large firms established in Germany and in Britain which proposed them and saw them through. Our Fig. *XVI* shows what already exists – the new Hampstead city, in the London area, the work of the Garden City Association. The plan was made and the buildings constructed by the most famous artists in Britain: Baillie-Scott, Barry Parker and Raymond Unwin, etc. (Built for well-off workers and others of slender means, the City was designed to [sentence breaks off.]

[LCdv 340] 14//2a 3
in the adjacent masses. These bodies, invoked to become a powerful means of expressing our current desires, will have close ties to public administrations, the active mechanisms for the population's security. Their forward march is supported by the major constitutional body, and at the outset each citizen is – and will increasingly be – called on to have frequent contact with public administrations. Elsewhere the public services – contiguous links in a long, long chain – have shared points of contact. They are fellow members in a complex whole. Thus they would also gain greatly from any centralisation.

Hence the solution to cohesion emerges as: a solid block of all a town's social organisations. It is an eminently favourable solution, which would allow very efficient monitoring of all the services entrusted to people who bear no responsibility, which would enable the constant monitoring of one service by another, thus making for easier transactions along the often very lengthy administrative chain. For the citizen himself, frequently called upon to deal with one of the public offices, this would avoid the constant setbacks which often rightly exasperate him as he is constantly sent from one building to the other.

{[In the margin:] page 3*}

The savings would be considerable

see the notes taken from Montenach on the subject of silhouette, loose sheet

[LCdv 341] goes up to 14 2ba$_3$

Montenach page 188

"...One thing which astounds me is that this marvellous collection of interwoven lines, some at right and some at acute angles, a form which I call the *silhouette* of a city, is given so little consideration nowadays, is studied so insufficiently, championed so poorly.

[...]

The aesthetic value of a town or city lies at least as much in the general impression which it gives as in the 1,000 splendid little details there are to discover.

[...]

I must mention here the quest for a silhouette, which involves designating certain plots for certain buildings, with certain heights to be achieved at all costs.

Nothing is more sublime than an ancient statue, in dazzling white marble, at the end of an *allee* of cypress trees or under the colonnades of a triumphal arch. Conversely, nothing is more pitiful and grotesque than the grand gestures made by a bronze personage set between an omnibus office and a urinal."[5]

[LCdv 342] 14//3

[Following 2 paragraphs crossed out in full:]

Public services of all sorts, social care and assistance, the central police force, fire department, etc. etc., in short all the innumerable cogs in the administration of a state and a city and a district, which these days are spread across many buildings, should be brought together.

This would avoid the constant obstacles which do often face people who have to deal with the administration and are constantly sent from one building to the other. The services themselves, who so often have points of contact as contiguous rings in a long chain, would gain infinitely from this centralisation.

{[In the margin, mark indicating insertion from LCdv 340:] *}

The resulting savings would be enormous, as public buildings, always used as a pretext for architectural experiments, could – because they were grouped in a single cube – exchange 1, 2 or 3 of their luxurious façades for a purely utilitarian façade. The principle of grouping public buildings were adopted, one could assume the growth likely to occur, one could design on a template all the services which would be grouped there in line with the close connections between them. The site deemed the most practical would be indicated, which would allow the most beautiful solution, and building would begin as

---

5 Montenach, *Pour le visage aimé de la patrie*, p. 188.

and when required. The years would pass, bringing new buildings or successive floors, and all would respect the template as adopted. The work would complete itself, taking on a complexity as a unit due to the nuanced styles that reference the progress or regression during the periods when they were created. Then, finally, a powerful block would be born –

[LCdv 343] 4//
this beauty, admired everywhere in famous cities: variety in an imposing unity. Thus the dimensions of this cube with multiple purposes would become colossal. The city would once again have its acropolis, once again its piazetta, once again its Burg [__] – and depending on the architects' imaginations, with lower expenses – but as everyone agreed on a single desired goal, the city could be proud of itself. Then true patriotism would re-emerge, with roots made of reality and not of old ramblings. {[In the margin:] Yes?}
Sitte page 157[6]
our current methods, the new materials… which withstand strain and fire, our capital, our organisation, allow us to realise these beautiful projects. {[In the margin:] Only one thing is missing in this area: belief, and everywhere also a will.}
[Following 2 paragraphs crossed out in full:] But one must have that will! One must understand how to faithfully recognise the errors, and to rid oneself of them at a stroke. The further we advance in our study, the more clearly we can discern these errors. Soon, we will denounce them. But first
{[In the margin:] Let us say again a few words on the respect due to the existing objects, created by artists in a harmonious atmosphere.}

[LCdv 344] 14//14 a//M//1
The matter of respect when the objects in question are ancient works was touched on when we studied the cathedral square in Ulm. The lack of subtlety during a wretched period has been underlined by repair measures which were recently taken in this city. The case of Ulm is indeed typical; nobody will be surprised that it can be seen repeated across Europe, constantly. For the pillaging of ancient cities' artistic heritage has been conducted with alarming gusto throughout the 19th century. It took vehement protests in the art world to put the brake on these ravages. We must recall the brilliant campaign led by artists from all countries when foreign initiatives wanted to undertake a reconstruction of the Parthenon.
The concept of respecting ancient artworks is ill-defined and forgotten by the public, who do not know what to decide. Those at each extreme have theoretical precepts which are equally valuable. Who, then, can state the ideal solution in a steady voice?
{[In the margin:] Must subsequent eras *consolidate* the old works that have become weakened or crippled, or *restore* them, or add to them or even reconstruct them, thus risking all their poetry and their true spirit being lost, and committing the most serious of errors in taste and tact? Or must they let them, the old works, die their beautiful death gently, without troubling them in their death throes?}
This is the current opinion of our administrations, at least nowadays: if large buildings are planned on a site occupied by old houses, the old must fall without hesitation in the face of the *more beautiful* object that is planned. An admirable principle of strength and

---

6 Jeanneret is referring to Camille Martin's translation of Sitte, *Der Städtebau*.

self-confidence; in the lovely eras[7] in which art climbed from strength to strength towards dazzling heights. But today a frightening principle, today poor taste, a lack of artistic education and tact often prevail among those who hold the aesthetic destiny of a city in their hands!

[LCdv 345] 2

Thus gradually the models of *convenance* and beauty are disappearing: when one speaks of re-adapting inconvenient buildings to our current needs, the question changes. It is at least less categorical in terms of consequences than the question of complete destruction. Subtlety will be required here, and what man standing alone, in these days of looking for one's true self, will dare to claim his designs are sound? The cities of Germany have felt this danger. Ulm, with so many others, served to [__][8] and {when the question is a thorny one,} a new system was installed, the results of which are certainly the best obtained to date. This is the system of public competitions, open to all. Each entrant proposes the solution he deems best for conserving that which makes the building in question beautiful. And admittedly it will be easier to construct one's opinion given the number of solutions proposed than where a single project is proposed by a single individual. {[In the margin:] juries are formed of modernist men who have attracted attention through their work, because without the choice made by these juries such competitions would not have the right impact.} The beauties in these cities are therefore at less risk, and this system will often allow major talents to bring forth unexpected solutions, full of beauty.

A case presented itself in Munich where the old Augustinerstock church, which gives the street a grand character and provides a foreground for the Frauenkirche and a companion piece for St. Michaelskirche (see our Fig.[__]), was facing ruin. The large buildings which extend behind the church in question were to be demolished and replaced with a huge building for public administration (a police building).

[LCdv 346] 14 a//3

A competition was launched. Projects arrived from all over Germany. A jury, selected – as is the fashion in Germany nowadays – from among the artistic notables of the modern movement – correctly distinguished the qualities and faults of each project, and in the end performing the work was entrusted to a man whose high level of skill ensures he is beyond reproach. The Augustinerhof [Augustinerstock] was saved and it will always bring the street the strict beauty of its great walls shot through with great circular eyes.

The journal *Städtebau* is always publishing the results of similar competitions. The city of Lübeck had a square – in front of the town hall, if I am not mistaken – to which German renaissance buildings, against the sky for which they were created, brought a paradoxical charm from cut-out gables [**90**]. Two of these tall buildings in the grand style were connected by a small house whose proportions were unsatisfactory. Help was therefore supplied: an adaptation in adequate modern style, this new frontage which was to bring a *respectful* tone to the square. Certainly, in other countries things would have

---

7 Ironically, Jeanneret describes these as 'les belles époques' although the time of writing would later be known as 'La Belle Epoque'.

8 "garder à voir": we cannot translate this.

Fig. 90 Town hall in Lübeck. Postcard, owned by Jeanneret (LC 105-1112-28 BV)

happened more quickly. Either the two large, stylish buildings would have teased the administrative designers so much that they would have knocked them down, or the middle building would have been planned

[LCdv 347] 4
{[In the margin:] delete the competitions, skip}
by whoever, any which way. Once again we see here the effectiveness of public competitions when the prizes are large enough to be worth the effort of wanting them and the jury is made up of major artists with new concepts, and not people to whom the subject is alien, as is regularly the case in Switzerland, or people full of everyday prejudices, as always in France.

We have also seen the lack of tact from administrations when they permit themselves to complete unfinished work from past eras. Once again, this is feasible, but once again, the competitions have to date proven the surest method, *provided the juries are skilled*. The façade of Santa Maria del Fiore in Florence shows precisely how useless competitions are if the jury is incompetent.

The craze for '*freeing up*' ancient buildings has allowed us to see the irreparable mistakes made by people whose inadequate artistic education condemns to making many mistakes. We cited the case of Notre-Dame in Paris, not as the most typical – for there have been other, more flagrant lacks of delicacy in other cities – but as the most painful because the *most beautiful* masterpiece of the glorious mediaeval age found itself devalued.

[LCdv 348] 14 a//5

Administrative peril strikes again in the regularisation of streets in old towns. In the course of this study, we have seen the deep reasons which dictated their layout. Reasons as current today as they were then, because it is the site which was the primary cause of their design.

Little by little, barbaric regularisation takes effect. Nobody suspects a thing, as it happens too slowly. These are constant, senseless sacrifices, for no acceptable reason, offered up to the 'bureaucratic Moloch' every day; curved streets are straightened under a utilitarian pretext, squares strain into perfect geometric shapes, using beauty as an excuse!

The administration no more respects art than it respects the site. Both are incompatible with the way it is currently organised.

We have seen that the systems employed today will not bring about a respect for the site. Neither the working method nor the administrative concepts will allow a city to one day shed its ugliness.

A city such as the old Carlsbad [Karlovy Vary], Fig. XI [**91**], which shows instinctive adaptations of the street plan to the relief of the site, cannot be understood by your average geometer. Schultze-Naumburg and others assure us that while certain modern towns sometimes astonish with

Fig. 91 Carlsbad (Karlovy Vary). Drawing by Jeanneret, copied from Merian, *Topographia Bohemiae*, plate after p. 16 (B2-20-361 FLC)

[LCdv 349] 6

{[In the margin:] abbreviated}

their overly straight streets, impractical for cars, we can be sure that this is not a matter of an especially unfavourable site, but rather of design by a poor dilettante. No longer do either a respect for the beauty of land or a respect for what that land requires instil fear in our geometers, blinded by unacceptable procedure. We say that the beauty of a town, the fruit of properly adapting all utilitarian, public well-being and aesthetic requirements, can only be realised by artists: men who feel the deep-seated responsibility of a vocation where men are passionate about this cause.

Germany and sometimes Britain have permanently removed the question of developing towns and cities from the hands of the unsuited and irresponsible administrators, placing it back in the active, modernist hands of architects who are today at the forefront of the art movement.

[LCdv 350] 15//D//1

For planning cities is an entirely new role; with the most practical strategies at his disposal to lighten his heavy load, anyone given responsibility for presiding over the future advancement of a city will need not only to call on his memory, on all the lessons he has learned from studying earlier works, but must also be cut from artistic cloth, have creative power, poetry.

In planning a vaster building, deciding with the very lines of this plan how this large building's façades will appear, he is a great designer. And – as we said at the beginning – he holds in his hands the beauty or ugliness of the block. If the block itself is not beautiful, all the artists on earth could gather and still be unable to elicit *Beauty*. They might create the most exquisite things, the best-proportioned, the richest, the most colossal, but they would never generate emotion as their plastic edifice would rest on an ugly pedestal.

Equally a sculptor who would only be able to create the detail of a figure, even one who could do so admirably, who did not know the art of grouping things, or even who for reasons unknown was forbidden to design all 10 or 15 figures for the monument on which he was to work; this sculptor who came to create the most beautiful

[LCdv 351] 2

plastic details on top of poorly proportioned volumes, could not for one moment dream of eliciting emotions. His talent is useless; all beauty he adds will accentuate the impression of disharmony, every day he labours will be one more step towards ugliness.

That is the nerve centre of art, *that law of harmony*; it must be understood. Beyond that, all efforts are in vain.

{[In the margin with an arrow pointing up:] See above page 28{6}}

In order to undertake this arduous task, men must have noble souls. For their thankless labour demands a constant sacrifice. Their work will not be completed until years after they designed it. And having applied all the strength in their beings, they will only taste the fruit [of their labour] much later, when they are preoccupied by new concerns. In order to foreshadow a town's future, to discern the sense of forward progress and to satisfy it, they need the spirit of the age with modernist ideas, and a broad imagination. If we are to both change and respect the leftover beauty from ages past, then extreme tact and great knowledge of the laws of beauty will be required. In order to design beautiful streets, beautiful squares, to dictate the proper building height and proportions, to design those moving screens of buildings with changing perspectives, to balance the cubes of buildings in a proper relationship, in mutual interrelation and in a proper quantity given the voids of the walls, squares and gardens,

[LCdv 352] 15/15//3
one needs a painter's sensibility, a sculptor's power.

A brief word will sum it up: the matter of city development must be put back into *living, responsible* hands. It must finally emerge from the administrative mire where all is sterile, *anonymous.* {Sitte 145 *}

{[In the margin:] *This vote is truly important, because it confirms the impossibility of achieving the goal with the help of administrations alone. Why not have historical pictures painted ...[9]}

{end of part I}

[Following paragraph crossed out to the end]

It is making a process, bureaucracy from this substance. We have arrived at this conclusion because each page of this study pushed us to. We had to make it short and not very technical so that everyone can read it.

We did not intend when beginning this study that our conclusions would need to be so categorical, but now having brought the question back to reality, that is to a question of utilitarian aesthetics, to our modern life, the repeated research which was needed prevents us from softening the verdict. There is a risk here. In Switzerland today, the time to follow the German administrations in their evolution is now or never. The future of a city is a question.

page 145 (Sitte)

{[In the margin:] too much of a live issue to be resolved by a dead organisation. Sitte in a conclusive page will dispense with the need for any further comment.}

[LCdv 353] [MA 242]
The Art of Building Cities[10]

[...] the fact that through official channels one cannot design a monumental church building, or paint a historical scene, or compose a symphony.

This is just as true as the fact that through official channels one cannot design a monumental church building, or paint a historical scene. Works of art cannot be created by a committee or through office activity, but only by a single individual; an artistically effective city plan is also a work of art and not merely an administrative matter. This is the crux of the whole situation. Granting that each individual member of a municipal building office, by virtue of his ability and knowledge, his numerous travels and other studies, as well as his innate artistic sensibility and lively imagination, could design an excellent city plan, yet several in association in the office will never produce anything but dry, pedantic stuff that smacks of the dust of documents. The head of the

---

9 Quotation not attributed by Jeanneret, from the French translation of Sitte's Städtebau, *L'Art de Bâtir les Villes. Notes et réflexions d'un architecte traduites et completées par Camille Martin* (Genève: Eggiman, 1902), p. 146.

10 Jeanneret mentions p. 145 in the French translation of Sitte's book *Städtebau* by Camille Martin; in the English translation by Crasemann-Collins, this part is on page 260. Collins/Crasemann-Collins, *Camillo Sitte: The Birth of Modern City Planning*, p. 225. Jeanneret notes down and attaches the quotation, see LCdv 353-354.

office has, of course, no time to do the job himself, because he is inundated with meetings, reports, committees, administration, etc.; his subordinate,

[LCdv 354]
on the other hand, would not dare to have ideas of his own; he must stick to the official norms, ... and his personal ambition, his individuality as a creative and sensitive being, and his enthusiasm for a thing for which he alone will be responsible before the world do not, for reason of his official function, enter into the matter. –
(Camillo Sitte (page 146) –

Material for '*On Possible Strategies*'
[LCdv 355] 5
The sphere of city planning, very particularly that of the major capitals, with its infinitely complex requirements, provided the motivation to create special classes at the fine art academy (Seminar für Städtebau an der Königlichen Hochschule Berlin, Prof. D. J. Brix and Felix Genzmer, Hofbaurat). This is proof of the urgent need for more satisfactory solutions than those with which we had believed we could be content.
Many of the more interesting submissions consisted of architectural proposals made by architects to the municipal authorities in various towns and cities. One could sense the will from all quarters to bring taste into administrative matters. Thus a proposal was accepted from a Darmstadt architect to build a church along with all the neighbouring buildings.[11] Thus a building for which laudable effort was expended was united with its surroundings.
{[In the margin:] thus he succeeded in something rare these days, in putting the building he dreamed up into a perfectly harmonious atmosphere.}
Pick up from 5 a
Here at the *Ton-Kalk-Zement Ausstellung*, an exhibition of prime importance for demonstrating the plastic qualities of the most modern materials, we found gathered together a whole series of plans for water towers, reservoirs, aqueducts, in which the heads of the new school showed the capacity for beauty in these new edifices, habitually left in the very practical but insufficiently artistic hands of engineers.

[LCdv 356] 6
But here, in a room at the *Städtebauausstellung* were plans of very particular interest. These were being exhibited by the *Berliner Waldschutzverein* (Berlin society for forest protection) in the aim of showing the unfortunate way in which until now the very characterful forests surrounding Berlin have been destroyed.[12] And those few leaves of paper, which launched an appeal to the providence of those who have any love for their city, make us think that we really need a local society for the protection of trees and the natural beauty immediately surrounding our towns, in the aim of opposing depredations and vandalism by our bureaucrats or individuals. Collective protests would often manage

---

11 *Le Corbusier – Carnets de Voyage d'Allemagne 1910–1911*, ed. Giuliano Gresleri (Milan: Electa, 1994), Carnet 1, p. 74: "Prof. Putzen, Darmstadt planned a church and all the surrounding buildings. 1170." The numbers are catalogue numbers; Putzen's project is the Darmstadt Lutheran church.
12 *Le Corbusier – Carnets de Voyage d'Allemagne 1910–1911*, Carnet 1, p. 77: "There is a *Berlin Waldschutz Verein* 234 (we probably have a *Bäumeschutzverein* ourselves)."

to intimidate these overly [__] administrations and to save what little beauty unfortunate designs have thus far allowed to remain.

On all the advertising columns this last week of the exhibition for art in the cities, we could see appeals to the people of Berlin: "Berlin made beautiful by flowers![13] Call for entries! Competition to decorate balconies with flowers. Berlin is renowned for possessing many balconies. The competition provides the possibility of showing residents and outsiders what a powerful and joyous effect can be obtained by generally decorating balconies, windows and also whole street fronts on business premises. That is why the *Gross-Berlin* administration urges its population to create and maintain beautiful decorations, not only so that beautiful street images are created, but also in order to procure for the people, after work, intimate corners for recreation. It is why the administration hopes all citizens will grasp with joy the opportunity to beautify their home towns by their own means and in so doing confirm Berlin's reputation as one of the world's most beautiful cities ... ... (the jury will be formed of architects, gardeners, artists and writers)" ... Such competitions have already been held and have had a remarkable educational force. Nowhere have we seen, as in Berlin, an opportunity to admire the perfect taste, distinction and strength of using flowers in support of architecture.

[Several lines illegible]

[LCdv 357] 7
[In front of the whole paragraph up to "original atmosphere" is: "put at the end".]

Collective efforts! That is the major force in the era. In Germany, Britain and Austria there is the will to work together, instead of the craze for outrageous individualism which reigns among Parisian architects and which makes them exhaust themselves and flag, spreading their efforts too thinly, drowning in the mass of banal products, this disharmony giving them the seal of insignificance. Huge capital, mobilised by [__] stock companies, significant sites of some hundreds of hectares are bought by either municipalities or limited companies so they are shielded from speculation. (*Put a note at the bottom of the page, the case of Ulm). The greatest architects are therefore called upon to work together.[14] They accept with joy: this matter is worth studying as it aims to resolve the issue of felicitous housing, a happiness due to and obtained by an entirely original atmosphere.

---

13 *Le Corbusier – Carnets de Voyage d'Allemagne 1910–1911*, Carnet 2, pp. 104–106: "Berlin im Blumen Schmuck Aufruf Balkonschmuck Wettbewerb [Berlin decorated with flowers, Call for decorated balconies, Competition]. Berlin already holds the reputation for having the most balconies of all cities. The competition provides an opportunity to show residents and outsiders what an excellent and joyful effect can be achieved by general decoration of balconies, windows as well as the buildings and façades of businesses. That is why the private Greater Berlin administration is calling for beautiful Schmuckanlagen [decorative features] to be maintained, not simply to beautify the city overall but also to procure for the people, after their day's work, corners for recreation. That is why the administration hopes all bourgeois [we suspect this is a calque on German 'Bürger', i.e. all citizens rather than just the bourgeoisie] will gladly seize the opportunity to beautify their Vaterstadt [home town] by their own means and in so doing confirm Berlin's reputation as one of the world's most beautiful cities. Competition 3 M.[ark] to register. Enter orally or in writing before the 15 August. Judging will take place from 29 August to 3 September. Jury of garden architects, artists, writers."

14 Jeanneret finds the 'Ulm case' in: Hans von Berlepsch-Valendàs, *Bodenpolitik und gemeindliche Wohnungsfürsorge der Stadt Ulm* (Munich: Reinhardt, 1910). In this 46-page book, Berlepsch-Valendàs uses his knowledge of new English workers' settlements to demonstrate how the city of Ulm runs its land policy and creates new residential areas for workers.

Thus in the areas surrounding major cities, London, Berlin, Munich etc., vast garden cities where everything that makes for a comfortable life is available, where the most modest of working men can raise his family in guaranteed conditions of happiness and hygiene. What an admirable and eminently philanthropic problem of the common good these garden cities address. This is where the Swiss public authorities should act with vigour to protect the most advantageous sites against often shameless speculation. The trailblazers were – essentially practical – British people. Today the trail is [___]: and the effort of several noble economists assisted by valiant artists has been acknowledged.

[LCdv 358] 8

But to study garden cities would require a new booklet and here we can only alert the authorities and ask that they deal with this question, a particularly urgent question in industrial cities (*as a note the opening of the first congress in Britain): The *Städtebau-Ausstellung* in Berlin dedicated entire halls to garden cities. We noted in particular those at Hampstead in England (catalogue N° 433), the Krupp foundation in Essen (*as a note catalogue 467), the modern city of Hellerau on the immediate outskirts of Dresden. (225) The catalogue states on the issue of the latter: The extent of the intended site for the garden city of Hellerau is 140 hectares extending [___] to the north of Dresden: designed by Prof. Riemerschmid (from Munich), will be decorated architecturally by the best artists. The land and buildings remain the property of the [garden city] society, which will devote 4% interest on the growing cumulative profits to good works. Homes with a rent of between 280 and 3,000 marks will be for rent only.

The garden city society is established as a GmbH whereas the Landesversicherungsanstalt is liable for the building association which will construct the small houses up to a rental value of 600 marks. Of the model on display, the streets Pillnitz-Moritzburg and am Grünen Zipfel have been built. Besides that, in other places 2 groups of small houses by Hermann Muthesius were erected, and 1 group by Henri Tessenow, as well as villas by Theodor Fischer, Hermann Muthesius, Baillie-Scott, and Henri Tessenow. The marketplace and the hotel which includes [Sentence breaks off here.]

[As material for On Possible Strategies, see also LCdv 447–449.]

Part II

Critical Application

La Chaux-de-Fonds

[LCdv 359] IInd PART//Critical Application.//La Chaux-de-Fonds.

[LCdv 360] 1
The town of La-Ch. de Fds.//Its current development and its extension plan.
Comparison of the strategies employed with those set out in part I.
"The word sounding the death knell to the harmonious aspects of cities is regularisation."
This is how Schultze-Naumburg puts it: "At the same rate as an understanding of beauty is
disappearing, the grace of cities is also going. – Anyone who has benefited from reading the
above pages will know how necessary it is to soften rigid lines, how much an exception
appears beautiful and pleasing. The prime cause of all this regularisation is that any trace of
sentiment, of love for living and local things, has disappeared in the councils which adminis-
ter our towns and cities. These councils no longer wish to acknowledge their own good old
natural town with its special customs and beauty; these upstarts are ashamed of what they
call its nudity: its unvarnished simplicity. Their only dream is to make it exactly resemble
the universal model of the city. So they want it to be all straight and regular, and they cannot
attain this magnificent goal by any route other than their great straight streets. For as long as
the street front adopts a living form, they cannot make buildings line up like soldiers along
a front. And then the streets must also be as wide as those in cities, for the image of a great
brouhaha in the capital city is the one that rumbles and buzzes around their heads."[1]
"That is why in the provinces the mania for regularisation and degradation rages. Each
little village wants its new, well-defined straight street

[LCdv 361] 1a
and there are even states where the procedures for drawing with a tracing-line are firmly
established, even down to the tiniest village. This is an everyday occurrence with streets,
which for no valid reason are straightened up and drawn perfectly straight. And if
a building unfortunately finds itself on the new route, the planners will not stop for anything so minor. They will take the street straight through the block."[2]
Indeed this is a widespread problem.

---

1 Jeanneret translates from Schultze-Naumburg, *Kulturarbeiten. Vol. IV Städtebau* (Munich: Callwey, 1909),
  p. 165/168f.; cf. LCdv 406–408.
2 Schultze-Naumburg, *Kulturarbeiten Städtebau*, p. 170, cf. LCdv 405–408.

La Chaux-de-Fonds was a mountain village which had developed peacefully over the centuries, until 5 May 1794. A terrible fire broke out which destroyed everything and the development plan still applied today must be traced back to that very date, 1794.

The population was wiped out as this terrible misfortune took hold. Yet action was needed, a new town had to be made to rise from the ashes. Nobody thought themselves worthy of taking the initiative to plan the new town. 9 days after the fire a petition was sent to the government in Neuchâtel, asking it to send men capable of drawing up a new street plan; 8 days later, engineers from Neuchâtel submitted the new plan to the local authority and it was accepted. That was on 22 May 1794.

The new plan was for the town hall square and the streets opening onto it, up to the Hôtel de la fleur de Lys in one direction and the Rue St Pierre in the other. The streets remain more or less unchanged to the present day.

Of all the existing streets, these are the best designed. And yet they have a crippling inherent

[LCdv 362] 2)

flaw. Geometers from Neuchâtel {so strangers not at all familiar with the challenging climate and land} planned them in *a few days*. And their plan was an administrative plan in which only the set square played a role. It was an unfortunate design because it dictated all the town's subsequent development. Now the development in question is the most flagrant nonsense one can imagine.

There will be no need to discuss this matter extensively.

Nobody in La Chaux-de-Fonds is under any illusion: it has been established, and we have accepted, that the town is ugly; not knowing who was at fault, people have ended up giving credence to the axiom that only the climate is at fault, that architecture and fine art have no place at 1,000 metres' altitude. An unprecedented lie which has been lent credence by people acting in their own interests.

In the meantime, the town is developing intensively. Industrialism is bringing with it a whole trail of woes, and no compensation will make the situation more tolerable. The fact is becoming more widespread these days that those who have worked and made their fortunes then desert this ugly land and go to live elsewhere, taking with them the riches extracted from the land. Yet 45,000 souls live on these streets and, according to the forecasts in the new extension plan, later perhaps 80,000 could not find a nicer place to live.

Let us study the master plan, Fig. [**92**]. The first design by the outside engineers has been drawn in solid black, including the country lanes and roads which led to the village. Those lanes and roads which will be sacrificed to the new extension plan, but which still exist, are indicated by a wide black dashed line.

[LCdv 363] 3)

All the public buildings, i.e. those that might justify an aesthetic approach, are marked by a black dot with white stripes.

We mentioned 'nonsense' above; it is only right that we state the reasons why.

There is not a single street that is not perfectly straight, and it was the geometer's constant concern to lengthen them as far as possible. *On the whole map of La Chaux-de-Fonds there is not a single layout which creates beautiful views. But there are plenty that* bring with them *boredom and ugliness*, to tell the truth these are the only layouts there are. {[In the margin:] Examining the map does nothing to temper this assessment.} The principles which guided the geometer throughout his work are so rudimentary they can be summed up in 3 clauses: exclusive use of the chequerboard, oblique intersections,

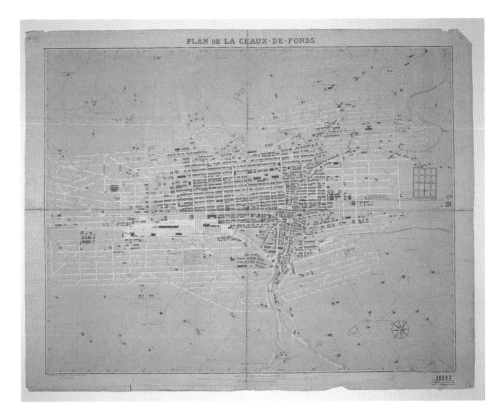

Fig. 92 Town map of La Chaux-de-Fonds, 1908 (FLC 30283)

open squares. There is nothing besides these: geometers have never concerned themselves with placing emphasis on a building. In the whole town, there is *not a single public or private building which is presented in the favourable conditions which we set out in Part I.* Except the Temple National which is the oldest building.

But there is a more serious matter.

Logical planning models did exist. On such hilly land, farmers had made roads with a curve which was perfectly in keeping with the nature of the land. These roads have all but disappeared; those that remain, marked as dotted lines on the map, are due to disappear when the planned streets are built.

It will further be noted that these roads all cross the administrative diagrams at a diagonal. This is typically instructive. The absolute mania for having only straight lines is perfectly characterised by the streets which climb hills (the slopes of Le Pouillerel, Les Cretêts, or Les Arètes), which are *all* designed to climb *as directly as possible.* And we ask ourselves how heavy cars will reach some districts, especially: Les Mélèzes; the one above La Combe Grieurin; and Le Réservoir.

[LCdv 364] 4)

Architects who have been involved with building in the Rue de la Montagne and Les Tourelles districts know how teams of horses suffered on these streets with the steepest slopes.

At La Chaux-de-Fonds everyone laments the rigours of the climate which mean the trees struggle to grow and only reach any size when they are a hundred years old.

On our map we have drawn all the *allees* of large trees which have to date resisted vandalism by both individuals and geometers. Not one will remain standing. Everything is being sacrificed. All the trees will fall, and everyone will lament it, but no-one will protest.

In the entire town, there are 3 parks and gardens which, being jealously guarded by their owners, have thus far been sheltered from expropriation. However the planning office has already laid out the streets which will dismember them. La Loge park – in the centre of our map – will have 2 streets cross it. Le Chalet park – to the right of the map – has already taken a hit in the plans. The Les Crêtêts park (to the left on the map), almost entirely planted by a passionate nature lover some 50 years ago, will also be skewered if its owners make one false move, as a street which will cut it in two is already being planned.

The superb square arrangement of large limes to the top left of our map, made beautiful by the enormous shade, a plateau which in the past was admirably situated but is now completely compromised by the large apartment blocks commissioned on its south side, will fall at the first hurdle. The *allee* of young, already large trees flanked with 2 superb plane trees, which leads up to Les Mélèzes (to the bottom left of our Fig. [__])

[LCdv 365] 4a

will go to make way for a street layout most lamentably adapted to its terrain.

Now place on page 5A. Then take up 5 again above, with illustrations next.[3]

[LCdv 366] 5

{[In the margin:] A}

We provide a series of views of La Chaux-de-Fonds which we contrast with those taken in other towns and cities which applied artistic considerations. We always try to contrast the solutions to 2 similar problems. And as a general rule we carefully avoid views of rich, sumptuous monuments as we would like to prove that a goal can be achieved with the same financial means. We would have liked to take only those lessons that our beautiful Swiss towns teach in abundance, so as to stay within a very local setting. To that end we

[LCdv 367] 6)

approached over 20 Swiss municipalities to obtain several good shots and some situation plans which could provide effective demonstrations. Yet the outcome of this was rather poor. The views we were sent were merely postcards, not sufficiently well made, which we deemed impossible to use. We were therefore obliged to fall back on our own resources, and that is why we used our travel photographs. Please excuse their limited success.

As for the views of La Chaux-de-Fonds itself, those are not taken in the ugliest parts of town – we do not wish to play such a childish game – but instead in the largest

---

3 In line with Jeanneret's instructions, manuscript pages MA 198 (bottom) and MA 199 (top to middle) follow here, then MA 198 (top) and MA 199 (bottom), numbered LCdv 366–371.

streets and the newest districts. The lesson learned from comparison with the streets in other towns will be so brutal that we will once again be accused of having shown bias. We would be wrongly accused, as the published views of La Chaux-de-Fonds reflect reality, and it is precisely *this reality* which is at fault, and not the lens on our Kodak.

page 5. What does the future have in store for us? . . . . . . etc.

[LCdv 368]

What does the future hold in store for us? Hundreds of straight streets, and all of uniformly, eternally equal width. On both sides of the valley, all the streets form perspective lines, never enclosed, and continue to be oriented exactly in the direction of the very strongest wind: west-east. In summer, everyone complains about the swirls of dust which rage on days when the foehn blows. In winter, nothing stops the flurries of snow. Quite the reverse, the streets channel the wind which sweeps through without encountering the least obstacle. We have seen that, in all the towns where enclosed aspects had created comfort and beauty, straight streets of medium width were very short. 500-metre lengths were rarely seen.

Here are several planned lengths for absolutely rectilinear streets; lengths likely to be increased yet further with a future extension plan:

Rue du Progrès 1800 metres in straight line currently 600m

Rue Numa Droz

Rue

Rue

Rue

Rue

[LCdv 369]

List of streets:

Rue du Progrès:	2,740 m in straight line, currently 1,400m
Rue du Temple Allemand	1,900 " " " " " 1,280m
Rue du Nord	1,700 currently in 2 sections of 440 left (Le Locle) 680 right
" Numa Droz	1,840 due to be extended, with a slight, insignificant bend, to 2,560m. by the new Rue Breguet and thanks to the demolition of a building.
Rue Leop. Rob[ert]	1,680 m extending in a straight line into a narrower street of indeterminate length (road to Le Locle.)
New *Rue de la Réformation*	2,160 [m] planned.
" " " " République	2,070 [m] "
" Rue des Crétêts	2,000m approx. and extending further –

[LCdv 370]

and we must add that in order to follow the layout adopted on the geometer's drawing board, expropriations and the demolition of buildings add up to: [__]

(a solution which is really uneconomical, for everyone knows that this type of operation is never beneficial to local areas)

[LCdv 371]

Fig.s *ABCDEF* show the views of our largest streets running lengthways. Not one is closed off at the end. Many have public buildings, but none of these beautifies the view for a moment. Fig. *A* (Rue de la Serre) [**93**], the Hôtel Communal cannot be seen on the left. Further down, 2 buildings which motivated very special architectural experiments, the Synagogue and the Contrôle Fédéral are absolutely invisible. Once again these same 3 buildings should feature in Fig. *B* [**94**], yet the top of their roofs can scarcely be seen.

[LCdv 372] 7)

The Rue du Parc, Fig. *C*, has the rear façades of the latter two buildings discussed immediately above. They still fail to stand out in the street silhouette. The Rue de la Paix, Fig. *D* [**95**] only offers its staccato and ever-interrupted line of façades, ending in a slight depression on the Place du 1er Mars, which is flanked to the worst possible effect by buildings which the area of fully parallel streets forces to spring up around the square in complete isolation from one another.

La Rue Numa [-Droz] has 2 very large secondary schools, another smaller one and finally a church. Once again, none of these 4 buildings is obvious in the street view.

We pass by the following streets – [Rue] du Progrès with 8 large public buildings – 3 very large secondary schools, 3 churches, 1 chapel, 1 school with a large astronomy

Fig. 93 Synagogue in the Rue de la Serre, La Chaux-de-Fonds. Photo, ca. 1900 (AS-P2-28 BV)

Fig. 94 Rue de la Serre in La Chaux-de-Fonds. Photo, ca. 1900 (AS-P2-48 BV)

dome – the view of this (*Q*) highlights its problematic contribution to beauty. – La Rue du Temple Allemand with 6 public buildings, of which we believed it was pointless to provide a view since the 5 previous images will suffice to illustrate the unsuccessful use of plastic strategies, ends the area of straight streets. Finally, Fig. *E* shows a street parallel to the previous ones (La Rue du Nord) which is currently enclosed, but with a line of perspective that will be revised in a few years by the proposed demolition of the 2 old buildings which enclose it! (One of these buildings is a rare specimen of our national architecture.)

The largest street in town, where all the most expensive buildings are gathered, suffers the same fate as its poorer relations. Fig. *F* [**96, 97**] in fact shows the eternal perspective narrowing of the 2 parallel, infinitely long street fronts. Buildings that cost an enormous amount such as the Nouvelle Caisse d'Épargne,

Fig. 95 Rue de la Paix in La Chaux-de-Fonds. Postkarte, 1912 (CP-438 BV)

[LCdv 373] 8)

Federal bank, new Post office – an enormous 2 million [Franc] building – and the The-atre, old Post office, so many private buildings on which no expense has been spared, try in vain to make this street into a grand artery. The result remains absolutely poor, for none of the buildings stands out. The street continues in a straight line for some hun-dreds of metres (in fact, because its continuation into the ancient route cantonale was slightly curved, its curve was corrected a few years ago). – Then here is what the geom-eters plan to finish off 1,500 metres of rectilinear route: a Y-shaped fork, i.e. one of the ugliest strategies imaginable.

Illustrations *A B C D E F* to be placed here

(*Then text:*) But let us study the large cross streets, those that climb the slopes along the 'fall line'.

Fig. 96 Post office in the Rue Léopold-Robert, La Chaux-de-Fonds. Postcard, ca. 1900 (CP-1934 BV)

Fig. 97 Rue Léopold-Robert in La Chaux-de-Fonds. Postcard, ca. 1900 (CP-1396 BV)

Fig. 98 Rue du Collège Primaire in La Chaux-de-Fonds. Photo, ca. 1900 (HP-P2-86 BV)

Here the inflexible chequerboard strategy provides views the more the streets are cut through. For where the blocks have a very elongated rectangular shape, the longitudinal streets benefit from their relative continuation in the long sides of the rectangles. Here, from the bottom to the top of the [cross] street, there will be a rather ugly succession of individual, straight façades, each separated by an empty space double the width of the fronts.

Fig. *G* [**98**], Rue du Collège Primaire is successfully enclosed by the façade of a secondary school, a façade which would have stood out if it were high, but which here only has a mediocre effect because it only extends

[LCdv 374] 9)

widthways. We wanted to contrast these unsatisfactory enclosing walls, which do not succeed in continuing the line of buildings, with a very typical and simple example taken from [Schultze-] Naumburg.

But in Fig. *H*, the street [Rue de l'Avenir?] comes to an end against a sudden increase in incline, with no provision for any of the mitigation which we discussed in the first part of this work. The street in Fig. *I* [Rue de l'Avenir] is closed at its end, which is good, but is once again subject to the disadvantages of the chequerboard and appears cut through in an ugly way. The Synagogue which could have become a splendid motif enters awkwardly into the overall view and merely creates a disagreeable, unbalanced impression. As for the – surely costly – enclosure which surrounds the building in the foreground, it could have given rise to more architecturally advanced experiments.

Finally, we would like to note in Fig [*K*] the successful ending of an awfully ugly street, Rue du Ier Mars. We would contrast this with the view of the neighbouring street [Rue du Stand?] where the most beautiful plastic elements, stairs, supporting wall, and to top it all off a large building, have been absolutely neglected by a total lack of both thinking in the round and harmony. The same slacking and infringing the laws of beauty are stark in Fig. *L* where the monumental stairway, flanked by its large supporting walls and dominated by a building

[**LCdv 375**] 10)
enclosing the view, would have provided a renaissance architect with the opportunity to create the purest of masterpieces.
Fig. *G. H. I. J. [K] L*
(Then text.)
Land which is as hilly as that in La Chaux-de-Fonds would allow very varied and very splendid solutions. But the incomprehensible adoption of the chequerboard strategy on such unruly land has killed everything and instead heaped ugliness upon ugliness.
Fig. *M* [**99**] shows a very well designed street, it was an old route cantonale that existed before the fire and which due to special considerations the local authority geometers were obliged to preserve. But even if a street is good in itself, how can one assess the plan which obliges straight and fully parallel streets to cut across it every 60 metres, making the tops of housing blocks line up as depicted in our Figure?

Fig. 99 Rue de la Balance towards Rue du Versoix in La Chaux-de-Fonds. Photo, ca. 1900 (AS-P2-39 BV)

{[In the margin:] Set against with drawing of Nuremberg}

It is here, drawing on the very ill which created this unfortunate chequerboard, that use could have been made of façade projections, as discussed.

Yet the type of lot adopted by the geometers in La Chaux-de-Fonds is the one with the disadvantages stated on page [LCdv 66]. This approach had been adopted some 60 years ago when space was not in short supply, and when buildings were only constructed in isolation from one another. Enclosing and retaining walls were required, and one cannot criticise those walls strongly enough – at that time, they lacked emphasis because they lacked trees to be their crowning glory. Figure *N* shows the old architecture, not at all bad: quite the reverse. It feels infinitely less parvenu than everything else which for the past 20 years has grown up without a care for tradition. Thus enclosing walls should be subject to special care and attention from master builders.

Fig. *M N*

{Then text.}

[LCdv 376] 11)

Which public squares exist now, and which will in future? Firstly there are the two old ones: the town hall square Place de l'Hôtel de Ville is the most beautiful, although it is already excessively interrupted. The 'marketplace' is not badly planned, but its construction has allowed all sorts of buildings which are hardly harmonious.

Fig. 100 Place de l'Ouest in La Chaux-de-Fonds. Photo, ca. 1900 (AS-P2-88 BV)

There are the recent squares, like Place de l'Ouest; all the squares required in future will be like this. For the extension plan *does not make provision for even a single public square.* These squares will be made in the same way as the square with which we are currently concerned, a view of which is shown [**100**] in Fig. *O*. One of the plots which was intended for building will be used, simply by taking out the buildings at its core. Neither the land nor the orientation nor the buildings which border it have been considered. These will arise by chance, as everything else has arisen.

The Place de l'Ouest provides the least advantageous plan we have identified for a small town square, and its fountain placed in the geometric centre is a sort of signature for official building works. Hence all future squares in La Chaux-de-Fonds will be of this type, where 8 streets open up all 4 corners of the square.

One square of the same type, called Jacquet Droz, Fig. *P* [**101**], shows that the beauty which the voting office building seemed (on paper) bound to bring has, quite simply, robbed it of its character as a square. As this experiment has nevertheless seduced the administrators of our streets, the marketplace saw a strange little building arise in the middle 3 years ago; the beauty it brings remains problematic, as are its use and the purpose of the dormer windows which 'decorate' its roof.

Fig. *O. P*

Fig. 101 Place Jaquet Droz in La Chaux-de-Fonds. Photo, ca. 1900 (P2-501 BV)

[LCdv 377] 12)

That brings us to the subject of emphasising buildings.

Just as no public squares were planned here, equally no plans have been made for siting monumental buildings. The chequerboard extends its rows across peaks and troughs, and all public buildings will be sited just as those already built have been, i.e.:

if the building is of major importance, in the geometric centre of a lot. This was the case with all the large secondary schools: Ouest, Charrière, Primaire; for the Grammar School, the Synagogue, the Contrôle [Fédéral]. The building will therefore need 4 decorated façades, costly stone plinths; large cornices must run round all 4 sides. Then the great size of the void surrounding the building will give it a shrunken, denuded feel. What is more it will never play a part in the street view: take for example the large Grammar School building, to the left of Fig. *Q*. [**102**].

The building will occupy the outside edge of the lot, like the Mechanical Watchmaking School to the right of Fig. *Q* [**103, 104**]. Once again, 3 or 4 of its façades will by necessity be similar, and once again no such building will play a role in the street view. This is how the current churches have been sited: the [Temple] Indépendant, Catholic Church, La Croix-Bleue and l'Église de l'Ouest. This is how all churches will be sited in future. {[In the margin:] put Temple Allemand on photo as good [example] [**105**]}.

The building will appear squashed between 2 adjoining buildings. Only 1 or 2 façades will be required here, but once again this façade will never

Fig. 102 Collège Industriel in La Chaux-de-Fonds. Photo, ca. 1900 (AS-P2-76 BV)

Fig. 103 Ecole d'Horlogerie in La Chaux-de-Fonds. Photo, ca. 1900 (AS-P2-74 BV)

Fig. 104 Ecole d'Horlogerie in La Chaux-de-Fonds. Photo, ca. 1900 (B2-4663 BV)

Fig. 105 Temple Allemand in the Rue du Collège Primaire, La Chaux-de-Fonds. Photo, ca. 1900
(AS-P2-86 BV)

[LCdv 378] 13)
in any way benefit the street view. That is the case for the Palais Judiciaire.

All these buildings erected at great cost, which are often the source of more or less successful plastic experiments, *do not in any way at all benefit the beauty of the town* because no
street curves inwards to emphasise the buildings' façades, because no square is planned
according to a procedure which allows one to *see* buildings. There isn't a single view in the
whole town of La Chaux-de-Fonds which differs from that of a long rectilinear corridor with
open doors, and the vanishing line of the street fronts means one cannot see [the façade]
which covers them. The Temple Indépendant, Fig. *R* [**106**] cannot be seen from any street. It
is only at the point when one is on its doorstep that one can see it, isolated in empty surroundings, [apparently] shrunken. In Augsburg, the cathedral admirably encloses the street
view. [**107**]. The new Hôtel des Postes does not bring the Rue Léop[old] Rob.[ert] any new
beauty, it merely lends the area of its façade to the impression of perspective vanishing [**96**].
But on the issue of this enormous edifice, one might be permitted to ask how the station
square will be finished off, flanked as it is by the new station, the new post office and
the excessively tall apartment block Hôtel de la Gare. These 3 buildings alone cost
almost 8 million and the result is an awful, inconsistent square where the total lack of an
overview hits home. Fig. *S* [**108, 109**]

Fig. 106 Temple Indépendant in La Chaux-de-Fonds. Photo, ca. 1900 (AS-P2-83 BV)

Fig. 107 St. Ulrich in Augsburg. Photo by Jeanneret, 1910 (LC 108-315 BV)

Fig. 108 Place de la Gare in La Chaux-de-Fonds. Photo, ca. 1900 (P2-43 BV)

Fig. 109 Place de la Gare with Hôtel de la Poste in La Chaux-de-Fonds. Photo, ca. 1900 (P2-83 BV)

Fig.s *Q. R. S.*
But let us finish this study with a look at what the current realities allow us to foresee in future. For this purpose, we will satisfy ourselves with several views of that district – which seems to be the district of the future: l'Ouest. The expensive land is there. The luxury villas are there, and the sun, proximity to major arterial roads, as well as the countryside. The past 5 years have allowed us to foresee that the new La Chaux-de-Fonds will be there. Let us move through the streets of this new

[LCdv 379] 14)
place.
Fig. T_1 was taken from the future construction site, looking towards the workers' district built over the past 15 years. [**110, 111**]. On the very edge of this area of large tenement blocks are the richest villas in town, Fig. T_3, those on which hundreds of thousands of francs have been spent. In the centre of Fig. T_1 we can see two of these villas. It shows them surrounded by enormous new apartment cubes which speculation has erected there comfortably. Let us now turn to the new terraces, and take the view T_2. Right in the middle of this land, virgin scarcely 5 years ago, where an admirably organised district could have been built, rises the enormous chimney of an enormous electricity plant. The plant and all its corollaries, plume of black smoke, pylon and other accompaniments. We move on to view W_1 through this future land, on which speculation has already erected something frightful, and we end with Fig. W_2, the very centre of this beautiful expanse, so well situated, which this business-focused town could have made into the loveliest of districts. In such an atmosphere, how can one hope that a bit of beauty may be born?
The excess of freedom here is precisely what has created slavery. The most tyrannical dependency of the least wealthy on the most wealthy, or the boldest or the least scrupulous.

Fig. 110 New buildings above the town centre, La Chaux-de-Fonds. Photo, ca. 1900 (P2-806 BV)

NO. 65 · SCHÜTTEL, ÉDITEUR, CHAUX-DE-FONDS   La Chaux-de-Fonds - Les Tourelles

Fig. 111 Les Tourelles in La Chaux-de-Fonds. Photo, ca. 1900 (CP-49 BV)

Fig.s T_1 T_2 W_1 W_2
Above the first villas we just discussed, the land rises sharply and forms a natural terrace which 10 years ago – when the site for this area was still fields – had all the hallmarks of being suitable for building villas. The edge of the terrace was crowned with small houses where the living was peaceful and the atmosphere provided a rest from the arid city streets. Yet nothing could stop the

[LCdv 380] 15
tenement blocks already advancing from the valley floor. Improvised constructions: former builders or former bureaucrats perpetuated the defacement of the town calmly and without the shadow of a doubt or protest, even on the most beautiful sites. The tide rose higher, Fig. V_1, and stopped at the very foot of the terrace crowned with villas; but before getting their breath back and overrunning the small villas and extending their invasion higher still, the self-appointed master builders erected the ghastly mess shown in our Fig. V_2 in front of the wealthiest villas. This was allowed to happen, then when it was all done people became outraged. It was a bit late then, and the occupant of the villa – seeing, instead of a beautiful mountain chain adorning his horizon, nothing but horrid rooftops and chimney stacks – had to pack his bags to go and build higher up. We have seen this in our study of La Chaux-de-Fonds. Freedom reigns within its great rectilinear avenues. {[In the margin:] The difficulty is:} "Freedom in city planning is anarchy, and as long as the public authorities fail to act, the little" [text breaks off here]. {does not follow any relief plan}

Appendix: Material for *Critical Application*, II

[LCdv 381]

Henry Provensal, page 299[1]

Everything is false, everything shouts ostentatiously, and the late nineteenth-century bourgeois has resolved the terrific problem of inexpensively procuring 'luxury' buildings where, in poor bric à brac taste, astonishing and ephemeral furniture clashes with lacklustre copies inspired by the great eras of style.

Chx-de-Fds

[LCdv 382]

Ch de Fds II

Speaking of the classification of Swiss bourgeois housing being undertaken by the 'Société des Ingénieurs et Architectes', Montenach says: "I hope that from all this effort a great reform movement will emerge, which will give us a fresh taste for local architecture and stop the cosmopolitan infiltration threatening to alter not only the exterior character of our towns, our villages, the setting for our daily lives, but also our customs, our habits, our spirit." 385[2]

It must be said that, although they are very lovely, there are very few of our farms remaining; their farmers *are no longer proud* because, faced with the invasion of poor taste, they have lost the ability to commune with that beauty which they touch every hour of every day. –

They must at all costs be listed so as to preserve them, as in a few years or due to fire there will be nothing left of these *living* witnesses to tradition – concrete symbols of experience.

[LCdv 383]

"The town has a considerable action on the countryside, and the countryside, with its primitive elements, has no less influence in return. In the end, the ugly town is a host for aesthetic contamination which spreads to the entire country.

We will shelter our natural monuments and sites from destructive undertakings by welcoming home beauty, victorious, by unifying art and the people." Montenach page 130 5 and 6 §[3]

---

1 Notes of excerpt from Henri Provensal, *L'Art de Demain* (Paris: Perrin, 1904).

2 Georges de Montenach, *Pour le visage aimé de la patrie. Ouvrage de propagande esthétique et sociale* (Lausanne: Sack-Reymond, 1908), p. 385.

3 Montenach, *Pour le visage aimé de la patrie*, p. 130f.

"Almost always, it is the natural environment that initially caused [towns] to be established. It is also the environment we have to thank for their taking one or other direction, one or other shape." Ditto. 131 III §[4]

La Chaux-de-Fonds

"The industrial occupations which the inhabitants pursue have a considerable influence on the evolution of towns and cities, and these occupations almost always originate from specific crops or materials being found locally. The degree of civilisation, the political system, the religious denomination, the customs, needs, habits and tastes are all elements in

[LCdv 384]
producing this social milieu which is very subtle, very hard to pinpoint but leaves an impression on everything." Montenach 135 § 2 ½[5]

[LCdv 385]
Chaux-de-Fonds
Chap. II.

Say that there is no education in schools, that local architecture is not understood because not publicly revealed – quite the reverse – that many readers in La Chaux-de-Fonds will smile when they hear us state: cubic buildings without sculptures are beautiful, and they are beautiful in our town.
See sheet

Instead of going to gather prime aesthetic triumphs from far-flung lands – triumphs which will seem incomplete because we are largely ignorant of the life which these arts merely reflect – a study and an understanding of the beauty in our part of the world would provide

[LCdv 386]
such a source of education in taste and such a thirst for beauty and such a love of our part of the world, where we have lived and which our ancestors understood and shaped.
Thus an awareness of harmony, of *convenance* will emerge and thus the principles of indigenous art will be revealed; we must attempt this work in our youth, for grown men are already taken up with and absorbed in the struggle for their daily bread.
page ~~300~~ 45

A town must be an individual
Page 11 cahier City III quote *Le visage aimé*, p. ~~44~~

[LCdv 387]
§2. La Chaux-de-Fonds

"The axiom may be stated that our Swiss towns will always have greater aesthetic value when they are rural – I use this term in a broad sense – that is to say when they clearly display our land, our climate, our rustic customs.

---

4 Montenach, *Pour le visage aimé de la patrie*, p. 131.
5 Montenach, *Pour le visage aimé de la patrie*, p. 135.

Sadly, not only do our towns not stay rural, but instead our villages become like cities. In fact, buildings erected everywhere appear to have been borrowed from cosmopolitan boulevards. Everywhere, in the fields, by every bend in our roads, we see details with a pronounced urban character. Nothing does more to make a whole landscape ugly than these repeated little deformations of their natural countenance." Montenach 150/III[6]

"'We receive ready-made impressions and our tastes are quietly established from a distance of five hundred leagues, by people who understand nothing of our spirit, our traditions, our way of seeing, understanding and feeling. Tyrannical, absurd and unconscious fashion dominates our preferences; our personality is self-effacing, the contours of our character are disappearing. We are slipping, paralysed and sterile, into grey uniformity, into banality, and we are losing our historic and social soul.' This is something we must react against: we must remove

[LCdv 388]

this rekindling of local activity from the realm of beauty; it could still produce the same results as in the past, for in the past it never shunned the laws of necessary progress." page 153 2 ½ §[7]

"In a town there is but a single soul and a single spirit, which generates aesthetic unity." ~~165~~ 161 1 §[8]

"The socialists claim that it was speculation, an inordinate love of money and profit which above all caused beauty to be shunned in our towns and cities, caused the masses to be indifferent to it; which caused shoddy wares to be used in all matters." 160 last §[9]

[LCdv 389]
[On] Modern Strategies or Ch-de-Fds II

"Every town must have a standard type, something which distinguishes it from others. It is an essential condition for a town. The true mission of those who deal with the aesthetic of towns and cities, their area of work, is knowing how to distinguish this standard type, to tease out the traits it embodies from everything else which, by superimposing itself on them, has erased them. Once this first job is done, they must impress this rediscovered local type upon all new things done in the town. If they move away from this mission, they risk being lost in unproductive efforts and merely aggravating the problem they wished to avert." (Montenach 374)[10]

– "The Belgians also felt the considerable influence which municipal regulations exercised over the aesthetics of the town and the street, and they saw that it was due to the inadequacy of these, to their outdated, narrow spirit, that many things are poorly executed, and many others which would be excellent are not executed at all. They therefore endeavoured to have these regulations revised, to broaden their tolerance, so as to allow connecting routes to become more picturesque and lively again.

---

6 Montenach, *Pour le visage aimé de la patrie*, p. 150f.
7 Montenach includes the quotation without stating his source. Montenach, *Pour le visage aimé de la patrie*, p. 153f.
8 Montenach, *Pour le visage aimé de la patrie*, p. 161.
9 Jeanneret misattributes this passage; it is actually from Montenach, *Pour le visage aimé de la patrie*, p. 164.
10 Montenach, *Pour le visage aimé de la patrie*, p. 374.

With the same aim, they also redoubled their efforts to enshrine in law the principle of *aesthetic obligations*. These, they stated, must

[LCdv 390]

have the same status as the requirements inspired by hygiene, cleanliness and public safety needs." Montenach 375[11]

"For my part, I am convinced that a comparative study of our Swiss council regulations would reveal disconcerting gaps and bad habits." (M. page 376)[12]

["I am convinced that, in our Swiss towns, where citizens are still very strongly attached to their birthplace and where the small-town mentality is so very much alive, our authorities would achieve marvellous results if they took the trouble"] "– each time a new district is to see the light of day, each time a major transformation is in question – to bring together interested parties, to enlighten them, inform them, suggest to them certain ideas and certain sacrifices." 377[13]

"Current practice, which consists of an all-too-brief examination of each individual plan, will never procure us the advantages that broad cooperation would in terms of grace and beauty."[14]

[LCdv 391] [MA 233]

"The modern architect and entrepreneur want their constructions to come in at a cheap price, while appearing to be expensive. They achieve this through insincerity and ostentatious trompe-l'œil, both of which are inimical to art. If however the men tasked with building, decorating, furnishing our homes no longer had any interest in deceiving us as regards the value of the materials employed and work supplied, then pretentious, showy, glaring banality would vanish from our habit. If skilled and grasping dealers no longer speculated on our inborn desire to decorate our dwellings by attracting us to their creations where the old is remade as new, then the sense of beauty, of taste would spread quickly and in turn have a favourable impact on production. And we might hope to live in a décor that did not resemble a comic opera, or a café-concert. Then we might at the very least be reacquainted with simplicity, without which no art is possible." page 167 III § Montenach extract from Mr. Charles Albert, Conference on Art and society.[15]

[LCdv 392]

["In one of his weekly columns in the *Journal de Genève*, Mr. Philippe Monnier wrote the following lines and, in reproducing them here, I not only lend weight to the reflections I have just expressed, but also come to the very best conclusion. 'I do not know the extent to which – as Mr. Fatio assures us – we have a national architecture; truthfully, if one observes all the influences we have experienced, if one recognises the ties of similarity which bind us to influences in Burgundy or Savoie, I doubt it somewhat. At the very least, we share with some others a way of being, living and building walls.'"]

---

11 Montenach, *Pour le visage aimé de la patrie*, p. 375f. Jeanneret foreshortens "au meme titre et au meme rang" to "au meme rang", which we translate as 'have the same status'.
12 Montenach, *Pour le visage aimé de la patrie*, p. 376.
13 Montenach, *Pour le visage aimé de la patrie*, p. 377.
14 Montenach, *Pour le visage aimé de la patrie*, p. 378.
15 Charles Albert, *L'Art et la société, Conférence faite le 27 juin, 1896* (Paris: Bibliothèque de l'Art social, 1896), quotation from Montenach, *Pour le visage aimé de la patrie*, p. 167f.

"'At the very least we have, here and there, the local, domestic, indigenous building, which expresses the genius loci, springs from and continues the land, and merges with it. So why not look to this building as a source of beneficial inspiration? Why not let our dreams linger a while at the foot of these modest remains which are full of examples and learning? And why, in both town and country, so many heterogeneous models, so many paradoxical buildings, so many Norwegian, Swedish, English, Russian houses; houses from Berne, from Fribourg, but never from Geneva? What are these foreign imports doing here in Geneva? What needs do they meet? What anarchy they launch into the countryside and our troubled hearts!

And since it is necessary for all living organisms to adapt, and since we must also adapt or die, why not adapt ourselves in accordance with our lineage, that line which the past has traced and which has behind it all the weight and prestige of a tradition? Do we no longer have clean hearts, now that we scrape a living from loans and ventures? Has our spirit become so humdrum that we are content with buildings which might be in any climates and any country, which cannot be tolerated as shared places?'" Montenach page 53, extract from Philippe Monnier in the weekly columns in the Journal du Genève.[16]

[LCdv 393]

La Ch-de-Fonds part II* [asterisk refers to LCdv 389]

In a strange aberration the residents of our province have managed – following the example of the big cities, influenced by the 'pâtisserie' stucco towns from Piedmont as well as the pompous specimens from the École des Beaux-Arts in Paris and other prestigious institutions, all of them suspect places which destroy our national taste – to believe even the standard types of their own native architecture ridiculous. ChEJt

[LCdv 394]

La Chaux-de-Fds. Chap. II

"By chance, the fashion here is the old Swiss style... [which has brought about some interesting restorations, unfortunately mostly shocking as out of place.]

... (Since), with a fundamental perversion of aesthetic sensibility, there is an exchange taking place between town and country. In the former, some keen amateurs are now erecting chalets, true farmhouses, which in the middle of perfectly aligned avenues have the same effect as a cow does dancing the quadrille. In order to compensate, they erect multiple apartment blocks in the middle of fields and meadows, with successive storeys, decorated with narrow balconies, which would appear to have fallen there by accident from a basket carried by goodness knows which travelling daemon!" Montenach page 52 paragraph III[17]

[LCdv 395]

Ch. de-Fds Chap. II

On the subject of laws to preserve the countryside, but state this with particular regard to buildings

"Given the very nature of the objects to be safeguarded and the sometimes contradictory interests present, it is very clear that private initiatives, however strongly they appeal to

16 Montenach, *Pour le visage aimé de la patrie*, p. 53.
17 Montenach, *Pour le visage aimé de la patrie*, p. 53.

public opinion, will not bear fruit unless they receive assistance and backing from the state." Montenach p. 118 paragraph III[18]

Say that remarkable farms in the countryside should be listed, as historical monuments are in France.

[LCdv 396]

L. Ch. de. Fds. II. Montenach 44.

"It is the marble from the Greek countryside which produced Scopas, Praxiteles and Lysippos; the old trunks of our oaks and walnuts produced the naive sculptors of saints on the altar, [the cabinetmakers] who chiselled the sides of chests. The acanthus leaf made the Corinthian capital, and the Egyptian column was the product of papyrus and palms. All Japanese art moves between the slender bamboo stems, the water lily and the lotus flower. Everywhere, man's works, however many transformations they have undergone, have their roots deep in the soil from which they spring!"[19]

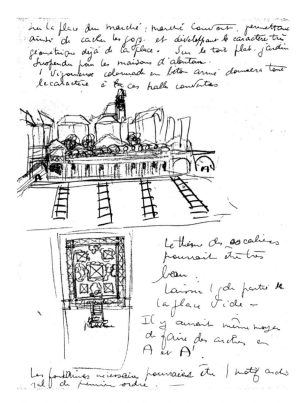

Fig. 112 Jeanneret, designs for the Place du Marché in La Chaux-de-Fonds (LCdv 398)

---

18 Montenach, *Pour le visage aimé de la patrie*, p. 118.
19 Montenach, *Pour le visage aimé de la patrie*, p. 44.

[LCdv 397]
[Two small, quick sketches in the margin (a square and streets leading onto it), the subject is L'Eplattenier's monument for the Place de l'Hôtel de Ville in La Chaux-de-Fonds].
3
...they said that the monument should be placed at the geometric centre of the square, as they deduced triumphantly that this ensures it is seen from all the streets, even from a long way away it will be seen from *a b c d* and *e*. And this is in line with the goal of power, it will be the elegant square for a monument worthy of admiration. And they forgot that the very principle which they followed, of gripping, 'amazing' the viewer, would then be irrevocably compromised because that first impression would have such a limited prospect. The artist wanted to give his normally-sized work the maximum possible appearance of power. And remembering that people have always been careful to contrive such effects (cathedrals and their squares, their small and large doors, naves, etc. etc.), he sought out a precise point from which his monument could not be seen from either *a*, *b*, *c* or *d* but only from as close as possible, that is from [text breaks off here.]
[As material for the chapter Critical Application, see LCdv 405–408, 418–420, 438].

[LCdv 398] [Drawings: Designs for La Chaux-de-Fonds – Place du Marché with market hall, view and plan] **[112]**

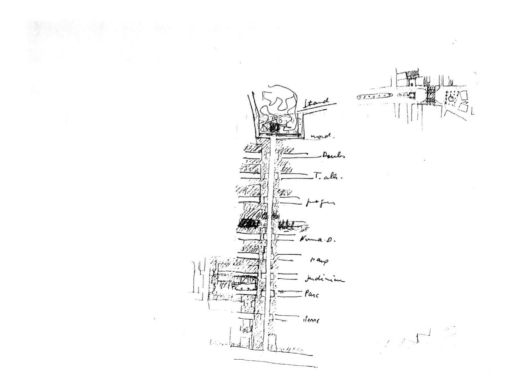

Fig. 113 Rue Léopold Robert in La Chaux-de-Fonds. Sketches by Jeanneret (LCdv 399)

On the marketplace: covered market, allowing the latrines to be hidden and enhancing the already highly geometric nature of the square. On the flat roof, hanging garden for the surrounding buildings.

A strong reinforced concrete column will give these covered halls plenty of character.

[Sketch]

[Sketch]

Stairs could be a very beautiful subject.

Leave a large part of the square empty –

There would even be a way of making arches from *A* to *A'*.

The necessary fountains could be a first-rate architectural motif. –

[LCdv 399] [Two street layout sketches for La Chaux-de-Fonds] **[113]**

[LCdv 400] [Three town planning sketches for La Chaux-de-Fonds, draft for optical enclosure of the Rue Léopold Robert] **[114]**

A sort of little terrace *closing off* the promenade pavement. A stand of trees from *a* to *b*, trimmed box trees showing the building at the end to advantage.

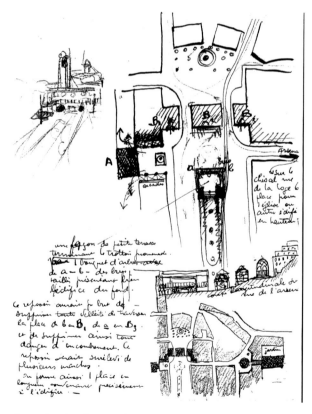

Fig. 114 Jeanneret, design for the closure of Rue Léopold-Robert in La Chaux-de-Fonds. (LCdv 400)

This altar of repose[20] would aim to remove any inclination for people to cross the square between *b* and *B*, or *a* and *B3*, and thus remove any risk of congestion. This altar of repose would be raised up on several steps.

__ thus forms a long square exactly suited to the building. –
On the lot Rue de la Loge 6, square for the church or other tall building
Longitudinal section of Rue de l'Arsenal.

[LCdv 401] [Sketch: Design for station square in La Chaux-de-Fonds]

[LCdv 402] [Sketch: Design for station square in La Chaux-de-Fonds][**115**]

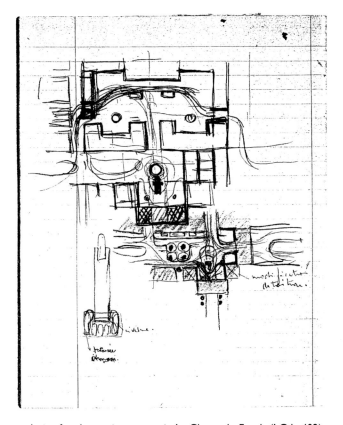

Fig. 115 Jeanneret, design for the station square in La Chaux-de-Fonds (LCdv 402)

---

20 In urban design terms, Jeanneret's design of this 'terrace' works like an altar of repose or the elevation of the choir, seen from the nave of a church.

Materials: Notebooks

Notebook C.2 – City II *Bridges*

[LCdv 403]
Englisches Haus. – CITY II BRIDGES. Ch. E. Jeanneret 3 Lotzbeckstrasse [III]

[LCdv 404]
Ask L'Ep.[lattenier] for photos of La Ch-de-Fds
Wangen an der Aare   (maybe)   stretch of road
Yverdon the street with castle (maybe)   "
(must write to Valangin, write to Lugano, San Lorenzo –
Neuchâtel, La place des Halles
Use my photo of Solothurn, of the clock tower and fountain.

Typical: in Berne. Cathedral square. Monument now in the geometric centre. Previously a fountain in the corner. (See perspective overview drawing)

The passageways for faster transit could be equipped with well-liked, chic shops –

...But the most magnificent of buildings was [by] Timur Beg (or Tamerlane). His warfaring successes in Russia, in the Caucasus, in Persia, in Asia Minor and the Indies, gave him abundant materials with which to adorn

[LCdv 405] 2
his capital Samarkand. Many caravans brought rich spoils there. When a city was taken by force, the order was given to spare the architects, painters, skilled workers, who Tamerlane then used to execute his projects. Tamerlane was very hard to satisfy, constantly playing a very active part in his constructions; he often ordered that an already-finished monument be altered and personally oversaw the rebuilding he had ordered. –
The Meciti, the Mosques of Samarkand[1] [followed by two lines in pencil, illegible]

{[In the margin in pencil:] Chaux-de-Fonds} *From Schultze Naumburg.* "Thus in the countryside the craze for regularisation and degradation reigns. Each little village wants its new, well-defined streets in vanishing perspective, and there are even states where

---

1 Izdamie imperatorskoj archeologiceskoj Kommissii: *Meceti Samarkanda.* (Les Mosquées de Samarcande, published by la commission impériale archéologique), Volume: *Le Gour Emir*, St. Petersburg: Éxpédition pour la confection des papiers d'état 1905. Text in Russian and French.

[for] construction plans this way of drawing with a tracing-line is already firmly established right across the land.

[LCdv 406] 3

One hears the story as shown in Fig. 94 [**116**] in which some street may for example be made straight without any convincing reason. But unfortunately on its route is a farmer's house. This means absolutely nothing to the planners; they take the street straight through the farmyard which sacrifices the building needlessly. This is clearly a typical example. Yet however a sufficient number of similar cases can be found, in the [___] of [___] own development plans, systematic, lebensfeindliche schemes [hostile to life]."[2]

Before that: "the word sounding the death knell to a harmonious city layout is called: *regularisation*. At the same rate as our understanding of beauty and of the excellent practices of our ancient arts are disappearing, or even more so, a bloody end has come[3] for

[LCdv 407] 4

the Begradigung [straightening out] of our towns. Anyone who has read the previous chapters attentively will know how necessary it is in most cases to soften coldly rigid lines and how beautiful an apparently arbitrary exception appears —[4]

[whole paragraph crossed out]. If it is a matter of large new Anlagen [areas of planning], people will therefore think[5] that the old must go and some new, more beautiful object

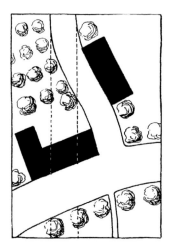

Fig. 116 Street regularisation. From Schultze-Naumburg, *Kulturarbeiten Städtebau*, fig. 94

2 Jeanneret translates Paul Schultze-Naumburg, *Kulturarbeiten. Bd. 4 Der Städtebau*, 2nd ed. (Munich: Callwey, 1909), pp. 170f.

3 Jeanneret misunderstands "so kam die Gepflogenheit in Blüte", the habit flourished, as "a bloody end has come".

4 Jeanneret notes beside the text: "Introduction to La Chaux de Fds + 0 + Chaux de Fonds"; he clearly wants to use parts of this text in his *Critical application: La Chaux-de-Fonds*.

5 Schultze-Naumburg: "it will be accepted".

will arrive in its place. As for regularising our streets, it is not a question of new, imposing creations, but of miserable sacrifices offered up to the bureaucratic Moloch as
a senseless *fait accompli*."[6]
"The main cause of all this regularisation is that the town fathers have lost any vestige of
feeling for living forms, and with the new times[7] they no longer recognise[8] their old
home towns

[LCdv 408] 5 [+ sign in the margin, with a curly bracket covering the whole paragraph
below:]
but instead like true parvenus they are ashamed of its bareness, coarse simplicity and no
longer dream of anything other than exactly resembling the major city model. They
imagine that this is all straight and regular. This magnificent goal cannot be achieved
other than through[9] vanishing lines. For as long as the vanishing lines take a living
form, the buildings cannot be lined up like a front of soldiers.
And besides that the streets must be as wide as those in big cities, for *Grossstädtischer
Verkehr* [traffic in large cities] is the image which rumbles and buzzes all around their
heads. –

All the owners in L. Ch. de Fds should be required to plant trees in the courtyards in
front of their houses. (small trees, which in 20 years will be big and beautiful –

[LCdv 409] 6
[First line illegible]

[Next to two small sketches:] To be added, plan [of a] square [with] trees on two levels.
It is the Rathaus.
Add to the Ulm case [opening up space around Ulm Minster] that buildings can play the role of
a screen. Like trees, something *imponierend* = impressive is often used to lend a colossal feel.

Insist on galleries with large shops {8 metres or 7m}, street fronts and almost 100m of
interior shop-window frontage. [Next to this, ground plan sketch for one such gallery].
[Fragments, cannot be translated]

[Whole paragraph crossed out] "The primary way of removing all sense of scale from
a building is to place it in the middle of a square, that is to isolate it. The poor 19th
century way of building employed this method relentlessly.
They even went further and removed the context framing old buildings which

[LCdv 410] 7
the ancients, with their reliable artistic sense, had incorporated into a group of buildings,
they 'freed' them but also removed their sense of scale. Then when the municipal gardener came to give the building its garden design, this work was completed and everything that could benefit the building was cancelled out."[10]

---

6 Jeanneret translates Schultze-Naumburg, *Der Städtebau*, p. 165.
7 Schultze-Naumburg: "in the traits handed down to them".
8 Schultze-Naumburg: "anything of merit in".
9 Schultze-Naumburg: "new".
10 Jeanneret translates Schultze-Naumburg, *Der Städtebau*, p. 133.

One of the surest means of giving grandeur is to place the building on one of the narrowest sides of the square or on the corner.[11]

On streets climbing a slope. The steep slope of certain streets can cause astonishment. When this is the case, we can be sure that this is not due to an especially unfavourable site, but rather to a design by a poor dilettante.[12] –

The two illustrations I made of these gardens. State that the administrations prefer the poor one because they will not imagine

[LCdv 411] 8

such beautiful motifs. [__] create overhanging gardens on the one hand and gardens below on the other.

[Underneath: 2 sketches similar to Fig. 114 in Schultze-Naumburg, with text:] The opposite to make a wall of trees. Superb roads.

"Undulating land often brings the need for bridges of various heights passing over other roads. This is a beautiful motif with varying[13] attractiveness.[14]

Paul Schultze-Naumburg Kulturarbeiten Vol. IV Städtebau published by Kunstwart

General Considerations. Say that we have selected many images which might in certain cases be more typical, because they will serve several purposes.

[LCdv 412] 9

Place des Vosges 140m square; made with similar buildings with similar, 3-storey houses built in the Franco-Dutch Henry IV style. An arcade all around the ground floor. Statue Louis XIII 1639. Bronze on a white marble plinth, the inside area of the square enclosed by splendid wrought-iron railings, cut through by 2 gravel paths into a cross shape with 4 lawn areas. It was here that for the first time vegetation was used in an urban square. The colour of the architecture, white paths, contrasting with the black statue of the horseman, gave the square a very distinguished character despite its simplicity.

The square plan, the Geschlossenheit, the similar building heights, the one axis accentuated, bring a sense of restful volume, with such clarity as is seen in the palace courtyards of the Italian Renaissance.

"The revolution razed the Louis XIII monument to the ground and the systematic destruction of the square began, and continues to the present day. Two lines of trees were planted along the railings, which hid the agreeable ensemble of façades. The railings which were destroyed have been replaced by cast [__]. In place of the bronze statue stands a marble statue which is hidden by a few more twisted trees. The lawn areas are cut into 4 little triangular parcels in the middle of which stand

[LCdv 413] 10

4 fountains, all alike. Wooden sheds, a bandstand emerged, the children of the working classes play in the sand."[15]

---

11 Jeanneret paraphrases Schultze-Naumburg, *Der Städtebau*, p. 139.

12 Jeanneret part-paraphrases, part-translates Schultze-Naumburg, *Der Städtebau*, p. 184.

13 Schultze-Naumburg: "manifold".

14 Jeanneret paraphrases Schultze-Naumburg, *Der Städtebau*, p. 206.

15 Jeanneret first summarises, then translates, Albert Erich Brinckmann, *Platz und Monument* (Berlin: Wasmuth, 1908), pp. 93ff., on the Place des Vosges.

The Gattamelata: Vasari tells us how Donatello, while working the space which it would occupy, considered how he shrouded himself in the greatest secrecy in his workshop so he did not hear incompetent judgements. The Gattamelata was also produced for the place it occupies, and above all its staging confers its full beauty on it. Donatello imagined the views available to him and which made up the square, and reckoned with the conditions for effectiveness of the bronze.
(Wirksamkeitsbedingungen) Brinckmann page 11[16]

[LCdv 414] [Back of loose sheet]
a constant building height allows us to establish a ratio between the height of the façades and the diameter of the square, the first figure gives the diam. of the square. The second the building height. Etoile = 1: 1/50 Victoire 1: ¼
[Several fragments, cannot be translated]
{[Written upside down above the lines below:] *BRIDGES*}
To round off this study of the square, please note: in certain eras, peoples taken with beauty created 'squares to glory'. We do not consider this name to be out of place, since when we evoke these towns and cities it presents a sumptuous picture, of great nobility or gleaming with splendour: these peoples' glory appears straight away in the objective form of heritage.

[LCdv 415] [Back of loose sheet]
Write [about?] Viollet-le-Duc. Russia. [Underneath, a draft letter to the mayor of Cahors, partly illegible:] I am currently writing a book on [__] in which a chapter on [__] to study bridges. I found in a French archaeology manual by Mr. Camille Enlart a view of the Pont Valentré in Cahors, this bridge seems [__] publish a view in my work. [__] I have taken the liberty of sending you a tracing from the Enlart book [__]

[LCdv 416] [Back of loose sheet]
Lib[rary] gde encyclopédie
Date Place Dauphine.
   "   "   St. Peter's, Rome
   "   Cour du Louvre {a.k.a. cour carrée} 122 m/124
Pierre Lescaut first plans 1539
Claude Perrault Colonnades 1667–80
Percier and Fontaine finished the courtyard
from 1806–1813
Pont Neuf by Cerceau Jacques
     1578
First bridge in Paris
which was not covered
    in buildings.

[LCdv 417] [Loose sheet, drawing] **[117]**
Das Sendlingerthor. in ~~18~~ 1570 Süddeutsche Bauz[eitung] page 218. 1903[17]

---

16 Jenneret paraphrases Brinckmann, *Platz und Monument*, p. 11.
17 Sendlinger Tor in Munich. Drawing by Jenneret, copied from *Süddeutsche Bauzeitung* 13 (1903), p. 218.

Fig. 117 Sendlinger Tor, Munich. Drawing by Jeanneret, copied from *Süddeutsche Bauzeitung* 13 (1903), p. 218 (LCdv 417)

[LCdv 418] [Sketches for La Chaux-de-Fonds railway station, etc.]
Trees on all three levels thanks to reinforced concrete, streets with walkways accessed via steps running lengthways. Street goes under a block of old buildings through passageways.

[LCdv 419]
In an old town, it would be possible to design wide 'commercial' streets which were almost or completely straight, and passed through blocks of housing. Straight through, using passageways driven through the buildings situated on the street's route – and no longer dumbly demolishing the precious encyclopaedia of a town's tradition.
Why not plant a tree or trees at half-height or at the very top of a building? Large and powerful trees and Virginia creepers and ivy etc. In the past, materials prevented this because the stones would be dislodged by the growing roots. Today, reinforced concrete permits it and allows all conceivable combinations.
Say that the art of city planning is a desert nowadays whereas

[LCdv 420]
the rising tide of progress could have made it a lush forest. Thus one hardly dares speak of an oasis, when one should be calling stridently for a full forest, complete

with birdsong, flowers, the poetry of its sunsets and the murmuring lullaby of its inner life.

Cahier C.3 – *Cities III* (Materials for *Blocks, Streets* and *Squares*)

[LCdv 421]
CITIES III // K

[LCdv 422] [Loose sheet: lending slip from RBL, Munich]
[Munich,] 4 June 1910 // Thiéry // Üeber geometr. Täuschungen // Leipzig // 1895 // Ch. E. Jeanneret // Math. A. 2^{38n} [bears library's stamps: "15-JUL" and "5-7-10"].

[LCdv 423] [Loose sheet: lending slip from RBL, Munich]
[Munich,] 23. Oktober 1910 // Brückenbauten // von der Staats-Bau-Verwaltung // M. // 1906. // Ch. E. Jeanneret // 4° / Bavar. / 1775 f. [bears library stamp: "I. 24. SEP."]

[LCdv 424]
1
Proposition. (a) philosophical point of view. (b) satisfaction point of view.
(a) in which there is a dream of shared living to make [___] easier (b) listing the plastic, utilitarian, hygienic and moral characteristics.
La Ch-de-Fonds before the fire   }
The town created over the past 20 years   } critique
Conclusion   Proposed new features.
                        remedies
The Chapallaz Stotzer job
Debschitz Kaiserplatz 2
4–5
exhibition at École des Beaux-Arts from Saturday
graphische Jahresausstell[ung] Kunstgewerbeschule, 14–16 July
until 17, at the Rathaus

[LCdv 425]
The procedures prescribed are to replace a chequerboard town. But then (and only then) will the straight street be back in its rightful place: a place of the greatest beauty. The elegant line par excellence in nature, but also the rarest, is the straight line. The solemn columns of high pine forests; the horizon over the sea; the vastness of the plain; the grandeur of the Alps seen from a summit, as all violence melts away into a wide horizontal expanse.
There are two possible aims for a straight street: grandeur or beauty. Grandeur first: it is not unique in a city [___] striking and if the dimensions are huge, out of all proportion, and if possible on a slight slope. Then we would have the Champs-Elysées.

[LCdv 426] 3 [IV]
Books to consult:

Camillo Sitte.
Claudel: L'Arbre (la Ville)

V. Cousin. Le vrai, le beau, le juste. [*Du vrai, du beau et du bien*]
Henrici Aesthetik im Städtebau. 47$^{\underline{id}}$
Berlepsch-Valendàs. Eine Studie über Städtebau in England.
Muthesius das Englische Haus. –
buy G. Le Bon. Psychologie de l'éducation, Baedeker Süddeutschland 2.50 [illegible]
von der Tann)

[LCdv 427] 5

A	Proposition	B
1 Men gather in the aim of benefiting from it.		1 What is a town or city?
2 The weakest can find support.		a) Useful
3 Consistency: creating laws.		b) Hygienic
4 Security – and as a result: pleasures, aspiring to beauty		c) Beautiful
		a
		easy-to-use streets, – allocate blocks – districts – according to their use. Measures strict from now on.
6 This is the ideal town or city. Which *did exist.* –		*b*
		Buildings in the sunlight, fresh air – but not through draughts. Stinking factories confined and combined according to the wind.
7 But 19th century, and prev. abuse. Then industrialisation,		Similar measure for those that are noisy. Reserve the good building lots for housing and protect them
social crises. Current imbalance.		*c*
8 Do not therefore conclude from current state of play that any effort useless.		Impression of comfort, calm. for housing; greenery around the houses. – A glorious place, with accumulation of beauty. Give several plans of past towns and cities. Summary.
10 The 20th heralds the power of shared institutions. All will come to participate in public life – then in intellectual life. Hence:		The 3 cities: their limits and crossover, their shared life. their plan

11 Municipality: buildings
for the community, meeting rooms
concert halls. Promenades

~~12~~ Beautiful streets and squares. Beautiful
schools and colleges since taste
must be taught from childhood.

12 Conclusion: Respect, mother country.
Hate dissipates. Elevation
of moral feeling.

2 Conclusion.
Local pride. {put at the end}
exaltation of patriotic
sentiment, possibility for
large movements of people.
for an ideal goal.
discuss the champions of the 3
categories
abc
which manage to completely
miss their target due to overly
large squares. –

[LCdv 428] 7

– Summary –

Sacrifice of self, for all. Current sacrifice of self-esteem, and frank admission of the error of our previous path.

Which leads us

to state

that the criticism below is meant well, and not in a proud and divisive spirit.

[LCdv 429] 9

Critical and practical study
La Ch-de-Fds 100 years ago.
Publish a plan and one or two perspective views, have these show the beauty and faults, if any. Conclude that instinct is accurate when *it comes naturally.*
La Ch-de-Fds today.
Critique of open streets. To plan streets one should at least have a site map with contours marked so they *create an image.* {[In the margin:] check how it's done nowadays}.
Those streets that are enclosed are poorly enclosed. Ugly squares.
Show on a *relief* plan what is planned for the districts of Les Crêtets, Crêtes des Olives, Réservoir, Recorne, etc.
Request a subdivision plan of [the Rue] du Point-du-Jour, [the Rue] des Armes-Réunies.
{[In the margin:] La-Ch-d-Fds built too open, but too high.} – Bridges: things that used to be beautiful. (Town hall, Le Trou d'Uri).
Station square, anarchy, millions at stake forfeited.
Fountains in the squares. (Place de l'Ouest, Place du Marché, (urinal)).
Public buildings failing to achieve the desired effect: post office façade should have faced onto the station square, Hôtel Judiciaire – public. – Place du Bois du Petit-Château.
Rue Léop[old] Robert.
The steps on the Rue des Armes-Réunies.
Église Indépendante. Rear view, Collège Industriel.
– Uhrendorf. The cemetery. Crematory oven.

Diagrams	Illustrations	Plan of Karlsruhe.
Squares	Rue de l'Horloge, Berne [Kramgasse]	~~Plan of Stuttgart~~
streets	Plan of Stuttgart	Plan of the Ring in Vienna.
several streets	Plan and overview of Nuremberg	
several squares	Plan of Siena (Palio square, longitudinal section of	The museum in Solothurn –
road junction	cathedral (baptistery square)	
crossroads.	Piazza Signoria Florence	
Sq[uares]	Pisa.	
	Cathedral square, Rouen.	
	New district of Stuttgart. (find, Zeitschriftensaal)	
	Strasbourg cath[edral].	Place N[otre]. Dame, Paris.
	Arches in Verona	
	Streets in Le Landeron	
	Place de l'Hôtel de Ville, Neuchâtel	
	Place de[l'] Arsenal, Solothurn	
	Place de Roland Brême. [Marktplatz, Bremen]	
	Stein am Rhein	
	Schaffhausen – Basel.	
	Lugano.	
	Curjel and Moser church	
	Street [by Max] Billing	

[LCdv 430] 11
[For the pages that follow this in the Cahier, C.3,57–63, see LCdv 10–16]

[LCdv 431] 23
Brinckmann page 107.
The formation of the *star-shaped square*
~~on the subject of the Place des Victoires, Paris~~
"The monument in the middle of a space should not only be sculpturally satisfying, but it must also belong in its situation, as with every other monument. The monument at the Place des Victoires tried to achieve this, as shown in the calculation (diameter of square 78m, over-all height of surrounding architecture 19m, of which 6m ground floor, 9½ first floor, 3½ upper floor, monument height 8m, of which pedestal almost 4m, figure 4m), its proportions and those of its architectural backdrop had been chosen so that whereas the pedestal stood out against the heavy ground floor of the street fronts, the sculpture appeared to people entering the square against the free arrangement of pilasters. This bringing together of sculpture and architecture is typical of France in the century that followed. (see plan)"[18]

Work on the Place de l'Etoile in Paris began under Napoleon and ended in 1836.

18 Jeanneret copies out this passage in German from Albert Erich Brinckmann, *Platz und Monument* (Berlin: Wasmuth, 1908), p. 104.

[LCdv 432] 2

Bindings

The books that are used a great deal are bound at the Bibliotheca Regia Monacensis in thick, light ultramarine linen, of a quality similar to my rug. The cardboard is 22½mm thick. The cloth covers the spine and the boards and the corners, which are rounded to a radius of 7mm.

[LCdv 433] 25 / 3

A "The ideal way to complete the monumental star-shaped square would be to end the radiating streets – well proportioned in relation to the space of the square – with significant architecture at an appropriate distance, rather than to leave it to convention to enclose the view and resolve the shape pictorially. Even for squares whose Raumbild is poor, a good impression of Raum would be achieved, and perhaps this shape still has a future." Brinckmann 108.[19]

B id. 108. Louis XIV bought an hôtel and its grounds to build a large geometric square in its place, according to plans by J. H. Mansard, with the library, academies, mint and ambassadors' palace. –[20]

C Books from which Brinckmann draws constantly

P. Patte, Mémoire sur les objets les plus importants de l'architecture, Paris 1759 –
M. A. Laugier, Observations sur l'architecture, The Hague 1765.

D Before Napoleon I no freestanding fountains in the centre of squares. But only since N., and even then the proportions are rarely favourable for the surroundings. Fontaine de la Paix on place St Sulpice, obstructs the portico of S. S., which it blocks, and is insufficiently strong. The architect wanted 2 fountains, 1 on either side of the façade, in Roman style. The trees planted since are even more destructive, have destroyed everything.

[LCdv 434] 4

Note that Raumgefühl changes with the times, middle of page 153[21]

[LCdv 435] 27 / 5

Brinckmann page 131 shows that "regularity in street layout began as early as ~~Louis XIII~~ {Colbert Richelieu} with the influence of Italian theorists, at the same time that the need for fortified towns provided the impetus for a systematic ordering, so that 'one must not neglect anything if as much regularity as possible is to reign in the square's interior (in der Festung). This applies to the distribution of streets, of bourgeois housing, to siting the guards, barracks, etc.'"[22]

La Théorie et la pratique du jardinage, Paris 1747, Daviles et d'Argenville[23]

"With a few beautiful, well-positioned buildings, one can immensely improve the overall impression a town makes. 'A beautiful building is multiplied, and decorates a town, as many times as you provide different points from which to view it, whereas a building

---

19 Jeanneret copies out this passage in German from Brinckmann, *Platz und Monument*, p. 108.

20 Jeanneret paraphrases Brinckmann, *Platz und Monument*, p. 108.

21 Cf. Brinckmann, *Platz und Monument*, p. 153.

22 Jeanneret paraphrases Brinckmann, *Platz und Monument*, p. 130f.; Brinckmann quotes Bélidor, *La Science des Ingenieurs* (Paris, 1729) in French.

23 Cf. Antoine-Joseph Dézallier d'Argenville, *La théorie et particque du jardinage* (Paris: J. Mariette, 1709).

which is only seen from a single point will only ever be a single building.'"[24] (Situation of Odéon)

Rue de Tournon and the [Palais/Jardin du] Luxembourg [Sketches]

[LCdv 436] 6

{page 140} Laugier said: "There must be regularity and whimsy, relationships and oppositions, chance elements that lend variety to the tableau, *precise order in the details*, and confusion, chaos and tumult in the whole."[25]

"The conditions for a competition {to improve St Petersburg} which Catherine the Great held in November 1763 were published in the Gazette de France January 1764."[26]

In Wiesbaden's districts of villas and Landhäuser, it was necessary to accommodate the workshops and workers required for the districts themselves. Therein lies the difficulty of these matters, islands were therefore created (Inseln geschlossener Bebauung) so that these services could be accommodated here along with their staff. (Hubatschek page 7)[27]

Finish the first part with a list of measures to be taken, in Munich division into 9 zones, 1 is the current city in which there are no restrictive measures. Then the 8 others determined by the number of storeys in the buildings, of which 4 were built using the geschlossene and 4 the offene pattern. One of the most important points is the placement of the major buildings. The buildings

[LCdv 437] 29 / 7

[paragraph deleted] were not placed in a single district but the most favourable street was created for all the special considerations relating to that building, and then one chose the district. It was {Theodor Fischer} [and] {under his leadership} Bauamtmann Bertsch who undertook all development of Munich in this vein.[28]

Die bautechnischen Aufgaben einer modernen Stadt, Joh.[ann] Hubatschek. Druck und Verlag E. Mareis (Linz)

[Paragraph crossed out] He says that Verkehr [traffic] no longer has any place in the square and that for cars and all the modern [___], streets are sufficient. There must be a peaceful area in a square, perhaps even a complete quiet, a calm must prevail so that people may talk, play or look at a statue there, while the Verkehr is allocated the streets (page 9, first paragraph). This makes me think that one could make beautiful squares from which cars are banned. I had already dreamed and thought of the quiet [___] in Venice, and of the ugly sight of omnibuses on the Piazza della Signoria in Florence.[29]

Du sens chromatique dans l'antiquité

---

24 Jeanneret copies out the first sentence in German from Brinckmann, *Platz und Monument*, p. 138; the following phrase by Laugier, published in the Mercure de France, July 1748, is quoted in French by Brinckmann.

25 Jeanneret copies out Laugier's dictum in French from Brinckmann, *Platz und Monument*, p. 140.

26 Jeanneret copies out this passage in German from Brinckmann, *Platz und Monument*, p. 140.

27 Jeanneret paraphrases Johann Hubatschek, *Die bautechnischen Anlagen einer Stadt* (Linz: E. Mareis, 1905), p. 7.

28 In this paragraph and at the end of LCdv 436, Jeanneret paraphrases Hubatschek, *Die bautechnischen Anlagen einer Stadt.* p. 7.

29 Jeanneret paraphrases Hubatschek, *Die bautechnischen Anlagen einer Stadt.* p. 9. It is unclear whether the end of the paragraph is a quotation or Jeanneret's own thoughts.

by Dr. N-P Bénaky.
Paris, publisher A. Maloine
21 place de l'École de Médecine, 1897

After the Empire, Klazissismus. ... Brinckmann ... The siting of monuments (in previous eras) disappeared, but the regular lines remained – instead of changing views, the same

[LCdv 438] [Loose sheet, drawing: Design for station square in La Chaux-de-Fonds]

[LCdv 439] 8
Straßenbild always appeared: the abstraction of classicism had a cost in terms of the Ödigkeit of the später Städtebau [bleakness of later city planning].[30]

In Karlsruhe 32 avenues fanning outwards. Dated 1715 by Bagnetti and Retti. 2 Italians

The trees planted in regular squares destroy everything. Place des Vosges and cite Louvre Tuileries

[Paragraph crossed out] Brinckmann. "The modern French star-shaped square with many straight streets extending far into the distance is called 'Verkehrsplatz' [square for traffic] despite the fact that the concentration of strongly increasing Verkehr has the greatest disadvantages for its rapid dispersal, and indeed further complicates [the situation] instead of lösen (providing a solution). Only a star-shaped space with the diameter of Place de l'Etoile in Paris, having a large raised central section, can still bring order to modern Verkehr. A raumkünstlerisch value [value of artistic volume] is not generated by such squares lined with disharmonisch [discordant] apartment blocks. Despite more than one advantage, the diagonal system shows a similar lack of aesthetic culture (crudeness) to

[LCdv 440] 31
the Rechtecksystem ['right-angled' system]; it has only been thought through in terms of area, and not of Raum."[31]

Ch. Buls. Esthétique des Villes Bruxelles 1893

"The purely theoretical cleverness of some architects planning cities, like stepped and sawtooth streets (Hénard Paris), hexagonal blocks, America, are hardly worth mentioning. This playing with the plan is worthless."[32]

During the 18th century the feeling also arrived in Germany of the princes being sovereign, they raised up public statues to themselves in the open. The usual position of the monument was the middle of the square, but without the fine detail of relationships with street openings, of proportion, and of links to the volume of the square (Platzraum) to which attention had been paid in France... for example: – Kassel Berlin etc.[33]

A new book by Brinckmann has come out which is apparently very good (Theodor Fischer says).

30 Here and in the last paragraph of LCdv 437, Jeanneret paraphrases Brinckmann, *Platz und Monument*, p. 145.
31 Jeanneret translates Brinckmann, *Platz und Monument*, p. 156.
32 Jeanneret copies out this passage in German from Brinckmann, *Platz und Monument*, p. 157.
33 Jeanneret paraphrases Brinckmann, *Platz und Monument*, p. 158f.

[LCdv 441] 10

[Paragraph deleted] At the beginning of my work, where I stated Carl Henrici's opinion of Sitte: add "In conclusion, we will look at Brinckmann's opinion of Sitte." Having spoken somewhat vehemently, I must now calm down and conclude, say that now we are convinced a wrong has been done, we should not content ourselves with a new formula as this would only substitute one wrong for another, but we should instead be interested in and excited about and follow the comings and goings of the leaders of the [reform] movement.

The last chapter in Brinckmann
N$\underline{^o}$ 35 is characteristic of him.
Moderne Bestrebungen

[Paragraph deleted] Conclude that, due to the totally different life in the city over the last 50 years, we cannot build new cities according to the old formulas. But as we have an infinitely rich palette comprising everything the history of our city streets and squares has supplied, with colours which evoke feeling, let us create – on a canvas of today's needs – a work of harmony, the city plans for our time.

[LCdv 442] 33 / 11

What we need is to drop an affectation: art with its various vanities. State in conclusion that even if opinions are contradictory, it is good that they are aired. Recommend reading Brinckmann etc.

[Paragraph deleted] Public life in daily newspapers, markets without artistic needs, purely ornamental fountains.

To recap, the true modern square today is none other than a meeting of several streets which make spending time on squares uncomfortable [___] and make it impossible to produce an enclosed impression. {Hubatschek} B (B of which it seems to me one must do less)

[Paragraph crossed out] "[Assumption that, even today,] chance would bring beauty all on its own, as in the olden days: grave mistake, for today there are no longer, as in the past, solid artistic traditions among the populace, und ein wildes Durcheinander die Folge wäre [and a confused pell-mell would be the result]."[34]

"A town or city must not merely be agreeable and hygienic to live in, and meet the needs of industry and commerce; it must not only be beautiful, but it shall also be *characteristic*; it must be

[LCdv 443] 12

an individual in and of itself, so that it can be essentially distinguished from other towns. For only then will it be pleasant for residents and interesting to strangers."[35]

Translate Theod. Fischer page 16
Hubatschek

---

34 Jeanneret translates from Hubatschek, *Die bautechnischen Anlagen einer Stadt.* p. 11.
35 Jeanneret translates from Hubatschek, *Die bautechnischen Anlagen einer Stadt*, p. 14f.

[Paragraph crossed out] Broad streets in cities with heavy Verkehr [traffic] are beautiful and imposing, but in towns one may more or less travel the length of the streets in half a day, [and they merely] increase still further the towns' deserted aspect and tedium [to 'as evidence']

[Paragraph crossed out] It is therefore preferable to keep a sufficiently hygienic street width, wide front gardens, wide Baufluchtlinien [building lines] and practical Bürgersteige (pavements) which meet the needs of the comings and goings and of hygiene.

As proof that traffic does not utilise great street width, London's streets with most traffic – such as London Bridge, which is 16 metres wide with daily Verkehr of at least 25,000 cars and 125,000 people.[36]

[LCdv 444] 35 / 13
To be recommended as street width: 10 metres for residential streets, 18 m approx. for streets with traffic.[37]

[Paragraph crossed out] Good practical implementation of a regularisation plan, once created, includes above all a good *building law* as well as a good *expropriation law* and creating both these laws to cover all cases will be a big issue for modern towns and cities in terms of technical construction].[38]
Page 25 translate.[39]

"'Propose what can be done,' they never stop repeating to me. It is as if I were told, 'Propose doing what is done,' or at least, 'Propose some good which can be allied with the existing evil.' Such a project, in certain matters, is much more chimerical than mine. For in this alliance the good is spoiled, and the evil is not cured." (Emile page VII)[40]

[LCdv 445] 14
Emile page 9. line 13

The Stadtbaudirektor in Dresden is Fritz Schumacher (catalogue Städtebauausstellung [urban design exhibition] page 26 N° 122).

Em v. Seid[l]: catalogue Städtebau 212, Map of new zoological garden for Munich, scale 1:500. For the first time, the moment best expressing the wissenschaftlich [scientific] goes together with artistic action and creates characteristic images, and surprising impressions are always used for expression.

Enclosed and open development patterns in utility §2 I part – 1. –

Title: Der Städtebau und die Grundpfeiler der heimischen Bauweise – zum Verständnis für die Gebildeten aller Stände namentlich aber für Stadtverordnete, Baumeister, Architekten, Bauherren, etc. by Jos. Aug. Lux, Verlag von Gerhardt Kühtmann – Dresden.

---

36 In these last three paragraphs, Jeanneret paraphrases Hubatschek, *Die bautechnischen Anlagen einer Stadt*, p. 20.
37 Jeanneret paraphrases Hubatschek, *Die bautechnischen Anlagen einer Stadt*, p. 20.
38 Jeanneret paraphrases Hubatschek, *Die bautechnischen Anlagen einer Stadt*, p. 23.
39 It is not clear what Jeanneret is referring to here.
40 Jean-Jacques Rousseau, *Emile, Or, On Education*, edited by Christopher Kelly, translated by Allan Bloom (Hanover, N.H. University Press of New England, 2010), p. 158.

[LCdv 446] 37 / 15
I should find a joint-stock company which would build a block of villas on a slope, each seeming to produce the other and forming a monumental monolith.

Inspired by book Renaissance- und Barockvilla in Italien. Bernhard Patzak, Verlag Klinkhardt & Biermann, Leipzig

---

l'Hôtel de Bouillon, Quai Malaquais, recent annex to l'École des Beaux Arts – by François Mansart 1598–1666.
Jules Hardouin Mansart [1646–1708], great-nephew of [arrow to F. Mansart above] started to become famous at 20 years old. At 26 he built Château Clagny for Louis XIV in 1672, and handled [the building by Louis le Vau of] Versailles from 1678 until 1708 when he died.
Dôme des Invalides 1693–1706.

[LCdv 447] 16
Le Nôtre 1613–1700.

Finish off *On modern strategies* thus. If we must change the street then so be it, but where the street is part of the buildings, the most delicious combinations, the finer points which will make new plans – not using a new formula but using a work of art – can only be designed as a beautiful volume if the buildings to be erected there have a beautiful volume. Now a building, a city, a room, these are all simply applications of a taste for beautiful *volume*. It is this volume which we must teach the general populace to understand, and the architects to create. They will make a room, and then a house; and then a street, then a square, with the right volume, with beautiful volume. Let us conclude with what Mr. Brinckmann summarises perfectly in his book.[41]

[LCdv 448] 39 / 17 [118]
To plan cities is to arrange volumes, using buildings as material! (Städte bauen heißt: mit dem Hausmaterial Raum gestalten!) {further down:} the historian need not respond to the curious (impertinent) question of objectivity in relation to the *new shape*. As with any art, city planning is not a construct of abstract ideas, which triggers its own decline, but rather it is sensible[42] thought: thought about the material, only artistic strength can shape this abstraobjective[43] process into a measured creation. See [__] Brinckmann.[44]
City planning and architecture are closely related. They relate to one another more or less as the plan of a house relates to its architecture. The divisions for a house of isolated rooms and rooms grouped together according to certain requirements corresponds to the division of the town into

[LCdv 449] 18
rooms for living, recreation, and industry; the communication between various rooms using corridors corresponds to the arrangement of various roads and, just as architecture, when establishing its foundation plan, constantly thinks of how it will be realised

---

41 Cf. Brinckmann, *Platz und Monument*, p. 169f.
42 Brinckmann: "sensory".
43 Sic, Jeanneret's translation of the German "geistig-körperlich", literally "mental-physical".
44 Cf. Brinckmann, *Platz und Monument*, p. 170.

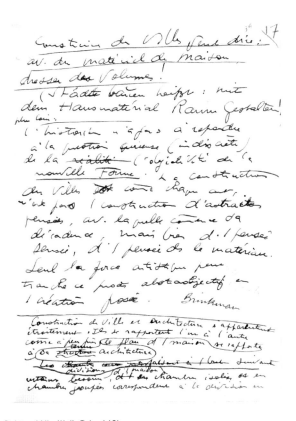

Fig. 118 Page from Cahier *Ville III* (LCdv 448)

aesthetically in elevation, so city planning is influenced while laying out its streets and squares by their aesthetic side, by the way they present as volume.

The exhibition also made a strong impression on great swathes of the public who until now hardly knew anything about city planning. They felt very well that it was no longer a matter of a twist on different styles. Beyond knowing if [the period from] the Middle Ages to the Renaissance should be our model, if we have to more or less adhere to old styles, *the battle for art, for the future will still be fought in city planning.* Taken from Berliner Architektur in a brief account of the exhibition.[45]

Cahier C.11 – *City J* Theodor Fischer (Berlin, October 1910)

[LCdv 450] City. // J

[LCdv 451] [Loose sheet; lending slip from Royal Library Berlin (RLB), filled out by Jeanneret] [119]
Reading room

---

45 Throughout these last three paragraphs, Jeanneret paraphrases Walter Lehweß, "Architektektonisches von der Städtebau-Ausstellung zu Berlin", in *Berliner Architekturwelt*, Vol. 13 (1910), pp. 123–125.

Fig. 119 Lending slip from the Royal Library Berlin (LCdv 451)

Die Entstellung unseres Landes // by Schultze-Naumburg // Flugschriften des Hei-
matschutzbundes 2
Ch. E. Jeanneret // architect // Dessauerstr. 36
[Stamp: "Not for loan". On the reverse, stamp: "K. Bibliothek 20.-OCT.-10*9".]

[LCdv 452] [Loose sheet; lending slip from RLB, filled out by Jeanneret]
Berlepsch-Valendàs. // Die Gartenstadt München- // - Perlach
Ch. E. Jeanneret
architect // 83 Stahnsdorferstr. // Neu-Babelsberg.

[LCdv 453] [Loose sheet; lending slip from RLB, filled out by Jeanneret] **[120]**
A. E. Brinckmann. // Spätmittelalterliche Stadt= // anlagen. Berlin 1910
Ch. E. Jeanneret // architect // 83 Stahnsdorferstr. // Neu-Babelsberg.
Ch. E. Jeanneret
[Stamp: "On loan". On the reverse, stamp: "K. Bibliothek 29.-OCT.-10.*6".]

[LCdv 454] [Loose sheet; lending slip from RLB, filled out by Jeanneret]
Reading room.
Jos. Aug. Lux. // Die Stadtwohnung // Charlottenburg 1910 //
Ch. E. Jeanneret // architect // Dessauerstr. 36
[Stamp: "Not for loan". On the reverse, stamp: "K. Bibliothek 20.-OCT.-10*9".]

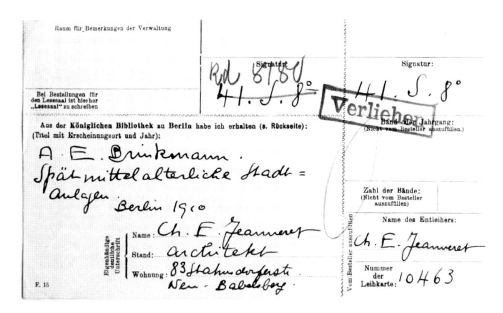

Fig. 120 Lending slip from the Royal Library Berlin (LCdv 453)

[LCdv 455] [Loose sheet; lending slip from RLB, filled out by Jeanneret]
A. E. Brinckmann. // Die praktische Bedeutung der Ornament // stiche für die deutsche Frührenaissance // Strasbourg 1907 ["Stud z. dtsch. Kunstgesch. 90" added by librarian]
Ch. E. Jeanneret // architect // 83 Stahnsdorferstr. // Neu-Babelsberg.

[LCdv 456] [Loose sheet; lending slip from RLB, filled out by Jeanneret]
Alt-Holland // by Jos. Aug. Lux // Leipzig 1908 [added by librarian: "Stätten der Kultur 10"]
Ch E. Jeanneret // architect // 83 Stahnsdorferstr // Neu-Babelsberg.

[LCdv 457] 1
Gliederung der Massen nach Herrschendem und Beherrschtem ist eines der wichtigsten Kunstmittel im Städtebau. [Separating masses into the dominant and the dominated is one of the major mechanisms in city planning.] Fischer, Stadterweiterungsfragen. Lecture by → [Arrow points to 'Fischer'] Stuttgart 27 May 1903.
2nd principle. Thus although we were just talking about Gliederung der Massen [articulation of masses] with a view to unity, we will now state a 2nd rule: "die Steigerung des Charakteristischen" [Enhancing characteristic qualities].[46]
The beautiful and characteristic hills which rise up all around the valley have sadly been left denuded. This is "so as not to destroy the picturesque view", as if it would be preserved because one allowed the herd of houses to climb up and cover the dominant [hill] up to its neck.

---

46 Cf. Theodor Fischer, *Stadterweiterungsfragen* (Stuttgart: DVA, 1903), p. 8.

The opposite is true, which takes our way of thinking in a different direction, that of heightening the characteristic: that which is high must be raised up higher.[47]

[LCdv 458]

The hills must be raised higher by urban edifices, certainly not by apartment blocks with no roofs, but by impressive buildings with strong silhouettes, by public buildings or equally by private buildings, if this raises rich people's spirits and causes them to regain prosperity... I do not think that the city of Stuttgart could regain its rhythm and posture by any other means than by city planning, making the hills rise up out of the valley.

He [Fischer] proposes examples/photos, hills crowned with groups of buildings.

In almost all these examples, it befits the nature of the question that the mountainsides between the built-up plain and the buildings which crown the top have preserved, as required, the picturesque nature which, when one considers it, is so natural and self-explanatory that one can never be astonished enough that the opposite idea could have arisen, to build on the slope and leave the summit free [underneath, a sketch of the urban design situation described].[48]

[LCdv 459] 3

... page 26 not only am I not asking that money be spent to improve beauty: I am going so far as to say that we could have everything at a much lower price if we made things more beautiful – and more simple.

More simple, and more fit for purpose! So walk through your town and see what, out of everything you see, is needed for it to be fit for purpose.

Consider the great width of the streets, which bears no relation to the Verkehr [traffic] (I am talking about residential streets), see the monstrous earth moving which will occur in the near future, merely to avoid some valley[49] or other. But look above all at the luxury, so often absolutely ridiculous, artificial and

[LCdv 460]

worthless, in the façades behind which poor housing is crammed in. Without any of that and without all this diversity[50], our streets would be incomparably beautiful and healthier, without this fake and impractical luxury, our city would be more distinguished in its own way and – all in all – we would have saved a large proportion of the money and with it could have created huge, healthy dwellings. Thus I seek to link aesthetics with economy (in the general sense (Oekonomie)) and hygiene, and I see that if most people thought like that, lots of Rechnerei und Schreiberei [calculations and writing] would be unnecessary. On 12/11/10[51]

[LCdv 461] 5

"Some have said: 'One must not make a curved street for no reason.' I reply to them: One must not make a straight street for no reason."[52]

(Th. Fischer.)

---

47 Jeanneret paraphrases Fischer, *Stadterweiterungsfragen*, p. 17f.
48 Jeanneret paraphrases Fischer, *Stadterweiterungsfragen*, pp. 19–23.
49 Fischer: "bend".
50 Fischer: "much more besides".
51 Here and on the previous page, Jeanneret translates Fischer, *Stadterweiterungsfragen*, p. 26f.
52 Jeanneret paraphrases Fischer, *Stadterweiterungsfragen*, p. 40.

Cahier C.12 – *Roland Fréart* (Berlin, October 1910)

[LCdv 462] Rolandus Fréart // Sieur de Chambray. // F

[LCdv 463] 1
He gave great impetus to public works.
Trajan made Rome more beautiful: he built a new forum, the Trajan Forum, with a large basilica as decoration, Basilica Ulpia, with Trajan's Column towering above.
Besides the port on the Danube which he commissioned in preparation for his war against the Dacians, he built the port of Alcántara on the Tagus River, which is considered one of the most beautiful monuments in Roman art.
Trajan's reign can be considered the zenith of that Empire. The Senate gave Emperor Trajan the soubriquet 'best prince' (princeps optimus); it would later wish each new emperor be more fortunate than Augustus and better than Trajan (felicior Augusto, melior Traiano). 53–117 AD
(Gde encyclopédie) –
Koenigliche Bibliothek Berlin 20 Oct 1910) –
Augustus {born 63 B.C. Died 14 A.D.} It is understandable that, having such a sum of money (his friends left it to him – around 4 billion sesterce – i.e. 8 to 900,000,000 francs) Augustus could more or less single-handedly have almost funded

[LCdv 464]
the complete reconstruction of Rome and the cities of Italy, more or less changing the face of the country totally. ... New aqueducts were built to supply the Eternal City with water. Magnificent monuments were raised: Marcellus' theatre, Statilius Taurus' ampitheatre (the 1st stone amphitheatre in the city of Rome), the Basilica Julia, Augustus' forum, Agrippa's pantheon, the Temple of Apollo Palatinus and the library, the temple of Mars Ultor, the Temple of Jupiter Tonans on the Capitoline Hill... To make it easier to access Rome, he took it upon himself to repair the Via Flaminia up to Rimini, and wanted each magistrate who was victorious to provide funds from their share of the spoils to build other roads. He rebuilt the temples which had fallen into disrepair or been consumed by fire, and he decorated them as well as other temples in the richest of ways. On a single occasion, he arranged for gold to the weight

[LCdv 465] 2
of 16000000 pounds, and 50,000,000 sesterces' worth of pearls and precious stones to be brought into the sanctuary of Jupiter Capitolinus.*
The same can be said for almost all the cities in Italy. →* in a word, as Augustus himself said, "he had found it built of brick and left it in marble."
Suetonius said "He also made Italy Rome's equal in right and honour."[53]
– [About] the man: I believe, despite the beautiful elogies and touching words which he elicited from Horace and Virgil, despite the sentimental phrases and declamations on which he rarely stinted, I believe that fundamentally he must have been horribly dry and cold; that he needed to weigh, to measure, to calculate everything in his life, his actions,

---

53 Suetonius, *Life of Augustus*, quoted in Greg Rowe, *Princes and Political Cultures: The New Tiberian Senatorial Decrees* (Ann Arbor: University of Michigan Press, 2002), p. 105.

his words: that there was not a single part of his conduct, however small, left for instinct, feeling, impulse, or his heart's desire. Everything was calculation and reasoning: of all the men in antiquity, Augustus is perhaps the man who knew the least about weakness and honourable sentiments.

(Camille Jullian. G[ran]de Encyclopédie)[54]

[LCdv 466] 3

...; The people to whom I am speaking will see straight away that they have rid themselves of a certain blind respect which long history and custom, even in the case of major excesses, ordinarily imprints onto most people's minds and preoccupies them such that they find it difficult to disabuse themselves of it later, because they are too deferential and almost dare not examine things that have enjoyed popular approval for a long time. (page 2)[55]

... As if the Pantheon, that marvellous and incomparable edifice which can still be seen in Rome today, were not the invention of its builder because he did not alter the Corinthian order according to which it is built in its entirety. It is not in the detail of individual parts that we can see an architect's talent; he must be judged by the

[LCdv 467]

overall range of his work. Narrow minds who are unable to achieve a universal understanding of art, or to embrace the full extent of it, must stop still, powerless, and grub around incessantly in these minutiae; thus as their studies are not directed towards anything else, and they are themselves already sterile, their ideas are so base and unsightly that they produce nothing but hideous figures, ugly cartouches and other ridiculous and similarly impertinent grotesques with which modern architecture is entirely infested. Others to whom nature has been kinder, and who have greater imaginations, can see that true and essential beauty in architecture lies not simply in each part taken individually, but instead results principally from symmetry, which is the union and

[LCdv 468] 4

overall combination of everything coming together to form visible harmony, which those of us with clear eyes enlightened by artistic intelligence take great pleasure in considering. The problem is that these fine geniuses are always so very rare, whilst everywhere is teeming with common workers. If the Greats would only slough off some of the mistrust they have for the arts and those who practise them, and consider the need which they themselves have, particularly for that which I will discuss, it seems very much that the arts might be revived even today, and might bring forth 'new antiquities'. Experience of this remained rather fresh during the reign of Francis the First, one of the most illustrious kings in history who, through the extraordinary love he had for virtue and higher matters, populated his government with the most exceptional

[LCdv 469]

figures of his century, who in turn had superb monuments erected in the memory of this great monarch. In my opinion this is the only remedy for restoring all the arts to their

---

54 Although one would expect Jeanneret to have used this source in the *Staatsbibliothek Berlin*, it cannot be found there.

55 Fréart, *Parallèle*, p. 2.

former glory, from which they were toppled through disregard. The Greeks invented the arts, and only they have perhaps seen them in their perfect state, have held them in such high esteem that their first Republics made professions of the arts, but not simply as hired hands; their works were rewarded with honour, and since they claimed as their reward glory and immortality for their names, they only produced great things. What we read of that nation would be hard to believe if the good intentions of their authors were not beyond reproach, and if there were not, even today,

[LCdv 470]

visible traces of the tales told about it. Page 3.[56]

...; for the excellence and perfection of an art lie not in the multiplicity of its principles; on the contrary, the simpler and fewer these are, the more admirable the art will be: we see this in the principles of geometry, which nevertheless forms the basis and general store for all the arts, from which that art is derived, and without whose help it would be impossible for it to survive.[57]

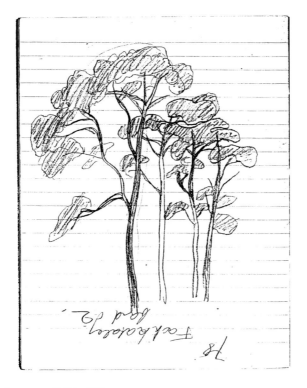

Fig. 121 Sketch by Jeanneret (LCdv 473)

56 Fréart, *Parallèle*, p. 3.
57 Fréart, *Parallèle*, p. 7.

[LCdv 471] 6
Doric intercolumniations. Parthenon 1 2/5 module (module = base of column or triglyph)

[LCdv 472] [Sketch with trees]

[LCdv 473] [Sketch with trees, under which, upside down:] **[121]**
78 Fachkatalog vol. 2

Cahier C.13 – *Laugier* (Berlin, January to March 1911)

[LCdv 474] Laugier. // G // Borrowed from the Koenigliche Bibliothek Berlin January 1911

[LCdv 475] 1 **[122]**
[Page text centred, in the shape of the title page of the second, expanded edition of 1755:]

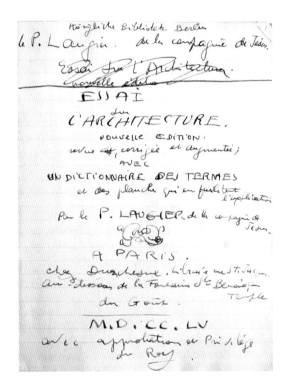

Fig. 122 Frontispiece of Laugier's *Essai*. Cahier C.13 (LCdv 475)

Königliche Bibliothek Berlin
Abbé Laugier, the Society of Jesus.
~~Essay on Architecture.~~
~~new editio~~
ESSAY
on
ARCHITECTURE.
New EDITION.
revised, amended and improved;
WITH A DICTIONARY OF TERMS
and plates which aid explanation
By ABBÉ LAUGIER, the Society of Jesus.
[Sketch of coat of arms]
IN PARIS
At Duchesne's Bookshop, Rue St. Jacques.
Above the Fontaine St Benoît, at the Temple
du Goût.
M.D.CC.LV
With the King's approval and
privilege. //

[LCdv 476] 3
II order 1 order 1/2 1 1
Nave of a church width to height 1 to 2 1/2, Laugier remarks that the impact of such height is singularly majestic.
He states:
"Perhaps one day, through study and reflection, I shall succeed in basing the science of proportions on more rational and firmer principles.
Up to now one went about this matter haphazardly. In a recent work, which amazes by its lavish display of engravings, the intention has been to throw light on this obscure part of the art. The author proves at length the necessity of proportions which nobody doubts but when he should have told us in what precisely they consist, he only repeats the arbitrary

[LCdv 477]
opinions of some authors of the past and gives us, even more arbitrarily, musical harmonies as rule."[58] (page XXIV foreword)
page XVI
"I should like to convince everybody of a truth in which I myself believe absolutely, namely that the parts of an architectural Order are the parts of the building itself. They

---

58 Marc-Antoine Laugier, *Essai sur l'architecture. Avec un dictionnaire des termes, et des planches qui en facilitent l'explication. Nouvelle édition, revue, corrigée, et augmentée* (Paris: Duchesne, 1755), p. XXVI; transl. into English as *An Essay on Architecture* by Wolfgang and Anni Herrmann (Los Angeles: Hennessey and Ingalls, 1977), p. 156.

must therefore be applied in such a way that they not only adorn but actually constitute the building. The existence of the building must depend so completely on the union of these parts that not a single one could be taken away without the whole building collapsing. If one imprints this reasonable and lucid principle well into one's mind one will easily recognize a host of errors arising from a practice which obstinately follows

[LCdv 478] 5

the opposite principle. No longer will these pilasters and these entablatures plastered over the solid mass of the building be taken for true architecture; they are so much decoration only that one can destroy the whole architectural layer with a blow of a chisel without the building losing anything but an ornament. On the other hand, free-standing columns which carry an entablature never leave one in doubt about the truth of the architectural display they present because one feels that none of these parts could be touched without causing damage and ruin to the building."[59]

Preface X [...] "I can truly say that my main intention is to suggest to the public, especially to the artists, that they should doubt, should make conjectures, and should never be easily satisfied.

[LCdv 479]

If, spurred by me to do their own research, they are led to find me wrong, to correct my inaccuracies, and to improve my reasoning, I shall be only too pleased.

This book is just an essay in which I really give no more than indications and clear the way. The task of applying my principles extensively I leave to others who may use a keen intelligence which I would not have."[60]

"The beauty and splendour of a town depends mainly on three things: its entries, its streets and its buildings. (page 210 The entries to a town must be (1) free and unobstructed; [(2) numerous, proportionate to the circumference of the wall;] (3) sufficiently ornate" page 211

He demands a straight, very wide street in front of the entrance, with as many benefits on the inside: "It is not enough that the avenue be wide and as far as possible without

[LCdv 480] 7

bend or deviation; the gate and the street inside, which corresponds to the avenue, must also have these advantages. It would even be desirable to find a large square opened up by several streets forming a fanlike pattern (*en patte d'oie*) at the entrance of a big town. The entrance to Rome at the Porta del Popolo is in this style;"[61] we have nothing like it in Paris. (page 213)

"The gateway of a great town must have décor and an air of magnificence and grandeur."[62] (214)

"Where the tollhouses now stand one should erect great triumphal arches on which the memory of the great deeds which made the reigns of our kings famous would be immortalized. Triumphal arches are the most fitting decoration for the entries of a town like

---

59 Laugier, *Essai* 1755, pp. XVIIf. / Herrmann, *Essay*, pp. 152f.
60 Laugier, *Essai* 1755, pp. XLIIf. / Herrmann, *Essay*, p. 4.
61 Laugier, *Essai* 1755, pp. 211f. / Herrmann, *Essay*, p. 123.
62 Laugier, *Essai* 1755, p. 214 / Herrmann, *Essay*, p. 124.

Paris. They proudly announce the place of residence of the conquering monarchs who filled the whole of Europe with their

[LCdv 481]

exploits."[63] "People are in difficulty about setting up monuments to the glory of the august princes who govern us: which monuments could be more worthy of them than triumphal arches? They provide a simple and natural way of passing on to posterity the memory of their great actions and, when placed at the entry to the town, right away display these actions to the stranger. That is how the Romans, a nation which had only noble ideas and always thought on a grand scale, honored their emperors. They did not think of creating immensely large squares merely to place at the center of each a solitary statue of one of these rulers of the world. They marked their greatness much better by erecting on several avenues of their

[LCdv 482] 9)

town superb arches which recall the military triumph, the climax of their great actions. By taking up the ideas of this admirable nation and giving to all entries into our capital this Roman air, this lofty style of decoration, we shall gain a twofold advantage. We shall create magnificent entrance gates capable of attracting the attention and holding the admiration of the stranger and will, without too much cost, set up monuments which will contribute both to the glory of our kings and to the edification of posterity."[64] 216.

217 "I imagine a great avenue, very wide and straight, lined with two or four rows of trees; it ends at a triumphal arch, similar to the one I have described;

[LCdv 483]

from there one enters a large place formed by a half-section of a circle, of an oval or of a polygon; several streets extend fanlike form it (*en patte d'oie*) of which some lead into the center, others to the outlying districts of the town and all with a vista of a beautiful work. All this combined will make it the most beautiful entry to a town imaginable. For a long time to come one cannot execute anything similar in a town like Paris. Too much must be pulled down, too much be rebuilt. But at least one can make the plan for it and order its execution step by step as the houses decay with age. What we will have begun, our descendants will conclude. Posterity, indebted to us

[LCdv 484] 11

for having imagined the scheme, will give us credit for a thousand masterpieces which, when executed, will recall in centuries of the most distant future the soundness and grandeur of our ideas."[65]

page 27

"[The author of the Examen opposes this principle...] 'Let us not,' he says, 'be slaves to primitive practices; let us not demand too strict a correlation with them in our formations when *the length of time and the force of an ancient habit have authorized these*' (underlined in the book). This means that irregularities can in time become legitimate, and that

63 Laugier, *Essai* 1755, p. 215 / Herrmann, *Essay*, p. 124.

64 Laugier, *Essai* 1755, p. 215f. / Herrmann, *Essay*, p. 124f.

65 Laugier, *Essai* 1755, pp. 219f. / Herrmann, *Essay*, p. 127.

whereas the ancients had the right to condemn certain abuses while they were novel, we are not allowed to proscribe them, since they have been sanctioned by the length

[LCdv 485]

of time and the force of habit. This way of thinking which makes what is right simply dependent on custom seems to me a very easy expedience for ignorant and lazy artists but it obstructs the progress of the arts too much to be generally adopted. I have always believed that what is originally an abuse does not cease to be one by having become customary. In matters of reason and taste, what has once been condemned should always be condemned. [...] If only arbitrary rules are wanted for the arts one can insist on custom, but if the processes of art must go back to

[LCdv 486] 13)

fixed principles it is necessary to appeal to reason against custom and to sacrifice to the light of one the force and sway of the other."[66]

Preface XXXIII

"It seems to me that in those arts which are not purely mechanical it is not sufficient to know how to work; it is above all important to learn to think. An artist should be able to explain everything he does, and for this he needs firm principles to determine his judgments and justify his choice so that he can tell whether a thing is good or bad, not simply by instinct but by reasoning and as a man experienced in the way of beauty."[67]

[LCdv 487]

page 209 "Most of our towns have remained in a state of neglect, confusion and disorder, brought about by the ignorance and boorishness of our forefathers. New houses have been built but neither the bad distributions of the streets nor the unsightly irregularity of the decorations, made at random and according to anybody's whim, are changed. Our towns are still what they are, a mass of houses crowded together haphazardly without system, planning or design. Nowhere is this disorder more noticeable than in Paris. The center of this capital has hardly changed for three hundred years; there are still the same number of little, narrow and tortuous streets

[LCdv 488] 15)

smelling of dirt and filth where the encounter of carriages causes constant obstruction."[68]
"Its avenues are miserable, the streets badly laid out and too narrow, the houses are plain and banal, the squares few in number and insignificant and nearly all palaces badly placed – in short, it is a very big, disordered town where one encounters few striking objects and is much surprised to find nothing that is in accordance with the idea one had formed of it or that comes anywhere near to what one has seen in more than one less famous town."[69]
... page 222... "the streets are [mostly so narrow that one cannot pass through them without danger and] so winding and so full of senseless bends

66 Laugier, *Essai* 1755, pp. 27f. / Herrmann, *Essay*, pp. 21f.
67 Laugier, *Essai* 1755, p. XXXIIIf. / Herrmann, *Essay*, p. 1.
68 Laugier, *Essai* 1755, pp. 209f. / Herrmann, *Essay*, p. 121.
69 Laugier, *Essai* 1755, p. 210 / Herrmann, *Essay*, p. 122.

[LCdv 489]

and corners that the way between one place and the other becomes twice as long."[70]

222 "One must look at a town as a forest. The streets of the one are the roads of the other; both must be cut through in the same way. The essential beauty of a park consists in the great number of roads, their width and their alignment. This, however, is not sufficient: it needs a Le Nôtre to design the plan for it, someone who applies taste and intelligence so that there is at one and the same time order and fantasy, symmetry and variety, with roads here in the pattern of a star, there in that of *patte d'oie*, with a featherlike arrangement in one place, fanlike in another, with parallel roads further away and everywhere *carrefours* of different design

[LCdv 490] 17

and shape. The more variety, abundance, contrast and even disorder in this composition, the greater will be the piquant and delightful beauty of the park. [...] Let us carry out this idea and use the design of parks as plan for our towns. [...] There are towns with perfectly aligned streets, but since the plan was made by uninspired people, a boring accuracy and cold uniformity prevail which makes one miss the disorder of towns of ours that have no kind of alignment at all; everything is related to a single shape, to a large parallelogram transversed lengthwise and crosswise by lines at right angles. Everywhere we have only

[LCdv 491]

boring repetition of the same objects, and all quarters look so much alike that one is mistaken and gets lost. [...] Above all, let us avoid excessive regularity and excessive symmetry. [...] Whoever does not vary our pleasures, will not succeed in pleasing us.

It is therefore no small matter to draw a plan for a town in such a way that the splendor of the whole is divided into an infinite number of beautiful, entirely different details so that one hardly ever meets the same objects again, and, wandering from one end to the other, comes in every quarter across something new, unique, startling, so that there is order and yet

[LCdv 492] 19)

a sort of confusion, and everything is in alignment without being monotonous, and a multitude of regular parts brings about a certain impression of irregularity and disorder which suits great cities so well. To do this one must master the art of combination and have a soul full of fire and imagination which apprehends vividly the fairest and happiest combinations."[71] (end of sentence bizarre and incomprehensible ChEJt)

"[...] What happy thoughts, ingenious turns, variety of expression, wealth of idea, bizarre connections, lively contrasts, what fire and boldness, what a sensational composition!"[72]

[LCdv 493]

page 225 "So many provincial towns, with meagre resources, have had the courage to contemplate rebuilding the town on a new plan, hoping to achieve it with the help of

---

70 Laugier, *Essai* 1755, pp. 221f. / Herrmann, *Essay*, p. 128.

71 Laugier, *Essai* 1755, pp. 221f. / Herrmann, *Essay*, pp. 21f.

72 Laugier, *Essai* 1755, p. 225 / Herrmann, *Essay*, pp. 129f.

time and patience. [...] The greatest projects demand only resolution and courage provided they meet no physical obstacle."[73]

It might be stated in the chapter on La Chaux-de-Fonds that this is the youngest town in Francophone Switzerland – and the ugliest to boot. It has no past whatsoever; besides, the past becomes an encumbrance where it persists in places which continue developing as events unfold (Geneva, Lausanne, Berlin etc.).

[LCdv 494] 21

So, what a magnificent dream, to make this oh-so-modernist town of La Chaux-de-Fonds into the most beautiful new town in Francophone Switzerland.

"Nothing would be more worthy of a nation as bold, ingenious, and powerful as the French than to start on a new plan which in time will make Paris the most beautiful city in the universe."[74]

"When he is consulted (the architect), he must only propose what is fitting. If he has reputation at heart he will not look for dazzling designs to flatter the vanity of people to whom splendour is not at all fitting and who themselves are often too inclined →} [Arrow to: "to go beyond the limits"]

→ never forgetting this true principle

that a beautiful building is not one that has any kind of beauty (*beauté arbitraire*), but one that, considering the circumstances, has all the beauty that is befitting and none beyond."[75]

to go beyond the limits. An architect, knowing well what is fitting to each person, will elaborate or restrain his plans according to his judgment,→ [Arrow to: "never forgetting"]

[LCdv 495]

26 January 1911

Laugier begins his chapter thus: On the decoration of buildings:

"When the plan of a town is well mapped out, the main and most difficult part is done. It remains, however, to regulate the exterior decoration of the buildings. If one wants a well-built town, the façades of houses must not be left to the whim of private persons. Every part that faces the street must be determined and governed by public authority according to the design which will be laid down for the whole street. It is necessary to settle not only the sites where it will be permitted to build but also the style in which to build."[76]

229. ... "As to façades of houses, they need regularity and much variety. Long streets where all houses seem to be one single building,

[LCdv 496] 23

because one has observed a rigorous symmetrical scheme, are a thoroughly boring sight. Too much uniformity is the worst of all faults."[77]

---

73 Laugier, *Essai* 1755, p. 225 / Herrmann, *Essay*, p. 130.
74 Laugier, *Essai* 1755, p. 225 / Herrmann, *Essay*, p. 130.
75 Laugier, *Essai* 1755, pp. 27f. / Herrmann, *Essay*, pp. 99.
76 Laugier, *Essai* 1755, p. 227 / Herrmann, *Essay*, p. 130.
77 Laugier, *Essai* 1755, p. 227 (sic) / Herrmann, *Essay*, p. 131.

Comparison with a painting, gradation of light, colour, then brutality in one place etc., next: "Do we wish to decorate our streets in an exquisite style? Then we must not use ornament in profusion; let us apply much that is simple, a little that is casual together with elegance and magnificence. As a rule one [...] should occasionally proceed abruptly from one extreme to the other using contrasts the boldness of which attracts the eye and produces strong effects, abandon from time to time symmetry and give in to caprice and eccentricity;

[LCdv 497]

blend the soft with the hard, the delicate with the rough, the elegant with the rustic, (1) and never depart from the true and natural (2)."[78] (This last proposition (1) to (2) seems to me not very conclusive in itself.) page 230

He comes back to perfectly aligned streets:

"I wish that this scheme of embellishment, of which I have outlined the principles and have fixated approximate rules, would find connoisseurs who appreciate it, devoted citizens who kindly consent to it and intrepid magistrates who seriously consider it and make efficient preparations to having it executed."[79]

GARDENS.

One form of imitation became widespread, that of

[LCdv 498] 25

substituting real gardens, planned tastefully, for insipid orchards, gardens... with grace, filled with all those happy objects which until then had only existed in poets' imaginations.

"If wealth of bronzes and marbles, if nature stifled and buried under such an exaggerated display of symmetry and pomp, if a strange, extraordinary, stiff, and bombastic style makes up the beauty, then Versailles deserves to be preferred to all others. [But judged by our impressions what do we find when walking in these stately gardens?[80]] "At first astonishment and admiration but soon sadness and boredom."[81]

"...we shall then note" (in Versailles) "many faults which, by depriving a garden of the delightful and graceful, deprive it of its most essential beauty."[82]

"There will never be pleasant

[LCdv 499]

gardens unless places already embellished by nature are chosen, delightful places where the eye will fall on a landscape adorned with a thousand rustic charms and where contemplation will give rise to those moments of sweet reverie which hold the soul in happy repose."[83]

A second fault is the overly methodical regularity of these gardens (Versailles).

78 Laugier, *Essai* 1755, p. 230 / Herrmann, *Essay*, p. 132.
79 Laugier, *Essai* 1755, pp. 27f. / Herrmann, *Essay*, pp. 99.
80 Jeanneret omits this sentence and places a question mark at the end of the previous sentence.
81 Laugier, *Essai* 1755, pp. 236f. / Herrmann, *Essay*, p. 136.
82 Laugier, *Essai* 1755, pp. 236f. / Herrmann, *Essay*, p. 136.
83 Laugier, *Essai* 1755, pp. 237 / Herrmann, *Essay*, pp. 136f.

This fault... "diminishes their enjoyment to such an extent that for pleasant promenades one has to leave these groves where art is too conspicuous and go and look for *la belle nature* amidst the open country adorned with artless naiveté."[84]

(A tendentious train of thought, which would soon lead one to Jean-Jacques Rousseau.)

"When given the choice, the man of genius will always prefer the uneven

[LCdv 500] 27

to the even ground. On uneven ground, he will find a thousand ways to invent new spectacles, form enjoyable contrasts, produce delightful surprises, avoid any kind of monotony, place everywhere something which is singular and picturesque and retain the true and natural look of everything. On level ground, on the contrary, he must force his mind not to give in to insipid symmetry; he may well have his dreams, yet will be driven to follow convention and repeat himself endlessly.

A third fault of the gardens of Versailles is that one feels too much hemmed in. One goes into a garden to breathe fresh air and be at ease. Here, one always seems to be within four walls."[85]

"The unpleasantness of

[LCdv 501]

these green walls was felt. Quite rightly one took a dislike to them and sought means by which to enjoy shade without losing the view and to escape the heat of the sun without being confined between two walls. In this one succeeded through planting trees with the trunks left free and unencumbered and the crowns joined together; they form the desired cover in a thousand different ways. Hence the charming *quinconces* which provide cool shade without obstructing the view and arcades and bowers that form a vault of greenery supported by as many columns as there are tree trunks. [...] The gardens of Versailles are like the paintings of Caravaggio in which black predominates excessively or like modern music where the profusion of dissonances badly affects the senses."[86]

He then accuses the greenery of lacking liveliness, an accusation

[LCdv 502] 29

which no longer counts now that the great, monumental foliage almost has a certain, solemn something. (ChEJt.)

"The only beautiful parterres are parterres *en gazon*;

[...] to let the gardener decide not only on the right place for these flowers but also on the particular kind of flower suitable"[87]... (246)

"A gardener ought to be an excellent painter or, at least, have a good knowledge of that part of painting which has to do with complementary colors and with the different tones of the same color. He could then arrange the green so as to create surprise and enable us to enjoy unusual pleasure."[88]

84 Laugier, *Essai* 1755, p. 240 / Herrmann, *Essay*, p. 138.
85 Laugier, *Essai* 1755, pp. 242f. / Herrmann, *Essay*, pp. 139f.
86 Laugier, *Essai* 1755, pp. 243f. / Herrmann, *Essay*, p. 140.
87 Laugier, *Essai* 1755, pp. 245f. / Herrmann, *Essay*, p. 141.
88 Laugier, *Essai* 1755, pp. 247f. / Herrmann, *Essay*, p. 142.

[LCdv 503]
What is a garden without water?
– This overly superb and not at all delightful garden (Versailles)

On what is seemly in churches: "Nude figures in particular must be strictly banished from painting and sculpture. It is surprising to see them even on altars making them almost indecent and scandalous."[89]
La Place Royale (Place des Vosges) "the most spacious of all, could be beautiful, if the iron grille round the center, resembling a garden enclosure, were broken up, if the squat porticoes which run all the way round and are worth less than the worst cloisters of a monastery were bricked up, if the great pavilions which conceal the two main entrances were demolished, if the four corners were opened up by great streets – with all this done it would look like a square.

[LCdv 504] 31
As it is, it can only be taken for a courtyard the center of which has been turned into a garden. The Place des Victoires, although the smallest, is however the most beautiful because of the many wide streets leading to it. The Place Louis le Grand" (Vendôme) "is generally admired for its strict symmetry and rich architecture. [...] and the square itself is like an isolated court-yard to which no street leads directly and which is so well enclosed on all sides that, standing at the center, one would be led to believe that there is no way of getting out. For a square to be beautiful it should be a communal center from which people can make their way into different quarters [...] Porticoes are the right decoration for squares and if joined to these there are build-ings of different height and

[LCdv 505]
shape, the decoration will be perfect. Symmetry is necessary but also a certain disorder that varies and strengthens the spectacle."[90]
"One must go to Rome to develop a taste for beautiful fountains.
[...] it would be absurd to establish as a principle that every statue must have a square. In our days we have seen thoughtless people make a rash proposal to pull down eight or nine hundred houses to make room for a statue of Louis XV."[91]
...And why! Does a statue demand a square on principle? Is the position of Henri IV's statue on the Pont Neuf not a hundred times better than that of all the others?"
About clothing statues: "I do not know if the current way of dressing statues is the best and the most

[LCdv 506] 33
fitting one. Why mislead posterity? Why disguise our heroes under a dress that was not customary in our times? If the Romans had had this bizarre idea we would be very annoyed with them. To suppress or change what could in the eyes of future centuries characterize our nation and our century is acting dishonestly."[92] (169)

---

89 Laugier, *Essai* 1755, p. 156 / Herrmann, *Essay*, p. 91.
90 Laugier, *Essai* 1755, pp. 164–6 / Herrmann, *Essay*, p. 95.
91 Laugier, *Essai* 1755, pp. 166f. / Herrmann, *Essay*, p. 96.
92 Laugier, *Essai* 1755, p. 169 / Herrmann, *Essay*, p. 98.

On new building methods: "Even when the prejudice of the mind begins to disappear, it would still remain for the habit of the hand to be reformed. This second obstacle will always slow down success. It is not at all easy to make the workmen execute things which they have never done before. Their imaginations rebel, their ideas are confounded and their hands refuse to work. It needs an ardor and a patience, of which few people are capable,

[LCdv 507]

to drag the workman away from the ordinary routine and to lead him on a route which is completely unknown to him. One must endure from him much grumbling, engage with him in many quarrels, smoothe over many of his aversions. Only by overcoming all these difficulties have the architects of the fifteenth century brought about the revolution that gave the deathblow to Gothic architecture and restored over its debris the antique systems (*ordonnances*)."[93]
"If only arbitrary rules are wanted for the arts one can insist on custom, but if the processes of art must go back to fixed principles it is necessary to appeal to reason against custom and to sacrifice to the light of one the force and sway of the other."[94]
page 28

[LCdv 508] 35

"In short, everything that goes against nature may be peculiar but will never be beautiful. Every part of a building must be supported from the foundation upward. Here is a rule from which it is never permitted to depart."[95] (page 48)
Page 56 "For many centuries we have combined, always in a different manner, the seven tones of the musical scale and are still far from having exhausted all possible combinations. I say the same of those parts that are the essential elements of an architectural Order. They are small in number yet, without adding anything, one can combine them ad infinitum. It is a sign of genius to know how to avail oneself of these different combinations, this source of pleasing variety. An architect adheres to irrelevancies only because he lacks genius; he overloads his work

[LCdv 509]

only because he is not gifted enough to make it simple."[96]
... "it seems to me that we have really only three Orders: the Doric, the Ionic and the Corinthian. They alone are distinguished by inventiveness and individual character, [...] It is therefore true that architecture is only under moderate obligation to the Romans and that it owes everything that is valuable and solid to the Greeks alone. I am not going to speak here about the Gothic and Arabesque or Moorish Orders which ruled for too long. They are remarkable only the one for being excessively heavy, the other for being excessively light. Both of them show so little inventiveness, taste and accuracy that they are generally regarded as lasting proof of the barbarism which filled a period

---

93 Laugier, *Essai* 1755, p. 186 / Herrmann, *Essay*, p. 107.
94 Laugier, *Essai* 1755, p. 28 / Herrmann, *Essay*, p. 22.
95 Laugier, *Essai* 1755, p. 48 / Herrmann, *Essay*, p. 32.
96 Laugier, *Essai* 1755, pp. 56f. / Herrmann, *Essay*, p. 37.

[LCdv 510] 37

of more than ten centuries."[97] Page 62

"It has been noticed a long time ago that invention is not our strong point. We do better in perfecting and in surpassing the inventions of others."[98] 63.

"The three orders, understood in this way, appear to cover the whole range of art, satisfying all the needs and tastes. The Doric and Corinthian are two extremes beyond which one cannot go without falling either into a clumsy or a fragile style. The Ionic gives us, between these two extremes, the proper and happy medium. There, ingeniously accomplished, is the whole graduation from solid to delicate! It will, therefore, always be extremely difficult to add something new to such a fortunate discovery."[99] 64

[LCdv 511]

"The rectangle is the most common form of our buildings. However, this far too universal form has become hackneyed and is not interesting anymore. It is our nature to love novelty and variety; the fine arts must all be adapted to this inborn taste."[100] (This was written at the dawn of Louis XV's reign, it makes me think of the Baroque in Würzburg, Dresden, from that time.) further: ... this can be considered a proper mixture of straight lines and curves, (in plan) –

The first lines of the introduction; page 1. "Of all the useful arts, architecture demands the most accomplished talent and the most extensive knowledge. It needs perhaps as much genius, esprit and taste to be come a great architect as is needed for a first-rate painter or poet."[101]

[LCdv 512] 39

(Appreciation) "The Church of St. Sulpice is another monument where the coarseness of our work, has, unfortunately, been sanctioned. Did it need such heavy masses to give solidity to this building? Our architects will assert this, the public will be against them and I would only have to take them to Sainte Chapelle to confound them. The ancients were sparing with the use of stone and lavish with that of iron; in this way and with the help of level and plumb line they succeeded in joining the solid to the delicate. What would be the disadvantage of doing as they did? We understand decoration infinitely better than they did, but they were more skilled in construction than we are. If we want to improve, do not let us consult them in matters of decoration but let us never stop consulting them in those of construction."[102] (page 129)

[LCdv 513]

{page 17.} "I enter Notre-Dame, the most eminent of our Gothic buildings in Paris, though not by far as beautiful as certain others in the provinces which everybody admires. Nevertheless, at first glance my attention is captured, my imagination is struck by the size, the height and the unobstructed view (*dégagement*) of the vast nave; for some moments I am lost in the amazement that the grand effect of the whole stirs in me.

97 Laugier, *Essai* 1755, p. 62 / Herrmann, *Essay*, pp. 39f.

98 Laugier, *Essai* 1755, p. 63 / Herrmann, *Essay*, p. 40.

99 Laugier, *Essai* 1755, p. 64 / Herrmann, *Essay*, p. 41.

100 Laugier, *Essai* 1755, p. 111 / Herrmann, *Essay*, p. 65.

101 Laugier, *Essai* 1755, p. 1 / Herrmann, *Essay*, p. 7.

102 Laugier, *Essai* 1755, pp. 128f. / Herrmann, *Essay*, p. 76.

Recovering from the first astonishment and taking note of the details, I find innumerable absurdities, but I lay the blame for them on the misfortunes of the time. For all that I am still full of admiration when after my thorough and critical examination I return to the middle of the nave and the impression which remains with me makes me say: 'How many faults, but how grand!'"[103] (16 February 1911)

[LCdv 514]

"This *'essential'* beauty can be felt, and we find it hard to define: this is a charm which draws our interest. The impression of pleasure stays with us, the idea of the thing escapes us; our heart is sure of its facts, our mind on its own is not always able to yield to the truth of it."[104] Page 255

"Prejudice and fashion may make our eyes accustomed to failings, and they may soften our feelings about these in our spirits; but they are not able to engender beauty. The effect of prejudice or fashion always disappears, given thought; in its place, beauty is such that its sphere of influence increases with thought; one routinely leaves it behind through prejudice and fashion; one always returns to it through one's feelings and reasoning."[105] Page 256.

– "if there is no essential beauty, everything will become arbitrary in this most spiritual area of the arts" (architecture), [...]. "It will not matter if I praise or censure

[LCdv 515]

everything I encounter, or rather: I will be no more in the right to say that something is good than to say it is bad. I will be obliged to admit the wildest imaginings of a licentious artist. I will have neither principles with which to contradict him, nor limits to place upon him. The more capricious and bold he is, the better able he will be to triumph over established fashion, substituting in its place new ones, and making them succeed through their oddness."[106] (page 256)

"Firstly, I will not be able to convince myself that beauty in relation to the arts is merely an effect of prejudice born of nationhood or education, and has no constancy because it is merely founded on fashion."[107] (page 254 – therefore comes before the lines above).

"Modern architecture is architecture which was customary during barbarian times, and

[LCdv 516] 43

is commonly known as Gothic. It can be subdivided into two types, the old and the new Gothic. The old Gothic, as imagined by the first barbarians to be established on the lands of the Roman Empire, was a clumsy, rustic imitation of the ancient orders of architecture which these ignorant and clumsy people copied in the same way a village dweller today might copy a painting by Raphael."[108]

103 *Essai* 1755, p. 174 (!) / Herrmann, p. 101/ Laugier.

104 This and the following excerpts are from Laugier's response to Monsieur Frezier, as published in the *Mercure* in July 1754, but also inserted at the end of the 1755 *Essai*. Neither the 1755 translation (London: Osborne and Shipton), nor the translation we used above (by Wolfgang and Anni Herrmann) includes this response. It is therefore our own translation. Laugier, *Essai* 1755, p. 255.

105 Laugier, *Essai* 1755, p. 256.

106 Laugier, *Essai* 1755, p. 256.

107 Laugier, *Essai* 1755, p. 254.

108 Laugier, *Essai* 1755, p. 280, in "Dictionnaire des Termes", under "Architecture".

My impression of this book:
Laugier published it in 1755 at a time of reaction against Louis XIV style, when Hindu and Chinese ideas were beginning to be imported. He is a man cast

[LCdv 517]

in a Louis XIV mould, who therefore has in him everything he needs for a powerful, grand concept of architecture – without, it is true, having in him the extremely sensible mediaeval tradition. Having seen Louis' desires come to fruition in Versailles and in the squares of Paris, as well as in the provinces, he seeks even greater purity in this form entirely devoted to grandeur.

Yet feels that this bombastic habit was at times unsuitable. He laments, in the gardens at Versailles at the time, the excess artificiality. But I think that today, now that 180 years have allowed us to gain an overwhelming impression of the natural beauty there,

[LCdv 518] 45

huge foliage in free forms has taken over from the slender proportions of days gone by, to powerful architectural effect – this asserts itself everywhere, given the heights it now reaches, and the physical embodiment of space, contrasts, balance, harmony between restraint and folly, flowerbeds like embroidery and marble walls with a green patina from the vases, hedges and clipped box trees, the exuberant domes of chestnut trees, long *allees* laid out like the naves of cathedrals, etc. – I think that Laugier would alter his criticism to unrestrained praise.

His ideas about urban design are perfect for his era, and for art. Logical steps forward in [architectural] spectacle. Always striving

[LCdv 519]

for the *grand style [français]*, which is superior to the surprises and entertainment of the picturesque.

His star-shaped squares are perfect, due to their dimensions in both height and width, and the placement of the monuments is correct given the aim he pursues. It all accords perfectly with life in that era.

His ideas on the Gothic are comical but readily understandable – one might almost call them reasonable.

In the present day, when a reaction can be detected against the outdated principles of the mediaeval picturesque style developed by Sitte, Laugier speaks with uncommon force because he is of an era which has already tried and tested the *grand style*

[LCdv 520] 47

and which, having reached saturation point, but also emboldened by this extraordinary develop-ment, has turned towards charm and grace. We are emerging from our spinelessness, we have allowed ourselves to be deceived by a childish bout of romanticism and are now yearning for a style which – in order to enact the growing wisdom of our philosophy and science and the generosity of our dreams for society – adopts an adequate form of expression i.e. more abstract beauty than petty materialism, striving for *greatness*, a sign that the masses are marching in unison and overturning the picturesque, which is the mark of narrow, miserly individualism.

12 March 1911

Inventory

Tables of contents, overviews

[LCdv 521]

The government of the city of Florence 1294

~~TABLE OF CONTENTS~~

[LCdv 522]

Proposition:

1/2 General Considerations.

		Introduction
		Blocks
	Revise.	Streets
1/2 squares.		1/2 Squares
tree		Walls.
garden and Park.		
bridges		
cemetery		

1/2 useful strategies.   1/2 Useful strategies
    La Chaux-de-Fonds. black
    the style   white
    garden cities.
    Conclusion

[under which, upside down:]
Climatic conditions and finally finding a way to express our mountain-dwellers' tempera-ment. Very different to lowland buildings.

[LCdv 523] [Front of loose sheet]
blocks
squares → Streets. (1)
enclosure
       Bridges.
       the tree
   4   Gardens and Parks.
       cemeteries.
  ~~2~~   General Considerations
       5 Garden cities → [after 6.]
  3   useful strategies
       6   La Chaux de Fonds
           "   II
      ~~6~~ 7   Conclusion.

[LCdv 524] [Loose sheet]
Octave 5 M.   see also
Cemeteries.   catalogue
Bridges.   City planning
Gardens and parks   exhibition
Garden cities   and write
Japanese garden
allees

Write
~~Berlin 1908. 8. 17⁹~~
~~Brinckmann.~~
Go to Schenke for a representation
Go to see Dr. Jakobs

Overview tables of contents for 'On Squares'

[LCdv 525] [MA 152]

Planning of squares is unsatisfactory

classification	{I}		{I}
of	{II}	today	{II}< parade square recently
squares	{III}		{III}

{unity

Plastic elements {embodiment of space {feeling of enclosure
{emphasising special buildings, hence orientation of the square
{adding impressions with the presence of a monument

unity.   {through uniform style
{by respecting what came before. ("Progress owes a debt of respect to the things it replaces") {today by adopting a bizarre plan we allow a *variety* of buildings, which will be built {by various architects, specifically to create a unified whole from the lie of the land on the plan.
{Or by making the square completely [__] by a single architect, or at least to a single outline or in {a single style

enclosure   {opening
{analyse what one wants to do. 3 CD, 4AB
square for a building {select principles for emphasising a building. 4CE, 5A and 4D; 5B

	{building presents itself as a whole. 5.C		
various	{adjoining squares. 5D.		
	{Addition to architecture 2H,A. }		{dead point F
ornament	{integral part C2	}obligation	{
	{pleasing annex CE	} F2	{contrasts G{3A

various monuments in a group 3B.
Summary   {square to glory E5. cars banned
{hence pure geometric square 5.F {good 17th and 18th} Table and
{poor 19th. } comparison of diam[etres]
with building heights

Piazza della Signoria.   Summary. Square built as and when
~~Cities VI p 13~~ / /   requires a plan with lie of the land.
A square built all at once *allows*, and one must make the most of this,
{if financial resources permit} geometric solutions of a nobler order

place des Vosges
City II p. 9 City III p. 3 B City III p. 1

[LCdv 526]

Monuments   just as, if a living room contained
a [laboratory] retort or a blackboard
or a modern bedroom contained a Roman chair or _,
~~Let us begin again to compare the public~~ square to a bedroom
with furniture. //
~~monuments are the furniture.~~
~~2 types of room. the irregular design.~~   {which should
the ordered design.   {bear some
~~Replacing luxury furniture then, ornament {City VI p6A}~~ {intimate

signifying and plastic relation to the walls
definition of ornament
                        {Solothurn fountain City VI p. 6BD people were not aware
{a {disordered square   {Berne, cite Fribourg etc. }   of the [...]
its application {   {Donatello David Michelangelo} ~~1 monument — / 2 squares~~
{   {Vosges
{b ordered square   {Victoires City III p.1
1   {Louis XV
St Pierre. ~~Concorde~~. Stanislas Nancy
                                                {he allowed
shared obligation {dead point {the King does not oblige himself to   {himself to
City VI page 6C **2**   {all the more so since traffic
was so light and was not ___
~~lack of knowledge today City VI p.6 E Note.8}~~ very brief //

Additional restriction.
The question of monuments is a whole study in itself.   sheet *
The monument has become baroque stupidity   (notebook *trees* p.1)
in the modern day. **3** façade... was built
as and when. The concept of scale
is lost. Then there's an exaggeration and lack
of tact. Napoléon set the pace with Etoile
then everything else is a pale imitation
of it, table of relationship between area
of façade
table of [...] relationship between building
height and diameter.
Gattamelata. City II p.10
Monument in the middle City III p. 1
~~Berne Erlach[?] depression Note. II~~
~~Solothurn fountain Arsenal Swiss fountains in general Berne Fribourg etc. Note 11~~
~~the monument in line with a gateway which it crowds or in which it is lost Note 10~~
Traffic dead point Note 9
inevitability of the axis – for monuments. Michelangelo. Note 8
Michelangelo

[LCdv 527] 1)

unsatisfactory planning of squares

3 squares.

I   for its own sake.   )3 squares

II   for a building   ABC.

III   crossroads   page 1

  unsuitability.

Today: I   square for its own sake. p. 2   Today

    II   square for a building.   p. 3   A. B. C. // page 23 parade

    III   square for traffic p.=3   modern stupidity

no longer any <u>discussion</u> __ ____ //

~~Place~~ [...] {Analysis} of plastic elements 4 a   <u>plastic elements</u>

Various applications over the years   street <u>openings</u>

                                Simple example.   therefore one of the main

a) square [sketch of 'turbine square'] street openings   factors in the

                            enclosed by itself. p. 5   beauty of squares

                                It relates to the relationship

                                between

~~b)~~ corollary marketplace, Stuttgart   p. 8   the quantity of façades

  Hence there is also the matter of   Views and perspective narrowing

  Street openings.   6   of streets depend on

                                [Sketch here of   effect of a

                                marketplace, Grimma] square

  3 types of corner openings.   add   plus [...]

  openings in the middle of one side   6   although

                            application Stuttgart   of

  rectilinear openings {in a single direction} then   beauty of the

  closed   façades.

  opening with an arch.   6   and [...] embodiment of space

  opening with passageway into the block. Sienna Louvre. St [...]

  more perfect opening behind an

  arcade Vosges. forum Pompeii   7

[LCdv 528] 2

~~Openings Optical effect~~   the monument

~~Marketplace, Stuttgart.~~   is ornament

at the end.   A   An ornament is beautiful

<u>ornament ~~in~~ {in these} squares {for their own sake}</u>   2 cases of ornament

Poor procedures   {these squares we have always had {need}   strict and geometric

        to apply ornament as it was done   one which is more or less

        for items in daily use Crockery.   chance

        Rooms. Clothing.

A good typical example David Michelangelo   8

<u>Analysis</u>   B

  2 sorts

1) the monument was an integral part   C

of the square and laid out in one go with
the façades like {luxury} furniture in a

prestigious room thus monumental
the square is for the monument
2) the monument decorates a
square whose walls are given over for
various different initiatives, hence:
picturesque.
the monument is for the square.
1 annex

I {shared} obligation must not obstruct   9
the traffic.
        Dead point.
II obligation law of contrasts   10
a   Gattamelata
b   David Michelangelo
        and idiotic lack of knowledge
        of Michelangelo's wishes

{[... ...] the monument must
add something which the architecture
was unable to give: A
new feeling}
[This section has an arrow to 'Analysis']

[LCdv 529] 3)

c) Swiss fountains.
        Solothurn Arsenal enriching
        Berne. enriching {jewel in setting}   A
        street and square,
balanced impression of richness
on opposite sides of the square.   11

Lack of knowledge again.
Monuments in a group, Scaliger.   B

Square for a building.   13

Analysis: what is the cause
that accounts for the effect.   C
the aim: All for the building.
            b) All for the square due to
               the building
Analyse the nature of the impression

page I City III
    place des Vosges,
    people began
at that time to design
    squares all at once
        D monumental
            replacing the
            picturesque.
        E
            Definition
the monument
        is above all
        F an ornament.
– next an exposé of facts
Today lack of knowl-
edge: 1 exposé of facts,
        G then ornament
            if possible
            but some
subjects are anti-plastic
– hence hybridism
in some monum.s
            made by masters
        H the unbearable
ugliness of those made
by ___
Continued page 6

one wants to produce
       Is one doing it all for beauty
  or   All for utility
hence: is such a task suited to eliciting beauty
       Grand   D
  or   pretty
       Do such dimensions allow [a]
       colossal [approach]
  or   do they require [a] delicate approach.
       Will this material {work with}
       this effect?
       Will these surroundings complement
this impression?
is this façade [right] for this square   12
       or this square for this façade?

[LCdv 530]
In 2 typical examples we see
the realisation of 2 wishes   A
through the deployment
of all the favourable
factors.   12

Despite the completely opposing
characters of the 2 above-mentioned   B
works, formal laws
govern the external expression of   14
abstract feelings.
Sitte proves it.

Let us therefore study these
several principles and know how   C
to make strong combinations of them
as a strong unit to
make our wishes
a reality.
    Impression of dominance.   14
    Impression of brutality   14
       Rouen
       Palazzo Vecchio   D
because of the Street openings.   [indecipherable
                       notes made in pencil]

lack of knowledge today
hence the principle: if façade higher
than it is wide, narrow square   E
and conversely, if façade
wider than it is high,
wide square.

[LCdv 531] 5
Examples.

Always a deep logic		A
Hidden flying buttress	17	
lack of knowledge today.		
Ulm.		
Lack of tact. New spire		B
Florence new façade. –		

The ~~monument~~ building creates several   the building
squares thus ~~making~~ multiplying   21   presents itself to   C
the beauty its façades contribute   as a whole
Vicenza XLI 13
Lucca XLI 12
Salzburg
Bruges
Ulm XXI
Schweidnitz [Świdnica] IV
Piazza and Piazzetta

adjoining squares at different
levels   D

~~Parade square.~~   ~~23~~   put at the start
          perfect assembly of
                    2 previous types
Square to glory.
          Athens.   sq. to glory   E
          Jerusalem
~~Monuments in a group Scaliger~~   page 3 City III 2§
Geometric square ~~from~~   page 3 City III 1§   F
17th and 18th   [above this, in thick
                                                      pencil: 'sq. to glory at the time,
                                                      geometry = pinnacle»]

from 19th --→   page 8 City III
                                                      then table and some comparisons
                                                      of proportions with dimensions
and then monument

[LCdv 532] [Back of loose sheet]
I   in order to be dominant square must be smaller than façade. Rouen 14
~~Palazzo Vecchio~~
          to accentuate contribution made by street openings Rouen. 14

Palazzo Vecchio. Cathedrals in general.   15
Lack of understanding ~~in this era~~ today. 15
II   Another principle: If façade high, square deep } Fig.   16
                           If façade wide, square wide.   } Genoa
                                                            Verona 17
                                                            etc. __ __
                                                            flying buttr[ess].
Lack of understanding [in this/of the] era. { Ulm.   18
                                            { Florence   19.   = secondary branch
                                                        we note in passing: 19

III   The building presents itself   Vicenza 21
                                       Lucca XLI 21
                                       Salzburg 22
                                       Ulm.
                                       Schweidnitz
                                       San Marco
{ adjoining squares
{ a particular case, square on 2 levels

[LCdv 533] 38

The 20th century must partly correct the 19th and resolve the matter.   1
The 19th hygiene benefits.   1
The planner {as we have said, ideally [the] most perfect man.
The field he operates in {= the city. Some minimum levels hygiene traffic beauty} His
assistants are enemies.   2
programme.   factories in a group   2 and 3
              then he will have to reckon with noise from commerce.   3
              commercial grouped together.   3
              then Residential   3
To sum up choice of 3 sites   4
{once these outlines {areas} established}
Once that is done, meet traffic needs.   4
                          factories with trams   4, 5
                          practical grouping of public buildings   4
                          {acting at same time as a landmark}
to promote beauty by designing with beauty.
One single method. Regularisation plan definition.
what it includes   { enumerate
                    { End §1.
lack of correspondence between the methods and the current __ and street planning.
untenable situation. Because routes for everyone.
so seek network for vehicles, and shortest route for pedestrians,
    factory blocks and trams.
    public buildings, distribution and also orientation

Illustrations

[LCdv 534]

E I Parthenon E   II nd Part 43 photos w/plans
E I Piazza Pallio
E I Karlsruhe
N I Streets in [...] Ulm. XXI
P I block [sketch]
P I [sketch]
P I [sketch]
P I [sketch]
P I [sketch] may come together
P I schools S. Sitte
P I blocks [sketch] etc.
N I Nuremberg drawing plan
N I 4 Squares LX
N I Streets LVII
N I XXIV
N I LIX
N I XXVIII ~~IV~~
N I Antwerp VII
N I Weissenburg drawing XII
N I Altorf IX
N I XXX Drawing
N I Diagram curved streets
E I Piazzetta Venice
K I Place Dauphine
K I Schweidnitz drawing
K ? Various squares XLI
K I XLII Rathaus Stuttg[art] K I Salzburg squares
K I 3 small squares IXL
           LXL XXXVI
E I Place de l'Etoile
K I Poor modern squares
E I Forum Pompeii
R I Enclosure Rouen
M I Carlsbad drawing
B I Hampstead
B I Breisach
[All this row in brackets, preceded by: y°]

Bibliographic Notes

[LCdv 536]

AUTHORS Reference	BIBLIOGRAPHY	Publisher
Berlepsch-Valendàs	Bodenpolitik und gemeindliche Wohnungsfürsorge der Stadt Ulm. (with many illustrations) Munich	E Reinhardt

Ebenezer Howard	Garden Cities of To-morrow	
Jos. Aug. Lux.		
Metzendorf. Essen	Brochure on Margarethe [Krupp] Stiftung, Essen	
	Catalogue of Städtebauausstellung Berlin 1910	
	Journal: Städtebau Berlin	
Cahier M p16	Süddeutsche Bauzeitung – (journal)	
Cahier M p16	Gartenkunst (journal)	
Schultze-Naumburg	Kulturarbeiten	Kunstwart
		Munich

[LCdv 537]

Information:

~~Foundation Journal Städtebau Theodor Goecke. Camillo Sitte.~~

~~\Vienna- \Berlin \ Verlag von Ernst Wasmuth~~

Conclusion

[LCdv 538]

[…]

Read the Metzendorf brochure and the Städtebauausstellung catalogue.

The following talks were held following the Städtebauausstellung.

Ist Series:

Prof. Goecke, Landesbaurat: what hopes {expectations} can we have for the result of the Greater Berlin competition?[1]

[LCdv 539] [Continued from LCdv 538]

Geh. Baurat und Stadtbaurat Krause:

The question of traffic flow in Gross-Berlin

Prof. Dr. Eberstadt:

Workers' housing in Germany and Britain. (Projected images) –

Königlicher Baurat Schließmann.

The need for building regulations, their claim to power and the limits of their usefulness

Königlicher Oberbaurat Stübben.

Regularity and irregularity in city planning (projections)

Prof. Hoegg. Director of Gewerbsmuseum Bremen: Parks and cemeteries. (projections)

Fritz Stahl. The city ___ work of art (projections)

Prof. Blum. (On traffic).

Privatdozent Dr. Brinckmann. Aachen

On siting monumental sculptures (projection)

[LCdv 540] [Continued from LCdv 539]

~~II Series.~~

~~Prof. Cornelius Gurlitt. Dresden –~~

Geh. Baurat Prof. Genzmer.

Feeling of volume (Raumkunst) and Städtebau)

Geh. Reg. Rat Dr. Ing. [? Regierungsrat, Dr. of Engineering] Muthesius:

---

1 Jeanneret has translated the title "Welche Erwartungen dürfen wir an das Ergebnis des Wettbewerbs Gross-Berlin knüpfen?".

The garden city movement (projection)
Dr. Südekum: Residential law and custom (Wohnungswesen)
Prof. Diestel Königlicher Baurat Dresden.
Considering the new era when grouping buildings.
Obering[enieur] Petersen.
Traffic flow in cities (projection)
Dr. Hegemann: {Bestrebungen} Efforts in planning American cities (projection)
Geh. Baurat Eger.
Developing the Wasserstrassen in Gross-Berlin and other cities.
Architect. Hermann Jansen.
Gross-Berlin in the future (projection)
Garden city at Essen-Metzendorf will be remarkable for the way in which its master plan is drawn, in broad sweeps, and only the part currently built has small, defined streets. Städtebau July August [1910] Tafel 46[I].

Cahiers: Title Pages

[LCdv 28]
GENERAL // CONSIDERATIONS. // Text. // I

[LCdv 403]
Englisches Haus. – //
– CITY II // BRIDGES. //
Ch. E. Jeanneret // 3 Lotzbeckstrasse [III]

[LCdv 421]
CITY III // **K**

[LCdv 79]
CITY IV

[LCdv 233]
TREES. // **H** // MONUMENTS.

[LCdv 541]
CITIES VI // Les Places. // Gardens I // **L**

[LCdv 168]
part I // Chap. II // SQUARE. // Text. // §4 I

[LCdv 187]
part I // Chap. II // SQUARE // Text. // §4 II

[LCdv 542]
GARDEN CITIES // §10 // part I // Chap. II // I // §9 // **M** // CEMETERY

[LCdv 543]
GARDEN CITIES // II // CEMETERY // **i**

[LCdv 450]
City. // **J**

[LCdv 544]
Rolandus Fréart // Sieur de Chambray. // **F**

[LCdv 474]
Laugier. // **G** // Borrowed from the Koenigliche Bibliothek Berlin January 1911

Bibliography

Charles Edouard Jeanneret's bibliography reconstructed

Complete bibliography of all works listed and/or consulted by Jeanneret while writing *La Construction des villes* in 1910/11:

Albert, Charles. *L'Art et la Société. Conférence faite le 27 juin, 1896.* Paris: Bibliothèque de l'Art social, 1896.

Anonymous. "Treppe zu Kempten." *Süddeutsche Bauzeitung* 13, no. 22 (1903), pp. 169–170.

Anonymous. "Wettbewerb Augustinerstock München." In *Süddeutsche Bauzeitung* 19, no. 27 (1909), pp. 209–214, and no. 28 (1909), pp. 217–223.

Anonymous. "Wettbewerb zum Ulmer Münsterplatz." In *Süddeutsche Bauzeitung* 16, no. 50 (1906), pp. 393–396, and no. 51 (1906), pp. 401–403.

Bénaky, Doct. N.P. *Du sens chromatique dans l'antiquité.* Paris: A. Maloine, 1897.

Berlepsch-Valendàs, Hans Eduard von. "Eine Studie über Städtebau in England – Hampstead." In *Kunst und Kunsthandwerk* 12, no. 5 (1909), pp. 241–284.

Berlepsch-Valendàs, Hans Eduard von. *Bodenpolitik und gemeindliche Wohnungsfürsorge der Stadt Ulm.* Munich: E. Reinhardt, 1910.

Berlepsch-Valendàs, Hans Eduard von, and Peter Andreas Hansen. *Die Gartenstadt München-Perlach.* Munich: E. Reinhardt, 1910.

Braun, E. "Eine deutsche Stadt vor hundert Jahren." In *Der Städtebau* 6, no. 10 (1909), pp. 135–137.

Brinckmann, Albert Erich. *Die praktische Bedeutung der Ornamentstiche für die deutsche Frührenaissance* [Studien zur deutschen Kunstgeschichte 90]. Straßburg: Heitz, 1907, also PhD diss., University of Heidelberg, 1907.

Brinckmann, Albert Erich. *Platz und Monument: Untersuchungen zur Geschichte und Ästhetik der Stadtbaukunst in neuerer Zeit.* Berlin: Wasmuth, 1908. Reprint, with an afterword by Jochen Meyer. Berlin: Gebr. Mann, 2002.

Brinckmann, Albert Erich. *Spätmittelalterliche Stadtanlagen in Südfrankreich.* Berlin: Schenck, 1910.

Bruck, Robert. "Platzkonkurrenz für das Reiterdenkmal Ludwigs XV. in Paris." In *Der Städtebau* 5, no. 9 (1908), pp. 117–122.

Buls, Charles. *Esthétique des Villes.* Bruxelles: Bruylant-Christophe, 1893. Translated by Ph. Schäfer as *Ästhetik der Städte* (Gießen: Roth, 1898).

Burger, Fritz (ed.). *Die Villen des Andrea Palladio, Ein Beitrag zur Entwicklungsgeschichte der Renaissance-Architektur.* Leipzig: Klinkhardt & Biermann, 1909.

Cingria-Vaneyre, Alexandre. *Les Entretiens de la Villa de Rouet.* Genève: Jullien, 1908.

Claudel, Paul. *L'Arbre. Tête d'or. L'échange. La ville. La jeune fille Violaine. Le repos du septième jour.* Paris: Mercure de France, 1901.

Cousin, Victor. *Du vrai, du beau et du bien.* Paris: Didier, 1853.

Dézallier d'Argenville, Antoine-Joseph. *La théorie et pratique du jardinage*. Paris: J. Mariette, 4th ed. 1747.

Ebe, Gustav. "Brücken im Stadtbilde." In *Der Städtebau* 3, no. 12 (1906), pp. 159–162.

Eberstadt, Rudolf. "Die neue Gartenvorstadt in London-Hampstead." In *Der Städtebau* 6, no. 8 (1909), pp. 99–103.

Encke, Fritz, and Reinhold Hoemann. "Der Bremer Friedhofswettbewerb." In *Die Gartenkunst* 12, no. 4 (1910), pp. 51–57.

Enlart, Camille. *Architecture civile et militaire*. Part 1, vol. 2 of *Manuel d'Archéologie française*. Paris: A. Picard et fils, 1902–1904.

Fatio, Guillaume. *Ouvrons les Yeux! Voyage esthétique à travers la Suisse*. Geneva: Atar, 1904.

Fatio, Guillaume, and Georg Luck. *Augen auf! Schweizer Baukunst alter und neuer Zeit*. Geneva: Atar, 1904.

Fischer, Theodor. "Der Münsterplatz in Ulm." In *Süddeutsche Bauzeitung* 15, no. 16 (1905), pp. 125–128.

Fischer, Theodor. *Stadterweiterungsfragen*, lecture on 27 May, 1903. Stuttgart: DVA, 1903.

Fréart, Roland, Sieur de Chambray. *Parallèle de l'architecture antique av. la moderne*. Paris: Martin, 1650.

Fuchs, Ludwig F. "Garten und Park in künstlerischer Gestaltung." In *Süddeutsche Bauzeitung* 17 (1907), no. 36, pp. 281–285, No. 37, pp. 293–294, No. 38, pp. 301–303.

Gessner, Albert. *Das deutsche Miethaus. Ein Beitrag zur Städtekultur der Gegenwart*. München: Bruckmann, 1909.

Goecke, Theodor. "Allgemeine Städtebau-Ausstellung Berlin 1910." In *Der Städtebau* 7 (1910), no. 7/8, pp. 73–92.

Grisebach, August. "Max Längers Entwürfe zum Hamburger Stadtpark und zum Osterholzer Friedhof bei Bremen." In *Die Kunst – Angewandte Kunst* 22 (1910), pp. 489–503.

Hansen, Peter Andreas. "Baulinienplan für Marktredwitz." In *Der Städtebau* 6 (1909), pp. 57–60.

Hegemann, Werner (ed.). *Der Städtebau nach den Ergebnissen der Allgemeinen Städtebau-Ausstellung in Berlin, nebst e. Anhang: Die internationale Städtebau-Ausstellung in Düsseldorf. 600 Wiedergaben d. Bilder- und Planmaterials der beiden Ausstellungen….* Berlin: Wasmuth, 1911.

Henrici, Karl. *Beiträge zur praktischen Ästhetik im Städtebau. Eine Sammlung von Vorträgen und Aufsätzen*. München: Callwey, 1904.

Hocheder, Carl. "Gedanken über das künstlerische Sehen im Zusammenhange mit dem Ausgange des Wettbewerbes zur Umgestaltung des Münsterplatzes in Ulm." In *Der Städtebau* 5 (1908), no. 2, pp. 15–18.

Hofmann, Albert. *Geschichte des Denkmals*. Part 4, sub-volume 8, no. 2b of *Handbuch des Architekten*, Stuttgart: Kröner, 1906.

Howard, Ebenezer. *Garden Cities of To-morrow*. London: Swan Sonnenschein, 1902 (2nd edition of *To-morrow: a Peaceful Path to Real Reform*, 1898).

Hubatschek, Johann. *Bautechnische Aufgaben einer modernen Stadt*. Linz: E. Mareis, 1905.

Izdamie imperatorskoj archeologiceskoj Kommissii, *Meceti Samarkanda (Les Mosquées de Samarcande*, publié par la commission impériale archéologique), Vol.: *Le Gour Emir*. St. Petersburg: Éxpédition pour la confection des papiers d'état, 1905.

Königlich Oberste Baubehörde. *Von der Staatsbauverwaltung in Bayern ausgeführte Straßen, Brücken- und Wasserbautenrückenbauten*. 2 Vols. Munich: Piloty & Loehle, vol. I 1906, vol. II 1909.

Kuczynski, Robert René, and Walter Lehweß. "Zweifamilienhäuser für Großstädte." In *Der Städtebau* 7 (1910), no. 6, pp. 67–72.

Lambert, André and Eduard Stahl. *Die Gartenarchitektur. Handbuch der Architektur*, part 4, 10th sub-volume. Stuttgart: A Bergsträsser, 1898. 2nd edition Leipzig, 1910.

Laugier, Marc Antoine. *Essai sur l'Architecture. Avec un dictionnaire des termes, et des planches qui en facilitent l'explication. Nouvelle édition, revue, corrigée, et augmentée*. Paris: Duchesne,

1755. Translated by Wolfgang and Anni Herrmann as *An Essay on Architecture* (Los Angeles: Hennessey and Ingalls, 1977).

Laugier, Marc Antoine. *Observations sur l'Architecture*. La Haye/Paris: Desaint, 1765.

Le Bon, Gustave. *Psychologie de l'éducation*. Paris: E. Flammarion 1909.

Lehweß, Walter. "Architektonisches von der Städtebau-Ausstellung zu Berlin." In *Berliner Architekturwelt* 13 (1910), pp. 123–125.

Lux, Joseph August. "Alt-Wiener Vorgärten." In *Süddeutsche Bauzeitung* 17 (1907), no. 36, pp. 286–288.

Lux, Joseph August. "Die Gartenkunst und die Landschaftsgärtnerei." In *Süddeutsche Bauzeitung* 17 (1907), no. 3, pp. 21–23.

Lux, Joseph August. *Alt-Holland* [Stätten der Kultur 10]. Leipzig: Klinkhardt & Biermann, 1908.

Lux, Joseph August. *Der Städtebau und die Grundpfeiler der heimischen Bauweise – zum Verständnis für die Gebildeten aller Stände, namentlich aber für Stadtverordnete, Baumeister, Architekten, Bauherren etc.* Dresden: Gerhardt Kühtmann, 1908.

Lux, Joseph August. *Ingenieur-Aesthetik*. Munich: Lammers, 1910.

Lux, Joseph August, and Max Warnatsch. *Die Stadtwohnung. Wie man sie sich praktisch, schön und preiswert einrichtet. Ein prakt. Ratgeber*. Charlottenburg: Teschner 1910.

Merian, Matthäus. *Topographia Germaniae*, vol. 2: *Topographia Bohemiae, Moraviae et Silesiae*. Frankfurt/Main: Merian, 1650. Reprint: Kassel/Basel: Bärenreiter, 1960.

Merian, Matthäus. *Topographia Germaniae*, vol. 4: *Topographia Helvetiae, Rhaetiae et Valesiae, Das ist Beschreybung und eygentliche Abbildung der vornehmsten Staette und Plätze in der Hochlöblichen Eydgenossenschafft Graubündten Wallis und etlicher zugewandten Orthen*. Frankfurt/Main: Merian Erben 1654. Reprint Kassel/Basel: Bärenreiter, 1960.

Merian, Matthäus. *Topographia Germaniae*, vol. 7: *Topographia Franconiae, Das ist Beschreybung und eygentliche Contrafactur der Vornembsten Stätte und Plätze des Franckenlandes und deren die zu dem Hochlöblichen Fränkischen Craiße gezogen warden*. Frankfurt/Main: Merian 1649. Reprint Kassel/Basel: Bärenreiter, 1962.

Merian, Matthäus. *Topographia Germaniae*, vol. 14: *Topographia Alsatiae, &c. Completa, Das ist Vollkömliche Beschreibung und eygentliche Abbildung der vornehmbsten Städt und Oerther im Obern und untern Elsaß auch den benachbarten Sundgow Brißgow Graffschafft Mümpelgart und andern Gegenden*. Frankfurt/Main: Merian Erben 1663. Reprint: Kassel/Basel: Bärenreiter. 1964.

Metzendorf, Georg. *Denkschrift über den Ausbau des Stiftungsgeländes* [Margarethenhöhe]. Essen: Petersen, 1909.

Ministero della pubblica istruzione (ed.). *Elenco degli Edifici Monumentali in Italia*. Rome: Cecchini, 1902.

Montenach, Georges de. *Pour le visage aimé de la patrie. Ouvrage de propagande esthétique et sociale*. Lausanne: Sack-Reymond, 1908.

Muthesius, Hermann. *Das Englische Haus: Entwicklung, Bedingungen, Anlage, Aufbau, Einrichtung und Innenraum*, 3 vols. Berlin: Ernst Wasmuth, 1904–11. Translated by Janet Seligman as *The English House*. Edited and with an introduction by Dennis Sharp, preface by Julius Posener (New York: Rizzoli, 1979).

Patte, Pierre. *Mémoire sur les objets les plus importans de l'architecture*. Paris: Rozet, 1769.

Patzak, Bernhard. *Die Renaissance- und Barockvilla in Italien*. Vol. III, *Die Villa Imperiale in Pesaro. Studien zur Kunstgeschichte der ital. Renaissancevilla und ihrer Innendekoration*. Leipzig: Klinkhardt & Biermann, 1908.

Provensal, Henri. *L'Art de Demain*. Paris. Perrin, 1904.

Riat, Georges. *L'Art des Jardins*. Paris: L. Henry May, 1900.

Schmid, Max. "Baukunst und Innendekoration auf der Ausstellung für Christliche Kunst in Düsseldorf 1909." In *Moderne Bauformen* 8 (1909), no. 9, p. 388f.

Schultze-Naumburg, Paul. *Die Entstellung unseres Landes*. Vol. 2 of *Flugschriften des Heimatschutzbundes*. Halle: Gebauer-Schwetschke, 1905.

Schultze-Naumburg, Paul. *Der Städtebau*. Vol.4 of *Kulturarbeiten*. Munich: Callwey, 1906.

Seeck, Franz. "Neuzeitliche Friedhofsanlagen." In *Die Kunst – Angewandte Kunst* 20 (1909), pp. 521–536.

Sitte, Camillo. *Der Städtebau nach seinen künstlerischen Grundsätzen*, Vienna: Carl Graeser, 1889. Translated as *L'Art de Bâtir les Villes. Notes et Réflexions d'un Architecte traduites et complétées par Camille Martin*. Geneva: Ch. Eggiman & Cie/Paris: Librairie Renouard 1902.

Sitte, Siegfried. "Das Schulhaus im Stadtplane." In *Der Städtebau* 3 (1906), no. 10, pp. 130–133.

Speck, Arthur. "Die Kronprinzenbrücke über das Spreetal in Bautzen." In *Süddeutsche Bauzeitung* 20 (1910), no. 14, pp. 105–110.

Stübben, Joseph. *Der Städtebau. Handbuch der Architektur*, Part 4, sub-volume 9. Darmstadt: Bergstrasser, 1890. Translated by Adalbert Albrecht as *City-Building* (1911). This unpublished translation is available at the Frances Loeb Library, Harvard University; available online: https://urbanism.uchicago.edu/page/joseph-stübbens-city-building.

Thièry, Armand. *Über optisch-geometrische Täuschungen*, Leipzig: W. Engelmann 1895, also PhD diss., University of Leipzig, 1895.

Unwin, Raymond. *Town Planning in Practice: an Introduction to the Art of Designing Cities and Suburbs*. London: Fisher Unwin, 1909. Translated by L. MacLean as *Grundlagen des Städtebaues. Eine Anleitung zum Entwerfen städtebaulicher Anlagen*. Berlin: Baumgärtel, 1910.

Wasmuth, Ernst (ed.). *Führer durch die allgemeine Städtebau-Ausstellung in Berlin 1910*. Berlin: Wasmuth, 1910.

Werner, H. "Der Umbau der Stuttgarter Altstadt." In *Der Städtebau* 8 (1911), no. 2, pp. 20–23, Tafeln 10–12.

Werner, H. "Der Umbau der Stuttgarter Altstadt." In *Süddeutsche Bauzeitung* 20 (1910), no. 1, pp. 1–7.

Zell, Franz. "Die Münchner Friedhof- und Grabmalreform." In *Süddeutsche Bauzeitung* 17 (1907), no. 33, pp. 257–261.

Sources relating to Jeanneret's research

Behrendt, Curt Walter. *Die einheitliche Blockfront als Raumelement im Stadtbau: Ein Beitrag zur Stadtbaukunst der Gegenwart*. Berlin: Cassirer, 1911.

Behrens, Peter. "Kunst und Technik." in: *Peter Behrens. Zeitloses und Zeitbewegtes. Aufsätze, Vorträge, Gespräche 1900–1938*, edited by Hartmut Frank and Karin Lelonek, pp. 352–367. Munich: Dölling and Galitz, 2015. Originally published as "Kunst und Technik" in *Elektrotechnische Zeitschrift* 31 (1910), no. 22, pp. 552–555.

Ebe, Gustav. "Brücken im Stadtbilde." In *Der Städtebau* 3 (1906), no. 12, pp. 159–162.

Eberstadt, Rudolf. "Die neue Gartenvorstadt in London-Hampstead." In *Der Städtebau* 6 (1909), no. 8, pp. 99–103.

Goecke, Theodor. "Der Wettbewerb um Entwürfe für den Osterholzer Friedhof in Bremen." In *Der Städtebau* 8 (1911), no. 8, pp. 89–91.

Heicke, Carl. "Rückständige Gartenkunst." In *Süddeutsche Bauzeitung* 16 (1906), no. 46, pp. 64–367 and no. 48, pp. 379–383.

Heicke, Carl. "Was lehrt uns die Darmstädter Gartenbau-Ausstellung?" In *Die Gartenkunst* 11 (1905), no. 7, pp. 184–186.

Hénard, Eugène. *Etudes sur les transformations de Paris*, edited by Jean-Louis Cohen. Paris: Editions L'Equerre, 1982.

Gurlitt, Cornelius. *Handbuch des Städtebaues*. Berlin: Architekturverlag Der Zirkel, 1920.

L'Eplattenier, Charles. "Renouveau d'Art." In *L'Abeille*, La Chaux-de-Fonds, 20 February 1910.

L'Eplattenier, Charles. "L'Esthétique des villes." In [Résumé de l'intervention de Ch. L'Eplatt. à] l'Assemblée générale des délégués de l'Union des villes suisses réunis à La Chaux-de-Fonds à l'Hôtel de Ville, les 24 et 25 septembre 1910, in: *Compte-rendu des délibérations de l'Assemblée générale des délégués de l'Union des villes suisses, 1910*. Supplement to the Schweizerisches Zentralblatt für Staats- und Gemeinde-Verwaltung 11 (1910), pp. 24–31.

Mörsch, Emil. *Der Eisenbetonbau, seine Theorie und Anwendung.* 2nd edition Stuttgart: Wittwer, 1906. Translated as *Le béton armé: Etude théorique et pratique* by Max Dubois (Paris: Béranger, 1909).

Mörsch, Emil. *Concrete-Steel Construction.* Translated from the third German edition, revised and enlarged by Ernest Payson Goodrich (New York: Engineering News Publ. Co., 1909).

Nußbaum, Hans Christian. "Verdient die offene oder die geschlossene Bauweise den Vorzug?" In *Der Städtebau* 1 (1904), no. 1, pp. 29–31 and no. 3, pp. 42–45.

Patte, Pierre. *Monumens érigés en France à la gloire de Louis XV.* Paris: Auteur et al., 1765.

Pérelle, Gabriel. *Topographie de France.* Paris: Jombert, 1753.

Ritter, William. "De la prétendue laideur de La Chaux-de-Fonds." In *Feuille d'Avis de La Chaux-de-Fonds*, 17 and 24 March 1917.

Ritter, William. *L'Entêtement Slovaque.* Paris: Bibliothèque de l'Occident, 1910.

Storez, Maurice. L'Architecture *et l'art décoratif en France.* Evreux: Auguste Aubert, 1915.

Taut, Bruno. *Die Stadtkrone.* Jena: Diederichs, 1919. Reprint: Berlin, Gebr. Mann, 2002. An English version of Taut's own text in his anthology was translated by Ulrike Altenmüller and Matthew Mindrup, published in *Journal of Architectural Education*, 63, 1 (2009), pp. 121–134.

Wagner, Martin. *Das sanitäre Grün der Städte. Ein Beitrag zur Freiflächentheorie.* Berlin: Heymanns, 1915.

Wagner, Otto, *Die Großstadt: eine Studie über diese*, Wien: Schroll, 1911.

Wagner, Otto. *Moderne Architektur.* Vienna: Schroll, 1896. Translated from the 3rd edition 1902 by Harry Francis Mallgrave as *Modern architecture: a guidebook for his students to this field of art.* Santa Monica: Getty Center, 1988.

Worringer, Wilhelm. *Abstraktion und Einfuehlung. Ein Beitrag zur Stilpsychologie.* Neuwied: Heuser; also PhD Diss., University of Berne, 1907. Reprint Munich: Wilhelm Fink Verlag, 2007.

Relevant writings by Jeanneret/Le Corbusier

Emery, Marc Albert. *Charles-Edouard Jeanneret: La Construction des Villes.* Lausanne: L'Age d'Homme 1992.

Jeanneret, Charles Edouard. "L'Art et Utilité publique." In *L'Abeille, Supplément du National Suisse*, La Chaux-de-Fonds, 15 May, 1910.

Jeanneret, Charles Edouard. *Etude sur le Mouvement d'Art décoratif en Allemagne*, La Chaux-de-Fonds, 1912. Reprint New York: Da Capo, 1968.

Jeanneret, Charles Edouard. *A Study of the Decorative Art Movement in Germany.* Translated by Alex Thomas Anderson, edited by Mateo Kries. Weil am Rhein: Vitra Design Museum, 2008.

Le Corbusier – Carnets de Voyage d'Allemagne 1910–1911, edited by Giuliano Gresleri. Paris: FLC; Milan: Electa, 1994. English edition published 2002.

Le Corbusier – Carnets de Voyage d'Orient 1911, edited by Giuliano Gresleri. Paris: FLC; Milan: Electa, 1987. English edition published in 2002.

Le Corbusier. *Vers une architecture.* Paris: Crès, 1923. Translated by John Goodman as *Toward an Architecture*, with an introduction by Jean-Louis Cohen. Los Angeles: Getty Research Institute, 2007.

Le Corbusier. *Urbanisme.* Paris: Crès, 1925. Translated by Frederick Etchells as *The City of Tomorrow and its Planning* (New York: Payson & Clarke, 1929. Reprint New York: Dover, 1987).

Le Corbusier. *Précisions sur un état présent de l'architecture et de l'urbanisme.* Paris: Crès, 1930. Translated by Edith Schreiber Aujame as *Precisions on the Present State of Architecture and City Planning* (Cambridge, Mass.: MIT Press, 1991).

Secondary sources

Adshead, S.D. "Sitte and Le Corbusier." *Town Planning Review* XIV (1930), pp. 85–94.

Barrelet, Jean-Marc, and Jacques Ramseyer. *La Chaux-de-Fonds ou le défi d'une cité horlogère. 1848–1914.* La Chaux-de-Fonds: Editions d'En Haut, 1990.

Baudouï, Rémi, and Arnaud Dercelles. *Correspondance Le Corbusier. Edition établie, annotée et présentée par Rémi Baudouï et Arnaud Dercelles [Fondation Le Corbusier].* Gollion: Infolio, 2011–.

Bergdoll, Barry. "The Nature of Mies's Space." In *Mies in Berlin,* edited by Terence Riley and Barry Bergdoll, pp. 66–105. New York: The Museum of Modern Art, 2001.

Bergdoll, Barry. "Paris: Le Corbusier and the Nineteenth-Century City." In *Le Corbusier: An Atlas of Modern Landscapes,* edited by Jean-Louis Cohen, pp. 246–249. New York: Museum of Modern Art, 2013.

Blum, Elisabeth. *Le Corbusiers Wege.* Vol. 73 of *Bauwelt-Fundamente.* Braunschweig: Vieweg, 1988.

Borrmann, Norbert. *Paul Schultze-Naumburg, 1869–1949, Maler, Publizist, Architekt. Vom Kulturreformer der Jahrhundertwende zum Kulturpolitiker im Dritten Reich.* Essen: Richard Bacht, 1989.

Brooks, Harold Allen. "Jeanneret and Sitte: Le Corbusier's Earliest Ideas on Urban Design." In *In Search of Modern Architecture,* edited by Helen Searing, pp. 278 297. Cambridge, Mass.: MIT Press, 1982.

Brooks, Harold Allen. "Jeannerets Auseinandersetzung mit Sitte." In *Archithese* 2 (1983), pp. 29–32.

Brooks, Harold Allen. *Essays on Le Corbusier.* Princeton, NJ: Princeton Univ. Press, 1987.

Brooks, Harold Allen. *Le Corbusier's Formative Years. Charles-Edouard Jeanneret at La Chaux-de-Fonds.* Chicago/London: The University of Chicago Press, 1997.

Brucculeri, Antonio. "The Challenge of the 'Grand Siècle'." In *Le Corbusier before Le Corbusier,* edited by Stanislaus von Moos and Arthur Rüegg, pp. 99–107. New Haven/London: Yale University Press, 2002.

Cohen, Jean-Louis. "France ou Allemagne? Un Zigzag éditorial de Charles-Edouard Jeanneret." In *SvM. Die Festschrift für Stanislaus von Moos,* edited by Karin Gimmi et al., pp. 74–93. Zurich: gta, 2005.

Collins, George and Christiane Crasemann Collins. *Camillo Sitte: The Birth of Modern City Planning.* New York: Rizzoli, 1986.

Davey, Peter. *Arts and Crafts Architecture.* London: Phaidon, 1995. First published 1980 by Architectural Press.

Dennis, Michael. *Court and Garden.* Cambridge, Mass.: MIT Press, 1986.

Dercelles, Arnaud. "Présentation de la bibliothèque personnelle de Le Corbusier." In *Le Corbusier et le livre,* pp. 6–78. Barcelona: Collegi d'Arquitectes de Catalunya, 2005.

Duboy, Philippe. *Architecture de la ville: culture et triomphe de l'urbanisme. Ch. E. Jeanneret, «La Construction des Villes», Bibliothèque Nationale de Paris, 1915.* Paris: pour la ministère de l'urbanisme, du logement et des transports, 1985.

Duboy, Philippe. "Charles Edouard Jeanneret à la Bibliothèque Nationale." In *Architecture, Mouvement, Continuité* 49 (1979), pp. 9–12.

Duboy, Philippe. "L.C.B.N. 1915." In *Casabella* (1987), no. 531/532, pp. 94–103, 113–114, 120.

Dumont, Marie-Jeanne. *Le Corbusier. Lettres à ses maîtres tome I. Lettres à Auguste Perret.* Paris: Editions du Linteau, 2002.

Dumont, Marie-Jeanne. *Le Corbusier. Lettres à ses maîtres tome II. Lettres à Charles L'Eplattenier.* Paris: Editions du Linteau, 2006.

Dumont, Marie-Jeanne. *Lettres à ses maîtres tome III. Le Corbusier, William Ritter – correspondence croisée, 1910–1955.* Paris: Editions du Linteau, 2014.

Emery, Marc Albert. "Urbanisme." In *Le Corbusier, une encyclopédie.* Paris: Centre Pompidou, 1987.

Etlin, Richard A. *Frank Lloyd Wright and Le Corbusier: The Romantic Legacy*. Manchester: Manchester University Press, 1994.

Evenson, Norma. *Le Corbusier: The Machine and the Grand Design*. New York: Braziller, 1969.

Fehl, Gerhard (ed.). *Stadt-Umbau. Die planmäßige Erneuerung europäischer Großstädte zwischen Wiener Kongreß und Weimarer Republik*. Basel: Birkhäuser, 1995.

Fehl, Gerhard (ed.). *Kleinstadt, Steildach, Volksgemeinschaft*. Vol. 102 of *Bauwelt-Fundamente*. Braunschweig/Wiesbaden: Vieweg, 1995.

Gimmi, Karin, et al. *SvM. Die Festschrift für Stanislaus von Moos*. Zurich: gta, 2005.

Gresleri, Giuliano. *Le Corbusier. Viaggio in Oriente*, Venice: Marsilio Editori, 1984. Translated by Lydia Romana Höller as *Le Corbusier. Reise nach dem Orient*. Paris: FLC; Zurich: Spur Publishers, 1991.

Gubler, Jacques. "La Chaux-de-Fonds." In *Inventar der Neueren Schweizer Architektur. 1850–1920*, Vol. 3, pp. 127–218. Bern: Gesellschaft für Schweizerische Kunstgeschichte, 1982.

Helfrich, Andreas, *Die Margarethenhöhe Essen. Architekt und Auftraggeber vor dem Hintergrund der Kommunalpolitik Essen und der Firmenpolitik Krupp zw. 1886 u. 1914*, Weimar: VDG 2000 (also PhD Diss. Darmstadt, 1999).

Hilpert, Thilo. *Die funktionelle Stadt*. Vol. 48 of *Bauwelt Fundamente*. Vieweg: Braunschweig, 1978.

Hipp, Hermann. "Schumachers Hamburg. Die reformierte Großstad." In *Moderne Architektur in Deutschland 1900 bis 1950. Reform und Tradition*, edited by Vittorio Magnago Lampugnani and Romana Schneider, pp. 151–184. Stuttgart: Hatje, 1992.

Höffler, Karl-Heinz. *Reinhard Baumeister (1883–1917): Begründer der Wissenschaft vom Städtebau*, Karlsruhe: Institut für Städtebau und Landesplanung, 1976.

Jarzombek, Mark. "Joseph August Lux. Werkbund Promoter, Historian of a Lost Modernity." In *JSAH* 63 (2004), pp. 202–219.

Kerkhoff, Ulrich. *Eine Abkehr vom Historismus oder Ein Weg zur Moderne: Theodor Fischer*. Stuttgart: Krämer 1987; also PhD diss., University of Bonn, 1987.

Köhler, Bettina. "Architekturgeschichte als Geschichte der Raumwahrnehmung." In *Daidalos* 67 (1998), pp. 36–43.

Lampugnani, Vittorio Magnago. "Moderne, Lebensreform, Stadt und Grün. Urbanistische Experimente in Berlin 1900 bis 1914." In *Stadt der Architektur. Architektur der Stadt. Berlin 1900-2000*, edited by Thorsten Scheer, Josef Paul Kleihues and Paul Kahlfeldt, pp. 29–39. Berlin: Nicolai, 2000.

McLeod, Mary. *Urbanism and Utopia. Le Corbusier from regional syndicalism to Vichy*. PhD diss., Princeton University, 1985.

Mallgrave, Harry Francis and Eleftherios Ikonomou (eds.). *Empathy, Form, and Space: Problems in German Aesthetics, 1873–1893*. Santa Monica: Getty Center for the History of Art and the Humanities, 1994.

Meacham, Standish. *Regaining Paradise: Englishness and the Early Garden City Movement*. New Haven and London: Yale University, 1999.

Metzendorf, Rainer. *Georg Metzendorf 1874–1934: Siedlungen und Bauten*. Darmstadt: Selbstverlag der hess. histor. Kommission 1994, also PhD diss, Aachen 1993.

Metzendorf, Rainer. *Margarethenhöhe – Experiment und Leitbild. 1906–1996*, Bottrop/Essen: Pomp, 1997.

Meyer, Jochen. "Die Stadt als Kunstwerk." Afterword to *Platz und Monument* by Albert Erich Brinckmann, pp. 177–211. Berlin. Gebr. Mann, 2000.

Mönninger, Michael. *Vom Ornament zum Nationalkunstwerk: Die Schriften von Camillo Sitte zu Kunsttheorie, Pädagogik und Gewerbe*. Wiesbaden: Vieweg, 1998; also PhD diss., HfG Karlsruhe, 1995.

Moos, Stanislaus von. *Le Corbusier. Elemente einer Synthese*, Frauenfeld/Stuttgart: Huber, 1968. Translated as *Elements of a Synthesis*. Cambridge, Mass.: MIT Press, 1979. Revised and expanded edition of the English translation (Rotterdam: 010 Publishers, 2009).

Moos, Stanislaus von. "Urbanism and Transcultural Exchanges, 1910–1935: A Survey." In *Le Corbusier: The Garland Essays*, edited by Harold Allen Brooks, pp. 219–232. New York: Garland, 1987.

Moos, Stanislaus von, and Arthur Rüegg (eds.). *Le Corbusier before Le Corbusier*. New Haven and London: Yale University Press, 2002.

Nerdinger, Winfried. "Le Corbusier und Deutschland. Genesis und Wirkungsgeschichte eines Konflikts. 1910–1933." In *Arch+* 90/91 (1987), pp. 80–86.

Nerdinger, Winfried. *Theodor Fischer. Architekt und Städtebauer*. Berlin: Ernst & Sohn, 1988.

Oechslin, Werner. "Allemagne. Influences, confluences et reniements." In *Le Corbusier: une encyclopédie*, edited by Jacques Lucan, pp. 33–39. Paris: Centre Georges Pompidou, 1987.

Oechslin, Werner. "Le Corbusier und Deutschland: 1910/1911." In *LC im Brennpunkt*, edited by Werner Oechslin and Franz Oswald, pp. 27–47. Zurich: ETH and vdf, 1988.

Passanti, Francesco. "Architecture: Proportion, Classicism, and Other Issues." In *Le Corbusier before Le Corbusier*, edited by Stanislaus von Moos and Arthur Rüegg, pp. 69–98. New Haven/London: Yale University Press, 2002.

Petit, Jean. *Le Corbusier parle*. Paris: Forces Vives, 1967. Revised edition Lugano: Fidia Edizioni D'Arte, 1996.

Piccinato, Giorgio. *Städtebau in Deutschland 1871–1914*. Vol. 62 of *Bauwelt Fundamente*. Braunschweig: Vieweg, 1983. Translated by Michael Peterek. Originally published as *La costruzione dell' urbanistica, germania 1871–1914* (Rome: Officina, 1977).

Piguet, Claire. "L'Observatoire cantonal de Neuchâtel: une architecture et un ensemble décoratif Art nouveau entre terre et ciel." In *Revue historique neuchâteloise* 3–4 (2003).

Posener, Julius. *Berlin auf dem Wege zu einer neuen Architektur. Das Zeitalter Wilhelms II*. Munich/New York: Prestel, 1995 (1979).

Reiterer, Gabriele. *AugenSinn. Zu Raum und Wahrnehmung in Camillo Sittes "Städtebau"*. Salzburg: Pustet, 2003.

Rowe, Colin. *The Mathematics of the Ideal Villa and Other Essays*. Cambridge, Mass.: MIT Press, 1976.

Rowe, Colin. *The Architecture of Good Intentions*. London: Academy Press, 1994.

Rowe, Colin, and Fred Koetter. *Collage City*. Cambridge, Mass.: MIT Press, 1978.

Rüegg, Arthur, et al. *La Chaux-de-Fonds avant Le Corbusier*. Exhibition catalogue La Chaux-de-Fonds, 1987.

Sanderson, Kim. "In pursuit of the intangible: A translation on Le Corbusier's early urban planning work." https://www.academia.edu/8804938/In_pursuit_of_the_intangible_A_translation_on_Le_Corbusier_s_early_urban_planning_work?source=swp_. Translated as "À la poursuite de l'intangible" by Pierre Fuentes. *Traduire*, no. 227 (2012), pp. 47–52. http://journals.openedition.org/traduire/477; DOI: 10.4000/traduire.477

Schirren, Matthias. *Hugo Häring: Architekt des Neuen Bauens, 1882–1958*. Ostfildern-Ruit: Hatje Cantz, 2001.

Schneider, Uwe. *Hermann Muthesius und die Reformdiskussion in der Gartenarchitektur des frühen 20. Jahrhunderts*. Worms: Wernersche Verlagsgesellschaft, 2000.

Schnoor, Christoph. *La Construction des villes. Le Corbusiers erstes städtebauliches Traktat von 1910/11*. Zurich: gta, 2008.

Schnoor, Christoph. "Städtebau zwischen beauté und utilité. La Construction des villes von Charles-Edouard Jeanneret." In *Stadtformen. Die Architektur der Stadt zwischen Imagination on Konstruktion*, edited by Vittorio Magnago Lampugnani and Matthias Noell, pp. 252–265. Zurich: gta, 2005.

Schnoor, Christoph. "Soyez de votre temps – Le Corbusier et William Ritter." In *Le Corbusier. La Suisse, Les Suisses*, XIIIe Rencontre de la Fondation Le Corbusier, edited by Fondation Le Corbusier, pp. 104–127. Paris: Editions de la Villette/FLC, 2006.

Schnoor, Christoph. "Le Raum dans « La construction des villes » de Le Corbusier. Une traduction aux multiples strates linguistiques et culturelles." In *Traduire l'architecture. Texte et image, un passage vers la creation ?*, edited by Jean-Sébastien Cluzel et al., pp. 135–144. Paris: Picard, 2015.

Schubert, Leo. "Jeanneret, the City and Photography." In *Le Corbusier before Le Corbusier*, edited by Stanislaus von Moos and Arthur Rüegg, pp. 55–68. New Haven and London: Yale University Press, 2002.

Sekler, Patricia. "Le Corbusier, Jeanneret, Patented Ideas, and the Urbanistic cell." In *La ville et l'urbanisme après Le Corbusier*, actes du colloque des 23–26 septembre 1987, p. 123. La Chaux-de-Fonds: Editions d'en Haut 1993.

Simone, Rosario de. *Ch. E. Jeanneret-Le Corbusier. Viaggio in Germania 1910–1911*, Rome: Officina, 1989.

Sonne, Wolfgang. *Representing the State: Capital City Planning in the Early Twentieth Century.* Translated by Elizabeth Schwaiger. Munich: Prestel, 2003. Originally "Hauptstadtplanungen 1900–1914: die Repräsentation des Staates in der Stadt" (PhD diss., ETH Zurich, 2001).

Sonne, Wolfgang. "Ideen für die Großstadt: Der Wettbewerb Groß-Berlin 1910." In *Stadt der Architektur. Architektur der Stadt. Berlin 1900-2000*, edited by Thorsten Scheer, Josef Paul Kleihues and Paul Kahlfeldt, pp. 67–77. Berlin: Nicolai, 2000.

Spechtenhauser, Klaus. "The Mentor: William Ritter." In *Le Corbusier before Le Corbusier*, edited by Stanislaus von Moos and Arthur Rüegg, pp. 260–263. New Haven/London: Yale University Press, 2002.

Turner, Paul Venable. *The Education of Le Corbusier.* New York/London: Garland, 1977; also PhD diss., Harvard University, 1971.

Vaisse, Pierre. "Le Corbusier and the Gothic." In *Le Corbusier before Le Corbusier*, edited by Stanislaus von Moos and Arthur Rüegg, pp. 44–53. New Haven/London: Yale University Press, 2002.

Van Eck, Caroline. *Organicism in Nineteenth-Century Architecture: An inquiry into its theoretical and philosophical background.* Amsterdam: Architectura et Natura Press, 1994.

Vogt, Max Adolf. *Le Corbusier, the Noble Savage: Toward an Archaeology of Modernism.* Translated by Jacques Gubler. Cambridge, Mass.: MIT Press, 1998. Originally published as *Le Corbusier, Der edle Wilde. Zur Archäologie der Moderne.* (Braunschweig/Wiesbaden: Vieweg, 1996).

Wagner, Martin. *Das sanitäre Grün der Städte. Ein Beitrag zur Freiflächentheorie.* Berlin: Carl Heymanns Verlag, 1915.

Wyss, Beat. *Der Wille zur Kunst. Zur ästhetischen Mentalität der Moderne*, Cologne: DuMont, 1996.

Illustrations

List of essay captions (source in brackets)

List of captions manuscript (source in brackets)

77. Garden of Brickwall House in Sussex. From Muthesius, *Das englische Haus*, fig. 65

78. Garden by Thomas H. Mawson. From Muthesius, *Das englische Haus*, fig. 66

79. Trellis from the Decameron. Sketch by Jeanneret, after Riat, *L'Art des jardins*, p. 69 (B2-20-352 FLC)

80. Plan of a public garden in Cologne. Sketch by Jeanneret, copied from Stübben, *Städtebau*, fig. 841 (LCdv 269)

81. Tombstones on the Waldfriedhof, Munich. Sketches by Jeanneret, copied from Zell, "Die Münchener Friedhof- und Grabmalreform" (LCdv 274)

82. Cemetery design by Wilhelm Kreis at the exhibition for Christian art in Düsseldorf. From *Moderne Bauformen* 8 (1909), no. 9, p. 388f.

83. Cemetery design by Wilhelm Kreis at the exhibition for Christian art in Düsseldorf. From *Moderne Bauformen* 8 (1909), no. 9, p. 388f.

84. Cemetery designs. Sketches by Jeanneret (LCdv 298)

85. Entry to the garden suburb Margarethenhöhe in Essen. From Metzendorf, *Denkschrift*

86. Tramway bridge between Margarethenhöhe garden suburb and Essen. From *Der Städtebau* 7 (1910) no. 7/8, pp. 73–92, fig. 30.

87. Development plan of Margarethenhöhe garden suburb. From Metzendorf, *Denkschrift*

88. Breisach on the Rhine. Drawing by Jeanneret, copied from Merian, *Topographia Alsatiae*, p. 6 (B2-20-360 FLC)

89. Breisach on the Rhine. From Merian, *Topographia Alsatiae*, p. 6.

90. Town hall in Lübeck. Postcard, owned by Jeanneret (LC 105-1112-28 BV)

91. Carlsbad (Karlovy Vary). Drawing by Jeanneret, copied from Merian, *Topographia Bohemiae*, plate after p. 16 (B2-20-361 FLC)

92. Town map of La Chaux-de-Fonds, 1908 (FLC 30283)

93. Synagogue in the Rue de la Serre, La Chaux-de-Fonds. Photo, ca. 1900 (AS-P2-28 BV)

94. Rue de la Serre in La Chaux-de-Fonds. Photo, ca. 1900 (AS-P2-48 BV)

95. Rue de la Paix in La Chaux-de-Fonds. Postkarte, 1912 (CP-438 BV)

96. Post office in the Rue Léopold-Robert, La Chaux-de-Fonds. Postcard, ca. 1900 (CP-1934 BV)

97. Rue Léopold-Robert in La Chaux-de-Fonds. Postcard, ca. 1900 (CP-1396 BV)

98. Rue du Collège Primaire in La Chaux-de-Fonds. Photo, ca. 1900 (HP-P2-86 BV)

99. Rue de la Balance towards Rue du Versoix in La Chaux-de-Fonds. Photo, ca. 1900 (AS-P2-39 BV)

100. Place de l'Ouest in La Chaux-de-Fonds. Photo, ca. 1900 (AS-P2-88 BV)

101. Place Jaquet Droz in La Chaux-de-Fonds. Photo, ca. 1900 (P2-501 BV)

102. Collège Industriel in La Chaux-de-Fonds. Photo, ca. 1900 (AS-P2-76 BV)

103. Ecole d'Horlogerie in La Chaux-de-Fonds. Photo, ca. 1900 (AS-P2-74 BV)

104. Ecole d'Horlogerie in La Chaux-de-Fonds. Photo, ca. 1900 (B2-4663 BV)

105. Temple Allemand in the Rue du Collège Primaire, La Chaux-de-Fonds. Photo, ca. 1900 (AS-P2-86 BV)

106. Temple Indépendant in La Chaux-de-Fonds. Photo, ca. 1900 (AS-P2-83 BV)

107. St. Ulrich in Augsburg. Photo by Jeanneret, 1910 (LC 108-315 BV)

108. Place de la Gare in La Chaux-de-Fonds. Photo, ca. 1900 (P2-43 BV)

Index